THE AMERICAN PEOPLES ENCYCLOPEDIA

ENCYCLOPEDIA YEAR BOOK

ENCYCLOPEDIA YEAR BOOK

THE
AMERICAN
PEOPLES
ENCYCLOPEDIA

CONTENTS

The World in Review

Events of the Year

EDITORIAL DIRECTOR
LOWELL A. MARTIN

STAFF

EDITOR IN CHIEF   JAMES E. JARNAGIN
MANAGING EDITOR   JAMES E. CHURCHILL, JR.
ART DIRECTOR   BARBARA EFFRON

EDITORIAL

ASSOCIATE EDITORS   HALLBERG HALLMUNDSSON
    FRED D. MOORE
PRODUCTION EDITOR   HELEN RIEHL HITCHCOCK
STYLE EDITORS   J. M. A. RAIKES
    MARION LEE JOHNSON
RESEARCHERS   FERN MAMBERG
    SERGIO BARZANTI
INDEXER   KATHLEEN LEERBURGER
STAFF ASSISTANTS   ELEANOR C. WOOD
    DOROTHY BALDO
    RUTH E. NORTHLANE
    JANET H. RAMLOW

ILLUSTRATION

LAYOUT   GERALDINE F. SMITH
PHOTO RESEARCHER   MARGARET SHULL

MANUFACTURING

EDWARD C. McKENNA
RAYMOND H. LABOTT

CONTRIBUTORS

HELMUT A. ABT is an astronomer in charge of the 84-inch telescope at Kitt Peak National Observatory, Tucson, Ariz. He was formerly with Lick Observatory in California and the Yerkes Observatory of the University of Chicago.
ASTRONOMY

JOHN M. BAILEY is chairman of the Democratic National Committee. DEMOCRATIC PARTY

N. CARL BAREFOOT, JR., director of publications for the American Association of Museums, also edits the association's *Museum News.*
MUSEUMS

JACK STRALEY BATTELL, executive editor of *Chess Review,* has written many articles on chess and, with I. A. Horowitz, coauthored the book *The Best of Chess.* GAMES: CHESS

LIONEL BAXTER is vice president, Radio Division, Storer Broadcasting Co. He serves on the board of directors of the Radio Advertising Bureau. RADIO

WILF BELL, a reporter for *The Ottawa Citizen,* has been with that newspaper for 15 years.
OTTAWA

WILLIAM BENDER, music critic of the New York *World Journal Tribune,* contributes to numerous periodicals and writes regular criticism for his newspaper. MUSIC

BETSY TALBOT BLACKWELL began her career on the fashion magazine *Mademoiselle* in 1935. She has been its editor in chief since 1937.
FASHIONS

W. GRANGER BLAIR has been with *The New York Times* since early 1953, with U.S., Middle East, European and North African assignments highlighting his career. Presently he is stationed in London and covers Scandinavia for the *Times.*
SCANDINAVIA

RAYMOND C. BLISS is chairman of the Republican National Committee. REPUBLICAN PARTY

GEORGE A. W. BOEHM worked for *Scientific American, Newsweek* and *Fortune* before devoting all his time to free-lance science writing. He belongs to the National Association of Science Writers and the American Mathematical Association. BIOLOGICAL SCIENCES: MEMORY TRANSFER

ANTHONY BOUCHER reviews mysteries for *The New York Times Book Review* and edits *Best Detective Stories of the Year.*
LITERATURE: MYSTERY FICTION

ELSTON G. BRADFIELD, a staff member of the *Chicago Tribune,* is editor emeritus of two numismatic publications: *The Centinel* and *The Numismatist.* HOBBIES: COIN COLLECTING

BOB BROEG, sports editor of the *St. Louis Post-Dispatch,* has written articles for *The Saturday Evening Post, Sports Illustrated* and *The Sporting News.* SPORTS: BASKETBALL

WALTER J. CAMPBELL is editor of *Steel, The Metalworking Weekly.* STEEL

LEON CARNOVSKY, Ph.D., formerly managing editor of *Library Quarterly,* is a professor in the University of Chicago's Graduate Library School.
LIBRARIES

JOSEPH W. CARTER worked on the *St. Louis Post-Dispatch* and *The New York Times* before joining *Aviation Week & Space Technology* in 1964. AVIATION

JAMES CHACE was managing editor of *East Europe* magazine until late 1966 when he joined the soon-to-be-published *Interplay* magazine as managing editor. Mr. Chace contributes to *The New Republic* and is author of the book *The Rules of the Game.* EUROPE: EAST

JAMES E. CHURCHILL, JR., has worked on *Encyclopedia Year Book* for five years and is its managing editor. THEATER: DAVID MERRICK

HAROLD (SPIKE) CLAASSEN, assistant sports editor of The Associated Press, has written three books on sports. The most recent one is *The History of Professional Football.*
SPORTS: BOXING; GOLF; HIGHLIGHTS

RICHARD L. COE, drama and film critic of *The Washington Post,* has contributed articles to *The London Citizen* and the *Screen Producers' Guild Journal.* He is a guest lecturer at American University. MOTION PICTURES

ROGER CONANT, past president of the American Association of Zoological Parks and Aquariums and of the American Society of Ichthyologists and Herpetologists, became director of the Philadelphia Zoological Garden in early 1967. ZOOS

DANIEL I. COOPER, Ph.D., a nuclear physicist, is publisher of *International Science and Technology.* PHYSICS

PAUL CUNEO is book editor of *America* magazine, executive editor of *Catholic Mind,* and a member of the Catholic Book Club's selection board. LITERATURE

ROBERT E. DALLOS spent four years working on the *Wall Street Journal* before becoming a *New York Times* reporter in 1965. NEW YORK CITY

DEREK DAVIES, editor of *Far Eastern Economic Review,* lives in Hong Kong, where he also serves as correspondent of *The Financial Times* of London. INDONESIA; SOUTHEAST ASIA; SEATO; SUKARNO

PETER DESBARATS edits *Parallel,* a bimonthly magazine published in Montreal. A columnist for *The Montreal Star,* he has written two books: *The State of Quebec* and *Halibut York and More* (children's verse). CANADA: EXPO 67; MONTREAL

JACOB DESCHIN, photography editor of *The New York Times,* writes a regular column for *Popular Photography* magazine and has authored numerous books, *Your Future in Photography* and *Say It with Your Camera* among them. PHOTOGRAPHY

JOHN DORNBERG was born in Germany, grew up in the United States, and has lived and worked in Germany since 1956. He is Bonn-Berlin correspondent for *Newsweek.* BERLIN; ERHARD; GERMANY; KIESINGER

RICK DU BROW is the television critic of United Press International, which has syndicated his "Television in Review" column since 1962. He worked his way around the world as a newspaperman before settling in California. TELEVISION

JOSEPH A. DUFFY, executive director of the American Booksellers Association, has over forty years' experience in the book-publishing industry. BOOK PUBLISHING

WILLIAM J. EATON is Washington correspondent for the *Chicago Daily News.* CIVIL RIGHTS

JOHN O. ELLIS works as a meteorologist for the U.S. Environmental Science Services Administration. WEATHER

JAMES FERON has covered Israel and Cyprus for *The New York Times* since June 1965 and prior to that served in London and at the United Nations. MIDDLE EAST; NASSER

WILLIAM C. FOSTER is director of the U.S. Arms Control and Disarmament Agency. DISARMAMENT

BLAIR FRASER began working on *Maclean's* magazine in 1943 and has been its Ottawa editor, overseas editor and editor. CANADA

ORVILLE L. FREEMAN served three terms as governor of Minnesota before becoming U.S. Secretary of Agriculture in 1961. AGRICULTURE

STEPHEN P. FREIDBERG worked as director of research, European Community Information Service, Washington, D.C., before becoming assistant spokesman, Commission of the European Economic Community, Brussels. EUROPEAN ECONOMIC COMMUNITY

WILLIAM FRENCH won the President's Medal of The University of Western Ontario for distinguished ·magazine writing in 1965. He is literary editor of the *Toronto Globe and Mail.* DIEFENBAKER; MARTIN; PEARSON; TORONTO; VANIER

LAWRENCE GALTON has written two books as well as numerous pieces for *The New York Times Magazine, Reader's Digest* and *Popular Science.* He is a contributing medical editor to *Cosmopolitan* and *Family Circle.* MEDICINE

WILLIAM H. GERDTS, Ph.D., in 1966 left his post as curator of painting and sculpture at the Newark Museum to become an associate professor in the University of Maryland's art department. PAINTING AND SCULPTURE

FRANK GIFFORD, all-American back for USC and veteran of 12 seasons with the New York Giants, is WCBS-TV's director of sports. He also does a nightly 15-minute show on CBS radio and analyzes the Giant games on CBS-TV. SPORTS: FOOTBALL

JAMES L. GODDARD, M.D., was appointed commissioner of the U.S. Food and Drug Administration by President Johnson in January 1966. Prior to his appointment, Dr. Goddard served as chief of the Communicable Disease Center of the U.S. Public Health Service. DRUGS

CHARLES H. GOREN, one of the world's leading experts on bridge, has written many books on the subject. GAMES: BRIDGE

PETER GRAY, Ph.D., has headed the University of Pittsburgh's department of biology since 1947. He has published more than 40 distinguished science articles since 1926. BIOLOGICAL SCIENCES

STANLEY GREEN, an author and lecturer, contributes articles to *Reader's Digest, Saturday Review, The New York Times, The Atlantic* and other publications. RECORDINGS

PETER F. GREENE is editor of Dun & Bradstreet's *Exporters' Encyclopaedia,* a member of the National Foreign Trade Council and a director of the International Executive Association. INTERNATIONAL TRADE; TARIFFS

PHILIP GREER was assistant financial editor of the *New York Herald Tribune* before he became New York financial correspondent for *The Washington Post.* BUSINESS

STUART GRIFFIN lives in Tokyo, where he serves as East Asia correspondent for *The Observer* of London and The Observer Foreign News Service. A correspondent for NBC News, Foreign News Service, he also contributes regularly to *The Christian Science Monitor* and to *Business Week.* JAPAN; SATO; TOKYO

JAMES J. HAGGERTY has specialized in aerospace writing since 1948 and does regular columns for the *Journal of the Armed Forces* (weekly) and *Engineering Opportunities Magazine* (monthly). He is editor of *Aerospace Year Book.* MISSILES AND ROCKETS; SPACE

IRENE G. HAINES supervises the Pre-Historic Laboratory of The Oriental Institute at the University of Chicago. She has taken part in many archaeological digs. ARCHAEOLOGY

JOSEPH W. HALL, JR., with The Associated Press for more than 25 years, is on the news service's U.S. Senate staff.
CABINET; DIRKSEN; EISENHOWER; FORD; HUMPHREY; MCCORMACK; TRUMAN; WASHINGTON

DAVID E. HALVORSEN, of the *Chicago Tribune,* recently wrote for the paper a 16-article series on Chicago's progress and its future. CHICAGO

GEORGE B. HARTZOG, JR., is director of the U.S. National Park Service. PARKS

JOHN W. HAZARD has worked on *The Washington Times* and the *Wall Street Journal.* Co-author of *The Investment Business,* he is executive editor of *Changing Times,* the Kiplinger magazine.
BALANCE OF PAYMENTS

FRED M. HECHINGER lists *Pre-School Education Today* (1966) among his books. Education editor of *The New York Times,* he has received six honorary doctoral degrees and many literary awards. EDUCATION

GLADYS M. HELDMAN gave up competitive tennis to become editor and publisher of *World Tennis* magazine. With Pancho Gonzalez she wrote *Tennis.* SPORTS: TENNIS

DORIS HERING, associate editor and senior critic of *Dance Magazine,* is a member of the National Regional Ballet Board of Directors. DANCE

ARTHUR E. HESS, as director of the Bureau of Health Insurances of the Social Security Administration, oversees the U.S. Medicare program.
MEDICARE

MAYNARD K. HINE, D.D.S., is president of the American Dental Association. DENTISTRY

J. EDGAR HOOVER has headed the Federal Bureau of Investigation since 1924. CRIME

JOHN HUGHES, Far Eastern correspondent for *The Christian Science Monitor,* has published one book (*The New Face of Africa*). His articles have appeared in *The Atlantic, New Republic* and *The New Leader.* VIETNAM

ROBERT D. HURSH is editor in chief of Bancroft Whitney Co. in San Francisco.
LEGISLATION; SUPREME COURT

JOSEPH D. HUTNYAN specializes in writing about economics and finance. He is chief of the Washington bureau of the *American Banker,* a daily banking newspaper. BANKING; TAXATION

DOUGLAS HYDE has to his credit 14 books on world affairs, *The Mind Behind New China* and *Confrontation in the East* among them. Mr. Hyde spends much of every year in fact-finding travels.
MALAYSIA: COMMUNIST GUERRILLA PROBLEM

RAYMOND E. JANSSEN, Ph.D., is chairman of the geology department at Marshall University in Huntington, W. Va. GEOLOGY

DAVID R. JONES moved from a *New York Times* reporter job in Detroit to become the paper's Washington bureau labor reporter. LABOR

THOMAS O. JONES, Ph.D., director of the Division of Environmental Sciences of the National Science Foundation, worked on the foundation's Antarctic programs 1958–65. ANTARCTICA

RICHARD JOSEPH has been travel editor of *Esquire* for 20 years and a syndicated travel columnist for 7 years. He averages about 100,000 miles of travel annually. TRAVEL

JAMES S. KEAT is *The Baltimore Sun*'s New Delhi bureau chief. GANDHI; INDIA

EDWARD M. KENNEDY, Democrat from Massachusetts, was elected to the U.S. Senate in 1962. He is a member of the Senate Committee on Labor and Public Welfare. FIREARMS CONTROL

HELEN KITCHEN is editor in chief of *Africa Report,* the most widely read North American journal of African affairs, and author of *The Many, Not the Few* (1967). Mrs. Kitchen serves on the Department of State's Public Advisory Board on Africa. AFRICA

HERBERT KOSHETZ is assistant to the financial and business editor of *The New York Times.* A writer on business and financial subjects for more than 20 years, his specialty is the field of merchandising and textiles. RETAILING

HERMAN E. KRAWITZ, assistant general manager, Metropolitan Opera Association, had a major role in planning the new Met. He has been with the Metropolitan 12 years.
MUSIC: THE NEW METROPOLITAN OPERA HOUSE

CHARLES KURALT, CBS news correspondent based in New York, travels about the world covering stories for the network in Vietnam and Missouri, in Santo Domingo and Colorado. He was formerly CBS News' chief correspondent in Latin America and on the West Coast.
THE WORLD IN 1966

HARRY W. LAIDLER, Ph.D., directed the League for Industrial Democracy for nearly 50 years and is now its executive director emeritus.
SOCIALIST PARTIES

BENSON Y. LANDIS, Ph.D., edited the *Yearbook of American Churches.* Author of *Religion in the U.S.* and *World Religions,* Dr. Landis died in November 1966. RELIGION: PROTESTANTISM

JOSEPH COLLINS LAWRENCE teaches history at the University of British Columbia in Vancouver. CANADA: PRAIRIE PROVINCES; VANCOUVER

DAVID LIDMAN, stamp news editor of *The New York Times,* is chairman of the U.S. Post Office Department Stamp Advisory Committee and director-at-large of the American Philatelic Society.
HOBBIES: STAMP COLLECTING

ERNEST A. LOTITO is a reporter-editor with United Press International's Rome bureau. He did graduate work at Padua University in Italy in 1958–59. ITALY; MORO; ROME

FRANCIS L. McCARTHY, veteran of 35 years' service with United Press International, is the news service's Latin-America editor.
CUBA; DOMINICAN REPUBLIC;
LATIN AMERICA; OAS; PUERTO RICO

PAUL W. McCLOSKEY worked for the National Catholic Welfare Conference News Service in Washington, D.C., for 13 years before joining the Commerce Department in 1966.
PAUL VI, POPE; RELIGION: ROMAN CATHOLICISM

THOMAS F. McGARRY is special assistant for public affairs in the U.S. Bureau of Public Roads.
HIGHWAYS

RICHARD F. MAIN is a *Los Angeles Times* reporter. LOS ANGELES

MARK MANCALL, Ph.D., teaches history at Stanford University. He formerly taught at Harvard, where he was a research fellow at the university's East Asian Research Center.
CHINA; CHOU EN-LAI; MAO TSE-TUNG; TAIWAN

DAVID M. MASON has covered assignments in Africa, the Middle East and Great Britain. He is now news editor of the Paris bureau of The Associated Press.
DE GAULLE; EUROPE; FRANCE; NATO; PARIS

FRED D. MOORE, associate editor of *Encyclopedia International,* edited that encyclopedia's art and architecture content. He is also an associate editor on *Encyclopedia Year Book.* ARCHITECTURE

BRUCE MUNN joined United Press International in 1938 and has been its chief United Nations correspondent since 1949. In 1957 and 1958 he was president of the UN Correspondents Association. THANT; UNITED NATIONS

STAN MUSIAL, a star baseball player for the St. Louis Cardinals for 22 years, has been Consultant to the President on Physical Fitness since 1964.
PUBLIC HEALTH: PHYSICAL FITNESS

EUGENE R. NICOLAI, public information officer to the Secretary of the Interior, has worked in the Department of the Interior since 1941.
CONSERVATION

JOHN G. NORRIS was *The Washington Post*'s military reporter before he became assistant foreign editor for the paper in 1966.
ARMED FORCES; DEFENSE; NUCLEAR TESTING

LAWRENCE F. O'BRIEN is Postmaster General of the United States. POSTAL SERVICES

JAMES V. O'GARA, executive editor of *Advertising Age,* also teaches at Fordham University.
ADVERTISING

ARTHUR M. OKUN, Ph.D., holds a professorship of economics at Yale University but is currently on leave, serving as a member of President Johnson's Council of Economic Advisers.
ECONOMICS: A LOOK AT THE NEW ECONOMICS

FRED OLMSTED was city editor of *The Detroit Free Press* before becoming its automotive writer.
AUTOMOBILES

EDWARD P. PARKER, executive vice president of Parker Brothers, Inc. (a leading U.S. manufacturer of games), has been with the firm since 1934. GAMES: TRENDS AND TWISTS

LESTER B. PEARSON is prime minister of Canada. CANADA: EXPO 67 INTRODUCTION

ROGER V. PIERCE, a consulting engineer, is a past president of the American Institute of Mining, Metallurgical and Petroleum Engineers. MINING

HENRY POPKIN, Ph.D., professor of English at the State University of New York in Buffalo, edited *The Concise Encyclopedia of Modern Drama.* His pieces on drama have appeared in *Life, The Times* of London and *The Nation.*
THEATER

SHIRLEY POVICH is sports editor of *The Washington Post.* SPORTS: BASEBALL

HOWARD PYLE is president of the National Safety Council. ACCIDENTS; AUTOMOBILES: SAFETY

JOHN QUIRT covers Wall Street for CBS News and WCBS-TV, New York. As a financial writer he contributes regularly to national publications; prior to his radio-TV career he worked on *Forbes* magazine and the *New York Herald Tribune.*
STOCK MARKET

DALTON ROBERTSON worked on *Canadian Business* (the publication of the Canadian Chamber of Commerce) before joining *The Financial Post,* leading Canadian business newspaper.
CANADA: ECONOMIC REVIEW

ARTHUR M. ROSS is commissioner of labor statistics in the U.S. Department of Labor.
COST OF LIVING; EMPLOYMENT

WILLIAM L. RYAN is an expert on the Soviet Union and world communism. News analyst for The Associated Press, he has visited about 80 countries. BREZHNEV; COMMUNISM;
KOSYGIN; MOSCOW; U.S.S.R.

CHRISTINE SADLER, Washington editor of *McCall's,* has two books to her credit: *America's First Ladies* and *Children of the White House.*
JOHNSON (CLAUDIA)

ELI SALTZ, Ph.D. holds a professorship in psychology and directs the Center for the Study of Cognitive Processes at Wayne State University, Detroit, Mich. PSYCHOLOGY

DAVID SARNOFF is chairman of the board of Radio Corporation of America and a pioneer in the field of electronic communications.
COMMUNICATIONS: A LOOK AT
ELECTRONICS AND PRINTING

ROBERT J. SHAW is assistant to the executive secretary, Library Administration Division, American Library Association.
AMERICAN LIBRARY ASSOCIATION

SARGENT SHRIVER has headed the Office of Economic Opportunity since it was formed in 1964. He directed the Peace Corps from 1961 until January 1966.
POVERTY

GODFREY SPERLING, JR., is assistant chief of the Washington news bureau of *The Christian Science Monitor* and the chief national political writer for the paper.
ELECTIONS

NEAL STANFORD, Washington staff correspondent for *The Christian Science Monitor* since 1941, is a contributing editor to the Foreign Policy Association *Bulletin*. He also writes for the *Foreign Service Journal*.
FOREIGN AID

FRED B. STAUFFER, formerly transportation editor of the *New York Herald Tribune,* joined the staff of the new *World Journal Tribune* in 1966.
TRANSPORTATION

WILLIAM H. STEWART, M.D., an officer of U.S. Public Health Service since 1951, became surgeon general of the U.S. Public Health Service in 1965. In an earlier post he supervised the Division of Public Health Methods.
PUBLIC HEALTH

WILLIAM H. STRINGER is chief of *The Christian Science Monitor's* London bureau. Prior to this assignment he headed the paper's Washington bureau.
ELIZABETH II; GREAT BRITAIN; LONDON; WILSON

HAROLD SUSSMAN is Charles Kriser Fellow at New York University. He also lectures on anthropology at New York City's Cooper Union.
ANTHROPOLOGY

WILLIAM H. TAFT, Ph.D., author of two books on the history of Missouri newspapers, is professor of journalism at the University of Missouri.
MAGAZINES; NEWSPAPERS

J. F. terHORST has covered Washington since 1957 and has been Washington bureau chief of *The Detroit News* since 1961. Foreign assignments have taken him to the Middle East, Europe and southeast Asia. Mr. terHorst writes a twice-weekly column syndicated by the North American Newspaper Alliance.
JOHNSON (LYNDON B.); U.S.: THE WASHINGTON SCENE

JACK C. THOMPSON, for 36 years a meteorologist with the U.S. Weather Bureau, is now a professor of meterology at San Jose State College, San Jose, Calif.
METEOROLOGY

PATRICIA TOPPING is secretary of the research committee of the Arctic Institute of North America.
ARCTIC

JOHN P. TULLY, Ph.D., became oceanographic consultant to the chairman of the Fisheries Research Board of Canada in 1966. Dr. Tully also serves as secretary of the Canadian Committee on Oceanography.
OCEANOGRAPHY

JACK H. VAUGHN was appointed director of the Peace Corps in 1966. Previously Mr. Vaughn was assistant secretary of state for inter-American affairs and regional director of the Peace Corps, 1961–64.
PEACE CORPS

JERRY VOORHIS, author of *American Cooperatives*, is president and executive director of the Cooperative League of the U.S.A.
COOPERATIVES

A. JAMES WAGNER is research meteorologist in the U.S. Weather Bureau's Extended Forecast Division.
WEATHER: JET STREAMS, PLANETARY WAVES, AND WEATHER PATTERNS

JACK WAX is editor and publisher of the monthly trade magazine *Profitable Hobby Merchandising*.
HOBBIES

ROBERT C. WEAVER was appointed Secretary of Housing and Urban Development by President Johnson in 1966.
URBAN DEVELOPMENT

JUNE A. WILLENZ is executive director of the American Veterans Committee in Washington, D.C.
VETERANS

SHELDON WILLIAMS is London art correspondent for the international edition of the *New York Herald Tribune-Washington Post*.
PAINTING AND SCULPTURE: EUROPEAN

JOHN S. WILSON, a free-lance music writer, is author of several books including *Jazz: The Transition Years, 1940–1960*, published in 1966.
MUSIC: POPULAR

PAUL WOODRING, education editor-at-large of *Saturday Review,* is currently distinguished service professor of Western Washington State College, Bellingham, Wash.
EDUCATION: PRESSURES

MAX WYKES-JOYCE is a free-lance writer living in London who regularly contributes to such publications as the *London Times Supplement, Connoisseur, Truth and Books* and *Bookmen*.
LITERATURE: EUROPEAN

RICHARD YAFFE, manager of the American Bureau of the *London Jewish Chronicle* and editor of *Israel Horizons,* has served as special Eastern Europe correspondent for CBS and on the staff of the New York *Post*.
RELIGION: JUDAISM

R. M. YOUNGER, a free-lance Australian writer, is author of *Australia and the Australians: A Short History,* published in 1966. For four years Mr. Younger was director of the Australian News and Information Bureau in New York City.
AUSTRALIA; NEW ZEALAND

ILLUSTRATORS

GEORGE BUCTEL   GRAPHICS INSTITUTE
FREDERICK C. HOLMES   CHET RENESON

THE

WORLD IN REVIEW

THE WORLD IN 1966

By CHARLES KURALT
CBS NEWS CORRESPONDENT

A good case could be made for the proposition that 1966 was the year the world began to go mad. It was the year the United States mislaid a hydrogen bomb; the Chinese cut off one another's pigtails in a parody of *1984*; the Russians banned *Hello, Dolly!* and the Arabs banned Coca-Cola. In the United States it was the year young civil-rights activists demanded "black power," and the year young theologians exclaimed, "God is dead!", and the year a young woman told a Senate investigating committee, "Everybody I know uses LSD except my grandmother."

The principal fact of life during the year in Europe was a bitter quarrel among friends; in Africa, intertribal bloodletting; in Asia, the savage Vietnam war. Even in Latin America, of all places, an old-fashioned arms race began during the year.

There were shocking incidents of mass murder in every corner of the world: Thousands were killed in bloody outbreaks in Nigeria; tens of thousands were slaughtered following the downfall of President Sukarno in Indonesia; in the United States, in a two-week period of July and August, eight student nurses were slain by an intruder in Chicago, and an honor student at the University of Texas shot 46 persons, killing 16.

However 1966 history is recorded, it will not be as a reasonable or peaceful year.

War in Vietnam. The Vietnam war was the bloodiest conflict of all. It cost the lives of 15,600 U.S. and Allied troops during the year. In addition, it spoiled hopes for an improvement in U.S.-Soviet relationships; it served as a wedge of misunderstanding between the United States and its friends in Europe; and it threatened to divert funds from "Great Society" programs of President Johnson at home.

The war's escalation was relentless. For each new battalion of North Vietnamese troops which infiltrated into the South, the United States landed more soldiers of its own. By year's end, there were more than 350,000 United States troops in the field, not counting about 40,000 Navy men manning ships offshore, and thousands of airmen based in Thailand and Guam who daily bombed military

Wide World

The earth hangs in the sky alongside the moon's horizon in this Aug. 23 picture taken by Lunar Orbiter 1 camera.

and industrial targets in communist North Vietnam.

While pursuing the war, President Johnson searched urgently for a way to end it. Few were the foreign capitals which did not receive a visit from Secretary of State Dean Rusk, Vice-President Hubert H. Humphrey, Ambassador Averell Harriman or some lesser emissary on a Vietnam peace mission. In October, the President himself (who had made brief trips to Canada and Mexico earlier during the year) took off on a 17-day, flying visit to seven Asian and Pacific nations, including a summit conference in Manila, at which he pledged that the United States would withdraw from Vietnam within six months if North Vietnam would recall its troops from the battlefield. That offer was called "shameless humbug" by the Communist Chinese; and the North Vietnamese, in abusive terms, said the only basis for negotiation on the war was complete evacuation of U.S. military forces.

As the war grew in size, so did the debate on the rightness and morality of it. Protest demonstrations were held in several American cities in the spring and summer; and after public, televised Senate hearings on the war, Senator J. William Fulbright (D-Ark.), chairman of the Foreign Relations Committee, concluded that in Vietnam, "We are acting like a Boy Scout dragging reluctant old ladies across streets they do not want to cross." Senator Fulbright, a leading critic of the war, said he was concerned that the United States might be succumbing to the "arrogance of power." President Johnson replied that this country was using its power in Vietnam not willingly and recklessly, but reluctantly and with restraint. He spoke of "Nervous Nellies" and "those who will break ranks under the strain."

There was no doubt, however, that the strain was beginning to have its effect on the American people. President Johnson's personal popularity, as reflected in public-opinion polls, dropped greatly.

In South Vietnam, President Nguyen Cao Ky had his own popularity problems, and they took more dramatic form. For much of the year, Buddhists and other opponents struggled to bring his Government down, and for a time actually took over whole cities in a kind of war within a war. Ky hung on with U.S. support, and some steam was taken out of his Opposition by successful constituent-assembly elections Sept. 11, in which 80 per cent of the registered voters went to the polls. Such limited

China's Mao Tse-tung (foreground) takes a swim in the Yangtze River and reportedly breaks a record.

UPI

15

U.S. 7th Fleet lands amphibious tractors of 1st Bn., 26th Marines, near Ham Tam, Vietnam.

successes for U.S. goals, however, did little to ease American apprehensions that the war might drag on for years.

China. The fear that Communist China might enter the war was eased somewhat by abundant evidence that the Chinese had troubles of their own. A struggle for power within the government hierarchy pitted Communist Party Chief Mao Tse-tung and his heir apparent, Defense Minister Lin Piao, against apparently more conservative opponents. As a result, the Great Proletarian Cultural Revolution, di-

North Vietnamese leader Ho Chi Minh at Hanoi meeting.

rected by Lin Piao, purged dozens of officials suspected of "bourgeois" activities, among them Peking Mayor Peng Chen, who had been one of China's 10 top leaders. The young Red Guards, in support of the purge, declared their intention to sweep away "all old influences, ideas, culture, customs, and habits." From a modest beginning with traffic lights—red, they demanded, should henceforth mean "go"—they went on to cut off pigtails in the streets, destroy businesses they considered "bourgeois," enter private homes searching for Western books, break up Greek and Roman works of art, and strip people in public of their Western-style clothing. It was a kind of national hysteria that seems to have gone further than the Government intended. Western observers of China suggested that, for the moment, China was looking inward, not outward, and in the absence of a direct threat, did not seem likely to involve itself directly in an Asian war.

An ominous note for the future issued out of China during the year, however. The Chinese announced, and Western intelligence sources confirmed, that China had test-fired a medium-range ballistic missile armed with a nuclear warhead. The best guess of the missile's range was 400 miles—a range great enough to pose a threat to several noncommunist neighbors.

The neighbor of China with whom it was on the worst terms during 1966 was its most powerful one—the Soviet Union. The Chinese-Soviet split seemed irreconcilable; China rejected an invitation to the 23d Communist Party Congress in Moscow, with the accusation that the Soviet Union was in the hands of "revisionists" who "are working hand in hand with the United States in a whole series of "dirty deals." The Russians fired back, "The Chinese Government is guilty of adventurism, splitism, Trotskyism, nationalism, chauvinism and dogmatism." There were reports that both countries strengthened border defenses.

De Gaulle. The United States' quarrel with one of its own Allies was less virulent, less explosive, but no less real. France, while by no means an enemy, ended 1966 much less a friend. The reason was Charles de Gaulle, who on Jan. 8 began his second seven-year term as president. He declared, "The Western world is no longer threatened," and on that principle, he took France's military forces out of the North Atlantic Treaty Organization, and ordered NATO out of France. At 75, he traveled to the Soviet Union (where he became the first French head of state since Napoleon to sleep in the Kremlin), and to Asia (where he demanded U.S. withdrawal from Vietnam in a speech to 100,000 people in Pnompenh, Cambodia). De Gaulle angered British, as well as American, officials. British Defense Minister Denis Healey, in fact, had to apologize to the House of Commons for his outburst: "De Gaulle is a bad ally in NATO and a bad partner in the Common Market. . . . Nobody trusts him in Europe." But De Gaulle, determined that France live up to his idea of its grandeur, moved his country grandly forward on an independent course.

Great Britain. Britain, meantime, struggled through a maze of "end of Empire" crises. Prime Minister Harold Wilson's Labor Party won a landslide election victory March 31, increasing its parliamentary majority from three seats to 97. Prime Minister Wilson enjoyed few other victories. He was forced into agonizing, finally unsuccessful negotiations with the rebellious Government of Rhodesia after economic sanctions failed to sway the white Rhodesians to Britain's will. Britain's prestige, and the black Rhodesian majority, were the losers. England also suffered a 45-day merchant-seaman's strike, "an attack on the jugular," that idled more than a third of its ships and damaged its already weak economy. In an effort to shore up the economy, Mr. Wilson announced the most drastic restraints ever imposed in Britain: an absolute wage-price freeze for six months, and severe controls after that.

United States. Americans, too, had cause to worry about the economy. At the year's beginning, in his economic report to Congress, President Johnson said, "Perhaps our most serious economic challenge in 1966 will be to preserve the essential stability of costs and prices." And that is about the way it worked out. Before the year was over, housewives in dozens of cities had found a common enemy: the supermarket. Women picketed and organized boycotts in an effort to force food prices down—but food prices continued to climb,

French President de Gaulle (l), Belgian Prime Minister Paul Van Den Boeyants (r, foreground) and Belgian Foreign Minister Pierre Harmel discuss the Common Market and NATO.

UPI

along with prices of other basic commodities. A number of big strikes, including a 43-day strike against major airlines, added to the inflationary tendency of the economy. The administration took several moves intended to discourage investment and "shift the economy into lower gear." But the gears were still grinding a bit at year's end, and it was widely speculated that the President would seek a general tax increase early in the new year in a further anti-inflationary move.

The President stuck, however, to his contention that it was still possible for the country to have both guns and butter; that the Vietnam war should not be an excuse for cutting down on his social-welfare program at home. He sought, and got, a twelfth cabinet position, a Department of Transportation, to wrestle with the transportation problems of a mobile people. The administration also won from the Congress a measure to end water pollution in several river basins, a speedup of certain aspects of the "war on poverty," and a rise in the minimum wage for American workers to $1.40 an hour, beginning in 1967, with a further rise to $1.60 in 1968. The Congress also agreed to set safety standards for American automobiles after a furor stirred up by author Ralph Nader's *Unsafe at Any Speed*.

But the 1966 civil-rights bill, including a ban on discrimination in the sale or rental of hous-

Wide World
Budget director Charles Schultze, LBJ and the budget.

Ralph Nader, author *Unsafe at Any Speed*; (r) Secretary of Transportation Alan S. Boyd.

Photos UPI

ing, failed to pass. Many observers read this defeat as a white reaction against the steady gains of the civil-rights movement in recent years, and specifically against what many considered excesses in the movement. These were grouped under a rallying cry first heard in 1966: "black power."

The young chairman of the Student Non-Violent Coordinating Committee, Stokely Carmichael, refused to explain exactly what he meant by the expression, but National Director Floyd B. McKissick of CORE, in endorsing the concept, was more explicit. "As long as the white man has all the power and money, nothing will happen," he said. "The only way to achieve meaningful change is to take power." Other civil-rights leaders publicly disagreed, but the expression "black power" was heard frequently on such occasions as the march of James Meredith through Mississippi. Meredith, a Negro whose enrollment at the University of Mississippi in 1962 made him the focus of racial violence, attempted early in June to try to encourage Negro voter registration with a pilgrimage down a Mississippi highway. He was shot from ambush and wounded, whereupon other civil-rights leaders took up his march to the state capitol at Jackson.

Never before was racial rioting so widespread in the United States as in the summer of 1966. The smallest incident seemed suffi-

In person and in bronze: President Lyndon B. Johnson.

Atlanta, Ga., Negroes learn how to fill out voter-registration forms.

In Saigon conference are (l to r) Lodge, Ky, McNamara and Katzenbach.

cient cause for shooting and fire-bombing. In Chicago a policeman shut off the stream from a fire hydrant in which Negro youths had been playing; 2 Negroes were killed, scores wounded and 372 arrested in the 4 days of rioting which followed. In Baltimore a racist white preacher gave a speech, and teen-aged white gangs invaded a Negro section to cause trouble. In Grenada, Miss., the cause was the entrance into previously all-white schools of a handful of Negro children. A mob of whites attacked and beat the children and their parents with ax handles and chains as police, in some instances, looked on without interfering. There were other disturbances causing death or injury, and property damage, in Los Angeles, San Francisco and Oakland, Calif.; Atlanta, Ga.; Cleveland and Dayton, O.; Jacksonville, Fla.; Waukegan, Ill.; Detroit, Lansing and Benton Harbor, Mich.; Omaha, Neb.; Brooklyn and Troy, N.Y., and some 20 other American cities.

In the midst of this racial turmoil, it is worth noting, the United States got its first Negro cabinet member, Dr. Robert C. Weaver, who was appointed Secretary of Housing and Urban Development; and its first Negro Senator since Reconstruction, Edward W. Brooke, who was elected in Massachusetts.

It is also worth noting, however, that Mr. Brooke was elected as a Republican. With Vietnam, inflation and racial disturbances on their minds, the voters in the off-year election went heavily antiadministration. The Republican Party made a net gain of 47 seats in the House of Representatives, three seats in the Senate and eight governorships. Among the major GOP victories, film star Ronald Reagan was elected governor of California. Gov. George Romney was reelected easily in Michigan. Charles H. Percy defeated veteran Democratic Senator Paul H. Douglas in Illinois. All three were considered possible Republican presidential candidates for 1968. Spiro T. Agnew and Winthrop Rockefeller won the governorships of Maryland and Arkansas against white-supremacist opponents, and Mr. Rockefeller's brother, Nelson, was reelected governor of New York in a surprising landslide. The governorship of Georgia was left in doubt. Neither Lester Maddox, Democrat, nor Howard Callaway, Republican, won a majority of votes on election day. Weeks later, the U.S. Supreme Court ruled that Georgia's legislature could choose between them, and in the heavily Democratic legislature, Mr. Maddox, an extreme segregationist, was declared governor in January 1967.

International Developments. As nonpresidential election years go in the United States, 1966 was an interesting year. Politics in certain other countries was positively spectacular.

Two demagogic national leaders, one in Africa, one in Asia, were surprised during the year to find themselves out of office—President Kwame Nkrumah, of Ghana, known as "His Messianic Majesty," and "The Redeemer"; and President Sukarno of Indonesia, known as "The Eternal Leader."

Nkrumah was ousted *in absentia*. He was on his way to Peking when a group of Army dissidents led by Lt. Gen. Joseph A. Ankrah took

President Joseph Mobutu (Congo, Kinshasa) waves during parade.

over the country, promising to reduce the influence of communist countries upon Ghana and follow a policy of strict neutrality. Nkrumah was found to have amassed a fortune of more than $7 million, including personally owned newspapers, surburban houses and an office building. He took asylum in Guinea.

Sukarno also bowed to the strength of the army. He turned over power to Lt. Gen. Suharto, following weeks of violent anticommunist demonstrations. During the spring, some 400,-000 Indonesians who were suspected of communist sympathies, or who had declared themselves pro-Sukarno, or who were simply in the wrong place at the wrong time, were slaughtered in Jakarta and in the provinces, one of the worst bloodbaths in world history. Sukarno's former Foreign Minister Subandrio was sentenced to death after a trial. A political result of Sukarno's ouster was a peace agreement with Malaysia, which Sukarno had always threatened to "destroy." Sukarno stayed on in his country, under virtual house arrest.

In South Africa, Prime Minister Hendrik Verwoerd, 64, apostle of apartheid, was stabbed to death at a session of Parliament. His assassin was Dimitrio Tsafendas, whose complaint, ironically, was that Verwoerd was "doing too much for the nonwhites." The new prime minister was Balthazar Johannes Vorster, a pro-Nazi during World War II.

India's leadership changed during the year in a less flamboyant but no less important development. Prime Minister Lal Bahadur Shastri, 61, died in the Soviet Union one day after signing a political accord with Pakistan designed to end the armed struggle over Kashmir. Mrs. Indira Gandhi, 48, daughter of former Prime Minister Nehru, was elected to succeed Shastri and immediately plunged into her work with characteristic energy, visiting the United States, France, Britain and the U.S.S.R. to seek help for India's growing food problem.

South African Prime Minister Balthazar Johannes Vorster.
South African Information Service

There was even a small change in the Government of Spain during the year. Generalissimo Francisco Franco, most durable of the world's dictators, granted a charter which gave Spain a limited amount of democracy.

Problems of the past came back to haunt several governments during 1966: Ancient Arab-Israeli hatred exploded again in the Middle East. After suffering nuisance attacks on its borders, mostly directed from Syria, Israel struck back in November with an armed raid on a village in Jordan. The results: censure of Israel by the United Nations, pressure on Jordan's moderate King Hussein from his Palestinian subjects to retaliate, and the fear of a new outbreak of Arab-Israeli fighting.

Moroccan suspicion of the French, and vice versa, lay at the base of the complicated "Ben Barka affair," which caused France and Morocco to recall ambassadors from each other's capitals. Exiled Moroccan opposition leader Mehdi Ben Barka had been kidnaped and apparently murdered in Paris. France blamed Moroccan Interior Minister Mohammed Oufkir and two conspirators and demanded their return from Morocco for trial. Morocco rejected the demand initially, then in November sent Lt. Col. Ahmed Dlimi, head of the Moroccan State Security Service, to Paris to stand trial. The case was still unresolved at year's end.

Old U.S.-Soviet suspicions cropped up again in the case of Newcomb Mott, 27, an American textbook salesman convicted by the Russians of having crossed the Soviet border illegally and sentenced to prison. He died Jan. 20, and the Russians called his death suicide. But the belief of many Americans involved in the case was that he was murdered.

Yet another matter involving hard feelings of the past was simply a marriage: Crown Princess Beatrix of the Netherlands provoked wide criticism in her own country by choosing to marry a German who was a former member of the Hitler Youth, Claus von Amsberg. But marry him she did and the furor died away.

Black African governments went through the agonies of nationhood. The vast federation that is Nigeria suffered an undeclared tribal war between the majority Hausa tribesmen and the wealthier, better-educated Ibo tribesmen in the Northern Region. The massacre of Ibos continued until virtually all of them were either dead or evacuated from Hausa territory. Uncounted thousands of Ibos lost their lives, and two federal premiers were assassinated. Lt. Col. Yakubu Gowon, a Hausa, took power Aug. 1.

Violent changes of government also took place in Uganda, Burundi, Central African Republic and Upper Volta, but even in the midst of these alarms, three still newer African countries were created. Malawi became the British Commonwealth's ninth republic, with Dr. Hastings Banda as the first president. Bechuanaland became Botswana, and Basutoland became Lesotho, Africa's newest independent states.

Two new governments came into being in the Western Hemisphere: British Guiana became Guyana May 25 with Dr. Forbes Burnham as prime minister; Barbados won its independence Nov. 30. And the turbulent Dominican Republic tried again to make a go of it as a democratic country. Dr. Joaquin Balaguer was elected president and the last troops of the Inter-American Peace Force (mostly U.S. troops) who had been sent to Santo

In October, accord was reached between Iraq's President Abdul Rahman Arif (l) and Mustafa Barzani, leader of rebelling Kurdish tribesmen.

UPI

Above: Greece's new Premier, Ioannis Paraskevopoulos (r), and Foreign Minister, Pavlos Economou-Gouras. Right: At Moscow Airport (l to r) Patolichev, Gromyko, Wilson, Roderick (of British Embassy), interpreter and Kosygin.

Domingo in 1965 to restore order were removed.

Kurt Kiesinger, a Nazi in his youth, became chancellor of West Germany, succeeding Ludwig Erhard. Radical Leftist military men took over the Government of Syria, and resumed diplomatic relations with the United Arab Republic. Radical Rightist military men took over the Government of Argentina, and set about closing down universities and arresting people suspected of sympathy with former dictator Juan Peron.

In Canada, a member of Prime Minister Lester Pearson's Cabinet charged that several members of the Cabinet of former Prime Minister John Diefenbaker had been involved in liaisons with an East German woman "spy," Mrs. Gerda Munsinger. The resulting uproar permeated Canadian political life all year, and at one point very nearly brought down the Pearson Government.

In Latin America, Chile, Argentina, Venezuela and Peru competed hotly in the purchase of expensive jet fighters, mostly for reasons of national pride. Brazil sought to buy modern U.S. tanks.

The most peaceful international development may have been the change of Government in Australia, where Harold E. Holt replaced Sir Robert Menzies as prime minister without fuss or bother, after Sir Robert explained: "I am tired."

U.S.S.R.-U.S. Space Gains. Exploration of outer space yielded achievements of solid substance in 1966, and there was even an achievement of some magnitude on earth: the United States and the Soviet Union agreed on a treaty to ban weapons of mass destruction from outer space, and to prevent military exploitations of the moon and the planets. Since the two countries appeared to be in a neck-and-neck race to the moon, the treaty offered some hope that reaching it would be a cause for rejoicing on earth, rather than a source of apprehension.

Both U.S. and Soviet scientists sent unmanned scientific spaceships to the moon during the year. The Russian Luna 9 made the first "soft" landing Feb. 3 (really a bouncing, rolling landing) and after releasing a few elementary photographs transmitted by the craft, set off a brisk controversy about the nature of the moon's surface. Said Soviet scientist Nikolai Barabashov: "It is spongelike." Said Britain's Sir Bernard Lovell: "It is like pumice stone." Said America's Dr. Gerard P. Kuiper: "It is the consistency of crunchy snow." Four months later the United States' Surveyor 1 answered many of the questions by making a perfect soft landing on the moon, and, standing upright, sent back hundreds of photographs of the moon's surface, its own shadow, and even its own foot, anchored in moon soil. The photos showed a firm surface, peppered by micrometeorite bits, but with no loose dust. In the near distance, there was a boulder field, and in the far distance, a mountain.

In the meantime, men were mastering the skills necessary to reach and walk on that surface. The United States launched no fewer than five 2-man orbital space missions, which achieved a new altitude record (850 miles above the earth) and proved that men could achieve a rendezvous with other orbiting spacecraft and accomplish useful work while floating free outside a space capsule. The five missions completed the Gemini series of flights.

The Russians announced no manned flights in 1966, but both countries orbited photo ships around the moon to seek out landing places for their astronauts. The United States sent up weather satellites for advance information on weather movements. The Russians crashed a spaceship into Venus, the first man-made object to touch another planet.

Disasters, Law, Religion. The year had more than its quota of natural disasters. Among the worst were earthquakes in Turkey Aug. 19–23, which left about 2,300 people dead, 1,500 injured, and a staggering 100,000 homeless. Torrential rains brought terrible flood damage to art treasures and ancient buildings of Florence and Venice during November. An avalanche of coal slag crashed down on the Welsh village of Aberfan Oct. 21, engulfing a school and a row of miners' cottages and killing 144. January floods and landslides brought down several of the hillside shantytowns of Rio de Janeiro, killing 239. Bad weather also played a part in the year's worst air and sea accidents. Thick fog at Tokyo contributed to the loss of 321 lives in three separate air crashes there in February and March, and a storm at sea broke up the ferry boat *Heraklion* in the Aegean on Dec. 8, with a loss of some 234 persons.

In the world of law, there were several landmark decisions of the U.S. Supreme Court.

Richard Kiley in the musical drama *Man of La Mancha*.

Perhaps most important, the court issued what amounted to a list of dos and don'ts for police in dealing with persons suspected of crimes. Among other things, the court said, suspects must be advised of their right to remain silent and to have a lawyer present at their questioning. The court voided the poll tax in state elections as unconstitutional, and broadened the base of evidence (some said confusingly so) on which books can be judged obscene.

In the world of religion, unification of Christian churches came a step closer as Pope Paul expressed the wish that they might someday be joined, and the Archbishop of Canterbury and the World Council of Churches concurred. More than one church-state controversy entered the news. The Government of Poland refused permission for the Pope to enter the country for rites marking 1,000 years of Christianity there, so Stefan Cardinal Wyszynski presided over the ceremony, and 300,000 Polish Catholics attended. In the United States, Senate Minority Leader Everett Dirksen pleaded, "They teach the little children sex in the schools. They teach them about communism. They even teach them ballet! Why not God Almighty?" But Senator Dirksen's constitutional amendment to permit prayers in public schools failed to pass the Congress.

Arts, Medicine, Sports. In the world of the arts, there were two great literary controversies. In the Soviet Union, writers Andrei Sinyavski and Yuli M. Daniel, whose works branded "anti-Soviet" were published abroad under pseudonyms, received sentences of prison terms at hard labor, in spite of a public appeal from Soviet and Western authors and critics. In the United States, Mrs. John F. Kennedy sued to prevent publication by *Look* magazine and Harper & Row of certain parts of a book by William Manchester, *The Death of a President*, dealing with President Kennedy's assassination. Mrs. Kennedy found sections dealing with her own recollections of the event "tasteless and distorted," and, outside of court, won agreement that they be deleted.

Pulitzer Prizes were awarded *The Collected Stories of Katherine Anne Porter* (which also won the National Book Award for fiction) and to Arthur M. Schlesinger's history of the Kennedy administration, *A Thousand Days*. In the New York theater, the sellout hit of the year was *Mame*. Tony awards for plays went to the unorthodox drama *Marat/Sade* and to the musical *Man of La Mancha*. Oscar awards for motion pictures went to *The Sound of Music* and to actress Julie Christie for *Darling* and actor Lee Marvin for *Cat Ballou*. The Metropolitan Opera opened its 1966–67 season in a new $45 million opera house at New York's Lincoln Center for the Performing Arts.

In the world of medicine, a kind of revolution occurred in 1966. More than 17 million elderly Americans signed up for the voluntary medical-insurance section of the Medicare law, which went into effect July 1. Two types of partial "artificial hearts" were tried with limited success in Houston and in New York. Nobel Prizes for medicine went to Dr. Francis Peyton Rous of Rockefeller University, New York, and to Dr. Charles Brenton Huggins of the University of Chicago, for their research on cancer. Best publicized operation of the year: the removal of a small polyp from the throat of President Lyndon B. Johnson, and a repair of the scar from his old gallbladder operation.

In the world of sports, 1966 was the year the Yankees finished last. The Baltimore Orioles finished first in the American League and went on to beat the Los Angeles Dodgers four straight in the World Series. The Dodgers' great pitcher, Sandy Koufax, announced his retirement. The Green Bay Packers reigned as champions of the National Football League, the Buffalo Bills as champs of the American Football League. The leagues announced a merger, on the model of baseball's major leagues. The Boston Celtics won their eighth straight pro-basketball championship. Cassius Clay successfully defended his heavyweight boxing title five times. In golf, Billy Casper won the U.S. Open in a playoff with Arnold Palmer, and Jack Nicklaus won the Masters Tournament in a three-man playoff. Jim Ryun, 19, of the University of Kansas, became the first American mile-run record holder since 1934, by running a mile in 3:51.3. A horse named Kauai King won the Kentucky Derby and the Preakness. The most remarkable sports achievement of the year, by any yardstick, was brought to light in a Chinese announcement that Mao Tse-tung, to demonstrate his fitness, swam 15 kilometers in 65 minutes in the Yangtze River. His time was considerably better than the world's record.

A Strange, Marvelous Year. It is possible, of course, that these great events may not be the things most people remember about 1966 at all.

The people of the Spanish town of Palomares will no doubt remember 1966, instead, as the year the bomb fell out of the sky. After an American B-52 collided with the tanker refueling it over Palomares, one of the plane's hydrogen bombs was discovered to be missing. Weeks later, it was recovered from the nearby ocean and displayed, slightly dented, to newsmen.

Wide World
Dodger Sandy Koufax announces retirement from baseball.

The men of France will surely remember 1966 as the year they lost their status. The Government repealed parts of the 1804 Napoleonic Code, and gave wives the right to work or to have a bank account without the permission of their husbands—and suddenly connubial *fraternité* in France had more *liberté* and *egalité*.

Britons will remember 1966 as the beginning of the end of their ancient and familiar (and illogical) system of money which dated back to the Saxon kingdoms. After a century of debate, it was announced that Britain would institute a decimal system of pounds and pence in 1971.

And Americans? Well, for Americans it was the year uniform daylight saving time was voted in, ending a hodgepodge of summer time zones. It was the year theologians argued whether "God is dead," a theory most ordinary churchgoers failed to grasp. It was the year college students discovered the mind-transporting drug, LSD, in such great numbers that the Food and Drug Administration was forced to detour the LSD "trips" by cutting down on the supply. It was the year Dr. Sam Sheppard was finally acquitted of murdering his wife; the year Luci Baines Johnson, younger daughter of the President, was wed; and so were Frank Sinatra, 50, (to Mia Farrow, 21), and Supreme Court Justice William O. Douglas, 67, (to Cathleen Curran Heffernan, 23).

It was a strange and marvelous year. And if, near the end of it, the Secretary-General of the United Nations, U Thant, sadly decided that "the pressure of world events is remorselessly leading toward a major war," and announced his retirement, who could blame him?

But, in the end, even U Thant was persuaded to stay on, to try to make it through 1967 with everyone else.

THE MILITARY BALANCE SHEET 1966

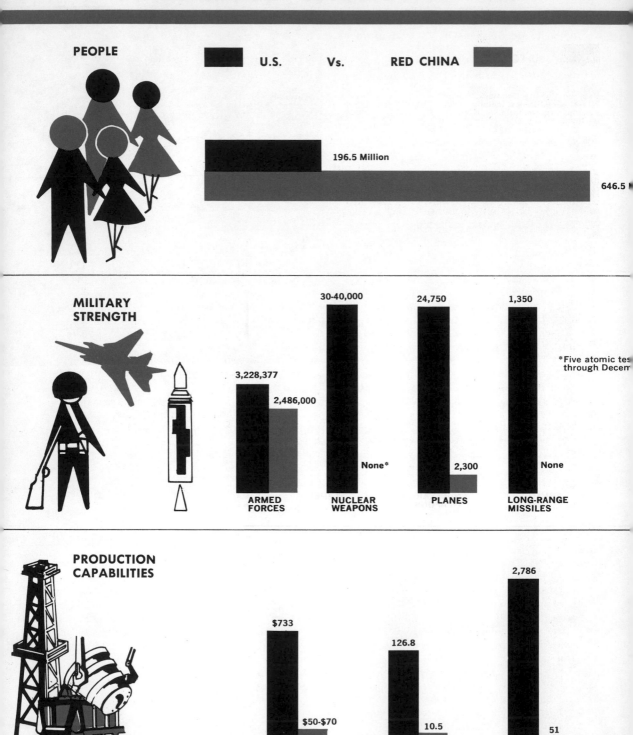

PEOPLE

U.S.   Vs.   RED CHINA

196.5 Million

646.5

MILITARY STRENGTH

*Five atomic tes through Decem

	ARMED FORCES	NUCLEAR WEAPONS	PLANES	LONG-RANGE MISSILES
U.S.	3,228,377	30-40,000	24,750	1,350
Red China	2,486,000	None*	2,300	None

PRODUCTION CAPABILITIES

	OUTPUT OF GOODS AND SERVICES (annual in U.S. $ billions)	STEEL OUTPUT (millions of metric tons)	OIL PRODUCTION (millions of barrels)
U.S.	$733	126.8	2,786
Red China	$50-$70	10.5	51

Sources: The Institute for Strategic Studies; United Nations

NATO **Vs.** **WARSAW PACT NATIONS**

Belgium, Canada, Denmark, France,
W. Germany, Greece, Iceland, Italy,
Luxembourg, Netherlands, Norway,
Portugal, Turkey, United Kingdom, U.S.

Albania, Bulgaria, Czechoslovakia,
E. Germany, Hungary, Poland, Rumania,
Soviet Union.

510 Million

335 Million

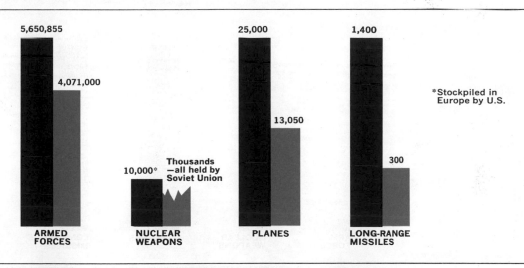

5,650,855

4,071,000

10,000* Thousands
—all held by
Soviet Union

25,000

13,050

1,400

300

*Stockpiled in
Europe by U.S.

ARMED FORCES **NUCLEAR WEAPONS** **PLANES** **LONG-RANGE MISSILES**

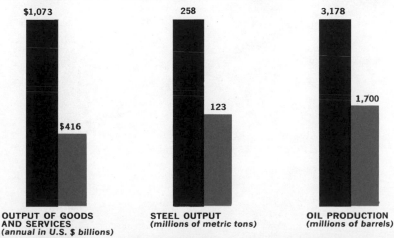

$1,073

$416

258

123

3,178

1,700

OUTPUT OF GOODS AND SERVICES
(annual in U.S. $ billions)

STEEL OUTPUT
(millions of metric tons)

OIL PRODUCTION
(millions of barrels)

1950-57 Years of agreement and good relations.

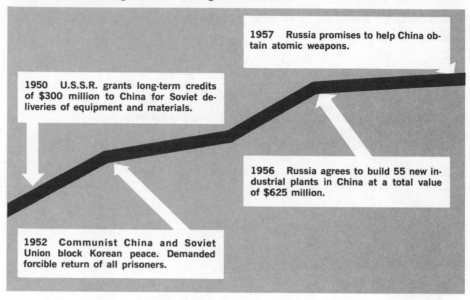

1957   Russia promises to help China obtain atomic weapons.

1950   U.S.S.R. grants long-term credits of $300 million to China for Soviet deliveries of equipment and materials.

1956   Russia agrees to build 55 new industrial plants in China at a total value of $625 million.

1952   Communist China and Soviet Union block Korean peace. Demanded forcible return of all prisoners.

1958-61 Agreement gives way to dispute.

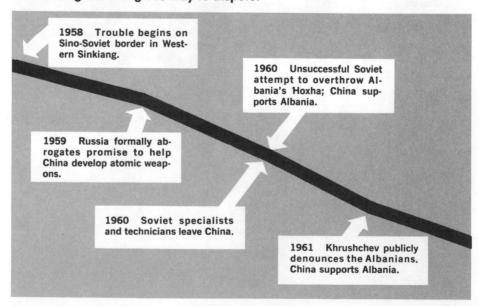

1958   Trouble begins on Sino-Soviet border in Western Sinkiang.

1960   Unsuccessful Soviet attempt to overthrow Albania's Hoxha; China supports Albania.

1959   Russia formally abrogates promise to help China develop atomic weapons.

1960   Soviet specialists and technicians leave China.

1961   Khrushchev publicly denounces the Albanians. China supports Albania.

1962-66 The dispute becomes a rift.

1965 Mar. China refuses to attend meeting of 19 Communist countries in Moscow.

1962 Apr. Gromyko visits Yugoslavia; China steps up criticism of Yugoslavia.

1963 Partial nuclear test-ban treaty signed; Chinese opposition to treaty.

1965 Nov. 45-country Afro-Asian Conference canceled because of Chinese threats to boycott the conference if Russia attended.

1962 Oct. Cuban crisis; China invades India.

1964 Mar. Khrushchev ousted as premier.

1966 Bulgaria, with Soviet support, calls for a conference of the world Communist movement to deal with the Chinese "heresy."

The effect of the rift on China-Soviet trade.

Communist China imports from Soviet Union   (U.S. $ millions)

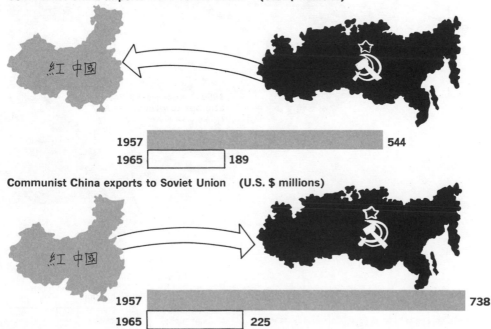

1957	544
1965	189

Communist China exports to Soviet Union   (U.S. $ millions)

1957	738
1965	225

MAJOR POLITICAL HIGHLIGHTS, 1966

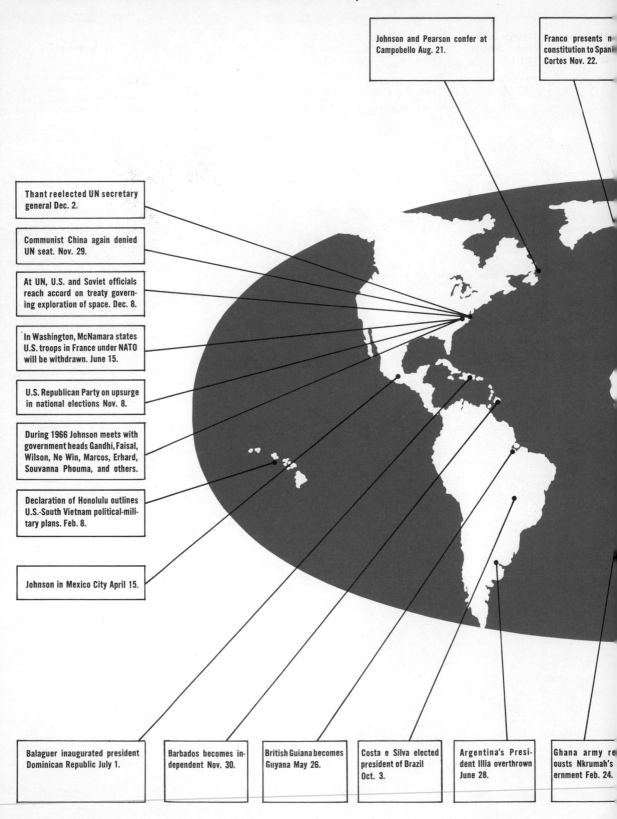

Johnson and Pearson confer at Campobello Aug. 21.

Franco presents n~ constitution to Spani~ Cortes Nov. 22.

Thant reelected UN secretary general Dec. 2.

Communist China again denied UN seat. Nov. 29.

At UN, U.S. and Soviet officials reach accord on treaty governing exploration of space. Dec. 8.

In Washington, McNamara states U.S. troops in France under NATO will be withdrawn. June 15.

U.S. Republican Party on upsurge in national elections Nov. 8.

During 1966 Johnson meets with government heads Gandhi, Faisal, Wilson, Ne Win, Marcos, Erhard, Souvanna Phouma, and others.

Declaration of Honolulu outlines U.S.-South Vietnam political-military plans. Feb. 8.

Johnson in Mexico City April 15.

Balaguer inaugurated president Dominican Republic July 1.

Barbados becomes independent Nov. 30.

British Guiana becomes Guyana May 26.

Costa e Silva elected president of Brazil Oct. 3.

Argentina's President Illia overthrown June 28.

Ghana army re~ ousts Nkrumah's ~ernment Feb. 24.

GROSS NATIONAL PRODUCT PER CAPITA[1]

Kuwait	$3,290	Lebanon	$390	Mauritania	$140
United States	3,020	Yugoslavia	390	Philippines	140
Sweden	2,040	Albania	380	Ceylon	130
Switzerland	2,030	Barbados	360	Cambodia	120
Canada	1,940	British Honduras	360	Korea (South)	120
Luxembourg	1,770	Costa Rica	360	New Guinea and Papua	120
New Zealand	1,760	Cuba	360	Sierra Leone	120
Australia	1,730	Portugal	340	Cameroun	110
Denmark	1,650	Surinam	330	Thailand	110
Iceland	1,550	Hong Kong	320	Vietnam (South)	110
France	1,540	Nicaragua	320	Nigeria	100
Germany, Fed. Rep. of	1,540	Guatemala	290	Vietnam (North)	100
Norway	1,520	Gabon	280	China (Mainland)	95
United Kingdom	1,500	Colombia	270	Malagasy Republic	95
Belgium	1,460	Peru	270	Sudan	95
Finland	1,440	El Salvador	260	Central African Republic	90
Netherlands	1,260	Guyana	260	India	90
Czechoslovakia	1,200	Malaysia	260	Kenya	90
Germany (East)	1,120	Iraq	240	Pakistan	90
Israel	1,070	Turkey	240	Yemen	90
Austria	1,020	Algeria	230	Afghanistan	85
Puerto Rico	980	Ghana	230	Gambia	85
Poland	930	Brazil	220	Swaziland	85
Hungary	890	Jordan	220	Togo	85
U.S.S.R.	890	Mauritius	220	Uganda	80
Italy	850	Dominican Republic	210	Haiti	75
Ireland	800	Iran	210	Niger	75
Venezuela	780	Korea (North)	210	Chad	70
Rumania	710	Libya	210	Congo, Dem. Rep. of	70
Japan	660	Rhodesia	210	Dahomey	70
Argentina	650	Ivory Coast	200	Guinea, Republic of	70
Bulgaria	650	Paraguay	200	Indonesia	70
Trinidad & Tobago	590	China, Republic of	190	Nepal	70
Uruguay	540	Ecuador	190	Tanzania	70
Cyprus	530	Honduras	190	Botswana	65
South Africa	530	Saudi Arabia	190	Burma	65
Spain	530	Liberia	180	Mali	65
Greece	510	Syria	180	Angola	60
Mongolia	480	Tunisia	180	Laos	60
Singapore	460	Morocco	170	Lesotho	60
Chile	450	Senegal	170	Burundi	50
Panama	450	Zambia	160	Ethiopia	50
Jamaica	430	United Arab Republic	150	Rwanda	50
Mexico	430	Bolivia	140	Somali Republic	50
Malta	410	Congo (Brazzaville)	140	Upper Volta	45
				Malawi	40

[1] Unofficial 1964 figures

Source: International Bank for Reconstruction and Development

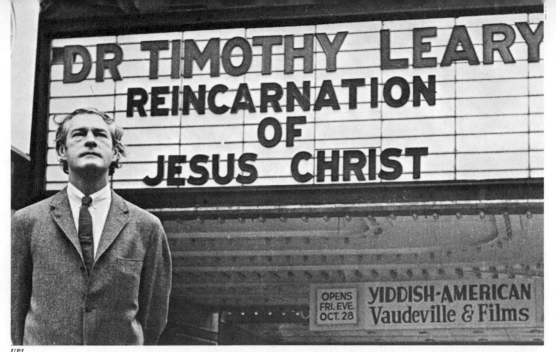

Dr. Timothy Leary, founder of the League of Spiritual Discovery. Dr. Leary calls the league an orthodox, psychedelic religion, and hopes its members will be allowed to use LSD and marijuana as their sacraments.

FACES IN THE NEWS

Illinois' Charles Percy and daughter Valerie during his campaign for U.S. Senate. Valerie was killed Sept. 18.

Wide World

On June 13, Jack Ruby enters Dallas hearing that found him sane. Ruby died of cancer Jan. 3, 1967.

Wide World

Under fire during 1966 for "irregularities," Rep. Adam Clayton Powell (D-N.Y.) was denied his House seat Jan. 10, 1967, pending an inquiry.

Betrothed royalty: Denmark's Crown Princess Margarethe and her fiancé, Count Henri de Laborde de Monpezat.

India's Reita Faria, Miss World for 1967, poses in London beside an Indian god called Trimurti.

Above: Prince Charles, heir to British throne, turned 18 on Nov. 14. Below: Bishop James A. Pike resigned as Episcopal Bishop of California May 12. Later the Episcopal House of Bishops denounced his theologizing as "irresponsible."

Above: Democrat John D. Rockefeller IV, elected Nov. 8 to West Virginia's House of Delegates. Below: *A Girl at the Window*, Rembrandt oil, part of a $7 million art theft Dec. 30 from Dulwich College Art Gallery, London. This and other paintings were recovered five days later.

Justino Diaz and Leontyne Price backstage on opening night of new Metropolitan Opera House in New York City. They sang title roles in *Antony and Cleopatra*.

Actor George Hamilton, friend of Lynda Bird Johnson, has preinduction physical at U.S. military hospital, Munich.

At a second trial, Dr. Sam Sheppard, Cleveland, Ohio, was acquitted Nov. 16 of the 1954 slaying of his wife.

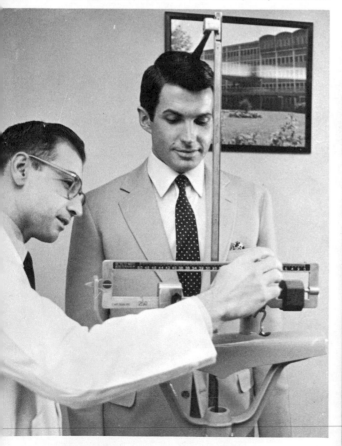

CARTOONS
OF
THE
YEAR

JANUARY

LePelley in
"The Christian Science Monitor"

FEBRUARY

LePelley in
"The Christian Science Monitor"

MARCH

"Says he's an expert on China
and wants to testify against it"

© 1966 Herblock
in "The Washington Post"

37

Little
in "*The Nashville Tennessean*"

"After you, Alphonse"

APRIL

Shanks
in "*The Buffalo Evening News*"

"I've got a touch of it myself"

MAY

JUNE

"War and Peace"

© Juhl—P.I.B., Copenhagen.

Yardley in "The Baltimore Sun"

Still the big fish

JULY

AUGUST

"I have a feeling I'm being shadowed"

SEPTEMBER

"Come back, darling, I'll try to be nicer"

Ed Valtman
in "The Hartford Times"

LePelley
in "The Christian Science Monitor"

Assorted summits

Gene Bass
Scripps-Howard Newspaper Alliance

"Oh, me? . . . I was run over by an elephant"

OCTOBER   **NOVEMBER**

"The trophy room is almost complete!"

DECEMBER

DIARY
OF
1966
NEWS
EVENTS

JANUARY HEADLINE HIGHLIGHTS

U.S. Seeks Vietnam Peace: U.S. envoys visited 34 world capitals in a "peace offensive" begun as 1965 ended. UN Ambassador Arthur Goldberg on Jan. 5 asked the United Nations to help promote a peaceful end to the Vietnam war. President Johnson said in his State of the Union Message Jan. 12: "We will meet at any conference . . . discuss any proposals."

As the United States extended a Christmas pause in air strikes against North Vietnam, sentiment in Congress ranged from "hawks"

Mrs. Indira Gandhi, daughter of India's late Prime Minister Nehru, is sworn in as prime minister of the world's most densely populated democracy Jan. 24.

Wide World

Some 6 million New York City bus and subway riders greet 1966 on foot. A Transport Workers Union strike halted public transportation Jan. 1-13. During the strike, New Yorkers walked, fought traffic or remained at home.

UPI

urging stepped-up military action to "doves" seeking a longer bombing lull. On Jan. 26 Secretary of State Dean Rusk said U.S. peace efforts had extended "from A to Z and almost through Z."

Peking called those efforts a "hoax"; the U.S.S.R. sent a mission to Hanoi, then pledged more aid to North Vietnam, whose President Ho Chi Minh later declared that "if the United States really wants peace," it must negotiate with the National Liberation Front.

On Jan. 31 President Johnson announced that U.S. bombing had resumed after a 37-day suspension.

India's New Leader: Indira Gandhi, daughter of India's first Prime Minister, Jawaharlal Nehru, was elected prime minister of India Jan. 19. She succeeded Lal Bahadur Shastri, who died of a heart attack Jan. 11 in Tashkent, U.S.S.R., shortly after he had signed an accord with Pakistan's President Ayub Khan, settling a dispute over Kashmir.

S EVENTS... NEWS EVENTS... NEWS EVENTS... NEWS EVENTS... NEWS EVEN

1 Central African Republic: President David Dacko is overthrown in coup led by Army Chief of Staff Col. Jean Bedel Bokassa, who proclaims himself chief of state.

3 United States: Congress of Racial Equality (CORE) names Floyd B. McKissick national director to succeed James Farmer, who resigned.

10 United States: Second session of 89th Congress convenes. **Guatemala:** Mexico's President Gustavo Diaz Ordaz starts six-nation trip—first visit of a Mexican chief of state to Central American countries—in Guatemala City.

12 United States: In his third State of the Union Message to Congress, President Johnson stresses U.S. support of South Vietnam and the "Great Society here at home."

13 United States: President Johnson names Robert C. Weaver secretary of housing and urban development, cabinet post created in 1965. **India:** Vice-President Hubert Humphrey and Soviet Premier Aleksei Kosygin confer for two hours in New Delhi.

15 Nigeria: Prime Minister Sir Abubakar Tafawa Balewa is kidnaped when dissident army units attempt overthrow of Government. **Cuba:** Sino-Soviet rivalry marks Tricontinental Conference of Asian, African and Latin-American Revolutionary Solidarity Jan. 3–15 in Havana. Decision on adding Latin America to the Afro-Asian Peoples' Solidarity Organization is postponed until 1968.

16 Nigeria: Maj. Gen. Johnson Aguiyi-Ironsi, Nigerian Army commander, accepts Council of Ministers' invitation to head a provisional Government.

17 United States: Sargent Shriver will step down as Peace Corps director to devote full time to the Office of Economic Opportunity, President Johnson tells newsmen. New Peace Corps Director will be Jack H. Vaughn, assistant secretary of state for inter-American affairs. **Luxembourg:** At first meeting of the six European Economic Community (EEC) foreign ministers since France's boycott of EEC in July 1965, French Foreign Minister Maurice Couve de Murville submits conditions for resumption of normal French-EEC relations.

20 United States: At Independence, Mo., ceremonies announcing creation in Jerusalem of the Harry S. Truman Center for Advancement of Peace, President Johnson proposes an international attack on disease, hunger and illiteracy—to extend former President Truman's Point Four Program of technical assistance to underdeveloped nations. **Australia:** Sir Robert Menzies, Australia's prime minister since 1949, announces that he will retire. Governor-General Lord Casey asks Federal Treasurer Harold E. Holt, Menzies' successor as Liberal Party leader, to form a Government.

21 Italy: Premier Aldo Moro and his Center-Left coalition Cabinet resign after secret ballot defeats state nursery-school bill.

22 Nigeria: Government announces that the body of Prime Minister Abubakar Tafawa Balewa, abducted Jan. 15, has been found on roadside 25 miles north of the capital.

23 South Vietnam: Fighting resumes after 78-hour truce for Vietnamese Lunar New Year.

24 United States: President Johnson submits $112,800,000,000 budget to Congress for 1967 fiscal year.

25 Soviet Union: First Secretary Leonid I. Brezhnev heads Soviet Communist Party commission to draft new collective-farm charter.

27 Switzerland: 17-nation disarmament conference resumes after four-month recess.

FEBRUARY HEADLINE HIGHLIGHTS

Vietnam Conference and Debate: In his first trip outside continental North America since taking office, President Johnson flew to Hawaii Feb. 5 for three days of meetings with South Vietnam's Premier Nguyen Cao Ky, Chief of State Nguyen Van Thieu and top U.S. political and military advisers.

A Declaration of Honolulu, issued Feb. 8, outlined future U.S.-South Vietnamese political and military policies. The three-part document, stating the "purposes" of the United States and South Vietnam and the "common commitments of both governments," stressed civil reforms as well as military efforts.

En route back to Washington, President Johnson conferred in Los Angeles with Vice-President Humphrey, who was to meet Premier Ky in Honolulu, and return with him to Saigon "to promote and carry forward" the programs discussed at Honolulu. From Saigon, Humphrey went to other Asian capitals, to New Zealand and Australia to explain what

Arriving in Honolulu Feb. 6 for top-level conferences with U.S. leaders, South Vietnam's Premier Nguyen Cao Ky (l) and Chief of State Lt. Gen. Nguyen Van Thieu are greeted by President Lyndon Johnson and Secretary of State Rusk. Mrs. Ky descends plane steps.

Wide World

was accomplished at the Honolulu conference.

Early in February, too, the UN Security Council voted to debate a U.S. request for negotiated settlement. And as the month progressed, debate on this issue was heard round the world. Focal point was a Senate Foreign Relations Committee inquiry into the aims and justifications of the undeclared war in Vietnam. But views of both "hawks" and "doves" at every level from top-level government officials to the man in the street were pitted against one another on television, in press conferences, magazine articles, demonstrations and marches in major U.S. cities.

As the month ended, there was general agreement in Congress that: there was no clear-cut alternative to waging a limited war; the ultimate goal should be a situation allowing the South Vietnamese people to choose freely their own Government; any role of the communist-led Vietcong in South Vietnam should be decided during peace negotiations.

VS EVENTS... NEWS EVENTS... NEWS EVENTS... NEWS EVENTS... NEWS EVEN

1 United States: President Johnson, asking Congress for $3,380,000,000 in foreign-aid funds for the 1967 fiscal year, proposes that the United States help only countries that are "determined to help themselves." **Great Britain:** Queen Elizabeth and Prince Philip leave London Airport for five-week tour of Caribbean.
2 Soviet Union: Premier Kosygin calls for a ban on use of nuclear weapons against nations with no nuclear weapons on their territory.
3 Soviet Union: Tass, official Soviet press agency, announces that an unmanned Soviet spaceship, Luna 9, has made a successful soft landing on the moon.
4 United States: President Johnson announces that an additional three million tons of U.S. grain will be shipped to India for famine relief.
7 France: German Chancellor Ludwig Erhard confers with French President de Gaulle at Paris Elysée Palace in sixth semiannual meeting under 1963 French-West German Cooperation Treaty.
11 Switzerland: Rev. Dr. Engene Carson Blake, stated clerk of the General Assembly of the U.S. United Presbyterian Church, is elected secretary-general of the World Council of Churches. **United States:** President Johnson announces the appointment of Lee C. White, special counsel to the President, as Federal Power Commission chairman, and Deputy Budget Director Elmer B. Staats as controller general. **Belgium:** After Feb. 10 resignation of 12 socialist ministers, King Baudouin accepts resignation of Premier Pierre Harmel's Government and asks Harmel to head caretaker Government.
16 United States: President Johnson announces an increase in the interest rate on U.S. savings bonds from 3.75 to 4.15 per cent, retroactive to Dec. 1, 1965.
19 Soviet Union: Plenary meeting of Soviet Communist Party's Central Committee approves 1966–70 five-year economic-development plan.
21 France: At first news conference since his reelection, President de Gaulle declares that by April 4, 1969—when the 15 North Atlantic Treaty Organization members may affirm or renounce NATO membership—"every foreign element stationed in France must be under the sole control of French authorities." **South Vietnam:** Premier Ky announces that he has reorganized his Cabinet.
22 Uganda: Prime Minister Milton Obote declares that he has assumed "all the powers of the Government of Uganda."
23 United States: Freedom House presents its National Freedom Award to President Johnson—first in its 23-year history to be awarded an incumbent president. **Italy:** In an attempt to solve Italy's 33-day-old government crisis, Premier-designate Aldo Moro presents a four-party coalition Cabinet to President Saragat.
24 Ghana: Army rebels, led by Lt. Gen. Joseph A. Ankrah, overthrow Government of President Kwame Nkrumah in coup while Nkrumah is en route to Peking. Ankrah heads ruling National Liberation Council. **Soviet Union:** British Prime Minister Wilson ends three days of "useful and constructive" meetings with Premier Kosygin and other Soviet leaders in Moscow. **United States:** Alabama's Governor George C. Wallace announces that Mrs. Wallace will be a candidate for governor in November elections since Alabama's constitution prohibits a governor from seeking a second consecutive four-year term.

MARCH HEADLINE HIGHLIGHTS

During historic meeting Pope Paul VI and the Archbishop of Canterbury, Dr. Michael Ramsey, sign an agreement March 24 committing the Roman Catholic and the Anglican churches to a program of contacts and collaboration aimed at unity.

Wide World

Wilson Wins Election: British Prime Minister Harold Wilson's Labor Party increased its parliamentary majority from 3 to 97 seats in national elections March 31. The Labor Party won 363 seats, the Conservatives 253, the Liberals 12 and the Irish Republican Labor 1.

Gemini 8: Six and a half hours after launch from Cape Kennedy, March 16, U.S. spacecraft Gemini 8, with astronauts Neil A. Armstrong and Maj. David R. Scott aboard, successfully joined with an Agena rocket—the first time that two vehicles had linked together in space.

However, shortly after the docking, the astronauts temporarily lost maneuverability of the craft, and it began to tumble violently at an altitude of 185 miles. By deactivating the entire maneuvering system and by firing the reentry rockets, the astronauts were able to regain control of the craft, but the flight was terminated on orders of Flight Director John Hodge in Houston.

S EVENTS... NEWS EVENTS... NEWS EVENTS... NEWS EVENTS... NEWS EVEN

1 Soviet Union: Unmanned Soviet spacecraft crashes into Venus—first man-made object to touch another planet.

3 United States: President Johnson signs into law Veterans Readjustment Act providing education, housing and other benefits for veterans who have served after Jan. 31, 1955.

4 United States: The United States recognizes Ghana's new military Government.

6 Austria: Chancellor Josef Klaus' Christian Democrats win narrow majority in national elections—first parliamentary majority since that held by the same party in 1945.

7 United States: Supreme Court upholds the constitutionality of the major provisions of the 1965 Voting Rights Act.

8 Australia: Prime Minister Holt says that Australia will increase its military forces in Vietnam from 1,500 to 4,500 men in June.

10 South Vietnam: The military Government's National Leadership Committee dismisses Gen. Nguyen Chanh Thi as commander-governor of the nation's five northernmost provinces. **Netherlands:** The wedding of Crown Princess Beatrix to Claus von Amsberg, 39-year-old German commoner, is marred by demonstrations by groups opposing the marriage because of the World War II nazi occupation of their country.

15 United States: Two men are killed and at least 25 injured as Negro teen-agers riot in Watts section of Los Angeles—where 34 were killed in August 1965 riots. . . . President Johnson signs tax bill speeding up collection of corporation taxes, increasing income-tax withholding rates and raising excise taxes on automobiles to 7 per cent, on telephone services to 10 per cent.

16 United States: David Dubinsky, president of the International Ladies Garment Workers Union since 1932, announces his resignation.

19 Belgium: King Baudouin swears in a Social Christian-Liberal coalition Cabinet with Paul Vanden Boeynants as premier.

22 Communist China: In a letter to Moscow the Chinese Communist Party declines an invitation to the 23d Congress of the Soviet Communist Party. **United States:** President Johnson names Robert Komer special assistant "for peaceful reconstruction in Vietnam."

24 Vatican City: Dr. Arthur Michael Ramsey, archbishop of Canterbury, and Pope Paul VI announce that they "intend to inaugurate between the Roman Catholic Church and the Anglican Communion a serious dialogue" to explore the possibility of eventual union. The announcement followed the first official meeting of heads of the two churches since a split in 1534.

27 Indonesia: President Sukarno announces a new Cabinet including the two leading anti-Communists—Lt. Gen. Suharto and former Defense Minister Gen. Abdul Haris Nasution.

29 United States: India's Prime Minister Indira Gandhi and President Johnson complete two days of formal talks. **Soviet Union:** The 23d Congress of the Soviet Communist Party opens in Moscow with representatives of 86 communist and Leftist parties attending. **Ecuador:** After the armed forces' high command overthrows the ruling military junta, representatives of Ecuador's political parties elect Clemente Yerovi Indaburo provisional president.

31 United States: President Johnson names as special presidential assistants Robert E. Kintner, former head of NBC, and Walt W. Rostow, chairman of the State Department Policy Planning Council.

APRIL HEADLINE HIGHLIGHTS

Vietnam Political Crisis: Antigovernment agitation spread to Saigon in April, following the March dismissal of Lt. Gen. Nguyen Chanh Thi as military commander-governor of South Vietnam's five northernmost provinces.

There were street demonstrations in major cities as militant Buddhist leaders demanded a return to civilian rule. At one point Premier Nguyen Cao Ky backed down in the face of open defiance by northern military leaders.

In midmonth Ky's Government called a national political congress to make recommendations for ending unrest and returning to constitutional government. The Buddhists boycotted the congress, but the meeting supported their demand for elections. The ruling generals agreed on April 14 to hold national elections for a constituent assembly.

Reports that Vietnamese troops were being diverted to police and security duty during the political crisis prompted new debate in the U.S. Congress on the Johnson administration's

An arch of balloons greets President Johnson, April 14, as he rides in motorcade from Mexico City's airport to presidential palace with Mexico's President Gustavo Diaz Ordaz. The 24-hour Mexican trip was Mr. Johnson's initial journey as U.S. president to a foreign capital.

Wide World

management of the Vietnam war. In response to a charge by House Minority Leader Gerald Ford (R-Mich.) that U.S. airmen were short of bombs, and there was a backup of supply ships in Vietnam, Defense Secretary McNamara denied the bomb shortage, and assured newsmen that the unloading of supplies in Vietnam was "normal."

The pace of the war slowed somewhat, early in April, as political unrest heightened. For the week ending April 9 the U.S. death toll was higher than that of the South Vietnamese for the first time since the war began: 95 Americans killed, 67 South Vietnamese.

As the month progressed, air activity increased. On April 23, U.S. jets met their first strong communist air opposition and had their first encounter with a North Vietnamese-manned, supersonic MiG-21, the U.S.S.R.'s most advanced fighter plane. Later U.S. Air Force Phantom jets clashed with MiG-17's, MiG-15's and a few of the faster MiG-21's.

S EVENTS... NEWS EVENTS... NEWS EVENTS... NEWS EVENTS... NEWS EVENT

4 Soviet Union: Soviet news agency Tass announces that Luna 10, a Soviet satellite launched April 3, is orbiting the moon.

5 Canada: By a vote of 143-112 the House of Commons rejects a resolution prohibiting capital punishment.

6 United States: In an address to the Pharmaceutical Manufacturers Association, Dr. James L. Goddard, U.S. Food and Drug Administration commissioner, states that some U.S. drug manufacturers are more interested in profit than in helping people get well.

7 Spain: A U.S. Navy undersea device recovers a U.S. hydrogen bomb missing since Jan. 17 when a B-52 nuclear bomber and a KC-135 refueling tanker collided off the Spanish coast near Palomares.

8 United States: New York's Nelson Rockefeller announces that he will seek a third term as governor.

9 United Nations: By a vote of 10-0 with 5 abstentions, the UN Security Council adopts a resolution authorizing Great Britain to use force to keep seaborne oil from reaching Rhodesia through Mozambique. **United States:** Secretary of State Rusk unveils a statue of Sir Winston Churchill in front of the British Embassy in Washington.

11 United States: The Government increases from 5½ per cent to 5¾ per cent maximum interest that can be charged on mortgages insured by the Federal Housing Administration and the Veterans Administration. The new rate applies to mortgages negotiated after April 11. . . . Jack Nicklaus wins U.S. Masters Golf Tournament, becoming the first to win the tournament two years in a row.

12 Indonesia: Hamengku Buwono IX, deputy premier in charge of economic affairs, pledges Indonesian Government's support of private enterprise, reversing the nation's recent socialist trend.

15 Mexico: In Mexico City to unveil a statue of Abraham Lincoln, President Johnson announces his endorsement of an Argentine proposal for a meeting of Western Hemisphere heads of state to examine "common problems" and "to give the Alliance for Progress increased momentum."

16 Iraq: A joint session of the Iraqi Cabinet and the National Defense Council elects Acting Chief of Staff Maj. Gen. Abdel Rahman Arif president of Iraq. Arif succeeds his brother, Abdul Salam Arif, who was killed in a helicopter crash April 13.

21 Great Britain: Queen Elizabeth II opens the fourth new Parliament of her reign—first parliamentary session to be televised.

25 United States: Jack J. Valenti resigns as special assistant to President Johnson to become president of the Motion Picture Association of America.

27 Vatican City: Pope Paul VI discusses the quest for peace, and other world problems with Soviet Foreign Minister Andrei A. Gromyko for 45 minutes. **United States:** The Interstate Commerce Commission authorizes merger of the Pennsylvania and New York Central railroads.

28 United States: President Johnson accepts "with regret" the resignation of Thomas C. Mann as undersecretary of state for economic affairs.

29 United States: The American Association of University Professors announces that salaries of U.S. college and university teachers increased by an average 7.3 per cent during the 1965–66 academic year.

UPI

HEADLINE HIGHLIGHTS

Vietnam Unrest: On May 15, South Vietnam's Premier Ky ordered loyalist troops into the northern city of Danang, which had been out of the Government's control since March. The action ended the political truce between the Unified Buddhist Church and the ruling junta.

Government troops seized most of Danang May 15 in a series of brief encounters with about 700 rebel defenders. Led by tanks, government troops on May 20 attacked the rebels' final stronghold, and by May 23 the last of

In May 23 address to 5,000 Buddhists in Hue, Buddhist leader Thich Tri Quang urges the military Government not to use force in suppressing rebel forces in the city of Danang.

On Guyana's independence day, May 26, the Duke of Kent hands new constitution to Prime Minister Forbes Burnham. Guyana was formerly the colony of British Guiana.

Wide World

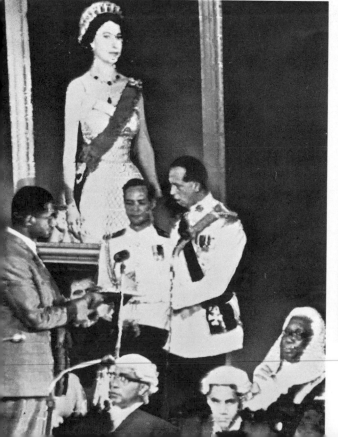

George Buctel

the antigovernment forces in Danang filed out of two pagodas and were taken to detention camps.

After losing Danang, the Buddhists switched the center of their struggle to Saigon, where they held a hunger strike in the main pagoda compound May 21. Demonstrations by thousands of Buddhists in Saigon May 20–23 were crushed by police using bayonets and tear gas.

Meanwhile in the northern city of Hue the "struggle movement" to depose Premier Ky's military junta continued. Thich Tri Quang, leader of the radical wing of the Unified Buddhist Church told his followers that he was ready to lead them in the "fight against military dictatorship." On May 27, Lt. Gen. Nguyen Chanh Thi, an ally of the Buddhists who was deposed March 10 as a military commander-governor of South Vietnam's five northernmost provinces, held a surprise meeting with Premier Ky on the "neutral grounds" of a U.S. Marine base in Chulai.

S EVENTS... NEWS EVENTS... NEWS EVENTS... NEWS EVENTS... NEWS EVENT

3 Great Britain: Chancellor of the Exchequer James Callaghan announces, in a budget address to the House of Commons, new measures to strengthen the pound and to slow down British inflation. He outlines the Labor Government's three major economic objectives as "a strong pound, a steadily growing industrial strength and full employment." **United States:** Mrs. George Wallace, wife of Governor Wallace (D-Ala.), wins Democratic nomination to succeed her husband.

5 Israel: Students and police clash during demonstrations at Hebrew University in Jerusalem protesting the visit of former West German Chancellor Konrad Adenauer.

7 United States: President Johnson names a National Advisory Committee on Health Manpower to recommend ways to alleviate a "critical shortage" of doctors, nurses and other health personnel. **United Arab Republic:** President Gamal Abdel Nasser and Yugoslavia's President Tito conclude five days of talks in Alexandria with a communiqué calling for "active preparation" for a disarmament conference which would include all nations.

9 Communist China: The Government announces that it has successfully exploded a device containing "thermonuclear material"—third in a series of Chinese nuclear tests. **Belgium:** Queen Elizabeth and Prince Philip begin five-day state visit.

10 Communist China: Hsinhua, China's press agency, reports that Mao Tse-tung, chairman of the Chinese Communist Party, has met with leaders of a visiting delegation from Albania. The report marked the first time that Mao's name had been mentioned in a Chinese public-events report since Nov. 26, 1965. **United Arab Republic:** Soviet Premier Kosygin begins official visit to Cairo. **Soviet Union:** Soviet Communist Party Chairman Brezhnev leaves Moscow for official visit to Rumania.

16 Great Britain: First strike by British merchant seamen in 55 years begins at 12:01 A.M.

23 United Nations: The Security Council rejects resolution calling for the use of force in Rhodesia to bring about the overthrow of the white-supremacy regime of Prime Minister Ian Smith. **Uganda:** A state of emergency with a dusk-to-dawn curfew is declared in Buganda, Uganda's richest kingdom, following a day of rioting and shooting. The King of Buganda had demanded that President Milton Obote remove his Government from Kampala, the capital, and from all of Buganda by May 30.

25 Great Britain: Prime Minister Wilson and West German Chancellor Erhard conclude two days of talks on NATO and other issues.

26 Guyana: The colony of British Guiana becomes the independent nation of Guyana—first new South American nation since Venezuela won independence from Spain in 1832. **United States:** President Johnson, in his first major speech on Africa as president, tells African ambassadors that the United States is "giving every encouragement and support" to United Kingdom and UN efforts to restore legitimate government in Rhodesia. "We will not support policies abroad which are based on the rule of minorities. . . ."

28 France: President de Gaulle arrives at Verdun to participate in ceremonies marking fiftieth anniversary of the World War I battle.

31 Czechoslovakia: Soviet Communist Party Chairman Brezhnev delivers statement to the 13th Congress of the Czechoslovak Communist Party, calling for the strengthening of the Warsaw Pact, East Europe's military alliance.

In Dominican Republic elections June 1, Joaquin Balaguer (r) is elected president over Juan Bosch.

After a 63½-hour flight, U.S. spacecraft Surveyor 1 completes a soft landing on the moon June 2. Below, Surveyor 1 photographs its shadow against moon's surface.

As the month of June ends, U.S. warplanes sweep over the North Vietnam cities of Hanoi and Haiphong, bombing North Vietnam oil facilities. The action immediately sets off increased worldwide debate over U.S. policy and involvement in Vietnam.

Civil-rights worker James H. Meredith, first Negro to graduate from the University of Mississippi, is shot from ambush June 6 while marching from Memphis, Tenn., to Jackson, Miss.

U.S. Space Feat: Gemini 9 astronauts Lt. Col. Thomas Stafford and Lt. Cmdr. Eugene Cernan completed a 3-day space flight June 6. The spacecraft achieved a triple rendezvous with an orbiting target vehicle, and Cernan set a space-walk record of 2 hours and 9 minutes. However, a scheduled linking of the craft with the orbiting target was canceled.

Mississippi March: James H. Meredith, first Negro to enroll at the University of Mississippi (1962), on June 5 began a 220-mile march from Memphis, Tenn., to Jackson, Miss., to encourage Negro voter registration. On June 6, Meredith was shot near Hernando, Miss. Aubrey James Norvell, a white man, was arrested and charged with the shooting.

With Meredith hospitalized, the march was continued by civil-rights leaders Martin Luther King, Jr., Floyd McKissick and Stokely Carmichael. On June 24, Meredith returned to lead the march to its conclusion with a rally at the State Capitol June 26.

VS EVENTS... NEWS EVENTS... NEWS EVENTS... NEWS EVENTS... NEWS EVEN

1 South Vietnam: The Government agrees to add ten civilians to its ruling committee of ten generals, and announces it is making "an effort to establish a people's armed-forces council" to advise the premier and the Cabinet. **Ireland:** Eamon de Valera, 83, wins reelection to a second seven-year term as president.

2 United States: Gov. William W. Scranton (R-Pa.) declares that he will never again seek election "for any public office under any circumstances." **Thailand:** At Bangkok airport, Indonesia's Foreign Minister Adam Malik reveals plans for a new southeast Asian union to include Malaysia, Indonesia, Thailand and the Philippines.

3 Communist China: The Government discloses that Peng Chen, mayor of Peking and member of the ruling Politburo, has been removed as first secretary of the Chinese Communist Party's Peking Municipal Committee. Peng was once considered a possible successor to Mao Tse-tung as party chairman.

5 South Vietnam: Electoral-law drafting commission recommends that election to a constituent assembly take place Sept. 11 with the assembly later drafting a constitution and having legislative power.

6 United States: Arthur M. Ross, commissioner of labor statistics, announces that the unemployment rate for May climbed to 4 per cent from 3.7 per cent in April—sharpest increase in 23 months.

8 Belgium: The foreign ministers of the 15 NATO nations, after two days of talks in Brussels, agree to refer to their permanent representatives on the Atlantic Council in Paris the future of French troops in West Germany, under NATO control through June.

13 Finland: Soviet Premier Kosygin arrives at Helsinki—his first visit as premier to a non-communist European nation. **United States:** A Supreme Court decision further limits the power of police to question suspected criminals in their custody.

15 United States: Secretary of Defense McNamara declares that all U.S. combat units in France will be evacuated in orderly stages within the next few months.

16 Rumania: Communist China's Premier Chou En-lai begins eight-day official visit.

18 United States: President Johnson names Richard Helms, a career intelligence officer, to succeed William F. Raborn as director of the Central Intelligence Agency.

20 Soviet Union: Beginning a 12-day state visit to the Soviet Union, French President de Gaulle declares that "France would like to see . . . a beginning of new relations toward relaxation, harmony and cooperation with the East European states." . . . Canada's Minister of Trade Robert Winters discloses that the Soviet Union has purchased 336 million bushels of wheat from Canada.

21 United States: President Johnson receives Saudi Arabia's King Faisal at the White House.

25 Yugoslavia: The Government and the Vatican renew diplomatic relations broken in 1952.

27 Australia: A three-day conference of the foreign-ministerial Council of the Southeast Asia Treaty Organization opens in Canberra.

28 Argentina: A three-man military junta overthrows President Arturo U. Illia, dissolves Congress, the Supreme Court and all political parties. Lt. Gen. Juan Carlos Ongania is named provisional president.

29 Great Britain: Leaders of the National Union of Seamen vote to postpone for one year the maritime strike begun May 16.

JULY HEADLINE HIGHLIGHTS

U.S. Riots: During July, riots erupted in Negro sections of many U.S. cities.

The first violence broke out over the July 4 weekend in Omaha, Neb., with the bombardment of a police car in the Near North Side area. Before the trouble ended July 5, 500 National Guardsmen were sent into the area, and 122 persons were arrested.

On July 12, in 100° heat, children on Chicago's Near West Side cooled themselves in water from a fire hydrant. A policeman turned the hydrant off; a man turned it back on and was arrested; violence ensued. By the time 4,000 National Guardsmen quelled the rioting and looting on July 15, at least 2 persons had been killed, 60 injured and 282 arrested.

Ohio's Gov. James A. Rhodes declared a state of emergency after Cleveland riots broke out July 18. The violence, lasting a week, claimed 4 dead and 50 injured, with 164 arrested. In the East New York section of Brooklyn, N.Y., an 11-year-old Negro boy died in a

Wide World

NEWS EVENTS... NEWS EVENTS... N

2 Tahiti: France detonates an atomic device off Mururoa atoll, 750 miles southeast of Tahiti. **United States:** President Johnson names a 20-member National Advisory Commission on Selective Service.

5 Indonesia: Stripping President Sukarno of his president-for-life title, the People's Consultative Congress authorizes Lt. Gen. Suharto to form a new Cabinet by Aug. 17. **United States:** Saturn 4B, a 29-ton satellite—the nation's heaviest to date—is launched from Cape Kennedy.

8 Rumania: Members of the Warsaw Pact issue an invitation to West European nations for

National Guardsmen patrol a section of Hough Street in Cleveland, Ohio, where rioting and violence broke out July 18. Building in background burned to the ground after snipers' gunfire forced firemen to evacuate area.

Diagram below depicts flight of Gemini 10. The craft containing Comdr. John Young of the Navy and Maj. Michael Collins of the Air Force was aloft July 18–21.

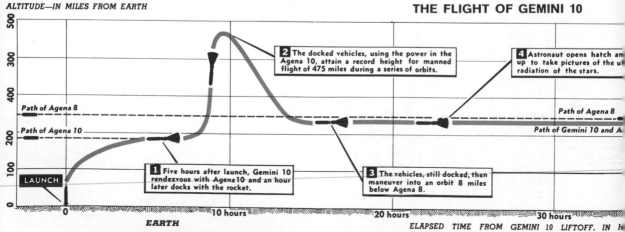

ALTITUDE—IN MILES FROM EARTH

THE FLIGHT OF GEMINI 10

Path of Agena 8

Path of Agena 10

2 The docked vehicles, using the power in the Agena 10, attain a record height for manned flight of 475 miles during a series of orbits.

4 Astronaut opens hatch an up to take pictures of the u radiation of the stars.

Path of Agena 8

Path of Gemini 10 and A

LAUNCH

1 Five hours after launch, Gemini 10 rendezvous with Agena 10 and an hour later docks with the rocket.

3 The vehicles, still docked, then maneuver into an orbit 8 miles below Agena 8.

10 hours   20 hours   30 hours

EARTH

ELAPSED TIME FROM GEMINI 10 LIFTOFF, IN H

July 21 street clash. Other U.S. cities affected by outbreaks of racial violence during July included San Francisco, Philadelphia, Pa., South Bend, Ind., Jacksonville, Fla., Des Moines, Iowa, Grenada, Miss., Baltimore, and Amityville, N.Y.

Commenting on the riots in an Indianapolis speech July 23, President Johnson declared: "Riots in the street . . . make reform more difficult by turning away the very people who can and must support reform."

U.S. Airline Strike: A strike by the International Association of Machinists against 5 major U.S. airlines—United, Trans World, National, Eastern and Northwest—began July 8. Each day the strike affected some 150,000 travelers and 4,100 flights in 231 U.S. cities and 23 foreign countries.

On July 31, members of the machinists' union rejected a new contract worked out July 29 by union leaders, the airlines, and the Johnson administration.

NTS... NEWS EVENTS... NEWS EVENTS... NEWS EVENTS... NEWS EVENTS...

a "general European conference for the discussion of questions related to insuring security in Europe."

9 Communist China: In a speech to the African-Asian writers' conference on Vietnam, Premier Chou En-lai declares that "unless U.S. troops are withdrawn" from Vietnam, "the reconvening of the [1954] Geneva conference [on southeast Asia] is entirely out of the question."

12 United States: President Johnson, in his first major policy speech on China as president, declares that for peace in Asia "reconciliation between nations that now call themselves enemies" is essential.

Soviet Union: India's Prime Minister Gandhi arrives in Moscow to present her views to Soviet leaders on the search for peace in Vietnam.

14 United States: Eight student nurses are killed in a dormitory located on Chicago's Far South Side.

16 Soviet Union: British Prime Minister Wilson arrives in Moscow for official visit.

18 The Hague: The International Court of Justice dismisses a complaint by Ethiopia and Liberia against the imposition of racial separation, apartheid, in the mandated territory of South-West Africa.

20 Great Britain: In an effort to save the British pound, the Labor Government raises taxes $500 million a year, stiffens installment-buying terms and establishes curbs on traveling expenses. The Government also asks for a six-month standstill in wages, and says that it will cut $280 million from the Government's foreign expenditure.

21 West Germany: French President de Gaulle arrives at Cologne-Bonn Airport for semiannual talks with German Chancellor Erhard.

23 North Vietnam: Hanoi radio announces that the North Vietnam Government has established an official 11-member committee to investigate U.S. war crimes in Vietnam.

24 Belgium: After three days of meetings in Brussels, foreign and agricultural ministers of the six Common Market nations reach an agreement on agricultural prices and subsidy arrangements.

26 Soviet Union: UN Secretary-General U Thant holds "a free, frank exchange of views" with Premier Kosygin in Moscow.

27 Belgium: Paul Henri Spaak, former Belgian premier and foreign minister and a founder of the European Common Market, announces his retirement from political life.

29 United States: British Prime Minister Wilson discusses the Vietnam war and Britain's economic crisis with President Johnson at the White House. **Nigeria:** Maj. Gen. Johnson T. U. Aguiyi-Ironsi, leader of Nigeria since a January 1966 coup, is seized in a mutiny by dissident army troops.

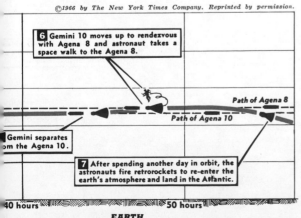

©1966 by The New York Times Company. Reprinted by permission.

6 Gemini 10 moves up to rendezvous with Agena 8 and astronaut takes a space walk to the Agena 8.

Path of Agena 8

Path of Agena 10

Gemini separates from the Agena 10.

7 After spending another day in orbit, the astronauts fire retrorockets to re-enter the earth's atmosphere and land in the Atlantic.

40 hours   50 hours

EARTH

UPI

HEADLINE HIGHLIGHTS

Airlines Fly Again: On Aug. 19, the 35,000 members of the International Association of Machinists voted by a margin of 2 to 1 to end the longest and costliest U.S. airline strike in history. Within hours of the settlement the 5 airlines on strike since July 8 were flying again.

The Aug. 15 settlement provided wage increases of between 5 and 6 per cent, considerably above President Johnson's noninflationary wage-price guideposts of 3.2 per cent.
De Gaulle on Tour: French President Charles

The wedding of the year: President Johnson's daughter Luci and Patrick Nugent walk down aisle of Shrine of the Immaculate Conception after their Aug. 6 nuptials.

Cambodia's Khmer Guards stand by as Prince Norodom Sihanouk welcomes French President Charles de Gaulle and Mme. de Gaulle to capital city Pnompenh Aug. 30.

Wide World

de Gaulle began a 27,000-mi., 19-day around-the-world tour Aug. 25. The President's first stop was Djibouti, the capital of French Somaliland, France's last African possession. At Djibouti, De Gaulle was met by a group of African nationalists demanding "total independence" from France. From Djibouti, De Gaulle flew to Addis Ababa, Ethiopia, for talks with Emperor Haile Selassie.

On Aug. 30 he was greeted at Pnompenh, Cambodia, by Prince Norodom Sihanouk, Cambodia's chief of state. The next day, De Gaulle discussed the possibility of peace in Vietnam with Nguyen Thuong, chief of North Vietnam's diplomatic mission in Cambodia. From Cambodia the President was scheduled to go to Nouméa, then to the New Hebrides, Tahiti and Guadeloupe.

In a U.S. Senate speech Aug. 29, Senate Majority Leader Mike Mansfield suggested that President Johnson meet De Gaulle in Guadeloupe to discuss southeast Asia.

S EVENTS... NEWS EVENTS... NEWS EVENTS... NEWS EVENTS... NEWS EVENT

1 United States: Charles J. Whitman, a 25-year-old student, shoots 14 persons to death from the top of a tower at the University of Texas in Austin. **Nigeria:** Lt. Col. Yakubu Gowon, Army chief of staff, announces that he heads Nigeria's new regime following a July 29 army mutiny.

3 Thailand: Foreign Minister Thanat Khoman urges Malaysia and the Philippines to join Thailand in forming an Asian-sponsored peace conference on Vietnam.

6 United States: Luci Baines Johnson, younger daughter of President and Mrs. Johnson, marries Patrick John Nugent of Waukegan, Ill.

10 Great Britain: Prime Minister Wilson reshuffles his Cabinet. Economic Minister George Brown and Foreign Secretary Michael Stewart exchange jobs. **United States:** The Treasury Department announces that it will discontinue printing $2.00 bills.

11 Indonesia: Malaysia and Indonesia sign a peace agreement formally ending an undeclared war begun in 1963.

12 North Korea: The Communist Party of North Korea declares itself independent of both Chinese and Soviet leadership of the communist world. **Communist China:** The Central Committee of the Chinese Communist Party ends 12 days of meetings in plenary session—first such meetings since 1962.

13 United States: Gen. William C. Westmoreland, commander of U.S. forces in Vietnam, reviews Vietnam war situation with President Johnson.

15 United States: The *New York Herald Tribune* newspaper is formally discontinued. **United Nations:** Secretary-General U Thant submits a record UN budget of $128,227,800 for 1967.

17 United States: In a speech celebrating fifth anniversary of the Alliance for Progress, President Johnson declares that the United States believes that "effective unity—and not separation—is vital to the needs" of Latin America's expanding population.

18 United States: The President's Advisory Committee on Labor-Management Policy issues a report calling for a more flexible national wage-price policy.

19 United States: President Johnson begins two-day tour of five northeastern states—New York, Rhode Island, New Hampshire, Vermont and Maine. **Turkey:** Eastern Turkey is hit by a devastating earthquake.

21 Canada: Prime Minister Pearson and President Johnson hold an "exceptionally friendly and frank" discussion of international affairs at Campobello Island, New Brunswick.

26 Canada: About 115,000 railroad workers go on strike against seven Canadian railroads. **United States:** In an Idaho address during tour of three western states, President Johnson urges the Soviet Union to "abandon the dogmas and vocabularies of the cold war" and join the United States in "rational acts of common endeavors." . . . Dr. Martin Luther King, Jr., chairman of the Southern Christian Leadership Conference, announces that street demonstrations supporting housing integration in Chicago will be halted. The announcement followed an agreement between civil-rights workers, Chicago civic authorities and real-estate representatives designed to end discrimination in residential renting and sales.

28 United States: Wisconsin Governor Warren P. Knowles calls out National Guard to hold back crowd of two thousand white youths heckling civil-rights demonstrators marching through the Milwaukee suburb of Wauwatosa.

SEPTEMBER
HEADLINE HIGHLIGHTS

Vietnam Elections: A total of 80.8 per cent of South Vietnam's registered voters went to the polls Sept. 11 to elect a 117-member constituent assembly. The assembly faces the task of drafting a constitution for South Vietnam and restoring civilian government in 1967.

Gemini 11: Shortly after launch Sept. 12, Gemini 11 met and linked with an Agena target vehicle. Astronauts Comdr. Charles Conrad, Jr., and Lt. Comdr. Richard F. Gordon, Jr., chased, rendezvoused and docked with the target vehicle during the first revolution—a new space achievement.

On the fifteenth revolution Comdr. Gordon began a 107-minute scheduled space walk, cut short due to heat and physical exhaustion. Gemini 11 set an altitude record of 850 miles, and marked the first time that man had created artificial gravity at an altitude of 185 miles.

The astronauts also used a computer, for the first time, to automatically steer the craft to a safe and accurate landing Sept. 15.

South Vietnam voters receive ballots in a Saigon suburb polling station Sept. 11. The voters elected a constituent assembly that will draft a constitution for South Vietnam.

Riots: During September, incidents of Negro rioting broke out in various U.S. cities.

On Sept. 1, over 900 National Guardsmen were called up to restore order in a Negro area of Dayton, Ohio. In the Chicago suburb of Cicero, about 250 civil-rights demonstrators met with harassment as they staged a 2-hour march through the all-white community Sept. 4.

Turbulence broke out in Atlanta, Ga., Sept. 6 when police wounded a Negro suspected of being a car thief. On Sept. 8, Atlanta police arrested Stokely Carmichael, Student Nonviolent Coordinating Committee chairman, on charges of inciting the riot.

Later, San Francisco Mayor John Shelley requested 2,000 National Guardsmen to quell rioting and looting. By the time order was restored, 51 were injured and over 200 arrested.

In St. Louis, youthful Negroes demonstrated for 6 nights after a white policeman had killed a Negro armed-robbery suspect.

EVENTS... NEWS EVENTS... NEWS EVENTS... NEWS EVENTS... NEWS EVENT

1 Cambodia: Addressing a crowd of 100,000 in Pnompenh, French President de Gaulle urges the United States to withdraw its forces from Vietnam. **United Nations:** In a written statement to the 117 UN delegations, Secretary-General U Thant declares that he has "decided not to offer" himself "for a second term as secretary-general."

2 Canada: Some Canadian railroads run again following a week-long railroad strike. Canada's Parliament passed a mandatory back-to-work law Sept. 1.

3 United States: President Johnson calls for an international "Water for Peace" conference to be held in Washington, D.C., in 1967.

6 South Africa: Prime Minister Henrik F. Verwoerd is assassinated while attending a meeting of Parliament in Cape Town.

8 United States: President Johnson welcomes Burma's chief of state General Ne Win to the White House.

9 United States: President Johnson signs into law the National Traffic and Motor Safety Bill and the Highway Safety Bill.

12 United States: Keith Funston announces that he will retire as president of the New York Stock Exchange when his contract expires Sept. 10, 1967.

13 South Africa: Minister of Justice, Police and Prisons Balthazar J. Vorster is chosen as South Africa's prime minister.

14 Great Britain: A communiqué issued by the Commonwealth Prime Ministers' Conference states that members of the conference "remain unanimous on the objective that the rebellion in Rhodesia must be brought to an end speedily." **United States:** Philippines' President Ferdinand E. Marcos arrives at White House for two-week state visit to the United States.

...The U.S. Senate fails to cut off filibuster against the 1966 civil-rights bill.

16 United States: Mrs. Lyndon B. Johnson attends opening night of the new Metropolitan Opera House at New York City's Lincoln Center.

18 United States: Valerie Jeanne Percy, 21-year-old daughter of Illinois Republican Senate candidate Charles H. Percy, is stabbed to death at her home in Kenilworth, Ill.

19 Vatican City: Pope Paul VI issues encyclical letter calling for peace in Vietnam.

20 United Nations: The 21st session of the UN General Assembly opens; Abdul Rahman Pazhwak of Afghanistan is elected assembly president; Guyana is admitted as the UN's 118th member.

21 United States: President Johnson announces that Attorney General Nicholas deB. Katzenbach will succeed George W. Ball as undersecretary of state.

23 United States: President Johnson signs bill increasing minimum wage to $1.60 by 1968.

24 North Vietnam: Czechoslovakia's Premier Josef Lenart arrives in Hanoi for talks with President Ho Chi Minh.

27 United States: President Johnson accepts invitation to attend a conference on Vietnam in Manila in late October. Leaders of South Vietnam, the Philippines, South Korea, Thailand, Australia and New Zealand are scheduled to attend the conference. . . . Following two days of meetings, President Johnson and German Chancellor Erhard agree to undertake a "searching reappraisal" of the needs and costs of European defense.

30 Botswana: The African colony of Bechuanaland officially becomes the independent nation of Botswana.

Split reaction by Australians in Melbourne to President Johnson's Oct. 21 visit to their city: (above) large crowd greets the President in a downtown area; antiwar demonstrators splatter Secret Service man and bubbletop limousine with paint (below).

OCTOBER

Manila Conference: "To advance the cause of peace and human progress" President Johnson began a 17-day trip to southeast Asia and the Far East Oct. 17.

The high point of the trip was the Manila Conference at which President Johnson and the leaders of South Vietnam, the Philippines, Thailand, Australia, New Zealand and South Korea —all of whom have sent troops or supplies to South Vietnam—discussed the Vietnam situation. A communiqué issued on the conference Oct. 25 stated that allied forces in Vietnam "shall be withdrawn after close consultation, as the other side withdraws its forces to the North, ceases infiltration and the level of violence thus subsides. . . ."

Prior to the Manila Conference President Johnson had visited Hawaii, American Samoa, New Zealand and Australia. After the conference he went to Thailand, Malaysia and South Korea. On Oct. 26 the President made a 2½ hour trip to Vietnam to visit U.S. troops.

S EVENTS... NEWS EVENTS... NEWS EVENTS... NEWS EVENTS... NEWS EVEN

3 Soviet Union: Tass, the official Soviet press agency, announces a new Soviet economic and military aid program for North Vietnam.

4 United States: French Foreign Minister Maurice Couve de Murville meets with President Johnson at the White House. **Lesotho:** British colony of Basutoland becomes new African nation of Lesotho.

7 United Nations: President Johnson and Secretary-General U Thant confer at UN headquarters in New York City. **United States:** President Johnson declares that to achieve the unification of Germany the United States must "achieve a reconciliation" with East Europe. The reconciliation will mean "a shift from the narrow concept of coexistence to the broader vision of a peaceful engagement."

9 United States: The Baltimore Orioles win baseball's World Series by defeating the Los Angeles Dodgers in four straight games.

10 South Vietnam: U.S. Secretary of Defense McNamara and Undersecretary of State Katzenbach arrive in Saigon "to review the progress of military and other operations" in Vietnam.

13 United States: President Johnson holds conference with Laotian Premier Souvanna Phouma in New York City.

14 The Netherlands: The 18-month-old Cabinet of Premier Joseph Cals falls after the lower House of Parliament rejects the Cabinet's budget for 1967. **United States:** The General electric Company and 11 labor unions agree to new contract averting a threatened strike.

15 Soviet Union: Soviet Communist Party Chairman Brezhnev declares that "if the United States wants to develop mutually beneficial relations with the Soviet Union—in principle, we also would like this—then it is necessary to clear major obstacles from the path. The piratical bombing attacks against. . . [North] Vietnam must be halted and the aggression against the Vietnam people stopped." **United States:** President Johnson signs bill creating the 12th U.S. Cabinet post, a department of transportation.

16 Lebanon: The Government orders a three-day bank holiday.

22 United States: Second session of 89th Congress adjourns. **Soviet Union:** Leaders of the Soviet Union, East Europe, Cuba and Mongolia end conference in Moscow with communiqué.

24 India: At the conclusion of four days of talks in New Delhi, Yugoslavia's President Tito, United Arab Republic's President Nasser and India's Prime Minister Gandhi call on the United States to halt its bombing of North Vietnam "without any preconditions."

25 Indonesia: Foreign Minister Subandrio is sentenced to death for conspiring to overthrow Indonesia's Government.

27 United Nations: The UN General Assembly adopts resolution ending South Africa's League of Nations mandate to administer South-West Africa. According to the resolution, "South-West Africa comes under the direct responsibility of the United Nations." **West Germany:** The four Cabinet members belonging to the Free Democratic Party resign destroying West Germany's coalition Government.

28 Communist China: Hsinhua, the Chinese Communist press agency, announces that "on Oct. 27, 1966, China successfully conducted over its own territory a guided-missile-nuclear-weapon test."

30 Italy: Delegates from Italy's two Socialist parties, the Italian Socialist Party and the Italian Democratic Socialist party, formally proclaim a merger.

NOVEMBER HEADLINE HIGHLIGHTS

Crisis in the Middle East: Early on Nov. 13, Israeli forces supported by jets and tanks moved into the Hebron area of Jordan, killing 15 Jordanian soldiers and 3 civilians and destroying several homes. The Israeli Government said that the raid was in reprisal for the killing of three Israeli soldiers whose truck had passed over a land mine planted by Arab terrorists.

On Nov. 25 the UN Security Council censured Israel for the raid and warned Israel that any further military actions would not "be tolerated." The Council warned that such acts would lead to "further and more effective steps" to end them.

U.S. Elections: In national elections Nov. 8, the Republican Party gained a total of 8 governorships (with the race in Georgia still in doubt at month's end), 3 U.S. Senate seats, and 47 seats to the U.S. House of Representatives. The 90th session of Congress will consist of 64 Democrats and 36 Republicans in the Senate,

Newly reelected Republican Governors George Romney of Michigan (left) and Nelson Rockefeller of New York enjoy postelection holiday in Puerto Rico.

David Acevedo "Time" magazine, © Time Inc.

and 248 Democrats and 187 Republicans in the House.

In races that drew national attention, Gov. George Romney (R-Mich.) and Gov. Nelson Rockefeller (R-N.Y.) were reelected; Ronald Reagan (R) defeated incumbent Edmund (Pat) Brown (D) for the governorship of California; Charles Percy (R) was elected to the Senate in Illinois over Sen. Paul Douglas; Edward Brooke (R-Mass.) became the first Negro ever elected to the Senate by popular vote;

Gov. Mark Hatfield (R-Oreg.) was elected to the Senate; and Mrs. George C. Wallace succeeded her husband as governor of Alabama.

President in Hospital: President Johnson underwent a 53-minute dual operation on his throat and abdomen at Bethesda Naval Hospital Nov. 16. Later that same day, Dr. James C. Cain, the Johnson family's personal physician, said that the President "could not be better."

President Johnson left the hospital for his LBJ Ranch in Texas Nov. 19.

S EVENTS... NEWS EVENTS... NEWS EVENTS... NEWS EVENTS... NEWS EVEN

1 United States: The Justice Department announces that the Kennedy family has placed autopsy photographs and X rays of the late President Kennedy in the National Archives in Washington, D.C. **South Korea:** A number of soldiers wearing "communist North Korean uniforms" launch a hand-grenade attack, killing 6 U.S. soldiers and a South Korean Army man. The attack occurred eight hours before President Johnson left South Korea.

2 United States: President Johnson arrives at Dulles International Airport, ending 17-day trip to southeast Asia and the Far East.

4 Italy: Devastating rains and winds sweep Italy, causing severe floods and landslides. Florence, noted for its art treasures, is particularly hard hit.

6 United States: President Johnson names Undersecretary of Commerce Alan Boyd secretary of transportation, a newly created cabinet post.

7 Soviet Union: Representatives of Communist China walk out of festivities in Moscow's Red Square commemorating the 49th anniversary of the Bolshevik Revolution.

10 Great Britain: Prime Minister Wilson declares that Britain would like to join the European Economic Community if "our essential . . . interests can be safeguarded."

11 United States: Following launch from Cape Kennedy, Gemini 12—with astronauts Capt. James A. Lovell, Jr., and Maj. Edwin E. Aldrin, Jr., aboard—links up with the nose cone of an Agena target vehicle.

12 Communist China: Representatives of the Soviet Union and its East European allies walk out of a Peking rally marking the centenary of the birth of China's revolutionary leader Sun Yat-sen. **United States:** President Johnson signs

$5,000,000,000, two-year extension Food for Peace bill.

13 India: Prime Minister Indira Gandhi reshuffles her Cabinet.

15 United States: Gemini 12 lands in the Atlantic Ocean, 700 miles from Cape Kennedy.

21 United States: A Mississippi circuit court sentences Aubrey James Norvell to five years in the penitentiary (three years suspended) for assault and battery with intent to kill civil-rights worker James Meredith in June.

22 Spain: Generalissimo Francisco Franco presents a new constitution to the Spanish Cortes (Parliament). The constitution, which the Cortes approved by acclamation, emphasizes social justice and is an important step toward a more liberal political system.

23 United Nations: Canada's External Affairs Minister Paul Martin proposes that Communist China be seated as permanent member of the UN Security Council, and that both Communist China and Nationalist China be represented in the UN General Assembly.

26 Australia: General elections give the coalition Government of Prime Minister Harold Holt another term in office.

28 Burundi: Premier Michel Micombero announces the overthrow of King Ntare V by military coup and declares himself president of the new republic.

29 United Nations: UN General Assembly defeats resolution that would replace Taiwan with Communist China in the United Nations.

30 South Vietnam: The Government announces that its troops and the troops of its allies will observe brief periods of cease-fire at Christmas and during both the solar and lunar New Years. **Barbados:** Caribbean island of Barbados becomes new independent nation.

DECEMBER HEADLINE HIGHLIGHTS

British-Rhodesian Impasse. The UN Security Council voted Dec. 26 to impose mandatory economic sanctions on Rhodesia. On Dec. 5 the white-minority Government of Prime Minister Ian Smith had rejected British terms for settlement of the Rhodesian independence crisis.

Smith and British Prime Minister Harold Wilson met over the Dec. 2–4 weekend on the cruiser *Tiger,* off Gibraltar. They produced a "working document," calling for (1) Rhodesia's Gov. Sir Humphrey Gibbs to appoint a broader Government headed by Smith and including nonwhites; (2) dissolution of Parliament; (3) a four-month transitional period for determining whether a new constitution was acceptable to the people "as a whole."

South Africa's Prime Minister Balthazar Vorster announced his country would disregard the sanctions.

New Bonn Coalition. By a Bundestag vote of 340 out of 472, Kurt Georg Kiesinger (minister-president of Baden-Württemberg) became

Wide World

Left: Richard Goodwin and attorney Simon Rifkind (rear) accompany Mrs. John F. Kennedy to *Look* magazine offices to discuss serialization of *The Death of a President.* Below: Rhodesian Prime Minister Ian Smith (r) and British Prime Minister Wilson leave cruiser *Tiger* Dec. 4. *UPI*

Chancellor of West Germany on Dec. 1, replacing Ludwig Erhard. Kiesinger heads a coalition of the Christian Democratic Union and the Social Democratic Party of Willy Brandt, vice-chancellor and foreign minister.

Space Treaty. On Dec. 8, U.S. and Soviet officials accepted terms of a UN treaty to govern exploration of outer space. The treaty, which must be ratified, prohibits the orbiting of nuclear weapons, and installation of such weapons on spatial bodies.

Book Battle. Mrs. John F. Kennedy filed suit in New York State Supreme Court Dec. 16 to block publication of *The Death of a President*. Accord was reached with *Look* magazine, owner of serial rights, but illness of author William Manchester delayed settlement of the suit against him and his publisher, Harper & Row. Although she had authorized Manchester to write the official story of the assassination, Mrs. Kennedy claimed that it would cause her "irreparable injury."

EVENTS... NEWS EVENTS... NEWS EVENTS... NEWS EVENTS... NEWS EVENTS

2 United Nations: UN General Assembly unanimously reelects U Thant of Burma to another term as secretary-general. In September, Thant had said that he would not offer himself for reelection, but the "overwhelming weight of opinion" forced him to reconsider.

3 Mexico: President Gustavo Diaz Ordaz and President Johnson inspect Amistad Dam at Ciudad Acuña, a joint U.S.-Mexican construction effort. **Japan:** Prime Minister Sato appoints a new 19-member Cabinet.

9 France: Soviet Premier Kosygin concludes eight-day state visit to France.

10 United Arab Republic: Concluding a four-day meeting in Cairo, the Arab League's Defense Council decides to install Iraqi and Saudi Arabian troops in Jordan within two months.

12 United States: The Supreme Court rules that Georgia's legislature may constitutionally elect the state's next governor. Neither of the candidates, Lester Maddox (D) and Rep. Howard Callaway (R), received the necessary majority vote in Nov. 8 general elections.

13 Soviet Union: Tass, the Soviet press agency, charges that U.S. pilots in Vietnam have bombed residential areas within the city limits of Hanoi for the first time.

14 United States: Bill D. Moyers announces his resignation as press secretary and special assistant to President Johnson. Moyers will become publisher of the Long Island, N.Y., newspaper *Newsday*. George C. Christian, a member of the White House staff, is named press secretary. **Spain:** Spanish electorate overwhelmingly approves new constitution, drafted by the Franco Government. **France:** Members of NATO, meeting in Paris without member France, agree to establish a permanent nuclear planning group of seven nations.

19 Soviet Union: Soviet Communist Party Chief Brezhnev is awarded the nation's highest military honor, the title of Hero of the Soviet Union.

20 Turkey: Premier Kosygin becomes first Soviet premier to visit Turkey. **United Nations:** The 21st session of the UN General Assembly adjourns.

22 Greece: Ioannis Paraskevopoulos is installed as premier, replacing Stephanos Stephanopoulos who resigned Dec. 21. **Jordan:** Premier Wasfi al-Tall forms a new Cabinet.

24 South Vietnam: A 48-hour Christmas ceasefire in the Vietnam war goes into effect. **Soviet Union:** Tass announces that Luna 13, a Soviet automatic research station, has landed on the moon and is transmitting information back to earth.

26 United States: Defense Department issues statement reemphasizing that it is U.S. policy to bomb only military targets in North Vietnam and that "all possible care is taken to avoid civilian casualties." However, according to the statement, "it is impossible to avoid all damage to civilian areas."

27 United States: Former President Eisenhower leaves Walter Reed Army Medical Center after 19 days of hospitalization for gallbladder surgery.

28 Communist China: Hsinhua, the Chinese press agency, announces that Communist China "successfully conducted a new nuclear explosion."

30 South Vietnam: A five-day strike by South Vietnamese longshoremen ends. **Great Britain:** Eight paintings, valued at over $5 million, are stolen from the Dulwich College Art Gallery in London.

31 South Vietnam: A 48-hour New Year ceasefire in Vietnam war begins.

EVENTS
OF THE YEAR

ACCIDENTS. In the first 9 months of 1966, accidents of all types took the lives of 82,900 persons in the United States. This represented a 6 per cent increase over the 1965 total and indicated a full year's toll of more than 112,-000 fatalities. The greatest increase by accident classes was in the motor-vehicle category, followed by home and work accidents.

National Safety Council statisticians computed that if the percentage change for the entire year was the same as for the first 9 months, the 1966 rate would be 57.9 accidental deaths for every 100,000 population. This would be higher than in any other year since 1953, when the rate reached 60.1. Earliest years for which rates are available are 1903–07, when there was an average annual death rate from accidents of 88.9. As late as 1936 the rate was 85.9, but it has generally been falling since then. Despite this fact, accidents are still the leading cause of death among persons between ages 1 and 37 and rank fourth as a cause of death among persons of all ages. Motor-vehicle accidents alone rank fifth.

By the end of 1966 it seemed probable that the motor-vehicle death toll would surpass 53,000 for the year, another all-time high. On a rate basis, motor-vehicle deaths reached their peak in 1937—30.8 per 100,000 population. After that the rate generally fell through 1960 —despite multiplying numbers of drivers, automobiles and miles driven—since which it has increased annually. For 1965 it was 25.3, and if the 1966 death toll reached 53,000, the rate would be 27.1. New Federal auto-safety legislation should have an increasingly greater effect on these figures. As for full effect of new automotive-safety features, however, it will be 10 years before safety features required on new models will be present on nearly all cars.

The first 9 months of 1966 saw increases in deaths from home accidents for persons of all age groups. In the public-deaths category, the 0-4 and 65-and-over age groups had decreases; all other age groups had increases.

In the first 10 months of 1966 the National Safety Council's Defensive Driving Course was taken by 157,678 persons across the country. This was 122,426 more persons than took the course in 1965 but considerably short of the council's eventual goal of 1 million trainees a year. By Sept. 30, a total of 192,930 persons had taken the course.

A second National Drivers Test, with national audience participation, was telecast by CBS News in 1966, and a third is planned for 1967.

HOWARD PYLE
President, NATIONAL SAFETY COUNCIL

ADVERTISING. As 1966 ended, some U.S. advertising leaders feared that the Federal Government might initiate measures aimed at restricting advertising expenditures. Their concern stemmed from statements attributed to Donald F. Turner, antitrust chief of the U.S. Department of Justice. He reputedly had spoken of the possibility of limiting promotional expenditures. Sources at the Justice Department denied this, saying that their chief had referred to the possible limitation of advertising expenditures by companies found guilty of illegally dominating a market. In any case, advertising men feared that this might mean restrictions on promotional expenditures.

Meanwhile several of the nation's top advertisers were reportedly being investigated with the intent of determining whether an antitrust action could be brought against any of them. If such an action ensued, the penalty to be sought would be a limitation on the promotional expenditures of the defendant.

Advertising expenditures, meantime, maintained their upward curve in 1966, when an estimated total of $15,600,000,000 was spent. The outlook for 1967 was that another new record would be established. Taking the long view was Arno Johnson, respected senior economist of the J. Walter Thompson Co., who predicted that by 1975 advertising volume would amount to some $30,000,000,000.

In 1965, the country's top 125 national advertisers alone expended $4,000,000,000 to advertise their products. *Advertising Age* reported that 650 advertising agencies had combined billings of $7,200,000,000, a new high. The world's largest agency again was the J. Walter Thompson Co., with billings reported at $530.1 million. Outside the United States, 451 foreign agencies had aggregate billings of $2,900,000,000.

While the 1966 advertising scene was affected by the extended newspaper strike in New York City, action by the Federal Government attracted most attention. It passed a bill designed to enforce "truth in packaging." A Supreme Court decision held that the Borden Co. must cite costs to justify a price discrepancy between its branded milk and Borden-produced, private-label milk. The Food and Drug Administration charged that the drug industry was irresponsible and that it should stop using "the language of advertising to make drugs sound more effective than they are." Finally, a National Commission on Food Marketing criticized advertising as stimulating product proliferation and increased cost.

JAMES V. O'GARA
Executive Editor, ADVERTISING AGE

AFRICA

By HELEN KITCHEN

Editor in Chief, AFRICA REPORT

Speaking to the founding conference of the Organization of African Unity (OAU) in May 1963, Tanzania's President Julius Nyerere articulated the buoyancy and optimism of the 30 presidents, kings and prime ministers meeting in Addis Ababa on that historic occasion: "If, when the nations of the world reassemble at the United Nations, they approach the problems of the world in the same spirit of goodwill and cooperation as the nations of Africa assembled here have approached their African problems, then the human race ... shall have taken an immense step toward universal brotherhood."

At the third annual OAU Assembly in November 1966, the Tanzanian President's address again reflected the prevailing mood of Africa, but this time it was weariness, frustration and disappointment. Returning to Dar es Salaam a few days later, Nyerere summed up the accomplishments of the bickering and sparsely attended third summit meeting. "Africa," he said, "is in a mess."

The painful fact that Africa's visionaries had to face in the latter days of 1966 was that the continent was now further from its goal of a new and genuinely African social, political and economic order than it was at the beginning of the decade. For 1966, like 1965 before it, was a dreary sequence of military coups and countercoups; of reported plots and counter-plots; of bitter words between "radicals" and "moderates"; of desperate measures to try to balance unbalanceable budgets; of unfulfilled economic targets; of declining world market prices for African agricultural exports and rising prices for vital imports; of aid cutbacks in Washington, London, Paris and Moscow; of escalating arms races in North Africa and the Horn. Above all, it was a year in which it became evident that the world had concluded that African unity was an illusion. In practical terms, this meant that the fragmented continent could not now muster enough leverage to move any of the major powers of East or West to direct action on Africa's behalf—notably in bringing an end to white minority rule in the southern third of the continent—when such action would conflict with that power's economic, or political, or military priorities.

This sense of impotence was reinforced by the increasing inability of many of these primarily agricultural nations to feed themselves. In newly independent Botswana, one fifth of the total population was being fed by the Government under the Food and Agriculture Organization World Food Program, and at least half of the independent states were feeding significant portions of their populations with U.S. Public Law-480 grain from the United States. Six years of worsening drought conditions were an immediate cause of food shortages, but a more intractable factor was the continuing exodus of the young from the land to urban centers.

The Decline of Pan-Africanism

The leaders of most of the states that predominated in OAU policy-making councils in

In a July meeting at Nairobi (Kenya) Airport, six heads of African states (l to r): Léon M'Ba, Gabon; Ahmadou Ahidjo, Cameroun; Jomo Kenyatta, Kenya; Nicholas Grunitsky, Togo; Jean Bedel Bokassa, Central African Republic; and Julius Nyerere, Tanzania.

UPI

its early days—notably Ghana, Guinea, Algeria, Mali and the United Arab Republic—believed that the end of direct colonial rule was only "half a loaf," and that genuine decolonization would not take place until Africa could be transformed from a "plantation" functioning only in relation to European needs and pressures into an integrated self-sufficient economic entity.

The key point in the so-called radicals' line of argument is that the prices of Africa's raw-materials exports (chiefly peanuts, palm oil, palm kernel oil, cocoa, coffee, oil, copper and iron ore) tend to rise more slowly than the prices of the manufactured goods still almost exclusively imported from abroad. It follows that the gap between Africa and the economically advanced countries could only widen as long as the economies remained structured as they were in colonial times. In view of the lack of private African capital at the end of the colonial era and the spottiness of the continent's natural resources, the radicals believed that creation of highly centralized, socialist states leading to pan-African unity was the logical way to bring Africa to its overriding goal of economic, political and psychological parity with the rest of the world.

There are sharp differences of opinion about the reasons for the eclipse of the major revolutionary figures, and the weakened influence of those still onstage. One current of analysis is that the social movement for revolutionary decolonization is genuinely representative of African aspirations, and that two primary factors are responsible for the recent turn to what is disdainfully described as *embourgeoisement*. The first is that too many prospering members of the managerial class were unwilling to make the personal sacrifice necessary to break the dependent relationship with the West and rebuild their societies from the ground up. The second is that Soviet-American moves toward a relaxation of tensions, beginning in 1963, destroyed Africa's bargaining position. Without the goad of Soviet pressure, this argument runs, the West was able to adopt an increasingly aloof attitude toward governments trying to set an independent course outside the Western orbit and toward liberation movements in southern Africa.

At the other end of the spectrum, the explanation is offered that Africa's moderate leaders awakened belatedly to the fact that their own governments, as well as the Organization of African Unity, were being subverted by a small minority of magnetic personalities who only claimed to have the masses behind them, and that the moderates thereupon launched a counteroffensive to take control of Africa's destiny. According to this thesis, the uniquely prosperous and unashamedly European-oriented Ivory Coast emerged from its "splendid isolation" in 1964 to become the aggressive quarterback of the moderate bloc. Acting initially through such regional and functional groupings as the five-state *Conseil de l'Entente* (Ivory Coast, Niger, Dahomey, Upper Volta and Togo) and the larger grouping of French-speaking states in the *Organisation Commune Africaine et Malgache,* Ivory Coast President Félix Houphouet-Boigny encouraged the moderate states to throw off their defensive attitudes and to stand forthrightly for an evolutionary route to African development in cooperation with the West. Other explanations of recent trends fall between these two poles.

Evidence of the Rightward Shift

Although it is too early to devise a fully satisfactory analysis of the shift to the Right, or to predict if and when Africa may resume a revolutionary course, the evidence of the shift is easily recited.

Of the eight military takeovers in Africa in 1965 and 1966, six (in the conservatively governed states of Congo [Kinshasa], Dahomey, the Central African Republic, Nigeria, Upper Volta and Burundi) were notably lacking in ideological content and demonstrated only the fragility of all African governments and the low level of force required to upset them. The overthrow of President Kwame Nkrumah, and the subsequent dismantling of the political structure he had created, brought Ghana back to ideological dead center. Algeria under Colonel Boumedienne has made no effort to export the Algerian revolution.

In Kenya the venerable President Jomo Kenyatta successfully isolated and neutralized a burgeoning radical splinter group in 1966. The Somali Republic, with an eye to each new Ethiopian acquisition of military equipment from the United States, continues to accept all of the Soviet arms it can absorb into its military establishment—but the effect on Somalia's domestic and foreign policy making appears to be nil. In Sudan, the vigorous Communist Party lost its representation in the Cabinet and, in December 1965, was made illegal by parliamentary action. Pressures to declare Sierra Leone and Gambia republics, thus loosening post-independence ties to the British Crown, were shelved indefinitely.

In southern Africa, the end of white minority rule remains an elusive goal. Defying most predictions, the ruling white minority in Rhodesia survived a year of world censure and voluntary economic sanctions following its unilateral declaration of independence (UDI) in November 1965. They achieved this, thanks largely to an oil lifeline through South Africa and Portuguese-ruled Mozambique. Landlocked Zambia, whose copper industry is perilously dependent on some imported coal and transport to the sea, has had to play a painfully ambivalent role in relation to neighboring Rhodesia and South Africa. After six years of litigation, the International Court of Justice ruled in July 1966 that Ethiopia and Liberia lacked the "legal standing" to warrant a decision on their charge that South Africa was violating its League of Nations mandate by introducing apartheid into South West Africa. A subsequent United Nations General Assembly resolution terminated the mandate and established a committee to propose ways of implementing the UN's authority in the territory, but at the end of 1966 it was unclear how this could be done.

Two new independent African states were born on the borders of the Republic of South Africa during the year, when the former British High Commission territories of Bechuanaland and Basutoland became the Republic of Botswana and the Kingdom of Lesotho. Both are very poor countries headed by pragmatists who accept the inevitability of their position in the South African economic orbit and believe they cannot afford to take the risk of becoming staging areas for premature revolutionary action against the white citadel.

The low-key wars of liberation against Portuguese rule dragged on inconclusively in Angola and Portuguese Guinea, and the front, opened in late 1964 in Mozambique, succeeded only in tying down several thousand more Portuguese troops. The OAU's "Committee of Liberation," beset by budgetary problems and an uncertain mandate from its parent body, had no more success in 1966 than in 1965 in bridging fissures within nationalist movements of South West Africa, Angola and Rhodesia.

Why Military Coups?

There is no meaningful way of classifying the African governments that have succumbed to military coups, or those that are likely to do so in the future. Countries where military juntas have replaced elected civilian governments since 1964 include products of French, British and Belgian colonial conditioning. They include nations that are very poor in natural resources, and some that are potentially well off. They include the most populous country in Africa, and one of its smallest ministates. They include the highly centralized single-party state of Ghana, the flexible, multiparty

Federation of Nigeria and the hereditary Kingdom of Burundi.

Against this diversity, the armies that have come to power have certain characteristics and values in common, whatever their colonial backgrounds. Although they do not derive from any particular social background, they represent an identifiable professional group with interests transcending (at least initially) some factors that divided politicians they replaced.

Some other broad generalizations can also be made about military rule in Africa. Ironically, the stated goals of the military regimes —stability, order, national unity, egalitarianism, rapid modernization—echo the themes sounded by the civilian governments pushed aside. The first wave of interventions came only when the gap between the civilian government and the electorate had so widened—because of corruption and greed at high levels (especially when combined with growing demands for public sacrifice), the tendency of leaders long in power to listen only to sycophants in their entourage, or the simple inability of well-intentioned governments to cope with inherently impossible economic odds and popular expectations—that authoritarian methods were required to turn the wheels of government.

The potential for further civil and ethnic strife remains very high in all of the African states. With few exceptions—Tunisia, Tanzania, the U.A.R. and the Somali Republic appear to have gone further than most toward a sense of community purpose—they remain artificial creations of 19th-century European bargaining tables whose geographical, tribal and cultural components have been only loosely cemented into nationhood by a thin overlay of institutions. Where national institutions are so frail, and expectations that independence will bring the dawn of a new day are so intense, the deficiencies of leaders loom larger than they do in countries where the office has come to be regarded as bigger than the man.

By the end of 1966, moreover, a new factor had entered the picture: Armies throughout Africa had lost their innocence. The multiplying examples of easy take-overs could have a brush-fire effect, especially in those parts of Africa where the officer corps of neighboring states have links and rivalries that go back to the days when they served together in the army of a colonial power. The odds point toward more military governments by the end of 1967.

The "Cliff-hangers"

At year's end, there were several African situations that did not lend themselves to facile predictions.

THE 39 INDEPENDENT STATES OF AFRICA

STATE	YEAR OF INDEPENDENCE	MAJOR POLITICAL CHANGES DURING 1965-66
ALGERIA	1962	Civilian government of Pres. Ahmed Ben Bella displaced by military coup led by Col. Boumedienne, June 19, 1965.
BOTSWANA	1966	Former British High Commission Territory of Bechuanaland, became independent republic Sept. 30, 1966.
BURUNDI	1962	Prime Minister Pierre Ngendandumwe assassinated Jan. 15, 1965. Loyalist troops thwarted Hutu-led coup attempt Oct. 19, 1965. On July 8, 1966, following prolonged governmental uncertainty, Crown Prince Charles Ndizeye, 19, seized power from long-absent Mwami Mwambutsa IV. Some observers, noting new Prime Minister Micombero was senior army officer, suspected indirect army coup. This confirmed Nov. 28, when Micombero assumed full power.
CAMEROUN	1960	None
CENTRAL AFRICAN REP.	1960	Civilian government led by Pres. David Dacko displaced by military coup led by Col. Bokassa, Jan. 1, 1966.
CHAD	1960	None
CONGO, REP. OF	1960	Noumazaly appointed Prime Minister May 6, 1966, replacing Pascal Lissouba. Problem of a "dual executive" thus relieved.
CONGO, DEM. REP. OF	1960	Civilian government led by Pres. Joseph Kasavubu displaced by military coup led by Gen. Mobutu, Nov. 25, 1965. Mobutu became head of government and head of state Oct. 26, 1966, displacing Prime Minister Leonard Mulamba.
DAHOMEY	1960	Army forced resignation of civilian government of Pres. Migan Apithy Nov. 9, 1965. Following brief provisional civilian rule, Gen. Soglo, army chief of staff, became head of state and government on Dec. 22, 1965.
ETHIOPIA	Independent throughout its history except for Italian colonial period (1936-41)	On March 22, 1966 the Emperor increased the responsibility and authority of the prime minister and cabinet under the 1955 revised constitution.
GABON	1960	None
GAMBIA	1965	Feb. 18, 1965, Gambia became an independent member of the Commonwealth.
GHANA	1957	Government of Pres. Kwame Nkrumah overthrown by army/police military coup, Feb. 24, 1966. Dr. Nkrumah, who was in Peking on visit, subsequently took refuge in Guinea.
GUINEA	1958	Ghana's deposed Nkrumah named co-President in March, 1966, but title apparently nominal.
IVORY COAST	1960	None
KENYA	1963	None
LESOTHO	1966	Former British High Commission Territory of Basutoland, became independent state Oct. 4, 1966. King Moshoeshoe II was arrested by the Government Dec. 28 for assuming too much power.

After a long and bitter debate, the United Nations Security Council voted on Dec. 16 to impose selective, mandatory sanctions against the illegally constituted white-minority regime in Rhodesia. To the angry African delegates in New York, the resolution as finally passed was deficient on three crucial counts: (1) It did not make Britain specifically responsible for preventing oil from reaching Rhodesia (i.e., by naval blockade if necessary). (2) It did not condemn South Africa and Portugal for their support of the Rhodesian Government. (3) It did not call on Britain to withdraw all its previous compromise offers to the Salisbury regime and to declare categorically that independence would be granted only under majority rule.

Adding fuel to African suspicions, Rhodesia's Prime Minister Ian Smith—whose rejection of Britain's "final offer" had prompted the United Kingdom to take the Rhodesian issue to the Security Council—began to talk in Salisbury like a man who envisaged a reopening of the dialogue with Britain. Britain, which was militarily, economically and politically unable to make the decision to intervene with force to reassert its control over Rhodesia, continued to argue that the kind of sanctions voted by the UN would eventually bring down the Smith regime or drastically alter its bargaining position.

In the Horn of Africa, where President Charles de Gaulle offered self-determination to French Somaliland after an unexpectedly bitter demonstration on his arrival for a goodwill visit in August, a new dimension was added to the existing tension between Somalia and Ethiopia. The Somali Republic is pledged by its constitution to seek the peaceful union of all Somalis in the neighboring countries and in French Somaliland, the last remaining French colonial territory in Africa. Ethiopia, however,

STATE	YEAR OF INDEPENDENCE	MAJOR POLITICAL CHANGES DURING 1965-66
LIBERIA	1847	None
LIBYA	1951	Mazik appointed Prime Minister March 20, 1965, replacing Mohammed Muntasir.
MALAGASY REP.	1960	None
MALAWI	1964	Malawi assumed republican status within the Commonwealth on July 6, 1966, and established presidential regime.
MALI	1960	None
MAURITANIA	1960	None
MOROCCO	1956	On June 7, 1965, Hassan recessed Parliament indefinitely, dismissed his Prime Minister, and assumed full responsibilty over governmental operations.
NIGER	1960	None
NIGERIA	1960	Civilian government led by Pres. Nnamdi Azikiwe and Prime Minister Sir Abubakar Tafawa Balewa overthrown by military coup, Jan. 15-16, 1966. Resulting compromise government, led by Maj. Gen. Johnson T.U. Aguiyi-Ironsi, overthrown by second military coup, July 29, 1966. Lt. Col. Gowon, leader of the second coup, remained in charge of increasingly shaky federation at year's end.
RWANDA	1962	None
SENEGAL	1960	None
SIERRA LEONE	1961	None
SOMALI REP.	1960	None
SOUTH AFRICA	1931	Prime Minister Hendrik Verwoerd assassinated Sept. 6, 1966. Successor chosen by parliamentary vote.
SUDAN	1956	Mohammed Ahmed Mahgoub's coalition government fell on Constituent Assembly no-confidence vote July 26, 1966. Sadik al-Mahdi, 30-year-old descendant of the founder of the modern Sudan, replaced him. Both are Umma Party.
TANZANIA	1961	None
TOGO	1960	Attempted coup d'état on Nov. 21, 1966 (by persons loyal to late Pres. Sylvanus Olympio, assassinated 1963) put down by army.
TUNISIA	1956	None
UGANDA	1962	On April 15, 1966, Prime Minister Milton Obote proclaimed a new basic law establishing a unitary state, and announced he would take over the presidency from the Kabaka of Buganda. With army assistance, he quelled a May 23 rebellion in Buganda and the Kabaka fled the country.
UNITED ARAB REP.	1922	Premiership changed hands twice: On Oct. 2, 1965, Ali Sabri was replaced by Zakari Mohieddin, who in turn gave way to Mohammed Sidkyi Suliman on Sept. 11, 1966.
UPPER VOLTA	1960	Civilian government led by Pres. Maurice Yameogo displaced by military coup led by Lt. Col. Lamizana, Jan. 3, 1966.
ZAMBIA	1964	None

with a vital interest in free access to the port and railway terminus in the territory's administrative capital of Djibouti, declared in September that French Somaliland is historically an "integral part of the Empire."

And in Nigeria, where thousands of Eastern Region Ibos were massacred before they could escape from the Hausa-dominated Northern Region following the military countercoup of July 29, ethnic bitterness had reached such proportions that Africa's most populous nation seemed perilously close to disintegration into tribal states. If there were any reasons for optimism, they were that the break had not yet come, that Nigeria's competent senior civil service had risen to the occasion and was preventing administrative collapse on the Congo pattern, and that the interregional economic ties created over a period of half a century were proving remarkably strong and resilient and difficult to untangle.

If stability for Africa seems more remote than it did in 1960, it is perhaps because we have expected of African leadership a degree of wisdom for which there are few precedents at comparable stages in the history of developed nations. As Anthony Hartley observed in a perceptive account of a recent trip through West Africa, published in *Encounter* magazine: "Africa will continue to be enmeshed in a political web constantly woven and unraveled ... How that change will end is hard to foresee, but the metamorphosis at present under way is at least authentically African. ... For all the importance of aid, neither Europe nor America can live this experience for Africa. In history there is no substitute for failure. Throughout a vast continent the forests, the rivers, and the deserts, disease, superstition, and brutality await their true conquerors who, in defeating them, will confirm a victory over themselves. ..."

Secretary of Agriculture Freeman, center, examines crops in South Vietnam.

AGRICULTURE

By ORVILLE L. FREEMAN
U.S. Secretary of Agriculture

Among outstanding developments on the agricultural scene in 1966 were the disappearance of long-standing grain surpluses in the United States; a food crisis in India relieved by record U.S. grain shipments to that country; and the establishment of a Food for Freedom program proposed by President Lyndon B. Johnson.

The U.S. carry-over of wheat on July 1, 1966, was down to 536 million bushels, a drop of about one third from the preceding year, and a decline of over 60 per cent from the record carry-over of 1961. The feed-grain carry-over as of October 1, 1966, was about 47 million tons, compared with almost 56 million tons in 1965 and 85 million tons in 1961. The 1966 carry-over of feed grains was at about the level of reasonable reserves, while the carry-over of wheat was slightly below this level.

Thus for the first time in 12 years the United States had no grain surpluses, an objective previously expected to be achieved in 1968. While the crop-reducing feed-grain and wheat programs were partly responsible, the sharp expansion in grain exports, which reached a record high in fiscal 1966, also played a major role.

A severe 1965 drought led to a food crisis in India. At the beginning of 1966, evidence indicated that India's crop shortage would be unprecedented, and that grain-import needs would exceed the requirements of any other country at any other time. To ease the situation, the United States made a vast quantity of wheat and other grains available for purchase under Food for Peace provisions, and by the spring of 1966, U.S. grain was being shipped to India at the rate of about a million tons per month. During the year U.S. grain shipments to India totaled about 9 million tons, some 50 per cent more than was shipped to that country in 1965.

In addition to food aid, the United States stepped up its technical assistance to enable India to make better use of its agricultural resources. Department of Agriculture teams gave particular attention to long-range soil- and water-conservation programs, and demonstration projects illustrating the benefits obtainable by proper fertilization and use of quality seeds.

Food for Freedom Program

While the Indian crisis was the most spectacular international agricultural development, it was not the only indication of a tightening world food situation. A succession of poor crops in Russia, eastern Europe, and China, which caused these regions to import large quantities of wheat, also helped focus international attention on dwindling world carry-overs of grain.

It is now apparent that the greatest single challenge the world is likely to face in the last one third of the twentieth century is that of producing and distributing enough food to wipe out widespread hunger for a rapidly growing population. The problem is centered in the food-short developing countries of Asia, Africa and Latin America.

To help cope with the challenge, President Johnson proposed a Food for Freedom program designed to assure not only continued food aid to the developing nations, but more effective assistance in helping these nations develop their own agricultures. The Food for Freedom program, an outgrowth of Food for Peace but with far greater emphasis on self-help, was authorized by Congress in the fall of 1966.

Three sets of facts have important bearing on Food for Freedom operations.

1. The United States in 1966–67 will have ample supplies of wheat to meet all domestic and commercial-export demands and for a still-generous, if prudently adjusted, overseas food-aid program. With big surpluses no longer available, care will be exercised in programing the use of wheat and other grains for food assistance.

To get additional production the national wheat allotment for 1967 was raised to 68.2 million acres, an increase of almost one third over the 1966 allotment.

2. Other agricultural-exporting nations will need to give more assistance in meeting world food needs than they have been providing. It is neither desirable nor right that the United States alone should bear the overwhelmingly large part of food-aid programs. With a record 1966 world wheat crop in prospect, other wheat exporters should be in good position to take on additional food-aid commitments.

3. Less-developed nations will need to speed up and intensify their own efforts to improve food production. They must give agricultural improvement higher priority than in the past.

But these nations cannot do the job themselves. They need technical help, and Food for Freedom will emphasize this activity.

Even before the new program was established, the U.S. Department of Agriculture was rapidly expanding its involvement in international agricultural technical-assistance and training programs.

During fiscal 1966, 300 USDA technicians worked in 39 countries through programs sponsored by the Agency for International Development, compared with 194 technicians in 26 countries a year earlier. There were 23 long-term resident USDA teams operating in developing countries, as against 13 in fiscal 1965. And the department cooperated in 84 international agricultural-development projects, nearly double the 46 of fiscal 1965.

Training figures also showed sharp increases. During fiscal 1966, the department developed, supervised and evaluated training programs for about 5,000 technicians and other agricultural specialists from over 100 countries. Some 350 private companies and institutions cooperated with USDA and the land-grant universities in these training programs.

These activities are showing results. A USDA/AID team has been working in El Salvador since late 1963. Better seed varieties

A U.S. Department of Agriculture scientist at a Peoria, Ill., laboratory prepares soybean flour, which may help supply protein to areas lacking in animal-protein foods.
USDA

are being used; 2,000 farmers have been re-settled on their own farms; a marketing coop-erative has been organized; and a supervised credit program has been started.

The largest team—24 members—is in Brazil. Working with the Brazilian Government, they have developed a farm-market news service which is helping raise farm incomes and re-duce marketing costs in Brazil. Soil scientists on the USDA team are assisting the Brazilian Government in locating 75 million acres of land suitable for settlement and development in the western two thirds of that country. When completed, the survey will help the Govern-ment select sites for future villages where set-tlers from overpopulated sections will have a reasonable chance to succeed in agricultural and industrial development. Other USDA spe-cialists in Brazil are working on marketing cooperatives, farm credit, and price-incentive policies to stimulate farm production.

A special effort has been made to support the "second front" in Vietnam. A presidential mission to Vietnam recommended ways to help Vietnamese farmers increase agricultural pro-duction. A second USDA team followed up with specific plans for improved credit, fish-eries, fertilizer use, and government organiza-tion. In the summer of 1966 the department recruited 18 agricultural specialists for AID direct-hire, and the Federal Extension Service is recruiting some 40 county agents for service in Vietnam's provinces.

An important part of the Food for Freedom activities involves intensified efforts to develop new sources of protein foods for the world's malnourished people.

Protein deficiency is especially serious for children, the sick, and pregnant and nursing women. The brains of preschool children, for example, reach 90 per cent of their full weight before they are four years old. If these chil-dren lack sufficient protein in this preschool period, the brain never develops properly.

Since the underdeveloped nations cannot financially afford to get their protein from animal sources, the United States is seeking to convert vegetable proteins—such as soybean flour or cottonseed—into tasty food mixtures that will provide nutritionally adequate diets at low cost. Several such projects are under way. USDA researchers have developed a method of making high-protein diet supple-ments by fermenting cereals and soybeans. These foods resemble *tempeh,* a cakelike staple in Indonesia, but are more nutritious.

A nourishing flour—from two by-products of flour milling, bran and middlings, which up to now have been fed mainly to livestock be-cause of their high fiber content—also has been developed. The new flour has more pro-teins and vitamins than regular white flour and goes well in soups, gruel, and *pasta.* Another promising research project deals with finding strains of wheat that combine high yields with high protein content.

Scientists have recently developed a hand process for making soybean flour. With simple equipment available in almost any village, a hand-operated machine can be made which will produce soybean flour containing 40 per cent protein.

The Department of Agriculture also supports a large number of research ventures abroad aimed at improving diets in the food-short nations. One project in the Middle East re-cently developed a protein-rich baby food, made from low-cost crops such as chick-peas, sesame and soybeans that are readily available in the Middle East. This new food is rich in amino acids, B vitamin, calcium and iron.

Arrangements are being worked out also under which American business firms can help underdeveloped countries produce high-protein food from native crops. Such ventures could become profitable for locally owned and local-ly managed commercial ventures.

The Roman philosopher Seneca observed that "a hungry people listens not to reason, nor cares for justice."

This realization, exemplified in the Food for Freedom program, is surely among the most significant and hopeful agricultural develop-ments of recent years.

ALABAMA. In November elections Lurleen Wallace succeeded her husband, George C. Wallace, as governor, and John J. Sparkman (D) retained his U.S. Senate seat. . . . Negro voter-registration drives brought violence to Bir-mingham and other towns in January. . . . A three-judge Federal panel outlawed the poll tax in March. . . . Tornadoes ripped through the state March 3–4. . . . On June 17, TVA said it would build the world's largest nuclear-powered generating plant near Brown Ferry.

ALASKA. A disastrous fire struck Sitka, first capital of Alaska, Jan. 2. . . . Public Law 89-375 provided $4.6 million for U.S. participa-tion in 1967's Alaska Purchase Centennial. . . . Public Law 89-658 extended the fishery zone 9 mi. beyond the 3-mi. territorial sea limit. . . . Gov. William A. Egan's Proclamation of Re-apportionment and Redistricting was chal-lenged, appealed to the Alaska Supreme Court, and upheld in May. . . . The Governor lost to Walter J. Hickel (R) in a bid for reelection.

FROM U. S.	COUNTRIES	TO U. S.
Robert G. Neumann	AFGHANISTAN	Abdul Majid
John D. Jernegan	ALGERIA	Cherif Guellal
Edwin M. Martin	ARGENTINA	Alvaro Alsogaray
Edward A. Clark	AUSTRALIA	John Keith Waller
J. W. Riddleberger	AUSTRIA	Ernst Lemberger
Ridgway B. Knight	BELGIUM	Louis Scheyven
Douglas Henderson	BOLIVIA	Julio Sanjines-Goytia
John W. Tuthill	BRAZIL	Vasco Leitao da Cunha
Henry A. Byroade	BURMA	U Tun Win
Donald Dumont	BURUNDI	Francois Kisukurume[2]
Leland Barrows	CAMEROUN	Joseph Owono
W. W. Butterworth	CANADA	A. Edgar Ritchie
Claude G. Ross	CENTRAL AFR. REP.	Michel Gallin-Douathe
Cecil B. Lyon	CEYLON	Oliver Weerasinghe
Brewster H. Morris	CHAD	Boukar Abdoul
Ralph A. Dungan	CHILE	Radomiro Tomic
Walter P. McConaughy	CHINA (TAIWAN)	Chow Shu-kai
Reynold E. Carlson	COLOMBIA	Eduardo Uribe
G. McMurtrie Godley	CONGO, DEM. REP. OF THE	Cyrille Adoula
H. L. T. Koren	CONGO, REP. OF THE	Jonas Mouanza
Raymond Telles	COSTA RICA	Fernando Ortuño
Taylor G. Belcher	CYPRUS	Zenon Rossides
Jacob D. Beam	CZECHOSLOVAKIA	Karel Duda
Clinton E. Knox	DAHOMEY	L. Ignacio-Pinto
Katharine Elkus White	DENMARK	Torben Ronne
John Hugh Crimmins	DOMINICAN REP.	Hector Garcia Godoy
Wimberly Coerr	ECUADOR	Gustavo Larrea
Raul H. Castro	EL SALVADOR	R. de Clairmont-Duenas
Edward M. Korry	ETHIOPIA	Tashoma Haile-Mariam
Tyler Thompson	FINLAND	Olavi Munkki
Charles E. Bohlen	FRANCE	Charles Lucet
David Bane	GABON	Louis Owanga
William R. Rivkin	GAMBIA	(vacant)
George C. McGhee	GERMANY (WEST)	Heinrich Knappstein
F. H. Williams	GHANA	Abraham B. Kofi
D. K. E. Bruce	GREAT BRITAIN	Patrick Dean
Phillips Talbot	GREECE	A. A. Matsas
John G. Mein	GUATEMALA	F. Linares Aranda
Robinson McIlvaine	GUINEA	Karim Bangoura
Delmar R. Carlson	GUYANA	John Carter
B. E. Timmons III	HAITI	Ducarmel Bocage[2]
Joseph J. Jova	HONDURAS	Ricardo Midence Soto
J. K. Penfield	ICELAND	P. Thorsteinsson
Chester Bowles	INDIA	Braj Kumar Nehru
Marshall Green	INDONESIA	I. N. Djajadiningrat[2]
Armin H. Meyer	IRAN	Khosro Khosrovani
Robert C. Strong	IRAQ	Nasir Hani
Raymond R. Guest	IRELAND	William P. Fay
Walworth Barbour	ISRAEL	Avraham Harman
G. F. Reinhardt	ITALY	Sergio Fenoaltea
George A. Morgan	IVORY COAST	Charles Gomis[2]
Wilson Beale, Jr.	JAMAICA	Neville Ashenheim
U. Alexis Johnson	JAPAN	Ryuji Takeuchi
Findley Burns, Jr.	JORDAN	Farhan Shubeilat
Glenn W. Ferguson	KENYA	Burudi Nabwera
Winthrop G. Brown	KOREA (SOUTH)	Hyun Chul Kim
Howard Cottam	KUWAIT	Talat Al-Ghoussein
William Sullivan	LAOS	Khamking Souvanlasy

FROM U. S.	COUNTRIES	TO U. S.
Dwight J. Porter	LEBANON	I. H. El-Ahdab
Ben Hill Brown, Jr.	LIBERIA	S. Edward Peal
David W. Newsome	LIBYA	Fathi Abidia
Patricia R. Harris	LUXEMBOURG	Maurice Steinmetz
C. V. Ferguson, Jr.	MALAGASY REP.	L. Rakotomalala
	MALAWI	Vincent H. Gondwe
Marshall P. Jones	MALAYSIA	Tan Sri Ong Yoke Lin
James D. Bell	MALDIVE IS.	(vacant)
Cecil B. Lyon	MALI	Moussa Léo Keita
C. Robert Moore	MALTA	Arvid Pardo
George J. Feldman	MAURITANIA	Abdallahi Ould Daddah
Geoffrey W. Lewis	MEXICO	Hugo B. Margain
Fulton Freeman	MOROCCO	Ahmed Laraki
Henry J. Tasca	NEPAL	Padma Bahadur Khatri
Carol C. Laise	NETHERLANDS	Carl W. A. Schurmann
William R. Tyler	NEW ZEALAND	George R. Laking
Herbert Powell	NICARAGUA	G. Sevilla-Sacasa
Aaron S. Brown	NIGER	Adamou Mayaki
Robert J. Ryan	NIGERIA	N. Ade Martins
Elbert G. Mathews	NORWAY	Arne Gunneng
Margaret Joy Tibbetts	PAKISTAN	Agha Hilaly
Eugene M. Locke	PANAMA	Richardo M. Arias E.
Charles W. Adair, Jr.	PARAGUAY	Juan Plate
William P. Snow	PERU	Celso Pastor
J. Wesley Jones	PHILIPPINES	José F. Imperial[2]
William Blair, Jr.	POLAND	Zdzislaw Szewczyk[2]
John A. Gronouski	PORTUGAL	Vasco Vieira Garin
W. Tapley Bennett	RUMANIA	Petre Bălăceanu
Richard H. Davis	RWANDA	Celestin Kabanda
Leo G. Cyr	SAUDI ARABIA	Ibrahim Al-Sowayel
Hermann F. Eilts	SENEGAL	Ousmane Socé Diop
William R. Rivkin	SIERRA LEONE	Gershon B. O. Collier
Andrew V. Corr	SINGAPORE	(vacant)
Francis J. Galbraith	SOMALI REP.	Ahmed M. Adan
Raymond L. Thurston	SOUTH AFRICA	H. L. T. Taswell
William M. Rountree	SPAIN	Marquis de Merry del Val
Angier Biddle Duke		
W. H. Weathersby	SUDAN	Amin Ahmed Hussein
J. G. Parsons	SWEDEN	Hubert de Besche
John S. Hayes	SWITZERLAND	Felix Schnyder
Hugh H. Smythe	SYRIAN ARAB REP.	A. Galeb Kayali[2]
John H. Burns	TANZANIA	Michael Lukumbuzya
Graham Martin	THAILAND	Sukich Nimmanheminda
William Witman II	TOGO	Robert Ajavon
Robert G. Miner	TRINIDAD and TOBAGO	Ellis Clarke
F. H. Russell	TUNISIA	Rachid Driss
Parker T. Hart	TURKEY	T. Menemencioğlu
H. E. Stebbins	UGANDA	E. O. Allimadi
Llewellyn E. Thompson	U.S.S.R.	Anatoliy F. Dobrynin
Lucius D. Battle	UNITED ARAB REP.	Mostafa Kamel
Elliot P. Skinner	UPPER VOLTA	Paul Rouamba
Henry A. Hoyt	URUGUAY	Juan F. Yriart
Maurice Bernbaum	VENEZUELA	E. Tejera-Paris
Henry Cabot Lodge	VIETNAM (SOUTH)	Vu Van Thai
Harlan Clark[2]	YEMEN	Yahya H. Geghman
C. B. Elbrick	YUGOSLAVIA	V. Micunovic
Robert C. Good	ZAMBIA	Samuel C. Mbilishi

[1] As of December 1966; all diplomats have the rank of ambassador except those noted.
[2] Chargé d'affaires.

AMERICAN LIBRARY ASSOCIATION. Librarians must become more "active, even aggressive, partners" in education if they are to meet the challenging demands of today's society, Mary V. Gaver, the president of the American Library Association, declared at the inaugural banquet of the 85th ALA annual conference July 10-16, 1966. To meet the shifting and expanding educational demands of the nation, Miss Gaver outlined a four-point program for librarians: recruitment, instruction in the use of libraries, library education, and manpower utilization.

The 1966 annual ALA conference in New York City with over 9,300 delegates was the largest meeting of librarians in history. Foster E. Mohrhardt, director, National Agricultural Library, was elected ALA president-elect. He holds that position until the 1967 convention to be held in San Francisco.

A fourteenth ALA division, the Information Science and Automation Division, was created by council action at the 1966 ALA midwinter meeting. This division will concern itself with the development and application of electronic data-processing techniques and the use of automated systems in all areas of library work. It will also foster research, promote the development of appropriate standards, disseminate information and provide a forum for the discussion of common problems.

David H. Clift, executive director of ALA, announced the establishment, on Sept. 1, of a new Office for Library Education. The establishment of this office was made possible by a six-year grant, with matching ALA funds, from the H. W. Wilson Foundation.

A recommended basic plan for a national statistics program for libraries was set forth at the National Conference on Library Statistics, cosponsored by the National Center for Educational Statistics, U.S. Office of Education, and ALA's Library Administration Division.

The 1966 J. Morris Jones-World Book Encyclopedia-ALA Goals Awards was presented to the American Association of School Librarians for a revision of national school-library standards.

Standards of Quality for Public Library Service, a revision of the national public-library standards, and *Standards for Library Services for the Blind and Visually Handicapped* were adopted by the Public Library Association and the Library Administration Division respectively.

ROBERT J. SHAW
Assistant to the Executive Secretary
Library Administration Division
AMERICAN LIBRARY ASSOCIATION

ANTARCTICA. Several steps in the long-range objectives of the U.S. Antarctic Research Program were accomplished during 1966. High on the polar plateau, in an area more remote than any the United States had previously chosen, a small, compact station named Plateau Station was established. A small camp is located 1,000 feet from the main station for use in case of emergency. During the 1966 winter, eight men wintered at the station for the purpose of carrying out meteorological, ionospheric and medical research.

Plateau Station also served as the terminus of the second phase of the geophysical traverse from the South Pole into Queen Maud Land, one of the few remaining unexplored areas on earth. Traveling 725 nautical miles in Sno-Cats Dec. 15, 1965–Jan. 29, 1966, the 11-man traverse party made observations in glaciology, meteorology and geomagnetism. Continuous radio-frequency soundings as well as conventional seismic methods were used to profile the sub-ice rock surface, located at an average depth of 9,200 feet. Ice-surface elevations ranged from 12,198 to 8,214 feet. The traverse will resume its zigzag route toward the Princess Ragnhild Coast during the 1967-68 austral summer.

On Oct. 12, 1965, three members of a British expedition died when their tractor fell 150 feet into a crevasse 250 miles from Halley Bay. On Feb. 2, 1966, a U.S. Navy LC-47 aircraft crashed on the Ross Ice Shelf with a crew of six, all of whom were killed. Eleven days later, another member of the U.S. expedition was killed in a cargo-unloading accident at the South Pole.

The U.S. Antarctic Policy Group approved a conservation policy using as a guideline the Agreed Measures for the Protection and Conservation of Antarctic Fauna and Flora, which had been adopted at a 1964 consultative meeting of the Antarctic Treaty signatories in Brussels. The National Science Foundation inaugurated a system of permits for all U.S. Antarctic Research Program personnel in order to control the collection of indigenous mammals and birds.

The Japanese station Showa, closed since Feb. 8, 1962, was reopened with the aid of a newly constructed, powerful icebreaker, the *Fuji.*

Argentina conducted an oversnow traverse from its General Belgrano Station to the South Pole and flew three aircraft from Argentina via that base to the Pole.

T. O. JONES
Director, Environmental Sciences Division
NATIONAL SCIENCE FOUNDATION

ANTHROPOLOGY. In Pittsburgh, Pa., at their 65th annual meeting, members of the American Anthropological Association voted to establish a strong set of ethical guidelines for scholars working on government contracts. The decision was a response to a report by former association president Ralph Beals, criticizing attempts by U.S. intelligence agencies to use social scientists for undercover work in foreign countries. Beals' report was prompted by Operation Camelot, a U.S. Army-financed project undertaken by The American University, Washington, D.C., in 1965 to study insurgency and counterinsurgency in Chile. Though canceled by the State Department, the project produced sharp criticism of U.S. scholars in Latin America. In many countries it was suggested that U.S. scholars were U.S. agents.

The Wenner-Gren Foundation awarded its Viking Medal to French scholar Claude Lévi-Strauss. Dr. Lévi-Strauss received the medal following worldwide balloting by fellow members of his profession, many of whom consider him the world's foremost anthropologist. He has urged a marshaling of anthropologists throughout the world to rescue now-available data on primitive societies.

In Europe, Dr. Robert Heine-Geldern, an Austrian anthropologist, formed an International Committee on Urgent Anthropological and Ethnological Research. UNESCO supports this program in both funds and formal arrangements.

In early 1966 a Chicago meeting dealt with the problem of Man the Hunter. The conference was called to assess knowledge about the world's hunting-and-gathering peoples, and to make plans to acquire more essential data before these societies disappear. George P. Murdock, of the University of Pittsburgh, noted that 10,000 years ago the world's population probably lived by hunting and gathering. Growing archaeological evidence may cause Dr. Murdock to push his dating back by almost another 5,000 years.

However, he noted that by the time of Christ, almost 50 per cent of the earth's human population was engaged in agricultural or pastoral activities. By the time the New World was discovered, only 15 per cent of the world's population depended on hunting and gathering food. Now only isolated pockets of hunters and gatherers remain.

Physical Anthropology. It is one of the cherished theories of physical anthropology that only 1 hominid (manlike creature) could occupy a given area at a given time. However, there have been recent finds of 2 or more distinct hominids in Africa, contemporaneous in both time and place. The consensus is fairly strong that these 2 hominids are distinct at the genus or species level and coexisted during the first half of the Pleistocene (age of glaciers). Some anthropologists now feel this opens the possibility that 1 or more extinct branches of the Hominidae could be ancestral to *Homo sapiens*. It has been further suggested that the reduction to a single hominid line, from the mid-Pleistocene, may have been due to one manlike creature's developing the tool of language. The line that developed language would of course be more immediately ancestral to man, since only man is a culture-bearing, culture-transmitting creature.

HAROLD SUSSMAN
Charles Kriser Fellow, NEW YORK UNIVERSITY

ARCHAEOLOGY. The year 1966 saw the appearance of Volume 110, No. 2 of the *Proceedings of the American Philosophical Society*, given over to *Archaeology: Horizons New and Old*, an important assessment of where the science stood in 1966. Two valuable compendiums of worldwide scope also appeared: *Prehistoric Societies* by Grahame Clark and Stuart Piggott, and *La Préhistoire* by André Leroi-Gourhan et al. One further matter of general interest was the appearance of studies by physicists advising caution in accepting radiocarbon age determinations at face value.

Western Hemisphere. In the United States, at Ephrata, Penn., Dale Beiver and William Pilkanis excavated the site of Bethania, a monastery believed built in the 1740's. Digging in Lapeer County, Michigan, Warren L. Wittry, of the Cranbrook Institute of Science, found a mastodon possibly 10,000 years old. During

Near New Delhi an Indian archaeologist examines footprints carved into rock and dating back to the third century B.C.

UPI

Above: Near Sperlonga, Italy, archaeologists have uncovered a playground of Roman Emperor Tiberius, who ruled from A.D. 14 to 37. The buildings and pools presumably were buried centuries ago by a landslide. Below: At Cadbury Castle, near Yeovil, England, archaeologist Sir Mortimer Wheeler examines finds unearthed during search for Camelot, home of the legendary King Arthur. Sir Mortimer heads the Camelot Research Committee.

Photos UPI

1966, Earl H. Swanson, Idaho State University Museum, did further excavating of two rock shelters overlooking the Salmon River in Idaho. Radiocarbon dating puts the possible age of one shelter at 10,000 years and the other at 11,500 years.

The Royal Ontario Museum, University of Toronto, continued its diggings at Altun Ha in British Honduras. A "lost city" discovered in the mountainous jungles of northern Peru may turn out to be the fabled Gran Pajatan, great city of the Chachapoyas, a northern people whom the Incas defeated and banished. Along the northern coast of Peru, the National University of Trujillo is restoring Chan Chan, a mud city covering an area of seven square miles.

Eastern Hemisphere. Early in 1966, bulldozers preparing a construction site in Nice, France, turned up a very early open-air encampment. Dr. Henry de Lumley and his aides then located the remains of an oval-shaped building, 50 x 20 feet in size. From the collection of bones and teeth identified as those of rhinoceros, elephant, wild boar, deer and rabbit, it appears that this settlement existed from 200,000 to 300,000 years ago.

In July, British archaeologist Sir Mortimer Wheeler announced that findings near Yeovil, England, indicated it to be the site of King Arthur's Camelot, which legend dates back to around A.D. 500.

New research in the Indus Valley, western Pakistan, at the Harappa site of Mohenjo-Daro, suggests that this ancient center of civilization may have been drowned in mud. Tests show deep layers of silt and evidences of much rebuilding. At Haft Tepe in Khuzestan, south-western Iran, Ezat Negahban of Tehran University exposed a late Elamite tomb complex (probably 8th to 6th century B.C.). Higher on the Iranian plateau, a Canadian team from Toronto tested an important cave, an early village site and a large mound named Godin Tepe. While on a survey in western Iran, David Stronach and Cuyler Young came across two Seljuk tombs of the 11th century. These are among the finest decorated brick monuments found in Iran to date.

In Syria, at Mureybat, Maurits Van Loon, of the Oriental Institute, University of Chicago, excavated an early village revealing an accumulation of human remains but no pottery. Diana Kirkbride conducted a fruitful operation in Jordan at an early village site, Beidha. This village flourished about 9,000 years ago. The Israeli Government Antiquities Service, as usual, was deeply involved during 1966 in caring for antiquities exposed in building and engineering operations.

In Turkey, archaeological teams from Cornell and Harvard uncovered an ancient bazaar in Sardis, dating from the 7th century B.C. Study of the bazaar adds to the history of city planning. James Mellaart, London University, unearthed a Neolithic hunting shrine at Catal Huyuk in Anatolia. The walls of this 8,000-year-old building are covered with rich paintings of hunting scenes believed to be the oldest such paintings found in a man-made dwelling.

The normal programs of various national and foreign academies in Athens and Rome were followed in 1966. In the shadow of the Acropolis, remains of private houses on the fringe of the Agora were excavated. Work in the district of Pylos turned up what may be King Nestor's palace. At Peristeraia three newly opened tombs contained gold objects of a workmanship suggesting mid-16th-century origin. In central Sicily a team from Princeton University found one of the largest hoards of ancient Greek gold coins ever reported. The 44 coins, in fine condition, are from 22 to 24 centuries old.

IRENE M. HAINES
The Oriental Institute
UNIVERSITY OF CHICAGO

ARCHITECTURE. The new Metropolitan Opera House in New York's Lincoln Center made a glamorous debut on Sept. 16, 1966. Opening night revealed a richly gilded colossus that was acoustically excellent and a technological marvel. Aesthetically, the house, designed by Wallace K. Harrison, is less than a complete success, the main deficiency being a lack of dra-matic focus. The bland facade of five bays is backed by a transparent wall of busily divided glass, revealing a diffuse jangle of colors, forms, textures and lights behind.

The opera house brings the major areas of Lincoln Center to essential completion. The world's largest cultural complex is light and spacious, and with its promenading crowds, certainly a pleasant place to be. Nevertheless, the total has achieved only compromise-by-committee, neither-modern-nor-traditional prudence rather than a true distinction. The exception is the north plaza, where a massive figure by Henry Moore and its reflecting pool are handsomely integrated into the surrounding space.

Two other New York City buildings by distinguished architects were completed in 1966. The CBS Building by the late Eero Saarinen is a fitting monument to a brilliant career. The uncompromising sobriety of this structure only enhances the elegance of its forms and proportions. The edifice illuminates the crudity of most of the box-style buildings put up in New York over the past years.

The Whitney Museum in New York, by Marcel Breuer with Hamilton Smith, is undoubtedly the most unconventional building of 1966. Of gray granite, it has setbacks on the lower floors, so that the facade is in the form of an inverted staircase. This unusual arrangement, continuing below the sidewalk to a sunken sculpture court, exposes a glass-walled story beneath street level. The design represents an imaginative and effective use of the city lot the building occupies.

The year 1966 was one of numerous accomplishments for Edward Durell Stone. His art museum in Ponce, Puerto Rico, was completed, and his John F. Kennedy Center for the Performing Arts in Washington, D.C., was begun. The fanciful elegance that is the hallmark of his style was fully revealed in the Pakistan Institute of Nuclear Science and Technology at Islamabad, in West Pakistan. Stone also received the giant commission for the new Pakistani capital, Islamabad, and will design five government structures, including the presidential residence, for it. His General Motors Tower in Manhattan, fifty stories high and sheathed in marble, is yet to be built.

Louis I. Kahn displayed his penchant for rectangular shapes used in a romantic manner in his Eleanor Donnelley Erdman Dormitory at Bryn Mawr College in Pennsylvania. Kahn was the subject of a summer show at the Museum of Modern Art in New York, which presented a review of his buildings and works in progress.

Stone's Ponce Museum of Art, Ponce, Puerto Rico.

Courtesy, Edward Durell Stone

Saarinen's CBS Building, New York City.

CBS

Another major project of the year was the new campus of the University of Illinois in downtown Chicago. The architect Walter Netsch, of Skidmore, Owings & Merrill, designed the Air Force Academy's space-frame chapel in Colorado.

Well received critically in 1966 was the Houston concert hall—named for Jesse H. Jones—by the Texas firm of Caudill Rowlett Scott. Its rectangular exterior encloses a seashell-shaped auditorium.

Romaldo Giurgola, chairman of the Columbia University division of architecture, was awarded the Arnold W. Brunner Memorial Prize in Architecture by the National Institute of Arts and Letters. His designs include the new headquarters of the American Institute of Architects in Washington, D.C.

Plans Unveiled. In February, Philip Johnson revealed his model for the national shrine to be built on Ellis Island in New York Harbor. Johnson's concept is to utilize the two major buildings of the famous gateway to the United States, the immigrant station and the hospital, as romantic ruins. These are to be supplemented by a great reinforced-concrete memorial in the shape of a truncated cone, with ramps winding around both inside and out.

In November, new plans were announced for a monumental edifice that has been in progress since 1891. The trustees of the Episcopal Cathedral of St. John the Divine in New

Stone's Nuclear Science Institute, Islamabad, Pakistan.

Breuer and Associates' Whitney Museum, New York City.

York approved changes that would cap the crossing with a large cylindrical dome of stained-glass panels set between concrete louvers. The dome replaces a tall Gothic spire that had been planned earlier and never built. The two high Gothic towers that were to crown the front facade have also been abandoned. Thus a building that was begun in a Romanesque-Byzantine style, and in 1911 adapted to Gothic, has again evolved, reflecting both changing economics and aesthetics. The new plans are by the architectural firm of Adams & Woodbridge.

At the beginning of December, the University of Texas at Austin unveiled a model for the Lyndon Baines Johnson Library, to be built on a 19-acre extension of its campus. The architect is Gordon Bunshaft of Skidmore, Owings & Merrill, who also designed Yale University's rare-book library. The design contains two buildings, the LBJ library, a boxlike structure set upon a podium, and a long, low-lying school library and research center.

In August official approval was given for construction of the World Trade Center in Manhattan. The dominant feature of the 16-acre complex, designed by Minoru Yamasaki, is to be twin stainless-steel skyscrapers taller than the Empire State Building. The concept has generated considerable controversy.

Saved and Lost. The opulent new burnishing of a venerable French jewel was first displayed in June. The Grand Trianon, a palace on the grounds of the even vaster palace of Versailles, was ordered built by King Louis XIV in 1687. Its first restoration came under Napoleon I, who had it redecorated in the Empire style. It has now been completely refurbished as a museum and official guesthouse for heads of state. Original Empire furnishings have been supplemented by air conditioning, bathrooms and television outlets.

Also revealed during 1966 was the deterioration, and probably complete loss, of the most celebrated domestic structure of the 20th century. This is the Villa Savoye by Le Corbusier. The villa, completed in 1930, is located at Poissy-sur-Seine, some 25 miles from Paris. Untenanted for years, it has been allowed to become structurally unsound. Its goemetric design was a seminal influence in the development of modern architecture, and loss of the villa is not short of tragic.

In New York the continuing construction of the new Madison Square Garden and other structures has completely obliterated all trace of Pennsylvania Station. This building by the distinguished architect Charles Follen McKim was erected between 1904 and 1910. Its concourse, famous to a generation of students as a prime example of architectural eclecticism, was inspired by the ancient Baths of Caracalla in Rome.

FRED D. MOORE

ARCTIC. News developments in the Arctic were numerous in 1966. Among the important ones, barring those that referred primarily to Alaska or Canada, were the following:

Bilateral fisheries discussions between representatives of the United States and the Soviet Union ended in July. A number of agreements were to be referred to the two governments, including a meeting of U.S. and Soviet scientists to be held in Moscow on problems of conservation and rules of the road for fishing vessels. Other agreements dealt with restriction of Soviet fishing near the U.S. coast and exchange of observers aboard fishing and research vessels.

A research grant to study the world's population of polar bears and to make recommendations for international cooperation was given by the Conservation Foundation of Canada to Dr. Richard A. Cooley. He is associate professor of geography and public affairs at the University of Washington.

Expressions of international goodwill and a determination to conserve and rationally harvest a valuable marine resource keynoted the North Pacific Fur Seal Commission's ninth annual meeting in Ottawa. The four member nations are Canada, Japan, the United States and the Soviet Union.

The *Soviet News Bulletin* stated that the water in northern rivers and lakes contains little of the fluorine and calcium salts required by living organisms. To add the missing ingredients, the U.S.S.R.'s first pilot fluoridation and stabilization plant is planned for construction near the village of Molochnoye, Murmansk region, to treat the water of the River Kola. Sodium fluosilicate solution and milk of lime will be metered from special tanks into the water-supply system.

The Teploelectroproelst Institute of Novosibirsk solved a complicated problem while designing a fueled power station at Chita (Transbaikalia territory, Russian Federation). Because of a permafrost area in the region, construction of a large project is difficult and involves great outlays. The station was therefore built on a man-made island on Lake Kenon, under whose water there is no permafrost. The first turbine generator went into operation with a capacity of 50,000 kw.

For the first time, in 1966, Intourist offered trips via Borisoglebsk-Nikel-Murmansk and on to Petrozavodsk, Leningrad, Moscow and other cities. This northernmost tourist route passes through the Arctic Regions.

A group of scientists affiliated with the Cold Regions Research and Engineering Laboratory (of the U.S. Army) reached rock in a project to drill through the ice cap on Greenland.

Rock was reached under 4,562 ft. of ice, which had taken an estimated 10,000 years to accumulate.

PATRICIA TOPPING
Secretary of the Research Committee
ARCTIC INSTITUTE OF NORTH AMERICA

ARIZONA. A three-man Federal court in Phoenix invalidated the 1965 legislative-reapportionment law passed by the state legislature. . . . John R. Williams (R) defeated Gov. Samuel Goddard, Jr., for the governorship; Republicans also gained control of the state legislature in November elections. . . . Robert Benjamin Smith, 18, of Mesa, killed four women and one child in a Nov. 12 shooting spree. . . . On Apr. 18 the U.S. Supreme Court declared unconstitutional Arizona's loyalty oath for state employees.

ARKANSAS. On Nov. 8, Winthrop Rockefeller (R) defeated segregationist James D. Johnson in the race for governor. . . . Legislative reapportionment reduced membership in the state House from 75 to 44 and in the state Senate from 26 to 25. . . . Seeking desegregation of school districts for the 1966–67 school year, the Justice Department on Feb. 7 filed two suits in the U.S. District in Fort Smith.

Arkansas' Governor-elect Winthrop Rockefeller (r), his wife, and new Lt. Gov. Maurice Britt on election night.

UPI

ARMED FORCES. The big buildup of U.S. armed forces for the Vietnam war continued at a high level during 1966.

1967 Defense Budget. In the fiscal 1967 defense budget, President Johnson asked for $58,300,000,000 and a manpower end-strength of 3,093,000. Money requests made to Congress were based on an arbitrary assumption that the war would end by June 30, 1967, with limited supplemental estimates submitted short of obvious needs. This was aimed at permitting closer planning and avoiding a big backlog of supplies when the war ended, as had happened in Korea, Defense Secretary Robert S. McNamara argued.

Congressional leaders objected, however, that this misled the public as to the cost of the war, and delayed weapon procurement that would be needed. On Dec. 6, 1966, the President and McNamara announced that this policy would end, and that a supplemental $9,000,-000,000 to $10,000,000,000 would be submitted in early January, bringing fiscal 1967 defense spending to between $67,000,000,000 and $68,000,000,000. Official estimates of the Vietnam war costs during fiscal 1967 therefore were doubled—from $10,000,000,000 to $20,-000,000,000.

U.S. Military Strength. Earlier in the year the 3,093,000-man strength limit was eliminated, and 3,326,491 men were in uniform on Nov. 30. This total was expected to grow, but the expansion of U.S. forces in Vietnam—which doubled from 181,000 in January 1966 to 389,000 on Dec. 31, 1966—was expected to slow down in calendar 1967. The total, however, was due to approximate 400,000 early in the year. These figures do not count men of the U.S. Seventh Fleet or in air-force units in Thailand, engaged in the war.

On Jan. 1, 1966, there was the equivalent of five Army and Marine divisions in Vietnam. The buildup during 1966 gave to Gen. William C. Westmoreland, commander of the U.S. forces in Vietnam, the equivalent of some 8⅔ U.S. divisions, along with much larger air, helicopter, artillery and logistics support. U.S. forces—with the South Vietnam Army, two divisions sent by South Korea, and some Australian and New Zealand troops—conducted numerous "search and destroy" operations against the estimated 280,000-man communist army in South Vietnam. The 1966 Allied spoiling attacks cut the number of battalion-sized enemy offensives from a high of 7 a month in 1965 to an average of 1.7 monthly during the last half of 1966.

But the war was far from won. The Vietcong still controlled much of the countryside,

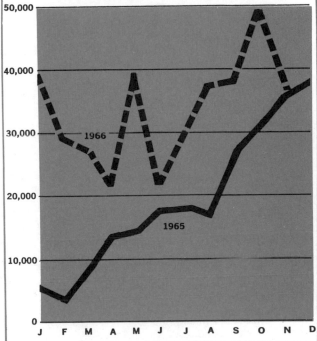

STEP-UP IN THE DRAFT
(Monthly inductions 1966 vs 1965)

and invariably moved back into hamlets after the Allied troops finished their "search and destroy" sweeps in communist areas. While by official estimates the "kill ratio" of communist to Allied deaths was 6.2 to 1, U.S. air operations against supply routes from North Vietnam could not prevent the enemy, through increased effort, from raising its infiltration of troops to 5,000–7,000 each month. Communist troop strength was believed growing, although infiltration of weapons, ammunition and supplies seemed down.

Late in the year a major decision was made to shift the main portion of the South Vietnamese Regular Army of 317,000 men (there are some 321,000 more in irregular forces) from periodic sweeps into enemy areas to "pacification" duties. Only by gradually taking over the 11,000 South Vietnamese hamlets, providing both night and day security for the peasants and winning their support through government help, can the war eventually be won, American and South Vietnamese leaders admitted.

In the war to date, American casualties in Vietnam, as of Dec. 31, totaled 6,664 dead and 37,738 wounded. During 1966, U.S. casualties were 5,008 killed in combat and 30,093 wounded. Also as of Dec. 31, the Pentagon

U.S. patrol boat searches Vietnamese fishing boat for enemy cargo.

Courtesy of "U.S. News & World Report"

had announced the loss of 841 aircraft of all U.S. services. This included 453 fixed-wing planes and four helicopters shot down over North Vietnam, and 145 airplanes and 239 helicopters in South Vietnam.

On Nov. 30 U.S. Army strength was 1,397,-971, organized into 17 divisions, ten separate brigades, and support units. Major combat units in Vietnam on Dec. 31 included the 1st, 4th, 9th and 25th Infantry Divisions, the 1st Cavalry Division (Air Mobile), the 1st Brigade of the 101st Airborne Division, the 173d Airborne Brigade, and the 196th and 199th Light Infantry brigades. Including support units, there were 244,000 Army troops in Vietnam. On Dec. 31 Army combat casualties totaled 4,156 dead and 23,561 wounded.

Overall U.S. Navy strength, as of Nov. 30, totaled 746,703 men and over 900 ships, including 16 attack aircraft carriers. All of the planned 41 Polaris submarines were afloat, with 40 of the total 41 already in commission. The powerful 7th Fleet, in the Far East, includes five attack carriers, three of which are always on the line, and which, with Marine aircraft, conduct almost half of the U.S. air missions against North Vietnam. Seventh Fleet ships fired approximately 200,000 projectiles in 1966 in support of operations ashore. A new nuclear-powered aircraft carrier is being constructed, but neither the Navy nor Congress has persuaded Secretary McNamara to build additional atom-proposed escort ships.

Marine Corps strength on Nov. 30 was 279,-354, including four divisions and three air wings. All of the 1st and 3d Marine divisions and 1st Marine Air Wing (reinforced) were in Vietnam, with a strength of 68,000 men on Dec. 31. Marine casualties were proportionately higher than in other services—2,027 killed in action and 12,366 wounded in the war to date.

The Air Force had a total strength of 902,-463 men on Nov. 30, and about 54,000 in Vietnam on Dec. 31. Strategic Air Command B-52's flew over 5,000 sorties against communist targets in Vietnam during 1966, thereby proving their effectiveness in a tactical role. SAC's first squadron of SR-71 2,000-mph reconnaissance planes was being formed. The planned force of 1,000 Minuteman ICBM's was expected to be operational by mid-1967.

The Selective Service Act expires in part on June 30, 1967, and a White House Commission reviewed the draft and prepared recommendations for changes. The act is expected to be reenacted with changes to make it more equitable.

NATO Nations. NATO's future grew more uncertain. France's President Charles de Gaulle ordered all foreign troops out of France, and there were demands in the United States (from former President Eisenhower, among others) that U.S. troop strength in Europe be cut to only a division or two. The Johnson administration publicly opposed any such move now, but McNamara reportedly favored some reduction, in time. A temporary cut in the 7th Army in Germany from 225,000 to 210,000 men was made in 1966, due to Vietnam war needs.

The United States moved its remaining air and logistics forces from France to England, West Germany and home, and NATO's political and military commands arranged to move to Brussels. West Germany's desire for a greater nuclear role was met in part by creation of a seven-nation nuclear-planning committee to permit nonnuclear NATO members to participate in nuclear planning and strategy. It is composed of the United States, Britain, Italy and Germany, with the other three spots rotating among Canada, Belgium, the Netherlands, Denmark, Greece and Turkey.

Another NATO problem was Britain's desire to cut further its 51,000-man army in Germany. Negotiations are under way between London, Bonn and Washington to avert this reduction. The end of the Malaysia-Indonesia confrontation permitted Britain to reduce its forces concentrated in that area, and a major, permanent reduction in British military forces east of Suez and elsewhere is planned. Britain's Labor Government wants to cut its $6,081,-000,000 defense budget and 437,600-man armed forces because of economic troubles.

The Government decided not to replace the Royal Navy's five aircraft carriers, and to rely instead on 50 American-built F-111A fighter-bombers ordered for the RAF. This brought resignations in the Admiralty. However, the Navy is taking over the strategic deterrent role from the RAF, with four Polaris submarines under construction. The Navy has six nuclear-powered attack submarines in service or planned, and 40 frigates for antisubmarine use.

While pulling its armed forces out of NATO, France remains a member of the Alliance, and 70,000 French troops will remain in West Germany under bilateral arrangements. France's armed forces total 522,500 men, including five divisions and 25–50 Mirage bombers equipped with atomic bombs. Under an increased $4,800,000,000 defense budget approved in October, the ambitious French program for a hydrogen missile force in underground silos and Polaris submarines goes forward.

Germany maintains a 440,000-man armed force, including 12 divisions, committed to NATO. Canada's armed forces are in an uproar over a government decision to combine the Army, Navy and Air Force into one service with one uniform.

Soviet Union and Red China. The Soviet Union, according to an admission by Secretary McNamara, has started building an antiballistic-missile system and is planning a larger ICBM force than anticipated, which seems certain to stimulate the arms race. New intelligence evidence suggests that Russia may have two to three times as many ICBM's by 1968—more than the 300–400 estimated now operational. This means that the United States no longer will have the present three or four to one ICBM margin as had been expected. McNamara, however, insists that the United States will retain a quantitative and qualitative superiority and be able to absorb a surprise attack and still inflict "unacceptable damage" on an aggressor.

Russia also is improving and "hardening" its ICBM force, and continuing to build nuclear-powered missile submarines, as well as maintaining some of them in the Atlantic and Pacific as a potential counter to the U.S. Polaris fleet. The official U.S.S.R. defense budget for 1967 was $16,000,000,000, up 8.2 per cent from the year before, but it was estimated by Western experts as actually over $35,-000,000. The armed forces reportedly total 3,165,000, and the Red Army apparently continues to maintain about 140 divisions, some half of them understrength. There were unconfirmed reports during the year that Moscow was considering withdrawing 5 of its 20 crack divisions from East Germany, and had strengthened its 17 divisions in the Far East.

Two somewhat conflicting movements featured military developments in Red China in 1966. There were three more Chinese atomic tests, including one of a 400-mile missile, indicating that Peking was pushing toward an operational nuclear capacity as fast as possible. It is estimated that China may have intermediate-range missiles, possibly some in submarines, in three to five years and ICBM's by 1975.

The other major development in Chinese defense was the apparent conflict between professional military chiefs and Chairman Mao Tse-tung and Defense Minister Lin Piao, his heir apparent. The military chiefs reportedly have been insisting that China must greatly modernize its armed forces, particularly the air force—a move that may require patching up Peking's ideological quarrel with Moscow in order to obtain Russian assistance. On the other hand Mao and Lin seem to be saying that men rather than matériel are all important, and that the 100 million-man militia, backing the 2.5 million-man regular forces, is all China needs for its defense.

JOHN G. NORRIS
Assistant Foreign Editor, THE WASHINGTON POST

ASTRONAUTS. From 351 applicants, the National Aeronautics and Space Administration selected 19 astronauts in 1966. The appointments brought to 50 the number of astronauts in the U.S. space team. Of the appointees, there are 4 civilians, 7 Air Force officers, 6 Navy officers and 2 Marine Corps officers.

For consideration by NASA, aspiring astronauts must meet these minimum requirements: U.S. citizenship; height not exceeding 6 feet; birth date on or after Dec. 1, 1929; bachelor's degree in engineering or in physical or biological sciences; 1,000 hours jet-pilot time or graduate of an armed-forces test-pilot school.

NEW ASTRONAUTS

Vance D. Brand . . . born May 9, 1931, Longmont, Colo. . . . civilian . . . B.S., U. of Colo.; M.B.A., UCLA . . . married.

John S. Bull . . . born Sept. 25, 1934, Memphis, Tenn. . . . lieutenant, USN . . . B.S., Rice . . . married.

Gerald P. Carr . . . born Aug. 22, 1933, Denver, Colo. . . . major, USMC . . . B.M.E., USC; M.S., Princeton . . . married.

Charles M. Duke, Jr. . . . born Oct. 3, 1935, Charlotte, N.C. . . . captain, USAF . . . B.S., U.S. Naval Academy; M.S., Mass. Institute of Technology . . . married.

Joe H. Engle . . . born Aug. 26, 1932, Abilene, Kans. . . . captain, USAF . . . B.S., U. of Kans. . . . married.

Ronald E. Evans . . . born Nov. 10, 1933, St. Francis, Kans. . . . lieutenant commander, USN . . . B.S., U. of Kans.; M.S., U.S. Naval Postgraduate School . . . married.

Edward G. Givens, Jr. . . . born Jan. 5, 1930, Quanah, Tex. . . . major, USAF . . . B.S., U.S. Naval Academy . . . married.

Fred W. Haise, Jr. . . . born Nov. 14, 1933, Biloxi, Miss. . . . civilian . . . B.S., U. of Okla. . . . married.

James B. Irwin . . . born March 17, 1930, Pittsburgh, Pa. . . . major, USAF . . . B.S., U.S. Naval Academy; M.S., U. of Mich. . . . married.

Don L. Lind . . . born May 18, 1930, Murray, Utah . . . civilian . . . B.S., U. of Utah; Ph.D., U. of Calif., Berkeley . . . married.

Jack R. Lousma . . . born Feb. 29, 1936, Grand Rapids, Mich. . . . captain, USMC . . . B.S., U. of Mich.; M.S., U.S. Naval Postgraduate School . . . married.

Bruce McCandless II . . . born June 8, 1937, Boston, Mass. . . . lieutenant, USN . . . B.S., U.S. Naval Academy; M.S., Stanford . . . married.

Thomas K. Mattingly . . . born March 17, 1936, Chicago, Ill. . . . lieutenant, USN . . . B.A.E., Auburn U. . . . single.

Edgar D. Mitchell . . . born Sept. 17, 1930, Hereford, Tex. . . . lieutenant commander, USN . . . B.S., Carnegie Tech.; D.Sc., Mass. Institute of Technology . . . married.

William R. Pogue . . . born Jan. 23, 1930, Okemah, Okla. . . . major, USAF . . . B.S., Okla. Baptist U.; M.S., Okla. State U. . . . married.

Stuart A. Roosa . . . born Aug. 16, 1933, Durango, Colo. . . . captain, USAF . . . B.S., U. of Colo. . . . married.

John L. Swigert, Jr. . . . Born Aug. 30, 1931, Denver, Colo. . . . civilian . . . B.S., U. of Colo.; M.S., Rensselaer Polytechnic Institute . . . single.

Paul J. Weitz . . . born July 25, 1932, Erie, Pa. . . . lieutenant commander, USN . . . B.S., Penn State; M.S., U.S. Naval Postgraduate School . . . married.

Alfred M. Worden . . . born Feb. 7, 1932, Jackson, Mich. . . . captain, USAF . . . B.M.S., U.S. Military Academy; M.S., U. of Mich. . . . married.

New astronauts are introduced at the Houston, Tex., Manned Spacecraft Center.

NASA

ASTRONOMY. With the forthcoming probability of transporting men to the moon, Mount Wilson and Palomar Observatories astronomer Fritz Zwicky predicted some advances in astronomy that could be made from a lunar observatory. One of the most obvious is that the lack of any lunar atmosphere would allow all types of radiation—ultraviolet light, X rays, gamma rays, and all types of radio waves—to reach the surface. The strongest radiation (Lyman alpha) from the most abundant stellar element (hydrogen) would be detectable. Because of the long lunar nights, the ability to observe during the days, and the absence of artificial lights, long exposures could be taken, reaching extremely distant galaxies whose red shifts would tell whether space is curved or not. Since there would be no distortion or fuzzing of star images by turbulent air, very high resolution photographs could be taken. The low magnetic field of the moon would allow cosmic rays to reach the surface unimpeded. The extreme lunar vacuum—exceeding anything attainable on the earth—would allow the growth of perfect crystals for lasers, and allow a more definitive measure of the speed of light and its possible changes. In the low-gravity field on the moon it would be possible to build larger rigid telescopes.

Stars. Most stars have roughly the same composition. Mild deviations exist: older stars have less metals like iron, titanium, chromium, and so on, than younger stars. The stars with extremely peculiar compositions are the magnetic stars, which have gross overabundances of rare earths and other heavy elements. Their average magnetic fields of several thousand gauss over their whole surfaces make it seem probable that the overabundances are due to magnetically induced nuclear reactions in their surface layers, much as in particle accelerators in physics laboratories. A star exceeding all known stars in unusual composition is the one called HD 101065, discovered by Australian astronomer A. Przybylski, who recently analyzed it. The star has so much holmium, a rare element never before seen in stars, that the absorptions by otherwise common elements like calcium could not be detected. The star is overabundant by factors of 100 or more in other rare elements like cerium, barium, and lanthanum.

The atmospheres of stars are known to be turbulent, and that turbulence broadens spectral lines, which are the narrow ranges of color taken out of the light from a star as that light passes through the star's atmosphere. These amounts of light removed are also a measure of the proportions of different elements present in the star's atmosphere. In recent years astronomers have interpreted weak lines in certain stars as being due entirely to deficiencies of the corresponding elements. However, Mount Wilson and Palomar Observatories astronomers P. S. Conti and A. J. Deutsch suggest that stars may differ in the amounts of turbulence in their atmospheres, giving fictitious indications of unusual abundances. This suggestion has been confirmed in certain cases. The cause of this turbulence in a star and the reason for differences between stars are not known at present.

Generally stars twinkle and planets do not. The twinkle is caused by small-scale inhomogeneities in our atmosphere that interrupt light beams coming from point sources like stars but not from objects having significant disks, like planets. The same principle has now been used to tell which radio sources come from pinpoint-size objects, like quasars, and which ones come from extended sources. In this case the interfering gas is the interplanetary medium, or solar wind. The giant 1,000-ft. radio telescope at Arecibo, Puerto Rico, has now separated point sources from extended sources for several dozen radio sources.

Radiation. Knowledge of objects outside the earth has been based primarily on the only kinds of radiation that can penetrate our atmosphere, namely the radiation around visible light and the radio waves. The corresponding fields of astronomy are now called optical astronomy and radio astronomy. But with the advent of rocket and space vehicles that rise above the atmosphere, we have the opportunity to detect other kinds of radiation, such as X rays. Small amounts of X rays come from the sun, but in recent years researchers have found a dozen places in the sky from which we receive X rays. The second strongest source is the Crab Nebula, the remnant of a supernova explosion A.D. 1054. However, the strongest source was a mystery until an accurate determination of its position was made in 1966 by scientists at American Science and Engineering, Inc. Identification with a 12th mag. star was made by Japanese astronomers at Tokyo Observatory, and detailed studies were made at Palomar Observatory. The object seems to be an old nova —a star that underwent an explosion more than a century ago and is still quivering from the experience. Several other X-ray sources have been identified as galaxies, although the fact that the X-ray energy emitted is 10 to 100 times greater than their total visible light and radio radiation energy will lead to serious problems concerning how these galaxies can produce so many X rays.

The radio waves coming from most extraterrestrial sources have a wide distribution of

One of the brighter Leonids lights the sky, leaving a luminous trail, during a meteor shower Nov. 17. Thousands of southern Californians witnessed this spectacular display.

A total eclipse of the sun cut a dark path across South America on Nov. 12. Left: the eclipse as photographed from U.S. Gemini 12 spacecraft; right: as seen from Lima, Peru.

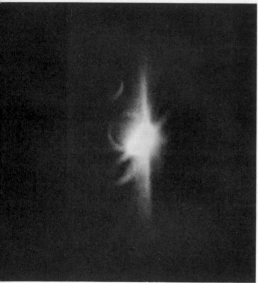

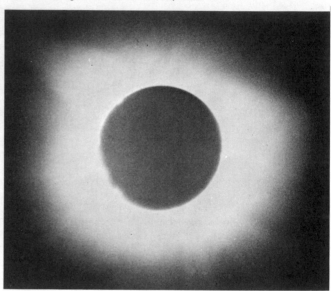

wavelengths, giving radio "noise," rather than a few individual "tones" or frequencies. Until recently the sole exception was the 21-centimeter radiation given off by neutral (or cool) hydrogen. It is with that single radiation that the shape of our galaxy and the distribution of its neutral hydrogen has largely been determined. Recently, though, other discrete wavelengths have been discovered. The most baffling are the four wavelengths near 18 centimeters given off by hydroxyl (OH) ions; these ions exist mostly in ionized (hot) hydrogen clouds, such as the Orion Nebula. Everything about these radiations is unexpected and unexplained. The radiation is strong in some nebulae and missing in others. The ratios of radiation strengths at the four wavelengths are not those predicted by atomic theory. The radiations are sometimes strongly polarized, and sometimes vary rapidly from day to day. Other discrete wavelengths from hydrogen and helium have also been discovered recently.

Mercury and Meteors. The planet Mercury is so close to the sun that one would expect its sunlit side to be exceedingly hot and the dark side cool. Dr. E. E. Epstein of Aerospace Corp. has monitored the planet with a 15-foot antenna receiving 3.4 millimeter radiation and reports, surprisingly, no difference between day and night temperatures: both are −130° F. What keeps the bright side of Mercury so cold is not known.

General Electric scientists have developed a chemical method for bringing out the submicroscopic tracks made by cosmic rays passing through meteorites. The method promises to give data on time meteors have been exposed in space to cosmic rays since they solidified.

HELMUT A. ABT
Astronomer, KITT PEAK NATIONAL OBSERVATORY

ATOMIC ENERGY COMMISSION. Dec. 31, 1966, marked the twentieth anniversary of the U.S. Atomic Energy Commission. Its activities during 1966 helped further the many uses of atomic energy. Developments included:

Power Reactors. The inauguration of new nuclear-power plants by electric utility companies—the largest a 786,000 kilowatt power plant making use of steam from the Commission's new plutonium production reactor in Richland, Wash.—forced upward the estimate of future nuclear facilities. By 1980 nuclear power is expected to generate between 80 and 110 million kilowatts, about 25 per cent of the total U.S. output.

Desalting. Water shortages have turned thought toward nuclear-powered desalting plants for seawater. In August, Congress authorized the AEC to participate in a $390 million facility to be located on a man-made island near Los Angeles.

Radioisotopes. Radioisotopes found employment in diverse fields, including snow measurement, valuable for flood and water-supply control. The first large-scale use of radioisotopes in sterilizing food took place at the Brookhaven, N.Y., National Laboratory. Fifteen tons of bacon irradiated there can be transported and stored for long periods of time without refrigeration.

Space. The first nuclear-power generator in space continued to supply supplementary power to its satellite as it marked its fifth anniversary. It had been developed by the AEC's SNAP (Systems for Nuclear Auxiliary Power) program. A SNAP 500-watt, nuclear-reactor space-power system being ground tested completed a year of continuously generating electricity. The NERVA (Nuclear Engine for Rocket Vehicle Application) rocket underwent a successful ground test, the engine first achieving full power in March. The NERVA reactor is considered man's best device for deep space exploration.

Medicine. The development of a radioisotope-powered cardiac pacemaker was begun by the AEC with the hope that it can be inserted into the body to stimulate a regular heartbeat. With a minimum life of ten years, it would greatly reduce the number of operations needed to replace a shorter-lived device.

Research. In December the AEC selected Weston, Ill., as site for its proposed 200,000,000,000 electron volt proton accelerator. The 200-BEV machine will be the largest, most complex instrument ever built for fundamental scientific research.

Abridgment, "Atomic Energy, 1966"
DIVISION OF PUBLIC INFORMATION
ATOMIC ENERGY COMMISSION

AUSTRALIA. In a year characterized by economic stability and sustained prosperity, Australia intensified defense preparations and held to a steady course in international relations.

U.S. Relations; Election. At the same time, Australia drew even closer to the United States in sentiment and policy. The triennial elections on Nov. 26 were fought principally on the issue of defense and foreign policy; Australia's direct and deepening military involvement in Vietnam, in step with U.S. participation there, was a central theme. The elections followed a month after President Johnson's whirlwind visit to the main Australian cities, where he and Mrs. Johnson were greeted with extraordinary enthusiasm by tremendous crowds.

The visit led some observers to link the strengthened vote for the U.S.-oriented Liberal-Country Party coalition with the widespread public response to the visit. Clearly, Australia's commitment to an active role beside the United States in southeast Asia was confirmed by the return of the coalition with a substantially increased parliamentary majority. There was a corresponding reduction in the strength of the Australian Labor Party—which, while supporting the Australian-United States alliance, trenchantly criticized the Government for sending draftees to Vietnam.

The marked electoral swing to the Government was a striking vote of confidence in 58-year-old Prime Minister Harold E. Holt, who in January succeeded Sir Robert Menzies on the latter's retirement after 16 years as prime minister. It was also a sharp rebuff for 70-year-old Opposition Leader Arthur A. Calwell, making his final bid, as head of the Labor Party, for power.

Vietnam Policy. Throughout the year, in close concert with New Zealand, Australia stressed the need to maintain forces in South Vietnam as part of a determination to prevent the spread of communism in the region, and the Government offered unqualified support for the U.S. bombing of North Vietnam targets as a military necessity to check infiltration.

Shortly after assuming office, Holt announced that Australia's fighting force in South Vietnam would be trebled to approximately 4,500 men. In April, Holt visited Vietnam and other countries of the region for on-the-spot discussions with political and military leaders. On his return to Canberra he said that southeast Asia had become "a crucial battleground for free people everywhere," adding that should the region fall under communist control, Australia would face a future in which its security would be in jeopardy. Subsequently Holt expressed his Government's belief that Australia

Prime Minister Holt and wife, relaxing at home.

UPI

was "more directly involved in South Vietnam even than the United States itself."

On Dec. 20, Prime Minister Holt announced that Australia would increase its number of troops in Vietnam.

Defense and Diplomacy. The closer involvement of Australia and New Zealand with the strategic problems of the whole Indo-Pacific region was brought into focus with the visit to Canberra in February of Britain's Defense Minister, Denis Healey, who held discussions there with Australian and New Zealand leaders. Subsequently there were grounds for fearing that Britain was considering a military withdrawal east of Suez. There was speculation on the possibility of Australia's providing a naval/military base, to which Britain and the United States would have access, as an alternative to Singapore.

Two weeks after the talks with Healey, U.S. Vice-President Hubert Humphrey visited Canberra, and once again speculation turned upon Australia's pivotal position in relation to the defense of the western Pacific and Indian Ocean region.

Other important diplomatic activity in Canberra centered around the meeting in June of leading members of the Southeast Asia Treaty Organization, followed immediately by a meeting of the ANZUS Council, bringing together the foreign ministers of Australia, New Zealand and the United States. Soon after these conferences, Prime Minister Holt visited Washington for discussions with President Johnson, and at the President's request he made a second U.S. visit on his way back to Australia from London. The very close identity of interest between Washington and Canberra was again confirmed in the joint statement issued at the conclusion of the talks. Subsequently Australia was one of the countries represented at the Manila Conference of nations with military forces backing South Vietnam.

Australia became a foundation member of the nine-nation Asian and Pacific Council, created in June.

More active parliamentary interest in the affairs of Asia was reflected in the visits by two seven-man groups of parliamentarians—one group going to Thailand, South Vietnam, Malaysia and Singapore and the other to India, Pakistan and adjoining lands. The visits were part of an effort to develop closer contact with the people and institutions of the noncommunist countries of the area.

Australia welcomed the settlement during the year of the long-standing dispute between Indonesia and Malaysia/Singapore, and the consequent end to "confrontation" which came in the wake of the political realignment in Jakarta. Following the Indonesian Government's abandonment of violently anti-Western policies, there were discussions in Canberra on prospects for developing closer economic contacts between Indonesia and Australia.

Holt attended the Commonwealth Prime Ministers' Conference in London in September. At its conclusion he deplored the heavy concentration of attention on the Rhodesian issue and expressed concern at what he termed "an unsatisfactory feature" of the conference: development of an Afro-Asian caucus system. Holt said he would want to look closely at the agenda for any future Commonwealth conference before deciding whether he would attend.

The Economy. During the year, the Australian economy remained remarkably sound throughout, but the pattern of economic activity underwent subtle but important change, as defense outlays made increasing claims upon resources. Easing of the overall growth in gross national product reflected the switch of resources from consumer goods into a heavier rate of investment in defense and capital programs. What one commentator described as "the crunch of defense" was apparent in the reduced tempo of expansion.

Among other factors contributing a dampening effect was a severe drought which afflicted important rural areas and cut output back sharply. The drought not only reduced farmers' incomes but also trimmed exports. A compensating factor was the record inflow of investment capital, which eased the balance-of-payments situation. Among expansionary features

Australian News and Information Bureau

Reverse sides of new Australian decimal coins, designed by Stuart Devlin, Melbourne.

was a high immigration intake. The increased number of new settlers arriving from abroad helped maintain activity and sustain demand.

Good rains after midyear improved prospects for farmers in some of the dry areas and made possible an excellent wheat crop. In marginal grazing areas, recovery in the livestock industries was slower than with grain growing.

The carefully planned changeover to decimal currency took place in February with a minimum of disruption. The basis for the conversion was £A 1 equals $A2.00 (the new Australian dollar being equivalent to $1.12 in U.S. dollars). Notes and coins were issued in the new currency denominations and new-value postage stamps were released.

In the year to June 30, overseas reserves showed little change, finishing at around the same satisfactory figure of more than $A1,-300,000,000 ($1,450,000,000) where they began. The Federal Government's total cash receipts for the fiscal year proved equal to its record disbursements. Domestic price levels were relatively stable, though many service charges moved upward. Wages were generally higher. Unemployment was at minimal levels.

An improved export result was achieved in spite of lowered returns for the main rural exports. Earnings from wool were down slightly. Wheat exports were lower, while falls also occurred in export returns from sugar, meat and butter. However, factory products of various types were exported in greater volume. Manufactured goods contributed a greater share (about 15 per cent) than ever before to export earnings.

Throughout the year businessmen were expressing some disappointment at the sluggish nature of the economy. They pointed to a sharp decline in sales of motor vehicles (down 10 per cent), appliances and other goods, as evidence that there was need for government action to stimulate recovery at the consumer level. Company results were uneven, and news of business activity was often mixed with disconcerting reports of investigations of earlier company failures. A resulting lack of confidence was reflected in dull trading on the stock exchanges, where prices showed a slight drift over the year. Meanwhile, new horizons for

development were opened as a result of important new mineral discoveries. New discoveries included major deposits of silver, lead and zinc in the Northern Territory, a high-grade nickel deposit in Western Australia, phosphate deposits in Queensland and lesser finds.

The Budget and Technological Changes. The budget presented in August for the fiscal year 1966–67 provided for a record expenditure of $A5,936,000,000 ($6,648,000,000)—an increase of some 11 per cent over the 1965–66 expenditure. It included $A1,000,000,000 ($1,-120,000,000) for defense outlays, representing an increase of 34 per cent. Payments to state governments rose substantially to $A926 million ($1,037,000,000) and the Federal program of capital works—largely in communications and transport—was set down at $A471 million ($527 million). A new feature of the budget was the provision of $A6 million ($6.7 million) in grants to encourage industry to undertake more research and development work. Provision was made for a total of $A103 million ($115 million) to be expended on external aid in various forms (including an initial contribution to the Asian Development Bank).

Some upward adjustments were made in social-security payments. Taxation rates were unchanged, but all but 10 per cent of the budget outlays were to come from revenue. Allowance was made for a credit of $A114 million, secured in the United States to cover defense items purchased there, and a total cash deficit of $A270 million ($302 million) was anticipated. Overall, the budget was designed to be mildly expansionary with the object of providing some stimulus to the economy.

Technological change accelerated during the year. Outlay on office machines increased considerably as, coinciding with the introduction of decimal currency, businesses adopted more efficient techniques and increased their use of office equipment. A special division was set up within the Federal Department of Labor to survey the impact and implication of technological developments within Australian industry in general, and to develop methods for coping with associated employment changes.

R. M. YOUNGER
Author, AUSTRALIA AND THE AUSTRALIANS

AUTOMOBILES

By FRED OLMSTED
Automotive Writer, DETROIT FREE PRESS

Despite headaches and hassles, the automobile industry wound up with another year in the 9 million range in new-car sales in 1966. The headaches resulted from a fairly sharp drop in the stock market after 5 years of unparalleled rise in the market. The hassles were over safety, which gave signs of being a worrisome subject for some time to come.

But neither the headaches nor hassles appeared to be any great handicap. Some production cutbacks resulted after the market slipped in April. The car makers also lengthened the period for changeover to new models to help cut the inventory backlog, which reached a record 1.7 million cars. They also advanced by a week or two the introduction of the 1967 models. But before the new models appeared, the market was back at the 9 million annual rate. And the new models provided impetus that seemingly assured a market at the 9 million "plateau" first reached by the record 9.3 million of 1965. However, 1966's total output was only 8.6 million.

The 1966 auto-market dip was attributed mainly to the unsettling effects of the war in Vietnam, high interest rates and a tightening of credit, and a stock market which reached new lows after the Dow-Jones industrial average soared close to the 1,000 level. The car-safety discussions also were blamed for an adverse effect on the market.

After a strong first quarter, a softening in the market was reflected by financial results for the next 3 months. General Motors reported earnings of $546 million, a drop of nearly 13 per cent from the all-time high of the same period a year earlier. But GM's sales for the quarter were off only 2.7 per cent. For the first half, GM earnings of $1,100,000,000 were down 10 per cent from the peak for the same period of 1965, but its sales were off only .1 per cent.

Ford Motor Co.'s sales for the first half were $6,500,000,000, up 9 per cent, but its net of $427 million was off 2.5 per cent. Chrysler Corp. totaled record first-half sales of $2,800,000,000, up 9 per cent, and a net of $117 million, off 1.2 per cent.

As the year advanced, sales generally held up better than profits. All Big Three companies reported sharp drops in third-quarter earnings, a low period because of model change-

overs. They blamed increased labor and material costs. GM reported a third-quarter net of $99.5 million, compared to $264 million a year earlier. Its worldwide sales for nine months were off 500,000 units, but its nine-month dollar volume was $14,500,000,000, compared to a $14,900,000,000 record in 1965.

Ford's nine-month net was $492.9 million, down from $540.2 million a year earlier. But Ford's sales total for that period was a record $8,800,000,000, up from $8,300,000,000 for nine months of 1965. Chrysler's sales for three quarters totaled a record $4,012,000,000, up from $3,681,000,000 in the same period of 1965. But its net for nine months was $123.4 million, compared to $136.4 million for a like period of 1965.

American Motors, struggling to regain the market it enjoyed in the compact-car era of the late 1950's, reported a net loss of $4.1 million in the first 9 months of its fiscal year (starting Oct. 1, 1965).

Studebaker Corp. got back on the profit side with a net of $8.3 million for the first half. But the company finally phased out its automotive operations, which it had consolidated in its Canadian plant late in 1963. The windup of Studebaker's Canadian auto production ended a 114-year history of Studebaker production of transportation vehicles, including farm wagons and the famed prairie schooner.

Studebaker declared a dividend of 25 cents on common stock in the third quarter—its first since 1954. Its earnings for nine months were $13.4 million, up from $7.4 million in the same span of 1965.

Still, in spite of difficulties in some areas, the industry faced 1967 with the expectation of a continuing 9 million car-sales rate. Most industry leaders agreed that truck sales would remain at the record rate of 1.7 million a year.

In a statement at new-model-introduction time, Frederic G. Donner, GM board chairman, and James M. Roche, president, said that if expansion of the economy continues, and consumer confidence remains high, the 1967 model year could be the third year in a row with total vehicle sales, including imports, exceeding 10 million units.

"There are currently some imbalances apparent in the economy," they said. "Nevertheless, business generally, as measured by production, employment and income, continues to establish new record levels. The expectation is that these important measures of economic growth will continue to rise in 1967."

1967 Models. Sales of the 1967 models, which reached the market in late September

1967 Camaro Super Sport Convertible.

Above: 1967 Cadillac Fleetwood Eldorado; below: front and rear views.

Photos from General Motors

and early October, appeared to bear out such predictions. The new models represented styling and engineering changes—plus some brand-new specialty models—that altogether cost an estimated $1,000,000,000-plus to bring to market.

Chevrolet introduced a new family-sports model named the Camaro (French for comrade, or pal) to compete with Ford's Mustang, which added up a million sales in its first two years on the market. Lincoln-Mercury added some intramural competition for the Mustang with a slightly larger luxury version, the Cougar.

Cadillac also departed from its conservative pattern by adding a front-wheel-drive model called the Eldorado with somewhat different styling but generally comparable with Olds-

mobile's Toronado, introduced in 1965 as the first front-wheel-drive American car in 30 years.

There was still a noticeable trend toward more horsepower and size, plus an emphasis on the top-of-the-line models and luxury options, including air conditioning, which was headed toward a 3 million annual installation rate.

Safety Items and Higher Costs. But with the new models came new and higher prices. The companies explained that most of the added cost resulted from the addition of safety items needed to conform with government demands. The companies said they made no allowance, or only partial allowance, for increased cost of labor and materials.

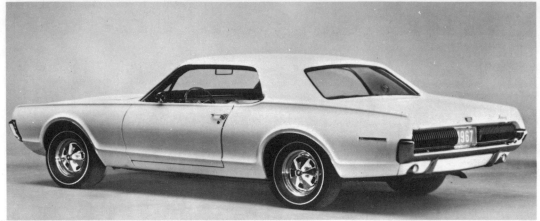

Two-door, hardtop Mercury Cougar.

Ford Motor Company

Plymouth's 1967 Sport Fury.

Chrysler-Plymouth

The Cavalier, a four-door of subcompact dimensions.

American Motors Corp.

Principal among the safety items were a dual braking system, with front and rear brakes served by different master cylinders, and a collapsible element in the steering column to eliminate a leading cause of accident injuries and deaths. But the companies also added some other safety items on their own: for example, Ford's padding of the windshield pillars, and industry-wide adoption of the lane-changer signal, which flashes the turn signal momentarily with a slight pressure while a motorist switches from one lane to another.

The new pricing was the signal for a brief industry skirmish. Ford and Chrysler announced prices first. Then General Motors came out with a lesser increase, averaging $56 a car, or 1.9 per cent. Ford, which had upped prices an average of $107 per car, or about 4 per cent, trimmed back to a $66 average, or 2.4 per cent. Chrysler, which averaged a $92 rise, or 3.2 per cent, cut back to $68 per car, also 2.4 per cent. American Motors' average increase was $79 per car, or 3.28 per cent. But it noted that it had trimmed prices an average of $70 with the 1966 models. The industry average was a rise of $69 per car, or 2.21 per cent.

The new-model introductions also formed the basis for some competitive maneuvering in the warranty field. The industry followed Chrysler's lead by adopting the same 5-year or 50,000-mile power-train warranty (engine, transmission, drive shaft, rear axle). Chrysler launched the "5-50" warranty with its 1963 models.

With its 1967 models, Chrysler boosted the warranty on the rest of the car from 1 to 2 years or 12,000 to 24,000 miles, the same as the rest of the industry. It also added steering and suspension components and wheels in its power-train warranty. The other companies followed suit.

Then Ford added a drive-train warranty on used cars back to 1964 models, with provision for registration of cars subject to the warranty program and payment of a $25 share of the cost by the car owner for each repair job under the warranty.

The warranty extensions left tires and regular maintenance items, such as spark plugs, as virtually the only items not warranted by the car makers. Tires are covered by the tire manufacturers' warranties.

The 1967 models featured larger-size tires in many instances, an evident response to tire-safety criticism in Washington. Tires also featured a wider and lower profile, with more rubber on the road for greater safety. Radial-ply tires were made available as optional equipment by some car makers. These tires, long in use in Europe, have cord plies placed at right angles instead of acute angles. The result is a somewhat harsher ride, but more stability and safer handling, plus up to twice as much wear due to a minimized "scrubbing" effect.

In response to accusations voiced in Washington, the tire industry made counterclaims, insisting that its product is better and costs less than 15 years ago. George R. Vila, chairman and president of the United States Rubber Co., noted that automotive engineers had "put ever-increasing demands on tires." At the same time, better roads and higher speeds for longer periods "impose additional demands," Vila said. But blowouts, he added, have been "nearly eliminated" since introduction of the tubeless tire 10 years ago.

Other Notable Developments. The year also brought several other notable developments. Ford introduced a new sodium-sulfur system for greater battery power in electric cars. The principal feature is a sodium-ion conducting ceramic tube with liquid sodium inside and liquid sulfur outside. A chemical reaction through the ceramic tube, composed largely of aluminum oxide, yields electric power several times that of conventional lead acid batteries and without the latter's deterioration. Ford said the system might be used in small cars for urban-suburban driving in 5 to 10 years.

General Motors demonstrated two operational electric vehicles, a converted Corvair powered by silver-zinc batteries, and a small van propelled by a hydrogen-oxygen fuel cell. But GM said any electric vehicle was probably 10 to 15 years away. The corporation also noted that it has been working for some time on a lithium-chlorine battery, which would provide more power, but indicated that such a power source was far in the future.

American Motors introduced a number of "idea cars," including a subcompact model with interchangeable doors and body panels for economy in manufacture and in making replacements and repairs. The company indicated it may move into manufacture of the low-cost car.

General Motors detailed a new and improved aluminum die-casting process, called Acurad, which it made accessible to industry despite patent rights it holds in the United States and abroad. The process, already used by GM in producing some components, yields aluminum parts with smoother surfaces and fewer internal flaws. Some experts foresaw the Acurad process as paving the way for a revival of the aluminum engines for automobiles.

AUTOMOBILES: SAFETY

By HOWARD PYLE
President, NATIONAL SAFETY COUNCIL

Nineteen sixty-six will undoubtedly be remembered as the year when a truly comprehensive program of traffic safety was initiated in the United States. On September 9, President Lyndon B. Johnson signed into law the National Traffic and Motor Safety Act and the Highway Safety Act. These Federal acts were the culmination of efforts by numerous individuals, organizations and committees of Congress acting out of great concern for the mounting death toll on U.S. highways.

Increased Death Toll. In the years just prior to 1962, it seemed possible that the yearly traffic death toll might be prevented from reaching 40,000. For the 10 years from 1951 to 1961, the number of traffic deaths had remained relatively stable (fluctuating between 37,000 and 39,000). During the same period the number of drivers increased by 24.5 million, and the total yearly vehicle miles of travel by 247,000,-000,000 miles. The traffic death rate dropped from 7.53 to 5.16 (deaths per 100 million miles of travel). The National Safety Council had been at work on the safety problem for many years, and the combined efforts of this and other safety-minded organizations and in-

South Bend students dramatize Indiana traffic death toll.
Wide World

dividuals were largely responsible for the accomplishment.

In 1962 and the years that followed, a variety of circumstances frustrated efforts to hold the traffic-deaths figure stable. There was, for example, an increased number of compact cars. There was also an increase in the average speed in a range where slight increases drastically increase the chances of fatalities. These and a large number of other factors known and unknown meant that after 10 years of relative stability, the death toll climbed past the 40,000 mark and just 3 years later threatened to pass 50,000 deaths.

Concern over the problem grew rapidly in many areas. Safety became front-page news when Sen. Abraham A. Ribicoff's Subcommittee on Executive Reorganization held open hearings on the Federal role in traffic safety. Ralph Nader, whose book *Unsafe at Any Speed* attacked the automotive and engineering side of the problem, testified at the hearings, and the National Safety Council testified, and presented a comprehensive, 18-point plan for dealing with the total traffic-safety problem. President Johnson's personal interest and the concentration of the news media on the traffic-safety problems further emphasized the need for official action. The 1966 bill resulted.

National Safety Agencies. The newly created National Traffic Safety Agency and National Highway Safety Agency will be responsible for the implementation of the acts. Dr. William J. Haddon, Jr., appointed administrator of the agencies, has long been identified with traffic safety. He has been quoted as saying that the agencies would "have a very energetic program that will be very carefully balanced and based on objective evidence rather than speculation"

The agencies will develop safety performance standards for motor vehicles and motor-vehicle equipment, establish performance standards for state and community highway-safety programs and assist in their implementation through a program of grants-in-aid. They will conduct and sponsor, through the National Traffic Safety Institute, research, development, testing and evaluation programs that are most needed by the Motor Vehicle Safety Performance Service and the Highway Safety Program Service.

The immediate concern of the agency is to provide the initial motor-vehicle-safety standards that the secretary of transportation is to prescribe by Jan. 31, 1967. Interim standards have already been proposed based on specifications the General Services Administration requires on government-purchased vehicles.

Before Jan. 31, 1968, these standards must be revised. The next concern of the agency therefore will be to carry out accident investigations to provide accurate knowledge on performance failures, and to provide the opportunity for persons and groups identified in the legislation to help set the standards.

State Programs. The new legislation will assist the various states to establish effective traffic-safety programs. There are many areas where the states need to concentrate:

> **Motor-Vehicle Inspection.** Increased efforts in this area would help eliminate or correct faulty equipment and prevent accidents.
>
> **Driver Education and Training.** Higher standards of classroom and behind-the-wheel instruction are needed. Although much can be done to engineer a safer vehicle, there is no substitute for the well-trained driver.
>
> **Traffic-Safety Data Systems.** Upgrading of the state accident-information systems (to the point where meaningful data are available) will make it possible for state and community safety-program planners to get the most for their safety money.

Other areas for state emphasis are: driver licensing and performance, accident investigation, emergency medical care and transportation of the injured, enforcement practices, pedestrian safety, roadway design and maintenance, traffic-control devices, school-bus safety, motorcycle safety, vehicle codes and court practices.

Research and the Future. Long-range research programs will have to be carried out in many of these areas before the final standards can be set up. Consequently the immediate motor-vehicle standards will be minimal. Also any features added to new models will not be on all cars until approximately ten years have elapsed. As a result of these factors, it will take some time before the full impact of the legislation is felt.

Similarly, in the area of highway-safety standards, there will also be a time lag. Road improvements are costly and slow, and again research and development must precede highway-improvement planning. The new demand for trained specialists will necessitate training programs to overcome personnel shortages in many areas.

The Congress has appropriated enough money for the agencies to operate, and the National Highway Safety Agency will complete a "cost of needs" study in 1968. Larger Federal aid, in the $1,000,000,000-to-$2,000,000,000-a-year category, is still in the future, and, hopefully, will be appropriated by the time the initial planning has taken place.

PROPOSED FEDERAL AUTO-SAFETY STANDARDS

On Nov. 30, Dr. William J. Haddon, Jr., administrator, National Traffic Safety Agency and the National Highway Safety Agency, proposed the following 23 auto-safety standards for 1968-model U.S. cars:

1. standard location and identification of certain controls.
2. braking effect for automatic transmissions.
3. windshield defrosting and defogging systems.
4. standardized windshield-wiping and washing systems.
5. assurance of adequate braking performance with hydraulic and parking-brake systems in case of partial system failure.
6. standards to reduce chances of brake failure due to fluid leakage from hydraulic hoses.
7. new safety glass requirements.
8. lamps, reflective devices and other equipment used for lighting and signaling.
9. standards for tire strength.
10. assurances that tires and rims will not be overloaded under reasonable conditions.
11. adequate rear-view mirrors.
12. protection of occupants from injury in any interior impact from instrument panels, seat backs, sun visors, arm rests and other protections.
13. head rests.
14. steering-control systems that will absorb force and minimize injuries from any impact wth the steering device.
15. standard steering column length.
16. protection against being thrown from windows.
17. standards to keep doors shut during crash.
18. assurance that seats are anchored securely.
19. installation of seat belts in all forward-facing seats.
20. specific standards for seat-belt assembly.
21. strong seat-belt anchorages.
22. ban against hazardous protections on wheel hubs.
23. improved fire standards.

Factors already positively affecting the traffic-safety picture are: spot-improvement programs designed to correct specific high-hazards areas of highways; increasing use of safety belts, and their appearance on all 1967 models as standard backseat and front-seat equipment; further construction of interstate highways, on which the death rate is lower than on other roadways; and increased acceptance of driver improvement and defensive driving training programs.

And so despite the mounting death toll, the events of 1966 give reasons to be optimistic. Nevertheless, sometime early in 1968 the total distance traveled yearly by motor vehicles in the United States will exceed one trillion miles. With this many miles traveled, even a slight increase in the death rate represents a large number of lives lost. It is important that private citizens and organizations get behind the present safety effort. In future the saving to the economic, intellectual and cultural communities will have a definite effect on the entire United States.

AVIATION. The U.S. aviation industry achieved notable advances in 1966, while experiencing sharp setbacks resulting from such diverse factors as labor-management discord and the war in Vietnam.

As the year ended, the industry awaited a decision by the Government on which of the two supersonic-transport-airframe designs was the winner—Boeing or Lockheed—and whose engines would power the aircraft—General Electric or Pratt & Whitney.

President Johnson, on Dec. 31, made the announcement that Boeing and General Electric were winners of the competition. Boeing's movable, or swing-wing, design calls for a 306-ft. plane weighing 338 tons, with an airspeed of 1,800 mph. Test planes are due to fly about 1970, although there are already worries about the project's cost, and the sonic-boom noise the craft will make.

TERMS OF THE AIRLINE-STRIKE AGREEMENT

Wages: Increases as follows—
- For 1966, raise of 5 per cent retroactive to last Jan. 1.
- For 1967, a second raise of 5 per cent, effective Jan. 1, 1967.
- For 1968, a third raise of 5 per cent, effective May 1, 1968.

Average pay raise: 56 cents an hour over the period 1966-68 for airline mechanics, making the mechanics' base rate $4.08 an hour.

Cost-of-living: Further raises, as much as an extra 6 cents an hour, if living costs keep rising.

Vacations: 3 weeks after 8 years' service, 4 weeks after 15 years. It's now 3 weeks after 10 years, 4 after 20. Changes effective partly next year, partly in 1968.

Holiday pay: 2½ times normal pay. Old rate: double pay.

Extra holiday: One additional holiday with pay—Good Friday.

Health, welfare: Starting next January, airlines will take over part of the cost of dependents' insurance now paid by employes.

Schedule of raises: A speedup in effective dates of the increases compared with earlier proposed settlements. Result: for the average worker covered, an extra $240 in wages above what had been promised by the agreement voted down by union members on July 31.

Employes covered: 19,000 mechanics, 16,400 others—ramp-service workers, cleaners, food-service employes, stores clerks.

Workers' total gains: Estimated at around 6 per cent each year of three-year contract. **Official guidepost on labor-cost increases:** 3.2 per cent.

A significant development for the air-transport industry was the passage of Congressional legislation establishing the nation's first cabinet-level department of transportation. President Johnson's choice of Alan S. Boyd, a former chairman of the Civil Aeronautics Board (CAB), to become secretary of transportation was generally welcomed by the airlines and related industries. Creation of the department represents a major advance for air and other forms of transportation in that the industry will now have a voice at cabinet level. Air-transport executives believe the department eventually can play a significant role in development of air transportation through its research activities.

Damaging to the aviation industry, particularly the five major airlines involved, was a 43-day strike during the summer by the International Association of Machinists. The shutdown of the carriers—Eastern, National, Northwest, Trans World and United—led to substantial financial losses for them and widespread inconvenience for travelers.

Statistics for the Year. For 1966 as a whole, the Air Transport Association (ATA), trade organization of the U.S. scheduled airlines, estimated the domestic trunk lines flew about 57,000,000,000 revenue passenger-miles within the 48 contiguous states. This represents a gain of 16 to 17 per cent over the 1965 record of 49,000,000,000 passenger-miles. Before the strike ATA officials were saying that the 59,-000,000,000 domestic-revenue passenger-miles predicted for 1966 by the CAB staff was conservative. The ATA estimated that 3,700,000,-000 domestic-trunk-revenue passenger-miles were lost during the strike, a figure that represents a substantial chunk of revenue.

The strike of course also adversely affected the air-cargo sector of the transport industry, which, however, continues to show a remarkable rate of growth. In the first nine months of 1966, scheduled airlines of the United States flew 1,120,000,000 ton-miles of cargo—freight, mail and express—compared with 910 million for the first three quarters of 1965, a gain of 23.2 per cent.

The present jet freighter fleet of the U.S. airlines represents an investment of about $439 million. It consists of 55 aircraft capable of all-cargo operations. In addition, there are 23 turboprops and 85 piston airplanes providing freight service. If these aircraft carried maximum loads, they could develop about 10 million ton-miles of cargo service a day, nearly four times the capacity available in 1960.

More than 100 jet freighters, valued at about $720 million, are on order, capable of producing an added 8 million ton-miles of service a day. Most of these are scheduled for delivery by the end of 1968.

The airlines now have, or are committed to purchase, jet freighter aircraft valued at about $1,200,000,000. As the ATA has pointed out, the gross investment in flight equipment of the entire U.S. scheduled airline industry totaled $1,200,000,000 as recently as 1955. Besides the freighter fleet, millions of ton-miles of capacity are available on more than 11,000 daily passenger flights.

To match the speed and efficiency of the jet freighters, the major airlines have embarked on multimillion-dollar programs of building highly sophisticated cargo terminals and have ordered mechanized supporting ground-handling equipment.

"The historic rate of growth of U.S. domestic and international airfreight over the past 15 years has been 14.5 per cent a year," according to Stuart G. Tipton, ATA president. He added that if the growth rate of 1963-65, which averaged 24.4 per cent a year, is projected, the freight volume for 1970 becomes 5,200,000,-000 ton-miles and for 1975, 15,300,000,000 ton-miles. "With the new technology of the 1970's, this last figure may be very conservative," Tipton added.

Introduction of the Boeing 727QC (Quick Change) aircraft in the summer of 1966 was a notable step. These airplanes can be changed from passenger to all-cargo configuration in 30 minutes or less, and back again to passenger status in the same length of time. The QC's carry passengers by day and cargo at night. Braniff International reported a daily utilization of the aircraft of 15 hours 45 minutes during initial operations.

A ruling by the U.S. Supreme Court upheld, in effect, a CAB order of 1964 granting domestic all-cargo airlines the right to sell blocked space to volume shippers at reduced rates. Three combination passenger-cargo airlines— American, Trans World and United—opposed the order unsuccessfully in the courts.

Under a blocked-space contract, the all-cargo carrier guarantees to move a specific minimum amount of freight between two terminals for a minimum period of 90 days. The minimum volume is 1,000 lb. per shipment. Under the agreement, a shipper can obtain a rate discount of 3 to 15 per cent. The all-cargo lines, Flying Tiger and Airlift International, foresee an increase in their traffic of up to 50 per cent annually as a result of the ruling.

Effects of the Vietnam Conflict. The war in Vietnam is bringing revenue to U.S. commer-

cial airlines, but it has created obstacles to production in the aircraft plants. Engine delivery delays ascribed to the need to meet military demands have resulted in slippages of delivery dates of civilian-transport aircraft by Douglas and Boeing. Both reported record-high backlogs of orders. For the first nine months of 1966, Boeing said its backlog stood at $4,890,-000,000. Douglas, in the first nine months of its fiscal year ended Aug. 31, 1966, reported a backlog of $2,990,000,000.

Boeing reported net earnings for the period of $60.3 million, while Douglas had a net loss of $16.4 million. Delivery delays of commercial transports by the two leading U.S. manufacturers prompted foreign carriers to consider canceling orders and to look to European manufacturers for new equipment.

The U.S. Air Force's Military Airlift Command will contract for at least $500 million in supplemental capacity from the commercial airlines during the 1967 fiscal year, about $400 million of it for international services. The total in fiscal year 1966 was $394.2 million. In fiscal year 1965 it was $231.3 million, when increased U.S. involvement in Vietnam started to make an impact.

Airlift Command officials say the need for sizable commercial participation in the military transport program will continue even after the conflict is over. They reason that the armed forces have become accustomed to swift service on priority items, and will keep on demanding such service.

Present and Future Developments. Another development of significance is the rapid growth of U.S. commuter airlines around major transportation hubs. These carriers, operating on a scheduled basis under air-taxi certification, link suburban areas with major airports. About 120 companies are operating in this field, using aircraft such as the Beech Model B80 Queen Airliner and the de Havilland Twin Otter.

Meanwhile, the boom in the general aviation industry continues. This category includes the private or corporate aircraft industry, the growth of which reflects the health of the national economy. Total deliveries of such aircraft in the first ten months of 1966 rose to 13,075 units valued at $341.7 million. Unit deliveries and dollar value both were up more than one third over the similar period in 1965.

With the advent of the supersonic transports less than a decade away and the start of service by the giant subsonic jets such as the Boeing 747 even nearer, airport operators are assessing their needs for the future. These new aircraft are bound to have an impact on terminal planning in such areas as passenger walking

Models illustrate size difference between new B-747 jet (r) and the present B-707. Pan American ordered 23 of the new 490-passenger jets and 2 similar-size cargo jets from the Boeing Co. Below, interior of the B-747, which will cruise at a speed of 596 mi. an hour.

distance, passenger ticketing and loading processes, baggage handling and air-cargo facilities. Simultaneous arrival of flights, each carrying 300 or more passengers, will further increase the strain on airport ground-access facilities— that is, the movement of travelers between home and job or airport. This is a problem now at airports serving metropolitan centers. It can only intensify as more cars use the highways and air travel continues to increase.

Late in 1966, Aeroflot, the Soviet airline, and Air Canada, the state-owned Canadian carrier, began a joint service linking Moscow and Montreal. It is the first time a North American airline has operated into the Russian capital on a scheduled basis, and the inauguration of the first Soviet commercial air service to North America.

The United States and the Soviet Union subsequently signed a bilateral air agreement, long deferred because of cold-war tensions. As a result, prospects were good that Aeroflot and Pan American World Airways would begin a transatlantic service between Moscow and New York in the spring of 1967.

JOSEPH W. CARTER
Associate Transport Editor
AVIATION WEEK & SPACE TECHNOLOGY

BALANCE OF PAYMENTS. On the surface, the United States' BOP looked pretty good at the end of 1966. But below the surface some ominous problems seemed to be boiling up.

BOP is the abbreviation for balance of payments. It represents the difference between the dollar value of what the United States spends, lends and invests outside the country and the value of what foreigners spend, lend and invest in the United States. If more dollars flow out of the United States than flow in, dollars build up abroad. Eventually, these surplus dollars tend to accumulate in foreign central banks. These banks, in turn, exchange some of their dollars for gold which the U.S. Treasury stands ready to sell for $35 an ounce.

Recent Deficits and Corrective Actions. For 14 out of the last 15 years the United States has shown a BOP deficit. Chief causes have been foreign aid, both civilian and military, plus heavy investments in foreign plants by U.S. businessmen, loans to and investments in foreign companies by American banks, big expenditures abroad by American tourists and spending on the Vietnam war. The resulting drain on the U.S. gold supply has reduced gold stocks from $20,000,000,000 in 1959 to around $13,000,000,000 in 1966—the lowest level since 1938.

The worst BOP deficit the United States suffered in recent years was in 1960 when $3,900,000,000 more dollars flowed out of the country than flowed in. During the next four years the deficit was held below $3,000,000,000. In 1965 it dropped sharply to $1,400,000,000 and in 1966 it was about the same.

The decline was due to strenuous Kennedy-Johnson-administration corrective action begun in 1963. A tax was imposed to discourage purchase of foreign securities by Americans. The amount of goods that American tourists could bring home duty-free was reduced. Then, beginning in 1965, American businessmen were asked voluntarily to cut back the amount they invested in foreign operations. And American banks were asked to limit loans to foreigners. At the same time, the Federal Reserve Board tightened up on credit to dampen inflationary forces. The resultant rise in interest rates— to the highest level in 40 years—tended to keep American investments home and to attract investments from abroad.

1966 Situation. By the beginning of 1966, the combination of these corrective actions had given administration officials hope that the end of the long struggle was at hand. The deficit had dwindled to its lowest level in eight years. Unfortunately, however, instead of disappearing in 1966, the deficit hung close to the level of the previous year. And disquieting evidences began to appear that in 1967 it might rise again. Thus, in December 1966, President Johnson, who at the beginning of the year had hoped that controls over lending and investing abroad might be relaxed or dispensed with by year-end, felt obliged to extend and strengthen them.

A complex interplay of forces caused this disappointing turnabout. For one thing, in 1966 U.S. merchandise imports rose more than exports. The difference between these two figures represents the balance of *trade,* as distinct from the balance of *payments.* The latter includes not only imports and exports but all other transactions for whatever purpose that result in an outflow or inflow of money. Traditionally, the United States has shown a balance-of-trade surplus. For example, in 1963, merchandise exports were $22,427,000,000 while imports were $17,140,000,000, leaving a surplus of $5,287,000,000. In 1964 exports were $25,671,000,000; imports were $18,684,000,000, leaving a surplus of $6,987,000,000. In 1965 exports were $26,567,000,000; imports were $21,366,000,000, leaving a surplus of $5,201,000,000. But toward the end of 1966 when the

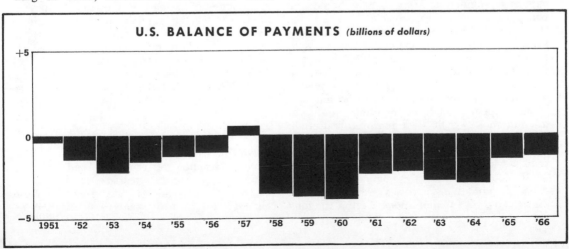

U.S. BALANCE OF PAYMENTS (billions of dollars)

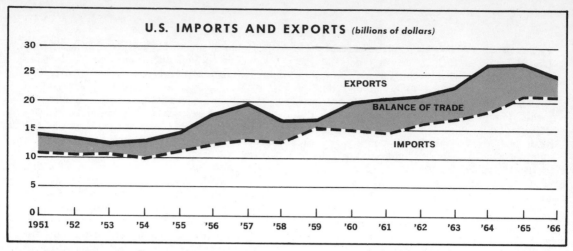

U.S. IMPORTS AND EXPORTS (billions of dollars)

EXPORTS

BALANCE OF TRADE

IMPORTS

1951 '52 '53 '54 '55 '56 '57 '58 '59 '60 '61 '62 '63 '64 '65 '66

President had to make his decision on continuation of controls, it appeared that although exports had risen, imports had risen even more, causing the 1966 balance-of-trade surplus to shrink to about $4,000,000,000. Since the balance-of-*trade* surplus had been the ballast that kept the balance-of-*payments* deficit from going through the roof, this shrinkage was disquieting.

The reasons for the sharp rise in imports were two. First, 1966 was an extremely prosperous year for Americans. Rise in the purchase of imported goods usually goes along with prosperity. And in 1966 imports got an added fillip because domestic prices were rising while prices of foreign goods were relatively stable. Second, American factories were running at near capacity. Shortages of materials and machinery had begun to appear and delivery times lengthen. As a result, businessmen tended to turn to foreign suppliers for goods they could not readily obtain at home.

Another factor that seemed to be turning less favorable toward the end of 1966 involved tight money and high interest rates. These had helped keep the BOP deficit fairly low in 1966. American businessmen, finding credit tight and expensive, tended to keep cash at home and bring in as much as possible from foreign subsidiaries. Also, they were able to raise capital abroad for foreign operations. As a result, banks and manufacturers actually loaned and invested less abroad than the voluntary government limitations called for. But at year-end— with the economy rising more slowly, and soft spots deepening in home building, auto production and other lines—it appeared that credit would ease. And easier credit in 1967 would mean of course the loss of one big weapon that had kept the BOP deficit down.

Also contributing to the administration's decision to continue controls was the fear that Americans, flush with money from a long period of prosperity, would troop abroad in unprecedented numbers, spending a record number of dollars in the process. The prospect even caused some talk of limitations on the number of dollars that American tourists might take out of the country. No action of this kind was taken, however, in 1966.

Lastly, at the end of 1966 the Vietnam war continued unabated and the administration predicted that military expenditures for the fiscal year July 1966 through June 1967 would be $7- to $10,000,000,000 over previous estimates.

Year-End Outlook. Thus by the end of 1966, indications that the BOP deficit had been licked appeared deceptive. True, it was expected to be the lowest in nine years. True, also, purchases of U.S. gold by foreign central banks appeared to have been drying up. France, for example, which had been converting around $34 million a month into gold, bought none from the U.S. Treasury in either October or November 1966, the explanation being that France had virtually reestablished its traditionally large reserve of gold against its outstanding currency.

Nonetheless, the ominous prospects of heavier military and tourist expenditures abroad, rising imports and an easing of tight money at home caused the administration to continue and even tighten its program of restrictions on business spending and lending to foreigners. In fact, although controls were nominally extended for only one year, President Johnson himself hinted that the program might have to be continued until the Vietnam war is over.

JOHN W. HAZARD
Executive Editor, CHANGING TIMES

BANKING. Rising interest rates usually trigger a chain reaction of economic and political effects somewhat like firecrackers popping on a string. When interest rates zoom to their highest level in forty years—as they did in

1966—the firecrackers take on the explosive intensity of bombs.

Consumers complain, politicians fret, businessmen are confused, and economists riffle through their manuals. Each contributes to the ebb and flow of agitation that washes across the economy. This was how it went in 1966 in the U.S. banking business.

Although rocketing interest rates received most of the attention, other events figured prominently in the dynamism that has been so characteristic of the banking system in recent years.

Congress liberalized bank-merger laws after a six-month conflict. The lawmakers also sought to lower the boom on the gray-flanneled bank robbers, those merchants of fraud who quietly buy into a bank, bleed its assets, and then get out before the government regulatory agencies discover that anything is amiss.

The year also marked the windup of the five-year term of James J. Saxon, comptroller of the currency. Further, it was a year when savings and loan associations and mutual savings banks, for the first time, were limited as to the amount of interest they could pay depositors. This was a direct result of the runaway interest-rate spiral, and the disruptive competitive ar that it caused among financial institutions.

Despite all of the attendant anxieties, the banking industry remained prosperous in 1966. Profits continued to inch upward, and institutions kept on pressing against the boundaries of traditional banking-business activity, most notably showing more interest in the credit-card field.

Bank-Rate Increases. For banking, the year 1966 was born on a note of conflict which was to send its rippling effect throughout the economy for the next 12 months. Late in 1965 the Federal Reserve Board ordered an increase in the discount rate from 4 to 4½ per cent and approved a rise in the interest ceiling on bank time deposits from 4½ to 5½ per cent.

The discount rate is the interest charge that banks pay to borrow from the Federal Reserve System; it is thought to have a catalyst effect on all interest rates. When the discount rate goes up, so do most other interest charges. The Federal Reserve Board, which manages the nation's money supply, said the bank-rate increase was needed to slow down demand forces in the economy which posed inflationary hazards. President Johnson disagreed, claiming the board had acted hastily and prematurely. The President feared that the board's move might set off an unnecessary interest-rate jump

which would work a hardship both on the consumer and the businessman.

The debate ranged hot and heavy during the early weeks of the 1966 Congressional session. However, it soon blew over, mostly because there was little either the Congress or the President could do about the new bank-rate increase. The Federal Reserve Board is a comparatively independent agency. The only overt control Congress can exercise over the board is to abolish or alter the law that created it. Apparently, the lawmakers did not feel that the controversial discount-rate increase was serious enough to require such drastic action.

As it turned out, the Federal Reserve Board's premonition of an approaching inflationary trend was completely accurate. The increase in the discount rate did little to stop it. Despite this rise in the cost of money, business continued to clamor for more capital.

To meet this crying demand for capital, banks increased the amount of interest which they offered to depositors. Since this pushed up the cost of the "raw material" in which banks deal—that is, money—the banks soon found they also had to raise the interest rate they were charging borrowers. It all began to resemble a frantic merry-go-round—business chasing the banks for more capital, and banks in turn pursuing depositors for more loanable funds. As the supply of money began to dwindle, the price went up. Suddenly the economy found itself helplessly caught in the clutches of a stratospheric interest-rate trend: by summer, rates had jumped to the highest level since the 1920's.

One side effect of this mad scramble for cash caused special concern in Congress. In their spirited campaigns to dig up every loanable dollar available, commercial banks began to entice thousands of millions away from savings and loan associations. Because these associations are traditionally a reservoir of financing for home construction, mortgage financing began to dry up. When voters have a difficult time buying houses they write to their congressmen, and the lawmakers pay attention to such letters—especially just before an election.

This, probably more than any other development, caused Congress to move to halt the interest-rate merry-go-round. Early in the fall, the lawmakers approved legislation authorizing Federal agencies to join in a coordinated effort to set ceilings on the interest that all financial institutions may pay depositors. The savings and loan associations were given an extra ¼ per cent competitive advantage in the hope

Montreal's Le Salon, the Bank of Montreal's exclusive new branch for women only.

that savers' funds would again start flowing into home construction. A weary Congress hoped that some semblance of stability might soon return to the money market.

Bank Merger Act. Although Congress was busy trying to resolve the interest-rate dilemma, it found time to enact other legislation of vital importance to the banking industry. The 1966 Bank Merger Act is a case in point. The banking industry long has argued that the Justice Department is too strict in its appraisals of bank mergers. The industry feels that since it already is regulated by the Government, the usual standards in adjudging monopoly are unrealistic.

As a result, the banks lobbied through Congress in early 1966 an amendment to the bank-merger law, intended to liberalize criteria for determining the legality of bank consolidations. Briefly, the law was supposed to stipulate that a bank merger could be legal, even if it had monopolistic tendencies, provided the merging banks proved the resultant bigger bank necessary to the "convenience and needs" of the community it would serve. This was the goal. What the new law actually did is a matter of dispute which will have to be resolved by the courts. The attempt to liberalize bank-merger law met bitter resistance from the Justice Department and Chairman Wright Patman (D-Tex.) of the House Banking and Currency Committee.

Statute for Federal Regulators. Another statute enacted by Congress in 1966 could have a profound effect on the banking business. This one was aimed at rooting out incompetence and corruption in financial institutions. President Johnson recommended the legislation after a series of Congressional investigations revealed that criminal activity figured in a number of bank failures.

The new law gives Federal regulators authority to issue cease and desist orders to stop unsound practices in banks and savings and loan associations before these policies actually bankrupt an institution. The new statute also permits Federal regulators to remove directors and officers guilty of "personal dishonesty." President Johnson hopes that added regulatory muscle will give the Government the means of nipping in the early stages those patterns of institutional and personal behavior which usually provide advance indications that a financial institution is en route to disaster.

Presumably, the legislation also will help the Government in its efforts to kick out of the banking business unsavory characters who make a handsome living by plundering a bank, and then turning it over to the creditors— usually the government agency which has insured it.

In the past, the Federal Government could thwart such swindlers only by closing a bank or a savings and loan association when the crooks moved in. Because this is considered drastic medicine which often injures innocent depositors, the agencies have been reluctant to use it except in extreme cases. The new statute gives the Federal Government the intermediate powers needed to put more stress on the "preventive" aspect of their responsibilities.

The new supervisory law also included an increase in the Federal insurance ceiling from $10,000 to $15,000, the maximum amount of each depositor's account which is insured by the Federal Government. A few days after Congress approved the extended protection for the public, the $97 million-deposit Public Bank of Detroit failed. However, depositors suffered no loss, since the institution's assets and obligations were purchased by the Bank of the Commonwealth in Detroit.

James J. Saxon. The year 1966 also will be remembered as the end of a colorful, contentious era in national banking which began in 1961 when President John F. Kennedy appointed James J. Saxon comptroller of the currency. As head of the national banking system, Mr. Saxon chartered more banks than any comptroller in history. He gave national banks exciting and controversial new lending and investment powers. He authorized member banks to set up branches in states which claimed their laws prohibited branching. To accomplish all of this, Mr. Saxon blasted years of tradition and centuries of protocol in an industry known for its abiding dedication to the *status quo*. Mr. Saxon's first deputy, William B. Camp, succeeds him.

If some of these events suggest an atmosphere of turbulence existed in the banking field in 1966, it is not reflected in the balance sheets. Banks, along with other businesses, continued to reap the fruits of the current five-year burst of economic prosperity. In 1965 the nation's insured commercial banks increased earnings by $1,800,000,000 to reach $17,200,000,000. Every indication is that this was topped in 1966.

JOSEPH D. HUTNYAN
Washington Bureau Chief
THE AMERICAN BANKER

BERLIN. The divided city, 110 miles inside East Germany, was both sadder and quieter in 1966 than at any time since the building of the Wall, which cuts through it like a jagged wound.

The tranquillity resulted from an unusual lack of incidents along the sector border as well as on the road, rail, canal and air corridors which are West Berlin's lifelines to the Federal Republic. Except for several minor disturbances on the waterways, and a brief harassment campaign (due largely to an East German epidemic of hoof-and-mouth disease) against truckers delivering fresh meat and vegetables from West Germany, traffic was largely unmolested.

But for the first time since December 1963, West Berliners were not permitted to visit their relatives in the city's Soviet sector at Christmastime. The three-year-old *Passierschein* (visiting permit) agreement was not renewed when, in last-minute negotiations on Dec. 13, East German authorities demanded formal diplomatic recognition and a third-state status for West Berlin as the price for opening the Wall again.

For nearly six months Horst Korber, the West Berlin representative, and Michael Kohl, his East German counterpart, negotiated at least once weekly in an effort to make a new deal. Finally, on Oct. 6, they arrived at a compromise solution that renewed the agreement for emergency visits until Jan. 31, 1967. But talks on an overall pact for Christmas, New Year's, Easter and Whitsuntide proved futile and on Dec. 13 were suspended indefinitely.

There is hope in the city, however, that for all the cool winds blowing from Walter Ulbricht's East German regime, contacts with the Soviets themselves will ultimately improve and indirectly thaw the atmosphere. Mayor Willy Brandt took important steps in this direction by meeting four times during 1966 with the Soviet Union's Ambassador to East Germany, Pyotr A. Abrasimov, who functions as Soviet high commissioner for East Berlin. One of the visits, on Oct. 12, took place in the U.S.S.R.'s Embassy on Unter den Linden; the other three at specially arranged receptions in West Berlin.

Otto Bach, president of the West Berlin Parliament, listens to Mayor Heinrich Albertz' Dec. 14 policy speech.
UPI

For West Berliners, the most important political development in 1966 was the appointment of Brandt as West Germany's new vice-chancellor and foreign minister, and his resignation as governing mayor, a job that is akin to the governorship of a U.S. state. His successor and longtime deputy, Heinrich Albertz, 51, a former Protestant pastor, was elected with a majority of 99 to 41 votes in the Berlin assembly on Dec. 14. Albertz, though a far less powerful and colorful figure than Brandt, who leads West Germany's Social Democratic Party, is expected to pursue his predecessor's policies vis-à-vis both the East Germans and the Western Allies, who technically still occupy the city.

Though there were no major incidents involving either the Soviets or East Germans, Berliners in 1966 were consistently and increasingly plagued by Russian and East German jet maneuvers, with their sonic booms.

And on April 6 one of these jets, a two-man, two-engine Yak-28 fighter-bomber, crashed in West Berlin's Stoessen Lake. The plane was the first of its kind to fall into Allied hands; shortly after the accident, a group of Soviet officers and an armed-guard platoon from the Soviet War Memorial in West Berlin marched to the scene to secure the plane. There was a tense confrontation with British officers, in whose sector the craft had crashed, before the Russians retreated. Though the bodies of the two crewmen and the plane itself were eventually returned to Soviet authorities, observers assume British and American intelligence experts gave it a detailed examination.

While East Berlin was the site of propagandistic celebrations and displays of military might on Aug. 13, the fifth anniversary of the building of the Wall, West Berliners commemorated that day by laying wreaths at the spots where refugees have been shot by Ulbricht's border guards.

Yet, for all the dismay caused by the collapse of the permit negotiations, 1966 did end on a happy note for West Berliners. After two years of work and many more of planning, the autobahn bridge at Hof, on the main road between West Berlin and Munich, was finally rebuilt following its destruction by the Nazis in 1945. The project, undertaken jointly by West and East Germany, was finished in November, and the bridge, which cuts 18 miles and 45 minutes off the trip between Berlin and Bavaria, was formally opened for traffic on Dec. 19. The first motorist to use it: Berlin's new Governing Mayor Heinrich Albertz, who had flown to Nuremberg the day before so he could drive toward the divided city.

JOHN DORNBERG
Bonn-Berlin Correspondent, NEWSWEEK

West Berlin children at play ignore Berlin Wall, five years old in August 1966.

UPI

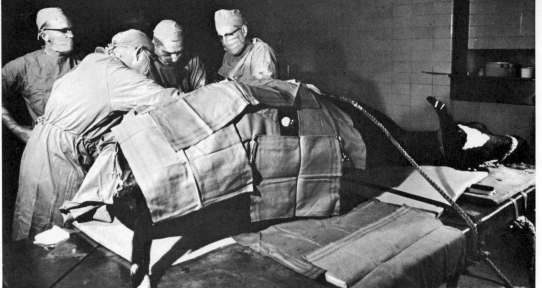

Doctors at University of California School of Veterinary Medicine insert tube inside cow in an experiment involving injection of viruses, cells or drugs.

BIOLOGICAL SCIENCES

By PETER GRAY
Andrey Avinoff Professor of Biology
UNIVERSITY OF PITTSBURGH

Evolution and Education. An event of outstanding interest to biologists in 1966 was a legal test of a high-school teacher's right to discuss the theory of evolution with her students. The last legal test of this was the famous 1925 Scopes trial, more of a circus than a legal action, which ended in Scopes' conviction for breaking a law in teaching evolution. His conviction was subsequently thrown out of court on a technicality. The present case, conducted with much more restraint, was started by Mrs. Susan Epperson of the Little Rock, Arkansas, Central High School. In January, she petitioned the court to declare the Arkansas antievolution law unconstitutional so that, when she started to teach evolution, she would not be guilty of a legal offense. At the hearing in April, she was joined by Mr. H. H. Blanchard, a parent, who wished his children to learn the theory of evolution as part of their college preparation.

The petitioners were opposed by a large number of ministers who presented the view that belief in the Bible is incompatible with the study of the theory of evolution. In June, Judge Murray O. Reed declared that Arkansas' antievolution law, passed in 1928, was unconstitutional. In presenting this judgment he said, "The truth or fallacy of arguments on each side of the evolution debate does not diminish the constitutional right of teachers and scientists to advance theories and to discuss them." This judgment, of the utmost importance to all teachers and students of biology, will be appealed by the state and may ultimately reach the Supreme Court.

Experiments on Living Animals. Biologists also became involved in another highly controversial legal issue—the right of scientists to conduct experiments on living animals. In March, John Barry Fugere, a high-school student in Newark, N.J., was, together with the East Orange Board of Education, taken to court by the New Jersey Society for the Prevention of Cruelty to Animals on the ground that his injection of tumor-producing cells into some chickens in the course of a high-school biology project involved needless cruelty. So important was this issue that the National Society for Medical Research and numerous prominent biologists and physicians intervened at Barry Fugere's trial in April. Judge Charles S. Barrett, Jr., ruled, in acquitting the defendants, that "Cruelty to my mind is the unjustifiable infliction of pain with the act having some malevolent or mischievous motive."

Unfortunately, this decision set off a national furore with the result that numerous bills attempting to limit or control experiments with living animals have been introduced both in state legislatures and in the U.S. Congress. Most of these bills, which seek to license and restrict animal experimenters as has long been done in England, are still under discussion. Two of them, HR10049 and S2576, go further than British legislation and would, in the opinion of most medical and biological research workers, sound the death knell of many vital research programs. In a closely related field, the so-called petnaping bill was passed in August. It requires inspection and registration of research facilities but, in the opinion of the National Society for Medical Research, will not seriously hamper investigators.

Legislation. Not all 1966 biological legislation was controversial. Senate bill S1446 designated five unpolluted streams as the beginning of a National Wild River Preservation System, and pending bills will endeavor to expand this. The Department of the Interior has asked that legislation be inaugurated that will place oysters, crabs and alligators under Federal protection. Legislation is, however, of no use without wide public support; and it is discouraging that a survey published in June by the University of Tennessee at Knoxville showed that only about 20 per cent of landowners in that state had any interest in the conservation of wildlife, although an additional 30 per cent said that they could be persuaded to take an interest if they received financial aid for doing so.

Water Resources. The handling of water resources remains one of the touchiest of conservation problems. Thus, on the one hand, LaMar Price of Fort Ord, Calif., pointed out that army multipurpose dams are of great value in the conservation of wildlife. On the other hand, plans for the enormous Rampart Dam on the Yukon River in Alaska have been discontinued following a report that almost incalculable damage would be done to fish and many other forms of wildlife if this construction were carried through.

Overdrainage can be as great a problem as overstorage; and Dr. Ira N. Gabrielson, president of the Wildlife Management Institute, pointed out that politically inspired financial assistance to farmers who wish to drain land results in more land being drained than the farmers can profitably utilize, even though the drainage destroys potentially valuable natural resources.

The almost continuous yearlong controversy over the water supply of Everglades National Park has brought some welcome publicity to this type of activity.

Conservation of Wildlife. The Soviet Government's official report on its game and wildlife preserves discloses that in the U.S.S.R. only about 0.2 per cent of the total land area is being set aside for conservation, compared to 1.0 per cent in the United States, 4.0 per cent in Great Britain and 4.25 per cent in Japan.

The conservation of individual species presents a much more cheerful picture. In February, U.S. Secretary of the Interior Stewart L. Udall directed that one square mile around any bald-eagle nest in national wildlife refuges be closed to all but refuge personnel. The directive further forbids the cutting of timber within half a mile of any nesting site. The Oregon Museum of Science and Industry, Portland, has set aside $1,000 for the study of the eagle's nesting habits. The Humble Oil and Refining Company has encouraged by every possible means the nesting of egrets and herons in the water-conservation lagoons around the company's plant at Baytown, Tex., and Harvard University has established a wildlife research center for the study of ducks, geese and owls near Concord, Mass.

The polar bear of North America's Arctic region is threatened with extinction by plane-flying hunters. The Canadian Government limits polar-bear hunting licenses to three hundred hunters per year. To get an idea of how many bears there are, and to learn more about their habits, Dr. Vagn Flyger of the University of Maryland fits captured bears with radio transmitters before freeing them. Signals from the transmitters will be picked up by orbiting satellite. Dr. Richard A. Cooley of the University of Washington has received a grant from the Conservation Foundation to explore the possibility of international cooperation among all countries having Arctic territory.

The Canadian Wildlife Service is trying to repopulate the Mawdesley Wildlife Management area, once the home of many buffalo, by the importation of a herd of twenty from the United States. In Australia, action by the Victorian Royal Society for the Prevention of Cruelty to Animals has forced the government of Victoria to rescind an order that all seals be killed because they interfere with fisheries. Australia's kangaroo, variously regarded as a pest or as a source of cheap meat for export, is in considerble danger of extinction. Dr. R. E. Dasmann of the American Conservation Foundation has urged that the Australian Government intervene and protect the species.

Aircraft are threatening fish as well as bears. A New Zealand commercial company employs helicopters to set up to fifty miles of fishing line and fifty thousand hooks each day and also to spread nets and lobster pots. The supply of fish is not inexhaustible, and Dr. M. E. Vinogradov of the Moscow Oceanographic Institute pointed out at the Second International Oceanographic Congress that from 1953 to 1963 the world's annual catch of fish increased from 23 million to 50 million tons. Many countries are now endeavoring to culture marine fish. At the same conference Dr. David Cushing of the Lowestoft Fisheries Laboratory in England described a method of rearing flounder, for subsequent liberation, in a walled-off fjord.

Dr. Frank J. Hester of the U.S. Bureau of Commercial Fisheries told a conference on "Exploiting the Ocean" (held at La Jolla, Calif., in June) that undersea farms may soon become a necessity. He suggested that some fish might be trained as "sheep dogs," and areas of the ocean walled off with fences of bubbles. The ever-increasing scarcity of protein makes the utilization of all parts of fish necessary, and Dr. I. A. Parfentjev of the Institute of Applied Biology has patented a new method for preparing fish flour, suitable for human nutrition, from parts of fish usually regarded as waste.

Fish are not the only food source threatened. Dr. A. C. Neish of the Canadian Government Atlantic Regional Laboratory at Halifax pointed out that in Nova Scotia, New Brunswick and Prince Edward Island alone, more than $1 million worth of seaweed was harvested annually. This seriously affects coastal forms, and Dr. Neish suggested that it may be necessary to investigate the possibility of harvesting deep water seaweeds.

Attempts at increasing the population of edible marine animals may be difficult. Dr. Robert Clutter of the La Jolla Fishery-Oceanography Center has found that the opossum shrimp, and possibly other forms, have a built-in device that inhibits older female shrimps from breeding.

Animal Behavior. Mechanisms that control animal behavior are still under intensive investigation in the United States. One of the more extraordinary experiments is being conducted by Dr. Robert C. Stones and Douglas E. Smith

at the Argonne National Laboratory. They find that bats change their behavior pattern and body temperature—as humans may have to in space—in accordance with the pattern of light and darkness to which they are subjected and also according to various colors of light. These automatic reactions were once thought to be controlled by internal mechanisms, but a great deal of work by Dr. Frank A. Brown at Northwestern University seems to have established the fact that the 24-hour clock found in most organisms is controlled from outside the body. The planet earth itself has a 24-hour rhythm, not only in light, but also in radiation, geomagnetism and electrical fields.

In a recent experiment, in cooperation with Dr. Young H. Park and Joseph R. Zeno, Brown was able to correlate an activity rhythm in mice with an artificially produced radiation rhythm. The fact that life responds to changes in the earth's magnetic field has led Dr. Bruce Heezen of Columbia University's Lamont Geological Observatory to suggest that variation in the earth's magnetic field may be the cause of the hitherto inexplicable disappearance of many life-forms. Heezen was able to establish a direct correlation between the appearance and disappearance of various microfossils from layers of the ocean's bed, where he was also able to show that there had been a reversal of magnetic field when these disappearances took place.

It has become apparent, through a report from Dr. Kenneth S. Norris of the University of California at Los Angeles, that fish, and particularly the opaleye perch on which he worked, have a built-in thermometer and ther-

Scientists from Bureau of Commercial Fisheries experiment with free-swimming marine animals. Photo shows killer whales riding herd on some larger whales.

Frank J. Hester, U.S. Bureau of Commercial Fisheries

mostat, the latter set to about 78° F. It appears that this thermostat controls their rhythmic movement from open tide pools to concealment under rocks and also ultimately causes them to leave the pools for the oceans. Aquatic insects, on the contrary, according to Dr. N. H. Anderson of Oregon State University, respond to light and particularly moonlight, rather than to temperature changes. No explanation has yet been offered, however, for the synchronous flashing of thousands of fireflies to which Dr. John Buck of the National Institutes of Health recently drew attention. He found that at times as much as one tenth of a mile of Amazon riverbank would be illuminated by fireflies, all of which turned their lights on and off in unison.

There is, of course, no doubt that insects can communicate with each other, but this communication is in most cases with the aid of chemicals. For example, Drs. K. Vick, W. A. Drew and J. Young of Oklahoma State University, together with a team of chemists from the same university, have recently shown that the alarm substance of harvester ants is a ketone, both produced by frightened ants and causing normal ants to become frightened. Other chemicals produced by insects are used, as Dr. Thomas Eisner and Jerrold Meinwald of Cornell University recently pointed out, for defense and for mating signals. The honeybee still seems to be the only insect known to communicate by sight signals, a fact which may be correlated with its outstanding intelligence.

Homing and Migration. Visual communication is linked with homing and migration in higher forms. However, Dr. T. C. Williams, J. M. Williams and D. R. Griffin of the Rockefeller University and New York Zoological Society reported to the New York Zoological Society that something else may be involved in the homing of bats. Normal bats released in Trinidad returned to their home cave from as much as one hundred miles away, but a few, fitted with aluminum-foil hoods over their eyes, returned from short distances, in spite of their inability to see. Dr. Griffin, long known for his experiments on bird navigation and migration, has been appointed to head the Institute for Research in Animal Behavior which will be jointly conducted by the Rockefeller University and the New York Zoological Society.

A startling suggestion was made by Dr. Stephen T. Emlen of the University of Michigan at the American Institute of Biological Sciences meeting at College Park, Md. Dr. Emlen suggested that the indigo bunting, which annually migrates over two thousand miles, may recognize whole constellations of stars in navigation, rather than a single bright star.

The only unusual fact about migration recorded in 1966 was the British Trust for Ornithology notation that very large numbers of lapwings crossed the Atlantic from England to Canada for the first time in forty years. The sudden appearance of large numbers of North American bats in Iceland, reported by Dr. Carl F. Koopman of the American Museum of Natural History, appears to be due to high winds rather than to voluntary migration.

Origin of Life. Theories about the origin of life continue to form the basis of many discussions among biologists. The generally accepted theory, that life probably evolved from inorganic matter at an early stage of the planet's history, was detailed by Dr. Sidney W. Fox of the University of Miami Institute of Molecular Evolution at a symposium held in Paris. He pointed out that naturally occurring polymers could have become enzymes from which all life sprang. This theory has recently been sharply queried by Dr. Philip H. Abelson of the Carnegie Institute of Washington; he casts doubts on the postulate that the primeval atmosphere of earth consisted of the necessary carbon dioxide, water, methane and ammonia. Dr. Abelson suggested, instead, that the principal constituent of the early atmosphere was hydrogen cyanide, a gas that is poisonous to all forms of existing life, and that inhibits the action of almost all known enzymes.

The long-discarded theory that life drifted through space from another planet revived a little when Dr. John E. Hotchin reported that satellite-borne microorganisms survived for as long as 18 hours, including 6 hours of solar radiation. Nevertheless, no one has yet found life-forms in space. It is apparent, however, that space vehicles must continue to be carefully sterilized to avoid contaminating other planets. According to Dr. Constantine D. J. Generales, Jr., of the New York State Medical Society, this is particularly important for spacecraft directed at planets like Mars, where it is theoretically possible that earthlike forms might exist. Dr. Generales pointed out, however, that the crash landing of the Russian Venus 3 could not possibly contaminate any life that might be on Venus, since the conditions on this planet could themselves sterilize earthly forms.

The date for the first appearance of life continues to be pushed backward through time. Drs. Barghoorn and Schopf, of Harvard, have found bacterialike forms in African cherts 3,000,000,000 years old. This adds at least 1,000,000,000 years to any previous estimate. Even relatively advanced forms of life appear to be older than was thought, since Dr. Andrew H. McNair of Dartmouth College has discov-

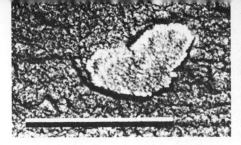

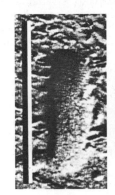

Drs. Barghoorn and Schopf of Harvard have found bacterialike forms (l) in African cherts 3,000,000,000 years old. Entomologist (r) inspects insect trap in field test.

ered clamlike and wormlike animals in rocks 720 million years old, which is 120 million years earlier than previous records. Drs. Wu Ju Kang, Chou Ming-Chen and Chia Lan-Po have found an unquestioned human skull of rather more than 500,000 years old; and Dr. Richard G. Klein of the University of Chicago has found evidence in the Ukraine that Neanderthal man, who appeared about 150,000 years ago and is said to have become extinct 70,000 years ago, may have evolved into modern man.

It is interesting that two supposedly extinct animals turned up in 1966. A pigmy opossum, presumably extinct for something close to a million years, was discovered sitting in a ski hut in the Australian Alps by Dr. K. D. Shortman. Also in Australia, a Gould League expedition rediscovered the paradise parrot, thought to have disappeared 50 years ago. The Tasmanian marsupial tiger, so close to extinction that the last trace of one was found 30 years ago, has been rediscovered by Dr. E. R. Guiler of Tasmania's Animals and Birds Protection Panel. Early settlers tried to wipe out this form of tiger, a dangerous predator of domestic animals.

Noxious Insects. Man's efforts to wipe out the noxious insect have, as usual, been far less successful. Dr. H. E. Smith of the University of North Carolina told the National Academy of Sciences that man was winning the war on insects hands down. But an exactly reverse point of view was presented by Dr. Ross E. Hutchins in his new book *Insects*. He believes that insects are adapting to chemical insecticides faster than man can invent new ones.

Indeed, most of the 1966 advances in pest control have been through the attraction of insects to traps, through biological control and through breeding. In the first category, Drs. William A. Jones, Martin Jacobson and Dial F. Martin of the U.S. Department of Agriculture have synthesized the male attractant odor of the female bollworm moth and are baiting traps with it, while the Texas agricultural station has developed a blue-green light which is fatally attractive to boll weevils. As methods of biological control, the Australian Government has imported a number of Hawaiian insects—two leaf miners and one root borer—in an endeavor to keep down the serious weed pest lantana. B. A. Franklin of the U.S.D.A. has discovered that a number of insect-destroying bacteria can be dusted onto tobacco plants.

An extremely interesting insect-control breeding program is being developed by the Australian Commonwealth Scientific and Industrial Research Organization. They are irradiating male noxious insects in an endeavor to produce mutants, the offspring of which will all be male. If sufficient numbers of such mutants are liberated, the males may come to dominate the environment to the extent that this particular kind of insect will become extinct. Finally, the Australians are trying to see whether insects can be discouraged by conditions that discourage humans. For instance, they have liberated immense numbers of artificially sterilized insects in the hope that the overcrowding will so discourage the fertile forms that they will abandon the struggle to survive.

BIOLOGICAL SCIENCES:

MEMORY TRANSFER

By GEORGE A. W. BOEHM

Free-Lance Science Writer

It is almost inconceivable that man will ever invent a machine nearly so remarkable as his own brain. Today's giant electronic computers can do arithmetic and look up names thousands of times faster than people, and far more accurately too. But compared to live brains the machines are stodgy and inflexible. The biggest and fastest of them can handle no more than a tiny fraction of the varied information in even the most forgetful human memory.

Stored somehow in a mass of nerve tissue scarcely larger than a pair of baseballs are multitudes of numbers and words and also many sorts of information that computers cannot cope with. A brain, for example, remembers a familiar face, and the appearance of the clothes a friend wore on a particular day. It remembers the sound of a voice and of a symphony orchestra. It remembers the odor of broiling steak and the softness of velvet, and hundreds of other sensations a whole roomful of computers could not recognize. Besides, a brain remembers certain techniques—such as ways of persuading people—that baffle computers. The most elaborate computer cannot remember anything that is not set down in numbers or simple words.

The capacity of a human memory is enormous—enough to fill many millions of books. Scientists who have studied the mind suppose that a brain contains everything its owner ever experienced plus some inborn instincts, such as the tendency to flinch from a blow. Forgetfulness comes about only through failure to recall memories that are firmly implanted in the brain.

The Brain and the Mind

One of the most fascinating problems in modern biology is to find how memories are stored and retrieved. Its solution would have far-reaching implications for medicine and education, and it might also lead to the design of supercomputers. The problem, as the ancient Greeks realized, amounts to discovering how the nerve tissue of the brain can contain the multitude of ideas we think of as the mind. To date, no one has come close to explaining the mentality of so simple a brain as that of a worm. Yet worms have vaster memories than the biggest computers.

Scientists interested in the relationship of brain to mind have long hoped for experimental ways to add or subtract specific memories. To this end, psychologists have devised many complicated experiments involving learning. The trouble has been that, although learning certainly calls for the addition of memories, it has little or no recognizable effect on the structure or chemical content of the brain. Other research men have cut away parts of the brains of laboratory animals, hoping to subtract specific kinds of memory. But while the animals have shown memory decreases, there has seemed to be no connection between what part of the brain was removed, and what sort of memory was lost.

Memory-Transfer Research

Men intent on finding the mechanism of the mind are now eagerly reviewing some astounding results from still another approach that has been tried repeatedly since the summer of 1965. Experiments performed in the United States and Europe have indicated that memory can sometimes be transferred from one animal to another, almost like an infectious disease of the brain. Untrained animals appear to learn "contagiously" from injections of extracts of the brains of trained animals. If this research lives up to its early promise, a chemical basis for memory may become clear to scientists.

The first step in this research applied to higher animals was taken by a team at UCLA, headed by psychologist Allan L. Jacobson. His group trained rats in box-cages to approach a cup whenever they heard a sharp click. Only after a click would they find food there. The rats were then killed. Their brains were ground fine and chemically treated to make an extract. This was then injected into the blood of untrained rats that had never been in the box-cages with the food cups. Immediately the untrained rats tended to interpret correctly the meaning of the click: that it meant food in the cup.

Similar experiments have been tried on mice, hamsters, pigeons, goldfish and other species. The animals have been taught that certain sounds, lights and other forms of stimulation have special meanings in terms of pleasant or unpleasant consequences. Then the researchers have tried to transfer this knowledge to other animals through injections of brain extracts.

114

Some of the experiments—though by no means all—have been strikingly successful. There has even been some apparent success in transferring memory from one species to another. Mice, for example, have learned from rat-brain injections to ignore a startling noise. And hamster-brain injections apparently have taught rats that a click promises food.

This transfer between species suggests that a memory, far from being strictly personal, may be stored in all animals in pretty much the same form. What could be the universal nature of memory? Is it chemical or physical or a mixture? These questions have aroused speculations among scientists who doubt that memory-transfer experiments are authentic.

Memory and the Chemical Agent

A number of experimenters suspect that memories are stored in the form of molecules of a chemical family called RNA (ribonucleic acid). RNA molecules are long and intricately twisted chains consisting of many thousands of atoms. Minor variations in the shape of such a molecule or the placement of a small proportion of its atoms could provide enough variability to account for all the memories a brain contains. Ordinarily, RNA is found in every living cell, where it controls the manufacture of proteins. Moreover, RNA helps to reproduce itself, sometimes in modified form. It is thus adaptable enough to be the raw material for newly formed memories, and also to preserve old memories indefinitely, even though the original RNA might deteriorate.

But how can such a large molecule get from the bloodstream into the brain? This question bothers many biologists, for the brain is usually protected by an invisible barrier that screens out foreign matter in the blood. For this reason some scientists rule out RNA in favor of smaller molecules: perhaps certain proteins or protein fragments, polypeptides.

Whatever the chemical agent may be, it seems to have a hard time penetrating the barrier between blood and brain, which may account for the failure of many transfer experiments. This is borne out by a series of notably successful experiments at Cornell University. At that time, it happened the rats were quite sick. Very likely the experiments went smoothly because the animals were suffering from brain damage that made the barrier leaky. If such is the case, present transfer techniques could scarcely be tried on humans, although less perilous methods might be worked out.

While most of the new research has concentrated on adding memories to untrained brains, some scientists have taken an opposite tack.

They have tried to suppress the formation of memory with injections of materials that block the formation of RNA or proteins or both.

This work has been less dramatic than memory transfer, but on the other hand it has been easier to duplicate and to interpret. Many experiments have been done on goldfish, which can be easily taught to swim to one end of a tank in order to avoid an electric shock.

How effectively memory is suppressed depends chiefly on when the chemicals are administered. Usually fish learn their lesson within a day and remember it well three days later. But if a little of a poisonous antibiotic called puromycin is injected immediately after the training period, the memory is soon lost. Puromycin is known to block the body's production of RNA; therefore it also halts production of some protein and polypeptides. Thus puromycin experiments shed no more light on the precise chemical nature of memory.

This work does show, however, that a memory is formed in stages—probably three or more distinct ones. In the first stage, memory is an "echo": a pulsating electric current that circulates among the brain's nerve cells. This is the kind of fleeting memory, soon discarded, that we use when we look up a telephone number there is no reason to retain for later use. This memory is immune to puromycin poisoning.

After a few minutes the electrical echo begins to change into a permanent form. Presumably this is because it leaves an imprint on RNA or some other substance with large molecules, for the transition to permanent form can be interrupted with puromycin.

A Look Ahead

Cautious scientists are not yet willing to accept memory transfer wholeheartedly. There are too many loose ends. To date, workers in this new field have been too busy exploring the exciting possibilities to dot every "i" and cross every "t." Now is the time for discovery; firm proof will have to wait. One source of confusion has been the impurity of the transfer extracts, all of which consist of numerous materials in varying proportions.

At this time practical applications seem remote. Nevertheless, it is tempting to speculate that memory transfer may someday fill classrooms with geniuses and improve the faulty memories of retarded children and old people. Even if the new techniques are never used in medicine or education, the research effort will prove worthwhile if it helps scientists understand how the puny brain contains the mighty mind.

BOOK PUBLISHING. A total of $2,500,000,000 in book sales was estimated for 1966. Sales of general trade books (fiction, nonfiction, reference and children's literature) to the public as well as to libraries and institutions climbed higher. Book-club, mail-order and subscription sales also showed gains. While paperback titles in the so-called "quality" group continued an upward trend in the number of titles published as well as in dollar volume, "mass market" paperback sales stalled short of 300 million units, a drop from 1965.

The boom in books was not without its handicaps. Lack of sufficient plant capacity to fill publishers' demands led to inordinate delays among printers and binders. Mergers and rumors of mergers among publishers and non-book corporations were reported throughout the year. Random House joined the communications combine headed by the Radio Corporation of America. The Los Angeles Times-Mirror Co. acquired Harry N. Abrams, Inc., while Bobbs-Merrill became an affiliate of IT&T.

The overseas sales of American books mounted, reaching the 250 million mark.

On the censorship front early in the year, the Supreme Court sentenced Ralph Ginzburg to five years in jail and fined him $28,000. The court ruled that salacious advertising could be a determining factor of guilt in the publication of questionable material that might otherwise be allowed. At the same time, the

Supreme Court overruled the Massachusetts court ban and permitted the sale of controversial *Fanny Hill*. In a California election-ballot referendum the so-called CLEAN bill was decisively defeated by popular vote. The bill sought to strengthen California's penal-code provisions regarding the sale and distribution of pornographic literature.

JOSEPH A. DUFFY
Executive Director
AMERICAN BOOKSELLERS ASSOCIATION

BREZHNEV, LEONID. The title "General Secretary of the Communist Party of the Soviet Union" was conferred upon Leonid Ilyich Brezhnev in March during the 23d Soviet Party Congress, and to some there seemed an ominous note in the resurrection of the office held by Joseph V. Stalin. But neither as general nor as "first" secretary did Brezhnev wield anything approaching the authority of Stalin, or for that matter, of Nikita S. Khrushchev, whom Brezhnev succeeded in October 1964. Nevertheless, Brezhnev appeared to be a man determined to use efficiently what power he had, and able, when the occasion warranted, to be tough about his job of directing party affairs.

Brezhnev's keynote speech to the 23d Congress, while pitched in a minor key and without fireworks, contained some significant features, notably admission of failures in agriculture and some other sectors of the economy, for which the blame, by implication, was placed upon his predecessor. He insisted that Soviet planners place primary importance upon the development of agriculture. Apparently he was determined to avoid recurrence of such an embarrassing situation as the Soviet grain crisis under Khrushchev which had forced the U.S.-S.R. to turn westward for wheat.

On the diplomatic side, Brezhnev began the year with a spectacular thrust aimed at the Soviet Union's big neighbor, Communist China, once hailed as its eternal friend. Brezhnev headed a high-powered delegation to the Mongolian People's Republic (Outer Mongolia), the buffer communist state where the Chinese had been attempting to subvert the Soviet influence. There Brezhnev signed a treaty of friendship and mutual defense and apparently nailed down Soviet influence, to the obvious discomfiture of the Red Chinese. For their part, the Chinese shortly thereafter sourly and insultingly turned down a Brezhnev invitation to send a delegation to the Soviet Communist Congress.

The Chinese also spurned Brezhnev's appeal to join in a united front with all communist

---

SOME BEST SELLERS OF 1966

FICTION

Capable of Honor	Allen Drury
Tai-Pan	James Clavell
The Adventurers	Harold Robbins
The Double Image	Helen MacInnes
The Embezzler	Louis Auchincloss
The Secret of Santa Vittoria	Robert Crichton
The Source	James Michener
Those Who Love	Irving Stone
Up the Down Staircase	Bel Kaufman
Valley of the Dolls	Jacqueline Susann

NONFICTION

A Thousand Days	Arthur Schlesinger, Jr.
Games People Play	Eric Berne
How to Avoid Probate	Norman Decey
Human Sexual Response	W. H. Masters and V. E. Johnson
In Cold Blood	Truman Capote
Kennedy	Theodore Sorensen
Rush to Judgment	Mark Lane
The Last Battle	Cornellus Ryan
Unsafe at Any Speed	Ralph Nader
With Kennedy	Pierre Salinger

nations to deal with the question of Vietnam. In published statements Brezhnev insisted the Soviet Union wanted better relations with both China and the United States, but China, at any rate, received these gestures with cold scorn.

In April, Brezhnev carried a step further the Soviet campaign to increase Moscow influence in North Vietnam and thus assert Moscow's stake in whatever might develop in Indochina. He met in the Kremlin with Le Duan, first secretary of the North Vietnamese Communist Party, and thereafter Moscow-Hanoi relations seemed to improve. Hanoi, though often appearing on the fence in the Soviet-Chinese dispute, frequently had leaned in the Chinese direction.

Brezhnev had other troubles in the communist world. Rumania, for example, had been displaying a strong tendency toward independence of action on both party and government levels. Brezhnev went to Bucharest in May on what obviously was a trouble-shooting mission. He talked for three days with Rumanian leaders, but the evidence was that a major policy dispute was unresolved. Brezhnev also journeyed to Prague to attend a Czechoslovak Communist Party Congress and, also at midyear, met with leaders of all East European communist nations except Albania in a session of the Warsaw Pact military alliance at Bucharest. Once again there was evidence of disaffection, particularly among the Rumanian leaders.

In September, Brezhnev undertook a tour of Bulgaria, Yugoslavia and Hungary for talks with the leaders of those countries. Moscow brushed aside Western speculation that a principal topic was the Moscow-Peking feud over control of the world communist movement.

Then in November, Rumania again struck a discordant note. At Sofia, Bulgaria, Brezhnev endorsed what obviously was a Moscow-inspired Bulgarian call for a world communist conference, its purpose to chastise the Red Chinese. Rumania balked, insisting that efforts continue to produce at least a facade of world communist unity. In any event, among communist parties haunted by doubts and fears, such a conference was not easy to arrange.

Brezhnev was determined to push ahead with the project. At the end of November, he returned to Budapest, to take part in the Hungarian Party's Congress. There he won majority support of other delegations for a world conference some time in 1967. Brezhnev, indeed, might have been justified in considering that the quarrel and its abrasions on the world movement could endanger his own position at the top of the Soviet collective leadership.

UPI

Soviet President Podgorny presents Chairman Brezhnev with two of the U.S.S.R.'s highest honors Dec. 19.

On the domestic scene, Brezhnev headed a new commission to prepare for collective-farm-system reforms. He consistently stressed the importance of higher living standards as a goal of the Five-Year Plan.

On his sixtieth birthday Dec. 19, the regime conferred on him the nation's highest civilian award, Hero of the Soviet Union, along with an Order of Lenin and a gold medal. The Supreme Soviet (Parliament) gave him two unusual standing ovations.

Brezhnev exhibited annoyance with some manifestations among Soviet intellectuals and the nation's youth. He maintained stony silence when he received an appeal from Soviet intellectuals pleading for guarantees against a return to any aspects of Stalinism. Under the party's direction, plays too critical of the Stalin era were removed from theaters. Brezhnev fretted about lack of party spirit among youth and called for a better job of indoctrination. In particular, he urged youth to stop admiring things foreign and to reject Western attitudes.

WILLIAM L. RYAN
Special Correspondent, THE ASSOCIATED PRESS

Herblock in "The Washington Post"

BUSINESS

By PHILIP GREER
New York Financial Correspondent
THE WASHINGTON POST

The longest peacetime business boom in U.S. history just managed to roll through its sixth straight year in 1966. Economic activity rose to new records during the year, but slowdowns in several key sectors indicated that the expansion might be coming to an end. Problems that had begun to appear in the latter part of 1965 grew to major proportions in 1966 and, by the end of the year, many economists were wondering whether the United States was headed for an economic pause or a recession.

Chief among the problem areas, of course, was the fighting in Vietnam. Aside from the toll in human life and property, the supply requirements created pressures that the economy was hard pressed to meet. At the same time, record levels of consumer income bolstered by production for Vietnam stimulated demand for civilian goods, and, for a time, the

economy was thought to be in serious danger of "overheating."

By the end of the year, the worries had swung from an overheated economy to one which was faltering in more and more areas.

The Economy in 1966

Gross National Product. Measured by the gross national product—the value of all goods and services produced in the United States—the year set new records. The GNP rose to an estimated $738,000,000,000, an 8.5 per cent increase over the previous record, $681,200,-000,000, established in 1965. Of that gain, 3.5 per cent was accounted for by price increases. But, as an indication of the prevailing mood at the end of the year, economists were predicting a much smaller advance in 1967.

Disposable income in the hands of consumers rose to $504,000,000,000 from the $469,100,-000,000 of 1965, and taxes paid by individuals increased to an estimated $75,000,000,000 from $66,000,000,000 the year before. Total income of U.S. wage earners was estimated at $579,-000,000,000 compared with $535,100,000,000 in 1965.

In all these areas, new records were being forecast for 1967, although the growth was not expected to be so spectacular.

The reverse, however, was true on the corporate side of the ledger. Corporate profits (after taxes) rose to $48,500,000,000 in 1966 from $44,500,000,000 the year before. But by the end of the year, the feeling was that after-tax profits by corporations would reach only $46,000,000,000 in 1967. Dividends paid by corporations climbed to $21,100,000,000 during the year, from $19,200,000,000 in 1965, but here, again, the expectation was that this total would rise much less in the new year.

Taxes and Interest Rates. All these predictions were based on the assumption that President Johnson would not ask Congress to increase personal and corporate income taxes in 1967—and that was nowhere near a certainty. In fact, the question of taxes and of government fiscal policy was the major economic question of 1966, and, as the year rolled to an end, there was no clear indication of what the answer would be.

At the beginning of 1966, the problems facing the economy were real enough. But, with business activity rolling at a record pace, there were few people who feared an early end to the boom. The U.S. consumer, after all, who provides the ultimate base for all economic activity, had plenty of money in his pocket and, from all indications, was anxious to spend it. At the same time, the demands of Vietnam seemed to assure sufficient government ordering to fill any air pockets that might develop.

But this same combination, strange as it seems, piled onto the economy burdens that finally began to have their effect. First, money for loans at the nation's banks began to get scarce. With that, interest rates began to rise, and the prime rate—the interest banks charge their biggest and best customers—climbed to 6 per cent in August. This was the highest the prime rate had been since the early 1930's.

As the prime rate rose, of course, interest rates were climbing all down the line. The home-building industry, which had been in the doldrums for several years, pulled in even further to the lowest level since World War II. Housing starts in 1966 dropped to 1,200,-000 from 1,540,000 in 1965.

Automobiles and Steel. The automobile industry, possibly the single most important industry in the United States, which had posted record sales for three consecutive years, reported its first downturn early in May. This sag was caused as much, perhaps, by intense publicity given a book that charged autos were unsafe—and the Congressional hearings that followed—as by the difficulty consumers had in borrowing money to finance new purchases.

Whatever the cause, the industry was never able to recover the lost momentum, and finished the year with a total production of 8,600,000 autos, down from 9,300,000 cars in 1965.

The slowdown in auto production affected the steel industry, which relies on the car manufacturers for approximately 25 per cent of its shipments. At the beginning of the year, steel users were still working off the inventory that had been accumulated as protection against a feared strike in the steel industry in 1965. The strike did not materialize, but new orders for steel were held back until the supplies on hand were used up. After only a few months of maximum production, steel mills were also forced to reduce their output, and steel production for the year came to 134,041,00 tons, only a small rise from the 131,000,000 tons produced in 1965, when the inventory building was in progress. Because of the stockpiles in the hands of steel users, actual shipments of steel during the year slipped to about 90,000,-000 tons from the 92,660,000 tons shipped in 1965.

Banking Picture. The shortage of cash affected the entire economy. The Federal Reserve, seeking a means of restraining expansion through monetary policy, as long as the admin-

Active day at New York Stock Exchange: Aug. 29, 1966.

Wide World

istration did not see fit to increase taxes and thus exert restraint through fiscal policy, kept a tight rein on the supply of money at the nation's banks.

The banking squeeze reached its most critical point in August. In the major New York City banks, more than 70 per cent of deposits was committed to loans, an extremely high percentage. At the same time, the Federal Government was financing its mounting debt, and corporations were withdrawing short-term funds they had loaned to banks in the form of certificates of deposit. For a while, it seemed as though the most critical banking crisis since the early 1930's was in the making.

At this point, the Federal Reserve, which had been urging a go-slow policy on loans, stepped in to supply the money the banking system needed, but also laid down hard-and-fast rules to keep the supply of credit from expanding further.

As a result, the crisis was avoided and, by the end of the year, interest rates had begun to ease slightly. But there was little doubt that credit was still extremely tight, and there was no indication of any significant easing in the Federal Reserve's tight-money policies.

Prices. Unlike 1965, when the Federal Government used pressure to keep manufacturers from increasing prices, the inflationary effects of record demand from all sectors pushed prices steadily higher in 1966. The wholesale commodity-price index of the Bureau of Labor Statistics rose to 106 per cent of its 1957–59 average, up from 102.5 per cent the previous year. Consumer prices rose to 113.1 per cent of the average of the same years, up from 109.9 per cent in 1965. In other words, items that added up to a total cost of $10 in 1957–59 cost $11.31 in 1966. These price increases, of course, accounted for a large part of the tremendous increase in the nation's gross national product.

The Stock Market. For the U.S. stock markets, one of the most sensitive barometers of the economy, the year was a mixed blessing. Volume on the New York Stock Exchange rose to new records, with 1,900,215,874 shares traded, compared with the previous record of 1,556,300,000 in 1965. On the American Stock Exchange, volume totaled a record 690,762,585 shares, up from 534,221,999 in 1965.

But on the other side of the coin, stock prices, as measured by the Dow-Jones Industrial Average, suffered one of their worst plunges on record. Entering 1966 in a strong uptrend, the Dow reached an all-time high of 995.15 on Feb. 9, then turned down and never approached that level again. By Oct. 7, the Dow

had tumbled to 742.42, a loss of more than 25 per cent. Against its 1965 close of 969.26, the average finished 1966 at 785.52, for a net loss of 183.74 points. By the end of November, the market value of all shares listed on the NYSE had fallen to $475,427,000,000 from $480,884,000,000 the year before.

"Tight money," of course, played its part in the stock market's fall. Interest rates on savings accounts and investment bonds, pushed higher by business' demand for new financing, proved extremely attractive to investors and siphoned money out of the equity markets. At the same time, mutual funds, wary of the economy's course, held back on investing $2,500,000,000 they took in on new share sales.

As the market fell, bearishness took hold in Wall Street. The short interest, reflecting the number of borrowed shares sold by traders in expectation of buying them back later at lower prices, soared to new record levels. On Dec. 15, the short interest on the New York Stock Exchange stood at 14,620,000 shares.

The biggest stock-market news of the year, though, came in the mutual-fund field. In February, Gerald Tsai, Jr., a well-known fund manager, sold shares in a new fund. The initial sale of $279,000,000 was the largest underwriting ever seen in Wall Street, eclipsing the $192,000,000 sale by the One William Street Fund in 1957. But Tsai's Manhattan Fund, issued at $10 a share when the stock market was at its all-time high, fell to almost $7 a share before recovering to finish the year at $8.60 a share.

Then, in December, the Securities & Exchange Commission released its long-awaited report on mutual funds. Four years in preparation, the report criticized many of the selling and investment practices of the industry. It recommended that Congress impose a ceiling on sales charges for fund shares, and a ceiling on the fees charged by fund-management companies. It also recommended an overhaul of the New York Stock Exchange Commission structure to provide lower costs for large-scale investors.

The fund industry withheld comment on the report, but indicated that it would strongly oppose the SEC when its proposals are presented to Congress in 1967.

Major U.S. Industries

Plastics and Nonferrous Metals. Despite the slowdowns that hit some key industries, others recorded banner years in 1966—and for some the indications were that business would get even better in the future. The plastics industry, for example, produced a record 13,-

500,000,000 pounds of raw materials, a 15.6 per cent increase over 1965.

Nonferrous metals enjoyed extremely strong demand, spurred by the needs of U.S. troops in Vietnam. Aluminum shipments reached a record 4,500,000 tons, up 10 per cent from 1965. Demand for the metal was so strong that the industry had to purchase 342,000 tons—about 7.5 per cent of total supply—from government stockpiles. Copper was extremely scarce. Although the domestic price finished the year in the area of 36 to 38 cents a pound, prices for copper for future delivery soared to 54 cents a pound on the London Metal Exchange, providing a glimpse of what may happen to prices in the future. U.S. mills also turned out 1,110,000 tons of zinc and 477,000 tons of lead in 1966. Consumption of these metals, though, was even higher. Zinc use rose 5.1 per cent to 1,413,000 tons, and lead consumption reached 1,150,000 tons.

Transportation. The big news in railroads was the approval by the Interstate Commerce Commission of the proposed merger of the New York Central and Pennsylvania Railroads. The merger, which would create the largest rail system in the country, was strongly opposed by competing roads, notably the Norfolk & Western. Despite ICC approval, legal challenges to the merger kept it from being consummated as the year closed. There was some doubt it would ever take place.

With Vietnam again providing the major impetus, the aerospace industry set new sales records in 1966. Total industry sales rose to $23,800,000,000 from $20,700,000,000 in 1965. The industry-wide backlog of unfilled orders climbed to $27,100,000,000 at the end of the third quarter from $18,700,000,000 at the same time in the previous year.

The biggest news in the aerospace industry was the competition for the Federal-government contract to build a supersonic commercial transport. Boeing and Lockheed were the two prime competitors for the job of building the plane itself, while General Electric and United Aircraft sought contracts to build the engines.

Design proposals for the plane, which will carry up to 350 passengers at speeds up to 1,800 miles per hour, were submitted to the Federal Aviation Agency in September, and the agency's recommendations went to President Johnson in December. On Dec. 31, the President chose Boeing to produce the plane and General Electric to manufacture the engines, but the program seemed to be stalled because of its high cost.

For the winning company, the project represents a $4,500,000,000 contract. Estimates of

Wide World

Treasury Secretary Fowler (l) and Commerce Secretary Connor discuss balance-of-payments deficit May 18.

the total market for the airship, which is expected to be in commercial service in 1974, range as high as $43,600,000,000 over the next 20 years. The biggest hitch in the program emerged with the realization that the "sonic boom" created by planes flying faster than sound might prohibit using the craft over land areas and, therefore, restrict the potential market.

Airlines also enjoyed a banner year, despite a mechanics strike that shut down five major trunk lines for 43 days in July and August. Passenger traffic rose to 80,000,000,000 revenue-miles with a total of 110,000,000 passengers.

Air-freight flights logged 2,100,000,000 ton-miles (one ton flown one mile) and mail traffic, largely to Vietnam, jumped a huge 62 per cent to 783,000,000 ton-miles.

Aircraft delivered to the airlines cost $1,500,-000,000, although delivery problems encountered by the two largest producers of commercial craft—Boeing and Douglas—slowed shipments for most of the year.

Financial Indicators

Administration Guidelines. As prices rose in many industries, wage demands by organized labor also broke through the Government's 3.2 per cent guidelines in 1966 and, in fact, forced the administration to change its approach.

Gardner Ackley, chairman of the President's Council of Economic Advisers, said during the year that wage increases should be tied to increases in productivity. The 3.2 per cent figure, he said, might not apply in all industries and should not be considered the only yardstick.

Nevertheless, factory wages overtook productivity toward the end of the year. The unit cost of labor compiled by the Census Bureau reached 102.4 per cent of the 1957–59 average in November, its fourth straight monthly increase.

Employment. One of the major reasons for increasing labor costs was the scarcity of skilled labor. Many industries found themselves unable to meet demand simply because they could not find enough experienced craftsmen. Unemployment dropped to its lowest levels of the postwar years. By the end of 1966, only 3.8 per cent of the work force was not employed, down from 4.6 per cent at the end of 1965. The number of jobs rose by 2,200,000 to more than 75,000,000 and the average income of a family of four went from $9,772 in 1965 to $10,304 by the end of 1966.

Gold. Older problems also continued to disturb the national business picture. The U.S. gold supply slipped further, despite the fact that France, which had been the most consistent purchaser of American gold, stopped buying toward the end of the year. At the end of 1966, the U.S. Treasury reported gold assets of $13,158,419,865.42, compared with $13,807,104,915.19 at the end of 1965.

Balance of Payments. The balance of payments, a consistent headache to American money managers for years, continued on the minus side, although the deficit was caused entirely by the Vietnam war. Spurred by presidential pressure to cut their foreign spending, U.S. corporations stepped up exports while putting a lid on imports. Still, although the export-import balance showed a favorable ratio of $29,300,000,000 in exports and $25,400,-000,000 in imports, the heavy spending in Vietnam indicated that the balance of payments for the year as a whole would be little changed from the loss of $1,300,000,000 recorded in 1965.

The Consumer. And the consumer, who still held the key to the future of the U.S. economy, also showed more caution in 1966. During the third quarter of the year, individuals saved $9,500,000,000, up from $5,100,000,000 in the second quarter. Retailers reported that Christmas sales, although showing an increase over 1965, were not nearly so brisk as they had hoped. Retail sales in the Christmas period rose 3 to 5 per cent from 1965, compared with anticipations of a 10 per cent rise.

It was clear as the year ended that both in their business and personal lives, people in the United States were uncertain of what the future contained, and they were no longer expanding their living standards at the breakneck pace of the previous four years.

After signing legislation Sept. 21 aimed at limiting rising interest rates, President Johnson gives pen to Federal Reserve Board Chairman William McChesney Martin, Jr.

UPI

GROSS NATIONAL PRODUCT

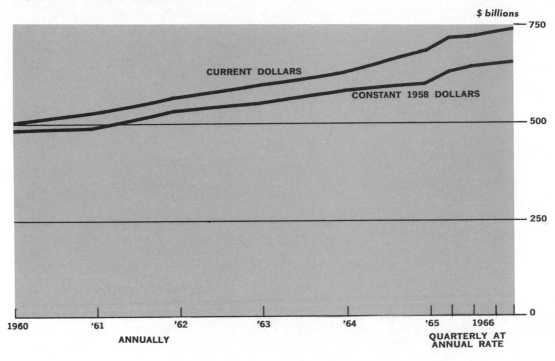

$ billions

CURRENT DOLLARS

CONSTANT 1958 DOLLARS

750

500

250

0

1960   '61   '62   '63   '64   '65   1966

ANNUALLY   QUARTERLY AT
                            ANNUAL RATE

EMPLOYMENT

in millions

INDUSTRIAL PRODUCTION

(1957-1959 = 100)

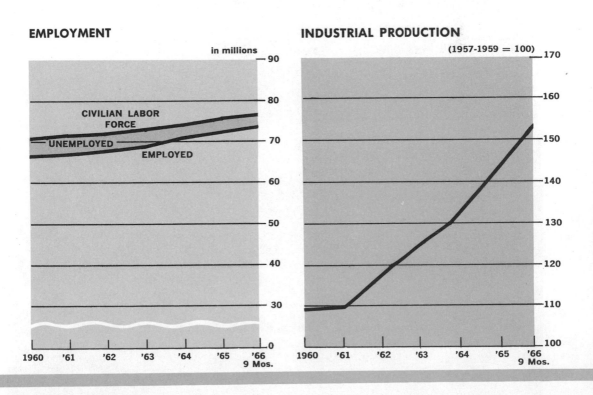

CIVILIAN LABOR FORCE

UNEMPLOYED

EMPLOYED

90
80
70
60
50
40
30
0

1960 '61 '62 '63 '64 '65 '66
                            9 Mos.

170
160
150
140
130
120
110
100

1960 '61 '62 '63 '64 '65 '66
                            9 Mos.

Source: Economic Indicators

Because of Vietnam, defense expenditures are up...

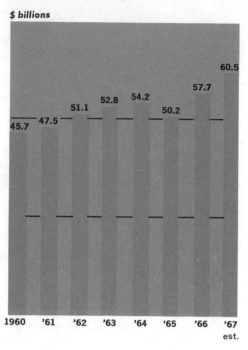

$ billions

45.7 47.5 51.1 52.8 54.2 50.2 57.7 60.5

1960 '61 '62 '63 '64 '65 '66 '67 est.

but effort is taking less of our total output than Korea.

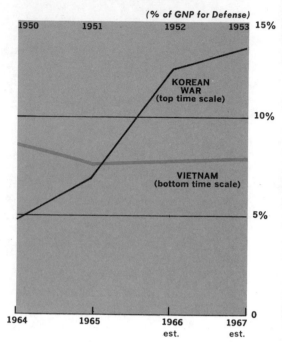

(% of GNP for Defense)

1950 1951 1952 1953 15%

KOREAN WAR (top time scale)

10%

VIETNAM (bottom time scale)

5%

1964 1965 1966 est. 1967 est. 0

Because of increased demand, industry continued to build up capacity and modernize its facilities.

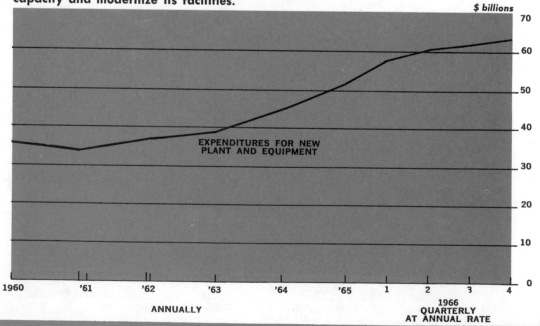

$ billions

70

60

50

EXPENDITURES FOR NEW PLANT AND EQUIPMENT

40

30

20

10

1960 '61 '62 '63 '64 '65 1 2 3 4 0

ANNUALLY

1966 QUARTERLY AT ANNUAL RATE

THE BATTLE FOR PRICE STABILITY

CONSUMER PRICES INCREASED AT FASTER RATE IN 1966

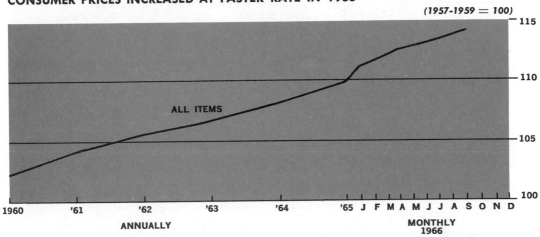

THE TREND FOR MAJOR ITEMS THAT CONSUMERS BUY

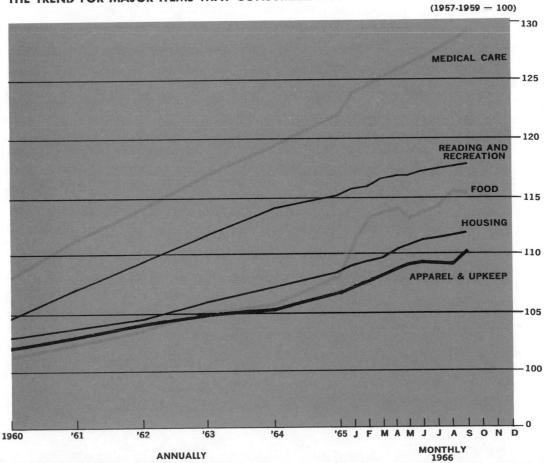

CONSUMER INCOME, SAVINGS AND SPENDING

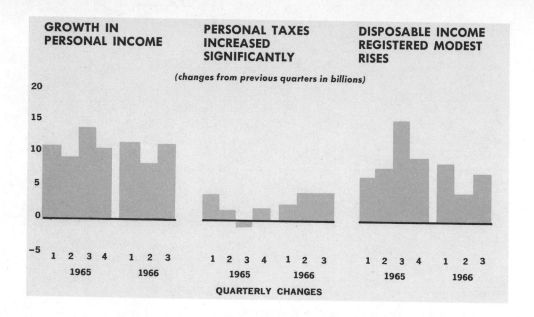

GROWTH IN PERSONAL INCOME

PERSONAL TAXES INCREASED SIGNIFICANTLY

DISPOSABLE INCOME REGISTERED MODEST RISES

(changes from previous quarters in billions)

QUARTERLY CHANGES

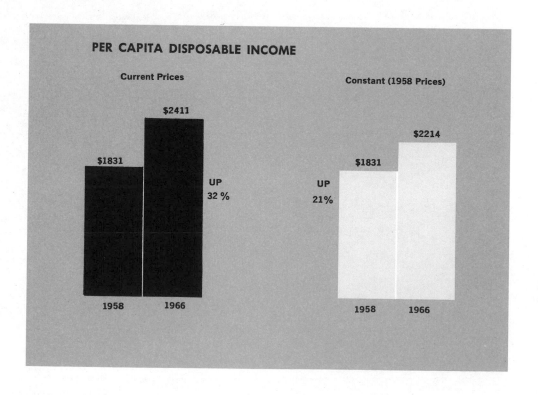

PER CAPITA DISPOSABLE INCOME

Current Prices

$2411

$1831

UP 32 %

1958   1966

Constant (1958 Prices)

$2214

$1831

UP 21%

1958   1966

Source: Economic Indicators; Survey of Current Business

CONSUMER SAVINGS
(As a Percent of Disposable Consumer Income)

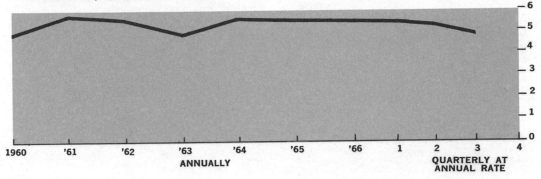

1960 '61 '62 '63 '64 '65 '66 1 2 3 4

ANNUALLY   QUARTERLY AT ANNUAL RATE

CONSUMER SPENDING FOR MAJOR CATEGORIES

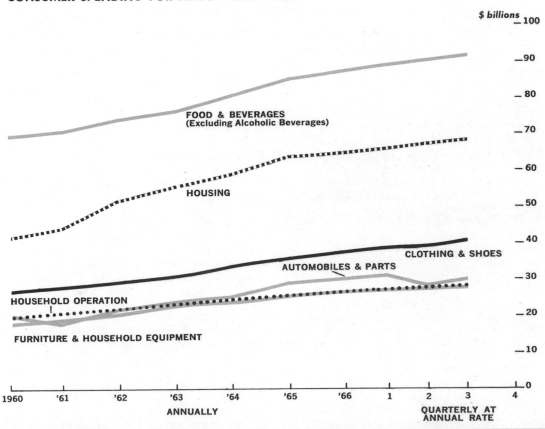

$ billions

FOOD & BEVERAGES
(Excluding Alcoholic Beverages)

HOUSING

CLOTHING & SHOES

AUTOMOBILES & PARTS

HOUSEHOLD OPERATION

FURNITURE & HOUSEHOLD EQUIPMENT

1960 '61 '62 '63 '64 '65 '66 1 2 3 4

ANNUALLY   QUARTERLY AT ANNUAL RATE

CABINET, U.S.

By JOSEPH W. HALL, Jr.

Washington Bureau, THE ASSOCIATED PRESS

President Johnson appointed secretaries during 1966 to head two newly created cabinet departments, bringing the number of cabinet members to 12.

Robert C. Weaver, the first Negro ever to serve in the Cabinet, was named in January to direct the Department of Housing and Urban Development. Alan S. Boyd, a Florida attorney and undersecretary of commerce, was selected in November to run the Department of Transportation.

The President created a cabinet vacancy in September by moving Attorney General Nicholas deBelleville Katzenbach from the Justice Department to the State Department where he became undersecretary. Johnson had not made known his choice for attorney general as the year ended.

Secretary of State. Secretary of State Dean Rusk spent most of his 1966 energies on problems of Vietnam, defending U.S. policy at Congressional hearings and in other forums. He went to Saigon in January and declared the United States was determined to do everything in its power to insure the safety, freedom and property of South Vietnam. Reportedly the Secretary offered fresh assurances to South Vietnamese leaders that President Johnson's drive for peace talks would not undermine their country's vital interests. In April the Secretary said he saw no "fatal inevitability of war with Communist China." He added that he was willing to have wider unofficial contacts between the two countries.

Rusk sought in June to stem the tide running in favor of troop reductions in Western Europe, asserting that he opposed cuts in North Atlantic Treaty Organization forces unless corresponding reductions were made by the Communists.

The Secretary was with President Johnson at the Manila Conference in October and joined in drafting the pledge to withdraw from South Vietnam within six months after North Vietnam disengaged itself from the war.

When Rusk left Washington in June for a trip to Australia, his department announced he had become the travelingest secretary of state in history, with a total of 592,913 miles since he took office in 1961. John Foster Dulles held the previous record. Rusk said in August he would have to quit his job when he runs out of money: his savings are used up, and he lives entirely on his $35,000 salary.

Secretary of the Treasury. Secretary of the Treasury Henry H. Fowler won from Congress three major pieces of tax legislation during 1966. One, passed in March, provided an additional $6,000,000,000 of funds for the Vietnamese war in the months directly ahead, by speeding up tax collections from individuals and corporations and by rescinding excise-tax cuts on autos and telephone service. The second, sent to the White House in October, suspended two major tax incentives to business to increase spending for new machinery and equipment and for construction. The third, long a pet project of Fowler's, increased tax incentives for foreigners to invest in the United States.

The Secretary was under constant pressure through the year to say whether a general tax increase would be sought to help finance the war and cool off the economy. He continued to hold open the possibility of such action. But in October he advised the President that the economy was robust, with no prospect of recession.

Secretary of Defense. Secretary of Defense Robert S. McNamara presided over an increase of 200,000 in U.S. fighting forces in Vietnam during the year, and indicated that a steady buildup also was in prospect for 1967. The American forces reached a total of about 360,000 at the end of 1966; there were Pentagon reports this figure would go to 500,000 in 1967. Three days before Nov. 8 elections, McNamara visited President Johnson's Texas ranch and announced a cutback in draft calls for the next four months, saying the buildup in Vietnam would be at a slower rate for a while.

The Secretary, serving his sixth year in the Pentagon post, came under heavy Congressional fire in 1966. He was attacked for refusing to start construction of an antimissile system to protect U.S. cities, for failure to buy more big bombers, for what his critics said were the shortcomings of the TFX airplane, and for military-equipment disposal practices.

In a speech May 18 at Montreal to the American Society of Newspaper Editors, the Secretary proposed that every young person in the United States be asked to give two years of service to his country either in the military, Peace Corps or some other voluntary work. But he indicated later he was only trying to point up a moral obligation to serve, not a legal obligation.

McNamara made his eighth visit to South Vietnam in October. He was mobbed by students at an appearance at Harvard University on Nov. 7. Some of them yelled "murderer" at him. But the Secretary said he would defend the right of student protests against Vietnamese policy because it showed "free discussion is so vigorous on the American campus today."

He called for increased Federal, state and local taxes to meet the nation's pressing social problems, not the Vietnamese war. On Nov. 10 he advised Johnson that Russia was erecting some antimissile installations; he held open the question of whether the United States should start building such a system.

Attorney General. Former Attorney General Nicholas deBelleville Katzenbach's decision in September to leave the Justice Department and the Cabinet for the post of undersecretary of state caused considerable surprise in Washington. There was immediate speculation that he might be in line to succeed Dean Rusk when the Secretary of State decided to retire.

Deputy Attorney General Ramsey Clark, the son of Supreme Court Justice Tom C. Clark, was serving as acting attorney general at year's end.

Postmaster General. Postmaster General Lawrence F. O'Brien operated in a dual role throughout 1966, serving as the Johnson administration's chief lobbyist with Congress, as well as heading the Post Office Department. He praised the record of Congress highly after it had adjourned in October, contending that the administration won approval of the great bulk of its program.

O'Brien also undertook to aid Democrats in the fall election campaign. After the election, he conceded that Republican gains were greater than he had expected.

The Postmaster General came under criticism in October as mail jams developed in several post offices over the country. He obtained a $30 million budget advance and put to work 150,000 temporary Christmas employees ahead of time to try to clear up the tremendous mail rush.

Secretary of the Interior. Secretary of the Interior Stewart L. Udall devoted much of his efforts throughout the year to advancing beautification and conservation programs in Congress and across the nation. He took part in the fight for a Redwood National Park in northern California.

On March 31 he started a drive in Congress to establish a nationwide system of scenic trails, beginning with the Appalachian Trail in the East and South. Udall declared in a speech at Chicago Sept. 15 that the nation could not afford to delay any longer in stopping the creeping corruption of its public waters. On Oct. 22 he said that Federal officials were taking a second look at proposals to build dams that would flood a part of the Grand Canyon.

Secretary of Agriculture. Secretary of Agriculture Orville L. Freeman came under Republican attack during 1966 on charges that he was ignoring the problems of farmers. He conceded in May that some administration actions to check rising food prices had "caused a strong reaction among farmers." But he insisted that, nevertheless, they were benefiting from a steady increase in farm income.

In February, Freeman flew to South Vietnam for a tour of its agricultural areas; the Secretary promised Premier Ky that he would try and get more fertilizer for Vietnam farms.

On April 13 he warned in a New York speech that famine may "truly stalk the earth" by 1984. Freeman helped win passage by Congress of a food-for-peace bill which marked a major shift in the 12-year-old program; under the legislation, more of the American farm products shipped abroad will come from current production and less from surpluses which have grown progressively smaller in recent years.

Secretary of Commerce. Secretary of Commerce John T. Connor was busy with problems of a booming economy and inflation throughout 1966. On Oct. 12 he said President Johnson stands ready to request wage and price controls if necessary to support the military effort in Vietnam. But the Secretary added that he saw no indication these were needed at the time. On Nov. 6 Connor said "a tax increase certainly is going to get our serious consideration" in 1967, commenting, "We are going to have to pay our bills."

The Secretary, in a speech at Durham, N.C., on April 1, said the failure of the Negro to enjoy equality in education and jobs was costing the nation $23,000,000,000 in 1966.

Secretary of Labor. Secretary of Labor W. Willard Wirtz spent a frustrating year trying to get his program through Congress. He won adoption of a minimum-wage bill increasing the ceiling from $1.25 to $1.60 an hour and bringing an additional 8 million workers under the law, but failed on the two other major pieces of administration labor legislation. One of these would have repealed section 14(b) of the Taft-Hartley law which allows states to ban the union shop. The other would have broadened the unemployment-compensation law to include Federal standards for the payments.

Wirtz said in October that the increase of productivity of U.S. workers had risen to 3.8 per cent, suggesting that the 3.2 per cent administration guideline figure for wage increases to hold down inflation could be increased.

Secretary of Health, Education, and Welfare. Secretary of Health, Education, and Welfare John W. Gardner came under continuing attack from Southern governors and members of Congress throughout the year because of school and hospital desegregation guidelines issued by his department. But he declared April 14 that the guidelines "call for very substantial progress" in achieving desegregation and that "there can be no substitute for such progress."

On April 26 the National Academy of Sciences awarded Gardner its public-welfare medal "for eminence in the application of science to public welfare." Gardner was successful in helping to win passage of three major education bills in the 1966 Congressional session—an extension of the elementary-and-secondary-school act, a higher-education measure, and an international-education bill.

Secretary of Housing and Urban Development. President Johnson announced Jan. 13 that he would name Robert C. Weaver as the first Negro cabinet member, taking over direction of the Department of Housing and Urban Development created late in 1965.

Weaver helped put through Congress one of the most significant measures of 1966—the Demonstration Cities Bill designed to help cities clean up their most blighted areas. He also won from Congress funds to start on an important program of rent subsidies for low-income families. Speaking Nov. 10, on the first anniversary of the creation of his department, the Secretary said, "We are on the threshold of a new kind of revolution in the treatment of urban problems."

Secretary of Transportation. Secretary of Transportation Alan S. Boyd was selected on Nov. 6 by President Johnson to fill the newly created 12th cabinet post. The choice was no surprise, since Boyd had served as undersecretary of commerce for transportation and had been the chief administration witness for the Department of Transportation Bill at the Capitol. However, since Congress had adjourned in October, Boyd's appointment was awaiting Senate approval at year's end.

A 44-year-old Florida lawyer, Boyd entered Federal government service in 1959 when he was named by former President Eisenhower to the Civil Aeronautics Board. President Kennedy appointed him chairman of the board in 1961; President Johnson shifted him to the Commerce post in 1965.

Boyd heads a department with more than 90,000 employees gathered from 35 separate units and with an annual $6,000,000,000 budget. He said soon after his appointment that he would move cautiously in developing his department's program and that he anticipated a shakedown period of a year or so.

CALIFORNIA. Ronald Reagan (R) won a decisive victory over incumbent Edmund G. Brown in November's gubernatorial race. . . . Los Angeles, Orange, San Bernardino, Ventura, Imperial and Riverside counties formed a regional-planning group—the Southern California Association of Governments. . . . An epidemic of Asian flu raged through the state in February. . . . The California Supreme Court in a May 10 ruling prohibited racial discrimination in disposal of property. . . . A mountain fire started June 11 and blazed for a week in Los Padres National Forest. . . . Los Angeles, San Francisco and Oakland were the scenes of race riots. . . . U.S. Supreme Court refused to review a state Supreme Court ruling that a ban on pay-TV violated freedom of speech.

Dec. 31, 1966: Prime Minister Lester Pearson puts torch to centennial flame.

CANADA

By BLAIR FRASER
Ottawa Editor, MACLEAN'S MAGAZINE

Canada approached its centennial year, 1967, with strangely mixed feelings. The economy was booming: national output nearly 7 per cent higher in real terms than in 1965; exports over $10,000,000,000 from $8,750,000,000 a year before; unemployment averaging only 3.7 per cent; total employment not only the highest in history but showing the highest percentage increase of any year since World War II. Yet the prevailing mood as 1966 ended was one of uncertainty, with an expectation of more unemployment, less capital investment, lower corporate profits and a general leveling off in 1967.

Political Situation

Outlook. Politically, the opposite was true. A year that began in near chaos, with the revival of a five-year-old scandal and the reduction of both major political parties and of Parliament itself to a nadir of public esteem, ended with the minority Pearson Government in firmer control of public affairs than it had ever been. Prime Minister Pearson himself was enjoying a serenity of power that had been denied him by a succession of perverse circumstances ever since he took office in April 1963.

Provincial Developments. One reason for Pearson's serenity was the trouble that overtook his competitors. For several years, through 1965, it had appeared that Prime Minister Pearson and his Federal Government were on the defensive and in frequent retreat before brash, powerful figures in various provinces—most notably Jean Lesage of Quebec and Cecil Bennett of British Columbia.

Lesage was the leader of the so-called Quiet Revolution in French Canada, the self-proclaimed spokesman of that one third of Canadians whose mother tongue is French, the man whose assertion of Quebec's autonomy and near-sovereignty carried the implicit threat that if his demands were not met Quebec might separate from Canada. Bennett's threats of separatism were not so clearly voiced but were even more seriously regarded, because (unlike Quebec) British Columbia probably could be admitted to membership in the United States if it wished, providing, as it would, a land connection between Washington and Alaska.

Both premiers were demanding more money, more authority, more autonomy at the expense of the central Government in Ottawa. Both called provincial elections, considerably earlier than was necessary, in order to get massive majority support for the expected confrontations with Ottawa. Both lost ground as a result.

Lesage was turned out of office altogether, in the political upset of the year. Opposition Leader Daniel Johnson, a French-Canadian despite his English name, was generally regarded as a hopeless underdog when the campaign began. Heir of the scandal-ridden Duplessis regime, which had been defeated and disgraced only six years before, Johnson

Quebec's Union Nationale leader Daniel Johnson and wife.

Wide World

seemed to have no program at all to match the Lesage government's impressive achievements and still more impressive plans. But by quietly capitalizing on local grievances, which Lesage had imprudently ignored, and especially by appealing to farmers disgruntled by the higher taxes required to finance the Quiet Revolution, Johnson and his Union Nationale won a small majority of seats in the provincial legislature with slightly less than a majority of the popular vote, and settled into five years of power as premier of Quebec. The lordly Liberals consolidated their own defeat by an outburst of mutual recrimination.

Bennett in British Columbia was not defeated, but instead of the massive majority he had requested, he came back with fewer seats than he had before the unnecessary election. His right-hand man in the Cabinet, Attorney General Robert Bonner, was defeated in his own constituency and had to beg a seat from a more fortunate but less important member of the Social Credit Party.

Meanwhile in Ontario, where Conservative Premier John Robarts had seemed impregnable, the spectacular failure of two finance companies ruined many small investors and cast doubt on the vigilance and the competence of provincial regulation of securities. There was no hint of any scandal involving politicians or officials, but the obvious failure of supervision put the Robarts government on the defensive, almost for the first time, and left it looking weaker than it had ever been before.

In Prince Edward Island another seemingly impregnable regime, the Conservative govern-

ment of Premier Walter Shaw, was turned out by the Liberals under 32-year-old Alexander Campbell, who became the youngest government leader in Canada. In Manitoba, Premier Dufferin Roblin, long regarded as a leading contender for national leadership of the Conservative Party, came limping back from an election with a loss of 5 seats, his majority reduced from 15 to 5. New Brunswick's Liberal Premier Louis J. Robichaud did not have to face the electorate directly, but went through a bruising battle in his own legislature to put through his scheme for reorganization of county and municipal governments. In general, the erstwhile strong men of the provinces were considerably subdued by the events of 1966.

Scandals. In Ottawa the Pearson Government had its own troubles, but these were matched and perhaps exceeded by those of the Conservatives. For both parties a major cause of distress was the scandal known as the Munsinger Case, a Canadian equivalent of the Profumo affair that rocked Britain in 1963.

The Canadian scandal broke almost by accident. A Vancouver postal clerk named George Victor Spencer, who later admitted having sold information to Soviet agents, was declared to be under surveillance by the Royal Canadian Mounted Police (RCMP) but had not been charged or brought to trial. The Conservative and the socialist oppositions both made an issue of the Spencer case, attacking the Pearson Government's security procedures in general, and its handling of the Spencer case in particular. A Royal Commission, appointed in March, absolved the Government and the RCMP of all blame (finding among other things that the RCMP, far from persecuting the miserable Spencer, who died April 10, had been his only friend in the last years of his life), but by that time the fat was in the fire. Goaded beyond endurance by personal attacks from the Conservatives, Justice Minister Lucien Cardin had countered by a reference to the Conservative handling of the Munsinger case five years before, which he said was "worse than the Profumo."

Bizarre details began to leak out. Gerda Munsinger was an immigrant from Germany who, it was said at a subsequent inquiry, had once worked for the Russians in Berlin and had been barred from the United States as a security risk. Later she got into Canada under her married name, and became friendly with some Canadian politicians—very friendly with one in particular, Pierre Sevigny, associate minister of defense in the Diefenbaker Cabinet.

Cardin believed, when he mentioned the case, that Gerda Munsinger was dead. Within

Photos UPI

The Ottawa Citizen (r) reports on the Gerda Munsinger Case, a scandal that rocked all Canada. Among the involved was Pierre Sevigny of Diefenbaker Cabinet.

days she was found in Munich, very much alive, by a *Toronto Star* reporter, Robert Reguly. The Government appointed Supreme Court Justice Wishart Spence as a one-man Royal Commission to look into the whole affair. RCMP witnesses and others gave evidence that confirmed, in general, what Cardin had said. The Spence report in late September sharply criticized the former Prime Minister, John Diefenbaker, for having retained Sevigny in his Cabinet after learning that this escapade had made Sevigny vulnerable, at least theoretically, to blackmail by Soviet agents.

Meanwhile, even before the Spence report was published, the national president of the Conservative Party, Dalton Camp, had called publicly for a leadership convention. At the party's annual meeting in November this demand was put to a vote; Camp, who had been reelected president over a pro-Diefenbaker nominee, carried his point with the rank and file and thus dealt a serious blow to his party's leader. At year's end Diefenbaker was still in office as leader of the Opposition, but his party was badly and bitterly split, and the Pearson Government correspondingly strengthened despite its minority position.

Legislative Standstill. All this fell far short of giving the Pearson Government a happy issue from all its afflictions. Its legislative program was badly delayed. Unification of the armed services, the pet project of Defense Minister Paul Hellyer, ran into fierce opposition from senior and retired officers and from the Conservatives in Parliament. Revision of the Bank Act, which should have been made

in 1964, had not been accomplished as 1967 began. The new Broadcasting Act, an urgent necessity since both top executives of the Canadian Broadcasting Corporation were about to retire, and no successors could be appointed until new legislation is passed, had not even been introduced. Major changes in transportation, forecast as imminent for years, were still be to enacted. In addition to these difficulties the Government was harassed throughout the year by a series of major strikes, one of which —a railway strike—required a special summoning of Parliament to pass a special law to end it.

Foreign Policy

In foreign policy, too, Canada had a year that was busy rather than fruitful. Canadian activity centered mainly on the questions of Vietnam, Rhodesia and the representation of China in the UN. All remained substantially unchanged despite Canada's efforts.

Vietnam. Canada has been a member of the International Control Commission (ICC) in Vietnam, along with India and Pakistan, ever since the Geneva Agreements of 1954 brought the Indochina war with France to an end. Canada has always hoped the ICC might play a role in bringing the Vietnam belligerents to the conference table, and 1966 saw a number of initiatives to this end.

In February, Secretary of State for External Affairs Paul Martin told Parliament that Canada's chief representative in Vietnam, Victor Moore, had had "a very fruitful" discussion with North Vietnamese officials in Hanoi. In March and again in June, Chester Ronning, who was the last Canadian diplomat to leave mainland China after the communist take-over in 1949, and who has many personal contacts both in Peking and Hanoi, paid visits to the North Vietnamese capital to explore any avenues for peace that could be found. Nothing came of these excursions, beyond the demonstration that a channel of communication did exist if either side wanted to use it.

In August, President Johnson visited Campobello Island, off New Brunswick, and Prime Minister Pearson went down to greet him. Vietnam was one of the topics they discussed, but again nothing concrete emerged.

Rhodesia. Prime Minister Pearson attended conferences of Commonwealth prime ministers in Lagos, Nigeria, in January and in London in September. At both, the main topic discussed was the "rebellion" in Rhodesia (which had unilaterally declared its independence of Britain in November 1965). At both, but especially in London, Pearson played a vigorous role in seeking a middle ground between Africans demanding drastic action against the Rhodesian "rebels," and the British and Australians urging caution and compromise. He managed to draft a final communiqué which both parties were willing to sign, and which committed the Africans to more patience and the British to more determined action than either had been willing to promise at the outset. At year's end, the Rhodesian issue was still unsettled, however, and the final effect of the September meeting remained in doubt.

Communist China. At the UN General Assembly Nov. 24, Paul Martin suggested that Communist China might replace Nationalist China on the Security Council, and that both might sit in the General Assembly. This revival of the "two Chinas policy" got a hostile reception in both Taipei and Peking. (The Communist Chinese were so offended that they canceled a scheduled visit to Peking by the Canadian trade commissioner in Hong Kong, which had been authorized for December.) On Nov. 29, Canada abstained from instead of voting against, as in previous years, the usual Albanian resolution that Communist China should replace Nationalist China in the UN. Vague rumors persisted in Ottawa that Canada might recognize Communist China during 1967, but they were unconfirmed at the end of 1966.

Nevertheless, despite trials at home and frustrations abroad, Canada and its Government could look back on a fairly good year.

Thriving Vancouver is Canada's third-largest city.

UPI

Logs at Port Alfred, Ont., part of pulp-paper industry.

Wide World

CANADA: ECONOMIC REVIEW

By DALTON ROBERTSON

Associate Editor, THE FINANCIAL POST

Expansion Continues. Canada's economy emerged from 1966 with a string of remarkable new gains to its credit. The long business expansion, which began early in 1961 and raised living standards by an impressive 25 per cent in only five years, gave every indication of continuing right through the country's centennial year of 1967 and on into the following year as well.

Total output of goods and services (GNP) will probably show at least a 10 per cent rise in value from year-earlier levels, when 1966 totals are finally tallied up. This will be the third very big year in a row when annual GNP increases ranged around the 10 per cent mark. It reflects a pace fast enough to keep unemployment down to about 3.5 per cent of the work force, absorb a population increase larger than most in the industrial world and leave another 4.5 per cent to add to real output per capita.

Within 1966 itself, however, very distinct shifts took place in rates of growth and in the climate for growth.

The economy plunged into the year at a clearly unsustainable and inflationary pace. The volume of overall activity in the first quarter of 1966 was 3 per cent higher than in the fourth quarter of 1965, a rise in three months as large as in the previous six. Prices, under this pressure in an economy already operating close to capacity, went up 1.4 per cent, or by more than in any quarter since the beginning of the business advance in 1961.

The expansion then flattened out with a fractional rise in the volume of second-quarter activity, a barely perceptible decline in the third quarter and a mild gain in fourth quarter. Price increases, in this more stable situation, tended to become smaller, quarter by quarter. The economy's inflationary fires were substantially dampened down, and a firm base for further growth had been reestablished by year-end.

Government Policy. Behind the slowing of Canada's long boom was a clearly visible and highly successful experiment in the so-called new economics. The Federal Government deliberately juggled its mix of credit and tax policies to skim off excessive activity without bringing about a rise in unemployment or precipitating a recession. With prices responding by year-end, and employment still high, it appeared that Ottawa, with a very precise sense of timing, had applied just the right amount of pressure to the brakes.

First evidence that the Government considered the business pace too fast for price safety came a few months before it did in the United States. During late September and early October of 1965, the Bank of Canada (the Canadian counterpart of the U.S. Federal Reserve) slowly switched away from easy-money policies. Through its open-market operations, money supply was increased at a slower and slower pace, and generally prevailing interest rates were encouraged upward. Credit restraint was the order of the day throughout 1966. Money supply and general bank loans advanced at only half the pace they did in 1965. The yield on a typical short-term government bond rose from 3.8 per cent to 5.8 per cent in the first several months of the year, and rates on prime conventional mortgages went from 7 per cent to as much as 8 per cent or 8¼ per cent.

Tax policy was also redrawn to back monetary policy in its posture of restraint. The need for a double-barreled approach was obvious. In a 15-month period through 1965 and into early 1966, consumer prices rose more than they had in the previous 46 months of business expansion. Wholesale prices for industrial materials climbed 4.2 per cent in the same period, again as much as they had in the previous four years. Unit labor costs were also rising in contrast to their relative stability in the early 1960's.

New Budget. In the face of these inflationary facts, Finance Minister Mitchell Sharp brought down a springtime budget frankly and specifically aimed at stretching out the boom.

Among his measures were: Modest reductions in some cost allowances; a slight upping of personal-income-tax rates; a small pullback in Federal spending on capital projects; and, especially significant, a temporary 5 per cent levy on corporate profits, refundable after 18 months. Coupled with these moves were guarantees of lower sales taxes in the future, a promise plainly designed to encourage business to put off, where possible, large new building or modernizing projects. The net result was to shift the effect of government activities on the economy from expansionary influence to restraining force.

Inflation. Many observers thought that not enough pressure was being exerted to damp down the forces of inflation. But as the year wore on, it was clear that Mr. Sharp had managed to cut the economy's momentum without tipping the country into recession. Industrial production after a strong, first-quarter rise flattened out and did not pass its April peak until August. Consumer costs, while still nearly 4 per cent higher than year-before levels, rose during the later months of 1966 at only one third or one quarter their previous rates. Raw industrial materials prices actually declined 4.6 per cent between February and October, bringing the level back to that of early 1965. During the slow-it-down period, employment rose in step with the growth of the work force and unemployment did not increase appreciably.

Construction. Canada's year of restraint had its more rapid and obvious effect in the field of construction—the area of steepest cost increase in recent years. Housing starts, which had been rising strongly through to the fall of 1965, zigzagged downward through 1966. Reflecting a scarcity of mortgage money and higher interest rates, it is estimated that only 135,000 starts were made in 1966 as against 166,500 the year before. Business, industrial and engineering construction contracts suffered a similar fate. These ran below year-earlier totals through much of 1966, portending a smaller-than-usual rise in building activity in 1967. Engineering construction contracts were the most depressed by tight-money conditions, while industrial contracts, reflecting the underlying drive of Canada's manufacturing boom, held up reasonably well.

New Plants and Equipment. Tight money also combined with higher costs and narrowing profit margins to slow down actual spending in 1966 on new plant and equipment. This was

a key objective of Federal government policy. The year 1966 was the third in succession to see a very large increase in capital-spending plans, and the pressures generated by the boom in capital spending intensified the economy's scramble for men, money and materials.

At the beginning of the year, it was expected that private and public expenditures on new facilities would top $14,546,000,000. That represented a 14 per cent increase in a year, and it came on top of advances of 17 per cent in 1965 and 16 per cent in 1964. The largest increase, 16 per cent, was expected to take place in business investment, with goods-producing industries spending 18 per cent more in 1967 than in 1966. Corporations planned to double iron-mine and potash-mine expenditures, while outlay for facilities in the non-ferrous area would rise by 50 per cent. Spending intentions in the "social capital" field were up 15 per cent. Looked at another way, business and government construction outlays would rise 12 per cent; spending on machinery, 17 per cent.

Later in the spring, the year-to-year advance in total spending intentions was revised upward to a clearly inflationary 17 per cent, with business outlays alone up 23 per cent. But the deflationary forces of 1966 will probably hold the overall increase down to 15 per cent. Machinery and equipment expenditures, for instance, registered only small increases in the first and second quarters of 1966 and declined in the third quarter. These outlays probably will stay on a plateau until the cut in sales taxes, promised for April 1967, offers a new incentive for expanded spending. Outlays

Chinese-Canadians at work in a market garden in southern British Columbia.

for nonresidential construction dropped substantially in the third quarter, although big year-to-year gains in construction (as in machinery) expenditure will still be registered.

The Consumer. Ottawa's rein-in policies reached through to the consumer front as well. Consumer installment credit outstanding, which rose by more than 13 per cent through 1965, registered a bare 3 per cent advance through the first seven months of 1966. Retail sales peaked in March, subsided for a few months and took till late autumn to regain the lost ground. Consumer spending overall, however, still ran a healthy 9 per cent higher than a year earlier. Outlays for nondurable goods and services were up 10 per cent from year before, while a mild slump in auto sales held the rise in durable sales down around 5 per cent.

These year-to-year spending gains reflected the fact that higher wages and more Canadians at work pushed total labor income (64 per cent of total personal income) nearly 13 per cent above 1965 levels. Wage rates alone averaged very close to 6 per cent higher than a year before—a source of some concern among producers and another reason for Ottawa's policies of mild restraint.

Because Canada's current expansion is basically a capital-spending boom, the fastest growing area was business investment in new facilities. This, for all its quarter-to-quarter variations under tightening credit conditions, appears to have made a 19 per cent year-to-year gain. But one other sector, exports, also contributed heavily to year-to-year growth.

Exports and Imports. Canada's sales abroad moved by a remarkable 19 per cent in 1966. The most notable increases appeared to be in wheat (huge sales to communist countries), pulp and paper, metals and metal products and a striking gain in auto exports. Bigger auto exports were triggered by the U.S.-Canada auto-production pact and in good part offset by higher auto and auto-part imports. The long-term advantage, however, should be in a rationalization of North American auto production and economies of scale, particularly for Canadian producers. Imports rose 16 per cent, and a small trade surplus in Canada's favor helped bring its overall deficit in goods and services down slightly.

Profits. Profits, in this mixed climate where big year-to-year sales gains were coupled with tight money, made no significant gains in 1966. Declines of more than 10 per cent were registered by the textile, paper and transportation industries, while most others showed modest increases. Although on a year-to-year basis profits were unchanged, the effect of the heightened wage-cost squeeze was obvious in the fact that overall earnings declined during the second and third quarters of 1966, while in the same period in 1965 they rose.

Outlook. Two developments late in 1966 suggested that another shift in policy, this time away from restraint, was in the making. In the last few months of the year, the central bank was less rigid in pursuit of monetary snugness, and the chartered banks, as a result, found they had a little more room for maneuvering. Ottawa's supplementary budget in December, long advertised as one which would attack inflation, turned out to be a mild affair. Sales-tax increases were only large enough to offset higher welfare payments, and the effect of government activities on the economy remained unchanged. The Finance Minister also made it clear at that time that he would move swiftly to stimulate or restrain the economy, should conditions in 1967 require such action.

Certainly any easing, especially in credit, would spur the Canadian economy forward once again. The pause in business spending on new plant and equipment is temporary. It was brought on by tight money and will end with easier money. The outlook for growth in final markets at home and abroad from now until 1970 is bright.

There is no excess capacity in the country's manufacturing industries, despite the culmination of the longest capital expansion in Canadian history. Nor at year-end were inventories up enough to discourage outlays in new capacity or more efficient machinery and equipment.

Certainly Canada is not without its problems. Its Economic Council, a public but independent adviser on economic matters, points out that skill levels in Canada are shamefully below those in the United States. Productivity is substantially lower and the country's competitive position is weakened as a result. Union demands for wage parity with U.S. workers are mounting—although such a development when there is no comparability in productivity could cause either devaluation or unemployment. If parity spread from highly efficient to less efficient industries, Canada would be pricing itself right out of its foreign markets and find itself less able to cope with import competition.

But these problems are not likely to bring about serious troubles in the medium range. And between now and the early 1970's is the prospect of very fast-rising family formations and a work force growing considerably faster than any in the industrial world. The outlook is for heightening demand on both business and consumer fronts.

ENROLLMENT
(in Millions)

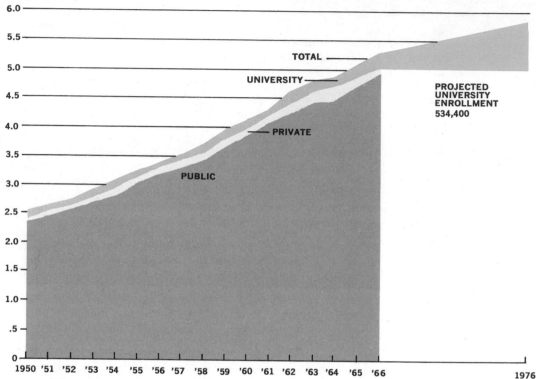

TOTAL

UNIVERSITY

PROJECTED
UNIVERSITY
ENROLLMENT
534,400

PRIVATE

PUBLIC

1950 '51 '52 '53 '54 '55 '56 '57 '58 '59 '60 '61 '62 '63 '64 '65 '66   1976

HOW FAR DO THEY GO IN SCHOOL?
(Total Population 15 years of age and over)

male

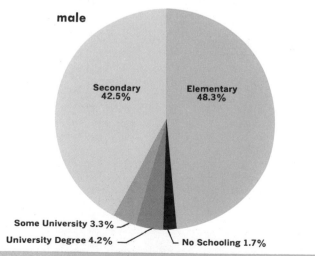

Secondary
42.5%

Elementary
48.3%

Some University 3.3%

University Degree 4.2%

No Schooling 1.7%

female

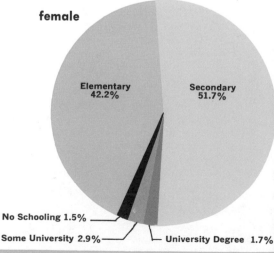

Elementary
42.2%

Secondary
51.7%

No Schooling 1.5%

Some University 2.9%

University Degree 1.7%

Source: Dominion Bureau of Statistics

SCHOOL CONSTRUCTION INCREASES TO KEEP PACE WITH RISING ENROLLMENT
$ millions

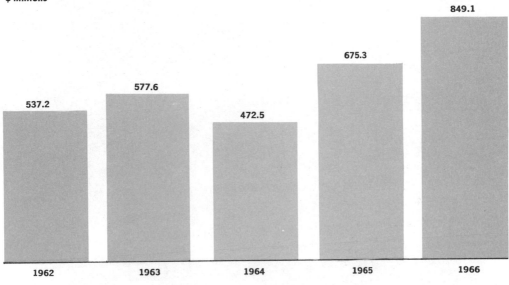

1962	1963	1964	1965	1966
537.2	577.6	472.5	675.3	849.1

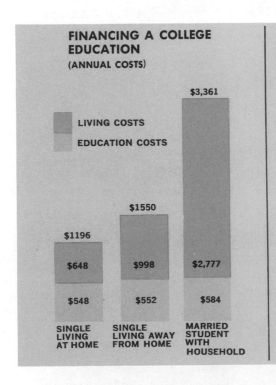

FINANCING A COLLEGE EDUCATION
(ANNUAL COSTS)

LIVING COSTS
EDUCATION COSTS

$1196
$648
$548
SINGLE LIVING AT HOME

$1550
$998
$552
SINGLE LIVING AWAY FROM HOME

$3,361
$2,777
$584
MARRIED STUDENT WITH HOUSEHOLD

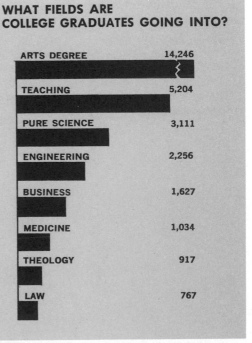

WHAT FIELDS ARE COLLEGE GRADUATES GOING INTO?

Field	
ARTS DEGREE	14,246
TEACHING	5,204
PURE SCIENCE	3,111
ENGINEERING	2,256
BUSINESS	1,627
MEDICINE	1,034
THEOLOGY	917
LAW	767

A model of Expo's Canadian Pavilion.

CANADA: EXPO 67 INTRODUCTION

By THE RIGHT HONORABLE LESTER B. PEARSON, P.E., O.B.E., M.P.
Prime Minister of Canada

Throughout 1967, Canadians will be "hosts to the world" as we celebrate the 100th anniversary of our nation's Confederation. A magnificent array of Centennial celebrations will go on throughout the year in every part of our country, but the highlight will be the 1967 Universal and International Exhibition—Expo —which will run for 6 months, starting on Friday, April 28, on Expo's specially built islands in St. Lawrence River at Montreal.

More than 70 nations will participate in this exhibition, an all-time record for which Canada is deeply gratified. The truly international flavor of this participation will bring to life the exhibition's theme, "Man and His World."

It was in 1960 that this country first applied to The International Exhibitions Bureau in Paris for permission to mark our 100th birthday by staging what the bureau classes as a "first category" exhibition. It was not until November 1962 that we were awarded the right to stage Expo—the first time that this right to a first-category exhibition had ever been awarded anywhere in the Americas.

Almost immediately, on December 20, 1962, the Canadian Parliament established the Corporation for the 1967 World Exhibition. Its job has been to organize and manage Expo, and the success with which it has carried out this task will soon be attested to by millions of visitors from across the world.

The net cost of the exhibition is being shared by the Government of Canada (50 per cent), the Government of the Province of Quebec (37.5 per cent), and the City of Montreal (12.5 per cent). Montreal, the seventh-largest city on the North American continent and the second-largest French-language city in the world, was selected as ideally accessible by land, sea and air.

Expo's thousand-acre site is on a complex of islands, largely man-made, located in the St. Lawrence River opposite Montreal Harbor.

In addition to the 70 nations participating, the 10 Canadian provinces, 3 American states, 4 international organizations, 5 noncommercial organizations, various cities and private companies are taking part. The corporation itself is devoting some 20 acres to the development of Expo's theme.

We have invited the world to help us celebrate our Centennial. We are confident that it will establish new world exhibition records.

A model of the U.S. Pavilion.

expo67

By PETER DESBARATS
Editor in Chief, PARALLEL

First-Category Exhibition. Its official title is the 1967 Universal and International Exhibition. The short form is "Expo 67." But regardless of the title, which has caused a great deal of confusion outside Canada, the exhibition which opens in Montreal on April 28, 1967, is in many respects the largest, most diversified and most ambitious world's fair in history.

It involves more countries than any previous world's fair—70 participating nations. About 55 countries took part in the 1964–65 New York World's Fair, 25 were represented at the Seattle exhibition in 1962 and 42 nations took part in the exhibition at Brussels, Belgium, in 1958. Expo 67's 1,000-acre site on two largely man-made islands in the St. Lawrence River is the largest and most spectacular setting ever created for a world's fair. And the Montreal exhibition is the only "first-category" world's fair ever held in North America.

This classification (Seattle was a second-category exhibition) was assigned to it by the International Bureau of Expositions in 1962 when the 1967 World's Fair was awarded to Canada. The previous first-category exhibition was at Brussels in 1958 and the next will be held in Osaka, Japan, in 1970.

In the eyes of the International Bureau of Expositions, created in 1928 to eliminate con-

flicting "world's fairs," the 1964–65 fair in New York was an "outlaw" exhibition. This, and the controversial reputation of the New York fair, explains Canada's decision to adopt a completely fresh title (Expo 67) and approach to the largest international project in its 100 years of nationhood.

Canada's first bid for the 1967 exhibition was unsuccessful. It was given to the Soviet Union, which wanted to stage a world's fair in Moscow to mark the 50th anniversary of the Communist Revolution. When Russia later backed down, Canada made a second and successful attempt for a fair to coincide with the 100th anniversary of Confederation. It was in 1867 that British colonies north of the United States joined forces to create the Canadian nation.

A world's fair is an almost overwhelming project for a nation of 20 million people, even when that nation has the second highest standard of living in the world. From the start, Canada counted on three factors to make Expo 67 a success.

Scope of Expo 67. The first was a decision to emphasize the scientific and cultural achievements of mankind while maintaining the "carnival" attractions normally associated with a world's fair. Experience at previous fairs had shown that scientific and cultural displays drew larger crowds than light entertainments or exhibits geared mainly to commercial or national propaganda. Five of the

The Canadian Pulp & Paper Association Pavilion.

A model of Alexander Calder's sculpture *Man*.

most dominant exhibition areas at Expo 67 are "theme pavilions" built by Expo itself to illustrate aspects of the overall theme of the exhibition: Man and His World. Four of these buildings will show the achievements of man as Creator, Explorer, Producer and Provider while a fifth will be devoted to Man and the Community. Canada has drawn on experts in all participating nations for help in creating these major pavilions. Some idea of the scope of these pavilions can be gained from studying the plans of one: Man the Explorer. This pavilion will house displays showing polar exploration, underwater exploration, subterranean work and research, the history of flight, space exploration and man's effort to explore his own physical and intellectual processes. The centerpiece of the Man the Creator pavilion will be an international fine-arts exhibition. The exhibit will include over 150 famous works of art from all ages and from a variety of cultures.

U.S. Tourists Beckoned. The second factor in Canada's optimistic approach to the fair was the geographical closeness of the United States to Canada. Previous world's fairs had shown that three quarters of all visitors came from homes within 500 miles of the exhibition site. The largest concentration of population within that distance from Montreal is not in Canada at all but in the northeastern United States, primarily in the New York area. Of an estimated 30 million paid admissions to Expo 67 by an estimated 10 million visitors—most people spend two or three days at a world's fair—about 55 per cent will be U.S. visitors. This is why the bulk of Expo's $25 million publicity budget is being spent on efforts to attract U.S. tourists to Montreal in 1967. Promotion for Expo tickets or "passports," as they are called, advertises not only the six-month world's fair but

the "foreign" attractions of Montreal, a city where three quarters of the residents are French Canadians and which bills itself as the home of more French-speaking people than any city other than Paris.

The traditionally close relations between Canada and the United States also ensured strong official participation by the "Americans." One of the largest national pavilions, exceeded only by the Canadian pavilion and the pavilion of the Soviet Union, is the $9 million U.S. pavilion—a 20-story transparent geodesic "bubble." Designed by R. Buckminster Fuller, it encloses 7 million cubic feet of exhibition space. In addition, the states of New York, Maine and Vermont, which touch the Canadian border within a few hours' drive of Montreal, are sponsoring separate pavilions.

International Lure of Expo 67. The third factor in Canada's decision to undertake a world's fair was the favorable Canadian "image" in most foreign countries. Not powerful enough to pose a threat to any country, yet rich enough to influence world affairs and assist underdeveloped nations, Canada since World War II has earned many friends around the world. It has successfully balanced its close alliance to the United States with fairly rapid development of trade and cultural contacts with communist countries, particularly Russia, Cuba and the nations of Eastern Europe. An indication of this is the fact that Russia joined Canada's traditional allies—the United States, Great Britain and France—as a major participant in Expo 67. The Russian pavilion will cost $15 million to build and equip. A 138-foot-high glass-walled structure supported only by two massive V-shaped struts, it is the most advanced Soviet building erected outside Russia. It will house the most extensive Russian

The Israeli Pavilion.

exhibition ever seen in North America and will include a complete planetarium to illustrate space achievements.

The Russians also will play a large part in the World Festival of entertainment which is part of Expo 67. The Bolshoi Ballet will be joined by the Bolshoi Opera, making its North American debut, as well as the Red Army Chorus and a number of smaller choral and dance groups. The United States will present the New York City Ballet, Mormon Tabernacle Choir, New York Philharmonic and other groups. The list of international attractions also includes Sir Laurence Olivier's National Theater Company of Britain, Milan's La Scala opera, as well as the Vienna and Hamburg state operas and the Stockholm Royal Opera (many of them appearing in North America for the first time), the Paris Opera Ballet, Amsterdam Concertgebouw Orchestra, the Théâtre de France—right down to the North American debut of Tunisia's "Troupe National Folklorique."

Because Expo 67 is a government-sponsored project operated by a nonprofit state corporation, and the centerpiece of a spectacular array of centenary celebrations being held in every Canadian city, town and hamlet in 1967, it will attract a parade of visiting heads of state. Queen Elizabeth of Great Britain, who is also the Queen of Canada, will be at Expo 67 about July 1, 1967, the official birthday date of the centennial year. President de Gaulle of France is also expected to visit the exhibition.

Expo 67's Island Site.   As the host country, Canada has erected the most elaborate national pavilion at Expo 67. Dominated by a 108-foot-high inverted pyramid called the Katimavik, a name derived from an Eskimo word meaning "the meeting place," the pavilion and exhibits will cost a total of $21 million. Quebec and Ontario will have their own pavilions and the

four Atlantic provinces and the four Western provinces will each sponsor joint pavilions. But the most impressive Canadian "exhibit" is the Expo 67 site—1,000 acres of islands, canals, bridges, lagoons, parkland and harbor created by dumping 25 million tons of earth and rock into the St. Lawrence River. The island site of the world's fair is only 10 minutes' drive from the center of Montreal, only a few minutes away by Montreal's brand-new subway which travels two miles under the St. Lawrence River with a special "Expo station" halfway along the route. To solve the problem of transportation within the huge exhibition ground—no private cars will be allowed—Expo 67 has built a three-and-a-half-mile railway which will carry visitors in air-conditioned coaches at no charge to five stations throughout the site.

This "Expo Express" will be complemented by a variety of secondary transportation systems ranging from "minirails"—scaled-down monorail systems—to gondolas which will carry visitors through the canal network.

There will be 38 restaurants and 67 snack bars on the site, serving a wide variety of national foods. The Russians alone are importing 20 chefs to staff their restaurants. Many of the restaurants will be in the La Ronde amusement area, which includes a 40-acre amusement park, an 18-acre lake and a 26-acre marina for visitors who prefer to travel to Montreal and to Expo by boat.

Canada's contribution to Expo 67 also includes Labyrinth, a $1,290,000 experimental film theater designed to accommodate new multiscreen films made for Labyrinth by the National Film Board of Canada, and Habitat 67. The latter is a 158-unit prefabricated futuristic apartment block in a pyramid shape constructed so that the roof of each unit forms a garden for another unit on the floor above.

Two of Alberta's main industries: an oil well in the midst of a wheat field.

CANADA: PRAIRIE PROVINCES

By JOSEPH C. LAWRENCE
Department of History
UNIVERSITY OF BRITISH COLUMBIA

Sparsely populated western Canada has always felt at a distinct disadvantage vis-à-vis eastern Canada, which controls the nation's political and economic life. The policies of Canadian railroads, banks, mortgage companies and national political parties seem to be made in the East, largely to suit eastern needs. Canada's Prairie Provinces—Alberta, Saskatchewan and Manitoba—are especially resentful that national trade policies governing the export of grain, oil, gas, beef, lumber and pulp from western Canada are made by the dominant manufacturing urban East.

The Political Situation

Western resentment and frustration are reflected in ambivalent political behavior which has led to the breakdown of the national parties on the provincial level. In Alberta, for example, the Social Credit government, now led by E. C. Manning, has held power since 1935. The Saskatchewan Liberal Party under Ross Thatcher, who won an uncertain victory over the 20-year-old socialist government in 1964, has barely maintained itself in power by behaving like a Social Credit government even to the point of constantly hectoring the Liberal Government in Ottawa. In Manitoba the Conservative regime of Duff Roblin was returned in 1966 but with a reduced majority of only 5 seats.

In national politics the Prairie Provinces differed sharply with the nation in the 1965 Federal election, which Liberal Prime Minister Pearson won. The Prairies elected 1 lone Liberal member of Parliament out of 48 seats. Nearly all the rest went to the Conservatives, who had initiated the much-favored policy of selling grain to the communist world. Many prairie voters obviously reason that they can safely reject the national parties on the provincial level, where their influence is dominant. But the voters also feel that they must compromise on the Federal level, where their representation in the Parliament is only 48 out of 265 seats, by voting for the old and well-established national parties.

A conference of western Liberals held in Saskatoon in August 1966 emphasized the distress of the old parties, burdened with national policies which seem to ignore the needs of the West. Thatcher, who presided, warned that the West was lost to third parties unless the Liberals adopted a national policy of lower tariffs, freer trade, and relaxed restrictions on foreign investment, especially American investment. The economic growth of the Prairie Provinces largely depends on U.S. investment.

The Economic Situation

The determination of the West to gain a greater control over its own economic life has been further emphasized by the unsuccessful struggle of W. A. C. Bennett, the Social Credit premier of British Columbia, to establish two independent banks in Vancouver, and the success of James Coyne in establishing the Bank of Western Canada with headquarters in Winnipeg. All of these measures have been opposed for years by eastern members of Parliament, dedicated to the perpetuation of eastern financial control over the economic life of the whole nation.

Thatcher's formula to repair the fortunes of the Liberal Party in the West is well calculated to appeal to voters in the rapidly changing Prairie Provinces. Until World War II the region was overwhelmingly agricultural, and crop failures meant the total collapse of the regional economy. Since then remarkable strides have been made, especially in Alberta and Saskatchewan, to so diversify the economy that a breakdown in one sector is compensated for by the relative prosperity of another. The rise of the oil industry offered the most striking opportunity to diversify. It began with a rich strike at Leduc, near Edmonton, Alta., in 1947, followed in rapid order by others in the Woodbend, Redwater, Lloydminster and Wainwright areas.

The 200 million barrels (1966) of crude oil produced annually by such strikes have helped to make Alberta the most prosperous of the Prairie Provinces, just as Saskatchewan's 81 million barrels annually are materially improving its economy. The development of natural-gas and oil industries and the building of pipelines now allow western Canada to export more than $360 million worth of these commodities to the Pacific Coast and mountain states, and the returns from sulfur, a by-product of the industry, are attaining significant dimensions.

Another important new industry is potash. Saskatchewan has recently discovered that it has over ½ of the world's recoverable potash;

Above, a natural-gas plant at Rimbey, Alta. Below, a potash mine at Esterhazy, Sask. Natural gas and potash are two of the Prairie Provinces' principal exports.

Annan Photos

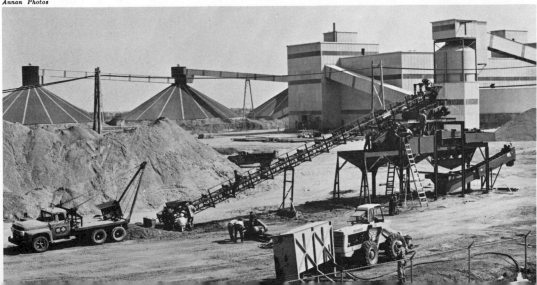

Prairie Farm Rehabilitation Administration

Aerial view of vast Saskatchewan River Dam project which began operation in 1966.

moreover, it is of a very high grade. Three mines, all subsidiaries of U.S. parent companies, produced 3.2 million tons of the fertilizer in 1965; 5 additional mines were about to go into production in 1966 and should produce about 2.4 million tons worth $54.4 million. Both sulfur and potash are shipped to Vancouver for transshipment to Japan, India and other overseas points.

Successful efforts have also been made to increase the value of processed goods within the region—to export more processed beef rather than cattle, flour rather than grain, lumber rather than logs, paper rather than pulp, petrochemicals and refined oil rather than crude oil. The program has proved remarkably successful. Between 1950 and 1965 the value of such manufacturing rose from about $300 million to $1,134,000,000. This provided employment for prairie people who would otherwise have been forced by farm mechanization to emigrate to urban British Columbia or to the urban East.

The diversification of the economy has called for the production of large volumes of cheap power. Fortunately the entire region is exceedingly rich in potential hydropower, and the provincial and Federal governments have cooperated well in developing it. The Saskatchewan River Dam project, costing $112 million, began operating in 1966 with 2 units. It is now producing 250,000 horsepowers and the second stage to be completed by 1969 will add another 400,000 horsepowers for the farms and industries of Saskatchewan. The project will provide

such additional benefits as flood control and irrigation. Manitoba is now spending $1,000,-000,000 to harness the Nelson River, the flow of which is greater than that of the Columbia or the Missouri. The $325 million first phase involves the diversion of the Churchill River into the Nelson, with Lake Winnipeg to be used as a great storage reservoir, and the construction of a 1 million-kilowatt generating station at Kettle Rapids with twin 580-mile transmission lines connecting with Winnipeg. The ultimate production of the Nelson project will exceed 5 million kilowatts of low-cost power.

Despite the success of the diversification effort, agriculture remains the prime industry of this vast region, accounting for more than $1,000,000,000 a year to the farmers. A series of bumper crops since 1960 combined with realistic grain-selling policies on the part of the Ottawa Government have meant unprecedented prosperity for wheatgrowers. New customers, like the Soviet Union and Communist China, account for upward of one third of the near-billion-dollar-a-year wheat sales. The communist nations are expected to remain more-or-less steady customers for years to come.

For several decades the region, like the adjoining plains area of the United States, has been an exporter of population to the Pacific Coast. Industrial expansion has slowed the process down, but not enough to offset the reduction in farm population caused by farm mechanization. The tide turned between 1956 and 1961, when high immigration offset normal population losses of 30 to 35 thousand people annually to record an annual gain of around 3,000. Winnipeg remains the largest city and perhaps the cultural center, but it no longer holds the preeminence it enjoyed between the 1880's and 1947. Rich gas and petroleum developments in Alberta combined with new modes of transportation (such as pipelines, roads and air) have shifted the focal point of activity from railroad- and grain-dominated Winnipeg to gas- oil- and beef-dominated Calgary and Edmonton.

The prairie region today is rapidly regaining the promise it displayed in the first decade of this century, and this time it is unlikely that drought and the collapse of the international grain market could abort it.

CANADA: PROVINCES AND TERRITORIES

ALBERTA. Grant MacEwan succeeded J. Percy Page as lieutenant governor, the Queen's provincial representative. . . . R. C. Clark became minister of the new department of youth, and A. O. Fimrite succeeded Ira McLaughlin as minister without portfolio and chairman of the Northern Alberta Development Council. . . . New oil discoveries in the Rainbow Lake area stepped up northern development. . . . Calgary campus of the University of Alberta became the independent University of Calgary.

BRITISH COLUMBIA. As a result of Sept. 12 general elections, the Social Credit Party of Premier W. A. C. Bennett was reelected, and the new provincial legislature is composed of 33 members of the Social Credit Party, 16 New Democrats and 6 Liberals. . . . Three pulp and paper mills were completed, and three others were being constructed. . . . The fourth British Columbia International Trade Fair is scheduled for Vancouver in 1967.

MANITOBA. General elections for Manitoba's Legislative Assembly were held in June. The Conservative Party won 31 seats, the Liberal Party 14, the New Democratic Party 11 and the Social Credit Party 1. . . . The legislature established a boundaries commission to make recommendations concerning local-government and school-district units.

NEW BRUNSWICK. The provincial legislature passed Premier Louis J. Robichaud's reform program which calls for a great many local services—in education, health, welfare and the administration of justice under provincial control. . . . As part of a single tax system projected for January 1967, the sales tax was raised from 3 to 6 per cent. . . . School districts were reduced in number from 400 to 34. . . . The economy expanded at a growth rate of 6 per cent.

NEWFOUNDLAND. In Sept. 8 general elections Premier Joseph R. Smallwood—a Liberal in power since 1949—was reelected. The Liberals won 39 House of Assembly seats, and the Conservatives 3. . . . Work began on a $57 million newsprint and pulp mill at Come-By-Chance and on a $65 million linerboard mill at Stephenville. . . . New construction at Memorial University included a $1 million Marine Research Laboratory and six student residences. . . . During 1966 the province's Come Home Year tourism rose by $14 million.

NORTHWEST TERRITORIES. Total mineral production reached an estimated $90 million in 1966. . . . Tourism—becoming a major industy —brought in approximately $1.8 million during the tourist year. . . . The Territories had fully representative government as of September 1966. At that time, three territorial councillors were elected; they represent the new constituencies of Keewatin, Central Arctic and Eastern Arctic.

NOVA SCOTIA. Canada General Electric Ltd. announced that it would build a $65 million heavy-water plant at Point Tupper. . . . The Nova Scotia legislature revised the provincial Assessment Act and the Social Assistance Act, and passed the Housing Development Act. . . . The Atlantic Development Board began a thorough study of transportation in the Atlantic Provinces. . . . Major new office buildings and apartment houses were under construction in Halifax.

ONTARIO. The Ontario legislature, which met for a record 111 days, passed bills providing for a free legal-aid system, an Ontario Medical Services Insurance Plan, a Consumer Protection Act, and a Securities Act. The provincial government also increased various taxes, including the retail sales tax and the gasoline tax. . . . During 1966, Ontario was hit by strikes in the fields of transportation, packaging, construction, nickel and steel, and manufacturing. . . . The Ontario Farmers' Union led a protest demonstration against milk and dairy prices.

PRINCE EDWARD ISLAND. Liberals won control of the government in July 11 elections, ending seven years of Conservative administration. The new Premier is 32-year-old Alexander B. Campbell. . . . Cabinet membership was increased from nine to ten in a special session of the legislature. . . . Work began on approaches of the island-mainland causeway.

QUEBEC. In provincial elections June 5, Daniel Johnson of the Union Nationale Party defeated Premier Jean Lesage of the Liberal Party. Lesage had been premier of Quebec since 1960. . . . Kruger Pulp & Paper Ltd. announced construction of a $30 million newsprint mill at St. Félicien. . . . A strike by 1,600 civil-service workers began May 9; Quebec's hospital workers were on strike from mid-July until Aug. 3; and teacher strikes broke out in various cities and towns throughout the year.

SASKATCHEWAN. In September the Saskatchewan Power Corporation and the Oil, Chemical and Atomic Workers Union were unable to reach a new contract agreement, and a major strike followed. . . . In a 1966 by-election Alex Mitchell, a Liberal, was elected to the Legislative Assembly, representing the Bengough constituency. . . . National Resources Minister John Cuelenaere left the provincial Cabinet in October.

YUKON TERRITORY. More than 300 delegates from Canada and Alaska attended the Second Northern Resources Conference in Whitehorse in March. . . . Total road mileage (including Alaska Highway) in the Yukon Territory is 2,139 miles. . . . Timber production reached its lowest mark in 10 years. . . . The territory realized some $5 million from tourism during the 1965–66 season.

CHICAGO. Businessmen of Chicago heralded 1966 as one of the greatest in the city's history. The Chicago Association of Commerce and Industry reported that the metropolitan area has an average family income of $11,400 annually, the highest in the United States. The city with 3.7 per cent of the nation's population produced 5.3 per cent of the gross national product. An acute shortage of skilled labor developed as unemployment dipped below 3 per cent.

The building boom that started in 1961 continued unabated. A state Supreme Court decision cleared the way for a massive new development over the Illinois Central Railroad property south of the Chicago River along the eastern edge of the Loop business center.

Picasso gave this 50-ft. sculpture to Chicago in 1966.
Public Building Commission of Chicago

Voters approved a $195 million bond issue in June, the largest in Chicago's history, for urban renewal, rapid transit in the Kennedy and Dan Ryan Expressways, street and alley lighting, and new police, fire and other municipal buildings.

The bright picture of a prosperous Chicago was dimmed by a summer of tragic crimes and racial disorders. On a pleasant night in July, a prowler broke into a south-side town house and murdered eight student nurses. A ninth escaped to tell of the horror-filled night that was called the "crime of the century." In September, Valerie Jeanne Percy, 21, the daughter of Charles H. Percy, who was then the Republican candidate for the United States Senate, was murdered in her bed in the Percy home in suburban Kenilworth.

During the summer, riots broke out unexpectedly in the Puerto Rican quarter on the city's northwest side, soon to be followed by a violent outbreak in predominantly Negro neighborhoods on the west side. The National Guard was mobilized by Governor Otto Kerner to restore order to the west side.

Dr. Martin Luther King, Jr., had selected Chicago as a target city for his northern freedom movement. His followers, demanding open housing, marched in all-white neighborhoods. It created a tense city as violence erupted, and hundreds were arrested and a score injured. Dr. King planned a march into the racially explosive suburb of Cicero, but an agreement was reached on open housing, and the march was canceled.

DAVID E. HALVORSEN
General Assignment Reporter, CHICAGO TRIBUNE

Mao Tse-tung (standing, first car) reviews members of the Cultural Revolution.

CHINA

By MARK MANCALL
Department of History
STANFORD UNIVERSITY

Developments in Communist China in 1966 were dominated by the convulsions of the so-called Cultural Revolution and the activities of its chief agents, the Red Guards. Important changes took place in China's leadership, new economic policies appeared to be in the making and a general ideological purge was under way. At year's end, the Cultural Revolution was still in full swing and the Red Guards were the most prominent feature of the Chinese political landscape. However, the Chinese Government yet had to make any official explanation of these events and information available to outside observers was scanty at best. But certain hypotheses appeared to be supported by the information available.

Internal Politics

Three Grave Problems. In September 1965, basic policy questions were debated at a very important meeting in Peking of the Chinese Communist Party's Central Committee. The meeting was also attended by regional and provincial party officials. China faced three grave problems. First, the American buildup in Vietnam was interpreted in Peking as posing a serious military threat to China's security. That buildup continued during 1966, and Peking continued to be obsessed by the fear that the United States might attack China. China's nuclear explosions during 1966 did not assuage that fear. Second, the 1965 Central Committee meeting made decisions about the economic policies to be pursued during the Third Five-Year Plan. The plan came into operation in January 1966, but it was not published. Third, China had suffered, in 1965, a series of grave setbacks in foreign policy, necessitating a reassessment of its overseas relations, particularly with the Afro-Asian world.

The Cultural Revolution, with the Red Guard movement, can in one respect be interpreted as a means of resolving differences of opinion that appeared at the September 1965 Central Committee meeting, or at least as a technique for destroying the opposition to resolutions made at that time. In response to the American buildup in Vietnam, the Cultural Revolution has placed China on a war footing by thorough mobilization of all sectors of the population. One of the most important issues in domestic debate over economic policies for the last fifteen years has been the question of "Red, or expert?"; in other words, whether basic technical and economic decisions at all levels should be made by the Communist Party, because of its adherence to the "general line" of Maoist thinking, or by technical personnel who are thoroughly educated in the subject matter of their specialization but not necessarily ideologically pure. To put it another way, is politics or rational economic development to occupy the prime position in the Government's overall policy-making process?

The Cultural Revolution appears to be a device for deciding the issue in favor of "Red" over "expert." Maoism considers the human element and "revolutionary correctness" more important than professional or technical training; to depend on the latter is styled a remnant of "bourgeois thinking,"—a prime target of the Cultural Revolution and the Red Guards. Similarly, a line of hard, unyielding foreign policy, regardless of the cost, appears to have won out

149

over a policy of compromise with antagonistic elements on the international scene.

Opposition Within the Party. Late in 1965, apparently realizing that opposition to his policies was mounting in the party, Mao Tse-tung "disappeared" from public sight for several months. Evidently he was planning the Cultural Revolution movement aimed at destroying those who disagreed with his policies, and aimed at placing China back in the revolutionary mainstream envisioned in his theories. Because of opposition within the party and because he believed the party had become too highly bureaucratized, Mao felt that the Communist Party was not suitable as an instrument to purge Chinese society. Instead, he turned to the Army, whose Chief of General Staff, Lo Jui-Ching, had been purged.

It also seems clear that Mao felt he had to draw the main strength for the Cultural Revolution from the countryside, which he knew well and in which he had fought twenty long years for victory in the Chinese Civil War. The cities, where pressure for bourgeois consumer goods and stability is greater than in the countryside, were in part conceived of as the enemy.

Apparently, the Cultural Revolution has also provided a setting for the resolution of regional and personal conflict. Within the party and government hierarchy, Southerners are rapidly moving up, replacing Chinese from other areas of the country, and there is considerable evidence that personal animosities have also played an important role in the determination of individual political fortunes.

Origins of Cultural Revolution. The current Cultural Revolution traces its origins to the "Four Cleanups" movement of the summer and autumn of 1964, when mass energies were applied to "cleaning up and 'capital construction' in the political, economic, ideological and organizational fields." As one observer has pointed out, the Cultural Revolution is the application of the Four Cleanups movement to the urban areas; the decision around April 1966 to carry the "Great Proletarian Cultural Revolution" to the cities was based on its evident success in the countryside.

The movement began in the cities with attacks on bourgeois outposts in the cultural field; work teams were sent to Peking University and, later, to other universities and schools of higher learning in the capital and the provinces. The movement embraced the press when the editorial boards of Peking's three leading newspapers, including the Peking *People's Daily,* the official organ of the party, were dismissed. Significant numbers of leading personnel in national and provincial propaganda organs, including Lu Ting-yi, the minister of culture, were removed from office. Many of the attacks on university and propaganda personnel were carried out by large groups of preuniversity-age children, brought to universities, ministries and newspapers for that purpose.

Called the "Red Guards," a name first used by Mao Tse-tung to describe the soldiers on the historic Long March in the mid-thirties, these groups of children and adolescents appear to have superseded the Young Communist League, the party's youth organization, as the most important organization for young Chinese, and as the major instrument for the Cultural Revolution. The Red Guards made their first important appearance in August 1966 at Peking University, and from there they spread the Cultural Revolution throughout Chinese society. Mao's wife, Chiang Ching, appears to have emerged a powerful leader of the Cultural Revolution.

Part of the indoctrination program of the Red Guards includes a visit to Peking, where Mao Tse-tung reviews them in the Square of Heavenly Peace. On Oct. 1, the anniversary of the establishment of the communist regime in Peking in 1949, the largest rally in Chinese history was held in the square, when perhaps 3 million Red Guards passed in review before Mao. In the latter part of 1966, between 9 and 11 million Red Guards demonstrated in the square on various occasions.

The Government faced serious problems in controlling the Red Guards, because at times they appear to have run wild through Peking and other cities, destroying whatever seemed to them "bourgeois," including priceless art treasures. They also caused the suicide of numerous leading figures, among them Lao She, one of China's greatest novelists. Consequently, as the movement spread through China in late August and early September, a 16-point program was sent down from the Government; according to reports, it was enthusiastically accepted by the Red Guards. Open opposition to the guards appeared in some areas; some were assaulted and murdered; and on occasion Red Guard groups fought among themselves—perhaps indicative of policy disagreements at the highest government and party levels. By mid-September, Peking itself admitted that widespread opposition to the guards had developed in more than seven large cities. At year's end, therefore, Peking's leaders confronted the problem of bringing the Red Guards under tighter control, and of coordinating their activities with those of the Army and other "revolutionary" groups in Chinese society.

Mao's Probable Successor. The most important single political development in China in 1966 was the final emergence of Lin Piao, the defense minister, as Mao's probable successor and the second most powerful man in China. Peng Chen, mayor of Peking and member of the Politburo, had been considered a possible successor to Mao, but he fell into disgrace in the spring. Now Lin is described in official statements as Mao's "close comrade in arms," and as the only member of the leadership who has "creatively applied the thought of Mao Tse-tung." In November, rumors circulated abroad that Lin had achieved his preeminent position by means of a coup that had partly miscarried, and that the Cultural Revolution and the Red Guards were created by him primarily as an instrument to ensure his control of power. True or not, the Cultural Revolution is intimately involved with the struggle over the succession to Mao.

In an authoritative table of Chinese leadership drawn up by the *Far Eastern Economic Review* (Sept. 29, 1966), comparing the Chinese leaders as listed in the *People's Handbook* of 1965 and as they have appeared at recent rallies, Lin Piao moved up from sixth to second place; Chou En-lai maintained his position in third place; and Liu Shao-chi, ostensibly the head of state of Communist China, moved from second to eighth place.

Lin Piao's rise to preeminent power is closely related to one of the more obtrusive aspects of the Cultural Revolution—the glorification of Mao Tse-tung. During 1966, the press and radio in China were swamped with quotations from Mao's writings, and with stories about the beneficial results obtained in practical work through the application of Mao's thought to specific problems. All the Red Guards carry small, plastic-covered red books containing quotations from Mao's works.

It appears that Mao, feeling that the end of his life may be near, is trying to impress upon China the necessity of maintaining his political line. At the same time, a new group of leaders is emerging in Peking, adhering to a strict interpretation of Maoism, and using the Maoist slogans as a source of power for themselves.

Economic Priorities

Peking has taken great precautions to prevent the Cultural Revolution from interfering with economic development. However, it has made public absolutely no information concerning the progress of the Third Five-Year Plan, and some Western specialists even doubt the existence of "a fully comprehensive plan." They believe instead that only "a general framework and a set of priorities" may exist. The Peking *People's Daily* editorial for Jan. 1, 1966, indicated what those priorities may be. Agriculture is to provide the foundation, and industry is to be the leading factor of the economy. The major task of the industrial sector is to provide support for agriculture, which appears to mean that the plan envisages important developments in the production of agricultural machinery and fertilizers.

The editorial stressed, however, that political and ideological work was more important than all other tasks, which may explain the failure to publish specific goals and progress reports. The Cultural Revolution appears to have interfered with work in some factories, mines and research institutions, with the notable exception of those connected with atomic-energy research, where an American-trained physicist figured prominently in the major Chinese nuclear explosion of the year. One of the aims of the Cultural Revolution is to create the truly universal revolutionary man—the revolutionary worker-peasant-soldier-poet in one personality.

Agriculture. Weather plagued Chinese agriculture in 1966, and drought dominated the rural scene in North China. While some areas seriously hit by drought reported declining harvests, large parts of the country claimed that 1966 crops equaled those of 1965. With the normal expected growth of China's population, such reports cannot be welcome in Pe-

Chairman Mao followed by #2 man, Lin Piao.

Eastfoto

Eastfoto
Autumn rice harvest of the Hungchi People's Commune.

Banners proclaim newly named Anti-Revisionism Street.
Wide World

king. Acreage planted in rice, particularly early rice, was expanded in 1966, partly as an emergency measure. This included the planting of rice in areas of North China previously not used for that crop. The same was true of the cotton crop, where the amount of land under cultivation was expanded and cotton was grown in areas, particularly in the northeast, not previously brought under cotton cultivation. As a precaution against disrupting what was already a fairly precarious agricultural situation, the *People's Daily* on Sept. 7 instructed teachers, students and Red Guards to refrain from going "to the countryside to hinder production." Conditions in the countryside, the paper said, were "different, and interruptions could disrupt work during the harvest period."

Industry. Reporting on industrial production was as meager in 1966 as was public information on the Five-Year Plan itself. Nevertheless, there were indications that steel production in the Anshan and Wuhan iron and steel complexes increased sharply. There were gains in coal production, too. In January, a new mine with an annual capacity of 900,000 tons, went into production in Shansi Province, and another large mine, largely automated, went into operation in Anhwei Province in June. The Hsinhua news agency reported that production of fertilizer surpassed set targets by 500,000 tons in the first five months of 1966. The Chinese oil industry reported in July 1966 that it had overfulfilled its production quota—for the first six months of 1966—of crude oil, gasoline, kerosene, diesel oil and "other major products." Increases in automobile production, machine building and the construction and output of hydroelectric power stations were also reported.

Foreign Trade. China's foreign trade apparently kept pace with that of 1965, though there were some indications of a falling-off in the growth rate. In July, foreign companies trading with China reported an observable slowdown in business, but this trend reversed during the following two months. By September, China's imports from its eight most important trading partners had increased by less than $100 million, as compared with a 1965 increase of more than $200 million over the same 1964 period. Export increases showed a similar downward trend to $90 million, as opposed to $190 million for 1965.

This slowdown in the expansion of foreign trade may be the result of the expansion itself, i.e., China may be reaching a "natural level" of foreign trade, given its program of industrial and agricultural development. While Chinese grain imports from Australia declined due to a bad harvest in the latter country, its imports of grain from Canada increased. Most notable were the increases in imports of machinery, iron and steel, and scientific and precision instruments, from Britain, West Germany and Japan. Japan improved its trade with China by some 41 per cent during the first six months of 1966, as compared with the same period of 1965, doing far better than any other single trading partner of China. Within the Soviet bloc, Eastern European nations and the Soviet Union exported primarily industrial products to China, and received agricultural and mineral products in return, though China did begin exporting manufactured freight cars to East Germany during 1966.

Foreign Affairs

The Vietnam war and China's argument with the Soviet Union continued to preoccupy Peking's attention during 1966. The Cultural Revolution brought renewed promises of aid to Vietnam, if the North Vietnamese or the Vietcong requested it. Western correspondents, traveling in China to visit the May Day celebrations in Peking, reported that anti-American propaganda was widely and actively spread throughout the population in an apparent campaign to prepare the population for some move in Vietnam, if it seemed necessary. The Cultural Revolution also brought the Sino-Soviet dispute to new levels of acrimony when the Soviet Embassy in Peking was besieged by tens of thousands of Red Guards, and Soviet and other East European diplomats in Peking were openly vilified and attacked on the streets. The Red Guards changed the name of the street on which the Soviet Embassy is located to Anti-Revisionism Street, a direct slap at Moscow. Moscow kept up its barrage of criticism against the Cultural Revolution, and at the end of November, *Pravda* published an editorial calling for resistance to Maoist extremism inside China by reasonable Chinese party leaders, and for an end to the Cultural Revolution. However, at the Hungarian Communist Party Congress in Budapest at the end of November, Soviet leaders denied that they intended to expel China from the international communist movement.

In November the UN General Assembly decisively defeated the annual motion to admit Communist China to the UN in place of Nationalist China. The motion was defeated by a vote of 57 against Peking to 46, with 17 member nations abstaining. Since the 1965 vote had been 47 to 47, with 20 abstentions, the motion was generally considered a victory for U.S. policy toward Communist China.

Wide World
Chou in Bucharest with protocol chief Dionisie Ionescu.

CHOU EN-LAI. Chou En-lai, the premier of Communist China, retained his position as third man in the Chinese Communist hierarchy and his rank as premier during the purges that characterized political life in China in 1966. Chou, whose ability to survive politically has been widely noted, has often been characterized as a moderate in economic and foreign policy, but his security in his political life has been maintained more often than not by his ability to compromise with changes in the Chinese Communist Party's policies.

During the year Chou made several important speeches. In January he gave an "important report" to the conference of the General Political Department of the People's Liberation Army. Other important conference reports were made by the party's Secretary-General, Teng Hsiao-ping, and by Peking party leader Peng Chen, who has since been purged.

In February, Chou was host to President Kwame Nkrumah of Ghana, who arrived in Peking for a state visit on Feb. 24. It was during this visit that Nkrumah was overthrown in Ghana, which represented a severe blow to Chinese foreign policy, always active in Nkrumah's support.

The most important Chinese visit abroad in 1966 was made at the end of March, when head of state Liu Shao-chi, since demoted to eighth place in the Chinese hierarchy, and Foreign Minister Chen Yi made a state visit to West Pakistan. Chou En-lai, an inveterate world traveler, did not go on this trip. By and large Chou was politically less active both internationally and at home than he had been in previous years, evidently preferring to stay out of the limelight while waiting out the storm of the Cultural Revolution.

MARK MANCALL
Department of History, STANFORD UNIVERSITY

153

Civil-rights marchers and state troopers clash near Canton, Miss.

CIVIL RIGHTS

By WILLIAM J. EATON
Washington Correspondent
CHICAGO DAILY NEWS

The drive for the Negro's full civil rights slowed considerably in 1966 from the rapid pace of the two preceding years. Negro riots in many Northern cities, a new and divisive "black power" doctrine and white resentment over housing-integration demands combined to check the progress toward racial equality. Fear of a "white backlash" at the polls in the off-year elections accounted for Congressional coolness to civil-rights legislation in the House and Senate. Federal courts continued to advance the Negro's cause, however, and Negroes in the South added considerably to their power at the polls through voter-registration campaigns. A Negro was elected to the U.S. Senate for the first time in a century, and other Negroes were the first of their race to serve in a president's Cabinet, and on the Federal Reserve Board of Governors.

As racial barriers were dismantled, however, civil-rights organizations increasingly turned their attention to monumental problems of poverty, unemployment, inadequate education and low skills that plague the Negro community. The organizations began to demand a Federal "freedom budget" of $18,500,000,-000 each year for a decade to overcome the economic barriers confronting many Negroes emerging from a segregated society.

Civil-Rights Measure Defeated. Perhaps the major development in 1966 was the death by filibuster of President Johnson's four-part civil-rights measure that would have put the problem of racial discrimination literally on the doorstep of people in the North for the first time. Its most controversial provision called for a ban on discrimination in the sale, rental or financing of any home or apartment by a real-estate agent or the owner himself. As outlined in Mr. Johnson's State of the Union Message to Congress on January 12, the bill also contained new machinery to ensure fair selection of juries in Federal and state courts, primarily to prevent exclusion of Negroes. Other provisions would have made it a Federal crime to attack or intimidate civil-rights workers, and would have given the attorney general broad powers to file suits to enforce constitutional rights of individuals.

Even before the hearings began, however, the seeds were being sown that would contribute to modification and eventual killing of the measure. Dr. Martin Luther King, Jr., chairman of the Southern Christian Leadership Conference, had announced January 7 that his forces would launch their first sustained "Northern movement" to attack housing discrimination in Chicago.

The Congress of Racial Equality picked a militant attorney, Floyd B. McKissick of Durham, N.C., as its new national director. In May, the Student Nonviolent Coordinating Committee switched leaders, dumping John Lewis, 26-year-old chairman, in favor of Stokely Carmichael, 25, an exponent of Negro self-help who became the best-known advocate of a "black power" route to equality.

And in Watts, the scene of destructive racial rioting in 1965, violence erupted again in mid-March. Two persons were dead, 20 injured and 19 buildings damaged before 200 police managed to bring the mob under control. (It was about then that the U.S. Census Bureau made public a study showing the average annual buying power of a family in Watts had dropped by $400 in the past 5 years while the average Negro's ability to buy went up 24 per cent.)

Riots occurred in Negro areas of Jersey City, N.J.; Pompano Beach, Fla.; Bakersfield, Calif.; Dayton, Ohio; Jacksonville, Fla.; Omaha; San Francisco; Cleveland; Chicago; and Brooklyn, N.Y., before the House started debate on the measure. By that time, Johnson administration officials had agreed to compromise the open-housing section of the bill in deference to the go-slow mood of whites in the North and pressure by real-estate lobbyists.

The House Judiciary Committee agreed on a modified version authored by Rep. Charles McC. Mathias, a Republican moderate from Maryland, that excluded 60 per cent of the nation's homes and apartments from the bill's coverage. It did this by exempting the sale of individually owned homes and the rental or sale of owner-occupied apartments with 4 units or less—i.e., up to a 4-flat building. The Mathias compromise also would allow the owner to instruct a real-estate agent not to sell or rent to Negroes.

Wide World

Floyd McKissick, Martin Luther King, Emanuel Celler and President Johnson hold civil-rights meeting. Below: Stokely Carmichael, "black power" advocate.

UPI

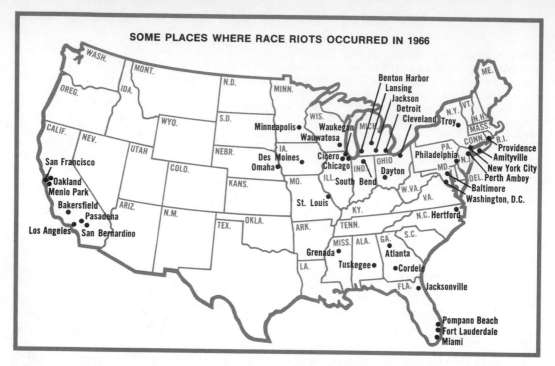

SOME PLACES WHERE RACE RIOTS OCCURRED IN 1966

On the House floor, the Mathias modification slipped through by 1 vote—180 to 179. A move to delete the entire provision on housing discrimination was rejected by a relatively close vote—198 to 179. The opposition was bolstered by the House Republican Policy Committee's objections to the open-housing section as "unworkable." McKissick and Carmichael, speaking for CORE and SNCC, denounced the bill as "racist" and "worthless."

The mood of the House was shown when it adopted, by a 389 to 25 vote, an amendment by Rep. William C. Cramer (R-Fla.) to make it a Federal crime to travel across state lines to incite a riot. Cramer said he wanted to give Congress a chance to show how it felt about the "fires, looting, vandalism, violence and death" associated with the riots in major cities.

The measure, also weakened in its section on school-desegregation suits, was passed on Aug. 9 after 12 days of debate by a vote of 259 to 157.

In 1964 and 1965, civil-rights bills sailed through Southern opposition in the Senate with the aid of the Republican leader, Everett McKinley Dirksen of Illinois. But 1966 was different, despite President Johnson's appeals, and Dirksen joined the Dixie filibuster. He objected that the ban on discrimination in housing sales was unconstitutional and found serious flaws in the procedures for jury selection.

The bill's supporters were ineffectual and poorly led. They could not even produce a quorum for 2 days, and then failed by 10 votes on 2 separate efforts to shut off the delaying debate. Ending a filibuster requires ⅔ of the senators present and voting. Administration forces barely mustered a majority—54 to 42 on September 14 and 52 to 41 on September 19—and gave up the fight.

Resistance, Violence and Schism. It was clear that white resistance to Negro pressure for change was stiffening. The calling of the National Guard to suppress rioting in several states dramatized the threat to public safety. In an Indianapolis speech July 23, President Johnson warned: "Riots in the streets do not bring about lasting reforms. . . . They make reform more difficult by turning away the very people who can and must support reform."

Attorney General Nicholas deB. Katzenbach, testifying before a Senate subcommittee in mid-August, said he found no evidence to show the riots were started or controlled by Left-Wing extremists, Communists or black nationalists. Rather, he said, the real causes were "disease and despair, joblessness and hopelessness, rat-infested housing and long-impacted cynicism." A review indicated that most were touched off by police questioning or arrests in Negro areas where the residents resisted this show of authority. Detroit, Lansing, Muskegon and Ypsilanti, Mich.; Minneapolis, Minn.; Perth Amboy, N.J.; and Waukegan, Ill., later suffered from Negro riots. So did Atlanta—a city which prided itself on its record of racial moderation and harmony. It was there that Stokely Carmichael was accused of inciting a riot by falsely accusing Atlanta police of killing a handcuffed Negro suspect. Moderate white

Mayor Ivan Allen was toppled from the roof of a police car when he tried to calm the crowd.

The wave of violence virtually nullified the impact of the White House Conference on Civil Rights in Washington June 1-2. It attracted 2,400 Negroes and whites from a wide variety of callings—sharecroppers, bankers, athletes, labor leaders, industrialists. Carmichael's group boycotted the meeting, charging that the President was not serious about civil rights, but McKissick came and nearly disrupted the meeting by demanding a vote on his resolution for withdrawal of U.S. troops from Vietnam. It was overwhelmingly rejected as "out of order" in one of 12 panels where voting was permitted.

The President, making a surprise appearance, pledged in a moving speech, "We shall not turn back!" but made no new commitments in the drive for equality.

Two widely separated events illustrated the Negro's different dilemmas in the North and the South. The nation was shocked June 6 when James H. Meredith, first Negro to graduate from the University of Mississippi, was shot from ambush as he walked on U.S. Highway 51 near Hernando, Miss. Meredith, 32, was on his own voting-rights march from Memphis, Tenn., to Jackson, Miss., to dissipate fear among Negroes in the state, and encourage them to use the ballot newly guaranteed by Federal law.

President Johnson and Mississippi Gov. Paul B. Johnson denounced the shooting, and the Governor promised to prosecute Aubrey J. Norvell, an unemployed hardware clerk from Memphis, who was arrested and charged with attempted murder.

Civil-rights leaders rushed to Memphis, and continued what they termed the "march against fear." Before it got to Jackson, June 26, the march stimulated the voting registration of 4,000 Negroes, and at least 10,000 Mississippi Negroes temporarily joined the procession. Although state police once fired tear gas at the marchers to move them off a school campground, the highway troopers generally provided protection from hostile whites.

The Mississippi march, a potential rallying point for all civil-rights groups, led to deep splits between them. The National Association for the Advancement of Colored People and the National Urban League refused to participate because they felt a march manifesto was too critical of President Johnson. Meredith, recovered, added to the grumbling.

Dr. King, who seemed in control for a while, lost leadership to the "black power" advocates who first chanted their slogan on that trek through Mississippi. Its meaning remained unclear and somewhat scary to the nation's white majority. Carmichael and others defended the concept as a means to solidify Negro organization in Negro areas, without white help, and denied it implied racial separation. The NAACP, Urban League and civil-rights patriarch A. Philip Randolph opposed the concept. Dr. King rejected the slogan but seemed more receptive to the appeal for racial pride and the application of Negroes' collective strength to civil-rights problems.

Open Housing and School Desegregation. In Chicago, the King organization led open-housing marches into all-white areas on the Southwest and Northwest sides, while angry white crowds jeered and threw rocks and bottles at his supporters. Dr. King was hit by a stone on one occasion, and he said: "I have never seen such hate—not in Mississippi or Alabama —as I see here in Chicago."

The tension became so great that Mayor Richard J. Daley and the city's business leadership worked out a ten-point agreement, pledging their efforts to open up housing to Negroes in return for King's cancellation of demonstrations. Some civil-rights advocates contended

An open-housing march in Chicago.

Wide World

the agreement was a "sellout" and marched into suburban Cicero anyway—under protection of National Guard troops.

The Chicago experience and the death of the civil-rights bill showed how sensitive the open-housing issue could be. It started a "backlash" from white homeowners who feared loss of their property's value, or radical changes in the racial makeup of their neighborhood.

Resistance also stiffened in the South and border states against school-desegregation demands of the U.S. Office of Education under its Commissioner, Harold Howe 2d. His 1966 guidelines required a start on faculty integration, shutdown of inadequate Negro schools, and doubling the pace of desegregation.

Southern governors and congressmen, along with many from the North, rebelled, and Howe became a popular target in House and Senate debate. He was accused of trying to bus students against their will to achieve racial balance. Howe denied any such intention, but the Capitol Hill revolt clearly slowed his enforcement of the law. But the Federal Government did, for the first time, shut off U.S. funds to school districts in Deep South states that retained totally segregated schools.

A survey indicated, however, that only 16 per cent of Negro pupils were going to classes with whites in the Southern and border states more than 12 years after the Supreme Court school-desegregation decree.

In the North, nothing was done by Federal authorities to challenge *de facto* segregation, or separation of the races by sending pupils to schools in their own neighborhoods. Federal studies indicated that all-Negro schools were inferior, and their students scored progressively lower than whites on achievement tests. There was high resistance to plans for bussing students outside their district to achieve better racial balance, however.

Similar problems were disclosed by the Equal Employment Opportunity Commission in a study of Negro hiring and promotion. "Only minimal gains have been made," the commission said.

U.S. Elections and Civil-Rights Trends. In voting, more progress was achieved. Negroes qualified to cast ballots in the South increased from 687,000 in 1964 to 1,151,000 by 1966. They voted in record numbers, electing sheriffs and other officials in several counties where Negroes form a majority of the population.

The Supreme Court voided the poll tax as prerequisite to voting, in a 6–3 decision March 25, eliminating the levy for state elections in Virginia, Texas, Alabama and Mississippi. It had tended to curtail Negro voting.

Alabama Democrats, recognizing the growing ballot-box power of Negroes, dropped their traditional "white supremacy" slogan.

The November 8 elections indicated perhaps that the "backlash" was not so strong as political observers expected. Edward W. Brooke, Negro attorney general of Massachusetts, easily won election to the U.S. Senate. George P. Mahoney, who won the Democratic nomination for governor of Maryland by dramatizing his opposition to open-housing laws, was defeated by Republican Spiro T. Agnew. Chicago-area congressmen who feared the sting of white resentment from the housing demonstrations squeaked through to victories. One possible casualty was Miami Mayor Robert King High, who lost the Florida governor's chair to Claude R. Kirk, Jr., a Republican who was clearly less liberal on racial issues.

In Georgia the voters balked at the Democratic candidacy of Lester Maddox, arch-segregationist. He failed to get the required majority in the traditionally Democratic state in a race against Republican Howard Callaway, also segregationist-minded but less extreme. The U.S. Supreme Court ruled Dec. 12 that the Georgia legislature decide the winner.

Another sign of antiextremist sentiment was the investigation of the Ku-Klux Klan by the House Committee on Un-American Activities. It resulted in conviction, for contempt of Congress, of Robert M. Shelton, imperial wizard of the United Klans of America.

The White House remained a symbol of civil-rights leadership. The President named Robert C. Weaver, 58-year-old great-grandson of a slave, to be his secretary of the Housing and Urban Development Department.

One of the most sweeping changes in civil rights—virtual desegregation of Southern hospitals—was achieved quietly in the preparation for the Medicare program. The Federal government could withhold funds unless hospitals complied with antidiscrimination rules.

Yet the dominant civil-rights theme of 1966 was a slowing of the integration pace while the white majority paused to examine new doubts and old fears.

COLORADO. Gov. John A. Love (R) and Sen. Gordon Allott (R), both incumbents, were reelected in Nov. 8 elections. . . . By boycotting five food chains in the Denver metropolitan area in mid-October, housewives touched off a nationwide drive against rising food prices. . . . In midyear a $3.8 million campaign was launched for a new Denver Art Museum. . . . A major new ski area near Glenwood Springs neared completion.

COMMUNICATIONS:

A LOOK AT ELECTRONICS AND PRINTING

By DAVID SARNOFF

Chairman of the Board

RADIO CORPORATION OF AMERICA

More than five thousand years ago, man developed writing as a way to give his words enduring form. In the 15th century, Johann Gutenberg vastly extended the reach of the written word and the means of transmitting information through the development of movable type. Today, a third revolution in graphics communications, electronic in nature and potentially as significant as writing and printing, is gathering momentum.

Gutenberg broke words into letters that could be reproduced in great quantities with speed and economy. Electronic devices break letters into patterns of tiny dots that can be transmitted over any distance, re-created in thousandths of a second, and ultimately reproduced at a fraction of usual printing costs.

Electronics in printing made one of its earliest appearances in 1962, in the composing room of newspapers, where its job was to set type by computer. In this process, news or advertising copy is fed into a computer which arranges the text into lines of column width, including the hyphenation of words, for automatic typesetting. To prepare text to fill a 21-inch newspaper column by this process takes only 17 seconds.

The following year, news copy originating in Brazil was flashed 5,000 miles via a Relay communications satellite to a computer in Camden, N.J., where it was instantly fed directly into teletypewriter circuits to hundreds of U.S. newspapers. The demonstration showed that it was possible to transmit for reproduction the entire news content of a typical newspaper—about 90 columns—from continent to continent in 5 minutes.

But the computer, working at speeds of thousands of words a minute, was driving mechanical devices capable of setting only a hundred or so words a minute.

In 1966, the first electronic graphics system was introduced, completely bypassing mechanical typesetting. Instead of passing copy from the computer to a typesetting machine, the system draws upon typefaces which are stored in the form of electronic signals in the com-

©*Karsh Ottawa*

David Sarnoff, 1966 recipient of an Overseas Press Club award for his pioneering work in electronic journalism.

puter's memory. As letters are needed to set copy, they are retrieved from the memory in thousandths of a second and displayed on a cathode-ray tube, comparable to the television picture tube. The words on the face of the tube are then exposed through a lens directly onto sensitized film or paper, ready for transfer to the printing plate. In this entire sequence nothing moves except electrons.

Videocomp, as this electronic composition system is called, can store any typeface or symbol in its memory—from Chinese ideographs to scientific equations. It can set up to nine hundred lines of type a minute—equal to the output of one hundred mechanical typesetting machines. Moreover, it will be possible within a few years electronically to reproduce photographs and drawings as well as text.

In the future, it will be possible to go from text and illustrations to printing in one integrated electronic process. Laser beams of light may take the electronically composed pages

159

Above: An engineer inspects a punched paper tape used in Video-comp, an electronic type-composition system. Left: Type-setting old and new, with new electronic type held above old wooden type.

and transfer them directly to a printing plate. Later, mechanical printing may be eliminated entirely, and text and illustrations would be transposed directly onto sensitized paper ready to be read.

As these processes take form, newspapers may no longer be published in a single location. They might be transmitted through computers to regional electronic printing centers that would turn out special editions for the areas they cover. Local news and advertising would be inserted on the spot. Since there is no limit to the distance electronic impulses can travel, newspapers also could be printed simultaneously on different continents.

Eventually newspapers may be printed in the home through a small copying device attached to a home communications center, and it should be possible to do the same with magazines and books.

There are special circumstances relating to textbooks, which account for almost one half of the more than 1,000,000,000 books published each year. The element of textbook obsolescence requires that the books be sup-plemented by a professor's mimeographed notes, and other special study materials. Much of this represents valuable intellectual activity which is limited in distribution to a few hundred copies. Computers will make it possible to catalogue this information and to reprint it upon demand, thereby vastly increasing the reservoir of available knowledge.

The same electronic information retrieval and copying system can also be employed by doctors, lawyers, and other professionals seeking the latest specialized information, by business executives, government officials and ordinary citizens. The material would be available on a worldwide basis, stored by regional computers on every continent, and instantly transmitted for copying in the home or office through space and terrestrial communications.

The significance of the third great revolution in written communications is not merely in the new reproduction techniques that are being developed. It lies in the fact that as never before, electronic printing will make information the most readily available and useful tool for human progress.

COMMUNISM. The year 1966, just a decade after Nikita S. Khrushchev exorcised the terrifying ghost of Joseph V. Stalin, found communist parties around the globe in a situation of burgeoning confusion and the world communist movement in a condition of diminishing strength. If the Soviet party ever really had hoped to establish world communist unity under its leadership, that hope now lay in shattered ruins. The split had widened to the point where the Chinese publicly pictured the Russians as their enemies. The ever-growing hostility between Moscow and Peking was reflected in divisions and squabbling among extreme Leftists in many noncommunist nations.

Global Confusion. For the Chinese party, numerically the world's biggest, it was a year of upheaval, purge and often political chaos. With the era of Party Chairman Mao Tsetung's personal leadership about to end, top Chinese party figures obviously were locked in a grim struggle for power. A phenomenon called the Red Guards—teen-age mobs inspired by the currently dominant Politburo faction—presented an incredible spectacle to the outside world of a party and nation in wild confusion.

There were new reverses in Africa, the most notable of which was in the overthrow in Ghana of President Kwame Nkrumah, one of communism's most valued allies on that continent. In Latin America, a splintering of the movement, plus growing confidence and stability among governments, contributed to a weakening of forces of the extreme Left. In Fidel Castro's Cuba there was an open clash between pro-Soviet and pro-Chinese elements at a Tricontinental Solidarity Conference.

Castro, totally dependent upon Moscow for Cuba's economic and military health, apparently succumbed to Soviet pressure and made a statement disassociating himself from Peking policy. He sharply criticized China's trade relations with Cuba. Peking called him a liar for saying that China broke a rice-sugar trade agreement. The eruption produced tension and discord at what was to be a meeting primarily concerned with denouncing the United States. Parties also were badly divided in Peru, Guatemala, Venezuela, Brazil and elsewhere.

In Asia it was much the same story. India's party remained split between Soviet and Chinese wings. The Japanese party leadership, evidently appalled at the Red Guard spectacle, turned to a neutralist attitude and as a result brought itself some internal woes. The Chinese brand of communism suffered sharp setbacks. The most painful was in Indonesia, where a party which once boasted 3 million members was broken up and destroyed in a bloodbath, a direct result of the abortive 1965 Red attempt to seize power in that archipelago nation of 105 million.

Among influential parties outside the Soviet orbit, there was an increasing tendency toward independence of action, apparently based on the assumption that if a half century of Soviet leadership had failed to lift them to power, it was time, as one prominent Italian Communist put it, to "seek reasons for its failure."

The Italian party was a distressing problem, at times, for Moscow. Led by mavericks, it displayed impatience with Moscow's internal and external policies which, some Communists apparently felt, damaged the Red cause in the West. The sentiment was infectious. Even the French party, once the most Stalinist and retrogressive, was coming around to the view that Moscow tended at times to be more an embarrassment than a help to French communist ambitions.

Within the bloc of nations ruled by communist parties, Kremlin authority was wearing thin. Rumania's party persisted in defying Soviet leadership, and its success in this was noted elsewhere. Its line was one of independence both on party and government levels. Red Chinese hostility to Moscow had provided another pole of authority which made expressions of independence less risky and less difficult for parties which in the past had faithfully reflected every Kremlin whim, flip and flop. Nationalism and national interests came more and more to the foreground.

Soviet Diplomacy vs Peking Aims. Soviet diplomacy leaped forcefully into Asia to counter Peking aims. Soviet Premier Aleksei N. Kosygin met in January at Tashkent in the Uzbek S.S.R. with leaders of India and Pakistan and produced an agreement for a pullback from the perilous Kashmir confrontation. The watching Chinese were enraged. But at that moment, in contrast with China, Russia's national interest seemed to require peace and stability in the vast Indian subcontinent.

Before the ink was dry on the pact, top Soviet leaders headed by Leonid I. Brezhnev, now General Secretary of the Communist Party, went to the People's Republic of Mongolia (Outer Mongolia) to hammer out a treaty of mutual assistance "ensuring the defense potential of both countries" and pledging joint measures, including military ones, "with the aim of insuring the security, independence and territorial integrity" of both. The obvious question was: Defense against what? The prospect of a U.S. attack on Outer Mongolia was farfetched. It could be assumed the pact with that

Huge portrait of Lenin dominates session of 23d Soviet Communist Party Congress.

buffer state—long a satellite of Moscow and a target of Red Chinese subversion—represented insurance against Peking aims. The Chinese, at any rate, chose to read it that way.

In February, the Soviet communist newspaper *Pravda* urged Peking to "return to the path of friendship." The theme was repeated by Brezhnev at the party's 23d Congress which opened late in March. But the bid came at an awkward moment. It became known that the Soviet party also had circulated a letter among many of the world's communist chiefs, claiming that the major aim of Chinese policy was to provoke a military clash between the Soviet Union and the United States. China scornfully rejected a bid to send a delegation to the Congress. It seized upon the letter—whose existence Moscow did not deny—and blasted the Kremlin as plotting to sell out communism in Vietnam and encircle China in a "filthy deal with the U.S. imperialists."

The party of Albania (Peking's sole ally in Europe) and those of Japan and New Zealand, whose leaderships until then were strongly anti-Moscow and "antirevisionist," also ignored the invitations. China's later upheaval, however, would lose her the support even of the "antirevisionist" Japanese.

23d Congress, Its Influence. There were 77 foreign communist delegations present when the Congress opened in Moscow, March 29. It was a dry, humdrum affair. Representing a Soviet party membership of 12,472,000 were 4,260 voting delegates and 325 alternates. The speeches they heard laid heavy stress on the Soviet economy and internal affairs.

The Congress did little to polish the Soviet party's image among foreign parties. In fact, it produced misgivings about the future course of Kremlin internal policies. It renamed the ruling party Presidium the Politburo, a term unused since Stalin's time. It conferred on Brezhnev the title of General Secretary, instead of First Secretary, which had signified a sort of *primus inter pares*. Stalin was the last to hold the title of General Secretary. Fears of a renascent Stalinism had been fanned in advance of the Congress. A month before, a Moscow court had sentenced two writers, Andrei D. Sinyavsky and Yuli M. Daniel, to hard labor on charges of having sent anti-Soviet writings abroad to be published.

On the eve of the Congress, a group of Soviet intellectuals wrote Brezhnev that any step toward rehabilitating Stalin would "lead to a new split in the ranks of Communists" and be interpreted as Soviet weakness before Red Chinese demands. Later, 63 Soviet intellectuals bitterly protested the sentences. The case was a blow to the Soviet party's image in the advanced world, and drew denunciations even from communist parties in the West, whose own fortunes had been hurt by it.

Nikolai G. Yegorychev, chief of the Moscow party organization, sought at the Congress to allay fears of Stalinism or Khrushchevism. But obviously there would be an attempt to play down the wave of attacks on the Stalin era. Yegorychev warned against attempts to "cross out the heroic history of our people who, under the guidance of the party for almost half a century, have passed along a difficult but glorious path of struggle and victories."

Brezhnev displayed deep worry. He complained, at the Congress, of "hack artists and writers" who "smear our order and slander our heroic people." He was disturbed about waning faith among youth in communism after 49 years of party power. The young, he said, had not been hardened like the oldsters in revolutionary struggle. They were subject to contamination by bourgeois ideas and ideological infection. And after all, he pointed out, half the Soviet population in 1966 was under 26.

The Congress lasted 11 days. Little sensational came of it. But abroad there were, from Moscow's viewpoint, unwanted results. Western parties had been questing for respectability in European eyes. Europe was not the Europe of 20 years before, staggering from the blows of World War II. It was fat and prosperous. Outworn dogma was losing its appeal, notably among the young. Communists sought more logical roads to political power and adopted bourgeois devices to lure young people.

In a display of independence from Moscow, leaders of 15 West European communist parties met in Vienna for three days in May. According to the participants, Soviet and East European parties were not informed of the Politburo-level meeting. It probed possibilities of alliances with noncommunist organizations, dialogues with Christian Democrats and Socialists, bridges to noncommunist labor and related matters in which the Italian party long before had taken a strong lead.

Moscow's problems were compounded by attitudes within the Soviet bloc. The United States seemed ready to take advantage of shifting winds and moved to improve relations with the bloc. At least some East European regimes were anxious for trade with the United States and the West. National interest was pushing to the fore. Soviet-Rumanian differences were reflected by a July summit meeting of Warsaw Pact members. Moscow had sought to tighten control over the alliance. Rumania insisted on louder voices for the junior partners. The meeting became a sort of Rumanian-Soviet confrontation which was not resolved for the remainder of the year.

China's Red Guard. The real shock to the movement, however, came from a China which seemed seized by sudden madness in late summer. Terror in the form of swaggering, uniformed, arm-banded teen-agers, on the prowl in mobs of many thousands, stalked the streets of cities in search of victims who represented the "four olds." The Red Guards, The Red Flag Fighting Teams, and even preteen-agers called The Red Scarves were to strike down old customs, old habits, old ideas and old culture, to root out all "monsters and freaks," all "revisionists" and "those in power who took the capitalist path." They had the hearty approval of Defense Minister Lin Piao, the saturnine 59-year-old army marshal who had moved into second place in the hierarchy behind Mao Tse-tung, and was a leading contender in the struggle for Mao's power.

The call went out. Young people, instead of going to school, would help "carry through the Great Proletarian Cultural Revolution," as the purge movement was called. At the start the Cultural Revolution had been based on the 9-million member Young Communist League. The league had an 8-day meeting in July at which it was exhorted by Li Hsueh-feng, successor to the purged Peng Chen as head of the Peking party committee, to lead the movement. But the league was destined to be bypassed. Evidently its members—whose age goes all the way up to the 40's—were considered too mature to serve as violence-minded vigilantes for Defense Minister Lin and his group.

Suddenly in August the Red Guards of Defense (Hung Wei Ping) burst on the scene. None of the youths were over 18. All were products of indoctrination from infancy. Their appearance followed the Party Central Committee's 11th Plenum in early August which produced a 16-point communiqué to guide the Cultural Revolution. One of the main points was "to topple those who are in power but who follow the capitalist road." Immediately thereafter, Red Guards streamed into Peking's streets, bent on mayhem, proclaimed by the press to be "the iron broom that sweeps away all kinds of freaks and monsters." Lin Piao admiringly likened them to "bamboo shoots after a spring rain."

The victims were countless thousands of educators, students, writers, artists, even military men and party politicians—and thousands of ordinary people deemed to dress wrongly or have the wrong sorts of haircuts. Anything smacking of foreign or "bourgeois" ways was a target. Stores were emptied of cosmetics and perfumes. Foreign books were burned, foreign music destroyed. Buddhist temples and Christian churches were sacked and priceless treasures destroyed. "Mao Tse-tung's thinking" reigned supreme.

One day an enormous portrait of Mao blocked access to the Soviet Embassy, while students demonstrated and renamed the thoroughfare Antirevisionism Street. The Russians were denounced and vilified, and a new shockwave rippled through the communist world.

Party after party—even some which in the past had been on the Chinese side of the quarrel—denounced the phenomenon and the persistent vilification of the Russians. Behind Lin Piao, the Red Army high command, purged of dissident officers, appeared gaining control over the nation. But the purge was far from ended and appeared at times to have encountered considerable resistance.

The Chinese leaders' preoccupation with the upheaval, however, tended to make it all the more cautious in its approach to Vietnam, where it appeared to want anything but a showdown with U.S. power. At the same time, the leaders badgered and harried the Russians, complaining that Moscow was giving only "sham help" to the Vietnamese Communists and that it plotted with the Americans to establish peace and encircle China.

U.S.S.R. Denounces China. Moscow had exercised restraint under the torrent of abuse, but its patience neared the cracking point. By November, Moscow was pressing other parties around the world to agree to a conference at which China could be condemned. Evidently, Moscow viewed China by now as a threat to its security. The Soviet party carried the campaign for a world conference to Sofia, Bulgaria, where leaders of 74 parties attended the 9th Bulgarian Party Congress. A number of parties balked at the conference bid. These included Rumania, Italy, Yugoslavia, Cuba, North Korea and North Vietnam.

The Russians carried the campaign to Budapest, and the 9th Hungarian Party Congress attended by leaders of 32 parties. The opposition persisted but it appeared there would be some sort of world conference in 1967, which

would, however, fall short of attempting to excommunicate the Chinese from the party.

On the eve of the Hungarian Congress in November, Moscow denounced Mao Tse-tung by name in strong language. The Russians accused Peking of duplicity, and a *Pravda* editorial called on parties everywhere to condemn China and the Cultural Revolution as distorting Marxism-Leninism.

Communism's Loss of Strength. While in a few areas communism may have grown, overall it lost much strength around the world, during 1966. At the beginning of the year, membership in communist parties in noncommunist countries, according to the best available estimates, was 40 per cent less than in 1964. Total hard-core membership for 78 parties outside the communist blocs in 1966 was reported by intelligence sources at only 2.6 million, a sharp drop.

In Europe, the strongest party both in terms of influence and numbers was the Italian, which had become a bellwether for dissenters from total Moscow domination. Italy's Communist Party claimed 1,350,000 members. The French party, once considered most influential of all outside the red bloc, had 280,000 members.

At least in the advanced countries, dogmatic communism was losing ground all the time. Yugoslavia underwent a political upheaval in which President Josip Broz Tito purged his wartime comrade-in-arms, Vice-President Aleksandar Rankovic, and others, including secret-police figures, on charges of plotting to gain power. The development underscored to what extent old Yugoslav diehards were on the run and how new ideas steadily were pushing to the fore.

The same ferment was easily detectable in other communist-ruled nations of Europe and in the Soviet Union itself. Leaders could expect even more difficulty in the coming years as they attempted to stem a tide of sentiment in favor of liberalization.

WILLIAM L. RYAN
Special Correspondent, THE ASSOCIATED PRESS

CONNECTICUT. Gov. John Dempsey (D) was reelected Nov. 8. . . . Total personal income for Connecticut for the fiscal year ending June 30 was $10,251,600,000. . . . The *Pargo* nuclear submarine was launched at Groton Sept. 17. . . . The state purchased 350 acres of Talcott Mountain in Simsbury, Avon and Bloomfield for future park and recreational development. . . . Construction began on a $47 million University of Connecticut Medical-Dental School at Farmington.

CONSERVATION. On Feb. 23, 1966, President Johnson sent a special message to Congress on "Preserving Our National Heritage." The President's message, which emphasized the need for renewed attacks on air and water pollution, established the framework to be followed by the Federal Government during 1966 in the realm of conservation.

Pointing out that losses due to pollution cost the United States thousands of millions of dollars a year, the President called for a clean-rivers demonstration program "to clean and preserve entire river basins from their sources to their mouths." He asked for more research in air and water pollution control, stronger enforcement programs, establishment of a National Water Commission, creation of new recreation areas, development of a nationwide system of trails, and programs to save more forested areas.

President Johnson's proposal to transfer the Federal Water Pollution Control Administration from the Department of Health, Education, and Welfare to the Department of the Interior became a reality May 10. Interior immediately scheduled a series of antipollution-enforcement hearings at Cleveland, Ohio, for Lake Erie; in the West for Lake Tahoe; and at Atlanta, Ga., for the Chattahoochee River.

Meanwhile, Congress began considering a multibillion-dollar Federal cost-sharing program to speed construction of new sewage-treatment works, improve existing systems and accelerate pollution research.

While emphasis was on pollution control, other conservation actions took place on an ever-widening front. Allotments under the Land and Water Conservation Fund to U.S. states for planning, acquiring and developing outdoor recreation areas—as well as to Federal agencies for similar activities—neared $80 million.

Secretary of the Interior Stewart L. Udall announced a series of Federal grants from the fund—first of their kind—to be used in cities across the United States to develop urban trails for bicycling, hiking or walking, horseback riding and nature study. The projects ranged from a nature trail in Manhattan to a 140-mile network of bicycle and horseback trails near Phoenix, Ariz.

Congress approved a third power plant for the Grand Coulee Dam in Washington. Costing $390 million, the plant will reestablish the Grand Coulee as the world's largest single producer of electricity, with a capacity of 5.6 million kilowatts as compared with a 1966 capacity of 2 million kilowatts. Simultaneously, work went ahead on the new extra-high-voltage

Water pollution, a growing U.S. problem, is reflected in this photograph of a fish-littered Delaware shore.
Photos U.S. Department of the Interior

Department of Interior researchers package fish protein concentrate, a low-cost, nutritive flourlike substance.

Bureau of Reclamation, U.S. Department of the Interior

Artist's conception of new $390 million power plant for Grand Coulee Dam in Washington. Two existing powerhouses are shown at right and left of spillway.

transmission circuits which will link the power resources of the Pacific Northwest and the South.

For the St. John River in Maine, Congress authorized the first Federal power installation in the East at the Dickey-Lincoln site at a cost of $227 million.

Water and Fish Research

Under a stepped-up saline-water-conversion research-and-development program, authorizing outlays totaling $185 million over a six-year period, the Department of the Interior awarded scores of contracts and grants to universities, institutes, government agencies and private industry. The program was established in an effort to lower cost of producing potable water from saline or brackish sources. Ground was broken for a new desalting plant at San Diego, Calif., to replace one which was transferred to the Guantanamo naval base in Cuba.

The Department of the Interior, the Atomic Energy Commission, the Metropolitan Water District of Southern California, the Los Angeles Department of Power and Light and two private power companies agreed to build a $390.9 million dual-purpose plant on a man-made island off the California coast. The project, which must be approved by Congress, will use atomic power to produce electricity and convert seawater to fresh. Such an installation would produce 150 million gallons of fresh water per day and 1,800 megawatts of electricity—enough water for a city of 750,000, enough power for a city of 1.8 million.

During 1966, Secretary Udall headed a National Resources Mission to Germany to observe air, water and land pollution-control programs. From this mission emerged a proposal for cooperative studies and other exchanges by West Germany and the United States in meeting common problems in these fields.

Hopes for developing a satisfactory low-cost, high-protein flourlike substance from whole fish became brighter. Interior-produced fish protein concentrate, which could supply a person's protein needs for 2 cents a day, was declared "safe, nutritious, wholesome and fit for human consumption" by the National Academy of Sciences. The product has yet to be approved by the Food and Drug Adminstration.

Secretary Udall estimated that if only the unharvested fish in United States coastal waters were made into such a concentrate, it would provide sufficient protein to balance the diet of 1,000,000,000 of the world's needy people for 300 days.

At year's end, plans were maturing for an international discussion on water—one of the basic factors of man's environment. The first International Water for Peace Conference, to be held in Washington, D.C., May 23-31, 1967, is expected to draw delegates from all parts of the world for discussion of water-supply problems of the present and the future, and methods for meeting ever-increasing demands.

E. R. NICOLAI
Public Information Officer
U.S. DEPARTMENT OF THE INTERIOR

COOPERATIVES. Governors of a score of U.S. states proclaimed October 1966 as "Cooperative Month." Numerous departments of the Federal Government joined the Department of Agriculture in officially observing the month. The Cooperative League and National Rural Electric Cooperative Association placed institutional ads in nationwide magazines, setting forth the values and benefits of cooperative enterprise. In practically every state, cooperative councils and associations sponsored observances. All of this gave the cooperative segment of the U.S. economy its widest recognition in history.

Block model of north and south sections of New York City's Co-op City, to be the world's largest cooperative project.

Herman J. Jessor, Architect

In 1966, ground was broken by Gov. Rocke-feller (R-N.Y.) and New York City officials for the largest single cooperative enterprise ever to be undertaken anywhere. This is Co-op City, a 15,500-unit cooperative housing project costing some $300 million. Prior to the groundbreaking, thousands of families had made their down payments, and had become members of the cooperative association that will own this new community. And United Housing Foundation, the developer of Co-op City, was carrying on an intensive education program preparing these families for their ownership responsibilities and opportunities.

Furthermore, progressive trends were evident among various new cooperative enterprises and services. For example, the Cooperative League prepared and issued a manual for the development of "Community Center" cooperatives, especially for smaller communities where the locally owned cooperative can become a major factor in revitalizing declining communities. Both urban and rural cooperatives responded to this concept. Among the new services were liquid-fertilizer distribution direct to farmers; increased distribution of fuels and auto supplies to both farm and town; home modernization; direct mail-order sale of packaged drugs and prescriptions; and travel, camping and other recreation aids.

In 1966, farmers' cooperatives further integrated services to their members. Cooperative Production Credit Associations, with outstanding loans of more than $2,500,000,000, provided in many cases lines of credit for farmers with the loans underwritten by their farm-supply cooperatives. Central Farmers Fertilizer Company, jointly owned by more than a score of regional farm-supply cooperatives, took steps to provide a fully integrated service for all three basic ingredients—phosphate, potash and nitrogen—to its members. All in all, regional farm-supply cooperatives

had more than $100 million worth of manufacturing facilities under construction.

Total estimated volume of business of farmers marketing and supply cooperatives in 1966 was about $15,000,000,000.

U.S. credit unions maintained their rapid growth, and, by mid-1966 boasted more than 17 million members with $8,000,000,000 of loans outstanding, $9,000,000,000 in share capital and more than $10,000,000,000 in total assets. CUNA International brought together a worldwide conference of representatives of people's savings and credit institutions in Jamaica in October.

In the same month, the Cooperative League of the U.S.A. celebrated its 50th anniversary with its 25th biennial Congress in St. Paul, Minn.

The rural electric cooperatives continued in 1966 to benefit rural America with rate reductions, especially in areas served by their own generating plants. The Department of Agriculture estimated in January 1966 that rate reductions by electric cooperatives had saved their member-customers more than $5.5 million over the previous five years. Meanwhile, recognizing their future need for far more financing than they can expect the Congress to authorize through the Rural Electrification Administration, the National Rural Electric Cooperative Association pushed for legislation to establish a Bank for Electric Cooperatives. The bank would be temporarily capitalized by a government loan but would also be able to raise funds in the private money market.

Cooperative insurance companies sought through a Commission on Cooperative Insurance Development to gear themselves to provide for a larger segment of the insurance needs of other cooperatives.

JERRY VOORHIS
Executive Director
THE COOPERATIVE LEAGUE OF THE U.S.A.

COST OF LIVING

By ARTHUR M. ROSS
Commissioner, Bureau of Labor Statistics
U.S. DEPARTMENT OF LABOR

The cost of living in the United States rose 3.7 per cent from October 1965 to October 1966.

Despite a general increase in wages, the purchasing power of the average wage earner dropped 1 per cent during that 12-month period. Most of the increase in living costs turned up in higher prices for food and services. Nondurables and services rose between 4 and 5 per cent from the year before.

Higher Food Prices. Many factors contributed to rising food prices. Milk prices—up 11 per cent—rose with a greater consumer demand for milk at a time when more animals were being slaughtered for meat. Milk prices had not gone up for several years prior to 1966, and dairymen in many instances reduced their herds and turned to the more profitable market for meat. Reflecting the change, by October 1966 all types of dairy products sold at higher prices, with cheese up 19 per cent and butter up 17 per cent over the previous year.

Bread prices also rose sharply during the year, indicating for the most part the rise in wheat prices. The year saw an increased demand in the United States for wheat to feed livestock. At the same time, large quantities of the domestic supply were shipped abroad— particularly in response to a famine in India. The higher demand for wheat occurred at a time when U.S. farmers, having created a surplus of wheat for years, cut back in wheat growing. Distribution costs for bakery products, and rising wages in the industry, also played a role in price increases to the consumer. Prices for white bread rose 9 per cent; whole wheat, 10.5 per cent over October 1965.

Meat prices in 1966 showed a long-term increase, with some reduction after August. Distribution of price increases was somewhat uneven, however, with hamburger up 7.2 per cent during the year, but porterhouse steak up only 5/10 of a per cent. In general, beef prices reflected rises in pork prices, which fluctuate with the corn/hog ratio. In 1966, higher prices for corn to feed livestock, and greater public demand for meat, sent prices up.

Left: Arthur M. Ross, commissioner, Bureau of Labor Statistics, announces a rise in U.S.'s consumer price index. Right: Women protest the rise in food prices.
Photos UPI

Poultry and fish prices also rose during the year. Highest price increases were asked for frozen shrimp and canned tuna. Fruit and vegetable prices fluctuated with changing weather and harvest seasons. Labor costs influenced an over-the-year increase in prices of most farm products.

Bills for food eaten away from home—restaurant meals or snacks—also rose 5 per cent during the year.

Higher Prices for Goods and Services. The public demanded—and paid more for—increased service in 1966. Mortgage interest rates, doctors' and dentists' fees, hospital-room rates, home-repair services, real-estate taxes and property insurance led consumer services with higher charges.

Medical-care-service prices went up 7.3 per cent from the previous October. Nurses—members of a profession generally recognized as being poorly paid—began in 1966 to seek better remuneration for their important work.

Public-transportation prices rose 6.6 per cent from October to October, largely because of increases in auto insurance. In New York City, higher transportation prices reflected the influence of a January transit-strike settlement. Private transportation went up less than 2.5 per cent, from October to October.

Technological advances in gas, electricity and coal industries helped to keep prices down in these areas. Gas and electricity prices rose only 1/10 of 1 per cent from 1965.

Overall housing prices—including utilities and fuel, rent and home ownership—increased 2.9 per cent over the year.

Apparel prices and upkeep rose 3.4 per cent. Wage increases for workers in clothing and related industries were partly responsible for the rise. The higher price of footwear—up more than 6 per cent from 1965—reflected a rise in hide prices and increased foreign demand during a period when Argentina stopped shipping hides. By year's end, however, the rise in shoe prices had slowed its pace.

Most durable items remained fairly stable during the year. Cars were among the major items showing little significant price rise. New-car prices went up only 7/10 of a per cent, and used-car prices rose only 1.2 per cent. There was considerably less consumer spending on cars than in previous years. Household durables went up 1.5 per cent. Home furnishings rose 1.9 per cent from October 1965 to October 1966.

Of five major U.S. cities, Detroit experienced the highest over-the-year rise in consumer prices—4.8 per cent. New York City followed with a rise of 4.2 per cent.

COUVE DE MURVILLE, MAURICE. France's Maurice Couve de Murville began 1966 by being renamed foreign minister in President de Gaulle's Cabinet. From that point on, the 59-year-old diplomat was almost constantly on the move: to Germany, to Washington, around the world. NATO and Vietnam figured largely in his diplomatic talks and travels.

Couve de Murville was with De Gaulle during both of his semiannual talks with then German Chancellor Ludwig Erhard in February and July. The Foreign Minister said in a taped West German television interview April 24: "If there is a desire on the German side for the French troops to continue to be stationed in Germany, I . . . have no doubts that this can be negotiated. . . . We certainly have no desire to maintain the French troops stationed in Germany, if the . . . Federal Republic does not desire it." In December, Couve de Murville and Germany's new Foreign Minister Willy Brandt exchanged letters in which Germany said it wanted the French troops to remain.

On March 28, Couve de Murville advised U.S. Undersecretary of State George Ball of French deadlines for withdrawing from the North Atlantic Treaty Organization. Later in the year he discussed Vietnam and NATO problems with President Johnson and Secretary of State Rusk. During this trip to the United States the Foreign Minister addressed the UN General Assembly on Vietnam. "For years now, France has been saying again and again that there is one way, and only one way, of putting an end to a war with no solution of itself, since neither the defeat of powerful America is imaginable, nor is the renunciation of a people who want their independence. . . . Since a political solution alone is conceivable . . . it is a matter of returning to the Geneva agreements through a negotiation."

April found the Foreign Minister in Rumania and Bulgaria for meetings with Rumania's Communist Party chief Nicolae Ceausescu and Bulgarian Premier Todor Zhivkov. And in July he and French Premier Georges Pompidou were in London for talks with British leaders on possible British membership in the European Economic Community.

Couve de Murville accompanied De Gaulle on two long trips. During a June visit to the Soviet Union, the French Foreign Minister and his Soviet counterpart, Andrei A. Gromyko, signed two French-Soviet agreements. One was on the peaceful use of outer space and the other dealt with scientific, technical and economic cooperation. Then in late summer Couve de Murville joined President de Gaulle on a trip around the world.

CRIME

By J. EDGAR HOOVER
Federal Bureau of Investigation
UNITED STATES DEPARTMENT OF JUSTICE

According to the FBI's Uniform Crime Reports figures, crime in the United States in the first six months of 1966 rose 8 per cent over the same period in 1965. An 11 per cent increase was recorded in suburban areas, 7 per cent in rural areas and 6 per cent in cities over 100,000.

Violent crimes were led by forcible rape, which was up 12 per cent, followed by aggravated assault up 11 per cent, robbery 6 per cent and murder 3 per cent. Property-offense increases were led by larceny $50 and over in value, which was up 11 per cent, with auto theft up 7 per cent and burglary up 5 per cent.

Mass violence marked the crime picture in mid-1966. On July 14, eight student nurses were brutally slain in their two-story dormitory in Chicago. Twenty-four-year-old Richard Speck was arrested shortly thereafter and charged with the crime. On August 1, Charles J. Whitman, a University of Texas student, killed his wife and mother; then climbed to the observation section of the University Tower in Austin, from which he began a shooting rampage resulting in the slaying of an additional 14 persons, including an unborn child. He also wounded 30 other individuals before he himself was killed by a policeman.

More than 2.75 million serious crimes were committed in the United States during the calendar year 1965, an increase of 6 per cent over 1964.

In the calendar year 1965, all crimes used by the FBI as an index to nationwide criminality registered increases, with murder, robbery, aggravated assault, and burglary each 6 per cent; forcible rape 9 per cent; larceny $50 and over, 8 per cent; and auto theft 5 per cent.

All city population groups had crime increases in 1965, paced by cities of less than 50,000 inhabitants with a 7 per cent increase. The sharpest rise occurred in the suburbs where crime jumped 8 per cent. Rural areas showed a 3 per cent increase. Crime rose 4 per cent in cities of over 250,000 inhabitants.

In 1965 the crime rate rose 5 per cent, and there were over 14 serious crimes committed per 1,000 population. In reality, this figure represents a "victim risk rate," since these crime counts do not represent the number of criminals but, more accurately, the number of victims of crime. Since 1960 the total volume of serious crimes reported in the United States has risen 46 per cent, with violent crimes showing a 35 per cent rise, and the property crimes a 47 per cent increase. In view of this 46 per cent increase in serious crime during a 5-year period in which our national population has risen 8 per cent, the volume of crime continues to outpace population growth by almost 6 to 1.

Arrests of persons under 18 years of age for serious crimes rose 47 per cent during the period 1960–65. This was more than double the percentage increase in the young age population during the same period. Police arrests in 1965 of persons under 18 comprised 21 per cent of the total police arrests nationwide for all offenses except traffic, and increased 3 per cent in 1965 over 1964. In the suburban communities, however, this young age group was represented in 32 percent of all arrests and in the rural areas 19 per cent.

FBI Accomplishments. Convictions in cases investigated by the FBI rose to 13,023 during the 1966 fiscal year, a record for any peacetime fiscal year. This represented convictions of over 96.7 per cent of all persons brought to trial. In the same period, the FBI recorded an all-time high of $253,634,881 in fines, savings and recoveries, a return of $1.50 for every dollar appropriated for the FBI.

In the course of the 1966 fiscal year, 14,323 FBI fugitives were located, an increase of 832 over the previous year.

During this 1966 fiscal period, the FBI laboratory received 218,265 specimens of evidence which necessitated a total of 284,304 examinations. In the same period, the FBI Identification Division received an average of 27,529 fingerprint cards for processing each working day. As the fiscal year closed, the FBI Identification Division had on file 179,775,988 sets of fingerprints representing an estimated 79,414,697 persons.

CUBA. Cuba stirred up a political storm in the Western Hemisphere in January 1966, when a communist-sponsored "Tricontinental Solidarity Conference" was held in Havana. Thirty-seven Latin-American delegations at Havana voted for the formation of a regional "Anti-Imperialist" organization, with headquarters in the Cuban capital, to "unify, coordinate and advance the struggle against Yankee imperialism."

Resolutions made public only after the end of the fortnight conference declared support of so-called national liberation movements in the Dominican Republic, Venezuela, Guatemala, Peru, Colombia and other unspecified nations of the hemisphere. They called for "self-determination" and "independence" for Puerto Rico, the Guianas, Martinique and Guadeloupe. The conference formed an "aid and support" committee for national liberation movements the world over.

Response to the conference's aim was not slow in coming. In February, all the Latin-American nations, with the exception of Mexico, filed a formal protest with United Nations Secretary-General Thant, protesting the Havana conference's advocacy of use of armed force by liberation movements, and energetically condemning the move to extend "wars of national liberation" to the Americas. In Washington, a Pentagon spokesman said the emphasis of U.S. military aid to Latin America in fiscal 1967 would be on development of counter-insurgency capabilities.

President Johnson, requesting Congressional approval of a $917 million military-assistance package on Feb. 1, said that about one fourth of the amount would be used "to strengthen the capacity to maintain internal security in countries where instability and weakness can pave the way for subversion."

In March a revolutionary tribunal sentenced five persons to prison terms ranging from 10 to 25 years at hard labor; they were convicted of conspiring to kill Castro. Two others were acquitted. In the same month the Castro regime fired Maj. Efigenio Ahmeijeiras, vice-minister of the armed forces, stripped him of his military rank and tried and sentenced him for activities against "revolutionary morals."

In May, Cuba's armed forces went on "battle alert" following a virulent attack by Castro on the United States for what he termed "thousands of provocations" by U.S. marines at the naval base at Guantanamo Bay.

In August, Castro reiterated that there was no chance of a Cuban reconciliation with the United States and vowed to continue "an implacable fight against imperialism." He indi-

Wide World
Havana marks 7th anniversary of Castro regime Jan. 2.

cated in a more than five-hour speech in Havana on Aug. 30 that he was under pressure to change or ease his policy toward the United States, either from within his own Cuban Communist Party or, perhaps, from Moscow,

In September, Castro fired 268 foreign-ministry employees, ostensibly because they were not sufficiently revolutionary-minded.

Hurricane Inez hovered over Cuba for three days in October, wreaking much damage to the Cuban economy, probably at its lowest point since Castro seized power in 1959. The sugar crop, at 4.5 million tons, was two million tons under prior Castro estimates. The year witnessed the break-off of trade relations with Red China. Cuban Premier Fidel Castro leveled charges of "economic aggression" against Peking for purportedly reneging on a big sugar-for-rice trade pact.

Also in October, 10 members of the Cuban National Ballet defected in Paris while touring Europe; it was the biggest single mass escape from Castro custody. In Miami, the same month, hundreds of Cuban refugees—the vanguard of an expected 70,000—applied for permanent U.S. residence, the first step toward obtaining citizenship under a bill liberalizing residence requirements. An estimated 50,000 Cubans were airlifted from Havana to Miami during 1966 under the Cuban-American agreement for evacuation of refugees.

On Dec. 29 the first 169 U.S. citizens and their families repatriated from Cuba arrived in New Orleans, La., from Havana via Merida, Mexico. The Mexican Government, which maintains relations with Cuba, arranged the new airlift following negotiations with Secretary of State Dean Rusk.

FRANCIS L. McCARTHY
Latin-America Editor
UNITED PRESS INTERNATIONAL

DANCE

By DORIS HERING
Associate Editor
DANCE MAGAZINE

Modern Dance. The modern dance has been acknowledged as America's unique contribution to the development of 20th-century dance. Yet even its most outstanding exponents have had an unceasing financial struggle.

Their status, while still precarious, took an upswing in 1966. Under the advisement of a specially selected dance panel headed by choreographer Agnes de Mille, the U.S. Government's National Endowment for the Arts awarded $23,000 to José Limón for the development of new works or the revival of old ones. Anna Sokolow received $10,000, as did ballet choreographer Antony Tudor. Paul Taylor, Alvin Ailey, Merce Cunningham and Alwin Nikolais each received $5,000. To Martha Graham the Endowment gave $40,000 for the creation of two new works, and a $141,000 matching grant to enable her to take her company on its first national tour in 15 years. The first part of the matching funds came to Miss Graham from Mrs. De Witt Wallace, co-chairman, *Reader's Digest*. The company began its tour on Oct. 2.

In the meantime, Paul Taylor, Alvin Ailey, Merce Cunningham, Alwin Nikolais and Murray Louis took stock of their respective situations. They discovered that although they were doing extensive European touring, they were making at best only sporadic trips in the United States. None could afford appearances of any substantial length in New York, the alleged dance capital of the world. They therefore formed a National Dance Foundation designed to foster a joint season in New York, with each company remaining intact, rather than its members becoming part of a repertory pool. The foundation was also to provide for a well-planned tour with equal bookings assured to each group.

There were other hopeful portents for the modern dance. The Rockefeller Foundation gave $370,000 to the University of Utah to form a touring modern dance company with Virginia Tanner as project director. And modern dance choreographers were increasingly sought out by ballet companies. For example, Joyce Trisler, Norman Walker and Anna Sokolow contributed works to the Boston Ballet. The Harkness Ballet acquired new works from Alvin Ailey and John Butler, and Mr. Butler staged his well-known *Carmina Burana* for the Pennsylvania Ballet. Merce Cunningham's *Summerspace* was acquired by the New York City Ballet.

Television took a serious look at modern dance when National Educational Television taped a program on the early days of some of today's great choreographers. The program included a specially made film of Doris Humphrey's masterpiece, *Passacaglia*, with Lola Huth and Chester Wolenski in the leading roles.

Ballet. The healthy trend toward decentralization in the U.S. dance was recognized in several positive ways. In the realm of regional, or nonprofessional (in the economic sense) ballet (which by the end of the year numbered some 250 companies), a Pacific Western Regional Association was organized. It held its first festival in Sacramento, Calif. The wheels were also set in motion for a new Midwestern Regional Ballet Association.

The Robert Joffrey Ballet, fortified by a Ford Foundation grant and the acquisition of a New York theater of its own, announced its intention to spend summers in residence at Pacific Lutheran University in Tacoma, Wash., and to follow each residency with a Pacific Northwest tour. The Ballet of Los Angeles made a summer debut with Stefan Wenta as artistic director, Yvonne Mounsey as ballet mistress and George Balanchine as artistic consultant.

Mr. Balanchine's own company, the New York City Ballet, inaugurated the new Saratoga, N.Y., Performing Arts Center in July, and in

Martha Graham as Clytemnestra.

Martha Swope

Martha Swope

Above: Merce Cunningham's *Summerspace* as performed by New York City Ballet. Morton Feldman did the score, while scenery and costumes are by the modern artist Robert Rauschenberg. Right: Gerald Arpino's *Sea Shadow,* danced by Lisa Bradley and Richard Gain of City Center Joffrey Ballet, is a mood piece about a creature from the sea and a human boy on the beach.

City Center Joffrey Ballet

the fall went on its most extensive national tour to date. The Saratoga repertoire included the world premiere of *Narkissos,* first choreographic effort of the company's leading male dancer, Edward Villella. One of the company's ballerinas, Violette Verdy, made her choreographic debut with the Dayton, Ohio, Civic Ballet.

A new ballerina, Lisa Bradley, emerged in the modest City Center Joffrey Ballet. Al-though she resembled a white anemone, she had a calm, sure grasp of the romantic style as typified by Joffrey's *Pas des Déesses.* She was the gently playful naiad of Gerald Arpino's *Sea Shadow* and the cold, cruel seductress in Arpino's *Nightwings,* premiered during the company's fall season.

The City Center Joffrey Ballet also premiered *These Three* by Eugene Loring, renowned for

Maya Plisetskaya in Act I of the Bolshoi Ballet's *Don Quixote.*

Wayne J. Shilkret Hurok Attractions

his "Americana" ballet, *Billy the Kid.* The dated choreographic style of *These Three,* which dealt with the three civil-rights workers killed in Mississippi, weakened its theme.

Astute publicity and spectacular dancing were earmarks of the American tour of Moscow's Bolshoi Ballet in the spring. The company presented a touching new version of Stravinsky's *The Rite of Spring,* staged by the husband-and-wife team of Vladimir Vasiliov and Natalia Kasatkina. It also exhibited a new and provocative, if sometimes excessively lavish, version of *The Nutcracker,* staged by Yuri Grigorovich.

Bolshoi ballerina Maya Plisetskaya, who relies more on aggressive bravura than on sensitivity, received much acclaim. Seasoned balletomanes, however, turned to the more tender and subtle dancing of Ekaterina Maximova and Natalia Bessmertnova. The male contingent, led by Vladimir Vasiliev, Mikhail Lavrovsky and Yuri Vladimirov, seemed endlessly prodigious in its supply of vital, virile performers.

Musical Theater. As with so much of dance, the evidences of growth on the Broadway scene were also more in organization than in creation. Only Bob Fosse, director and choreographer of *Sweet Charity* (with Gwen Verdon as the star), and Onna White, choreographer of *Mame,* retained the identity of their distinctly individual styles.

The most provocative Broadway news was a National Council on the Arts grant of $300,000 to Jerome Robbins to form an American Lyric Theater Workshop with the intention of, as he stated it, "providing a place for performing and creative artists to join, work on ideas, create new works, extend and develop the musical theater into an art capable of poetically expressing the events, deep hopes and needs of our lives." It was significant that the grant was made to a dancer-choreographer-director.

Also potentially significant was a grant of $25,000 by the Endowment for the Arts, with the intent of forming a national service organization for all aspects of dance. Called the Association of American Dance Companies, it was still defining its purposes and personnel as the year drew to a close.

DEATHS

Anselmo Cardinal Albareda, 74, Vatican librarian; Barcelona, Spain, July 20.

Florence Ellinwood Allen, 82, first woman judge on U.S. Court of Appeals (1934–59); Waite Hill, Ohio, Sept. 12.

Margery Allingham, 62, mystery writer; Colchester, England, June 30.

Ronald Armstrong-Jones, 66, father of the Earl of Snowdon; Carnarvonshire, Wales, Jan. 27.

Jean Arp, 78, French abstract sculptor-painter and a founder of the Dada movement; Basel, Switzerland, June 7.

William Waldorf Astor, 58, Viscount Astor of Cliveden, former member of Parliament; Nassau, the Bahamas, March 7.

Hugh Baillie, 75, president, United Press International (1935–55); La Jolla, Calif., March 1.

Art Baker, 68, actor, TV master of ceremonies (You Asked for It); Los Angeles, Calif., Aug. 26.

John F. Baldwin, 50, U.S. Representative (R-Calif., 1953–66); Bethesda, Md., March 9.

Maj. Charles A. Bassett 2d, 34, U.S. astronaut; St. Louis, Mo., Feb. 28.

Lucius Beebe, 63, author, editor; Hillsborough, Calif., Feb. 4.

Grover Cleveland Bergdoll, 72, notorious World War I draft dodger; Richmond, Va., Jan. 27.

Leslie L. Biffle, 76, longtime U.S. Senate employee until his retirement as secretary in 1952; Washington, April 6.

Sherman Billingsley, 66, nightclub proprietor (New York City's Stork Club); New York City, Oct. 4.

Smiley Blanton, 84, psychiatrist-author; New York City, Oct. 30.

André Breton, 70, father of surrealism; Paris, Sept. 28.

Arthur William Brown, 85, illustrator-caricaturist; New York City, Oct. 24.

Lenny Bruce, 40, comedian; Hollywood, Calif., Aug. 3.

W. Atlee Burpee, 71, retired seed-company executive; Philadelphia, Pa., Jan. 10.

Francis X. Bushman, 83, silent-screen star; Pacific Palisades, Calif., Aug. 23.

Montgomery Clift, 45, motion-picture actor (*From Here to Eternity*); New York City, July 23.

Edward Gordon Craig, 94, stage producer-designer, son of Ellen Terry; Vence, France, July 29.

Russel Crouse, 73, playwright-producer, with Howard Lindsay produced Broadway's *Life with Father;* New York City, April 3.

Dr. Peter J. W. Debye, 82, winner Nobel Prize for Chemistry (1936); Ithaca, N.Y., Nov. 2.

Morris De Castro, 64, Virgin Islands governor (1950–54); St. Croix, V.I., Dec. 9.

Charles Walter (Chuck) Dressen, 67, baseball manager; Detroit, Mich., Aug. 10.

Raymond Duncan, 91, artist, brother of dancer Isadora Duncan; Cavalaire, France, Aug. 14.

Hubert Eaton, 85, founder of Forest Lawn (Calif.) cemetery; Beverly Hills, Calif., Sept. 20.

Gus Edson, 65, cartoonist (The Gumps); Stamford, Conn., Sept. 26.

Aymar Embury II, 86, architect of New York City's Triborough Bridge and Lincoln Tunnel; Southampton, N.Y., Nov. 14.

Elizabeth Arden, 81, founder and owner of the Elizabeth Arden cosmetic firm; New York City, Oct. 18.
Wide World

Vincent Auriol, 81, president of France (1947–54); Paris, Jan. 1.
Wide World

Gertrude Berg, 66, actress-writer and creator of radio-TV's The Goldbergs, appeared on Broadway in A Majority of One; New York City, Sept. 14.
Wide World

Harry F. Byrd, Sr., 79, Democratic governor of Virginia (1926–30), U.S. Senator (1933–65); Berryville, Va., Oct. 20.
Wide World

Walt Disney, 65, cartoon and moviemaker, creator of Disneyland; Los Angeles, Calif., Dec. 15.
UPI

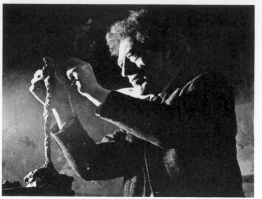

James E. (Sunny Jim) Fitzsimmons, 91, "grand old man of Thoroughbred racing"; Miami, Fla., March 11.

UPI

Alberto Giacometti, 64, Swiss-born sculptor, winner of Grand Prix de Sculpture of Venice in 1962, winner of the Grand Prix des Arts de la Ville de Paris; Chur, Switzerland, Jan. 11.

"Paris Match"

Theodore Francis Green, 98, Democratic Rhode Island governor (1932–37), U.S. Senator (1937–61); Providence, R.I., May 19.

Wide World

Eddie Erdelatz, 53, U.S. Naval Academy football coach during the 1940's; Burlingame, Calif., Nov. 10.

R. A. Emerson, 54, president, Canadian Pacific Railway (1964–66); Montreal, March 13.

Earl Barry Faris, 77, editor of International News Service (1916–58); Minneapolis, Kans., Nov. 6.

John Farrell, 75, chairman executive committee, Farrell Steamship Lines; Tokeneke, Conn., April 22.

Verna Felton, 76, movie and TV (December Bride) actress; North Hollywood, Calif., Dec. 14.

Joseph Fields, 71, coauthor of many Broadway hits (*Gentlemen Prefer Blonds* with Anita Loos); Beverly Hills, Calif., March 3.

Eric Fleming, 41, star of TV series Rawhide; Tingo Maria area, Peru, Sept. 28.

Kathryn Forbes, 57, author *Mama's Bank Account*; San Francisco, Calif., May 15.

C. S. Forester, 66, author, known for Horatio Hornblower novels; Fullerton, Calif., April 2.

Philipp Frank, 82, physicist and philosopher; Cambridge, Mass., July 21.

Lord Fraser of Allander, 63, British merchant, head of House of Fraser; Mugdock, Scotland, Nov. 6.

William Frawley, 72, stage, motion-picture and TV (I Love Lucy) actor; Hollywood, Calif., March 3.

Walter Gifford, 81, president, American Telephone & Telegraph (1925–48); New York City, May 7.

Maj. Gen. Harold Napoleon Gilbert, 70, U.S. Army and Air Corps recruiting chief (1938–41); Washington, Nov. 16.

Bernard F. Gimbel, 81, department-store tycoon; New York City, Sept. 29.

Gilbert H. Grosvenor, 90, editor *National Geographic* magazine (1899–1954); Baddeck, Nova Scotia, Feb. 4.

Moses Hadas, 66, classical scholar; Aspen, Colo., Aug. 17.

Virginia Hill, 49, famed for 1957 TV appearances before the Kefauver crime committee; Salzburg, Austria, March 24.

Richard Himber, 59, bandleader-magician; New York City, Dec. 11.

Gen. Cemal Gursel, 71, president of Turkey from 1960 until he suffered a stroke early in 1966; Ankara, Turkey, Sept. 14.

Wide World

Christian A. Herter, 71, Republican governor of Massachusetts (1953–57), secretary of state (1959–61); Washington, D.C., Dec. 30.

Wide World

Marguerite Higgins, 45, syndicated newspaper columnist and war correspondent, 1951 Pulitzer Prizewinner; Washington, D.C., Jan. 3.

Wide World

William Ernest Hocking, 92, philosopher and educator; Madison, N.H., June 19.

Gen. Courtney H. Hodges, 79, commander of U.S. First Army in Europe (1944–45); San Antonio, Tex., Jan. 16.

Malvina Hoffman, 81, internationally known U.S. sculptor; New York City, July 10.

Hans Hofmann, 85, painter and art teacher; New York City, Feb. 17.

Hedda Hopper, 75, Hollywood gossip columnist for 28 years; Hollywood, Calif., Feb. 1.

Albert W. Hull, 85, physicist specializing in development of vacuum tubes; Schenectady, N.Y., Jan. 22.

Mississippi John Hurt, 74, country blues singer; Grenada, Miss., Nov. 2.

Maj. Gen. Johnson T. U. Aguiyi-Ironsi, Chief of State of Nigeria; near Ibadan, Nigeria, July 29.

Col. James Jabara, 43, first U.S. jet-pilot ace (in Korean war); Delray Beach, Fla., Nov. 17.

Dr. D. C. Jarvis, 85, author of *Folk Medicine*; South Barre, Vt., Aug. 18.

Louis A. Johnson, 75, Secretary of Defense (1949–50); Washington, April 24.

Helen Kane, 62, "Boop-Boop-a-Doop Girl" singer of the 1920's and 1930's; New York City, Sept. 26.

K. T. (Kaufman Thuma) Keller, 80, president of Chrysler Corporation (1935–50), adviser to President Truman; London, Jan. 21.

Jan Kiepura, 62, Polish tenor; Rye, N.Y., Aug. 15.

Blanche Wolf Knopf, 71, cofounder of publishing firm Alfred A. Knopf, Inc.; New York City, June 14.

Hannes Kolehmainen, 76, Finnish distance runner who won four Olympic gold medals; Helsinki, Jan. 11.

Sergei P. Koroley, 59, Soviet designer of spacecrafts; Moscow, Jan. 14.

Henry Krajewski, 54, Poor Man's Party presidential candidate (1952–56–60); Secaucus, N.J., Nov. 8.

David L. Lawrence, 77, former Democratic governor of Pennsylvania, four-time mayor of Pittsburgh; Pittsburgh, Pa., Nov. 21.

Fulton Lewis, Jr., 63, radio commentator noted for conservative views; Washington, Aug. 21.

Murray D. Lincoln, 74, a founder and first president of CARE; Columbus, Ohio, Nov. 7.

Dr. Jesse T. Littleton, 78, Pyrex glassware developer; Fort Pierce, Fla., Feb. 24.

J. Howard McGrath, 62, U.S. Attorney General under President Truman; Narragansett, R.I., Sept. 2.

Lieut. Gen. Sir Iven Giffard Mackay, 84, Australian hero of World Wars I and II; Sydney, Sept. 30.

Patrick Vincent McNamara, 71, U.S. Senator (D-Mich., 1955–66); Bethesda, Md., April 30.

Dr. Louis L. Mann, 76, rabbi, founder of National Conference of Christians and Jews; Chicago, Ill., Feb. 1.

Herbert Marshall, 75, motion-picture actor; Beverly Hills, Calif., Jan. 22.

Alice G. Masaryk, 87, Czech patriot, daughter of first president of Czechoslovakia; Chicago, Nov. 29.

Alcoa

Roy A. Hunt, 85, pioneer aluminum producer and former president of Aluminum Company of America; Pittsburgh, Pa., Oct. 21.

Wide World

Hewlett Johnson, 92, "Red" Dean of Canterbury; Canterbury, England, Oct. 22.

Wide World

Joseph Francis (Buster) Keaton, 70, motion-picture comedian, star of silent films; Hollywood, Calif., Feb. 1.

Wide World

Sebastian Spering Kresge, 99, founder and head of Kresge chain stores; Mountainhome, Pa., Oct. 19.

Tony Lema, 32, U.S. professional golfer, winner of the 1964 British Open golf championship; Lansing, Ill., July 24.

Wide World

Gen. A. G. L. McNaughton, 79, "father" of the Canadian Army; Montebello, Que., July 11.

National Film Board

Dr. William C. Menninger, 66, psychiatrist and president of the Menninger Foundation in Topeka, Kans.; Topeka, Sept. 6.

Wide World

Adm. Chester W. Nimitz, 80, commander in chief, U.S. Pacific Fleet during World War II; San Francisco, Calif., Feb. 20.

UPI

Michael J. Quill, 60, president of the Transport Workers Union from 1935; New York City, Jan. 28.

UPI

Helen Menken, 64, radio and stage actress, president, American Theater Wing; New York City, March 27.

Stanislaw Mikolajczyk, 65, last noncommunist premier of Poland; Chevy Chase, Md., Dec. 13.

Ward Morehouse, 67, drama critic-journalist; New York City, Dec. 7.

Wyndham Mortimer, 82, a founder of United Automobile Workers of America and Congress of Industrial Organizations; Hawthorne, Calif., Aug. 23.

Anne Nichols, 75, author *Abie's Irish Rose*; Englewood Cliffs, N.J., Sept. 15.

Kathleen Norris, 85, prolific novelist and short-story writer; San Francisco, Calif., Jan. 18.

James T. O'Connell, 60, U.S. Undersecretary of Labor (1957–61); New York City, Oct. 12.

Frank O'Connor, 63, Irish writer noted for short stories; Dublin, March 10.

Sean T. O'Kelly, 84, president of Ireland (1945–59); Dublin, Nov. 23.

Alexander F. Osborn, 77, advertising executive and originator of "brainstorming sessions"; Buffalo, N.Y., May 5.

Walter Packard, 82, agricultural engineer, planner of Greek land-reclamation program; Berkeley, Calif., Oct. 31.

Gen. Pai Chung-hsi, 73, Chiang Kai-shek's leading commander; Taipei, Taiwan, Dec. 2.

Maxfield Parrish, 95, popular artist of the early 20th century; Plainfield, N.H., March 30.

Elizabeth Patterson, 90, motion-picture character actress; Los Angeles, Calif., Jan. 31.

Richard C. Patterson, Jr., 80, former U.S. diplomat and New York City official; New York City, Sept. 30.

Alice Pearce, 47, theater, motion-picture and TV comedienne; Los Angeles, Calif., March 3.

Jean-Pierre Peugeot, 70, French automobile maker; Paris, Oct. 18.

Joseph E. Ridder, 80, publisher; West Palm Beach, Fla., April 20.

Dr. Oswald H. Robertson, 79, a developer of the blood bank; Santa Cruz, Calif., March 23.

James Rorimer, 60, director, Metropolitan Museum of Art; New York City, May 11.

Robert Rossen, 57, Academy Award-winning director (*All the King's Men*); New York City, Feb. 18.

Mari Sandoz, 65, writer specializing in stories of the Old West; New York City, March 10.

Abraham Michael Saperstein, 63, sports promoter, founder-owner, the Harlem Globetrotters; Chicago, Ill., March 15.

Paul Reynaud, 87, French politician, and premier when France was overrun by Germans in 1940; Neuilly, France, Sept. 21.

Wide World

Billy Rose, 66, songwriter, Broadway theater producer, nightclub owner; Montego Bay, Jamaica, Feb. 10.

Wide World

Margaret Sanger, 82, founder of the birth-control movement; Tucson, Ariz., Sept. 6.

Wide World

René Schick-Gutierrez, 56, president of Nicaragua and foe of Castro regime; Managua, Nicaragua, Aug. 3.

Delmore Schwartz, 52, poet (1959 winner of Bollingen Prize), editor and critic; New York City, July 11.

Elliott M. See, Jr., 38, U.S. astronaut; St. Louis, Mo., Feb. 28.

Robert G. Shand, 70, 17 years managing editor, New York *Daily News*; New York City, Nov. 25.

Alfred P. Sloan, Jr., 90, former president and chairman of General Motors Corp., philanthropist; New York City, Feb. 17.

H. Alexander Smith, 86, U.S. Senator (R-N.J., 1944–59); Princeton, N.J., Oct. 27.

Lillian Smith, 68, novelist (*Strange Fruit*); Atlanta, Ga., Sept. 28.

Bob Swift, 51, American League baseball catcher and manager; Detroit, Mich., Oct. 17.

Helen Tamiris, 64, dancer and choreographer; New York City, Aug. 4.

Deems Taylor, 80, composer, author, critic, painter, translator; New York City, July 3.

Albert Thomas, 67, member, U.S. House of Representatives (D-Tex., 1937–66); Washington, Feb. 15.

Alexander Trachtenberg, 82, publisher and chief distributor of Marxist books in the United States; New York City, Dec. 16.

Randy Turpin, 37, world middleweight boxing champion 1951; Leamington, England, May 17.

Luis Turcios, 24, leader of Guatemala's Rebel Armed Forces; Guatemala City, Oct. 2.

Irita Van Doren, 75, editor (1926–63), *New York Herald Tribune*'s Sunday book review; New York City, Dec. 18.

Guy Warner Vaughan, 82, president, Curtiss-Wright Corp. (1935–49); New Rochelle, N.Y., Nov. 21.

Georg Von Hevesy, 80, Hungarian winner 1943 Nobel Prize for Chemistry; Freiburg, West Germany, July 5.

Count Felix Von Luckner, 85, German naval hero of World War I; Malmo, Sweden, April 13.

Wieland Wagner, 49, director, Bayreuth Wagner Festival, grandson of Richard Wagner; Munich, Oct. 16.

Mark S. Watson, 75, correspondent *The Baltimore Sun*, winner Pulitzer Prize and Presidential Medal of Freedom; Baltimore, Md., March 25.

Clifton Webb, 72, stage and screen star; Beverly Hills, Calif., Oct. 13.

Paul I. Wellman, 67, author; Los Angeles, Calif., Sept. 16.

Richard Whorf, 60, actor-director of stage, screen, TV; Santa Monica, Calif., Dec. 14.

C. E. Woolman, 76, former president, Delta Air Lines; Houston, Tex., Sept. 11.

Sir Evelyn Wrench, 84, founder of English-Speaking Union; London, Nov. 11.

Herbert J. Yates, 85, president, Republic Pictures Corp. (1935–59); Sherman Oaks, Calif., Feb. 3.

William Zorach, 79, Lithuanian-born American sculptor-painter; Bath, Me., Nov. 15.

Lal Bahadur Shastri, 61, prime minister of India from June 2, 1964; Tashkent, U.S.S.R., Jan. 11.

Wide World

Sophie Tucker, 79, vaudeville star, "Last of the Red-Hot Mamas"; New York City, Feb. 9.

UPI

Hendrik F. Verwoerd, 64, prime minister of South Africa from 1958; Cape Town, South Africa, Sept. 6.

Wide World

Evelyn Waugh, 62, British writer of satiric novels, author of *Brideshead Revisited*; Taunton, England, April 10.

UPI

Ed Wynn, 79, stage, motion-picture and TV actor; Beverly Hills, Calif., June 19.

Wide World

Dr. Fritz Zernike, 77, Nobel Prizewinner in Physics (1953); Groningen, the Netherlands, March 10.

UPI

DEFENSE. Debate over U.S. defense policy during 1966 centered in two major issues: Vietnam war strategy and whether to build a costly missile-defense system.

Antiballistic Missile System. The question of constructing an antiballistic missile (ABM) system—long in dispute—had cost some $2,000,000,000 by the end of 1966 in research and development funds, largely on the Army's Nike-X. Defense Secretary Robert S. McNamara and some military leaders favored continuing sizable expenditures on such development, but opposed actually producing and deploying the ABM. Their arguments were: (1) defensive missiles could not stop attacks of large numbers of ICBM's of ever-growing sophistication; (2) despite recurring reports, no solid evidence existed that Russia was actually building missile defenses, whereas construction of an American ABM system would start a costly and dangerous new arms race; (3) the ABM would cost $20,000,000,000 to $30,000,000,000—more expensive than any other weapons system; and (4) "the best defense is a good offense"—that is, the United States can more effectively offset the threat of thermonuclear attack by building better offensive missiles, with multiple warheads that could confuse and penetrate any defense system.

Late 1966 developments sharply altered the factual basis of the arguments. The Nike-X has been greatly improved. With its vastly improved radars, longer-range Zeus missiles that can hit ICBM's in space, and speedy Sprint missiles that can knock the ICBM's down once they have entered the atmosphere (where they can be distinguished from decoys), the Nike-X now probably can do a fairly effective job of destroying Russian missiles. Secret tests of

Nikes pitted against ICBM's demonstrated this to Pentagon skeptics. And of more immediate importance, Secretary McNamara acknowledged late in 1966 that there was considerable evidence—apparently gained from U.S. reconnaissance satellites—that Russia has begun to deploy ABM's around her major cities. This brings the United States face-to-face with the momentous decision on whether to go ahead with production and deployment of the Nike-X, or at least a skeletonized version of the system that could be expanded later into a $30,000,000,000 program if needed.

While the first two of the above arguments against the ABM have been weakened, the other two still are pertinent. Its cost, on top of the Vietnam war, would have great impact on President Johnson's Great Society programs and the U.S. economy. Moreover, McNamara stresses that planned improvements in U.S. missiles can assure that most of them get through Russia's ABM defense. Replacing the Polaris with the Poseidon missile, and an early model Minuteman with new versions, will continue to deter Russia from attacking, he argues. By the same token, the Secretary contends, the Soviets can offset an American ABM with more sophisticated ICBM's of their own.

ABM advocates concede that, judged by McNamara's "cost-effectiveness" standards, the long-standing deterrence concept may be the "best"—i.e., cheapest—way of countering Russia's missile force. But, they ask, what of the millions of Americans who would be killed if the logic of deterrence—the apparent certainty that an attacking country would be destroyed by the remaining U.S. missile force—does not persuade a half-mad or senile dictator of the Hitler or Mao Tse-tung type? Should

Combat operations center, North American Air Defense Command, Colorado Springs.

Wide World

Above: U.S. Army Sprint antimissile missile ready for firing, White Sands Missile Range, N.M. Right: Three generations of the Nike air-defense missile (l to r): Ajax, Hercules, Zeus.
Photos U.S. Army

not the United States try to save as much of the country as possible regardless of dollar costs? The Joint Chiefs of Staff and most of Congress, which approved an extra $167.9 million to gear Nike-X for actual production, believe so.

Complicating the problem is the rapid nuclear progress of Red China. McNamara says is will be 1975 before the Chinese could have long-range missiles threatening the United States, and that they could be handled by a modest ABM system.

In December, McNamara said that new U.S. intelligence estimates indicated that Russia is stepping up its ICBM production and may have a much larger force in 1968 than earlier estimates. While the former estimate of three-or-four-to-one margin in American to Soviet ICBM's now could be canceled, McNamara said that planned qualitative increases in the American missile force will assure continued U.S. superiority and safety from nuclear aggression.

Vietnam War Strategy. While American Vietnam war aims remained unaltered during 1966, there were significant developments in strategy. The buildup of U.S. combat units and logistics facilities continued, as did the bomb-

181

ing of North Vietnam, except for the 37-day pause which began in late December 1965.

President Johnson still was trying to bring the Communists to the conference table, to achieve a negotiated settlement which would end the North Vietnamese aggression in South Vietnam and permit U.S. troops to be withdrawn. While the bombing of the North was slowly accelerated and brought closer to Hanoi, it still was aimed at impeding the flow of men and supplies to the South and hurting Ho Chi Minh's regime without destroying it.

The debate between the hawks and the doves continued. The hawks were fearful that the White House might agree to a bombing pause without reciprocal communist action or a truce like that in Korea. Then the U.S. and South Korean forces had the Chinese and North Koreans on the run. The negotiations permitted the enemy to recover, and in the end caused far heavier American casualties. The doves continued to agitate for just the sort of steps that military leaders and hawks in Congress fear.

The United States expanded its troop strength in Vietnam by about 200,000 troops in 1966, and it was expected that about 400,000 U.S. troops would be there by early 1967, including the equivalent of eight army and marine divisions.

But the major change was in the role of U.S. and South Vietnamese land combat forces. Originally, the mission of American marine and army fighting units was to protect the major bases and cities and conduct limited patrols, leaving offensive operations to the South Vietnamese Army. Late in the year, however, after American troops had gradually stepped up their "spoiling" operations which blocked the enemy's offensives, came a decision to retrain and reassign most of the South Vietnamese army from "search and destroy" to "clear and hold" operations. American troops—with the elite South Vietnamese marines, paratroopers and rangers, as well as Koreans and Australians—took on the role of fighting the enemy Main Force units, which continued to grow as more men infiltrated down from the North.

The concept was that the war would last indefinitely if the pacification program could not be made to work. What was happening was that after the American and South Vietnamese troops concluded their "search and destroy" spoiling operations, and withdrew from contested areas, the enemy slipped back into control of the hamlets. "Pacification" was getting nowhere. Whether the new plan would help much was debatable, as the communist infiltration from the North continued and the enemy strength mounted despite heavy losses inflicted

by U.S. ground and air power. Administration officials said the U.S. buildup in Vietnam would level off in 1967, but there were skeptics. For, with the withdrawal of most of the South Vietnamese to static "clear and hold" duties, the skeptics predicted that more U.S. troops would be needed to fight the Red Main Force battalions.

U.S.-Soviet Space Treaty. On Dec. 8, the United States and the Soviet Union agreed on a historic treaty designed to keep the arms race from moving into space. If approved, the treaty, worked out within the United Nations, would prevent the military exploitation of the moon or other celestial bodies and ban mass-destruction weapons in space.

The effect is more psychological than immediate, as there are no known efforts to use space for military purposes. At this point, there seems no advantage to anyone in employing nuclear weapons from space. But the draft treaty does provide that the moon and stars will be used "exclusively for peaceful purposes," and thus bars any military bases or claims of national sovereignty in space.

Other Developments. There was continued debate, but little change, in some of the holdover defense-policy issues. McNamara resubmitted his controversial reserve reorganization plan, but Congress again rejected it. Many in Congress urged a call-up of the reserves, but the administration insisted that the reserves be held for a possible new emergency. McNamara still opposed the Air Force plan to develop a new heavy bomber, and dragged his feet on building nuclear-powered surface escort ships, despite Congressional pressure. There was growing criticism of the draft. President Johnson appointed a National Advisory Commission on Selective Service to study the entire draft system and make recommendations early in 1967.

JOHN G. NORRIS
Assistant Foreign Editor, THE WASHINGTON POST

DE GAULLE, CHARLES. President Charles de Gaulle in 1966 began his second seven-year term as France's chief of state, and although he passed his 76th birthday on Nov. 22, there was no public indication that he intended to retire before his new term expired.

NATO. De Gaulle, however, seemed to be acting like a man in a hurry. He moved quickly and firmly to divorce France from the North Atlantic Treaty Organization (NATO) military organization, thus, he said, ensuring France's independence of action on the world scene. He also made an 11-day tour of the Soviet Union and received Soviet Premier Aleksei N. Kosygin in France on a similar visit.

In Cambodia, Prince Norodom Sihanouk (l) and President de Gaulle enter Pnompenh stadium.

The actions against NATO and the exchange of visits between Paris and Moscow were closely connected in De Gaulle's historical vision, although even some of his closest allies doubted if his look into the future was sharp and clear.

De Gaulle shocked his NATO partners—particularly the United States—when in March he began a quickly paced series of moves to rid France of foreign—mostly U.S.—bases and NATO headquarters, by April 1, 1967. At the same time, he informed NATO that French forces would be removed from integrated NATO command July 1, 1966.

De Gaulle's allies did not reproach him so much for these blows against NATO as for his tactics. He had let it be understood that France would propose reforms for NATO, which all agreed were needed, but instead he handed out a *fait accompli*. De Gaulle contended that NATO, formed in 1949, was no longer necessary in its present form; that the threat from the Soviet Union had diminished; and that the whole Soviet bloc should be drawn closer to Western Europe, thus ending the cold war.

Travels. De Gaulle toured the Soviet Union with this *rapprochement* in mind and his reception was warm, both from officials and the public. He visited a Soviet missile-launching base and became the first foreign leader to see a Soviet rocket leave its pad. He and his Soviet hosts signed a common declaration calling for closer cooperation and regular consultation. The Soviet leaders responded with surprising speed to De Gaulle's invitation for a return visit to France, and De Gaulle used the occasion of Premier Kosygin's trip to preach his favorite theme of Europe from the Urals to the Atlantic—an appeal for the Soviet Union to break down its barriers with the West.

De Gaulle's most spectacular activity of a busy year was a three-week, round-the-world journey in August and September. There were three highlights to his trip, one unplanned. De Gaulle touched down first at Djibouti, French Somaliland, one of the few remaining chips of the once widespread French empire. He was met by rioting throngs, demanding independence. Shocked and surprised, De Gaulle withdrew his Somaliland governor and, back in Paris, promised a referendum by mid-1967 to let the residents of the African colony decide if they truly wanted independence—with a consequent cutoff of French aid—or whether they wanted to remain linked with France, with improved living conditions promised. The scheduled referendum quieted the independence fervor, at least momentarily.

De Gaulle then flew on to Pnompenh, Cambodia, using the little southeast Asian kingdom as a sounding board for his latest pronouncements on the Vietnamese war, just across Cambodia's border. Speaking in a sun-baked sports stadium, De Gaulle put the blame for the war squarely on the United States and said its forces must be withdrawn or the war could generate into a world conflict. De Gaulle made no such appeal to Hanoi, indicating that all the "aggression" in Vietnam had come from the American side. The Vietnamese, De Gaulle's thesis ran, should be let alone to settle their own affairs, without external intervention. Vietnam and all of southeast Asia would be given a status of neutrality, guaranteed by the world's great powers.

After dropping his explosive Pnompenh advice. De Gaulle winged on to the French nuclear-testing ground in the region of Tahiti. Waiting several days for weather conditions to clear on the atoll of Mururoa, De Gaulle witnessed the explosion of a French atomic bomb, pronounced himself satisfied and then returned to Paris, stopping in the French West Indies.

At his fourteenth news conference as president, convened six weeks after his return, De Gaulle again struck out at the Americans in Vietnam, sharply condemning their bombing attacks. But he had no fresh ideas as to how the conflict could be brought to the peace table.

De Gaulle used a large portion of his lecture to newsmen to deplore failure of West Germany to orient its political thinking toward Paris. De Gaulle noted bitterly that the French-West German cooperation treaty had remained largely a scrap of paper, with the Germans preferring links to Washington at the expense of Gaullist France.

DAVID M. MASON
Paris Bureau, THE ASSOCIATED PRESS

DELAWARE. On April 20 the Delaware River Basin Commission reported the Delaware River flow was the lowest ever recorded in April. . . . Former Sen. Daniel O. Hastings (R) died May 9, aged 92. . . . State NAACP leaders urged that Delaware State College (primarily a Negro institution) and the University of Delaware be consolidated. . . . On November 8 Republicans won control of both houses of the state legislature and Caleb Boggs (R) retained his U.S. Senate seat.

DEMOCRATIC PARTY. The Democratic Party during 1966 consolidated its 1964 victory at the polls by enacting into law 92 per cent of the party's platform as approved at the Democratic National Convention in Atlantic City.

The 1st and 2d sessions of the 89th Congress produced an unparalleled record of landmark legislation . . . in education, Medicare and social security, aid to Appalachia, improvement of cities, housing, recreational facilities, manpower retraining, minimum wage, voting rights, antipoverty programs and numerous other laws of long-term impact.

The National Committee undertook to support its members in Congress with special services to facilitate their use of all communications media. This included help with radio, television and audio-visual materials.

To enable candidates to run more effective election campaigns, the National Committee conducted two Candidates' Conferences calling together administration officials and political campaign experts to brief the Democratic office seekers on the techniques of political campaigning.

In addition to publishing *The Democrat* monthly, the National Committee produced numerous brochures and special campaign materials, including a 1966 campaign handbook entitled *Every One Counts,* a registration and get-out-the-vote manual entitled *Route to Victory,* and a detailed compilation of Democratic pledges and accomplishments entitled *1966 Democratic Fact Book.*

The Office of Women's Activities sponsored a Campaign Conference for Democratic women attended by some 3,600 delegates from 50 states. Other activities included the scheduling of Flying Caravan teams of prominent Democratic speakers who visited 17 states in the month of October. This division produced a 15-minute national television program entitled *Coffee with the First Lady,* featuring Mrs. Lyndon B. Johnson and Mrs. Hubert H. Humphrey.

Operation Support, an issues-education program, kept volunteers informed through a newsletter and papers prepared on special topics suggested by leaders appointed in 42 states.

In seeking broad support for programs of the party, the National Committee established a 40-state Dollars for Democrats drive aimed at stimulating direct local participation in party activity.

The Young Democratic Clubs of America, the official youth group of the party, climbed to a membership of 950,000 in 4,500 local clubs, with an additional 35,000 organized under the College Young Democrats on 700 campuses. The Democratic youth groups collected 100 boxcar loads of food, clothing, tools and medical supplies for South Vietnam.

The minority and nationality divisions of the Democratic National Committee held regional workshops for candidates and state and local party leaders. Several brochures were published, including *For the Dignity of Man* for the Negro groups.

The All Americans Council worked with various ethnic groups to broaden the base of understanding of administration programs. This council provided especially prepared information to 650 nationality newspapers and radio programs and helped create nationality sections in party headquarters of several states.

JOHN M. BAILEY
Chairman, DEMOCRATIC NATIONAL COMMITTEE

DENTISTRY. Like all professions connected with health, dentistry in 1966 was concerned with developing better methods of treatment, preventing disease and discovering causes of disease. The U.S. dental profession also took an increased interest in providing dental care for all segments of the population. Dental-insurance plans are being developed, and these, together with government-financed dental-care programs for the indigent, should make dental care more readily available.

Among the many dental problems undergoing scientific scrutiny were the prevention of caries (decay); cause and treatment of periodontal (gum) disease; improvement of oral-surgical techniques and filling materials; and early detection of oral cancer. Dentistry's scientific endeavors often extend into related health fields. For example, scientists have advanced the theory that saliva may serve as a valuable diagnostic tool. Early studies pursuing this hypothesis show that saliva appears to carry proteins indicative of some physical disorders, such as cystic fibrosis, diabetes, Paget's disease and certain circulatory disorders.

Decay Preventive. The year 1966 marked the 21st anniversary of the first installation—in Grand Rapids, Mich.—of fluoridation in a community water system. More than 80 million U.S. residents now drink fluoridated water. This dental-health measure remains the best-known decay preventive, reducing the incidence of decay in children by as much as 60 per cent.

Studies are being conducted to determine the combined effectiveness of fluoridated water used with topical applications of stannous-fluoride pastes and solutions, and fluoride dentifrices. Preliminary results indicate that each measure increases the preventive effect of fluoride.

Topical fluoride applications and fluoride dentifrices offer the possibility that adults may also experience a reduction in the incidence of decay. Examinations of U.S. Navy personnel after 6 months of such treatment disclose a reduction of decay of up to 63 per cent.

Oral Surgery. During 1966 several novel jaw-reconstruction experiments were performed. Bone grafts taken from the hip and little toe were used successfully to repair jaw fractures. Additionally, a plastic material was successfully used in animals as a replacement for the condyle—the ball-hinge and stem portion of the lower jaw.

Tooth transplantation has been attempted for many years, and researchers recently reported successful implantation of plastic teeth in animals, primarily monkeys and baboons. The plastic teeth did not cause immunologic reactions (the cause of foreign-tissue rejection); they did not require the use of antibiotics; they have maintained good function.

Filling Materials. New filling materials are being developed continually in an effort to find a material that will prevent recurring decay. One material, a translucent plastic, has demonstrated better sealing properties and longer durability. Additionally, ultrasonics has been employed experimentally to bond aluminum directly to tooth enamel, creating a solid union which prevents leakage.

Space-age technology has been used experimentally to develop stronger dental materials through a process which makes rocket parts lighter, stronger and more heat-resistant. This process involves the addition of tiny ceramic fibers—whiskers—to dental materials, increasing their strength up to 150 per cent.

Periodontal Disease. Special antibiotics and other drugs have been tested to determine their effectiveness in preventing formation of calculus—the hard, crustlike material on teeth which is a major factor in periodontal disease. Several antibiotics appear to inhibit the formation of calculus, an indication that perhaps certain strains of oral bacteria are involved in calculus formation.

Detection of Oral Cancer. Oral cytology, the taking of a smear of suspicious oral tissues, has been successfully used to detect oral cancer in its beginning stages. Dentists and public-health groups in many areas are conducting programs of early detection, and the American Dental Association has advocated the use of the cytology process by every dentist during routine oral examinations.

Cryotherapy—freezing of tissue—is being studied as a possible treatment for oral cancer, and animal experiments indicate that this treatment may have merit. However, only normal tissue has been used thus far in experiments, and studies are under way to determine the effect of cryotherapy upon tumors or abnormal tissue.

Scientists have found that oral cancers "sometimes seem to literally melt away" after injections of a certain drug—methotrexate—prior to surgery. They have emphasized that this new procedure cannot be considered a cure, since long-term survival has not been increased in the patients. However, the combination of the chemotherapy and surgery did delay recurrence of the oral tumor, appeared to reduce its size, and alleviated much of the pain associated with the tumor.

MAYNARD K. HINE, D.D.S.
President, AMERICAN DENTAL ASSOCIATION

DIEFENBAKER, JOHN G. The future of John G. Diefenbaker as leader of the opposition Conservative Party in the Canadian House of Commons was in grave doubt as 1966 ended. The former Prime Minister was rebuffed at the party association's annual meeting in November, when national president Dalton Camp, who urged a reappraisal of Diefenbaker's leadership, was returned to office by the 1,100 delegates, defeating Diefenbaker's candidate.

Diefenbaker vowed to fight on, although his chances of retaining the office appeared slim. The leadership issue caused a serious breach in the party, with older delegates—especially from rural areas—supporting Diefenbaker, and younger party members demanding a change.

The 71-year-old prairie lawyer suffered another humiliation during the year. A judicial inquiry, ordered by the Government and conducted by Justice Spence of the Supreme Court of Canada, found him negligent during his tenure as prime minister when he did not ask for the resignation of his Associate Minister of Defense, Pierre Sevigny, after learning that Sevigny was having an affair with a suspected security risk, East German immigrant Gerda Munsinger. Diefenbaker was stung by the inquiry's findings and came close to calling Justice Spence a political hatchet man. He refused to testify at the inquiry, arguing that it had been established as an act of political vengeance by the Liberal Government.

WILLIAM FRENCH
Literary Editor, TORONTO GLOBE AND MAIL

DIRKSEN, EVERETT McKINLEY. Senate Republican Leader Dirksen played such an active role in the 1966 Congressional session that some Democrats grumbled he actually was the majority leader. He was successful in his efforts to kill the bill repealing section 14(b) of the Taft-Hartley law, which allows states to ban the union shop, and the civil-rights bill with its open-housing provision. Dirksen led filibusters against both bills.

However, he failed to push through the Senate two constitutional amendments by which he set great store. They were aimed at controversial Supreme Court decisions. One would have allowed a state to apportion one branch of its legislature on factors other than population. The other would have permitted voluntary prayers in the public schools.

Dirksen maintained his close relations with President Johnson throughout the year and continued his firm support of Johnson's Vietnam war policy. He tried to cut back several of the President's spending programs in the Senate but had little success. In May the Illinois Senator fractured his right hip in a fall and underwent surgery at Walter Reed Hospital. Thereafter he hobbled around the Capitol on crutches but still managed to handle his customary heavy work load. In October he was operated on again to remove the pins placed in his hip. After the GOP gains in the Nov. 8 election, Dirksen predicted the ax will fall on Johnsonian spending in 1967.

JOSEPH W. HALL, JR.
Washington Bureau, THE ASSOCIATED PRESS

Canada's Opposition Leader John Diefenbaker, Feb. 13.

GOP leader Dirksen receives elephants as gift May 25.

Photos UPI

DISARMAMENT. In the field of arms control and disarmament, 1966 will certainly be remembered as a year of the most intensive efforts to negotiate a treaty to halt the spread of nuclear weapons. Although no concrete agreements were reached at the Geneva conference, which was in intermittent session from January to August, the session ended in an atmosphere of some optimism that was carried over into the ensuing debates of the UN General Assembly. Important differences between East and West still remain. But it is encouraging that each side has recognized publicly that the other is making a serious effort to reach agreement.

Thinking people in most parts of the world are haunted by the specter of possible failure in efforts to stop nuclear proliferation. There is no doubt that the spread of nuclear weapons to additional countries would, at best, lead to a far more troubled and unstable world environment than the one that we now know. At worst, it could lead to a kind of titanic battle in the dark, in which nations and their populations might be destroyed without ever knowing who the destroyer was.

One should not concentrate exclusively on the specter of failure in this aim. It seems at least as useful to contemplate the eventuality of success, for indeed there is a very real possibility of success.

The reason the United States has been concentrating so intensively on the negotiation of a *nonproliferation treaty* is that this seems the most logical next step, one which would create a very useful legal and psychological framework within which other measures could be carried out. If the remaining East-West differences can be bridged, and such a treaty comes into being, a number of factors will work in its favor.

The foremost of these is self-interest, the surest underpinning of any treaty. It is most unlikely that the existing nuclear-weapon powers, including Communist China, would wish to see any further dissemination of nuclear weapons. Such a treaty would also be in the interest of the nonnuclear-weapon countries, giving them at least reasonable assurance against nuclear "surprises" from their neighbors and rivals, and sparing them the tremendous expense of nuclear weapons development.

The Limited Test Ban Treaty has already been working in favor of nonproliferation since it was signed in 1963, by prohibiting all except the most difficult and expensive nuclear tests: the underground tests. Similarly the "safeguards" system of the International Atomic Energy Agency serves to halt the further

Wide World
William C. Foster, U.S. delegate to Disarmament Conference, arrives in Geneva Jan. 26 for arms-control talks.

spread of nuclear weapons. Where applied, these safeguards prevent the diversion of plutonium from peaceful to military purposes. Under the international safeguards system, a country wishing to violate a nonproliferation treaty *secretly* would encounter great obstacles. In nearly every conceivable case, moreover, the purpose of having nuclear weapons could only be served by advertising the fact.

The Inspection Problem. A nonproliferation treaty would not provide absolute assurance against the spread of nuclear weapons. It would, however, be a highly significant step, and doubtless many direct and indirect benefits would follow in its wake. But other measures also are necessary, including a comprehensive (all-environments) test ban, which would prohibit underground tests as well as the others.

The United States has been spending over $50 million a year on improving techniques for the distant detection and identification of underground nuclear explosions, and has made great progress in this field. Under the present state of technology it would be able in most (but not all) cases to distinguish between a natural earth tremor and an underground explosion. A comprehensive test ban therefore must provide additional assurance by allowing for a limited number of on-site inspections. It would not be necessary to send an inspection team to the source of every doubtful earth tremor. But the Soviets, not wishing to permit inspections on their territory, insist that "national"—meaning "distant"—means of detection are sufficient.

The problem therefore boils down to this: How long, in the face of such modern facts of life as mass education, mass communications and scientific intelligence gathering, can this ancient Russian obsession with secrecy hold out? The question is central, for even if the problem of identifying underground explosions is solved, the need for inspections will become increasingly important in those later stages of the arms-control process in which an attempt is made to halt the arms race among nuclear-weapon powers.

China. Communist China, of course, presents a special problem. Ultimately, if an international system of arms control and disarmament measures is to be effective, every militarily significant power, including mainland China, must subscribe to it. At present, however, even if China did not sign a nonproliferation treaty, this omission probably would not have any effect on the treaty's operation. And over the long haul, nonproliferation is as much in the interest of mainland China as of anyone else. More extensive measures of arms control and disarmament lie much farther into the future, at which time, hopefully, the present frenzy of China may have been replaced by a more pragmatic outlook on world affairs. Meanwhile, it is the task of other governments to build the edifice, as it were, so that there will be maximum pressures on China to enter into it, in its own self-interest.

Although the official definition of the term "arms control" is no less than a paragraph long, for most purposes it can be defined simply as *efforts to reduce the likelihood of war and to limit its scope if it occurs.* Stated another way, the advocates of arms control are trying to buy time until more satisfactory world peace-keeping arrangements can be evolved. While halting the further spread of nuclear weapons might in itself seem to be a limited objective, it is, of course, absolutely crucial. It should be remembered, also, that one peaceful initiative is apt to lead to another.

WILLIAM C. FOSTER
Director
U.S. ARMS CONTROL AND DISARMAMENT AGENCY

DISASTERS

JANUARY	7	Mozambique: After sweeping through Mozambique for four days, cyclone slashes into Rhodesia and South Africa; "several dozen" killed, 150,-000 homeless.
	11-13	Brazil: Rio de Janeiro hit by severe floods and landslides; 239 killed.
	14	Colombia: Avianca Airlines DC-4 crashes into shark-infested waters off Cartagena; 56 dead.
	24	France: An Air India Boeing 707 jetliner, bound for New York, crashes into a ridge near the three-mile-high summit of Mont Blanc; all 117 aboard dead.
	25	Indonesia: Indonesian state-oil-company ship *Permina* sinks near Belawan; at least 89 drowned.
		South Vietnam: U.S. Air Force transport plane crashes near Ankhe; 46 U.S. servicemen dead.
	28	West Germany: A Lufthansa Convair Metropolitan crashes while attempting to land at Bremen Airport; all 46 aboard killed.
	30	Pakistan: A passenger launch and a steamer collide at Chandpur Port in the Brahmaputra Delta region of East Pakistan; 80 killed, 38 injured.
	31	United States: Severe winter storms hit North Atlantic and southern sections of the United States; at least 166 persons dead.

UPI

FEBRUARY   4   Japan: Minutes away from Tokyo Airport, a Boeing 727 jet airliner plunges into Tokyo Bay; 133 killed.
         7   Kashmir: Indian F-27 airliner reported missing; 37 persons aboard.
      17   Soviet Union: A Soviet TU-114, the world's largest airliner, crashes on takeoff from Moscow; 48 killed.

MARCH   3-4   United States: A line of tornadoes smashes across Mississippi and Alabama; at least 62 dead 508 injured.
        4   Japan: A Canadian Pacific jetliner crashes at Tokyo Airport; 64 killed.
        5   Japan: A British Boeing 707 jetliner bursts into flames at foot of Mount Fuji; all 124 aboard killed.
      10   Jordan: Floods hit desert area of south Jordan; 57 dead, more than 3,000 homeless.
      11   Japan: Fire destroys two ski-resort hotels in Minakami; 31 killed.
      18   United Arab Republic: About to land at Cairo Airport, a Soviet-built Egyptian airliner crashes in sandstorm; 30 dead.
  20 & 22   Uganda: Series of earthquakes strikes Ruwenzori foothills; at least 79 dead.
      28   Brazil: Torrential rains in Rio de Janeiro area; about 40 persons lose lives.

APRIL   20   India: Explosion rocks passenger train at Diphu station; 55 killed.
      22   United States: A chartered airliner crashes into a wooded area of south Oklahoma; 81 dead.
      24   India: Another explosion occurs on a passenger train, west of Diphu; 40 killed.
      26   Soviet Union: Severe earthquake strikes Soviet city of Tashkent; about 8 dead, 35,000 families homeless, 28,000 buildings destroyed.
      27   Peru: Lansa Airlines Constellation crashes in Andes Mountains; 49 killed.
      30   Indonesia: Authorities report the eruption of Mount Kelut volcano in eastern Java; 82 known dead, 52 injured, 60 missing.

MAY   14   Ecuador: Landslide near Quito; 52 dead.
      18   Congo (Kinshasa): Earthquake strikes Beni in North Kivu Province; 90 dead, 20 injured.
   27-31   Brazil: Heavy rains cause severe flooding at Recife and nearby towns; 93 killed, 13,000 homeless.

JUNE   5-6   Honduras: Thirty inches of rain destroys western town of San Rafael; 73 reported killed.
      8   United States: Tornado strikes Topeka, Kans.; 14 known dead, more than 300 hurt, damage estimated at $100 million.
      13   India: Two suburban trains collide 9 miles outside of Bombay; 60 dead, over 106 injured.
      27   Nepal: Earthquake strikes mountainous area of western Nepal; about 100 dead, 20,000 homeless.
      28   Japan: Typhoon Kit sweeps across Japan's biggest island, Honshu; at least 32 dead.

In June, two weeks of heavy rains cause severe flooding in Hong Kong; at least 150 dead.

Rain-soaked coal waste slides down a mountainside at Aberfan, a small mountain village in Wales, Oct. 21; 144 persons, mostly children, killed.

JULY   15-26   South Korea: Torrential rains pound South Korea; 59 dead.

AUGUST   6   United States: A Braniff jet airliner crashes near Falls City, Neb.; all 42 aboard killed.
    19   Turkey: Devastating earthquake hits eastern Turkey; an estimated 2,300 dead, 1,500 injured.

SEPTEMBER   1   Yugoslavia: A Britannia Airways turboprop chartered by vacationers crashes while approaching Ljubljana Airport in northern Yugoslavia; 96 Britons killed.
    25   Japan: Two typhoons strike the area of Tokyo and southern Japan; 174 known dead, 140 missing, more than 700 injured.

OCTOBER   3   Cuba: A 24-ft. boat filled with Cuban refugees on way to the United States overturns in the Straits of Florida; 44 dead.
    10-14   Mexico: Hurricane Inez hits sections of Haiti, Cuba, Florida, Gulf of Mexico, eastern Mexico; at least 223 killed.
    17   Peru: Severe earthquake jolts Lima and Callao; an estimated 125 dead, 800 injured.
    26   Vietnam: Fire on U.S. carrier *Oriskany* in Gulf of Tonkin; 43 lost.

NOVEMBER   4-5   Italy: Sections of Italy—particularly culture-rich city of Florence—hit by worst floods in that nation's history; 113 reported dead, damage estimated at over $2,500,000,000.
    13   Japan: Japanese airliner en route to a honeymoon resort on Shikoku Island crashes while landing; all 50 aboard killed.
    18   South Africa: Bus plunges 200 feet into Jmhloti River near Ngomweni; at least 40 lost.
    24   Czechoslovakia: Tabso Airways Klyushin 18 crashes near Bratislava; all 82 aboard killed.

DECEMBER   8   Greece: A 16-ton refrigerator trailer, loosened from its mooring by a severe storm in the Aegean Sea, tears open and sinks a passenger ferryship; 234 drowned.
    24   South Vietnam: A four-engine U.S. cargo plane crashes near Danang air base; 111 dead, 18 injured, 13 missing.

DOMINICAN REPUBLIC. Joaquin Balaguer, 59, was sworn in July 1, 1966, as president of the problem-plagued Dominican Republic. Representatives of 33 nations, including U.S. Vice-President Hubert H. Humphrey, gathered for the inauguration, an event standing in sharp contrast to the despair and paralysis generated by the bloody civil war that began in April 1965. Balaguer was winner over former President Juan Bosch by a margin of nearly a quarter million votes. At year's end his chances for completing his four-year term seemed to rest largely in the hands of Bosch and his followers.

The United States, which poured $148 million in aid into the stricken nation during the 14 months of civil war, offered solid backing to the new Government. Vice-President Humphrey told the Dominicans: "I bring you the assurance that President Johnson has pledged the cooperation of the United States in mutual efforts under the Alliance for Progress program to advance the social and economic well-being of the Dominican people."

Balaguer's Reformist Party (PR) won 22 of the 27 seats in the Senate and 48 of the 74 seats in the Chamber of Deputies, further strengthening his hand in coping with urgent and critical economic and political problems.

Balaguer's Task. Unemployment, estimated at 30 per cent of the labor force, a huge foreign debt and stagnation of the economy—although it was in part alleviated by the massive injections of U.S. aid—rank as the most pressing economic problems.

Politically, wounds of the 1965 civil war have not healed completely, and a key factor will be the degree of success of Balaguer's government of "national unity," principally with Bosch and his Dominican Revolutionary Party (PRD), the only other major political party.

Balaguer, a bachelor, entered government service shortly after graduation from law school. He served as president in the last days of the late Rafael L. Trujillo's dictatorship, and for several months after Trujillo was assassinated in 1961. He was forced into exile in 1962.

In his first months in office, Balaguer launched a vigorous attack against a major national problem—an inflated, overpaid governmental bureaucracy. The main impact of the effort to streamline this sector was the reduction, on a sliding scale, of salaries of all public workers earning more than $200 monthly. For the majority of these employees, the new policy represented a pay cut of 15 to 20 per cent. At the top-heavy executive level, however, some salaries were sliced in half. The president's paycheck was reduced from $1,500 to $750 monthly.

The President also slashed electricity rates by 25 per cent to ease inflationary pressures against the poor, and imposed severe restrictions on automobiles and other luxury items.

Presence of Foreign Soldiers. Balaguer's first months in office were aided by the continued presence in the Dominican Republic of the Inter-American Peace Force (IAPF), which in late September ended nearly 17 months of service in the country. The controversial, six-nation force, whose "muscle" reached 30,000, left Santo Domingo during a 90-day period of staggered withdrawal—a method which enabled it to supervise the peace, after the elections.

Many countries that had voted for creation of the IAPF were unable to cope with political pressures at home, and failed to contribute troops. As a result, the United States bore the brunt of supplying the manpower involved, contributing some 23,000 troops. Brazil, Nicaragua, Paraguay, Honduras and Costa Rica supplied the remainder. In 17 months of peace-keeping services, the U.S. forces suffered 32 fatalities, although not all of them battle casualties.

Denounced by all Dominican factions as "occupation troops," the peace-force members nevertheless played a valuable role in the pacification of the country after the civil war. They not only halted hostilities between rival military factions, but established a buffer zone between them and, in their last months, preserved law and order while Dominicans secured their new constitutional government.

A month after the withdrawal of the IAPF, Bosch announced plans to leave the country and travel abroad, and hinted at possible retirement from politics. His PRD leadership was inherited by the Leftist element of the party, and the purge of pro-Bosch moderates that ensued may forebode political problems ahead for Balaguer's government of "national unity."

The Future. Dominican economists estimate that Balaguer will need a minimum of $100 million, and probably more, to consolidate his Government and get the economy moving—hopefully in 1967.

The United States is offering the country aid programs stressing economic development rather than budget balancing. Much of the aid supplied the country during the civil war went to balance the Dominican budget, and provide emergency funds to keep the country running.

FRANCIS L. McCARTHY
Latin-America Editor
UNITED PRESS INTERNATIONAL

DRUGS

By JAMES L. GODDARD, M.D.

Commissioner, U.S. FOOD AND DRUG ADMINISTRATION

Never before was interest and concern over public health greater than it was in 1966. Much of the concern was triggered by widespread publicity in the United States about the safety and use of certain drugs. What is being done to protect the consumer?

Drug Control

About 22,000 different drugs were available in 1966, and many more will be added each year. Drug manufacturers spent about $317 million in 1965 on research and development of drugs for human use. The drug industry and U.S. Food and Drug Administration share a joint responsibility: to ensure that the fruits of this work will benefit health and impose no hidden risks. How is this done?

The Food, Drug, and Cosmetic Act of 1938 required for the first time that drugs be proven safe before marketing. More than 90 per cent of the drugs now called for in physicians' prescriptions were developed after this requirement went into effect. Advances in drug therapy since 1938 have exceeded all previous advances. At the same time, many drugs believed promising in the early stages have been abandoned when required testing revealed that they could be injurious.

The Kefauver-Harris Drug Amendments of 1962 called for proof of effectiveness as well as safety and tightened other controls over drugs. The first step in FDA's controls over new drugs is in the Investigational New Drug (IND) process. During the IND stage, the sponsoring company learns whether the drug is safe and effective for human use, and whether, when manufactured in quantity, it will be stable and of uniform composition and activity.

Before the product is tested on human subjects, the sponsor must notify FDA. At that time, the sponsor outlines the plan for the proposed investigation, describes the composition and processing of the compound, and reports the results of previously conducted animal studies. FDA can stop the investigation for several reasons: if it finds that animal tests were inadequate or falsely reported, if the clinical plan is not sound, or if experience shows that continued investigation is unsafe. The sponsor must make periodic progress reports to FDA, and promptly inform the administration of any adverse effects resulting from tests.

Until 1962, FDA had no sure way of knowing how drugs fared in clinical testing. Some sponsors informed FDA scientists of the beginning and progress of tests, but in many cases the Government knew of the work only after its completion. Before the 1962 amendments, distribution of investigational drugs became more lax: there was an almost commercial distribution of some drugs labeled "For Investigational Use Only."

Competence and integrity of investigators are the key to safe new drugs. There have been cases of investigators who were not experts as claimed, or who turned their work over to inexperienced technicians. In other instances, studies reported were not actually carried out, and adverse reactions were suppressed. Such practices are a menace to public health.

In FDA control of drugs, the Investigational New Drug process is followed by the New Drug Application stage. In this stage, FDA scientists evaluate all experimental data on animal and human testing. The scientists study, as well, the drug's formula; a description of manufacturing procedures and controls; claims for the drug; directions and warning on package inserts and promotional materials. If the FDA scientists determine that the drug's usefulness outweighs its possible dangers, it goes on the market, usually as a prescription drug.

Following the New Drug Application stage comes Postmarketing Surveillance by FDA. Some undesirable effects of drugs do not show up until they are widely used. Therefore after the drug is marketed, manufacturers must report to FDA all new information on the drug, including any untoward effects that have been discovered. New drugs' labeling and advertising may then have to carry new warnings, and if a drug turns out to be dangerous, FDA approval is withdrawn.

FDA has a comprehensive program for collecting, evaluating and disseminating information about the reactions to every drug on the market. In 1966 (at the request of FDA) the National Academy of Science–National Research Council undertook a program to evaluate the effectiveness of 3,000 to 4,000 drugs introduced between 1938 and 1962.

Quality Control

Another requirement of the 1962 drug legislation is that drugs be processed, packed and held under adequate manufacturing controls. Prior to 1962, most U.S. drug manufacturers had exercised quality control to produce flawless drugs. Unfortunately, however, the staffs of some drug houses lacked proper facilities, equipment and technical competence. The life of the consumer was endangered. To protect consumers, "good manufacturing practices" provisions were enacted, and guidelines were set forth for drug companies to follow in construction, equipment, personnel, manufacturing methods, facilities and controls.

Two quality-control seminars have been held jointly by FDA, the Pharmaceutical Manufacturers Association and the University of Wisconsin School of Pharmacy and Extension Services in Pharmacy. Participants from all areas of the drug industry enrolled in the seminars. Another educational measure to improve quality control of drugs is FDA inspection of manufacturing plants at least every two years.

Despite general improvement in quality controls, both mechanical and human errors creep in. These errors require recall of marketed drugs; 538 were recalled between July 1965 and June 1966. Some explanations for faulty products lay in nonsterility, contamination with foreign substances, low or excess potency, decomposition, and label mix-ups. When errors do occur, the drug industry has the responsibility of correcting them; the Government has an obligation to see that the corrective actions are adequate.

Drug Abuse

Drugs properly used are a blessing to the sick. The same drugs are a curse to persons who become habituated to them. Congress enacted the Drug Abuse Control Amendments of 1965 because the abuse of certain drugs had become a major health problem.

The Food and Drug Administration has estimated that over 9,000,000,000 barbiturate (depressant) and amphetamine (stimulant) capsules and tablets are manufactured annually in the United States. About half of them are sold illegally, many by organized bootleg rings. High profits have attracted criminals. For example, amphetamines can be purchased wholesale for $1.00 per thousand, sold in the illegal market at $30 to $50 per thousand and peddled for as much as 10 to 25 cents each.

There are many legitimate medical uses for barbiturates, amphetamines and other, similar prescription drugs. However, the hallucinogenic drug LSD (lysergic acid diethylamide), which made headlines in 1966, has never been approved by FDA for distribution, except to a limited number of clinical investigators. Nineteen sixty-six brought a marked increase in the illicit use of stimulant and hallucinogenic drugs, particularly around educational institutions, and some unwisely experimented with the psychiatric effects of LSD.

Nonmedical use and abuse of hallucinogenic drugs and of central-nervous-system stimulants and depressants contribute to the rising death toll on the highways, to juvenile delinquency, violent and bizarre crimes, suicides, and other antisocial and abnormal behavior. Drug Abuse Control Amendments provided stronger regulation over drugs that have a potential for abuse. (Narcotics such as heroin and cocaine are controlled by the Treasury Department.) The law has established a system that requires clear identification of manufacturers, wholesalers and distributors. Legislation also provides for careful record keeping, which makes it possible to check and to account for the distribution of every pill manufactured.

ECONOMICS: A LOOK AT THE UNITED STATES' "NEW ECONOMICS"

By ARTHUR M. OKUN
Member, COUNCIL OF ECONOMIC ADVISERS

"The New York Times"
Two members of the Council of Economic Advisers: Chairman Gardner Ackley, right; member Arthur M. Okun, left.

The term "new economics" has been coined to describe the policy strategy of the Kennedy-Johnson administrations: the consistent and coordinated use of many policy tools to promote full and stable prosperity on a continuing basis. Under all four postwar presidents, economic policies have followed the precepts of the Employment Act of 1946, which charges the Federal Government to promote "maximum employment, production and purchasing power." But there have been important innovations in economic policy and performance in the 1960's.

The period of uninterrupted economic expansion since February 1961 has no parallel in U.S. history. Between the Civil War and 1961, the U.S. economy experienced 24 recessions or depressions. Intervals of economic expansion typically lasted 2 to 3 years, only to yield to a period of declining production and rising unemployment. Long-term growth formed a pattern of 2 steps forward followed by 1 step back. Recurrent recessions often were viewed as an inevitable fact of economic life.

Keynesian Concepts

It is a fundamental tenet of the "new economics" that recessions should not be accepted fatalistically. The Government does not always have the wisdom or the ability to prevent cumulative fluctuations. But policies should work continuously to sustain economic expansion, recognizing that a good offense is the best defense against recession. This strategy can be pursued without extending government control and without impinging on the freedom of private choice. For policies to sustain prosperity operate through the traditional responsibilities of government—to tax and spend for public needs, and to create money and regulate credit.

These traditional fiscal and monetary actions contribute to prosperity if they improve the balance of supply and demand. The nation enjoys stable prosperity when total demand for goods and services matches the productive capacity of its labor force and capital stock. When, however, demand sags below the level of supply capabilities, men are put out of work, and machines become idle. A weakening of

194

total demand tends to feed on itself, often turning into recession. On the other hand, when people try to buy more than the economy can produce, inflationary forces are unleashed in a boom which can easily turn into a bust. These principles were first set forth thirty years ago by the British economist John Maynard Keynes. They remain the basic guides for policy action to help maintain the overall balance between demand and supply.

Purchasing Power and Balance of the Economy

Taxes and government expenditures affect the economy's balance by changing the flow of purchasing power. Taxes cut into the income that individuals and business firms have available for buying goods and services. Higher taxes therefore mean lower levels of private demand, while lower taxes stimulate private spending. On the other side, government expenditures reverse the tax procedure, putting purchasing power into the hands of businesses and consumers. Thus the Government can increase total demand either by spending more or by taxing less.

The monetary policies of the Federal Reserve System affect demands for credit-financed expenditures by changing the costs and availability of funds. When money is tight, it becomes expensive and difficult to borrow, and this curbs spending for homes, household appliances, autos, business plant and equipment and inventories. Easy money turns the situation around and stimulates spending.

Because the "new economics" puts primary emphasis on the balance between supply and demand, it cannot give top priority to balancing the Federal Budget. Sometimes deficits are required to provide fiscal stimulus. At other times, the economy needs the restraint of budgetary surpluses. On this issue, the "new economics" clashed with a traditional view that balance of the Federal Budget was the first test of responsible fiscal policy. In the initial years of the Kennedy administration, the economy clearly had inadequate demand and excessive unemployment. A fiscal stimulus was needed. The administration waged an intensive educational campaign to convince the American public that balance of the economy deserved priority over balance in the budget.

From 1964 to 1966

The successful culmination of this educational effort and the most outstanding victory of the "new economics" came early in 1964. At that time, the U.S. Congress enacted the major tax cut that had been first proposed by President Kennedy in January 1963, and that was turned into legislative reality by President Johnson. The Revenue Act of 1964 lowered personal and corporate income taxes by $14,-000,000,000.

As economists had predicted, the income-tax cut showed up mainly in added spending in shops and markets. The increased consumer spending in turn provided many new jobs. With lower business taxes and stronger consumer markets, business investment spending expanded vigorously. Temporarily, the Federal deficit increased, but a mighty growth in tax revenues followed from the upsurge in individual and business incomes. The big tax cut was generally hailed as a success.

President Johnson continued the strategy, and Federal excise taxes were cut in June 1965. Fiscal policies were buttressed by other measures: the administration's wage-price guideposts for responsible private decisions, manpower policies to provide job training and information, and special techniques to improve the balance of payments. As of mid-1965 the economy was moving briskly ahead toward full employment while maintaining essential price stability.

At this point, the unexpected step-up in defense requirements for Vietnam stimulated economic activity. Employment and output rose rapidly in late 1965 and early 1966, and unemployment shrank to 4 per cent of the civilian labor force. But inflationary pressures rose.

For the first time, the "new economics" was confronted with a level of total demand that threatened to outrun supply. Stabilization policy demonstrated that it could and would work both ways. Monetary policy shifted strongly to restraint, after nearly five years in which it had actively supported expansion. In January 1966, the President held down the nondefense budget, and proposed several small, but cumulatively significant, tax increases.

Once the restraining actions took effect, a more moderate and satisfactory pace of overall economic advance was resumed in the spring of 1966. But excessive demands continued to strain the capital-goods industries. The President therefore returned to the Congress in September, requesting a temporary suspension of the investment tax credit on machinery and equipment and of tax provisions for accelerated depreciation on new buildings.

The blemished price record of 1966 testifies to the limitations of economic policy. But monetary and fiscal restraints on demand have worked to improve the outlook for prices. The basic health of the U.S. economy has been maintained with the assistance of the Government's active stabilization policies.

EDUCATION

By FRED M. HECHINGER
Education Editor, THE NEW YORK TIMES

Integration. The most heated controversy in education during 1966 involved the enforcement of guidelines for public school desegregation by the U.S. Office of Education. U.S. Commissioner of Education Harold Howe 2d became the target of outspoken attacks by Southern members of Congress, who charged that his field agents, in checking on compliance by local school districts, had been acting arrogantly. Mr. Howe defended his staff's actions before a special session of the House Rules Committee. He pointed out that his office was merely doing as Congress ordered, through Title VI of the Civil Rights Act of 1964. Under this law, no Federal money may be given to any facility that remains segregated by law.

The controversy revealed that prior to issuance of the guidelines in 1964, that is, during the 10 years following the Supreme Court ruling against school segregation, fewer than 1 per cent of the three million Negro children in the states of the former Confederacy had been enrolled in schools alongside white children. By contrast, between 1964 and 1966, as a result of the guidelines, the total had risen to 6 per cent. In 1966 it probably increased to above 10 per cent.

An amendment to the Elementary and Secondary Education Act, passed after heated Congressional debate, limited the period during which the commissioner may in future defer Federal funds. He may now do so only for 90 days before a hearing is granted to the district.

The controversy was not confined to the South. A number of communities in the North felt determined pressure by civil-rights groups to speed integration in areas where *de facto* segregated housing has created predominantly Negro schools. In New York City, a group of parents in East Harlem demanded that either the new Intermediate School 201 be integrated, or that they be given a significant measure of community control in the determination of the curriculum and even the selection of staff. The Board of Education appointed a task force of leading citizens from a variety of fields to determine how slum schools could best be improved, and how the community could be invited to participate, without endangering the integrity of personnel policies.

The integration and school improvement problem led to some significant experimentation. New York University announced plans to "adopt" a school in a predominantly Negro section of Brooklyn. It proposed to use professors from its School of Education and undergraduates from the university to work with the school's regular teaching force and, at the same time, revise teacher-training procedures.

In Hartford, Conn., and in Boston, Negro children from poor urban sections were enrolled in the schools of a number of privileged suburbs to which they commuted daily by special bus.

Enrollment. As during every previous year, all levels of U.S. education set new records. The overall enrollment was 56 million, a 2.6 per cent increase over 1965. Higher education saw the most significant rise—from 5.5 million to 6 million, or 9.1 per cent.

High school enrollments were estimated to be up 2.3 per cent, with a new total of 13.3 million students. Of these about 1.3 million were in nonpublic schools, the majority Roman Catholic parochial schools.

Kindergarten through eighth grade stood at 36.6 million, a 1.7 per cent gain. The nonpublic enrollment was 5.4 million, an increase of 100,000.

Preschool and Graduate Training. The pressure, despite these records, continued for even more schooling. In 1965 the Educational Policies Commission of the National Education Association called for the extension of free and universal schooling by two years beyond high school. This was to be achieved by community colleges. In 1966, the same policy group recommended that preschool education be made available to all children at age 4. The commission pointed out that of the 8.4 million youngsters in the 4- to 5-year age group, about 3.4 million are currently enrolled in private or public pre-

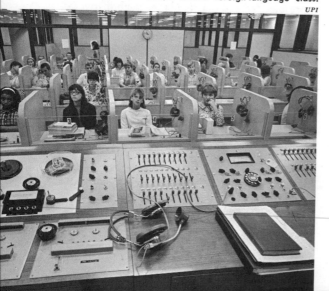

Nova School in Fort Lauderdale, Fla., is an educational test tube. Here students attend foreign language class.

school nursery or kindergarten classes. It called for similar privileges for any of the remaining 5 million whose parents wish them.

Preschooling also continued to be an important part of nationwide efforts to wipe out the handicaps of disadvantaged children. Summer Head Start programs, financed by the Office of Economic Opportunity, for the second year enrolled over 500,000 children in public and private centers. And the year-around Head Start program provided instruction for well over 150,000 children.

The preschool programs did not escape some sharp criticism, however. An evaluation report by Dr. Max Wolff, an urban sociologist, indicated that while the best of the preschool centers significantly raised the deprived children's learning readiness, the gains were quickly wiped out unless an equally effective kindergarten or school program followed.

One of the problems of year-around preschool programs was underlined in New York City. There 5,000 kindergarten applicants and 7,500 preschoolers found themselves stranded on a waiting list for lack of facilities. These Head Start growing pains merely bore out earlier warnings by Dr. Martin Deutsch, pioneer of the preschool movement, not to underestimate the need for careful preparation and teacher training. Nevertheless, all indications were that the concept of an earlier start would continue to be an important part of American educational thinking. Dr. Deutsch's experimentation and teaching were given added support when his entire research institute was made part of New York University.

While education for children before the traditional school starting age gathered momentum, an obverse trend continued to extend education beyond college graduation. Ten per cent more of the members of the class of 1966 than of 1965 were going on to graduate study. Amherst College reported that 90 per cent of its graduates were planning to go to graduate school, and at the College of the City of New York the total stood near 80 per cent. While the draft may be contributing to this trend, all indications are that the movement was well started before the beginning of conscription for service in Vietnam. And the 1966 class of girls at Radcliffe, who are not subject to military service, reached an all-time high of 75 per cent of graduate-school attendance.

Finances. It followed naturally that the new enrollment records have brought with them new highs in expenditures. Tentative government statistics indicated that during the 1965–66 year about $45,100,000,000, or 6.7 per cent of the gross national product, had been spent for

Office of Economic Opportunity
Migrant children in Head Start program, Eagle Pass, Tex.

education on all levels, public and private. This expenditure, it was predicted, will rise to $48,-800,000,000 in the 1966–67 fiscal year.

The Federal share of this total amount has risen to $6,100,000,000. As recently as 1964, the Washington contribution was only $2,300,-000,000.

Congress, in renewing the Elementary and Secondary Education Act, gave the schools $6,200,000,000 for two years, about $700 million more than President Johnson had asked. New authorizations for the Higher Education Facilities Act for a three-year period rose to $3,500,000,000. In addition, under the National Defense Education Act of 1958, Congress approved $190 million for college student loans in 1967 and $225 million in the following year.

The American Association of University Professors, in its study of the economic conditions of college teaching, disclosed that faculty salaries had risen by 7.3 per cent over those of 1965. Yet a wide gap remained between the richest and the poorest institutions. At the top-rated schools, full professors received average salaries of $23,290, while colleges at the bottom of the list were paying men of the same rank an average of only $7,160.

The rising cost of higher education was repeatedly underlined. The University of Pittsburgh, which had engaged in a crash program of academic self-improvement, as a result found itself with a $19.6 million deficit. It had to ask the state of Pennsylvania to assume greater responsibility for the institution's management and support.

In the South, the Ford Foundation launched a campaign of upgrading higher education and gave a number of universities grants totaling $33.5 million. This important move followed the disclosure by Dr. Allan M. Cartter in *An Assessment of Quality in Graduate Education,* published by the American Council on Education, that no Southern university had yet entered the "distinguished" category but that several of them stood on the threshold.

In New York, Columbia University launched a $200 million-fund campaign and announced that $75 million of the total would be used to endow 100 faculty chairs. The Ford Foundation simultaneously gave Columbia $35 million, but specified that $10 million would have to be used for efforts to involve the institution in urban and minorities affairs. It was the largest grant ever given to one single institution by the foundation. Previously, $25 million had been given to Stanford University, New York University and the University of Chicago.

The nation's public schools experienced a severe shortage of teachers, the most serious scarcity in a decade. A number of states, in order to man the classrooms, had to lower the qualifications for teacher licensing. Others appealed to college-educated housewives and to retired teachers to return to the classroom.

"Hi, Ma'am! I'm the future you're supposed to shape"
"The Kansas City Star"

Somewhat ironically, in view of the need for teachers, especially in the most needy districts, the newly created National Teacher Corps, originated to bring relief to such areas, ran into Congressional opposition. Because of appropriation cuts, the corps put only 1,200 teachers into the field in 1966, far short of its original goal of 4,000. Unless Congress provides additional funds, the $7.5 million given the corps for the 1967 academic year will barely last until June 30, and will not permit recruiting and training of a new group.

The Notre Dame University Press published an extensive survey of the conditions of parochial education in a volume, *Catholic Schools in Action.* The study indicated that not quite half of the nation's 11.5 million school-age Catholic children are enrolled in parochial schools. It also warned that, in order merely to hold the line at that proportion, a school construction expenditure of $721.6 million will be necessary by 1968.

Student Protest. The rebellion of U.S. college students was less strident in 1966 than in 1965. But the students' complaints, far from being forgotten, had already begun to effect some reforms of campus life and the curriculum. Two important books, outlining such reforms, were produced. At Columbia, sociologist Daniel Bell, acting as a one-man committee to stimulate faculty discussion on the necessity for change, wrote *The Reforming of General Education.* He urged that universities put an end to excessive specialization by undergraduates.

At Berkeley, Charles Muscatine, professor of English, produced a similar reform document, *Education at Berkeley,* in which he urged the creation of a special, high-powered board to bring about innovation and experimentation. The faculty senate quickly adopted the recommendation.

Finally, the U.S. Congress passed the International Education Act of 1966, which is intended to help schools and colleges improve instruction and research in this field. President Johnson moreover promised that he would create, by executive order and as a supplement to the act, a special center on international education within the U.S. Department of Health, Education, and Welfare. In this way the American education efforts abroad would no longer be linked with the State Department and thereby exposed to charges that they are mere extensions of American foreign policy. To underline the importance of education, the President also asked John W. Gardner, the Secretary of Health, Education, and Welfare, to organize a worldwide conference on the global problems of education.

EDUCATION: PRESSURES

By PAUL WOODRING

Education Editor at Large

SATURDAY REVIEW

1966 IVY LEAGUE APPLICATIONS

COLLEGES	APPLICATIONS	ACCEPTED	FRESHMAN CLASS SIZE	NEGROES ACCEPTED	NEGROES ACCEPTED LAST YEAR
Brown	4,950	1,050	625	30	30
Columbia	3,040	1,185	700	57	35
Cornell	10,450	3,575	2,300	85	70
Dartmouth	4,475	1,225	800	35	30
Harvard	6,700	1,345	1,200	40	40
Penn	7,895	2,981	1,700	75	46
Princeton	5,692	1,186	815	35	30
Yale	5,800	1,450	1,025	48	35
TOTALS:	49,002	13,997	9,165	405	316

Source: N.Y. Herald Tribune, April 15. 1966

U.S. public schools, perhaps because they are democratic institutions easily influenced by the fluctuating will of the people, are prone to correct their mistakes by swinging wildly to the opposite extreme. Only a decade ago many critics expressed alarm that our schools had grown soft—that they demanded too little of their students, and that consequently too little was being learned. Many parents said that too little homework was assigned, and that children were allowed to move up through the schools without gaining the intellectual discipline essential to sound education. Employers protested that high-school graduates were unable to use the English language properly and lacked a knowledge of simple arithmetic. Professors proclaimed that the students came to college unprepared for serious work.

The change in recent years has been dramatic. Now a growing chorus of voices protests that the academic work load placed upon children and adolescents is so great as to destroy the love of learning and to imperil the mental health of many. Some observers attribute the growing unrest among college students to excessive academic pressure. Psychiatrists, psychologists, and counselors have expressed fear that the pressures cause instability and neurosis.

Today many parents criticize teachers for demanding too much of students and for assigning too much homework. Teachers counter with the charge that the fault really lies with status-seeking parents who place an excessive emphasis on grades, and are satisfied with nothing less than A's because they want every son to be admitted to Harvard, and every daughter to Vassar. But the real causes of the new pressures lie deeper and can be explained only in the light of historical developments.

Origin of the Pressures

During the 35 or 40 years prior to 1955 there was a de-emphasis on academic learning in many U.S. schools, both public and private. During this period a new educational philosophy shifted the emphasis from the child's mind and his academic and intellectual learning to concern for his development as a well-rounded human being. These years were characterized by a growing permissiveness, both in the schools, and in the homes from which children came. Parents and teachers alike came to believe that children should not be pushed too hard—that individual interests rather than promises of reward or threats of punishment should be the motivation for learning. We came to accept the view that if a child was not properly motivated, the fault lay not with the child but with the teacher or the school.

The trend had many virtues. During the twenties and thirties the schools became more humane institutions in which children lived happier lives. No longer did children fear school or hate to return in September after a summer's vacation. The curriculum became more closely related to the interests of children. But, like all good things, the trend toward permissiveness and the child-centered school became ridiculous when carried to extremes.

In the fifties we saw a natural reaction to the excesses that had been carried on in the name of educational progressivism. This caused many parents and a considerable number of teachers to welcome the deluge of criticism to which the schools were subjected after World War II and to join in the demand for the re-establishment of standards for promotion, more academic emphasis and academic discipline. But it was the launching of Sputnik 1 by the U.S.S.R. in the fall of 1957 that turned the trick. Suddenly the American people came to the conclusion that their security was threatened by the scientific and technological talents of a nation that had previously been considered educationally backward. Perhaps the launching did not really indicate that Soviet science or Soviet education was superior to that in the United States, but that is the way that many Americans interpreted it. In any case, since it was not at all clear just how the Russians had gotten ahead of the United States, the schools offered a convenient scapegoat. U.S. people began asking why it was that their nation, with all its vast and expensive educational facilities, had failed to develop scientists who could launch a satellite into space ahead of other nations. They demanded higher standards in the schools, more intellectual rigor, and clearer evidence of results. Clichés such as "the whole child" and "life adjustment" lost their popularity. The new emphasis was on academic learning.

Lure of Prestige Schools

Concurrently another social change was at work. For the first time in U.S. history we faced the prospect of more students desiring higher education than the colleges were prepared to accept. The more highly prestigious institutions found themselves confronted with 5, 10 or even 20 well-qualified applicants for every vacancy in the freshman class. This made it possible for them to raise entrance standards far above those that had previously existed. Colleges that already were selective became more selective. Those that had once admitted students on the basis of family or social class now demanded high scores on entrance examinations no matter what prep school the students had attended. Inevitably the new entrance standards made it necessary for colleges to exclude some of the sons and daughters of their own alumni, who were as bright and well prepared as their parents had been.

Even the less-prestigious colleges, those that had once been willing to accept almost any high-school graduate, now began accepting only the upper half or upper third of the high-school graduating class. Understandably, parents became alarmed, and insisted that their sons and daughters make superior records in school in order that college doors might be opened to them. This is probably the most important single source of pressure in the high school. It made it possible for high-school teachers to set higher standards, make heavier assignments and grade more rigorously.

Proper Goals of Education

A new emphasis on hard work and more academic discipline was badly needed in many schools, because some had indeed grown soft. But excellence is not achieved merely by piling on more work. It is not a sign of excellence that school pressures are creating neurotic anxieties in parents and students.

The proper goals of education are not grades, honors, diplomas or degrees. These are but symbols. The academic disciplines, the bodies of knowledge, and skill in the three R's are essential ingredients of a sound education, and the mastery of these requires hard work. But these are means toward ends and should not be confused with goals. The ultimate goal of education for freemen in a free society is wisdom—the ability to make wise, independent decisions based upon accurate information, clear reasoning and sound value judgments.

The educated man is one who can plan a good life and conduct it properly. Educational pressures that help the individual to become this kind of an adult are legitimate.

It may be true that hard work never hurt anyone. But the fear of failure, the threat of failure or the awareness of failure have done great harm to many. And, as standards rise, the number of school children who fail to achieve the goals set for them by their parents, their teachers or their childhood associates must surely grow. The problem for both parents and teachers is to set goals for each child that will challenge him to learn but within the limits of his capabilities.

EISENHOWER, DWIGHT DAVID. Former President Eisenhower made a remark in October which was interpreted as meaning he favored use of nuclear weapons to win the Vietnamese war. But he later told an interviewer that, while he favored all measures necessary to end the fighting quickly, it would be silly to use massive atomic weapons in a guerrilla war such as the Vietnam conflict.

Through the year, Eisenhower continued to back President Johnson's policies in the Vietnamese war; in June the former President announced his support of Johnson's decision to bomb oil-storage facilities near Hanoi.

Eisenhower celebrated his 50th wedding anniversary with his wife, Mamie, on June 30. He passed his 76th birthday quietly Oct. 14 at his Gettysburg, Pa., farm. In the fall election campaign, Eisenhower conferred with many Republican candidates and gave them his endorsement, but he engaged in almost no active campaigning. In May the former President was treated for mild arthritis, and in December he underwent major gallbladder surgery.

JOSEPH W. HALL, JR.
Washington Bureau, THE ASSOCIATED PRESS

Former President Eisenhower just prior to 76th birthday.
Wide World

ELECTIONS, U.S.

By GODFREY SPERLING, JR.
News Manager, Washington Bureau
THE CHRISTIAN SCIENCE MONITOR

The Outcome. Election-year 1966 had something particularly important to say to the United States. The sharp Republican rebound, in Congress and in gubernatorial and state legislative races, was more than just a rebuff to the Johnson administration and a curb to further Great Society legislation. It was more than anything else another of those significant and recurrent proofs that the democratic processes are not out of kilter, that the two-party system is still a working and dynamic force in the U.S. society. Thus, the election said to all who could hear: the great Johnson landslide of 1964 and the Republican split that brought it about was to be a passing phenomenon.

Just as has happened on occasion in past years, a party that has seemed in absolute wreckage picked itself up and pulled itself together. Thus, although the Democrats still retained a healthy majority in both the Senate and the House of Representatives, the real mark of the GOP upsurge was this: President Johnson now appeared vulnerable in 1968. In the wake of his overwhelming victory in 1964 the President seemed absolutely unbeatable. Two years spelled a great difference. Two-party government now was back. Just as 1964 was a Democratic story, the 1966 election has to be told with strong Republican overtones.

The Winners. In either holding or capturing the governorships in the large population states—New York, California, Massachusetts, Pennsylvania, Michigan and Ohio—the Republicans placed themselves in possession of an important beachhead for 1968. Those are the states with the big electoral votes.

In George Romney, Charles Percy, Ronald Reagan, James Rhodes, Edward Brooke and Mark Hatfield, the Republicans have men who have now shown by impressive wins that they could effectively grace a presidential ticket. And New York's Governor Nelson Rockefeller has regained new luster.

The GOP upsurge rubbed off favorably on Richard Nixon too. His hard campaigning efforts in behalf of the GOP Congressional candidates gave the former vice-president a certain share in the glory. Thus, Nixon is in a stronger position in his bid for the nomination than he was before the election.

The big gainer was George Romney. By bringing in Robert P. Griffin to the Senate along with him, and in helping to defeat several Democratic Congressional incumbents, the Michigan Governor gained new standing. No longer was he a loner. Now he was a candidate who obviously was successfully working for the party. The presidential boom for Romney was on, with moderate GOP leaders across the nation starting to group behind him.

The Issues. What brought about this considerable shift in public sentiment between 1964 and 1966? Some of this change in voter thinking might well be called "normal." That is, since the days of Cleveland the "outs" have gained an average of about 40 seats in the House in off-year elections. In 1966 the gain was 47, not too much above that "norm." Yet another "norm" can be cited. Since Hoover the gain by the "outs" in the first off-year House

---

GUBERNATORIAL ELECTIONS

In November 1966 elections 35 states had gubernatorial races. Democrats won 12 governorships, Republicans 23. A list of governors of the 50 states follows.

ALABAMA: Lurleen Wallace (D)e	**LOUISIANA:** John J. McKeithen (D)	**OHIO:** James A. Rhodes (R)r
ALASKA: Walter J. Hickel (R)e	**MAINE:** Kenneth M. Curtis (D)e	**OKLAHOMA:** Dewey Bartlett (R)e
ARIZONA: Jack Williams (R)e	**MARYLAND:** Spiro T. Agnew (R)e	**OREGON:** Tom McCall (R)e
ARKANSAS: Winthrop Rockefeller (R)e	**MASSACHUSETTS:** John A. Volpe (R)r	**PENNSYLVANIA:** Raymond P. Shafer (R)e
CALIFORNIA: Ronald Reagan (R)e	**MICHIGAN:** George Romney (R)r	**RHODE ISLAND:** John H. Chafee (R)r
COLORADO: John A. Love (R)r	**MINNESOTA:** Harold LeVander (R)e	**SOUTH CAROLINA:** Robert McNair (D)e
CONNECTICUT: John N. Dempsey (D)r	**MISSISSIPPI:** Paul B. Johnson (D)	**SOUTH DAKOTA:** Nils A. Boe (R)r
DELAWARE: Charles L. Terry, Jr. (D)	**MISSOURI:** Warren E. Hearnes (D)	**TENNESSEE:** Buford Ellington (D)e
FLORIDA: Claude R. Kirk, Jr. (R)e	**MONTANA:** Tim M. Babcock (R)	**TEXAS:** John B. Connally (D)r
GEORGIA: Lester Maddox (D)e	**NEBRASKA:** Norbert T. Tiemann (R)e	**UTAH:** Calvin L. Rampton (D)
HAWAII: John A. Burns (D)r	**NEVADA:** Paul Laxalt (R)e	**VERMONT:** Philip Hoff (D)r
IDAHO: Donald Samuelson (R)e	**NEW HAMPSHIRE:** John W. King (D)r	**VIRGINIA:** Mills E. Godwin, Jr. (D)
ILLINOIS: Otto Kerner (D)	**NEW JERSEY:** Richard J. Hughes (D)	**WASHINGTON:** Daniel J. Evans (R)
INDIANA: Roger D. Branigin (D)	**NEW MEXICO:** David F. Cargo (R)e	**WEST VIRGINIA:** Hulett C. Smith (D)
IOWA: Harold Hughes (D)r	**NEW YORK:** Nelson A. Rockefeller (R)r	**WISCONSIN:** Warren P. Knowles (R)r
KANSAS: Robert Docking (D)e	**NORTH CAROLINA:** Dan K. Moore (D)	**WYOMING:** Stan K. Hathaway (R)e
KENTUCKY: Edward T. Breathitt (D)	**NORTH DAKOTA:** William L. Guy (D)	e = elected; r = reelected

Gov. Rockefeller (R-N.Y.) campaigns for reelection.

Lester Maddox (D-Ga.) is given election kiss by his wife.

Students in Everett, Wash., greet Sen. Robert Kennedy.

election after the president is elected for the first time is about 10. Measured against this, the 1966 GOP increases look impressive.

In many ways the big issue was the popularity of President Johnson himself. A President who has worked as hard as any president in history to help the needy and bring about social justice just was not able to evoke a warm response from the public.

Even those who benefit most from the record tide of legislation—Medicare, antipoverty, civil rights, urban renewal, aid to education, to name only a small part of the Johnson program—have been slow to find in the President a man they can love. In past years it has not been uncommon to find Roosevelt Democrats, Truman Democrats, Eisenhower Republicans, and Kennedy Democrats. But the political writer moves across the breadth of the United States and finds no evidence of those who now identify themselves as "Johnson Democrats."

This may explain as much as anything else the inroads Republicans made in 1966 among voters that have long been oriented with the Democratic Party, such as the Negro and

Lurleen Wallace succeeds husband as Alabama governor.

Edward Brooke (R-Mass.), a Negro, wins Senate seat.

Actor Ronald Reagan (R) defeats California Gov. Brown.

Gov. Romney (R-Mich.) stages successful reelection bid.

ethnic groups. Thus Romney gained good ground among the Negroes in Detroit, in a city that in the past would produce a near-saturation vote for such candidates as G. Mennen Williams. Williams, himself, went down before Griffin in this election.

Percy, too, won a good number of Negro and ethnic votes in Chicago, enough so as to make it impossible for that Senate institution, Paul Douglas, to amass the big-city majority he needed to win.

White Backlash. Obviously there were votes stemming from apprehensions about the open-occupancy issue, the black-power movement, and what some voters felt to be excessive protest activity on the part of the Negro community. The Reagan victory over Gov. Edmund (Pat) Brown in California seemed to be compounded, in part, of this white-protest ingredient. And there were evidences of this same voter resistance in several other areas, in Chicago and New York, for example.

Also, in the South there was evidence of heavy white-bloc voting. The win of Mrs. Lurleen Wallace in Alabama and the strong show-

Former Vice-President Nixon addresses an Indiana crowd.

In Illinois, Charles Percy (R) defeats Sen. Paul Douglas.

Mark Hatfield (R-Ore.) campaigns for Senate in Portland.

ing of Lester Maddox in Georgia were certainly a part of this pulling together of white voters. Yet, this could not, with any precision, be called "backlash." This was an expression of feeling by whites in the South that was there long before the outward expressions of Negro aspirations that have marked the last decade.

Pollsters noted, in advance of the election, that there was an unrest of unknown proportions among the voters. Also, the biggest undecided vote in years waited in the wings as election day moved near. Would these undecided voters be moved to actually get to the polls? And, if so, would they vote against the "ins"? On this imponderable rested the outcome of whether the GOP gains would be modest or impressive.

In the end the "undecideds" came out in droves. And the GOP upsurge was on its way. In the big cities, in New York, Chicago, Detroit, Philadelphia, Boston, Los Angeles, Baltimore, Memphis and Dallas, the Republicans cut strongly into the Democratic vote. In state legislatures across the country the Republicans made big advances too. And, in perhaps their most impressive performance, the GOP moved from 17 to a total of half of the 50 gubernatorial seats.

In both the Spiro T. Agnew victory in Maryland and the Winthrop Rockefeller win in Arkansas, the GOP governor triumphs came over Democrats appealing to the backlash and racism.

Seething beneath the surface and accounting for the GOP uprising was a growing anxiety among the people: anxiety over rising prices, over Vietnam, over the dipping stock market, and over the spate of terrible crimes of violence, many of which were unsolved. People in Chicago worried about the mass murders of the nurses and the murder of Mr. Percy's daughter. There was the "strangler" in Cincinnati. And there were similar crimes in almost every major city. And even in the quiet little towns people were becoming exceedingly cautious.

Such was the breadth of apprehension in the United States on the eve of the election. Running against it was a counterforce. Call it apathy. Call it contentment. Most people were still doing pretty well, making good money, having fine vacations.

In the end it was the current of anxiety that won out. That—together with a number of fresh, attractive GOP candidates—seemed to spell the difference. The Republicans were back in business again, with a victory that was resounding, particularly when one takes into account how far they had fallen in 1964.

Wide World

On Caribbean tour, Queen Elizabeth and Jamaica's Gov-

ELIZABETH II. The British royal spotlight shifted briefly in 1966 from Queen Elizabeth II to her eldest son and heir to the throne, Prince Charles.

The Prince of Wales' further education had become a matter of serious national interest. Opinion polls still reveal widespread British support for the institution of royalty, but there is also a feeling that royal individuals should work and "earn their keep." Reassurance was sought that Queen Elizabeth and Prince Philip were properly preparing Prince Charles, turned 18, for a useful life as monarch. It was widely felt that Prince Charles should participate prominently in decisions concerning his future.

General approval greeted the decision to send the Prince of Wales to Trinity College, Cambridge, for at least two years when he finishes school at Scotland's Gordonstoun in 1967. At Cambridge he would come under the experienced eye of Lord Butler, former British foreign secretary (who nearly became prime minister), who is Master of Trinity.

Queen Elizabeth meanwhile made several quiet royal trips which served to stress Britain's Commonwealth and European ties.

With the Duke of Edinburgh, she visited 14 Commonwealth countries and island territories in the Caribbean during February and March. She officiated at the state openings of Parliament in Trinidad and Jamaica.

In May the Queen visited Belgium, and at a state banquet declared that Britain earnestly

...ernor-General Sir Clifford Campbell listen to a local band.

desired to cooperate in building a wider European unity. These remarks, outspoken for a ceremonial occasion, suggested that the then Foreign Secretary, Michael Stewart, who accompanied the royal party, had had a prominent hand in drafting the Queen's speech.

In June the Queen opened Glasgow's new airport. In July she traveled to Belfast, in Northern Ireland, to open a river bridge, at a time when Ulsterite political feelings were running extremely high. A piece of concrete was thrown from a fourth floor and struck the hood of the Queen's Rolls-Royce. Later, the Queen said, "It is a strong car."

A Mass Observation poll, its results set forth in a book entitled *Long to Rule over Us?*, found that 7 out of 10 Britons were entirely or largely in favor of royalty. But 16 out of every 100 said they would vote for a republic, as compared with 10 in 100 in 1956.

WILLIAM H. STRINGER
London Bureau Chief
THE CHRISTIAN SCIENCE MONITOR

EMPLOYMENT. The U.S. labor force and employment increased continually throughout 1966. The total labor force, at 80.2 million in 1966, was up 1.8 million from 1965. Over the year, the civilian labor force expanded by 1.4 million. The increase in the armed forces amounted to 400,000.

The 1966 growth in total employment, 1.9 million, was much greater than the civilian

labor-force increase was in the United States. During the year, unemployment declined by some 500,000, to a figure slightly less than 3.0 million.

For most of the year, the unemployment rate remained below the 4 per cent level, reflecting the steady growth of the economy, and the effectiveness of training programs which upgraded workers' skills. The rate averaged 3.9 per cent in 1966, down from 4.6 per cent in 1965.

Employment Increases. All sectors of the economy, except mining, contributed to the large gain of 3.1 million in nonagricultural payroll employment.

Employment in manufacturing rose by more than a million to over 19 million—14 million of these were production workers. Of the 800,-000 increase in workers producing durable goods, some 240,000 occurred in electrical equipment. Employment in the production of machinery and transportation equipment, as well as in electrical equipment, grew to nearly 2 million in each industry.

Government—growing rapidly, especially at the state and local level—accounted for around ¼ of the year's increase in employment. Government workers increased by 750,000, to nearly 11 million.

Trade accounted for the third-largest gain in employment. Over 500,000 more persons worked in trade than had in 1965.

The service industries also had an employment increase of nearly half a million. The unemployment rate in this area dropped from 4.6 per cent in 1965 to 3.8 per cent in 1966.

Job openings continued to appear for highly skilled workers, while opportunities for those with no skills or little education actually lessened as the year wore on (evidence of a continually advancing technology). The unemployment rate for unskilled laborers was 2½ times as severe as that for skilled workers. The laborer rate was 7.3 per cent in 1966, down from 8.4 per cent in 1965.

Unemployment Decreases. With new housing starts down considerably from 1965, the number of construction workers began to fall steadily after the spring (midyear). Although the average unemployment rate in this industry was 8.2 per cent in 1966—down from 10.3 per cent in 1965—by the end of the year, it had risen to more than 9 per cent.

The Negro unemployment rate continued to be at least two times the rate for white workers despite the fact that it moved down in 1966 to 7.5 per cent. Negro workers suffered from the double disadvantage of lower educational attainment and from lingering discrimination as well.

Teen-agers also experienced a disadvantage (from lack of learning) in the job market, because they lack both experience and skill. The unemployment rate for this age group continued to be triple that for the nation as a whole. It was only slightly improved from 1965, at 12.0 per cent in 1966. The high rate of teen-age unemployment reflected the increasingly large numbers of 14- to 19-year-olds entering the labor force, many of whom are inadequately prepared to meet necessary job requirements.

The jobless rate for adult men was 2.5 per cent in 1966, the lowest rate since 1953. The rate for adult women was 3.8 per cent, down from 4.5 per cent in 1965.

By December, only 8 major areas in the nation were listed as having substantial unemployment—9 less than in 1965. These included 3 in California—Fresno, San Bernardino-Riverside-Ontario, and Stockton; 2 in Massachusetts —Fall River and Lowell; and 1 in Pennsylvania—Altoona. In these areas, unemployment ranged from 6.0 to 8.9 per cent. Two areas in Puerto Rico also remained on the substantial-unemployment list.

The number of major industrial centers with less than 3 per cent unemployment reached a record high of 65 by December. This represented an increase of 19 over the same period in 1965.

ARTHUR M. ROSS
Commissioner, Bureau of Labor Statistics
U.S. DEPARTMENT OF LABOR

ERHARD, LUDWIG. Since June 20, 1948, when he single-handedly rescinded rationing and price controls to trigger the German "economic miracle," Ludwig Erhard had been motivated by incurable optimism and an assiduous trust in the better side of human nature.

When he succeeded Konrad Adenauer as chancellor of the Federal Republic of Germany, Oct. 16, 1963, his faith became his tragedy. Erhard substituted it whenever political exigencies demanded decisiveness. He cringed from party infighting and appealed baroquely to statesmanship when the situation required knocking together politicians' heads.

On Dec. 1, after floundering badly in the job he had held for three years and 46 days, Erhard, 69, was forced to resign. He was succeeded by Kurt Georg Kiesinger, 62, until then minister-president of the southwest German state of Baden-Württemberg.

The events which led to Erhard's fall are a complex mixture of his own irresoluteness in the face of mounting domestic and foreign problems, exacerbated by deeply rooted rivalries in his Christian Democratic Union party and its semiautonomous wing in Bavaria, the Christian Social Union.

For the first few months of 1966, after he had led his CDU/CSU to a 47.6 per cent victory in the Sept. 19, 1965, election, it appeared as if Erhard, strengthened by the people's mandate, might catch himself.

Through careful compromises on agricultural and other economic problems, Erhard succeeded on Jan. 30 in ending France's seven-month boycott of the Common Market. A week later, when he visited French President Charles de Gaulle in Paris, there were faint hopes that the progressive estrangement between West Germany and France might be reversed.

On March 23, following a bitter fight within the party, Erhard was elected chairman and leader of the CDU, a post that until then had been held by 90-year-old Adenauer, who never made a secret of his dislike of Erhard.

But the victory was a Pyrrhic one. Less than four months later, on July 10, Erhard and his party suffered a scathing defeat in an election in North Rhine-Westphalia, Germany's largest state. Erhard had made the vote a test of his personal popularity and when the Social Democratic Party (SPD) won 49.5 per cent and 99 of 200 state legislature seats, the Chancellor's days were numbered.

A massive "let's dump Erhard" movement got under way within his own party which feared that his sinking prestige might cost them further state contests and the national election in 1969.

On Oct. 27 his coalition Government collapsed when the four ministers of the Free Democratic Party, on whose support he depended, withdrew from the Cabinet. Ostensibly, the FDP pullout was over a proposed tax increase to balance the 1967 budget. But there was no question in Bonn they had been maneuvered into their action by leading members of Erhard's own party, notably Majority Leader Rainer Barzel and Bavarian CSU chief Franz Josef Strauss, who were looking for a pretext to bring Erhard to fall.

At a caucus of his party's parliamentary group on Nov. 2, Erhard agreed to step down if it would help the CDU/CSU find a partner with whom to form a new coalition Government. One week later, on Nov. 10, the party nominated Kiesinger, who was sworn in as head of a coalition with the SPD on Dec. 1.

Erhard, still chairman of the CDU, will retain his seat as a Bundestag deputy and has said that he will remain active in politics.

JOHN DORNBERG
Bonn-Berlin Correspondent, NEWSWEEK

Europe's longest suspension bridge, linking Lisbon with the Tagus' south bank, was inaugurated in 1966.

EUROPE

By DAVID M. MASON

Paris Bureau, THE ASSOCIATED PRESS

Western Europe was marked in 1966 by one major political shakeup, a continued easing of tensions with the Soviet bloc and a costly natural disaster.

New German Chancellor. On Dec. 1, Dr. Kurt Georg Kiesinger, a longtime local politician hardly known outside Germany, became the Federal Republic's third chancellor, succeeding his Christian Democrat colleague, Ludwig Erhard. Erhard, given most of the credit for West Germany's postwar recovery, fell on worsening economic conditions at home, and setbacks in international affairs.

Kiesinger, who was able to overcome the stigma of Nazi Party membership, rose to lead a "grand coalition" of the moderately conservative Christian Democrats and the moderately Leftist Social Democrats. The Social Democrats' leader, West Berlin Mayor Willy Brandt, took over the foreign ministry. Franz Josef Strauss, a former defense minister in Erhard's Government, became finance minister under Kiesinger, and was generally tagged as the man to watch in the coalition, since many observers expected rough times ahead.

Almost as much attention was attracted by the budding Rightist National Democratic Party (NPD), which rang up startling legislative successes in Bavaria and Hesse during the power gap in Bonn. Critics labeled the NPD neo-Nazi, but party leaders denied the charge and said they were simply seeking Germany's deserved place in the world. That statement still recalled the early Hitlerian era, and the concern over the NPD was great enough to spark protests in France and elsewhere.

De Gaulle's Design. The iron curtain was still securely in place, dividing people and ideologies, but somehow the barbed wire and tank traps along the Czechoslovak borders and the ever more perfected Berlin Wall seemed to be moving into the past. The future was perhaps with President Charles de Gaulle's long-term design of a Europe united from the Ural Mountains to the Atlantic. De Gaulle, who visited the Soviet Union in midyear and greeted Soviet Premier Aleksei Kosygin in Paris in December, was taking the lead in breaking down barriers between East and West. Many expected that West Germany's new foreign minister would also press for more contacts between his country and the East.

But Germany, still split in two parts, remained the greatest obstacle to full *détente* with Moscow. The Soviet premier underscored this on his state visit to France, when he repeatedly struck warning notes about what he called the resurgence of fascism in West Germany. The Soviets, who still have vivid fear of and disdain for the Germans, emotions dating from World War II, firmly insist on continuing the crippling division of Germany, and become enraged at the thought of West Germany shar-

207

Left: Spain's Francisco Franco (r) greets Vice-President Gen. Agustin Muñoz Grandes. Center: Portugal's Premier Salazar turned 77 April 28. Right: Paul Henri Spaak of Belgium retired from public life July 27.

ing in any way the control of the West's nuclear force. However, 14 NATO members on Dec. 14 included West Germany in a nuclear-planning group set up to work out Allied nuclear strategy.

Disaster in Italy. While political change moved slowly over Europe, natural disaster struck Italy, and particularly Florence, one of the world's major depositories of painting, sculpture and other fine arts. Heavy rain sent River Arno floodwaters cascading into basement storerooms and even into church naves and through the streets of the city. A month after the early November floods, a tabulation of losses was still being made, but aid came from many parts of Europe and elsewhere in the Western world. The disaster struck a severe blow at Premier Aldo Moro's Government, undermining economic planning and bringing criticism for leaving the nation unprepared for nature's anger.

Spain and Portugal. Political stability, in the form of dictatorship, continued to characterize both Spain and Portugal. In Spain, Generalissimo Francisco Franco was, at 74, beginning to think of the time when he would no longer be at his country's helm. In late November, he announced a new constitution, providing for a king to succeed him, and for timid steps toward more freedom for Spaniards. Public worship by all religious faiths was permitted and laws banning labor strikes were relaxed. As another sign of liberalism, Franco decided to submit the constitution to the public for approval. The referendum was approved by about 90 per cent of the voters Dec. 14.

Portugal still held stubbornly on to its rumbling colonial territories in Africa, and at home

the Salazar regime remained firmly in power. There were occasional protests from intellectual circles, but these seemed to have little real effect on Portugal's largely closed and strictly governed society. One segment of that society was perhaps becoming a potential force of revolutionary tendencies. This was the thousands of unskilled and semiskilled Portuguese men and women who were leaving their country to fill employment demands in France and other more highly developed nations. Of course, the laborers took the bottom rung on the job scale in those countries but—more important—they were exposed to the luxuries and political freedoms they never dreamed existed before they crossed the borders of their own country. Would these experiences one day be translated into reforms at home? Many people thought so.

Britain and the Common Market. Great Britain remained well out in the economic cold as far as the European Common Market was concerned. As the year wore on, however, there were indications that Prime Minister Harold Wilson was moving off dead center and leaning toward serious consideration of complying with Common Market rules—basically the Rome Treaty—and applying again for membership. Wilson scheduled a series of trips to Common Market capitals, beginning with Paris and Rome in January 1967, to test the climate for British membership four years after the sharp veto by President de Gaulle.

But there seemed to be little latitude either in France's views toward Britain's ability to meet the rules, or in Britain's real desire to comply. Britain's agriculture would undoubtedly suffer severely from Common Market entry, unless special protection was provided, and

Crown Princess Beatrix of the Netherlands weds German diplomat Claus von Amsberg, March 10.

Britain's overall economy would suffer if Commonwealth trade preferences were wiped out, to be supplanted by the Common Market's closed-customs ring. A statement in late November by French Premier Georges Pompidou made it crystal clear that France's position had not moved a perceptible centimeter since the veto of Jan. 14, 1963.

Members of the British-led European Free Trade Association (EFTA) awaited results of Wilson's scheduled mission. Most of EFTA leaders are eager to join the Common Market, but realize that the ice must first be broken by Britain, the leading member. With American-European trade relations at stake, the new economic shape of Europe was, of course, of growing interest and concern to the United States.

Besides taking a new aim at the Common Market, Prime Minister Wilson spent most of 1966 wrestling with the problem of Rhodesia's determination to flaunt the dictates of London concerning treatment of the country's African majority. Prime Minister Ian Smith and Wilson met dramatically on the British cruiser *Tiger* off Gibraltar in December in a "final" effort to arrive at a solution which would guarantee the future of both whites and blacks in Rhodesia. When Smith, after a prolonged conference with his Cabinet back in Salisbury, rejected Wilson's shipboard proposals, the latter immediately sent emissaries to the United Nations to plead for more stringent economic sanctions against Rhodesia. But there was little likelihood that any new measures would be effective if South Africa continued to aid the Smith regime, particularly with the provision of petroleum products.

France, Scandinavia, Greece. De Gaulle's France continued to boom economically during the year, although its favorable trade balance had begun to decline by November. The most pressing needs of the nation remained adequate housing and extension of the country's tiny system of superhighways. France moved closer to becoming a thermonuclear power, with a first H-bomb test probably due in 1967, and with a missile-delivery system perhaps less than five years away.

In Finland, Communists won representation in the Government for the first time since 1948. Two months after the Social Democrats' victory in March, a coalition Government was formed with Communists holding the posts of first communications minister, second finance minister and first social affairs minister.

Sweden's ruling Social Democrats lost considerable ground in communal and municipal elections in September. The Social Democrats have ruled Sweden almost uninterruptedly for 34 years and turned the country into a welfare state.

On the other rim of Europe, Greece was still in seemingly endless negotiations with Turkey over the ultimate fate of Cyprus, where relative but ominous calm marked most of the year. Greece was shaken in early December by the sinking of the ferry boat *Heraklion;* 234 persons lost their lives. The Government of Premier Stephanos Stephenopoulos resigned Dec. 20. A new Cabinet, with Ioannis Paraskevopoulos as premier, was sworn in Dec. 22.

Political unity of Europe marked time during 1966, and one of its strongest proponents, Belgian Foreign Minister Paul-Henri Spaak, bowed out of public life.

French Foreign Minister Couve de Murville and Polish Foreign Minister Naszkowski sight-see in Cracow in May.

EUROPE: EAST

By JAMES CHACE
Managing Editor, EAST EUROPE

During 1966 the communist states of Eastern Europe greatly expanded their contacts with Western Europe. For people who had long considered Budapest as much a part of Europe as Brussels, this drawing together of the two Europes marked a new stage in attaining an overall European settlement. Indeed the Soviet bloc remained a bloc in name only. The Rumanians continued to assert their independence from Moscow, even to the extent of calling for an end to the Warsaw Pact (the Soviet-bloc counterpart to NATO). In a speech to celebrate the founding of the Rumanian Communist Party, the Rumanian chief Nicolae Ceausescu declared: "The existence of [military] blocs, as well as the sending of troops to other countries, is an anachronism incompatible with the independence and national sovereignty of the peoples and with normal relations among states."

Men who express sentiments like these cannot be treated as dependents, or expected to sacrifice what they consider the interests of their countries to some supranational requirements. Though Moscow has stated its willingness to abolish the Warsaw Pact in return for the dissolution of NATO, Bucharest's leading Communist did not put it quite this way; instead, by such a statement, Ceausescu echoed French President de Gaulle in his preference for the nation-state.

De Gaulle and East Europe. In fact the closing of the gap between Eastern and Western Europe was in good measure due to the efforts of General de Gaulle. With the United States deeply engaged in hostilities against the communist regime in North Vietnam, the relations between the East European communist states and Washington were at a standstill. The West European nations, however, showed little interest in the war in southeast Asia (and in the case of Paris were openly hostile to U.S. involvement) and were eager to broaden relations with the East Europeans.

In 1966, Maurice Couve de Murville, De Gaulle's foreign minister, completed trips to all the countries of Eastern Europe except East Germany and Albania. And in June the French President himself journeyed to the Soviet Union on a trip calculated to dramatize the unsatisfactory state of divided Europe, leaving behind him a Western alliance shaken by the withdrawal of French forces from NATO.

Moscow's policy toward Western Europe, which was generally supported by the other East European states, seemed to be a double one. The Russian leaders suggested that some kind of European settlement might be possible; at the same time, they warned against allowing West Germany to possess any nuclear arms. General de Gaulle could also endorse such a policy, believing that the problem of a divided Germany could only be solved as part of an overall European settlement, and that such a resolution would be possible if Bonn renounced nuclear weapons.

Hanoi and Peking. There was evidence then of a certain unity of approach among all the communist nations to the problems of Europe, and, as the year wore on, more cohesiveness in terms of overall foreign policy. Material aid to North Vietnam was made available; support for Hanoi was unstinting. The split with Communist China also widened, and even the efforts of the Rumanians, including a trip by China's Premier Chou En-lai to Bucharest, were in vain. By autumn, Rumania fell into line by at least tacitly supporting the critical line taken by Moscow toward Peking. At the 23d Soviet Communist Party Congress, the Soviet line was ratified by the East Europeans without much grumbling, primarily because Moscow put so little pressure on them.

However, at the Bulgarian party congress in mid-November, the Russians surprisingly forced all foreign delegations to stand up and be counted on the Chinese question. Bulgarian party chief Todor Zhivkov stated that "conditions are ripe for convening an international conference of the communist and workers parties"—a meeting that would surely be directed against the Chinese—and he was supported by the Soviet party chief, the Czechoslovak and Hungarian speakers. Despite the pressure, other Communists refused to go along with the idea of such a conference. The Rumanians made it clear that they were against any effort to impose a common program on the world's parties; altogether, fewer than half of the parties supported Moscow.

Internal Problems. If there was a certain steadfastness in foreign policy, stop-and-go approaches characterized internal problems. In economics, in the cultural sphere, in church-state relations, struggles between the old-line Communists and the new breed of technologists were taking place. Though there had been a definite movement toward liberalization of cultural life in the 1960's, the party showed its confusion and fears over exactly where this would all lead. Though strict "socialist realism" in the arts was no longer absolutely required, actual "artistic freedom" was forbidden.

In Russia, harsh prison sentences were imposed on writers Andrei Sinyavsky and Yuli Daniel for writing "slanderous" books about Soviet life and getting them published abroad under pseudonyms. This dogmatic attitude was also reflected in Yugoslavia, where the journalist Mihajlo Mihajlov was imprisoned on the grounds of spreading false information. While, in Yugoslavia, intellectuals are less controlled than in the other communist countries, the rule still applies: people must not speak, write or agitate against the interests of the party or state. Actually, Mihajlov deliberately provoked the authorities. He proposed to do something that under Yugoslav law is perfectly legal—publish a magazine. But it was to be a magazine in opposition to the policies of Tito's League of Communists and advocating democratic, multi-party socialism. This was going too far, and the party was ruthless in showing its hand.

And even in Czechoslovakia, which in recent years had made great strides toward allowing artists freedom of expression, the party clamped down. At the beginning of the year, an outspoken literary magazine, *Tvar*, published by the Writers Union for the younger generation, perished for lack of inhibitions. Demands by younger writers for their own organization were also shunted aside.

The situation in Poland continued to be gloomy. Year after year the party has tried to quench the spirit of freedom that was ignited in October of 1956 when the Polish party stood up against Soviet control. But by now most hopes have been crushed; writers have been imprisoned, censorship restored. In 1966 the well-known Marxist philosopher Leszek Kolakowski was ousted from the Communist Party after a speech he made at the University of Warsaw. He retained his seat at the university, however, even though he has frequently displayed his disagreement with current trends within Poland.

One outgrowth of the Kolakowski expulsion was the dispatch of a letter to high party authorities, signed by 21 Polish authors, all members of the party, protesting communist policies toward intellectuals. Though the letter did not mention Kolakowski by name, it was

Polish Council of Ministers Chairman Cyrankiewicz (l), Polish party leader Gomulka and Soviet party leader Brezhnev sign anti-Chinese Communist party declaration Oct. 15.

Sovfoto

Branch of state bank rises in Warsaw, almost completely rebuilt since end of World War II.

said to have echoed his criticism of the narrowing freedom of expression and artistic creation.

Although Albania has never displayed the slightest degree of liberalization in its meager cultural life, even the Albanian Communists showed themselves especially anxious to stamp out any signs of deviation from a hard party line. Classical plays were shut down; a novel by Dhimiter Zhuvani called *The Tunnel* was harshly criticized as "unworthy and revolting" at a time when "a revolutionary drive of the masses is under way." Apparently the only thing wrong with the novel in question was its deviation from the absolute strictures of "socialist realism," which demand that a novel portray the workers as heroic figures and bathe the whole story in the light of "inspired optimism."

Church and State. Not only was there an uneven picture of progress and retrogression on the cultural front, but also in the relations between the parties and the clergy. In Hungary, for example, relations between the Vatican and the party were more favorable than they had been for years, despite the fact that the Hungarian Cardinal Mindszenty remained in asylum in the U.S. Legation in Budapest. In Poland, however, the struggle between church and state reached a new intensity of bitterness. This was the year of the Polish millennium, celebrating one thousand years of Christianity in Poland, and a symbol for many Poles of Poland's connection to the West. The party saw in these celebrations a contest for the loyalty of the populace, and did everything possible to mitigate the religious observances.

Warsaw banned all foreign Catholic prelates from attending millennium ceremonies organized by the church. The ban went all the way to the top, including Pope Paul VI, who had reportedly considered a trip to Poland for just that purpose. Polish Primate Stefan Cardinal Wyszynski was also denied a visa to leave the country for a scheduled trip to the Vatican. Finally, during the celebration in April the Cardinal and the party chief rallied their opposing forces in Poznan to celebrate one thousand years of Polish history. On April 17 the Cardinal preached at Poznan Cathedral to a crowd that jammed the plaza and church. At almost the same time the party's First Secretary was addressing a rally in a nearby square.

The most significant clash occurred at the end of 1965 when the Polish bishops addressed to the German episcopate a letter which contained a long discussion of the thousand-year history of German-Polish relations and asked for an end of hatred, and a new dialogue between the peoples. The Communists never found anything substantially wrong with the letter, but it served as a basis for an antichurch campaign that went on for months. Editorials, speeches in the Parliament, and even demonstrations by students and workers were directed against what was termed the irresponsible, unpatriotic action of the clergy. The main theme of these attacks was that the Polish Primate was trying to reverse postwar Polish policy from alliance and friendship with the U.S.S.R. and to turn Poland into a "bulwark of Christianity" against the Russians. The year concluded with no sign of a truce between the two factions.

Economic Life. On the economic front, uncertainty prevailed. Here, too, the old-line Communists continued to obstruct the movement toward economic reform. In Yugoslavia, Tito's purge of the second-ranking Communist, Aleksandar Rankovic, was full of meaning for other communist countries as well. Rankovic, a typical man of the past, opposed the economic re-

Budapest's Chain Bridge, where Hungarian rebels surrendered to Soviet tanks in 1956.

form now being worked in Yugoslavia, in part because the new economic system will require new men to run it. Though his fall shows that the once-doctrinaire communist system may indeed evolve into something the founders never conceived, at the same time the purge is a warning that reforms that look good on paper may be sabotaged by those who are supposed to carry them out.

Bulgaria, Czechoslovakia and Hungary also found themselves in the throes of reforming their once highly centralized economic planning. In Sofia the shape of the country's re-organization was to go into effect at the beginning of 1967. The new program allows considerable freedom of action to the industrial enterprises. It stresses more reliance on profitability as a guide to production, expands the contractual right of the enterprises, and ties wages to production results. Like the reforms in Czechoslovakia and Hungary, it sees a three-tier system of fixed, limited and free prices. Factories will be allowed to finance production through their own savings and with the aid of bank loans, although the state will continue to aid heavy industry with capital investments.

Czechoslovak party chief Antonin Novotny won applause at the closing session of the 13th Czechoslovak Communist Party Congress when he said: "Let us have less useless and pompous talking and more responsibility and real work." The central theme of the conclave was the problem of the economy, and the need to implement the new economic system. Though there had been an upswing in the Czech economy since 1964, Novotny warned that this did not mean that new ideas and new methods were unnecessary. The Czech leaders stressed the fact that the elements of the reform—consumer orientation, the principles of personal profit

and reward for merit—do not represent "a single step backward, as our enemies wish to convey." Like the Yugoslav communist bosses, the Czech party leaders fear obstructionism by the old Stalinists who see in the reform a denial of the traditional tenets of Marxism.

However, ideology is something that can be gotten around; losing your job is another matter. The main problem bothering those who oppose the new reforms is simply that unemployment will result when the old Communists, whose main qualification as factory managers was party loyalty, will be shoved aside for the new-style technocrats. Economists in Hungary warned that at least one third of the industrial managers will lose their jobs after Jan. 1, 1968. Others will have to be retrained. Though the new system should improve market conditions and reduce prices through internal competition, the profit squeeze will temporarily create an unstable labor market. Income in the enterprises will depend on profits, and the more-successful concerns will be able to afford higher wage scales and thus attract more workers. Even in Rumania, where there has been no widespread economic reform, and the planning, production and prices are carefully controlled from the center, "material incentives" are to be offered.

The most crucial problem today in the eyes of the East European communist leaders is not the political tensions separating Eastern and Western Europe, or the "big brother" embrace of the Soviet Union, but the need to transform the highly centralized economies into something resembling a market economy. If the new economics proves successful, a new breed of technocrat, indifferent to ideology and impatient with the relics of the past, will have taken over and transformed the communist world.

EUROPEAN ECONOMIC COMMUNITY. The year 1966 was the most important for the European Economic Community since its establishment. The most serious crisis of the Community's existence came to an end in January, and the six member countries decided in July to complete the customs union 1½ years ahead of the Rome Treaty schedule.

Crisis Resolved. An extraordinary Council of Ministers meeting on Jan. 17–18 and 28–29 in Luxembourg brought to a close the crisis which had arisen with France's 1965 walkout from the Council of Ministers and subsequent boycott of Community institutions over agricultural and institutional questions. France and its five partners (Belgium, West Germany, Italy, Luxembourg and the Netherlands) agreed to continue to apply without change the Rome Treaty establishing the EEC. France, however, differed with its partners in stating that talks in the Council of Ministers must continue until unanimous agreement is reached, in contrast to the Rome Treaty's provisions for weighted majority voting as of Jan. 1, 1966.

On May 11 the Council of Ministers agreed on the agricultural financial regulation which provides for gradual Community take-over of all expenditures resulting from the common agricultural policy, and for sources of funds to cover the expenditures until the end of the EEC's transition period on Dec. 31, 1969. It is estimated that the agricultural policy will then cost EEC $1,300,000,000 annually.

The ministers also set July 1, 1968, as the date for completion of the customs union between the Six. On that date, all tariffs between the member states, which now stand at 20 per cent of their original 1957 level, will be eliminated, and the common agricultural policy, including common prices and market organizations, will be fully in place. In addition, the Community will apply as of July 1, 1968, a common external tariff on imports from the rest of the world.

At its July 24 meeting the Council approved market organizations and common prices for all major agricultural products except grains, whose price levels had been determined in December 1964.

The resolution of the Community crisis enabled the EEC to return as a full partner to the negotiating table of the Kennedy Round trade negotiations in Geneva. During 1966, the Council took many decisions on offers for industrial and tropical products which Commission negotiators discussed in Geneva. On July 27 and Dec. 22 the EEC ministers reached agreement on additional offers for agricultural products, some of which foresaw world commodity agreements.

Far-reaching Activities. The Community's relations with the rest of the world extended far beyond the Geneva negotiations. Nigeria was to become the first English-speaking associate member of the EEC, but the association agreement, signed on July 16 in Lagos, had not been ratified by the end of the year. Negotiations for an association agreement were begun with three East African countries: Kenya, Tanzania and Uganda. The Commission proposed negotiations with Algeria, Morocco and Tunisia for broad agreements in the commercial and financial fields.

Austria continued its negotiations with the EEC for a special relationship to mitigate the effect of the Community on Austria's exports. Israel, which signed a three-year trade agreement with the Community in 1964, requested the commencement of negotiations for an association. British Prime Minister Harold Wilson told the House of Commons in November that his Government favored entry into the EEC under the right conditions and that he would sound out the Community's member countries for a possible start of negotiations. The Commission also had discussions with representatives of the Latin-American countries, the Scandinavian countries, Spain and Ireland.

The EEC continued to experience a strong economic growth, with gross Community product increasing 4.5 per cent during 1966 and industrial production expanding 6 to 6.5 per cent. Internal trade rose 16.5 per cent, and exports increased 8.7 per cent, but the Community's trade balance with the outside world deteriorated to a 1966 deficit of $3,000,000,-000. The Commission submitted to the Council a five-year economic policy for 1966–70 predicting an annual 4.3 per cent growth and outlining tasks to ensure balanced economic development in member countries.

Several decisions of the European Court enabled the Commission to proceed with further development of the Community's antitrust policy, and to propose a regulation on exempting groups of agreements in the EEC from Community antitrust regulations. Work continued on draft conventions for the mutual recognition of companies in the member states, a European patent law, and a European company law. A Commission memorandum was sent to the member states' governments affirming the need for greater concentration of firms within the EEC to meet outside competition.

STEPHEN P. FREIDBERG
Assistant Spokesman, COMMISSION OF THE
EUROPEAN ECONOMIC COMMUNITY

FASHIONS

By BETSY TALBOT BLACKWELL
Editor-in-Chief
MADEMOISELLE

UPI

In 1966 the world of fashion was "in" fashion and everyone's topic for debate. It was Paris that set tongues wagging. Out of the august ateliers that spring came, among other items, dresses with cutout backs and cutaway middles, pea-jacketed pantsuits, a transparent chiffon shift pailletted in bikini places. And almost everything bared the knee. It appeared to many that Paris' great *couturiers* had swung to the world of ready-to-wear—to that group of French, English and American designers whose *boutique* fashions had started these trends two years before. Other viewers, unshocked by short skirts (which were hardly news elsewhere), saw much in the collections that was any woman's fashion, and thought that Paris had simply recognized the youth-oriented, jet-age speed of the sixties.

By fall, cutouts had disappeared; so had see-through dresses. But clothes remained short except for Dior's calf-length soldier coats (worn over miniskirts) and the midknee decreed by Balenciaga. The baffling extremes continued. From St. Laurent, for instance, both a series of pop-art dresses and subdued, elegant clothes. Féraud offered a microskirt (six inches above the knee); Cardin, frilled petticoats under barrel-shaped tweeds; Chanel, on the other hand, her perennial suits.

Where had fashion gone in 1966? If one searched for a look or looks, one found a fashion Tower of Babel. But if one searched for the year's shapes, one could find order at last.

The Year of the Dress. This was the year of the dress. It was small-shouldered, nipped-in at the rib cage. Its line was fluid. It was sometimes straight up and down, just grazing the hip; sometimes A'd with a flippy skirt; sometimes flaring into a tiny tent. Dresses were called skimps, skivvies, smalldresses, puptents. They had a spare shape in common, but a delicious variety of colors and fabrics divided them. One could collect a cache of prints copied from art: from Fauvism, Art Nouveau, thirties' moderne, pop and op. Color calligraphed flowers and swirls or blocked in bold geometrics. White was the new basic, all but replacing black. Knitted dresses were important and ubiquitous. An entire "horizontal closet" (knits fare better lying flat on shelves) could be built around them, from a skinny-ribbed sweater-dress to a silver-threaded party skimp.

Nineteen sixty-six saw the debut of paper dresses for day and evening. Ranging in price from a little over $1.00 to $10, they are designed to be worn a few times, then tossed out.

Coats. If 1966 was the year of the dress, it was the coat—narrow and small-boned—

215

Photographed by Gosta Peterson.

Photographed by George Barkentin.

"Mademoiselle," © *1966, Conde Nast Publications, Inc.*

UPI

Left: The pantsuit was among the most "in" of 1966's striking, popular fashions.
Center: In the "year of the dress," the sweater-dress was a particular favorite.
Right: Italian designer Pucci showed Oriental influence in designing lounge wear.

which proved the catalyst. This silhouette had appeared in 1965; to wear it one needed a dress that fitted underneath it. Soon coats and dresses were being designed to match, and then came the coat - plus - skirt - plus - pullover (or shirt). These coat combinations were so popular, some designers predicted that the suit might soon be obsolete. (Actually, suits stayed with us, but some of the best were knits, skinnied-down so they would slide under coats.)

By September, the smallcoat was rivaled by the tent, the puptent (a smaller version) and the strictly cut military coat. But again tops were taut, fullness controlled. Many coats were cozied with fur linings. Or if one wanted fur on the outside, the choice of pelt was enormous—mole dyed the color of ripe mulberries, and rabbit stenciled to look like hamster, to name but two. Most important: fur, any fur, was treated as fashion, not as an investment.

Pantsuits and Hip-Skirts. The 1966 girl was also the girl in the pantsuit. She traveled off to a college weekend in it; danced in it; even (a few) wore it shopping in the city. In the spring, pants belled, jackets were jacket-length.

Fall brought pipestem pants worn with tunic-length jackets or full-length (daytime) coats. Suitings were quite diverse: gray melton, chalk-striped flannel, shiny yellow vinyl.

Another shape in the 1966 closet was the hip-slung hip-skirt. It could be the quickest flip of fabric—the halfway-up-the-thigh mini-skirt or a mere inch or two above the knee. Worn either with a flower-printed T-shirt or a ribbed skivvy, the "hippy" was practically the summer uniform. Fall brought hip-skirts in fur with matching jackets, in kidskin, vinyl and cut velvet and in the more conventional wool plaids, flannels and coverts. The college girl wore her hippies with spare sweaters, knitted shirts, flowered or striped shirts and wide ties (never matching) copied from the boys' clothes sold on Carnaby Street in London.

Fabrics. Fabric often made the difference between a conservative look and a slightly mad one. It was a year for leather—smooth or sueded; for vinyls—flowered, tortoiseshell and fluorescent; for velvets and cut velvet; for double-faced wools (reversibles) and shetland;

216

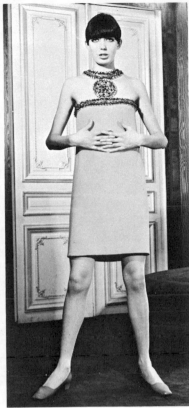

Left: This Christian Dior-N.Y. suit features a skirt slightly gathered at the waist.
Center: Cardin's cocktail dresses hit a new high, the hemlines hitting the thighs.
Right: Nina Ricci's cape design stood out in a season of stunning capelike creations.

for laces and crepe. It was also a year for metallics. Silver, bronze, pewter or gold threaded through knits; surfaced tricots (that looked like leathers), glittered in paillettes. From Paco Rabanne, a Parisian costume-jewelry designer, came plastic disks strung together in a dress shape—to slide over a body stocking or a silk slip. Another Rabanneism: a coat of cowhide triangles, gold-riveted onto shaker knitting.

Accessories and Other Items. Accessories were not mere addenda in 1966: the right shoes and stockings could finish or distort a line. The right shoes for short skirts were low-heeled. In this category: T-strapped sandals, Pilgrim-buckled pumps (the year's status shoe), chunky chained loafers, silver slippers, a raft of offerings in colorful patent leathers. More leg showing meant showier legs. Generally one pulled on tights, textured stockings, knee socks or over-the-knee socks. They came in nubby crochets, neutral fishnets, stripes, sweater cabling, point d'esprit, silver, and gold. The white stocking achieved a fashion status never before experienced. (Incidentally, leg makeups—like rouge and mouches for the knees—were showiest of all.) Boots were almost passé, then Paris revived them. The snazziest looked like high-buttoned shoes, or rose knee-high on tiny heels.

As for underwear, it looked like outerwear and was sometimes worn that way. Sleep clothes, too, could go out with the sun. A gaily striped slip slipped out to a discothèque; a sleeping shirt filled in with shorts. The lingerie shape was small and streamlined; the fabrics, noisy—a strong plaid, riotous flowers, pinstripes, a print simulating leopard or zebra. That last might match a real fur dress and coat. From Morocco and the East came jellabas and caftans for parties and for at-home lounging as well.

The face in fashion was subtly contoured with glowing blushers, glossy pale lipsticks, neutral eye shadows. The "in" hairdo was straight, long and thick. Almost everyone wanted a wiglet, especially a fall. (In real hair or Dynel, wefted to a small circular base, it took over the tasks of a full wig for young people.)

FIREARMS CONTROL

By EDWARD M. KENNEDY
Senator (D–Mass.), Member
JUVENILE DELINQUENCY SUBCOMMITTEE

A Menace to Society. The deadly potential of a firearm in the hands of the wrong person was brought home dramatically to the American people in 1966 by a series of shocking killings. In Austin, Tex., a deranged student climbed a tower, shot 14 people to death and wounded 32 others, before being killed himself; in Mesa, Ariz., 4 women and 1 child were killed, and a woman and child were wounded during a gruesome shooting in a beauty parlor; in New Haven, Conn., a man burst into an apartment with a carbine in his hand and shot 7 people, killing 5.

These spectacular mass killings suggest a fact which statistics bear out: America pays a drastic toll in lives each year for its attitude toward the possession and use of firearms. This attitude can only be described as irresponsible. Although every state in the Union has some kind of regulation on the use of firearms, the regulations vary widely from state to state and in the great majority of states are wholly inadequate. Furthermore, and more important, there is no Federal gun-control law which effectively regulates the sale and circulation of firearms in interstate traffic.

This combination of lax state laws and the absence of effective Federal laws to govern the interstate traffic of firearms does not provide adequate firearms control in the United States. A hunter or a marksman in this country can purchase a weapon with almost complete freedom, either over-the-counter or through the mail. But just as easily a criminal, a drug addict or even a child can purchase the same weapon.

The illegitimate use of firearms is now a distinct menace. About 17,000 Americans die each year from firearms, 600 of them children under 14 killed in gun accidents. In 1965, firearms accounted for 57 per cent of the nation's murders. A total of 278 police officers have been killed in the line of duty since 1960, and 96 per cent of them were killed by guns. Aggravated assaults by firearms totaled over 34,000 in 1965, and armed robberies committed with firearms totaled over 68,000. Sales of firearms through the mail reached a 1963 total of over 1 million; over-the-counter sales are estimated at 2 million each year.

These statistics are a source of continuing wonder to observers from foreign lands. Elsewhere in the world, gun-control laws are considered basic and the number of deaths by firearms in most other countries of the world is just a fraction of the carnage in the United States each year. Furthermore, many lethal weapons manufactured in foreign countries are not circulated in the country of their origin, but are sold instead in the United States. From 1959 to 1965, between five and seven million foreign weapons, old and new, poured into this country from abroad. It is estimated that from 75 to 90 per cent of the world's surplus war weapons are imported into the United States. England will not allow the importation of surplus military weapons, nor will Germany. But the United States will, and where there is a ready market there will always be someone to supply that market.

Some of our foreign critics like to explain America's high rate of firearm homicides with the suggestion that we as a nation still have the gun-happy mentality which has come to characterize our pioneer and Wild West history. This romantic notion is something less than the truth. One of the chief reasons so many Americans are killed or wounded by firearms is that firearms are so plentiful in this country and so easy to purchase. Some states, to be sure, have taken strong action to restrict the purchase of firearms within their borders. But how effective can these state laws be when guns can be purchased through the mails, or brought in from a nearby state whose laws are not so demanding?

Federal Control. If we are to make any progress, we must first establish a Federal framework of gun control. We must regulate interstate traffic in firearms, so that individual states can effectively enforce their own gun-control laws, without the disruptive effect of mail-order sales and gun traffic from other states.

This solution may be clear, but it is also very controversial. Continuing efforts to pass effective firearms-control legislation at the Federal level have failed because the opposition to such legislation is strong, united and well financed. The moving force behind this opposition is the National Rifle Association, and the hundreds of thousands of riflemen and hunters who see their way of life threatened by any attempt to pass a strong gun bill.

These citizens feel that the idea of Federal gun control is aimed at them. They say a Federal firearms law would cripple the rights of the law-abiding, the decent citizen who has a legitimate use for a firearm. Some even see in Federal gun control a plot by the Federal Government to register and eventually confiscate every firearm in the land, perhaps in preparation for a takeover by a foreign power.

Those of us who believe in Federal firearm legislation are faced with the task of calming these fears and explaining what such legislation would do and what it would not do.

There have, of course, been many gun-control bills proposed in Congress in recent years, and much disagreement on what constitutes a workable and effective law. But perhaps the one which best embodies the central aim of firearms control is the bill introduced by Sen. Thomas Dodd (D-Conn.), and reported out of the Juvenile Delinquency Subcommittee late in the second session of the 89th Congress.

The subcommittee bill would:

- Ban the mail-order sale of handguns.
- Regulate the mail-order sale of rifles and shotguns by requiring an affidavit.
- Require that firearms dealers be Federally licensed, and set license standards.
- Ban the sale of handguns to persons under 21, and rifles to persons under 18.
- Ban the over-the-counter sale of handguns by dealers to persons who reside in states other than the state of the dealer.
- Limit the importation of military surplus firearms and certain foreign-made firearms.

This bill would regulate interstate commerce in firearms to help keep guns out of the hands of those who would misuse them, and it would assist states in enforcing their firearms-control laws.

This bill would not interfere with the hunter. Nor would it interfere with the marksman, nor the gun collector, nor any citizen who had a legitimate reason for possessing a firearm. It would simply establish a Federal framework of basic firearms control.

There is no question that in this country today the rights of a citizen who has a legitimate use for a firearm are fully protected. What we must now consider is whether every citizen is protected against the irresponsible member of society who does not have a legitimate use and can yet purchase a firearm with ease and impunity. It is time that we look to the rights of the public, for it is the public that suffers from our failure to initiate responsible controls over the interstate traffic in firearms.

FLORIDA. Plans were announced in January for the razing of Miami Beach's famed Roney Plaza Hotel. . . . Tornadoes cut across central Florida Apr. 4, killing 10 persons and injuring over 300. . . . Hurricane Alma lashed Florida June 8–9. . . . Pompano Beach was the scene of a race riot June 21; similar disturbances occurred in July in Jacksonville.

Florida's new Republican Governor Claude Kirk.

UPI

FORD, GERALD R. House Republican Leader Ford, lacking the troops to block many Johnson administration bills in the 1966 Congress, spent much of the year campaigning for GOP gains in the Nov. 8 election. He proved a good

House Minority Leader Gerald Ford, January 1966.

Wide World

prophet, predicting Feb. 10 at Hampton, Va., that his party would win as many as 50 House seats: the gain was 47.

In a speech April 22 at Minneapolis, Minn., Ford declared that disunity among Democrats on U.S. Vietnam policy was "hurting the nation's war effort." Ford generally supported President Johnson's war policies through the year. However, he told a Springfield, Ill., audience Aug. 17 that Vietnam, violence in the cities and inflation were the issues which the Republicans would use to break down the Democratic "stranglehold" on Congress in November.

On Oct. 18, at Cincinnati, Ohio, Ford charged that the administration "has failed miserably in its handling of our economic problems," adding, "we are now faced with the highest interest rates in 45 years."

In late November, Representative Ford, and other Congressional leaders, met with President Johnson at the LBJ Ranch in Texas to discuss the economy and the forthcoming Federal budget. Ford called the meeting "extremely productive." He added, however, that he opposed a tax increase as a way of combating inflation.

Ford easily won reelection Nov. 8 in the 5th Michigan district to his 10th consecutive term in Congress. On Jan. 9, 1967, Representative Ford was reelected to serve as House minority leader in the 90th Congress.

JOSEPH W. HALL, JR.
Washington Bureau, THE ASSOCIATED PRESS

FOREIGN AID. The Johnson administration, for fiscal 1967, asked for $3,385,962,000 for foreign aid. The U.S. Congress authorized $3,-500,735,500. It appropriated $2,936,490,500.

The story behind these figures is interesting. This time the administration asked for less money for foreign aid than it ever had before in the 19 years of the program. It kept its request down for three major reasons: the Vietnam war, which was having its effect on all programs; a feeling that Congress expected a bare-bones figure minus all fat; recognition that Congress was getting fed up with the program in general.

But the sum finally appropriated was not the smallest sum ever voted. Nor was the percentage cut from the original request the smallest. In 1955 only $2,700,000,000 was appropriated; and in 1965 the percentage cut from the request was only 6.9 per cent, as against 1966's 13.3 per cent.

But there was a unique and surprising feature about Congressional action in 1966. It is customary for Congress to authorize less than the administration asks, and to appropriate less than it has authorized. But in 1966 it actually authorized more than the White House requested—$115 million more. But then it wound up by voting less than either authorized or requested. In the final figure of $2,936,490,500 the division between economic assistance and military assistance was $2,144,490,500 for economic help, $729 million for military assistance. (Funds for South Vietnam military assistance are not included.) This was about how the division had been running for some years.

It turned out that the final appropriation figure was the same net total as appropriated by the Senate. Normally the final figure is somewhere between what the Senate has appropriated and what the House has approved. But in 1966 the House accepted the Senate figure when conferees got together, a figure which was $110,575,300 below what the House had appropriated.

As sent to the President, the following foreign aid funds were appropriated for fiscal 1967:

Economic Assistance	
Development Loans	$ 500,000,000
Technical Cooperation and Development Grants	. 200,000,000
Alliance for Progress	
Loans	420,300,000
Grants	87,700,000
Supporting Assistance	690,000,000
Contingency Fund	35,000,000
International Organizations	140,433,000
American Schools and Hospitals Abroad	11,989,000
Administrative Expenses	
AID	55,813,500
State Department	3,255,000
Military Assistance	792,000,000
Total Foreign Aid	$2,936,490,500

U.S. FOREIGN AID SINCE WORLD WAR II—$125,000,000,000

	MILLIONS OF DOLLARS FISCAL 1945-65			MILLIONS OF DOLLARS FISCAL 1945-65			MILLIONS OF DOLLARS FISCAL 1945-65	
---	MILITARY	ECONOMIC	---	MILITARY	ECONOMIC	---	MILITARY	ECONOMIC
EUROPE	$16,192	$30,541	**FAR EAST**	$9,913	$16,191	Turkey	$2,635	$2,120
Austria	*	1,198	Japan	1,076	2,859	U.A.R. (Egypt)	None	1,081
Belgium-Luxembourg	1,255	732	Korea	2,291	4,011			
Denmark	621	302	Laos	*	419	**LATIN AMERICA**	925	9,425
France	4,261	5,141	Philippines	468	1,421	Argentina	68	639
Germany	952	4,043	Taiwan	2,531	2,225	Bolivia	13	414
Great Britain	1,035	7,924	Thailand	*	434	Brazil	270	2,519
Greece	1,780	1,890	Vietnam	*	2,378	Chile	110	1,014
Iceland	None	76				Colombia	78	646
Ireland	None	147	**NEAR EAST &**			Dominican Republic	14	190
Italy	2,311	3,742	**SOUTH ASIA**	6,265	17,324	Ecuador	42	206
Netherlands	1,243	1,230	Afghanistan	3	304	Mexico	11	1,019
Norway	853	402	Ceylon	None	91	Panama	2	157
Portugal	334	183	India	*	5,882	Paraguay	6	84
Spain	584	1,280	Iran	712	837	Peru	126	505
Sweden	None	109	Israel	28	1,046	Venezuela	93	
Yugoslavia	696	2,038	Jordan	37	474			
* classified			Pakistan	*	2,937	**AFRICA**	$186	$3,051

Reprinted from "World Journal Tribune," New York, Sept. 18, 1966.

The final bill provided $110 million for the Peace Corps, $250 million for the Inter-American Development Bank, $104 million for the International Development Assn., and $51 million for Cuban refugee relief.

As passed, the bill contained a provision allowing the President to transfer up to 10 per cent of development loan funds to the World Bank and its affiliates. It put an absolute ban on aid to countries selling, furnishing, or permitting any ships under their registry to carry any strategic or economically beneficial items to North Vietnam, or to Cuba as long as Castro ran the country. In previous years the President had been permitted to continue such aid if he judged that withholding it was against the national interest.

Debate during the year on foreign aid, and the sums authorized and appropriated, again pointed up the traumatic experience that debate on this subject brings to Congress. The legislative body is increasingly disillusioned with foreign aid and wishes it were possible to cut it out. (For one reason, countries receiving foreign aid have no constituents to vote in U.S. elections.) But at the same time Congress recognizes that not only does the need for foreign aid continue, but it seems to increase—not in Europe or industrialized countries but in the innumerable poorer and less industrialized countries of Asia and Africa.

It is possible that if the White House had made a more vigorous effort to salvage its full request from Congress it might have done bet-

Wide World

Congress appropriated $2,936,490,500 for foreign aid in 1966. Above: India's hungry benefit from the program.

ter in the final figure. But everyone agrees that President Johnson's preoccupation with the Vietnam war, with the Great Society, with the nation's economy and (some said) with the November elections resulted in the smallest aid bill in nine years and the first dip below $3,-000,000,000 in that period.

NEAL STANFORD
Washington Staff Correspondent
THE CHRISTIAN SCIENCE MONITOR

MILITARY NUCLEAR WEAPON STATIONS | URANIUM MINES | URANIUM PLANT | POWER PLANTS | RESEARCH CENTERS

"The New York Times"

FRANCE. France remained the most politically stable and one of the most prosperous states in Western Europe in 1966. Once again, its influence under the leadership of President Charles de Gaulle reached well beyond the numbers of its some 48 million inhabitants. But as De Gaulle began his second seven-year term in office and passed his 76th birthday in November, many feared that France's political solidity, and perhaps even its economic fortune,

Premier Kosygin, President de Gaulle confer in Paris.
UPI

would sharply falter when he leaves the scene. Some felt that he would not serve out his full seven years, although his health and determination seemed to be as vigorous as ever.

All through 1966, France's shattered opposition politicians, sidelined by De Gaulle when he returned to power in 1958, were attempting to situate themselves to benefit from the legislative elections expected to be held in March 1967. Two main groupings arose, headed by the two runners behind De Gaulle in the 1965 elections. They were François Mitterrand, an old-time political figure from the Fourth Republic days, who shaped the Federation of the Democratic-Socialist Left, composed of the Socialist Party, plus the Radical Party and other small groupings; and Jean Lecanuet, youthful, Kennedy-style former Christian Democratic party leader, who sought to project his Democratic Center group more advantageously.

Mitterrand, aware of the decisive importance of the Communists' 20 per cent of the vote, flirted with the Reds all year, finally reaching in December an agreement to jointly oppose Gaullism. Even if the loose character of the agreement does not make them the dominant factor in the electoral alliance, the Communists emerged from the virtual political isolation in which they had been kept since 1947.

A main feature of the compact concerns the withdrawal of candidates, after the first round of the elections, in which both parties—the Federation and the Communists—will present their own separate candidates in most of the electoral districts. If no candidate achieves an absolute majority, a second round is held; for this a simple majority suffices.

According to the terms of the agreement, the Leftist candidate with the least votes will pull out in favor of the other, when he has a reasonable chance of winning. The representatives of the two political groupings will meet immediately after the first round to implement the arrangement, through which they expect to reduce the preponderance in the National Assembly now held by the Gaullist Union for the New Republic. More important yet, the premises have been developed for a cooperation of the Left, even after the election. But many observers thought the alliance was too fragile to survive unless it scored clear electoral success —something very problematical.

Nuclear Development. Bolstering its status on the international level, France appeared to be moving rapidly toward thermonuclear-power status. Tests of atomic bombs and a "doped" bomb were conducted at a new Pacific test site on Mururoa atoll, in the region of Tahiti. The doped bomb had some thermonuclear

France honors Pablo Picasso on his 85th birthday with exhibition (above, mural *Parade*).

characteristics. Meanwhile on test ranges in southwestern France, short- and medium-range missiles were being perfected for the day when H-warheads will be ready. At the same time, France's force of supersonic Mirage IV atomic bombers numbered more than 50, each plane presumably with quick access to an atomic bomb. France continued to stress that it would be willing to join in a nuclear-disarmament scheme, but only if all the nuclear powers are prepared to accept a program that includes destruction of existing weapons stockpiles and the means to deliver them.

Economy.　France's prosperity seemed to be as secure as at any time in the past decade, with stores bursting with luxury items from the

NATO eviction notice will empty this Rochefort, France, harbor of U.S. ships.

On parade in Morocco are Gen. Mohammed Oufkir (l) and Maj. Ahmed Dlimi of the "affaire Ben Barka."

other five members of the European Common Market and from farther afield. Automobiles, another clear measure of prosperity, had become so numerous on the streets of the capital that authorities were considering vast new parking restrictions and ways to direct traffic through tunnels or along riverbanks. In Paris, where there was one car for every 3.5 persons, officials cautioned that the ratio would become even higher before streets and suburban highways could be adapted to accommodate the crush.

France's pitifully short superhighway system, shorter than even the smallest of her neighbors', was gradually adding new segments in the north and south. But drivers, who already pay the equivalent of about $1 a gallon for gasoline, are obliged to pay tolls to use some of the new stretches.

France disturbed the United States early in 1966 by cashing in excess dollars for gold. But in October and November, France ran low on dollars and the gold drain halted, at least temporarily. This depletion, which was far from serious at the end of the year, was a reflection of a developing unfavorable trade balance. In November, imports were covered by exports only up to 87 per cent, and it appeared that trade figures for the entire year would end in the minus column, in contrast to 1965. But despite this softening, Frenchmen seemed to be throwing caution to the winds

as the Christmas shopping season arrived. Three weeks before Christmas, big department stores were often so crowded that many shoppers were unable to get through doors and had to be content with examining window displays.

Housing. Despite many external signs of prosperity, France was still far from resolving its postwar housing crisis. Housing-ministry officials said at the end of the year that 20 to 25 per cent of France's 48 million inhabitants are in varying degrees badly housed. On an average, a Frenchman has one room to himself, a figure lower than that of most of western Europe. Despite mushrooming low-cost housing on the outskirts of many provincial cities and Paris, officials estimated it will take another 15 to 20 years to resolve the housing problem.

Crime. France's criminal case of the year, which spilled over the Mediterranean to Morocco, was the "affaire Ben Barka." Mehdi Ben Barka, the Leftist opposition leader in Morocco, disappeared from a Paris Left Bank street in late October 1965. The case finally got to trial in September after months of preliminary investigation. A half dozen defendants were in the box, and as many others were to be tried in absentia. After 39 trial sessions in which details of the case became more and more complex, the hearings were forced to a halt by the sudden appearance of Maj. Ahmed Dlimi, head of the Moroccan security police, who was accused in absentia of a role in the kidnaping. Dlimi said that he turned himself in to cleanse his country's name. President de Gaulle had accused Dlimi's chief, Interior Minister Mohammed Oufkir, of engineering the elimination of Ben Barka. A new trial was in prospect in 1967, but there seemed little chance of ever finding out what really happened to Ben Barka and who was responsible.

Colonies. France had a brief but ugly reminder during 1966 that it still had a colonial problem. When President de Gaulle went on a round-the-world trip in late August, he stopped first in Djibouti, French Somaliland, on Africa's eastern horn. He was met by mobs shouting demands for immediate independence. Rioting caused several deaths and scores of wounded persons, and forced France to envisage the possible loss of one of the few remaining parts of its once vast empire. De Gaulle scheduled a referendum for 1967, when residents of Somaliland will decide their political fate. Should they choose independence, the Somali Republic and Ethiopia would probably rush in to stake their claims.

DAVID M. MASON
Paris Bureau, THE ASSOCIATED PRESS

GAMES: Trends and Twists. During the twentieth century there has been an expansion of leisure time, a widening of the distribution of wealth, and an improvement in the general level of education. In the United States in particular, these factors have contributed in a large degree to the increased number of people who play games, and the increased number and types of games produced.

Although, over the last few years, there has been little new in basic game principles, game players have demanded more sophistication and more opportunity for decision than ever before. Much of what is popular today consists of a reshuffling of previously existing ideas, and a development of these ideas to make them compatible with everyday experiences. It is interesting to note that some games today, new and old, are being played against computers, and that when properly programed, the computer usually wins.

There has been a tendency in recent years toward inventing indoor games that include some physical action or manual dexterity. Booby Trap, Tippit and Hands Down are good examples. This tendency probably results from the ability of the manufacturers to use new techniques and new materials to produce at reasonable prices simple mechanical devices formerly impractical because of expense.

Of course there is always a place for fad games—games that create a momentary stir in the marketplace, then pass on and are heard of no more. For the most part, fad games are based on current events or fads in other fields, and they are generally promoted by television.

The favorite fad game of 1966 derived from Batman.

Perhaps the most unusual games development of 1966 was the Monopoly marathon. Throughout the United States, people played Monopoly for days on end. Two players found the game so fascinating that they played it for a record sixty hours without stopping. The record for team play, with members spelling each other and thus having a chance to sleep, was established at six hundred hours.

Of the trends in games, it seems likely that the trend toward sophistication will endure the longest. As scientists open up new worlds, and as more of the general population grasps the significance of these developments, today's marvels will become tomorrow's commonplaces. So it is with games. They will in future match the other wonders of everyday life. It is only a matter of time, for example, until the "new math" will be basic in game play.

EDWARD P. PARKER
Executive Vice-President, PARKER BROTHERS INC.

BRIDGE

Public interest in contract bridge increased in amazing fashion throughout 1966. Most attendance records at regional and national tournaments were broken, and capacity crowds sailed the seas on the famous Travel-with-Goren cruises that now carry bridge enthusiasts to almost every corner of the globe.

At the Summer Nationals in Denver, Colo., the American Contract Bridge League approved its 7,535th Life Master and the end

Staff members of Abt Associates, developers of educational games, play Manchester.

Abt Associates, Inc.

is nowhere near in sight with new adherents climbing on the "Master Point" bandwagon every day.

On the international scene a highly regarded North American team once again finished second to the apparently invincible Italians. Venezuela took third place, the Netherlands fourth and Thailand, competing in the international matches for the first time, finished fifth.

Winners of the American Contract Bridge League spring national tournament titles were:

Life Master Pairs—Hermine Baron, Meyer Schleifer, Los Angeles, Calif.

Open Pairs—Edgar Kaplan, New York City; Norman Kay, Philadelphia, Pa.

Men's Pairs—Barry Crane, Van Nuys, Calif.; Peter Rank, Walnut Creek, Calif.

Women's Pairs—Edith Kemp, Miami Beach, Fla.; Virginia Heckel, Chicago, Ill.

Women's Teams—Mrs. Frieda Arst, Chicago, Ill.; Mrs. Carol Stolkin, Wilmette, Ill.; Mrs. June Deutsch, Skokie, Ill.; Mrs. Sylvia Stein, Detroit, Mich.—tied with Mrs. Terry Michaels, Washington, D.C.; Mrs. Garner McDaniel, Houston; Mrs. John Gruver, Ellicott City, Md.; Mrs. David Sachs, Beltsville, Md.

Men's Teams—Edgar Kaplan, Philip Feldesman, New York City; Norman Kay, Philadelphia, Pa.; Richard Freeman, Atlanta, Ga.

Vanderbilt Teams—Lew Mathe, Los Angeles, Calif.; Robert Hamman, Van Nuys, Calif.; Philip Feldesman, New York City; Ira Rubin, Paramus, N.J.; Sammy Kehela, Toronto, Ont.

Spingold Teams—Ira Rubin, Paramus, N.J.; Bill Rott, New York City; Alvin Roth, New York City; Curtis Smith, Houston, Tex.

Blue Ribbon Pairs—Richard Zeckhauser, Great Neck, N.Y.; Charles Coon, New York City.

Mixed Pairs—Mr. and Mrs. Robert Sharp, Miami Beach, Fla.

CHARLES H. GOREN
Bridge Authority

CHESS

Tigran Petrosian of Armenia became the first world champion to successfully defend his chess title in postwar times. He defeated fellow U.S.S.R. challenger Boris Spassky of Leningrad by 12½–11½ in a cautious (positional) but hard-fought match with all of seventeen draws.

Spassky rebounded by winning the Piatigorsky Cup Tournament, sponsored by famous cello player Gregor Piatigorsky and his wife. He won what is for chess a fabulous first prize of $5,000, scoring 11½–6½, a half point ahead of U.S. Champion Robert J. Fischer of Brooklyn, N. Y., and well ahead of world champion Petrosian at 9–9. Fischer was at the bottom of the standings at the halfway mark, then surged to the top in a sensational spurt.

"Chess Review"

Havana chess match: Premier Castro vs. Bobby Fischer.

Soviet players won nearly all major tournaments in 1966. Spassky was tied for first by Wolfgang Unzicker of West Germany at Hastings, England; and Mikhail Tahl was tied by a comparatively unknown Yugoslav master at Sarajevo, Yugoslavia. But Lev Polugayevsky won at Beverwijk, the Netherlands; Vassily Smyslov at Santiago, Chile, and Mar del Plata, Argentina; and Mikhail Botvinnik at Amsterdam. Bent Larsen of Denmark alone surpassed Soviet players, winning at Le Havre, France, two points ahead of N. Krogius and Polugayevsky. Larsen also defeated the Soviet's Yefim Geller in a match, 5–4.

At Havana, Cuba, the Soviet team won its eighth straight world team title in the "Chess Olympics." Petrosian, Spassky, Tahl, Soviet champion Leonid Stein and alternates Korchnoy and Polugayevski ran up 39½-11½ game points.

Fischer won his seventh straight U.S. Championship, an all-time record. Pal Benko of Santa Monica and Robert Byrne of Indianapolis tied for the U.S. Open Championship in which Mrs. Mary Bain won the women's title. Jack P. Witeczek of Detroit took the first U.S. Open Postal Chess Championship. And Walter S. Browne of Brooklyn became the first (invitational) U. S. Junior Champion, and Charles Alden of Minneapolis came in first in the U. S. Junior Open Championship.

JACK STRALEY BATTELL
Executive Editor, CHESS REVIEW

GANDHI, INDIRA. Prime Minister of the world's largest democracy for all but three weeks of 1966, Mrs. Indira Gandhi still lives in the bungalow she occupied as a cabinet minister. Her decision not to seek more suitable quarters symbolized the uncertainty of her political tenure.

Few heads of government have assumed office with as many handicaps. Mrs. Gandhi was a woman prime minister in a nation where her sex is just beginning to emerge from millennia of discrimination. Although she came from a family long prominent in Indian politics, she had no following of her own. Neither did she inherit one, like Mrs. Sirimavo Bandaranaike, Ceylon's onetime premier.

Mrs. Gandhi became India's third prime minister on Jan. 24, 1966, following the death of Lal Bahadur Shastri. Her election was engineered by Kumaraswami Kamaraj, president of the ruling Congress Party, and a coalition of state leaders. They hoped to trade on memories of her father, Jawaharlal Nehru, India's revered first prime minister, and translate them into votes in the coming elections.

But the 48-year-old daughter surprised them. After an initially slow start, Mrs. Gandhi began charting a course of her own which often dismayed the politicians who put her in office. Once considered a member of the party's Left Wing, she gathered around her a small group of pragmatists who subordinated ideology to policies which would help break India's chronic economic stagnation.

By summer her control began to slip, however. Unpopular economic reforms, like devaluation of the Indian rupee, failed to show prompt results, leaving her vulnerable to charges she had knuckled under to foreign pressure. The rising tide of violent demonstrations, culminating in a riot in the capital in November, further damaged her Government's prestige. A second severe drought forced her again to seek additional relief from the United States.

Mrs. Gandhi's weakness derived from her lack of a personal following within the Congress Party. At one time or another she offended each of the leaders who had supported her, including Kamaraj. Her loyal followers had little political strength of their own. Their political vulnerability was exposed in November, when Mrs. Gandhi succeeded in dropping from her Cabinet only one of three ministers she attempted to eliminate.

Still, no one could forget Mrs. Gandhi was a Nehru. Occasionally she displayed some of her father's determination. Born at the family's ancestral home in Allahabad on Nov. 19, 1917, she grew up at the headquarters of India's independence movement. Widowed in 1960, Mrs. Gandhi spent most of her adult life serving as her father's hostess, traveling companion and political aide.

Although she served a successful term in 1959 as Congress Party president, Mrs. Gandhi did not accept public office until her father died in 1964. She joined Shastri's Cabinet as minister for information and broadcasting.

At year's end, Mrs. Gandhi was trying to recoup her fading popularity by going to the electorate over the party leaders' heads. Her advisers were counting on her personal appeal to stem dissatisfaction with the Congress Party and confirm her in office as its most effective vote getter.

James S. Keat
New Delhi Bureau Chief, THE BALTIMORE SUN

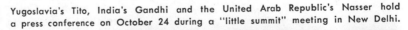

Yugoslavia's Tito, India's Gandhi and the United Arab Republic's Nasser hold a press conference on October 24 during a "little summit" meeting in New Delhi.

UPI

GEOLOGY. The year 1966 was one of the most active earthquake periods of recent times, with quakes occurring daily throughout the world.

Earthquakes. The most destructive earthquake in 98 years battered the central Asian city of Tashkent, capital of the Soviet Republic of Uzbekistan with a population of 1,127,000. Occurring on Apr. 26, it was followed by more than 600 additional shocks within the next three months, two of which were also quite severe. Soviet reports indicated 28,000 buildings destroyed, over 300,000 persons made homeless, 500 injured, but only 15 killed.

Severest of the earthquakes of 1966 was the one that occurred in easternmost Turkey on Aug. 19. It registered 7.5 on the Richter Scale (which measures an earthquake's intensity). It was followed by more than 100 aftershocks during the next two days, with spasmodic ones recurring for about a month. The Turkish Government officially fixed the death toll at 2,394, and the injuries at 1,747.

Numerous earthquakes occurred in the United States, but none was extremely severe. The strongest was the one that shook the High Sierra mountain region, centered in the vicinity of Truckee, Calif. With a severity of 6.5 on the Richter Scale, it was felt strongly in Reno,

Nev. Several other earthquakes also occurred in California, most of them associated with the San Andreas Fault in the southern half of the state. They displaced land a distance of four inches along the fault line in Monterey County. Several earthquakes were reported from Alaska, mostly from the Anchorage area, which had been hit by a devastating quake two years earlier. Moderate quakes occurred also in Utah, New Mexico, Virginia and West Virginia.

Japan reported the greatest number of earthquakes—an amazing 400,000 since August 1965. Most of these were centered in the area of Matsushiro, a town of 22,000 people in central Japan. Elsewhere in the Pacific Ocean area, earthquakes of strong intensity occurred off Vancouver Island, Canada; in the Philippine Islands; in the Solomon Islands and in central New Zealand.

A series of strong quakes, extending over a three-week period, shook a wide area in northern China, but communist reports lacked details. A series of quakes in Pakistan reportedly killed 11 persons and injured 40. Quakes also occurred at New Delhi and Shillong in India, as well as in Afghanistan.

In Europe, a series of more than 30 earthquakes of medium intensity shook the area of

Discovery well, Rainbow Lake Field, Alberta, Canada.

Gary Harker, "The Edmonton Journal"

Titograd, Yugoslavia. At Skopje, Yugoslavia, a long series of quakes continued. This series that began with the catastrophic quake in July 1963 now numbers well over 600. In Greece, more than 20 quakes occurred at various times throughout the year, but caused only one death and injured 20 persons. In Africa, severe quakes struck western Uganda and northern Congo, the latter reportedly killing 90 persons.

In South America, a violent earthquake occurred off the shore of Peru, causing buildings to collapse in Lima. It was felt as far away as Ecuador and Chile, and caused reported deaths of 125 and 800 injuries. A series of several shocks took place at Bogota, Colombia, claiming seven lives. Earthquakes also occurred in Venezuela and in the Central American country of San Salvador.

The U.S. Geological Survey announced that a series of about 1,000 minor earthquakes that had occurred in the vicinity of Denver, Colo., between April 1962 and November 1965 were found to have been man-made. The disposal of contaminated waste fluids from chemical operations into a 12,000-ft. well at the Army's Rocky Mountain Arsenal caused the quakes, the strongest of which was 4.3 on the Richter Scale. The well extended into highly fractured, relatively impermeable gneiss rock. When fluids were injected into the rock, slippage occurred along the fracture planes, producing the man-made earthquakes. With suspension of the waste disposal program, the earthquakes stopped.

A National Earthquake Information Center was established at the Coast & Geodetic Survey headquarters in Rockville, Md., which will report the occurrence of all earthquakes of medium magnitude (6.5 on the Richter Scale) or larger. It will also be the focal point of the Earthquake Emergency Plan to provide emergency and technical aid to areas damaged by earthquakes.

Volcanoes. Volcanic activity during the year was relatively minor, the only eruption of consequence occurring in eastern Java when Mt. Kelut erupted streams of lava and volcanic ash, resulting in reported deaths exceeding 100. Mt. Awu on the island of Sangir Besar near the Philippines also erupted with a reported loss of 28 lives, as did a volcano on Celebes Island where 28 persons were reported killed and 2,000 injured. Mt. Etna, on the island of Sicily, was reportedly active on three different occasions during the year. In Alaska, Mt. Redoubt, about 120 mi. southwest of Anchorage, exploded dust and ash to heights of 15,000 ft., its most active display in many years.

Minerals. One of the North American continent's richest oil fields was opened in northwestern Alberta, Canada. Known as the Rainbow Lake Field, situated 400 mi. northwest of Edmonton, it was estimated to have a reserve of 8,000,000,000 barrels. It is second in Alberta only to the Leduc Field, which set off the province's first oil boom in 1947. A rich oil and gas field was also discovered in Australia, 28 miles offshore from Victoria in the Bass Strait. Initial production was about 900 barrels of oil and 1 million cu. ft. of gas per day from the same well.

A new water-depth drilling record for the Gulf of Mexico was attained by the Humble Oil Co. and the Standard Oil Co. of California. The well, drilled jointly by the two companies, was situated below 4,345 ft. of water.

Enlargement of the diamond mining area of South Africa became imminent after diamonds were found in Mozambique, near the border of the existing Rhodesian diamond fields. The U.S. Geological Survey announced the discovery of a new gold field near Cortez, Nev.

Outer Space. Outer-space geology, particularly with respect to the moon, was promoted by soft landings of the Russian Luna 9 and American Surveyor 1, both camera-carrying vehicles that took the first pictures ever made directly from the moon's surface. These disproved the theory that the surface is covered by thick layers of dust, and revealed that it is of solid, jagged and porous rock similar to basaltic lava flows and pumice stone on earth. It is capable of sustaining rocket landings. This discovery supports a theory that the moon's interior was once molten, like the earth's.

Another American space vehicle, moving within a few dozen miles of the moon's surface, obtained pictures that indicated that the moon is not perfectly round. It has a quarter-mile bulge at its north pole, a quarter-mile depression at the south pole, and it bulges an eighth mile in between. The vehicle also confirmed the previously calculated gravity of the moon, which is about one sixth that of the earth.

RAYMOND E. JANSSEN
Chairman, Geology Department
MARSHALL UNIVERSITY

GEORGIA. U.S. Supreme Court ruled Dec. 5 that constitutional rights of Negro Julian Bond were violated when the state House of Representatives denied him his seat because he opposed the draft and Vietnam war. . . . Booming Atlanta's nonresidential construction has more than doubled since 1960. . . . September brought race riots to Atlanta. . . . In Nov. 8 elections neither Lester G. Maddox (D) nor Howard Callaway (R) won a majority. The state legislature ruled Maddox the winner.

Unidentified man peers over shoulder of Chancellor Kiesinger, flanked by his predecessors: Adenauer (l), Erhard (r). (R) Foreign Minister Brandt.

GERMANY

By JOHN DORNBERG
Bonn-Berlin Correspondent, NEWSWEEK

Nineteen sixty-six was a year that substantially revised the image that the Federal Republic of Germany has projected to the world since 1949. East Germany remained essentially the same, despite changes in its government.

West Germany

In West Germany the Government fell, its vaunted economy revealed serious cracks, three top generals resigned in a dispute over civilian leadership, relations with both France and the United States showed few if any signs of amelioration, and reunification with East Germany appeared more distant than ever. Worst of all, for the first time since 1951, an extreme Right-Wing party with neo-Nazi overtones scored significant triumphs at the polls.

Government. Chancellor Ludwig Erhard, 69, resigned Dec. 1. The 37 months of his administration were marked by incessant bickering between rival factions of his party. But despite the growing popularity of Berlin Mayor Willy Brandt's Social Democrats (SPD), Erhard, on Sept. 19, 1965, led his Christian Democratic Union party to an upset 47.6 per cent national victory. On March 23, 1966, he beat out 42-year-old Rainer Barzel, the Bundestag majority leader, for the chairmanship of the CDU. Nevertheless, Erhard's fortunes dwindled. He made the North Rhine-Westphalian July election a test of his personal popularity and policies, only to lose control of the state that

his party had ruled since 1946. The crisis came on Oct. 27 when the four Free Democratic ministers in Erhard's cabinet resigned in protest against a planned tax increase to balance the 1967 budget. For a week Erhard tried unsuccessfully to patch together the shambles of his Government. On Nov. 2 he offered to resign if a successor, capable of building a majority Government, could be found. On Nov. 10, at a tense caucus of his party's parliamentary group, Kurt Georg Kiesinger, 62, minister-president (governor) of Baden-Württemberg, was nominated with 137 of 244 votes as the CDU/CSU (Christian Social Union) candidate for the chancellorship.

Kiesinger was a dark-horse candidate, an outsider on whom the CDU/CSU leaders could agree only because he had stood aloof from their intramural disputes. But his equivocal record as a member of the Nazi Party and as an official in the Hitler foreign ministry made him an unlikely prospect for the chancellorship.

Instead, it seemed probable that the SPD, under Brandt, would form the next Government with the mercurial FDP of former Vice-Chancellor Erich Mende, 50. Between them the two parties would have had 251 Bundestag seats to the CDU/CSU's 245. This might have assured a stable administration, but it was not enough to insure a successful parliamentary coup against Erhard, for which they would have needed 249 votes. This impasse, coupled with the CDU/CSU's refusal to renew the old partnership with the FDP, left open the door for a "grand" coalition between two archfoes, SPD and CDU/CSU. When Kiesinger took office Dec. 1, he formed a Government that for the first time in 36 years included Socialists.

While the crisis changed the complexion of West Germany's Government, it also gave rise to a new, unexpected threat to democracy—the specter of extremism embodied by the rapidly growing National Democratic Party, founded on Nov. 28, 1964.

In two years the party has mushroomed from its original 473 to a force of more than 25,000 dues-paying members. After winning an insignificant 2.9 per cent of the national vote in September 1965, the NPD captured 103 city and county council seats in Bavaria's March 13 municipal elections. Then, on Nov. 6, undoubtedly buoyed by the crisis in Bonn, it won 7.9 per cent of the vote in the Hesse elections, sending eight deputies into the legislature. Two weeks later, on Nov. 20, it repeated this feat by winning 7.4 per cent of the vote in Bavaria, where it will now be represented by 15 deputies in the state assembly.

Economy. Though there had been indications as early as autumn of 1965 that Germany's postwar boom was leveling off, the immediacy of the trouble did not become apparent until a March 16 Bundestag debate disclosed that, since 1957, rising production costs, increased popularity of fuel oil and the pressure of cheap American imports had forced the shutdown of 74 out of 173 Ruhr coal mines and the layoff of 160,000 miners.

Then Germany's steel industry reported difficulties. Beset by rising costs and foreign competition, 30 of the country's largest mills applied to the Common Market coal-and-steel authority on May 23 for permission to merge their sales operations into four huge cartels and to set prices jointly.

What seemed at first to be a problem confined to the Ruhr soon turned out to be a more general instability.

By Aug. 30, prices had risen 4 per cent in 12 months, wages 8 per cent, productivity only 2.5 per cent. The Bundesbank (central bank) tried to meet inflation by raising the rediscount rate to 5 per cent. But government spending continued unchecked, and soon money was so tight that investment and construction projects had to be halted at midpoint. As pessimism spread, orders for consumer goods dropped.

On Dec. 9, Volkswagen, the largest car manufacturer, announced that it would go on short time, shutting down for a total of 16 days in January, February and March 1967 because of a five per cent drop in domestic demand. Other car makers and nearly every other industry followed suit within a ten-day period.

By Dec. 15, the number of unemployed (327,200) was higher than the number of job openings (318,000) for the first time since 1959, and economists predicted 700,000 jobless by the spring of 1967. These difficulties have been compounded by an expected $750 million budget deficit for 1967.

Foreign Troops. For Erhard, and now Kiesinger, another major headache has been the complex question of foreign troops in Germany. The initial difficulties arose on March 29, when French President Charles de Gaulle announced the withdrawal of his forces from the integrated NATO structure. Bonn's dilemma: what to do with the 60,000 French soldiers stationed on German soil. De Gaulle argued that, despite withdrawal from NATO, the troops had a right, deriving from postwar occupation statutes, to remain. Though Bonn actually wanted the French soldiers to stay—both for reasons of defense and Franco-German amity—the Erhard government insisted that their status be redefined so as to avoid the embarrassing impression that they were occupation forces. The dispute was not resolved until Dec. 15, when Foreign Ministers Brandt and Maurice Couve de Murville agreed on an exchange of formal letters in which Germany expressed a desire for the troops to remain,

Munich youths protest successes of Germany's neo-Nazi NPD Party.

and France assented to leave them on German soil only as long as Germany wanted them.

Two different troop problems jeopardized U.S.-German relations. One, unresolved at year's end, concerns Bonn's inability to pay Washington the $675 million it owes to offset the foreign-exchange costs of maintaining 225,000 American soldiers in the Federal Republic. The other difficulty arose at midyear when, because of commitments in Vietnam, U.S. Defense Secretary Robert S. McNamara announced that 15,000 of those soldiers would be temporarily withdrawn.

A related crisis involving the 51,000 soldiers of Britain's Army of the Rhine arose when West Germany announced that it could not pay in full the $240 million British foreign-exchange costs of maintaining the troops. A temporary compromise, which will prevent withdrawal of the forces, was reached on Dec. 14, when the United States agreed to meet part of the British costs by buying $35 million worth of weapons from the United Kingdom.

The German Military. West Germany was also plagued by mounting difficulties in its own fledgling Bundeswehr. On Sept. 14 one of its nine submarines sank in the North Sea with only one of its 20 crewmen rescued. On Nov. 28, the 65th of West Germany's 700 F-104G Starfighters crashed, and all of the planes were grounded until Dec. 20.

The F-104 crashes played an important role in the summer's abortive generals' revolt, touched off by the resignation of Luftwaffe Inspector General Werner Panitzki on Aug. 22 after he had had a bitter row with Defense Minister Kai-Uwe von Hassel. The next day, General Heinz Trettner, the Bundeswehr's top officer, resigned, as did Maj. Gen. Günther Pape, commander of the Third Military District. Ostensibly, the resignations were due to a long-running dispute between the generals and the defense ministry's civilian leadership. But at their root lay far more serious problems, not the least of which has been the attempt to build a new fighting force of "Citizens in Uniform," with officers trained in the Prussian tradition, and specialists who are not up to the demands of modern warfare or the sophisticated armaments which it requires.

Foreign Relations. Germany did not fare much better in foreign affairs than in domestic matters. Relations with the United States were strained because of the troop question and because of President Johnson's Oct. 7 speech, in which he gave relaxation of tensions in Europe priority over German reunification. Both Chancellor Kiesinger in his first government policy statement on Dec. 13 and Foreign Minister Brandt on Dec. 14 said that they intend to fill the Franco-German friendship treaty with new meaning and life, for relations with President de Gaulle had remained cool during the year.

A March 25 peace note, in which Bonn called for better relations with the communist countries, was met with rebuffs from nearly every Soviet-bloc country. The only bright note was the visit in Bonn by Rumanian Foreign Trade Minister Gheorghe Cioara on May 17, and Economics Minister Kurt Schmücker's return engagement in Bucharest on Sept. 4. It was the first visit to a communist country by a German cabinet-rank officer.

East Germany

If Bonn's relations with the Soviet bloc countries were, on the whole, cool in 1966, relations with East Germany (GDR) reached the point of deep frigidity. Yet, when the year began, there had been every reason to hope for a relaxation of tensions, for 1966 started as the year of the "great dialogue" between East Germany's Socialist Unity Party (SED) and West Germany's Social Democratic Party.

On Feb. 7, Walter Ulbricht, the chairman of the East German State Council and head of the SED, sent a letter to Willy Brandt and the SPD suggesting an exchange of views on the question of German reunification. For five months the SED and SPD corresponded, negotiated and raised hopes for a televised public debate. On June 29 the SED rescinded the offer, citing as the cause a safe-conduct law that the Bonn Government had passed to assure East German speakers and negotiators "immunity from prosecution for crimes committed at the Berlin Wall." Western observers believe this merely provided the SED a convenient excuse for pulling out of the talks in which it had never intended to participate.

The dialogue negotiations had one beneficial effect, however. While they were in progress, *Neues Deutschland,* the official SED party organ, twice published the full text of SPD letters, both of which were highly critical of the Ulbricht regime. It was the first time East Germans had an opportunity to see West German views stated without alteration in their own, usually manipulated press.

Economic Revival. On Aug. 13, East Germany celebrated the fifth anniversary of the building of the Berlin Wall with a fanfare of propaganda and a display of military might. While Ulbricht's claims—that the Wall had been built to ward off an American and West German invasion—seemed ludicrous enough, the event did give Western observers an op-

All photos UPI

Walter Ulbricht addresses rally commemorating fifth anniversary of Berlin Wall.

portunity to reflect on what the Wall had done for East Germany. By any yardstick one had to admit: quite a lot. Behind the Wall, and largely unnoticed by the West, East Germany has been flexing its industrial muscles and performing what many observers regard as a "second German economic miracle."

As the Communist bloc's second, Europe's sixth and the world's eighth most powerful industrial state, East Germany has become a force to be taken seriously. Not only has industrial productivity increased by approximately 6 per cent during 1966 and the standard of living improved tangibly, but East Germany today is a country in the throes of incipient nationalism. People point with pride to their achievements.

This pride in accomplishment is reflected in East Germany's continuing push for diplomatic recognition. On March 1, Ulbricht's regime made a formal bid for membership in the United Nations. On Sept. 26 the East German leader arrived in Yugoslavia for a week-long state visit, which, Western observers agreed, culminated in a marked enhancement of Ulbricht's prestige.

Cultural Suppression. Yet, for all East Germany's diplomatic coups and for all its improved living standard, intellectual and political freedom remained a distant dream in 1966. In contrast to other communist countries, where the reins on writers and artists are being loosened, restrictions in the GDR mounted.

The clampdown began at the 11th plenary meeting of the SED central committee Dec. 19–21, 1965, in East Berlin. Liberal, critical writers and poets such as satirist Wolfgang Biermann, novelists Stefan Heym and Christa Wolf and playwright Peter Hacks were chided publicly for deviating from socialist realism and proletarian values in their works. On Jan. 12, Cultural Minister Hans Bentzien was removed from office and replaced by his deputy,

Klaus Gysi, a man regarded as more responsive to party wishes.

Economic Relations with the U.S.S.R. Just as East Germany has been unable to free itself from the fetters of intellectual Stalinism, so it has failed to shake off the shackles of economic subservience to the Soviet Union.

The trade pact with the Soviets, which on Dec. 3, 1965, prompted East German planning chief Dr. Erich Apel, to kill himself in his Berlin office, has thrown its shadow over the GDR's economic development. Details and exact figures are not available, but East German industrial bosses do not deny that they are buying raw materials from Russia at highly inflated prices, 10 to 20 per cent above the world market average, and must sell finished products to the Soviet Union at rates below the world par. Ulbricht made a secret trip to Minsk in August and attempted to revise the terms, but apparently failed. A new trade agreement that ties the GDR even closer to the U.S.S.R. was signed Sept. 18.

Government. There have been a number of changes in government and the party. On Jan. 29, thirteen new cabinet ministers, in charge of a variety of economic functions, were appointed. On Sept. 23, at the start of the SED's 13th plenary central-committee meeting, two fast-rising pragmatists, Günter Mittag, chief of industry, and Gerhard Grüneberg, were promoted to full Politburo membership.

But despite the influx of new blood into the party's and regime's top leadership, the central power constellation in East Germany remained unchanged. As in the past, 1966 was a year full of rumors that 73-year-old Walter Ulbricht was in failing health and that his grip was loosening. His occasional absences from the public scene that gave rise to such reports were never long, however, and each time the spade-bearded leader returned, he seemed more powerful than before.

Keystone

UPI

Left: Queen Elizabeth II, Prince Philip and (l to r) Prince Edward, Prince Andrew and Prince Charles. Above: 16-year-old Princess Anne at Balmoral, in Scotland.

GREAT BRITAIN

By WILLIAM H. STRINGER
London Bureau Chief
THE CHRISTIAN SCIENCE MONITOR

A financially handicapped Britain found itself engaged in two crucial undertakings in 1966—the kind of ventures in which mankind's best efforts have often come to grief.

On the foreign front, Britain was attempting, through the doubtful device of economic sanctions, to topple a rebellious Rhodesian government, or to cause the white Rhodesians to afford the black inhabitants unhindered progress toward majority rule.

Sanctions, under the old League of Nations, failed to deter Italy from its aggression in Ethiopia.

At home, Britain was attempting to deflate an "overheated" economy—in which wage rises had vastly outdistanced productivity increases —and then to reflate that economy without touching off a new overheating.

Many Western nations, caught at various times in similar "stop-go" cycles, watched closely to see whether Britain could apply new formulas to break the cycle.

Meanwhile the Labor Government, reversing its former stance, was moving at the year's end to knock again at the door of the European Common Market, which had been slammed against Britain in 1963.

Domestic Scene

General Election. The year 1966 had dawned amid rumors of a new general election. The Labor Party's paper-thin Commons ma-

jority of three seats was obviously inadequate for handling grave issues looming ahead. In February, Prime Minister Harold Wilson called for an election in March. This Labor won handily, increasing its House of Commons majority to ninety-seven. Conservative Leader Edward Heath had campaigned vigorously, issuing jeremiads about the shaky economy and the need to "go into Europe." But Mr. Wilson shrewdly perceived that the electorate would be influenced by two main arguments: 1. That Labor had not had a fair opportunity to show its mettle, in less than two years of office. 2. That most wage earners, having recently won the biggest pay increases in postwar British history, were in a mellow mood. Mr. Wilson campaigned without definite commitments, and his perception was proved correct.

Wage Freeze and the Economy. Hardly had the votes been tallied, however, than the economic waves began to roughen, as Mr. Heath had predicted. A lengthy seamen's strike in spring, plus the overly mild prescriptions for bolstering the economy followed by Chancellor of the Exchequer James Callaghan, alarmed the international lenders and encouraged the speculators. The pound sterling came under heavy pressure. Mr. Wilson proclaimed that there would be no "devaluation," but this was a time for action, not words.

Finally, in July, the Prime Minister ordered into action a program of wage, price and credit freeze severe enough to impress even the international-banking fraternity—the "gnomes of Zurich." The austerity package included a total wage and price standstill for six months, plus six more months of "severe restraint." Added in were the heavier purchase taxes, restrictions on installment buying, income surtax, a hold-down on spending for travel abroad, deferred public

234

investment, and a £100 million cut in defenses "east of Suez."

The foreign lenders declared themselves satisfied, and the pound showed new health. But Britain's alarmed trade unions at first denounced the wage freeze, and deputy leader George Brown, heading the Department of Economic Affairs, threatened to resign. Alarm spread as the measures began to bite deeply, and unemployment began to rise—eventually to top the 600,000 mark.

However, Mr. Wilson managed to convince a majority of the unions that these tough measures were essential to save Britain and the pound, and a phalanx of the powerful unions at the Trades Union Congress annual conference went along with him. Bolstering the Government's position was the general British consensus that too many people were taking too much out of an inefficient economy: wages had gone up 9 per cent while productivity was rising a paltry one per cent.

The Government was able to persuade Parliament to place legislative compulsion behind its wage restraint, so that any wage or price boosts deemed out of line could be disallowed.

The freeze was unquestionably effective. Unemployment was especially high in the automobile industry. But soon the key question loomed: What policies would be followed in 1967 after the six-month freeze and after the period of "severe restraint"? Would the dammed-up wage claims come through in a flood, nullifying all the restraint? Or would a new brand of "socialism" take over, in which wage norms and permissive wage-price limits would be established, industry by industry, through a tripartite council representing the Trade Union Congress, the Confederation of British Industries and the Government? Wily Mr. Wilson avoided a clear-cut answer, but many authorities insisted that Britain could not revert to free-for-all collective bargaining again, under which inflation might move in rapidly. Some kind of restraint might have to be sold to both management and Labor's Left Wing, as the formula for the new Utopia.

Meanwhile Whitehall officials insisted that the studies undertaken patiently in a score of industries—by teams representing labor, management and Government—were beginning to root out restrictive work practices and other inefficiencies. But there was still anxiety whether British workers had learned the key lesson: that only through productivity increases can pay packets be permanently fattened.

The Government also promised, through tax favors and special grants, to expand investment incentive in export-conscious industries, such as electronics, machine tools, aircraft and computers. But many businessmen, noting the Government's preparations to nationalize the steel industry, and acquire controlling interests in the aircraft and possibly other industries, feared that the Labor Party had not really abandoned its ancient faith in government ownership.

By the year's end, although international payments were swinging into balance, it was still not clear how energetically Britain was progressing toward a truly *efficient* economy.

The Rhodesia Problem

Sanctions Ineffectual. Britain's other grave confrontation—with Rhodesia—had not yielded to statecraft at the year's end. Early in the year Mr. Wilson was promising the prime ministers of the Commonwealth, assembled at Lagos, that the sanctions chiefly on tobacco exports and oil imports, which Britain had slapped on Rhodesia, would cause the capitulation of the Ian Smith regime "in a matter of weeks rather than months." He seriously misjudged the temper of the white Rhodesians, who in November 1965 had proclaimed unilaterally their independence from Britain. Sanctions caused mild hardships, but the Rhodesians began to get their oil from South Africa and the Portuguese territories; they still sold tobacco to the United States, West Germany and other countries; and morale did not crack.

A British carrier plus destroyers turned back oil cargoes destined for Rhodesia via the Portuguese port of Beira, but the precious commodity came by truck and rail from the south.

Wilson-Smith Talks. By summer, however, both sides were ready for quiet talks to discover if the confrontation could somehow be ended. Nub of the British case was the demand that the Ian Smith regime should revise Rhodesia's constitution to imbed clauses which would guarantee more political representation for the black African majority of 4 million and insure the natives "unimpeded" progress toward majority rule. It was recognized that this political coming-of-age would require advances in education as well as political opportunity, and that the process might take from ten to twenty-five years.

For Rhodesia, Mr. Smith was insisting on a "braking" mechanism in the constitution, by which the political progress of the Africans could be slowed if they seemed unready for self-government.

Pressed by the nonwhite members of the Commonwealth at that organization's September session in London, Prime Minister Wilson agreed that if Rhodesia did not come to terms

Wide World

Prime Minister Harold Wilson en route to announce wage, price and credit freeze.

by December, Britain would go to the United Nations and ask the Security Council to authorize mandatory, but selective, sanctions against Rhodesia. (The previous sanctions had been permissive and covered only a few commodities.)

There ensued further talks and visits back and forth from Salisbury. Finally, when, close to the December deadline, Mr. Smith made some "modest concessions," Mr. Wilson met with him on board the British cruiser *Tiger* off Gibraltar. A working paper, covering both the assurances of "unimpeded" progress and the interim period while the new constitution was put to public approval by a Royal Commission, was developed. When Mr. Smith returned to Salisbury, however, his government rejected the paper—accepting the proposed constitutional changes but rejecting the plans for a broader-based interim government.

UN Support Sought. Thereupon Foreign Secretary George Brown went to the UN to ask for selective sanctions—on such items as chrome, meat, asbestos, tobacco, copper—and oil. Most countries, including the United States, stood ready to support the mandatory sanctions program. But the crucial question was whether South Africa would continue to nullify the key oil embargo by fulfilling Rhodesia's requirements from its own and Portuguese stocks.

The Labor Government's decision to go to the United Nations was by no means popular throughout Britain. The Conservative Party denounced the move. Opinion polls showed a majority opposing the use of force. To many Britons it seemed a pity that the Rhodesian discussions should fail when the constitutional changes had been agreed to by both sides and only the dispute over an interim government remained. But British officials dealing with Ian Smith described him as weak and vacillating and expressed doubt that his hard-lining colleagues of the Rhodesian Front would really cooperate at any time.

The vigorous demands of the nonwhite members of the Commonwealth caused some reassessment of the value of the Commonwealth as a racial bridge in today's world.

EEC

The third grave issue facing Britain was the timing of its bid to join the European Economic Community (Common Market). Throughout the year and even during the wage freeze, pressures built up, urging that the British Government move again along the course that was blocked by French President Charles de Gaulle in 1963. British industrialists were becoming convinced that only through larger continent-sized markets could British industry thrive. The Labor Party's opposing "Little Englanders" found themselves outnumbered in the Wilson Cabinet. The Prime Minister himself was seemingly convinced that much of the "supranationalism" to which Britain objected had drained out of the Common Market, thanks to De Gaulle's opposition to federalism in Europe.

By the year's end Mr. Wilson had announced that he and George Brown would visit the capitals of each of the six Common Market members, advise them of the British readiness for "going into Europe," and see what the prospects might be. This tour would be completed by March 1967. It was still widely anticipated that President de Gaulle would again veto the British bid, unless

Britain truly severed its "special relationship" with the United States. It seemed doubtful that Mr. Wilson would do this.

Other 1966 Highlights

Relations with Washington and Bonn. In 1966, Mr. Wilson continued to make the American alliance a cornerstone of British policy. He visited President Johnson again in late July, and discussed a wide range of topics headed by Vietnam. Foreign Secretary George Brown traveled to New York, the United Nations and Washington in October. When the United States bombed the outskirts of Hanoi and Haiphong, Britain "dissociated" itself from this action while continuing to support American Vietnam policy generally. The United States in turn vigorously supported the pound sterling during Britain's economic crisis, and approved British-proposed sanctions against Rhodesia.

President Johnson fulsomely toasted Mr. Wilson at a midsummer White House luncheon, coming close to comparing him to Sir Winston Churchill. This angered some Britons, but others realized that Mr. Johnson seldom uses a light touch. Britain earned American goodwill by retaining sizable forces "east of Suez" although socialist doctrine and budgetary considerations would have dictated early withdrawal from Singapore and the Persian Gulf. The demotion of Indonesia's President Sukarno reduced the need for British troops in Malaysia.

Throughout the year Britain engaged in inconclusive negotiations with West Germany, seeking to persuade Bonn to defray more of the foreign-currency costs of maintaining 51,000 British troops in Germany. Bonn agreed to account for £31,500,000 of the total foreign-exchange bill of £94 million. Britain threatened to pull out a third of its troops unless West Germany defrayed more of the costs. But Bonn, having balance-of-payments problems of its own, would not budge. Finally Washington persuaded London to postpone its threatened withdrawals until June 1967. By then the Americans, conferring with the British and Germans, hoped to have evolved new NATO strategies which took account of the general desire, among NATO nations, to thin out their troop contingents in Germany.

Cabinet Shuffle. Prime Minister Wilson reshuffled his Cabinet in August 1966, bringing mercurial, dedicated George Brown from the Department of Economic Affairs to head the Foreign Office; since his earliest governmental days Mr. Brown had hoped to follow in the footsteps of his mentor, Ernest Bevin, and become foreign secretary. Michael Stewart, schoolteacherish but effective foreign secretary, took over Mr. Brown's unenviable post at the Economic Affairs Department becoming responsible for operating the "wage freeze."

Mr. Brown undeniably brought a fresh breeze to the staid Foreign Office and was soon off to Moscow to discuss Vietnam and nuclear testing with Soviet Foreign Minister Andrei Gromyko. He found no "give" in the Soviet viewpoints, but late in the year London was able to announce that Soviet Premier Aleksei Kosygin would visit Britain in February 1967.

Fuel, Gibraltar, Crime. The year brought good news on the fuels front. The North Sea proved to be fairly prolific in potential gas wells. Oil was found nearby on British soil, and it began to appear that—what with natural gas available from North Africa, the Netherlands and the North Sea, and oil flowing in from all over the Middle East—Britain's perennial fuel shortages were at an end.

Annoyance came from another quarter when Spain, for reasons of national pride, stepped up its claims to Gibraltar. Madrid called it an affront that Britain still held this geographical bookend it had captured in 1704. London, finding 'that no Gibraltarians wanted to come under Spain's authoritarian rule, decided that Gibraltar was as British as the Bank of England or the royal family. Spain, rejecting the proposal to take its claim to the World Court, put "The Rock" under a tight economic squeeze.

On the crime front Britain abolished capital punishment and moved toward allowing majority verdicts (10-2) in jury trials. Lord Mountbatten was appointed to head a study into prison security after George Blake, a double-agent spy, escaped easily from a British prison. His report stating that "there is no

Conservative leader Heath campaigns in Harrow East.
UPI

really secure prison" in Britain was issued Dec. 22.

Parliament; Prince Charles. The Conservative Party kept up a running battle with the Laborites in Parliament. The Tories fought the steel bill line for line. They denounced the new selective employment tax as iniquitous and unworkable. They roundly criticized Mr. Wilson's handling of the economic crisis.

Tory Leader Heath developed a less wooden delivery during the election campaign and gained stature by his responsible discussion of vital issues. Later he devoted many months to revising Conservative programs and he reshuffled his "shadow cabinet" of alternate ministers.

The Liberal Party meanwhile rejoiced that it had boosted its Commons total from ten to twelve seats, but lamented that its share of the nation's popular vote had declined ominously. The fact that the Labor Party was crowding the middle of the political spectrum, while the Conservatives continued with their center-based programs, left the Liberals with little lebensraum in which to operate.

"Reform of Parliament" received desultory discussion throughout the year. The appointment of a lively debater, Richard Crossman, as Speaker of the House, suggested that reformist ideas would circulate more freely. But Parliament continued to amble along in its accustomed ways. Major policy was often made directly at Number Ten Downing Street. A proposal for an experimental televising of Commons sessions was rejected.

From Buckingham Palace came the decision to send Prince Charles—the Prince of Wales, who was eighteen in November—to Trinity College, in autumn 1967 for a period of at least two years. The prince's grandfather, King George VI, and his great-uncle, the Duke of Gloucester, went there. Prince Charles has been attending Gordonstoun, in Scotland.

At Year's End. . . As the year ended Prime Minister Wilson was criticized for not ringing up a very impressive nine months after the general election. The economic slump had caused the housing drive to falter, had postponed the motorways program. Rhodesia was not easily resolved. Mr. Wilson had taken a long while to decide to knock at the Common Market door. But if there was new criticism, his supporters, such as the *Daily Mirror,* said of the Prime Minister that "he is personally ambitious, stridently confident."

Whether Britain would find new greatness by "going into Europe" and whether it would finally triumph over its recurrent economic "stop-go" crisis and become a really efficient producer—these unresolved questions still faced Britain's first Labor Government in 13 years as 1966 ended.

HAWAII. In April the U.S. Supreme Court upheld a state Legislature plan for state Senate reapportionment. The ruling reversed an earlier decision of a lower Federal court. . . . Gov. John Burns was reelected Nov. 8. . . . Following the death of the Chief Justice of the Hawaii Supreme Court, Wilfred Tsukiyama, Gov. Burns appointed Lt. Gov. William Richardson to the post. . . . The U.S. Congress canceled Project Mohole, scheduled for the Pacific Ocean near Maui.

HELMS, RICHARD McGARRAH. Deputy Director of the Central Intelligence Agency Richard M. Helms was named director of the CIA by President Johnson, June 18, 1966, succeeding Vice Adm. William F. Raborn, Jr. Helms' appointment was unanimously confirmed by the Senate, June 28; he was sworn in at a White House ceremony June 30.

Born March 30, 1913, at St. Davids, Pa., Helms graduated from Williams College in 1935. He then served as a foreign correspondent for United Press and in 1937 joined the Indianapolis Times Publishing Company, becoming its national advertising manager. During World War II, Helms was assigned by the Navy to the Office of Strategic Services where he used his fluent French and German to full advantage. Upon being discharged from the Naval Reserve in 1946, he joined the Joint Strategic Services Unit of the War Department.

Helms became a member of the CIA immediately upon its formation Sept. 18, 1947. On Feb. 17, 1962, he was appointed deputy director for plans, and on April 28, 1965, he was named deputy director.

Central Intelligence Agency Director Richard Helms.
UPI

HIGHWAYS. Highway construction and improvement reached an all-time high during 1966 to keep pace with continued growth in vehicle ownership and operation. Federal, state and local governments invested $8,760,000,000 for road and street improvement during the year (plus $3,499,000,000 for maintenance and $2,631,000,000 for administration, police, safety, and debt interest and retirement). A total of 103 million licensed drivers operated 94 million vehicles 900,000,000,000 miles on the 3.7 million miles of roads and streets.

The major part of the improvements was financed through the $4,000,000,000-a-year Federal-aid highway program administered by the Bureau of Public Roads of the U.S. Department of Commerce. As of June 30, 1966, an estimated $9,940,000,000 worth of work was under way or authorized on the National System of Interstate and Defense Highways (90 per cent Federal, 10 per cent state), and $3,230,000,000 on Federal-aid primary, secondary and urban highways (50 per cent Federal, 50 per cent state).

During the fiscal year ending June 30, 1966, an additional 2,174 miles of the Interstate System were open to traffic, bringing the total in use by the public to 21,570 miles, or 53 per cent of the planned 41,000-mile system. Improvements were completed on 12,199 miles of Federal-aid primary, secondary and urban highways.

The Federal-aid highway program is financed through the Highway Trust Fund from special taxes on highway users, such as the motor-fuel tax. Total income to the trust fund in fiscal year 1966 was $3,924,786,000.

Increased emphasis was given to safety, beauty and social values in the highway program during 1966. The Bureau of Public Roads greatly accelerated its "spot improvement" safety program to eliminate hazards on older roads. It directed the state highway departments to inventory all such hazardous locations with high accident experience, and to establish a program to have them all improved by the end of 1969. As of June 30, 1966, the states had programed 1,548 spot-improvement projects, at a total cost of $291 million. The passage of the Highway Safety Act of 1966 and the National Traffic and Motor Safety Act of 1966 provided important tools to improve safety. They authorized the U.S. Government to establish vehicle-safety standards, a greatly expanded safety-research program, and a program of financial assistance to the states for safety programs.

The Highway Beautification Act, passed by Congress in the fall of 1965, provided for the

U.S. Bureau of Public Roads

New section of Interstate Highway System in Virginia illustrates major safety features: long sight distances, controlled access, acceleration and deceleration lanes.

control of billboards and junkyards along the Interstate and Federal-aid primary and urban highways. The act also provided for the use of unmatched Federal funds for roadside beautification. In addition, regular Federal highway aid was used extensively in 1966 for highway landscaping and the construction of roadside safety rest areas.

Federal Highway Administrator Rex M. Whitton took a number of steps in 1966 as part of a wide-ranging effort to ensure that the highway program is considerate of all human values and responsive to all its social responsibilities. These included regulations to require the considerate treatment and fair compensation for those dislocated by highway construction; the naming of a group of outstanding architects, landscape architects and urban planners to aid the Bureau of Public Roads in developing new guides and standards for urban freeways; and the publication of a checklist of practices to be followed to protect the comfort, convenience and safety of highway users and the neighboring public during highway construction.

Thomas F. McGarry
Special Assistant for Public Affairs
U.S. BUREAU OF PUBLIC ROADS

HOBBIES: New Developments. The hobby words for 1965 were "model-car (slot) racing." For the year 1966, the word was "handicrafts." Never in U.S. history had so many persons been so interested in learning how to make home decorations, gifts and craft objects for resale. An entire new national business began: a national craft business. Just what was this handicraft business?

Those who have been Boy Scouts or Girl Scouts, or who have attended vacation Bible schools are familiar with handicrafts. Those people have learned how to make papier-mâché; how to mold with clay; how to use milk cartons, paper cups and other expendable items to make party and patriotic decorations. Such activities, of course, continued.

But it was the tremendous increase of adult interest in handicrafts and the emergence of a national craft business which made the year 1966 unique in the history of hobbies. And what did adults learn to make? They created exotic things, such as liquid-resin grape clusters, liquid-resin pineapples (formed with glass balls used in Christmas decorations), beautiful Tiffany lamps, feather flowers of all kinds. Handicraft hobbyists also worked at gold leafing and decoupage, picture-frame sculpture from liquid metals, molding and modeling and decorating with all kinds of air-drying clays, paper craft in all its phases, making flowers with plastic pellets known as cooking crystals. The movement toward handicrafts was dramatically illustrated in July 1966 when *Life* magazine devoted ten pages to a study of contemporary handicraftsmen, and the work they have done.

As handicrafts emerged as the new number-one hobby, what happened to model-car racing? There was an inevitable decline in interest, following the wild surge of popularity during 1965. There were still plenty of racing centers, and the activity became far more organized—but the total participation appeared to have slackened, as young men looked elsewhere for their leisure-time activity.

Still extremely popular and even growing in 1966 was the hobby of model-kit building. More boys than ever before built model cars, planes and ships of plastic. Balsa model-plane flying may have been revitalized also, as more people learned that there are completely (or almost completely) silent airplane motors on the market which have not lost too much, if any, of their power. As more model-plane-flying clubs are formed, club members will need flying space. There will then doubtless follow head-on clashes with local laws that forbid noisy intown model-plane flying.

Scale-model railroading remained the second most popular adult hobby (after handicrafts) as the same influences that have sent craft interest soaring played their part in getting the adult male to "find something to do with his leisure time."

JACK WAX
Editor and Publisher
PROFITABLE HOBBY MERCHANDISING

COIN COLLECTING

For coin collecting, the year 1966 was marked by two developments: the official end of the U.S. coin shortage on July 6, and the tumbling of prices of common-date coins held by speculators. Both developments are of particular interest to coin collectors. Rare and scarce coins held steady or advanced.

Due to the coin shortage, changes in U.S. coinage were enacted by Congress in 1964 and 1965. Under the 1964 act, all new coins continued to bear the 1964 date. Under the Coinage Act of 1965, all 90 per cent silver coins (halves, quarters, dimes) were to continue to be stamped with the date 1964. Therefore all of these coins are dated 1964, even though they were struck in 1964, 1965 or 1966. The last of the 90 per cent silver quarters were minted in January 1966; dimes, February 1966; halves, April 1966.

Since the 1965 act required the clad coins to be dated not earlier than 1965, all clad coins made in 1965 and through July 31, 1966, are dated 1965. The first clad quarter was struck Aug. 23, 1965; the first clad dime, Dec. 6, 1965; the first clad half-dollar, Dec. 30, 1965. The first clad coin to enter circulation was the quarter on Nov. 1, 1965.

Reactivation of minting operations at the San Francisco Assay Office took place Sept. 1, 1965, with the striking of 1 cent pieces. From December 1965 through July 31, 1966, all 1 cent and 5 cent pieces were dated 1965.

Beginning on Aug. 1, 1966, all U.S. coins were stamped with the 1966 date. It is hoped normal dating on 1967 coins may be resumed Jan. 1, 1967.

The trend toward decimal coinages in the British Commonwealth continued throughout 1966. On Feb. 14, Australia converted to the decimal system. The Bahamas changed to decimals in May. Scheduled to "go decimal" are New Zealand on July 10, 1967; Western Samoa, Cook Islands and Tokelau Islands, July 1967; Zambia, 1968; Fiji Islands, Jan. 15, 1969; and Britain, 1971.

ELSTON G. BRADFIELD
Editor Emeritus, THE NUMISMATIST

STAMP COLLECTING

Postal administrations around the world during 1966 sought to outdo themselves and one another in innovations, or in their approaches to stamp issuance that were quite different from their normal pursuits in the field.

The United States, which issued its first Christmas-season stamp in 1962, a nondescript wreath-candle adhesive, and with rather uninspiring designs in the years that followed, in 1966 decided that a Christmas stamp should be a Christmas stamp. The Post Office Department issued a beautiful multicolored adhesive reproducing Hans Memling's *Madonna and Child,* which hangs in the National Gallery in Washington.

In its American Artists series, which had leaned toward western views, it issued a handsome 6-color reproduction of *The Boating Party.* It honored the works of Mary Cassatt.

Washington was the site of the only worldwide stamp show in 1966, and the U.S. Post Office Department created 3 outstanding philatelic souvenirs in honor of the Sixth International Philatelic Exhibition. There was a 6-color stamp, combining lithography with line-engraved printing, depicting colorful stamps on an envelope addressed to the exhibition, and the stamp was incorporated into a souvenir sheet that had as its design a view of the capital. There was an innovation in an 11 cents international airmail postal card, in which the imprinted stamp urged recipients to "Visit the USA." At the left side of the card 4 bicolor views of outstanding U.S. sites were depicted.

The first of a projected series of adhesives in homage to folklore characters was a stamp for Johnny Appleseed, who was really John Chapman. He had gained the nickname for his penchant for wandering around the country planting apple seeds during the nineteenth century.

The United States had a slight tiff with Poland over Washington's use of the royal, crowned eagle of Poland on a stamp that commemorated the millennium of Christianity in this now-communist-governed state. The Polish Government objected to the crowned eagle, their own insignia having lopped off the royal emblem.

Great Britain continued with an extensive program of commemoratives, including a series that depicted the Battle of Hastings based on the Bayeaux tapestry, the stamps commemorating the 900th anniversary of the 1066 battle. Britain also depicted native birds, marked the 900th anniversary of Westminster Abbey, and its 1966 victory in soccer's World Cup.

Canada, which celebrates in 1967 the centennial of its creation, issued a series of stamps for its provinces, and commemoratives of events leading to Confederation. Among the most striking stamps of 1966 was one from Czechoslovakia based on a work by Pablo Picasso that he painted soon after the Franco air force had destroyed Guernica during the Spanish Civil War of 1936–39. The original hangs in the Museum of Modern Art in New York City.

The year 1966 was the 20th anniversary of the United Nations Educational, Scientific and Cultural Organization, and many nations issued stamps to commemorate the event; as well as the opening of the World Health Organization's headquarters building in Geneva.

Several new states entered the albums—Guyana (British Guiana), Botswana (Bechuanaland), and Lesotho (Basutoland), all of which gained their independence in 1966. Cook Islands began production of its own stamps. The Soviet Union continued as the most prolific of stamp issuers, closely followed by Hungary, with France and Poland maintaining their usual large numbers of issues. The sultanates along the Persian Gulf, which took away from Britain the responsibility of their own stamp issuances a few years ago, also issued stamps for almost any occasion.

Although the Olympic Games will not be held until the summer of 1968 in Mexico City, the Mexican postal administration began its propagandizing of the games with a series of stamps late in the year.

DAVID LIDMAN
Stamps News Editor, THE NEW YORK TIMES

HUMPHREY, HUBERT HORATIO. For Vice-President Humphrey, 1966 was a frustrating year in many respects. He campaigned hard for his party through September and October, only to see Democrats lose many of the key races Nov. 8 in states which he had visited. President Johnson tapped him in February for a trip to South Vietnam and to other nations in the Far East. But this tour had the effect of tying him even more closely to the administration's war policies, a position which did not sit well with some longtime liberal supporters.

In his home base, Minnesota, the Democrat-Farmer-Labor Party which he helped build fell into disarray and lost the governorship despite the Vice-President's personal efforts.

Throughout the year, Sen. Robert F. Kennedy of New York showed a meteoric rise in popularity polls and won increasing mention as a possible vice-presidential nominee in 1968. If this were to happen, Humphrey would be displaced, although Kennedy insisted he was supporting a Johnson-Humphrey ticket in the next presidential election. Humphrey himself said on Sept. 17 that President Johnson had invited him to be his running mate again; the Vice-President noted that Johnson "is still at liberty to change his mind."

On his Far Eastern trip, Humphrey in Saigon on Feb. 11 forecast eventual victory over the Communists, and over poverty, disease and illiteracy in South Vietnam. The Vice-President also visited Thailand, Laos, Pakistan, India, Australia, New Zealand, the Philippines and South Korea.

On March 13, Humphrey urged that U.S. policy toward Communist China be one of "containment without necessarily isolation." He further said he was convinced there is much friendship for the United States among the mainland Chinese people.

The Vice-President ran into hecklers and demonstrators against the war while he was campaigning at Portland, Ore., in the fall. He acknowledged that "no war can be popular in a sane society." Appearing with Robert Kennedy on behalf of Democrats in New York, Humphrey said, "I'm very grateful to him for all he has done for the Democratic Party." The day after the election, the Vice-President said that "the election results for Congress fall within the normal pattern of off-year presidential elections."

In September, Humphrey sold the home in suburban Chevy Chase, Md., which he had occupied since he arrived in the capital in 1949, and moved with his wife to a fancy high-rise apartment on the Potomac River waterfront in southwest Washington only about a mile from the Capitol.

JOSEPH W. HALL, JR.
Washington Bureau, THE ASSOCIATED PRESS

Robert Humphrey, son of Vice-President and Mrs. Humphrey, marries Donna Erickson in Minneapolis Aug. 27.

Wide World

IDAHO. The U.S. Court of Appeals on Mar. 24 upheld a Federal Power Commission license granted (1964) the Pacific Northwest Power Co. for construction of a $257 million hydroelectric plant and dam on the Snake River at the Idaho-Oregon border. . . . An approved legislative reapportionment plan reduced state Senate membership from 44 to 35 and increased House membership from 63 to 70. . . . Donald Samuelson (R) won the governor's chair; Sen. Len Jordan (R) was reelected.

ILLINOIS. Chicago, Waukegan and Cicero were the scenes of racial outbreaks and civil-rights demonstrations during the summer. . . . On July 13, Gov. Otto Kerner signed an order barring real-estate agents from discriminating in the rental or sale of housing. Homeowners selling their own homes were unaffected by the order. . . . University of Chicago celebrated its 75th anniversary in January. . . . Charles H. Percy (R) won the U.S. Senate seat of incumbent Paul H. Douglas. . . . Richard F. Speck was arrested for the slaying of eight nurses in Chicago July 14, and Percy's daughter Valerie was murdered Sept. 18.

Soviet Premier Aleksei Kosygin (far right) consoles widow of Prime Minister Shastri.

INDIA

By JAMES S. KEAT
New Delhi Bureau Chief
THE BALTIMORE SUN

The year 1966 was India's blackest since 1947, its first year of independence. The surge of national unity that rose during the brief conflict with Pakistan in 1965 evaporated shortly after the New Year. Internal political divisions deepened with the death of Prime Minister Lal Bahadur Shastri. The halting pace of economic growth deteriorated, with a severe industrial slump in the spring, and a second disastrous drought in late summer.

By year's end, serious questions were raised over the ability of Prime Minister Indira Gandhi's administration to govern. Famine stalked Bihar State, eastern Uttar Pradesh and part of Madhya Pradesh. Riots over food shortages, rising prices, student grievances, political and religious issues challenged the Government's ability to maintain order. India-U.S. relations were strained.

The Political Situation. Internal troubles were aggravated by the approach of general elections early in 1967. The ruling Congress Party became engrossed in factional disputes which called into question its ability to give the country coherent rule. Their appetites whetted by divisions within the ruling party, opposition parties entered into agreements not to oppose each other in many contests in hopes of overcoming the Congress' superior political organization.

Politically the year began inauspiciously with Shastri's death in Tashkent, U.S.S.R.

early in the morning of Jan. 11, a few hours after he signed an agreement under Russian auspices to normalize relations with Pakistan.

Unlike the transition from Nehru to Shastri in 1964, there was no obvious successor. Kumaraswami Kamaraj, Congress Party president, maneuvered a coalition of state party leaders into backing Nehru's 48-year-old daughter, Mrs. Gandhi. For the first time, a challenger forced an open contest for the leadership. Morarji Desai, a leading conservative, was defeated 355-169 by the party's members of Parliament. Quickly rejecting the role of custodian pending the 1967 elections, which the party leaders had set out for her, Mrs. Gandhi attempted to infuse a fresh approach into the moribund party.

Many of Mrs. Gandhi's detractors, who considered her weak and indecisive, were confounded by midyear. On June 6 the Government devalued the rupee from 21 cents to a more realistic 13.3 cents. The decision, strongly favored by the United States and the World Bank, created an uproar among India's Leftists and dismayed even some conservatives. The sharp reaction to devaluation, which injured many Indians' pride at a time of declining confidence, halted Mrs. Gandhi's momentum. The initiative that marked her first four months in office degenerated into vacillation. She became increasingly defensive over charges she was selling out Nehru's principles for U.S. aid.

The Economic Situation. In the meantime the stagnant economy grew worse. For more than a year foreign-exchange reserves had been dropping sharply. By late 1965 they were barely enough to cover the statutory backing for India's currency. Then the United States, disturbed by both the conflict with Pakistan and lack of economic progress, froze all aid except for emergency shipments of food.

American economic aid was not fully restored until June. Industries that depended on imported raw materials or spare parts gradually cut production back by as much as half. Industrial growth was all but stalled in the winter and spring. At the same time, prices kept climbing.

Aroused by the economic crisis, the 10 Western nations that banded together as the "Aid India Club" under World Bank auspices came to the rescue with a combined offer of $900 million to finance imports of vital raw materials and equipment to keep factories operating. Although not all commitments had been formally made by year's end, the United States was expected to put up about 40 per cent of the loans. However, the exposure of India's continued abject dependence on foreign aid, combined with complaints about alleged "strings" attached to it, increased domestic controversy. The United States and the World Bank brought pressure on New Delhi to lower barriers against foreign private investment in badly needed fertilizer plants. In Indian eyes, these concessions to Washington did not bear the expected fruit. The full amount of aid was not immediately forthcoming. Potential investors hesitated to make new commitments. Worst of all, devaluation did not lead promptly to the expected increase in export earnings or stop inflation.

Uncertainty over foreign aid and domestic resources forced the Government to begin a new Five-Year Plan in April without a formal plan. An interim program for the first year was devised, and the outline of the full $31,600,-000,000 Five-Year-Plan was disclosed four months later. Doubts that the anticipated aid or internal financing would be realized forced officials to work quietly on a more modest, unpublicized program for the future.

Riots. The general sense of frustration which swept the country, fanned at times by opposition political parties, was translated into a series of riots which punctuated the year. Starting in Kerala in January and West Bengal the following month, Leftist-led demonstrations against food shortages and inflation turned into outbursts of violence. Mobs, mostly of young people, attacked public buildings and government-owned transportation facilities.

Another cause for rioting was the Government's decision, taken after a Sikh leader had threatened to immolate himself, to divide Punjab State into new Punjabi- and Hindi-speaking states. Rioting sparked by Hindu religious groups opposed to the partition spread to 5 Punjab cities. Seven persons were killed in a week of strife.

The climactic riot, and perhaps a turning point in the deteriorating law-and-order situation, occurred in New Delhi Nov. 7. About 125,000 orthodox Hindus, led by sadhus (holy men), marched through the capital to support demands for a nationwide ban on the slaughter of cows, the objects of veneration to Hindus. Whipped up by a politico-religious leader, the crowd clashed with police barring the gates of Parliament. Part of the mob ran amok, burning automobiles and smashing windows. Kamaraj's house was raided. Eight persons were killed, and more than 100 injured in 2 hours.

Aghast at the spectacle of rioting at the gates of Parliament, Mrs. Gandhi dropped the Home Minister, Gulzarilal Nanda, and reassigned major cabinet portfolios. Former Defense Minister Yeshwantrao B. Chavan, 53, succeeded Nanda and emerged as a potential

In drought-stricken Uttar Pradesh, work proceeds on an irrigation project.

UPI

prime minister. Mahomedali C. Chagla, former ambassador to Washington, became foreign minister. At the next threat of disturbance, the Government clamped down, averting trouble.

Developments in the North. Strife also marked the distant northeast corner. Occasional guerrilla raids and three train explosions marred the truce in the 12-year-old rebellion by members of the Naga hill tribes who have declared themselves independent of India. Mrs. Gandhi carried on intermittent negotiations with Naga political leaders, seeking a solution which would provide the Mongoloid tribesmen autonomy without independence.

The Nagas were joined in revolt by the Mizo tribe which inhabits the narrow strip of Assam State between East Pakistan and Burma. A large band of Mizos revolted in March, also demanding independence. Indian troops restored order in the major towns, but at year's end the tribesmen were waging a guerrilla war across the countryside. India accused Pakistan and Communist China of complicity in the Mizo revolt. Pakistan, for its part, denied it.

Foreign Relations. In contrast with the turbulent year in domestic affairs, India's foreign relations were relatively quiet, though not exactly serene. The Tashkent agreement with Pakistan, interpreted differently by the two nations, failed to bring on the hoped-for reconciliation. Indian and Pakistani cabinet ministers conferred in March on steps to restore good relations. They were unable to reach agreement when Pakistan insisted on some assurance of a solution to the 19-year-old Kashmir dispute.

India's menacing neighbor to the north, Communist China, periodically increased tensions in the Himalaya Mountains by intruding across the informal truce line which has divided the two countries since the border war of 1962. Peking's nuclear tests revived demands in India for development of atomic weapons, but New Delhi continued working instead for a nuclear disarmament treaty which would impose restrictions on the major powers as well as nonmembers of the nuclear club.

Fears that India under Mrs. Gandhi's guidance was slipping away from its traditional nonalignment between the Soviet bloc and the West led to a "little summit" at New Delhi in October. President Josip Tito of Yugoslavia and President Gamal Abdel Nasser of the United Arab Republic held four days of talks with Mrs. Gandhi. They reiterated the customary declarations of the neutral nations, including a call for an unconditional halt in American bombing of North Vietnam, but added little new to them.

Relations with the United States, strained

Wide World
A sacred white cow walks the streets of New Delhi.

at the beginning of the year, improved following Mrs. Gandhi's visit to Washington in March but deteriorated again late in the year.

Concern that India's plans to boost agricultural production by introducing modern farming techniques were not yielding the expected results rose again with the news that a second severe drought had damaged harvests in the east central region. The United States, which had supplemented India's 73 million-ton harvest in 1965–66 with shipments of 9.5 million tons of surplus wheat and other grains, faced equally great demands for 1967. Preliminary estimates indicated that the 1966–67 harvest would fall about 10 per cent below the target of 90 million tons of grain. Even that target was about 8 million tons short of the amount needed to maintain a reasonable standard for a predominantly vegetarian population of nearly 500 million persons.

At year's end, Bihar in particular faced a critical situation. Perhaps 30 million peasants were in need of relief. Drinking water and fodder for cattle had dried up, though winter rains eased their plight in some regions. Conditions were almost as bad in parts of Uttar Pradesh and Madhya Pradesh.

INDIANA. During 1966, Indiana celebrated its 150th anniversary as a state. . . . The 1965 Congressional Redistricting Act was held constitutional Feb. 2. . . . Groundbreaking for Burns Harbor, Lake Michigan, occurred Oct. 11. . . . A Federal bill creating Dunes National Park was passed in October. . . . In November elections, Republicans won 6 of Indiana's 11 seats in the U.S. House of Representatives. Republicans gained control of the state House of Representatives; Democrats retained control of the state Senate.

INDONESIA. The abortive communist coup of Sept. 30, 1965, proved a decisive turning point in the turbulent course of Indonesia's political history. The ensuing year saw the elimination of the country's extreme Left, the emergence of a "New Order" under General Suharto, Adam Malik and Sultan Hamengku Buwono, and the steady erosion of President Sukarno's power.

The Political Scene. The formal dissolution on March 12 of the PKI (Indonesian Communist Party), whose policies were closely identified with Peking, occurred at the peak of a wave of anti-Leftist—and specifically anti-Chinese—feeling which left hundreds of thousands slaughtered in its wake. The resulting political vacuum was filled, not by Indonesia's seven political parties, but by the students, organized into Action Commands, who emerged as the most dynamic new force within the country. To the students, Generals Suharto and Nasution and other leaders of the New Order appeared reluctant and indecisive. The new leaders' obvious avoidance of any open challenge to Sukarno left some grave question marks hanging over the political scene in general.

Not the least of these was the growing demand for an account of Sukarno's role in the events of late September 1965. The three trials of former leaders—Jusuf Muda Dalam, Dr. Subandrio and Omar Dhani—while confirming the extent of economic bungling and corruption under the old regime, had so far shed little light on Sukarno's suspected complicity in the affair itself. (In a written testimony presented during Dhani's trial, Sukarno simply denied any prior knowledge of the coup.) An even greater threat, however, was the growing tension between the more radical, impatient students—spurred by general public dissatisfaction over slow economic recovery—and the Army. Sporadic clashes between marines and students had already occurred. In early October, 62 student demonstrators were wounded by soldiers guarding the Merdeka palace.

International Affairs. The political changes wrought by the September coup at home were well matched by the complete reorientation of Indonesia's policies abroad. By late 1965 Indonesia had set itself on a course destined to isolate it more and more from the international sphere. Rigidly adhering to Sukarno's concept of opposing Necolim (Neo-colonialism, coloni-

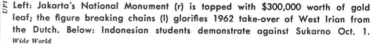

Left: Jakarta's National Monument (r) is topped with $300,000 worth of gold leaf; the figure breaking chains (l) glorifies 1962 take-over of West Irian from the Dutch. Below: Indonesian students demonstrate against Sukarno Oct. 1.
Wide World

alism and imperialism), Indonesia had embarked on a costly military campaign against Malaysia and had even withdrawn from the United Nations and all its associated agencies. Just one year later, however, by ending confrontation against Malaysia and rejoining the United Nations, Indonesia had normalized relations with the West, reasserted its long-cherished dream of Maphilindo (an economic and politic grouping of Malaysia, Philippines and Indonesia) and reestablished a positive role for itself in world politics.

True, Foreign Minister Adam Malik, in his foreign-policy statement to press and Parliament following the formation of the Ampera Cabinet in July, was careful to pay lip service to opposing the Necolim powers. But the subsequent ending of confrontation (Aug. 11) and reentry into the United Nations (Sept. 28) —in both cases over the protests of Sukarno— showed only too clearly just where the new leadership's foreign commitments lay. Even more dramatic evidence was the massive deterioration these steps cost Indonesia in its relations with China.

Russia, on the other hand, proved eager to avoid sharpening tensions with Indonesia despite the wave of anticommunist reaction gripping that country. Undoubtedly profiting from the Sino-Soviet rift, Malik won a moratorium on Indonesia's huge debt to Russia in late November. Malik's earlier 40-day mission in September—to India, Algeria, U.A.R., Yugoslavia, the United States and Japan—was aimed at attaining closer friendship with foreign countries. Despite Indonesia's nonaligned stance, it obviously stood to profit most from strengthening ties with the Western nations.

Economic Situation. The real key to the destiny of the New Order lay in how efficiently it could repair the shattered economy it had inherited. At the turn of the year, Indonesia's foreign debts amounted to roughly $2,500,-000,000, industrial production had ground almost to a halt, inflation was rampant, and export performance had dropped ($750 million in 1961) to $450 million. Average monthly incomes for workers and employees in the towns were considered sufficient to cover expenses for one week only. Despite drastic increases in wages, prices always ran far ahead, due to the galloping inflation.

It was in fact this situation—for which the Old Order was held responsible—that triggered the demands culminating in the signing of the March 11 Declaration (essentially entrusting Suharto with running the Government), the dissolution of the PKI and the purge of Leftist elements from the Cabinet (including Dr. Subandrio, then foreign minister, and Chairul Saleh, then 3d deputy premier).

But the measures to meet the demand for lower prices and the rehabilitation of the shattered economy, hampered by a lack of practical economic experience and the compromise character of the Ampera Cabinet, remained on the whole unsatisfactory. Although new edicts were passed to promote exports and to encourage both public and private production, little was done to halt the ever-spiraling inflation. The monthly export level dropped from $35-40 million in the first six months of the year to $4.4 million in September. More significant was the failure to avoid a catastrophe in food supply. Critical shortages of food were experienced in some rice-deficit areas.

One encouraging sign was the New Order's more sober, realistic approach to economic matters, highlighted by the remarkably honest analysis presented in April by Sultan Hamengku Buwono, prime minister for economy, finance and development. At the same time, Indonesia also officially acknowledged the need to seek a moratorium from its creditors. Efforts in this direction secured the agreement by eight major Western credit nations to an 18-month moratorium on its debts (followed later by the agreement with Russia). Missions dispatched to seek additional aid had also met with some success and by mid-October Finance Minister Frans Seda claimed that a total of $174 million "soft" credits had been promised.

Nevertheless, by late 1966, Indonesia's New Order was faced with the dilemma of not having consolidated its political power vis-à-vis the old leaders—Sukarno in particular—to the point where it could undertake the drastic structural reforms necessary to revive the economy. Frustration and impatience over the general lack of progress in this sphere threatened to erode the Government's popular support. Sukarno, who still enjoyed backing in various parts of the country, might well take advantage of this situation to try to win back his former prestige and power, making the threat of renewed civil strife still very real.

For the time being, Suharto's policy of slowly cutting the President off from his main source of power—the people—rather than forcing a showdown, continued to tie Sukarno's hands. The New Order was clearly hoping to ease political tensions "*à la Indonésie*"—through indirect maneuvers and prolonged discussions. But the time for such strategy was short.

DEREK DAVIS
Editor, FAR EASTERN ECONOMIC REVIEW

INTERNATIONAL TRADE. World trade, sparked by the desires of people the world over to improve their way of life, has grown rapidly in recent years. Trade of the free-world nations rose from $48,000,000,000 in 1948 to $160,-000,000,000 in 1965. During this period the United States, the world's leading trading nation, saw a record growth in its export trade. As 1966 opened, many observers questioned whether this impressive expansion, both in world and U.S. trade, would continue. While many were cautiously optimistic, there were indications that the year ahead would not be an easy one for world trade.

The U.S. Balance of Payments Deficit. In January, U.S. Secretary of Commerce John T. Connor reported that in 1965 American exports had topped $26,600,000,000, a 4 per cent increase over the previous year. At the same time, the Secretary said that export growth in 1966 would continue. What the Secretary did not say, but what was readily understood, was that a continued expansion in U.S. exports was vital to help reduce the deficit in the U.S. balance of payments (the difference between the outflow and inflow of all payments) that plagued the country.

Support for the Secretary's hopeful view on exports was furnished in late January by a number of knowledgeable trade experts (the Balance of Payments Group of the National Foreign Trade Council), who forecast that U.S. exports would reach a total of $29,100,-000,000 during 1966, against imports of $23,700,000,000. The resulting export surplus of $5,400,000,000 was expected to bring the deficit under $1,200,000,000. In 1965 it amounted to $1,300,000,000.

To achieve this trade expansion, U.S. exporters realized that they would have to redouble their efforts to sell more products to more markets. At the same time, they were aware that they would have to keep a watchful eye on the negotiations being held under the auspices of the General Agreement on Tariffs and Trade (GATT), which everyone hoped would be a major step toward greater world trade. These negotiations, involving the world's principal trading nations, seek to provide a more liberal climate for international commerce by reducing barriers to trade.

The importance of a continued growth in U.S. exports was underscored in February by a U.S. government spokesman who urged American companies not only to maintain their export efforts but to set aside a portion of their products for export. He cautioned that while U.S. exports had risen in the past year, the United States was failing to maintain its share of total world trade. The U.S. share of world exports declined from 20.9 per cent in 1960 to 18.9 per cent in 1965.

Not too many weeks went by before it was reported from Washington that there was mounting concern by government officials over signs that the deficit in the U.S. balance of payments might not be reduced, but rather might be increased in 1966. A government report in March indicated that, despite the expected increase in exports, offsetting factors such as growing imports, tourist spending abroad and overseas government expenditures (due in part to the conflict in Vietnam) would combine to increase the payments deficit to some $1,800,000,000.

The impressive growth in U.S. imports (one of the contributing factors to the expansion in world trade) during 1965, due to rising industrial activity and higher incomes in the United States, appeared likely to continue. In the first two months of 1966, imports expanded by nearly 11 per cent, while exports rose by only 4 per cent. However, there were indications that if they continued at this pace, exports would exceed the 1965 total by a good margin. By the time the June trade figures were released, exports were running at an annual rate of well over $28,000,000,000, about 8 per cent higher than the previous year.

Despite this good showing, the NFTC Balance of Payments Group, in issuing its mid-year review of the U.S. balance of payments, was less optimistic than it had been in January. The Group cut back its original export projection from $29,100,000,000 to $28,700,-000,000. They noted that although exports had shown substantial gains, they had also fallen somewhat short of earlier expectations. At the same time, the NFTC body increased its estimate for imports from $23,700,000,000 to $24,700,000,000.

Throughout the first half of 1966, while U.S. exporters and government officials worked to expand overseas sales, efforts continued in Europe to assure that progress would be made in GATT parleys to reduce trade barriers.

In July, U.S. imports rose again while exports declined. Administration spokesmen attributed the import rise partly to the war in Vietnam, noting that as domestic supplies became harder to obtain, companies had to step up imports to meet their needs. The booming domestic market was also responsible for the poor export showing. With demand remaining at a high level in the United States, suppliers were less able to provide products for export. It became more and more apparent that exports were not going to provide all the help toward reducing the balance-of-payments deficit that had been hoped for.

Although U.S. export trade was not moving ahead as rapidly as expected, world trade continued to advance. In September the International Monetary Fund reported that in the second quarter of 1966, world exports were running at an annual rate of $180,000,000,000. The report also noted that general world prosperity was continuing.

The importance of this continued prosperity to U.S. exporters was spelled out in late September by Secretary Connor, who observed that free-world trade was expected to hit $210,000,000,000 in 1975 and $365,000,000,-000 by the turn of the century. In urging American companies to keep up their efforts, the Secretary pointed out that in order to maintain their share of world trade, they would have to increase their sales abroad by 50 per cent in the next decade.

In August, U.S. exports picked up a bit, achieving a small gain over imports. In September, however, imports advanced again. Although exports were higher than imports for the month, the surplus was still too small for comfort. Washington continued to worry.

Late October brought the opening of the 53d National Foreign Trade Convention, a gathering of more than 2,000 international businessmen, bankers and government officials concerned with U.S. international business. At the close of their three-day meeting, delegates proposed a broad reappraisal of U.S. trade and shipping policies. In a declaration issued on the final day of the convention, they said that the expansion of U.S. exports was "a matter of vital importance," and called upon the government to "vigorously seek to remove the impediments to exports."

As the year drew to a close, it was clear that export expansion was extremely necessary, but that exports alone could not eliminate the U.S. balance-of-payments problem. A third-quarter government report on the payments balance, issued in mid-November, revealed that although exports had gone up by $300 million over the previous quarter, imports rose by $400 million. This gave rise to hopes in Washington that if everything went right in the final weeks of the year, the deficit in payments, even if it could not be eliminated, would at least be no more than it was in 1965.

PETER F. GREENE
Editor, Dun & Bradstreet's
EXPORTERS' ENCYCLOPEDIA

IOWA. Sen. Jack Miller (R) and Gov. Harold E. Hughes (D) were reelected Nov. 8. . . .

A tornado struck Belmond Oct. 14, killing six people. . . . Sargent Shriver announced Mar. 10 that General Electric would operate a women's Job Corps center at Clinton. . . . June 3–4 marchers on the Waterloo city hall demanded an investigation of alleged police brutality in the death of a Negro prisoner.

ITALY. The worst floods in Italy's history turned 1966, a year that had promised near-complete economic recovery, into a nightmare. Rain and raging rivers literally washed away the year's gains and cast uncertainty on the future. Nov. 4 and 5 were the black days that left the northern part of the nation crippled. Damage was estimated at $2,500,000,000, a figure that was still rising at year's end.

Moving quickly to recover, the Government of Premier Aldo Moro raised gasoline prices by 10 lire (1.6 cents) a liter. A week later Moro's Cabinet announced the sternest tax raises since World War II to finance an $800 million recovery program. They hiked all direct taxes by 10 per cent for 1 year, placing an extra heavy burden on a nation where taxes and social security take ⅛ of the national product, and where state and cities are weighed down by mountainous deficits.

Worst-hit Italian city was Florence, where the rampaging Arno River killed 27 people, inflicted millions in damage, and destroyed art works treasured by the world. Florence's art damage was estimated at over $15 million, and experts said it would take at least 20 years to repair. Cimabue's famed *Crucifix,* housed in the Basilica of Santa Croce, was reduced to mere paint. The Ponte Vecchio (Old Bridge), a symbol of art-rich Florence, remained standing but was seriously undermined. The damage list, including thousands of valuable books and documents, was enough to make art lovers despair.

The art world rallied to Florence's aid. Many nations established special committees to raise funds, and sent supplies and art-restoration experts to begin the long task ahead. Mrs. John F. Kennedy, widow of the late U.S. President and a supporter of the arts, was chosen honorary chairman of the U.S. Committee to Rescue Italian Art (CRIA). The restoration job would be monumental, but Florence and the world's art lovers were determined to succeed.

Political Activities. On another front, Italy's Socialists were equally determined to succeed. Their goal: a party big enough to challenge both the Christian Democrats and the Communists. The new United Socialist Party was chartered Oct. 30 under the dome of Rome's

Flood refugees leave Motta di Livenza (northeast Italy).

Sports Palace. It was the biggest political event in recent Italian history, and it brought the Socialists of Vice-Premier Pietro Nenni and the Social Democrats of President Giuseppe Saragat back together after 19 years of often bitter rivalry.

Elected president of the new party was Pietro Nenni, whose close ties with the Communists caused the schism, and whose subsequent break with them made the reconciliation possible. The balding, 75-year-old former Stalin Prizewinner vowed to seek "a socialist society founded on liberty and democracy." Nenni warned the Italian Communist Party, and the Christian Democrats, with whom the Socialists formed the Government's Center-Left coalition, that both were fair game in the 1968 general elections. In 1968 the Socialists hope to vastly improve their 1963 showing: 20 per cent of the vote, compared to 38 per cent for the Christian Democrats and 25 per cent for the Communists.

The Communists were obviously worried about losing some of their working-class vote. But their biggest problem was the split in their own party. Brewing for several years, the cleavage took place in Leghorn, birthplace of Italian communism, where a group of pro-Chinese-line dissidents formed their own party. Its name: the Marxist-Leninist Party of Italy.

The year 1966 opened with a government crisis for the coalition Government of Premier

Arno River floodwaters seep into Florence's Accademia. Center: Michelangelo's *David*.

Aldo Moro. The Premier, a Christian Democrat, was forced to resign in January after the Chamber of Deputies defeated a proposal for state-run nursery schools. A new coalition Cabinet, with Moro remaining as premier, was sworn in Feb. 24. On March 15 the Chamber of Deputies gave the new Cabinet a 347-251 vote of confidence.

A scandal that could help the Socialists against the Christian Democrats in 1968 took place in Agrigento, Sicily, a beautiful hilltop town overlooking a valley of ancient Greek temples. A large section of the town came tumbling down July 19—the result of over-building on poor foundation. The ensuing investigation turned into an indictment of the Christian Democratic Party for its slackness in allowing local electoral interests and pressures to prevail over honesty and discretion.

Italy also had its hands full with violent lawbreakers: the terrorists who want the German-speaking Alto Adige region returned to Austria. Relatively inactive in 1965, they stepped up bombings in 1966, taking the lives of six Italian outpost guards. Italy's outrage peaked in September when two guards were killed at the Malga Sasso border post near the Brenner Pass. Everyone from usually tranquil President Saragat to the man in the street blamed Austria and West Germany for harboring the terrorists. "The reply to this insulting challenge of neo-nazism to a democratic Italy is to fight with-out quarter against the criminals, their bosses, their accomplices," Saragat told the nation.

The nationwide outcry was the most vehement since the 1954 dispute with Yugoslavia over Trieste. It remained for Premier Moro to calm tempers in an hours-long address to Parliament. Moro promised to spare nothing in the battle against terrorism, at the same time urged continuing negotiations with Austria. Moro's year was packed with domestic problems, biggest of which were the floods. His only trip abroad was a five-day summer visit to West Germany for unity talks with Chancellor Ludwig Erhard and for a tour of Wall-split Berlin.

Tourism and Motion Pictures. Despite the late-fall floods, Italy's tourist traffic continued to boom, earning more than $1,000,000,000. The number of Italians touring their own country remained stationary, with a slight increase in the number vacationing abroad.

The year of the floods was also the year Dino de Laurentiis' epic film *The Bible* made its debut. Five years in the making, *The Bible* (actually Genesis) cost $18 million to produce, but De Laurentiis got back $15 million from Twentieth Century-Fox before the public even saw the picture. The film's director, John Huston, played Noah, hero of the greatest flood in the history of the world.

ERNEST A. LOTITO
Rome Bureau, UNITED PRESS INTERNATIONAL

A Florence square, filled with mud and stranded cars.

Restoration experts salvage flood-damaged ancient books. *UPI*

JAPAN

By STUART GRIFFIN
East Asia Correspondent
THE LONDON OBSERVER
FOREIGN NEWS SERVICE

The chief question students of Asia's most dynamic nation asked in 1966 was this: where will Japan's surging nationalism go? Of this nationalism, of its strength and velocity, there seems no harbored doubt. The "ism" traces to slender postwar beginnings indeed.

Japan surrendered unconditionally to the Allied Powers in 1945, and was placed under a seven-year, U.S.-dominated occupation unknown in over two thousand years of history. Overnight there was a collapse of the fanatic belief that Asia's sun-god-led "Holy Nation" had fought only for coprosperity of the Greater East Asia sphere against colonial exploitation of Asia by the West. Japan lay in biblical ruins, physically, spiritually burnt out.

Japan's Status. Twenty-two years later, fantastically, Japan has recovered, in industry, in commerce, in self-esteem and international recognition. Economically affluent, and thus politically stable, it seeks self-sufficiency socially, even as it seeks to join the world in all aspects. It looks to nationalism to effect these twin goals, in the belief that nationalism, a mystic Japanese driving nationalism, gave it prosperity and stability.

U. Alexis Johnson, new U.S. ambassador to Japan.
Wide World

Many Asians see Japan as area leader. This view is even shared by some Communist Chinese. But these Asians who give the palm to fellow-Asian nation Japan so proudly are more than matched by other Asians who view these islands, with their rising energetic population, with much misgiving.

Nationalism poises on a twin takeoff, somehow related: a reappraisal of Japan's postwar position of reliance on its chief benefactor and treaty ally, the United States; and a reappraisal, despite haunting fears of things thermonuclear, of Japan's attitude toward the bomb. These are related, since a nation atomically armed, as Japan has the potential and growingly the tendency to be, would scarcely require a dependent American relationship. In fact Japan would fear such a relationship, as indeed it already does, as a denial of sovereignty such as nationalism demands.

U.S. Ambassador U. Alexis Johnson approaches his new post in Tokyo doubtless aware of the legacy of outgoing envoy Dr. Edwin O. Reischauer: an incipient emotional rift between Japan and the United States in both political and economic spheres. Ambassador Johnson inherited the residual Japanese bitterness and fear, cleverly handled and bottled up during 1966 by Dr. Reischauer, the Japanese opposition to America's tough stance in Vietnam and bristling policy of "containment without isolation" vis-à-vis Communist China.

China in 1966, however, made all but the most intransigent Leftist wonder. First there were its Afro-Asian blunders, capped by the Indonesian debacle, the backfires from its do-nothing bluster over India-Pakistan and indeed over Vietnam. Then came the Great Cultural Proletarian Revolution, the Red Guard extremism, and the third, missile-borne atomic device.

A Look at 1966. The year 1966—and 1967 will doubtless continue in the same vein—saw Japan maintain a stoutly ambivalent policy toward both China and the United States.

Japanese respect the China which is their cultural progenitor; feel guilty toward the China which was their wartime victim; love the China which could with Japan's help develop Pan-Asianism; and fear the China which permits the rampages of the Red Guards and knows the secret of the atomic bomb and its pinpointed delivery.

Japanese, in turn, respect the America which brought Japan to defeat in war and then turned to restore it in peace; feel guilty at swiftly absorbing a culture long derided as commercial and crass; love the America which rebuilt

Boxlike streetcars dominate major streets of Hiroshima, a center of Japanese commerce.

Japan economically and led it back to international society; and fear the America whose war in Asia could embroil Japan in new ruin, even as it beats back the latest threat to Japan's peace and prosperity, ironically China.

Japan was determinedly Janus-faced, all things to all people, in 1966 and will doubtless so continue in 1967. It welcomed such people from the opposite political ends of the earth as U.S. Secretary of State Dean Rusk and Soviet Foreign Minister Andrei Gromyko, and, in between, statesmen, scholars, artists, businessmen, and tourists from all countries—the democratic, the communist, the neutral and uncommitted alike.

Japan talked of closer ties with the United Nations in 1966; then reaffirmed its policy of nondispatch of its Security Forces (i.e., Army, Navy and Air Forces), even on UN-sponsored missions. It talked of capital and trade liberalization; then dragged its feet throughout the year, notably at the annual binational economic talks with the United States. It said it planned further aid to developing nations, to redeem its pledge to the International Monetary Fund, World Bank, and Organization for Economic and Cooperative Development; then put up only 0.65 per cent of the minimum of one per cent of its gross national product, toward the development.

It prattled on self-satisfyingly about being "Workshop of Asia," "Third Pillar of the Free World" and "Leader of the Far East." Japan then watched, sometimes in dismay, as first the Philippines took the limelight by having Manila picked as site of the Asian Development Bank, then South Korea, by staging the Council of Asian Foreign Ministers meeting. And while Korea's infantry and marines battled in Vietnam to support the anticommunist struggle, and as Thailand gave increasing use of its bases and soil to support the war logistically and militarily, Japan hunched behind a do-nothing policy, of lukewarm support for the United States. Japan even let visiting President Lyndon Johnson fly past, visiting half a dozen Pacific-area capitals, ignoring Tokyo.

Many criticize the Japanese Government as no government, but rather a "consortium governing by consensus through compromise." But this is esoteric, compared with more voluble, realistic criticisms: by the United States that Japan was doing too little; by China that it was doing too much in Vietnam; and mostly, by the strident, Left-tipped antigovernment Opposition.

At year's end, a bedeviled Prime Minister Eisaku Sato was facing unpopularity as never before in newspaper survey polls and outright attack for a "black mist" Cabinet. The cabinet members were grilled for political favoritism, abuse of position for electioneering, tax evasions, fraud, corruption, intimidation and bribery.

Both the ruling Liberal-Democratic Party and the Socialist Party continued bogged down with factionalism. Both were forced to look at steady advances by the "third force"—and new proof of surging nationalism—the 4.5 million-household-strong Soka Gakkai, the militant, quasi-religious Buddhist movement. This movement is viewed as Right-Wing for all the

253

moderation currently expressed by its political arm, the Komeito, "Clean Politics" Party.

Japan seemed more than ever to want the cake it also sought to eat: of wanting UN support and a leadership role without help to UN causes with troops, or underdeveloped areas with aid funds; of wanting to be neutral politically but allowed to run rampant economically, especially in its Asian backyard; of wanting protection against even nuclear aggression, without paying proportional costs of its own defense; of wanting the United States specifically as a protector—and guarantor of economic prosperity—but of decrying the U.S. position of commitment, elsewhere in Asia, as involving and imperiling Japan.

It wants a free hand in doing volume business with China economically, yet it wants guarantees against China, politically and militarily, and from the very United States which would restrict its trading.

This confusion stems from the mood of nationalism. The ruling party and the Government are not alone in their confusion. Even more confused is the Left, the extreme Left. Japan's Communist Party, once shrilly pro-Peking, now opts for entente with Moscow. Leftists, too, fear the China of the Afro-Asian fumble, isolated even within the communist bloc; of the Great Cultural Revolution, the Red Guards, the bomb.

Here, too, nationalism was a factor. Japanese, though socialist, even communist, are Japanese, and could not brook Chinese interference in domestic affairs, dictating what line the party should follow, criticizing the party when it failed to follow prescribed guiding strings. Russia kept its own counsel, and Japan's Left moved quietly, solidly toward realignment with Russia.

A Look at 1967. Japanese, viewing 1967, know they must come to definite conclusions, or face the isolation from which they have emerged, and to which they fear a return. They must determine where Japan stands in Asia, in the world, with the communist bloc, the free world, the UN, the uncommitted countries.

Japanese talked in 1966 of having earth's fastest train, smallest transistor, longest tunnel, most effective drug, greatest shipbuilding industry, most populated city, cheapest steel-making process—obvious outgrowth of nationalism, itself hearkening back to the years of defeat, poverty, humiliation, occupation 22 years ago.

Many now urge fellow countrymen to hold the mirror before themselves; to embark on what Japanese call *jiko hansei*, a mood of "critical self-reflection"—to determine where Japan stands; where it is going, by what routes, and for what reasons.

Just as Japanese know political stability is paired with economic prosperity, thinking Japanese are aware that nationalism, however understandable, is suspect in a world growing international. In 1967 the nation's better intellectual leadership seems bent on fostering the nationalistic mood, but only if in the overall it helps and does not harm the international climate abroad, hopeful that the average Japanese will follow this new, quite difficult concept.

JOHNSON, CLAUDIA (LADY BIRD). Although Mrs. Lyndon B. Johnson said early in January that she would make fewer trips in 1966, her third year in the White House did not turn out as she had planned. She traveled more miles than in her previous two years and made three foreign trips: one to Asia and two to Mexico.

She visited such places as Pago Pago in Samoa and Lake Taal Volcano in the Philippines. She opened a school in New Zealand; addressed university students in Korea; received a coat trimmed with kangaroo in Australia; and spoke to the American Road Builders Association in Denver. She dedicated a dam on the Colorado River; gave a party in Mexico City; led a flotilla of 27 rubber rafts down the Rio Grande; and in one crowded week attended opera openings in both New York and San Francisco.

Nobody could have planned such a year. It grew like Topsy, and the agenda for it picked up steam along the way and day by day.

In early November—the quickly scheduled, 25,000-mile, 17-day trip to Asia completed—Mrs. Johnson's exhausted husband, the President, went to the hospital for two operations. The First Lady moved into a nearby room to write thank-you notes, and work out times to plant some more trees. "I'm beginning to feel the day won't be complete unless I plant a tree," she said.

In 3 years Mrs. Johnson's trips to promote interest in a more beautiful America have grown into spectaculars, so well covered are they by the press and TV. On her 2-day April trip to Texas' Big Bend National Park, 70 correspondents, photographers and TV cameramen went along. Counting White House and park personnel, a party of 137 donned boots, blue jeans and tennis shoes to follow her raft down the Rio Grande through the awe-inspiring Marsical Canyon.

A few days after this roughing-it experience, Mrs. Johnson and the President left for Mexico

Wide World

Mrs. Lyndon B. Johnson is welcomed to Offutt Air Force Base, Neb., June 15.

City to dedicate a statue of Lincoln. The visit turned into an enormous good-neighbor fiesta, but the First Lady found time to inspect some programs for children and do some plantings. (A Dec. 3 visit to Ciudad Acuña lasted only a brief four hours.)

In June she went to Nebraska on a history and beautification trip which had overtones of politics. She was the guest of Gov. and Mrs. Frank Morrison. He was seeking a seat in the U.S. Senate. Mrs. Johnson explored Omaha and Lincoln, visited Boys Town, and saw as much of the "Big Sky State" as she could in 15 action-packed hours.

That month she went also to Philadelphia to view restoration and garden projects in the old part of the city; received delegates to the National Youth Conference on Beautification at the White House; and attended her daughter Lynda's graduation from the University of Texas. (Lynda began a part-time magazine job in the fall, working in both Washington and New York.)

July was given mostly to plans and parties for Luci and her fiancé, Patrick J. Nugent,

whose wedding on Aug. 6 was a highlight event of the year. It was staged with the same meticulous attention to detail and warm hospitality which has marked all White House affairs since Lady Bird Johnson has lived there. No family friend was forgotten. The cake was eight feet tall, and the flower-laden house overflowed with happy guests. All the formalities were observed and no expense spared, but the atmosphere remained informal and friendly, like the First Lady herself.

September found Mrs. Johnson in the air again, ready for a three-day trip to three Western states, including California, where Democrats needed her help before the elections. In California she attended the opera; visited San Simeon; dedicated a scenic highway, a seaside park and a dam. The First Lady's trips are tiring to reporters and to her too, no doubt, but she truly enjoys each new experience. "Why, I'd have to be a vegetable not to," she has said.

Her "More Beautiful Capital" program is beginning to bear returns obvious not only to Washington's tourists, but to citizens who live

President and Mrs. Johnson watch Mr. and Mrs. Nugent cut their wedding cake Aug. 6.

in low-income areas, and Mrs. Johnson continues the work begun by Jacqueline Kennedy to beautify the White House. Proceeds from a book, *The Living White House,* published in November, will help buy more antiques and paintings.

CHRISTINE SADLER
Washington Editor, MCCALL'S

JOHNSON, LYNDON B. Time and the presidency have begun to take a physical and political toll of President Lyndon Baines Johnson. At 58, his face is deeply lined and his once-wavy black hair has given way to a receding gray line. The tall, trim Texan who ruled the Senate before 1961 and was vice-president until 1963 has become the hulking, slightly potbellied

Eskimo dancers greet President Johnson Nov. 1 as he arrives in Alaska after Asian tour.

Photos UPI

Vice-President Humphrey joins in celebrating the Johnsons' 32d wedding anniversary Nov. 17.

figure who occupies the world's most powerful, most awesome post. If the public-opinion polls are correct, 1966 was the year that President Johnson became one of the most unpopular, least-believed chief executives in many years. Yet, in one of the contradictions that abound in Lyndon Johnson, he remained the most active, physically restless, politically minded chief executive in the memory of White House watchers.

Voter Disenchantment. Voter disenchantment is no stranger to the men whom destiny summons to 1600 Pennsylvania Avenue, Washington, D.C. Harry Truman faced it in his time, and Dwight Eisenhower had his experiences with it. No less a popular hero than the late John F. Kennedy made its acquaintance in the third year of his tenure, too. Some of the qualities now so admired in the martyred Kennedy could not be detected with a magnifying glass by his critics a few weeks before the assassination. That voter disenchantment reached President Johnson in 1966 is no phenomenon, therefore, even though the fact of its happening had significant impact on the Congress, the country, the world and even himself.

When Mr. Johnson's year began, he had the popular support of 67 per cent of the American people. The overwhelmingly Democratic Congress of 1965 had enacted, at his insistence, almost every item on the liberal agenda for the past 30 years. The future looked bright indeed. Just 10 months later, in a massive switch of

sentiment, 54 per cent of the people disapproved his job performance. And the November elections posted a Republican victory for seats in Congress and the governorships of various U.S. states that was widely interpreted as a vote of no confidence in the Johnson administration.

Historians may disagree in years hence, but the short view was that President Johnson had become, in a word, unbelievable. The mantle inherited from President Kennedy no longer shielded him. His ranch-country style no longer amused, his long hours on the job no longer sufficed, his sincerity and effort no longer convinced.

Vietnam, Inflation, Civil Rights. The credibility of President Johnson suffered mainly on three counts. The man who had beaten Barry Goldwater in 1964 by promising to keep the Vietnam war at minimum-risk levels had nevertheless launched a major bombing offensive against North Vietnam in 1965 and, in 1966, there seemed no visible benefits from that escalation. The year 1966 began with about 190,000 American troops in Vietnam, many times more than were there at 1964 election time, and yet not enough to suit the President —or so it seemed to the American people. By election time in 1966, the number of GI's was nearly 400,000, more still were indicated, casualties were mounting inexorably and the end of the war was nowhere in sight. The January bombing pause and peace offensive, the February sessions with Vietnamese leaders in Honolulu and the seven-nation summit of Vietnam war Allies in Manila in October had produced only one paramount conclusion—the war was far from over.

Compounding President Johnson's war woes was the related problem of inflation. For sixty consecutive months, the nation's economy had boomed along at record levels. But in 1966—partly due to war, rising prices and wages—that old black spiral began plaguing Mr. Johnson as much as it plagued housewives, wage earners and bankers. He advised Congress and the nation not to worry; there was enough resiliency in the economy to afford guns for Vietnam, butter for the United States and no need for a tax increase. But as prices continued to climb and the war continued to escalate, the economic machine began to sputter and cough. Try as he did, Mr. Johnson simply could not convince everybody that the helmsman knew what lay ahead.

The third crisis was civil rights, an interlocking issue to which the President partly owed his 1964 election landslide and his esteem on Capitol Hill in 1965. But now the man who had electrified everyone by adopting the Negro cry "we shall overcome" as his own, found himself unable to sell a Democratic Congress on a civil-rights bill that would provide equal

President Johnson congratulates new Undersecretary of State Katzenbach after swearing-in ceremony on Oct. 3.

Wide World

housing opportunities for all. Where now was the heralded arm-twister of reluctant lawmakers?

Meanwhile, the plummeting consensus never really seemed to register with the man in the White House. The inner offices of his top aides were wired to the sound of Muzak and pleasing reports that contradicted critical press reports and dissenting Republicans. And wherever he went outside the White House, there were the ogling crowds.

Glimpses at the Man. President Johnson put big stock on his crowds in 1966, drawing from them a sense of approval that made the world seem right and, as he put it himself, "recharged the ol' battery." Why did the papers make so much fuss over Senator Robert Kennedy's squealing crowd in New England? It was not half so big a crowd as turned out for LBJ on Labor Day in conservative Battle Creek, Mich., now was it? Reporters had to agree, although one wondered if President Johnson was aware that he was the first president to visit there since William Howard Taft.

"Hey, Harold!" President Johnson had exclaimed aboard Air Force One to Australian Prime Minister Harold Holt after the wild welcome he received in Melbourne in October, "Did you ever see bigger crowds than that?"

Yet for all that seeming self-centeredness, the President many times displayed a warmth and human understanding that could be so totally disarming and so real it had to be believed. No Texan ever stood taller, no father ever was more proudly miserable than President Johnson when he walked down the aisle of Washington's Catholic Shrine of the Immaculate Conception on August 6 to give his beloved Luci in marriage to Patrick J. Nugent of Waukegan, Ill. There was the day he dropped by the Indian Embassy to pay a call on visiting Prime Minister Indira Gandhi, overstayed, and had to be invited to dinner.

Nor would anyone present forget the President's talk to the fatigue-suited American troops at Camranh Bay, on his surprise side trip to Vietnam in October.

Appointments. President Johnson was as full of surprises as ever in making appointments to high government office. When George W. Ball, the administration's conscience on Vietnam, resigned as undersecretary of state, the President disclosed Attorney General Nicholas deB. Katzenbach had been persuaded to "step down" into the number-two spot in Foggy Bottom. Had Robert C. Weaver lost his Washington luster as the nation's housing chief? In answer, the President made Weaver the first Negro ever to sit in the Cabinet by appointing him secretary of the new Department of Housing and Urban Development. Dr. James L. Goddard, tough-minded Public Health Service career man, became head of the U.S. Food and Drug Administration.

There were White House staff changes, too. Dapper Jack J. Valenti, 44-year-old Johnsonian confidant, quit to become president of the Motion Picture Association of America. George Reedy, longtime Johnson assistant and White House news secretary, resigned to enter private business. McGeorge Bundy, steel-trap mind on international affairs for both Mr. Kennedy and Mr. Johnson, left the White House to run the Ford Foundation. Walt Whitman Rostow moved over to the White House from the State Department's policy-planning helm. Robert E. Kintner, former board chairman of the National Broadcasting Co., was a surprise addition to the LBJ staff. Bill D. Moyers, White House press secretary, resigned in December, with George C. Christian named his successor.

Surgery; Future Plans. In November the President personally disclosed he was going back into Bethesda Naval Hospital for repair surgery on the incisional scar left by his gall bladder operation 13 months before. At the same time, he said, the doctors would remove a polyp, a small fleshy growth, from his throat. The surgery was a success, but doctors' efforts to slow him down were a flop.

Hardly was the President out of the anesthesia than he began summoning photographers, reporters and government officials to his bedside. Less than 24 hours later, he was out of bed and chatting in whispers with an unexpected visitor, General Eisenhower. By the second evening, he had tackled scores of official papers, posed repeatedly for pictures, huddled with a Congressional leader and presided at a hospital-suite celebration on his 32d wedding anniversary attended by half a hundred guests.

The President then hied himself off to the LBJ ranch in Texas. There he pondered what he would tell the American people in 1967 about the zooming cost of the Vietnam war and whether he would finally have to ask them for more income taxes as well as cutbacks in his Great Society programs. There was Johnson talk, too, of an early trip in 1967 to Latin America and a springtime visit to Europe. His popularity polls in 1966 may have been down, but President Johnson was far from counting himself out.

J. F. TERHORST
Washington Bureau Chief
THE DETROIT NEWS

KANSAS. Tornadoes ripped through Overland Park Apr. 19 and through widely scattered sections of eastern Kansas on June 8. President Johnson declared Topeka a major disaster area. . . . In July, plans for a multi-million-dollar air terminal at Kansas City's Mid-Continent International Airport were submitted to the city council. . . . Robert B. Docking (D) was elected governor, defeating incumbent William H. Avery. . . . In July, parts of the state were declared drought disaster areas.

KATZENBACH, NICHOLAS DEB. On Sept. 21, 1966, President Johnson named Attorney General Nicholas deB. Katzenbach undersecretary of state replacing George W. Ball, whose resignation became effective Sept. 30. The Senate approved the nomination Sept. 30. Katzenbach was sworn in at a formal White House ceremony by Supreme Court Justice Byron R. White Oct. 3.

Katzenbach had served in the Justice Department in various capacities since 1961. Prior to that he was a professor of international law at the University of Chicago and a member of the faculty of Yale Law School. A Rhodes scholar, the new Undersecretary of State was born Jan. 17, 1922, in Philadelphia, Pa.

KENTUCKY. The state House of Representatives defeated a bill to abolish capital punishment. . . . On Jan. 27, Gov. Edward T. Breathitt signed a state civil-rights bill. . . . Sen. John S. Cooper (R) was reelected by a landslide vote. . . . Louisville reported 16 deaths from pneumonia-influenza Feb. 28–Mar. 5. . . . Southern Illinois University's contract to operate the Job Corps center at Camp Breckenridge was not renewed when it expired July 1. . . . On May 4 an antipoverty grant of $395,-711 was announced for Louisville. . . . General farm income for 1966 was expected to be $800 million higher than that for 1965.

KIESINGER, KURT GEORG. Until he was named to succeed Ludwig Erhard as West German chancellor on Dec. 1, Kurt Georg Kiesinger, 62, was a little-known political outsider.

Though he had served in Bonn as a member of Parliament for nine years (1949–58), four of them as chairman of the Bundestag's foreign relations committee, Kiesinger's real climb to the pinnacle of German political power came through his eight-year tenure as minister-president (governor) of Baden-Württemberg.

A tall, silver-haired, good-looking man, Kiesinger has made a name for himself as a vote-getting, American-style politician. More-over, during his eight-year absence from the Federal capital, he had managed to stay aloof from the internecine strife that still jeopardizes his Christian Democratic Union (CDU) and its semiautonomous Bavarian wing, the Christian Social Union (CSU). As a dark horse, he was virtually the only man who could bridge the gap of regionalism, personal rivalry and ideology which divides his party.

One of seven children, Kiesinger was born April 6, 1904, in the village of Ebingen, 30 miles south of Stuttgart. He studied history, philosophy and law at Tübingen and Berlin Universities.

In 1933, Kiesinger joined the Nazi Party. He insists he was inwardly opposed to the National Socialists, following the murder of some of his friends during the June 30, 1934, purge of the storm-trooper (SA) movement, but he remained a party member until the end of the war.

In April 1940 he was inducted into the foreign service and assigned as a noncareer officer to the radio-political department of the foreign ministry, where his mission was to help conduct propaganda against the anti-Hitler allies. In September 1943 he was appointed deputy head of the department, a senior non-career post.

Kiesinger was interned for 14 months by American military government authorities after the war, then released. One 1947 denazification board classified him as a "follower," an appeal board in 1948 put him in the "exonerated" category.

In 1948 he resumed practicing law in Tübingen, where he now makes his home, became active in politics and was elected a deputy to postwar Germany's first national Parliament in Sept. 1949.

At a caucus of the CDU/CSU parliamentary group on Nov. 10, Kiesinger was one of four candidates nominated to succeed Erhard. On the third ballot he finally won as their candidate with 137 of 244 votes. Twenty-one days later, following a series of tough, nightlong negotiations, Kiesinger was elected head of a coalition Government with the Social Democrats by 340 of 472 votes in the Bundestag.

On Dec. 13, Kiesinger delivered his first government policy statement in which he outlined a number of economic measures designed to revive West Germany's slipping economy, and a foreign policy that will make Bonn more flexible in its relations both with France and the East European countries.

JOHN DORNBERG
Bonn-Berlin Correspondent, NEWSWEEK

KOSYGIN, ALEKSEI. Early in 1966, Premier Aleksei Nikolayevich Kosygin accomplished what was widely conceded to be a masterly diplomatic coup. The quiet, reserved man who succeeded the bombastic Nikita S. Khrushchev as chairman of the Council of Ministers of the Soviet Union, spent much of his year in diplomatic endeavors, though sharing these chores frequently with his opposite number in the Soviet leadership, General Secretary Leonid Ilyich Brezhnev of the Communist Party.

Kosygin distinguished himself in diplomacy in January by bringing together Prime Minister Lal Bahadur Shastri of India and President Ayub Khan of Pakistan at Tashkent, capital of the Uzbek S.S.R. There he persuaded the two to settle differences over disputed Kashmir. War had erupted there a few months before.

The Indian prime minister died suddenly at Tashkent after the agreement had been signed, and Kosygin traveled to India to represent the Soviet Union at the funeral. There, the Soviet premier met and talked with U.S. Vice-President Hubert H. Humphrey on matters of mutual concern to their two nations. These events did little to endear the Soviet leader to the Communist Chinese.

Back in Moscow, Kosygin had talks early in April with Shastri's successor as prime minister of India, Mrs. Indira Gandhi. Later he received Prime Minister Harold Wilson of Britain and also Secretary-General U Thant of the United Nations, who made separate peace-seeking missions to Moscow to talk, principally, about the Vietnam war. In May, Kosygin went to Cairo to visit President Gamal Abdel Nasser of the

Kosygin (c) and Wilson (r) visit exhibition in Moscow.
UPI

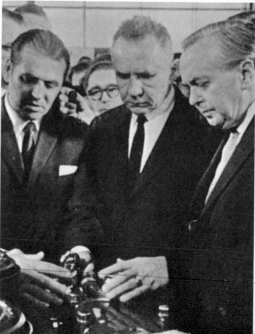

United Arab Republic and cement Cairo-Moscow relations. The trip produced nothing of a sensational nature. June found the Soviet premier in Finland to strengthen business ties.

In advance of the Supreme Soviet (Parliament) elections in June, Kosygin's speeches were relatively mild in tone with regard to the United States. He was critical of the American role in Vietnam, but also spoke of some "soberminded" U.S. leaders. He seemed to want to make clear that the Soviet Union did not wish to become any more deeply involved than it already was in the Vietnam conflict.

But toward the end of the year there were signs that pressure on him was beginning to have an effect. His tone became tougher, possibly reflecting the influence of Moscow's own hawks who, watching the performance of Soviet missiles and jets in Vietnam, were perhaps growing anxious about the effectiveness of Soviet defense weaponry. The pressures from a combination of military leaders and neo-Stalinists for more active involvement on behalf of North Vietnam conceivably could threaten Kosygin's position. There was some evidence that the Soviet premier hinted about this to his various peace-mission visitors.

On the domestic side, Kosygin at the February plenum of the Soviet Communist Party Central Committee—and a month later at the party's 23d Congress—played a significant part in the drive for economic reforms. Seemingly intent on a "Russia First" program, he pushed innovations in the field of agriculture and was instrumental in bringing about some radical departures for policies Khrushchev had pursued before his fall in October 1964. In August the Supreme Soviet confirmed Kosygin's reappointment as chairman of a council of about 85 ministers.

At year's end, in December, Kosygin emerged once again as the polished diplomat. This time he made a state visit to France, where he spent eight days. The government chief of the proletarian Soviet state was received with magnificent pomp by President Charles de Gaulle, who talked with him about a variety of subjects, including Vietnam and European security.

WILLIAM L. RYAN
Special Correspondent, THE ASSOCIATED PRESS

LABOR. The U.S. labor movement has had better years than 1966.

Labor and the Administration. The American Federation of Labor and Congress of Industrial Organizations began its second decade amid a spirit of unprecedented unity and hopeful of winning legislative triumphs from a friendly Congress. But by the time the year

had drawn to a close, some of labor's old internal strains had begun to show anew; it had suffered a serious legislative and political setback; and it was facing the possibility of the first new antistrike law in 20 years.

Organized labor, much to its surprise, experienced a rather difficult year with the Johnson administration and the liberal Congress. The first problem arose in January, when the President's Council of Economic Advisers held its guideposts for noninflationary wage settlements at 3.2 per cent. The guideposts normally would have risen to 3.6 per cent, but the council changed its formula for computing them in a bid to tamp down inflation.

Labor's relations with the Government were exacerbated when the Senate failed for the second time in 4 months to crack a conservative filibuster against its major legislative goal: repeal of section 14(b) of the Taft-Hartley Act, which permits states to ban the union shop. Relations ebbed further in February, when AFL-CIO President George Meany and the Johnson administration got into a public dispute over labor's second most important goal, the minimum wage.

Meany denounced the guideposts as unfair; hinted that labor would break its political alliance with the Democrats if it did not get its legislation; and warned the President publicly that he would face "a real quarrel" with labor if he did not meet its minimum-wage demands.

Meany and Johnson compromised their minimum-wage views in a bill expanding coverage to 8.1 million more workers and raising the minimum from $1.25 an hour to $1.40 an hour on Feb. 1, 1967, and to $1.60 an hour on Feb. 1, 1968. But this was scant comfort, because labor was defeated in Congress on its 2 other major bills: Federal standards for unemployment compensation, and the so-called "situs picketing" bill to ease restraints on construction-site picketing.

The AFL-CIO's legislative defeats were but a prelude to a more devastating setback in the November elections. Organized labor put on its biggest off-year political effort but sustained a net loss of 33 friendly House members. This forced the AFL-CIO to give up its hopes of winning major new legislation from the 90th Congress; put labor on the defensive to protect the gains already made; and raised questions about labor's political influence.

Gains, Strikes. This does not mean that 1966 produced no gains for labor. For one thing, AFL-CIO membership grew by 244,000 in fiscal 1966 to 13,385,000, the third rise in a row for the union.

Striking airline machinists in St. Louis, Mo., airport.

Above: George Meany, president, AFL-CIO; below: Walter Reuther, president, United Auto Workers.

The labor movement, after years of failure, finally achieved a significant breakthrough for migrant farm workers by winning a labor contract in the California grape region. There were signs that farm workers in Texas and Florida were moving toward unionization, and labor made important progress in organizing government workers, teachers and nurses.

Organized labor in 1966 also recaptured some of its past militancy and achieved some of its most impressive wage gains of the decade. The unions made a shambles of the Government's guideposts and by year-end were winning settlements of 5 per cent a year and more.

Labor was helped along to these big gains by a booming national economy, which produced soaring corporate profits, kept unemployment in the 3.7 per cent to 4 per cent range, and produced manpower shortages in some key skills. But the gains were undercut somewhat by inflation, which pushed up the cost of living by around 3.5 per cent.

The unions were forced to strike often to win their demands, and 1966 turned out to be the most strike-torn year since 1959. A New York City transit strike in January prompted President Johnson to say he would send a new antistrike bill to Congress. That never materialized, but Congress and the public began to clamor for new legislation when a machinists-union strike shut down five airlines for 43 days during the summer. President Johnson refused to back legislation that would send the strikers back to work, and the Senate-passed bill died in the House when the strike was settled. But public sentiment for legislation remained strong, and the President toward year-end set up a special panel to consider a new antistrike measure.

Meany vs. Reuther. Organized labor in 1966 remained a staunch supporter of the President's Vietnam policy. But differences over the AFL-CIO foreign-policy stance triggered an eruption between Meany and Walter P. Reuther, president of the United Automobile Workers union, who called the federation's Vietnam position "jingoistic" and "hysterical."

Reuther's attack broke almost three years of relative peace with Meany, and was rooted in deep philosophical differences that went beyond foreign policy. The auto union accused AFL-CIO of complacency, and said it would pursue an "independent course" on some basic issues. This seemed likely to strain AFL-CIO unity, probably erasing chances of Reuther's succeeding Meany as federation president.

DAVID R. JONES
Labor Reporter, Washington Bureau
THE NEW YORK TIMES

LATIN AMERICA

By FRANCIS L. McCARTHY
Latin-American Editor
UNITED PRESS INTERNATIONAL

Chiefs of State. Uruguayans in late November voted approval of a constitutional reform scrapping the nine-man Council of Government that had ruled the country since 1951, and replacing it with a single chief executive. In the same nation-wide balloting, Oscar D. Gestido, a retired Air Force general, was elected president on his 65th birthday to take office March 1, 1967. He called for austerity in a "modern, dynamic" society to solve the country's pressing economic problems.

The Uruguayan development highlighted sweeping political changes throughout the Western Hemisphere in 1966. The governments of nearly a dozen nations changed hands and one Latin-American president died in office. A repetition of the disastrous Bay of Pigs invasion of 1961 was narrowly averted in late November when the United States vetoed plans of a Haitian exile priest—Father Jean-Baptiste Georges—and a Cuban exile leader—Rolando Masferrer—to lead a mixed invasion force of 300 to 400 men against Haiti to eliminate the island's "President for Life," François (Papa Doc) Duvalier.

Victor Andres Belaunde, Peru's ambassador to the United Nations and a former president of the General Assembly, died Dec. 14 in New York. Belaunde, 82, was a noted Latin-American author and a former university professor.

President René Schick of Nicaragua died in Managua on Aug. 3. Following constitutional procedures, Lorenzo Guerrero, Interior Minister in Schick's cabinet, is serving until the term expires April 30, 1967.

In Costa Rica, Jose Joaquin Trejos was inaugurated president May 8 to replace Francisco J. Orlich, who had served out his full term.

In Argentina, on June 28 and 29, the armed forces deposed constitutional President Arturo U. Illia in a two-day bloodless coup. Lt. Gen. Juan Carlos Ongania was subsequently appointed president.

In the Dominican Republic, Joaquin Balaguer was inaugurated July 1, after his election a month earlier to the presidency, replacing provisional President Hector Garcia-Godoy. The latter was a compromise chief of state under an arrangement to end the 1965 civil war.

In Guatemala on July 1, Julio Cesar Mendez Montenegro was inaugurated to succeed Col. Enrique Peralta Azurdia, a *de facto* chief executive who headed a *coup d'état* that toppled the constitutional Government in March 1963.

On Aug. 6, Gen. René Barrientos was inaugurated president of Bolivia, replacing Gen. Alfredo Ovando, a *de facto* chief executive. Barrientos prior to his election had been a "copresident" with Ovando in a military Government that seized power. Barrientos resigned the copresidency to run for president in free elections.

In Colombia on Aug. 7, Carlos Lleras Restrepo was inaugurated president. He succeeded Guillermo Leon Valencia, who had served out his full term.

In Brazil, Gen. Artur da Costa e Silva was elected by the Congress on Oct. 3 to become president, succeeding Humberto Castelo Branco, a *de facto* chief executive. Costa e Silva takes office March 15, 1967.

In Ecuador on Nov. 17, a national constituent assembly selected Otto Arosemena Gomez as provisional president, pending general elections, to succeed Clemente Yerovi Indaburu. The latter acted as president after the ouster of the country's military junta on March 29.

Inter-American Cooperation. The hemisphere moved urgently throughout 1966 to strengthen the inter-American system to cope with ever-growing political and economic problems. First steps toward this end were taken at conferences in Panama and Buenos Aires. Diplomats of the Americas met to draft reforms to the outdated charter of the Organization of American States (OAS).

A hemisphere meeting of presidents scheduled for 1966 was put off until early 1967, possibly in April at Viña del Mar, Chile. The postponement came about after foreign ministers in New York for the opening of the United Nations General Assembly decided there was not enough time to work out an agenda. Substantive changes are to be made in the inter-American system. The chiefs of state did not want to come together to debate issues and adjourn without some major innovation to announce.

Failure of the foreign ministers to agree to a 1966 presidents' meeting created a logjam on the diplomatic calendar. Tentatively scheduled were the Third Special Inter-American Conference of Foreign Ministers, to amend the OAS charter; the 11th Meeting of Consultation of Foreign Ministers, to set the date and place of the summit meeting; and an Economic and Social Council (ECOSOC) meeting at the

UNITED STATES

MEXICO

GULF OF MEXICO

TROPIC OF CANCER

CUBA

DOMINICAN REPUBLIC

BRITISH HONDURAS
JAMAICA   HAITI
PUERTO RICO
HONDURAS
GUATEMALA
EL SALVADOR   NICARAGUA
CARIBBEAN   SEA

PANAMA CANAL ZONE
BARBADOS

COSTA RICA
TRINIDAD AND TOBAGO

PANAMA
VENEZUELA

GUYANA
SURINAM
FRENCH GUIANA

COLOMBIA

PACIFIC   OCEAN

EQUATOR

ECUADOR

Amazon River

PERU

BRAZIL

BOLIVIA

ATLANTIC OCEAN

TROPIC OF CAPRICORN

PARAGUAY

PACIFIC OCEAN

ANDES

CHILE   ARGENTINA   URUGUAY

ATLANTIC OCEAN

STRAIT OF MAGELLAN   TIERRA DEL FUEGO

LATIN AMERICA

0   500   1000   1500   2000 Miles
0   500   1000   1500   2000   2500   3000 Km.

BARBADOS

59°30'W

Speightstown
Mount Hillaby
1104 ft.   Bathsheba
Holetown
13°10'N

Bridgetown

BUCEL

0   5   10 Miles
0   5   10   15 Km.

ministerial level, to make the annual review of the Alliance for Progress. All of these were up in the air as late as Dec. 1.

The New York Times reported on June 20, however, that the United States and 19 Latin-American nations had reached a compromise resolution of differences over economic and social policies. This it termed an important achievement in inter-American relations.

According to the *Times* report, the United States agreed to put into treaty form a commitment to continue its long-term aid program, plus a pledge to help Latin America achieve economic integration and better access to world markets for its commodity exports. The *Times* also said Latin Americans had dropped their insistence that Washington be more specific about the kind and techniques of future assistance, and that it give Latin America drastic trade concessions.

The *Times* said Latin-American leaders had endorsed a series of self-help measures on policies against inflation and on effective tax systems, agrarian reform and education.

The compromise is to be embodied in amendments to the basic inter-American treaty, to be endorsed by the foreign ministers, the *Times* reported.

The newspaper's premise seems to have been supported by a speech by President Johnson on April 15 in Mexico City. He endorsed the Argentine suggestion of a summit meeting to discuss common problems and to decide how best to give the Alliance for Progress "increased momentum."

At that time, Johnson urged Latin-American nations to spend less on their armies and more on social programs, emphasized the need for rural reforms, pledged cooperation in expanding trade, strongly endorsed the concept of a Latin-American trade market and promised that the United States would speed work to finish the last link in the Inter-American Highway between Panama and Colombia.

In Mexico, on what he modestly described as a "neighborly visit" south of the border, Johnson called for joint efforts to "breathe new energy" into Latin America. "We will continue to concentrate our assistance mainly in economic and social fields—and to encourage our Latin-American neighbors, where possible, to limit their outlays for military purposes," Johnson said.

Lincoln Gordon, 52, was appointed by Johnson as assistant secretary of state for Inter-American Affairs on Jan. 18, 1966. On June 1 in Mexico City Gordon voiced "wholehearted" U.S. support of Latin-American economic integration.

Gordon, who succeeded Jack Hood Vaughn, named director of the Peace Corps, told the Inter-American Trade and Production Council (CICUP) that despite possible adverse effects on U.S. exports, "regional integration in the long run will bring benefits to all." He said that giving new impulse to Latin-American integration was at the top of the agenda for the 1967 meeting of hemisphere presidents.

The shaping of national development plans and policies is not, however, primarily a matter for the United States, he added. "It is to Latin America itself that we must look for the main initiative in determining the character of these programs and efforts," Gordon said.

In a press conference at Washington on June 20, Gordon confirmed that the United States had undertaken "a special commitment to Latin America" in supporting the economic and social norms drafted the week previous by the Inter-American Economic and Social Council (IA-ECOSOC).

Gordon said the United States will analyze any measure that might have adverse effects on the economies of Latin-American nations, will discuss the measure with the government or governments involved and will try to find some other way of solving the particular problem. This policy is not applied to any other part of the world, Gordon said.

He added, however, that if the United States found no other way to avoid using the measure without damaging "the national security or the economic balance" of a particular U.S. industry, the measure would be put into force anyway.

David Bronheim, deputy U.S. coordinator of the Alliance for Progress, who headed the U.S. delegation to the ECOSOC meeting, said the agreement reached on the reduction or elimination of tariff and nontariff barriers applied not only to Western Hemisphere trade but also to trade between OAS members and regional trade groupings. Bronheim said the United States undertook to work for the free access of Latin-American products to other areas of the world.

The Inter-American Committee for the Alliance for Progress (CIAP) estimated at its March meeting in Buenos Aires that Latin-American per capita gross national product (GNP) would rise 2.5 per cent in 1966; the value of exports, 3.9 per cent; and imports, 10 per cent.

U.S. sources estimated the 1966 per capita GNP increase for 19 Latin-American republics at about 2.7 per cent, compared to 2.8 in 1965 and 2.4 in 1964. Increase of GNP in all 19 nations was estimated at 5.6 per cent, as against increases of 5.7 in 1965 and 5.3 in 1964. This brought the total value to about $75,570,000,-000. Of this total, it was estimated, 88 per cent was from the following countries: Mexico, $18,900,000,000; Brazil, $15,260,000,000; Argentina, $12,230,000,000; Venezuela, $7,370,-000,000; Colombia, $5,400,000,000; Chile, $4,130,000,000; and Peru, $3,090,000,000.

Inflation. Brazil, Argentina, Chile, Colombia and Mexico continued to be plagued by inflation throughout 1966. In Brazil, living costs rose 35.2 per cent in the first nine months of 1966, as compared to 39.2 per cent in the corresponding period the preceding year. Total increase by year-end was estimated at under 42 per cent, compared to 45 per cent in 1965 and 85 per cent in 1964.

Argentine living costs in September were 20.2 per cent more than on Jan. 1, and 27.3 per cent over September 1965. Wholesale prices in June were 19.6 per cent over the same 1965 month.

Chile's wholesale prices rose by 13.6 per cent in the first six months of 1966, compared to a hike of 16.3 per cent in the January-June period of 1965. The official cost-of-living index went up by 23 per cent in the 12-month period ending in August.

Colombia's official living-cost index rose in the first 1966 half year by 9 per cent for salaried employees and by 9.7 per cent for manual workers, as compared to hikes of 5.6 and 2.6 per cent, respectively, in the same period of 1965.

The Mexican economy suffered further from built-in inflation. Recent practice has been to raise the minimum wage every two years. The last two such wage hikes each averaged 17 per cent. Further minimum-wage raises will bring continuing inflation. During 1966, car prices rose 8 to 10 per cent, newspapers 25 to 50 per cent. Prices on scores of industrial and consumer items, such as sugar and tobacco, also rose.

Financial Assistance. The preeminent position of Latin America as the most development-ripe part of the underdeveloped world was underscored in the annual statement of the World Bank and its affiliates, the International Development Association (IDA) and International Finance Corporation (IFC).

The statement showed that of the bank's total worldwide commitments of $839 million in the 1965–66 calendar year, $374 million, or more than 40 per cent, went to Latin America. These included $49 million to Brazil, $41.7 million to Colombia, $154 million to Mexico, $42.1 million to Peru and $58.3 million to Venezuela. Since the bank began operations in 1946, more than $2,500,000,000 has gone to Latin America in the form of 161 loans.

IDA credits of $7.5 million went to Paraguay for livestock development. IFC credits of $24.1 million went to Brazil, Chile, Colombia, Costa Rica, Ecuador, Honduras, Mexico and Venezuela.

The IFC, whose purpose is to promote the growth of private enterprise in the member countries, has financed Latin-American industry through more than $100 million in 69 different loans and equity purchases since its inception in 1956. This represents about 60 per cent of its total outlay for the 10-year period.

From the start of the Alliance for Progress through June 30, 1966, the Export-Import Bank assisted in financing $2,300,000,000 of U.S. exports to Latin America through direct financing, a bank-guarantee program and short- and medium-term insurance.

Agriculture. Total agricultural production in Latin America increased by 2 per cent in 1965–66, the United Nations Food and Agricultural Organization (FAO) said in a report released in Rome on Oct. 13. The FAO report attributed the increase almost solely to the recovery of Brazil's coffee crop from the frost and fire damage that it has suffered over the past few years.

The report indicated that while there was an increase in total agricultural production, there had been a 2 per cent reduction in food production in Latin America. The region's wheat production fell by more than 30 per cent during 1965–66. Drought in Argentina was mostly responsible for the decline.

Here are some other FAO comments on the 1965-66 Latin-American agricultural situation: The production of maize, the region's main grain crop, is estimated to have increased by about 5 per cent. . . . Sugar production rose by about 4 per cent. A slight fall in Cuban output, which had shown a sharp rise the previous year, was more than offset by larger harvests in Brazil and Mexico. . . . For almost all of the main products, there appeared to be little change in output at the regional level in 1965–66.

Economic Integration. A cornerstone for creation of a Latin-American common market was laid in Bogota in August at a "little summit" conference of five Latin-American nations: Venezuela, Peru, Colombia, Ecuador and Chile. Whether the cornerstone would result in construction of a fullscale structure, however, appeared still in doubt.

The germ for the economic integration of the nations was contained in a "Declaration of Bogota" signed at the conclusion of the conference. It called for the rapid cementing of common economic practices within the structure of the existing Latin-American Free Trade Association (LAFTA).

LAFTA was formed in 1960 by nine nations to improve trade among them. After a fairly good beginning, it became bogged down in bureaucracy and nationalistic prejudices.

The five nations responsible for new momentum are hoping their work will not follow the same course. To this end, they have already begun taking steps for their own regional economic integration while waiting for the other 14 countries in the area to react to their initiative.

Desire for regional economic cooperation has long been the dream of many Latin-American leaders. One of its foremost adherents, President Eduardo Frei of Chile, was one of three presidents who attended and endorsed the Bogota declaration.

As a beginning to the realization of a viable common market, the little-summit nations proposed a ministerial-level governing body for LAFTA to slice through red tape and get it back to its original momentum. Once LAFTA has begun functioning normally, the little nations feel it should merge with the thriving five-nation Central American Common Market (CACM). Later, the five countries not associated with either group would be brought in. Currently, however, only the five little-summit participants are on record as favoring the plan.

One major problem appears to be differences and rivalries between neighboring countries, which in the past have made almost impossible any long-term agreements. It is also questionable whether CACM would want to join the LAFTA-oriented group. CACM has been notably successful and might not care to align itself to LAFTA, which has failed to flourish.

Armaments. The issue of whether an "arms race" got under way in Latin America during 1966 was a controversial topic in the closing months of the year.

First spark came in President Johnson's April 15 speech in Mexico City, in which he urged Latin-American nations to spend less on their armies and more on social reform. Again, on Aug. 17, Johnson in a speech expressed concern that some Latin-American governments were diverting vital resources from important economic and social projects to the acquisition of expensive arms.

A rash of jet-fighter purchases by several Latin-American nations in the closing months of the year brought full controversy. Argentina girded itself with 25 A-4B fighter jets, bought from U.S. surplus stocks. Chile purchased 21 Hawker Hunter fighters from Britain. Brazil announced plans to purchase fighters from West Germany, which supplied 74 F-86 jets to Venezuela. Peru was negotiating with the United States and Britain for similar aircraft.

The apparent arms race among Latin America's developing countries brought a raft of criticism from both sides of the Rio Grande. *La Prensa,* Peru's top circulation paper, said in an editorial: "No Latin-American country— saddled with grave economic and social problems—can afford to submerge itself in the quicksand of a costly armaments race. . ."

In the United States, Senators Robert F. Kennedy (D-N.Y.) and Wayne Morse (D-Ore.) called for a halt to the U.S. sale of arms to underdeveloped Latin-American nations. Kennedy on Oct. 30 told an audience in Portland, Me., that sale of arms was a "wasteful and dangerous luxury." He said if the United States refused to sell Latin-American nations the arms they sought, and they turned elsewhere, "then we should take account of this waste in determining the amount of our economic aid to them."

But, on Nov. 18, U.S. Secretary of State Dean Rusk minimized the importance of the acquisition of jets by some hemisphere nations. Replying to a question at a Washington press conference, Rusk said the "arms race" had been "greatly exaggerated" and is "more on paper than on the ground." He added: "These countries are not going pell-mell into an arms race, and I think this term has been greatly exaggerated."

The Secretary pointed out that Latin America, as a region, spends less on defense than any other part of the world. As to the U.S. role, Rusk said the country provides only about 7 per cent of its aid to Latin America for military purposes. This is dwarfed, he said, by the amount of U.S. economic and technical assistance.

On Nov. 1, United Press International (UPI) quoted "U.S. officials" as disclosing that Latin-American governments approached have rejected suggestions they call a temporary halt to the acquisition of expensive arms. The officials reported the idea was quietly circulated by U.S. embassies in major Latin-American nations that indicated interest in modernizing and rebuilding their armed forces. Response to the idea was unfavorable, the officials said, and it was subsequently withdrawn by the State Department.

Officials explained that Latin-American armed forces are now in the process of a transformation, referred to as "rationalization," involving increased mobility, better communications and greater firepower.

Alliance for Progress. On Aug. 17, the fifth anniversary of the Alliance for Progress, President Johnson applauded the program's accomplishments, and charted a bold agenda for its future, including the economic integration of the 19 Latin-American republics and the raising of the 2.5 per cent annual per capita growth rate for the region from 4 to 6 per cent.

He said the main question confronting the Alliance now is whether Latin America wants to face the future "in unity or isolation . . . we are ready to work in close cooperation toward an integrated Latin America."

The President noted the success of the Alliance has shattered several venerable myths, including the notion that the *status quo* would not yield to evolutionary social progress, the idea that "inflationary spending is the royal road to rapid development" and the belief that "Communism in this hemisphere is the wave of the future."

The President acknowledged that the Alliance had only begun to meet present needs, while the tasks ahead are vast. By the year 2000 the hemisphere's population will reach 1,000,000,000, with nearly two thirds of the people in Latin America (present population, 248 million). Mr. Johnson noted that this extraordinary growth would require a 6 per cent annual increase in farm production, 140 million new jobs, 1 million new homes each year and more classrooms and doctors.

Johnson's answer to the forbidding growth prognosis was economic integration. He suggested these matters be given priority attention at the forthcoming conference of American presidents.

Other Developments. British Guiana, the only British dependency on the South American mainland, became independent on May 26 when it became known by its Amerindian name of "Guyana," or "Land of Waters." The country will remain in the British Commonwealth at least until April 1, 1969, after which it will be up to its Parliament to pass a resolution establishing a republic. In the meantime, Queen Elizabeth II will be represented by a governor-general, the first being Sir Richard Luyt, its last governor. Independence ended a British responsibility which began in 1796.

Barbados, Britain's oldest colony in the Caribbean, became an independent state Nov. 30.

Antigovernment guerrilla forces were active during 1966 in several countries, principally Colombia, Guatemala and Venezuela.

In October, the Government of President Raul Leoni of Venezuela quickly crushed a "vest pocket" revolt attributed to followers of ousted Dictator Marcos Perez Jimenez. The aborted coup did not threaten the stability of the country. Loyal troops suppressed the brief rebellion, which was centered at a National Guard school about 20 miles east of Caracas. An army lieutenant colonel who led the plotters was shot and killed. There was an unreported number of arrests. The Government officially shrugged off the incident as without importance.

In Guatemala City, in November, the Government imposed a 30-day state of siege (modified martial law) to cope with growing terrorism and subversion from both the political Right and Left. It was the third time in less than two years that Guatemala had been forced into a state of siege to cope with political violence.

Argentina devalued its peso by 12.4 per cent in November, the sharpest drop in the official rate for the national currency in 19 months. The step was taken in a government program to stabilize the economy. The Central Bank established a rate of 245 pesos for sellers and 255 pesos for buyers of U.S. dollars. It was the second drop in the value of the peso since the overthrow of the Illia regime in June, and the third in the year.

The peso, once exchanged at four to the dollar, has tumbled steadily since 1961. In a speech announcing the "liberalization" of the peso, President Juan Carlos Ongania said its ultimate freeing would lead to a stronger economy. He called on Argentines to hold their expenses to income and said the Government hoped to improve its own (and its people's) financial situation before 1968. Ongania said that many personal sacrifices would be expected from the workingman to help the nation's limping economy.

In Brazil the lame-duck regime of Humberto Castelo Branco won a smashing victory in nationwide Congressional elections in November, and assured the incoming Costa e Silva Government heavy majorities in both the Senate and Chamber of Deputies. Unofficial final results indicated Costa e Silva would have a 3-to-1 majority in the Chamber and a 2-to-1 margin in the Senate.

In Peru, President Fernando Belaunde Terry in November shook up his Cabinet for the ninth time during some three years in office. He made no essential change in the political makeup or policy of his government. The shakeup, involving replacement of four ministers, came after the Government eked out a narrow victory over the political opposition in nationwide municipal elections.

Wide World

Juan Carlos Ongania, 52, president of Argentina since June 1966.

UPI

Errol W. Barrow, 46, prime minister of newly independent Barbados.

LATIN-AMERICAN LEADERS

as of Dec. 31, 1966

René Barrientos, 47, inaugurated president of Bolivia, Aug. 6, 1966.

Artur da Costa e Silva, 64, elected president of Brazil, Oct. 3, 1966.

Eduardo Frei, 55, president of Chile since Nov. 3, 1964.

Wide World

Wide World

UPI

Carlos Lleras, 58, Colombia president since Aug. 7, 1966.

Jose Joaquin Trejos, 50, president of Costa Rica since May 8, 1966.

Fidel Castro, 39, premier of Cuba since February 1959.

Wide World

UPI

Wide World

Joaquin Balaguer, 59, Dominican Republic president, July 1, 1966.

Otto Arosemena Gomez, 45, president of Ecuador since November 1966.

Julio Adalberto Rivera, 45, El Salvador's president, July 1962.

UPI

Ecuadorian Ministry of Foreign Relations

UPI

Forbes Burnham, 43, prime minister of newly independent Guyana.

Julio Cesar Mendez, 50, president of Guatemala since July 1, 1966.

François Duvalier, 59, president of Haiti since Oct. 22, 1957.

Oswaldo Lopez Arellano, 45, president of Honduras, June 6, 1965.

Gustavo Diaz Ordaz, 55, president of Mexico since Dec. 1, 1964.

Lorenzo Guerrero, 66, president of Nicaragua since Aug. 3, 1966.

Marcos A. Robles, 61, president of Panama since Oct. 1, 1964.

Alfredo Stroessner, 54, president of Paraguay since Aug. 15, 1954.

Fernando Belaunde Terry, 53, president of Peru, July 28, 1963.

Oscar D. Gestido, 65, president-elect of Uruguay.

Raul Leoni, 61, president of Venezuela since March 11, 1964.

LEGISLATION IN 1966, MAJOR U.S.

PUBLIC LAW	SUBJECT	DESCRIPTION
89–528	AEROSPACE	**NASA Appropriation.** Appropriates $5,000,000,000 for National Aeronautics and Space Administration in fiscal 1967, including $2,970,000,000 for Apollo moon-landing project. Proposed by Miller (D-Cal.), approved Aug. 5.
89–670	COMMERCE AND TRANSPORTATION	**Transportation Department.** Establishes a new Cabinet department to consolidate the principal transportation operating programs of the Federal Government. Proposed by Holifield (D-Cal.), approved Oct. 15.
89–755		**Truth-in-Packaging.** Improves protection of the consumer by new standards of labeling and by providing for bringing order into the chaotic pattern of package size. Proposed by Hart (D-Mich.), Bartlett (D-Alaska), et al., approved Nov. 3.
89–750	EDUCATION	**Elementary and Secondary Education Amendments.** Extends for two years the Elementary and Secondary Education Act of 1965. Proposed by Perkins (D-Ky.), approved Nov. 3.
89–752		**Higher Education Amendments.** Extends for three years programs of assistance to higher education. Proposed by Staggers (D-W.Va.), approved Nov. 3.
89–583	FOREIGN POLICY	**Foreign Assistance Act.** Authorizes $3,500,735,500 for foreign technical and military assistance in fiscal 1967. Proposed by Morgan (D-Pa.), approved Sept. 19.
89–654	SAFETY	**Highway Safety Act.** Provides for coordinated national highway safety program through financial assistance to states. Proposed by Randolph (D-W.Va.), Cooper (R-Ky.), approved Sept. 9.
89–563		**Motor Vehicle Safety Act.** Provides for establishment of safety standards for motor vehicles in interstate commerce. Proposed by Magnuson (D-Wash.), approved Sept. 9.
89–472	TAXES AND ECONOMIC POLICY	**Public Debt.** Increases public debt limitation from $328,000,000,000 to $330,000,000,000. Proposed by Mills (D-Ark.), approved June 24.
89–368		**Tax Adjustment.** Provides for graduated withholding of Federal income taxes; increases excise taxes on automobiles and telephone services. Proposed by Mills (D-Ark.), approved Mar. 15.
89–754	URBAN DEVELOPMENT	**Demonstration Cities.** Provides financial and technical assistance to cities to plan, develop, and carry out programs to rebuild and revitalize entire areas of slum and to expand and improve social programs and services available to the people who live in such areas. Proposed by Muskie (D-Me.), approved Nov. 3.
89–358	VETERANS	**G.I. Bill.** Provides broad program of educational and other benefits for veterans of service in armed forces after Jan. 31, 1955. Proposed by Yarborough (D-Tex.), Hill (D-Ala.), et al., approved Mar. 3.
89–601	WELFARE	**Minimum Wage Law.** Increases minimum wage to $1.40 per hour, effective Feb. 1, 1967, and to $1.60 per hour, effective Feb. 1, 1968. Proposed by Debt (D-Pa.), approved Sept. 23.
89–487	MISCELLANEOUS	**Access to Government Information.** Establishes standards for guiding executive-branch agencies in making information available to the public. Proposed by Long (D-La.), Bartlett (D-Alaska), et al., approved July 4.
89–486		**Registration of Foreign Agents.** Provides for complete public disclosure by persons acting for and in the interest of foreign principals where their activities are, or border on being, political in nature. Proposed by Fulbright (D-Ark.) and Hickenlooper (R-Iowa), approved July 4.
89–387		**Uniform Time.** Establishes uniform dates for commencing and ending Daylight Saving Time in all states where it is observed. Proposed by Cotton (R-N.H.), McGee (D-Wyo.), approved April 13.
89–386		**Vice-President's Official Residence.** Authorizes planning, design, construction, furnishing and maintenance of official residence for vice-president of the United States. Proposed by Monroney (D-Okla.), Brewster (D-Md.), Hartke (D-Ind.), approved April 10.

ROBERT D. HURSH
Editor in Chief, BANCROFT-WHITNEY COMPANY

LIBRARIES.

LIBRARIES. Additional legislation and the creation of a National Library Commission in 1966 demonstrated President Johnson's and Congress' continued concern with improving libraries and library services throughout the United States.

On July 20, President Johnson signed into law the Library Services and Construction Act Amendments of 1966. The amendments, which extend the 1964 act, provide $575 million between 1966 and 1975 "to raise the physical standards of libraries, to replace outmoded buildings, and to help provide the 40 million square feet of library space still needed" in the United States. The amendments also provide $50 million to support interlibrary cooperation, and establish a $75 million grant program for library services for those persons physically handicapped or institutionalized.

At the time of the signing, President Johnson announced his intention of appointing a National Library Commission "to point toward an effective and efficient library system for the future."

The Higher Education Act of 1965 authorized library construction and a five-year program for library improvement generally. On May 13, 1966, President Johnson signed a supplemental appropriations bill making $10 million available for libraries under the act. He subsequently appointed an Advisory Committee on Library Research and Training Projects, as authorized by the act.

The rapid development of Federal libraries, each operating independently, has led to the creation of a Federal Library Committee of 18 members, designed to bring about a measure of coherence among the several libraries in Washington. Also at the Federal level, contracts were executed between the National Library of Medicine and the universities of Colorado, California (Los Angeles), Alabama and Harvard. These libraries will develop a network of regional centers for utilizing the National Library's operation of MEDLARS (Medical Literature Analysis and Retrieval System). The National Library of Medicine has also aided in establishing a British MEDLARS, operated jointly by the National Lending Library for Science and Technology, and Newcastle University.

The United States Information Libraries in Paris and London were closed for lack of funds. Subsequently, however, the Paris library reopened as a reference center only, with a sharply reduced book collection. Books formerly in the London branch were transferred to the University of London library.

A gift of $10 million came to the University of Chicago from the Regenstein Foundation for its projected new Graduate Research Library. The Regenstein Library will incorporate provisions for computers, high-speed equipment for printing texts, and electronic means of exploring recorded information.

LEON CARNOVSKY
Professor, Graduate Library School
UNIVERSITY OF CHICAGO

Julius Shulman, courtesy of A.I.A.

New libraries honored for their design by the American Institute of Architects in 1966 include the Swirbul Library at Adelphi University, Garden City, N.Y., (above) and Magnolia Branch, Seattle Public Library, Seattle, Wash.

Hugh H. Stratford, courtesy of A.I.A.

LITERATURE

By PAUL CUNEO
Book Editor, AMERICA MAGAZINE

Headline Makers. Throughout 1966, books made newspaper headlines. From January, when Truman Capote's *In Cold Blood* was published, until the end of the year, books made important news.

Capote called his meticulously researched and written book a "nonfiction novel," and not a few critics muttered about the phrase. The book is an account of the murder of a prosperous Kansas farm family—husband, wife, son and daughter—by two men who did not know them, and had no motive for the killing beyond the kinks worked into their personalities by heredity, environment and themselves. *In Cold Blood* was an instant best seller; Capote's picture appeared on the covers of magazines and the front pages of newspapers; and the book was endlessly praised and damned. It also produced the most spectacular literary feud of the year, when English critic Kenneth Tynan attacked Capote for making no effort to help the confessed murderers while busily taking notes for a book that would make him millions of dollars.

Not long after the appearance of *In Cold Blood,* a previously unknown writer named Ralph Nader published a book called *Unsafe at Any Speed.* The automobile industry was shaken by the author's charges that automobiles were manufactured with an almost total disregard for the driver's safety. So great was the furor raised by the book, and by the Congressional investigating committee that probed the subject, that when automobile sales declined in midyear, Detroit executives pinpointed Mr. Nader's charges as the primary cause.

When A. E. Hotchner published his sympathetic but candid account of his years of friendship with Ernest Hemingway, entitled

Papa Hemingway, Hemingway's widow tried to prevent publication of the book on grounds of invasion of privacy. Hemingway's name, Hotchner's revelations about Hemingway's mental condition in the months before his suicide, and his widow's efforts to obtain an injunction to stop the book all added up to more front-page news.

A spate of books questioning the accuracy and trustworthiness of the Warren report on President Kennedy's assassination brought this subject into the headlines. Edward Jay Epstein's *Inquest,* Mark Lane's *Rush to Judgment,* and Leo Sauvage's *The Oswald Affair* combined to present a disturbing number of charges, and raised doubts that Lee Harvey Oswald could have carried out the assassination alone. At the same time, a strange little book by novelist and short-story writer Jean Stafford, titled *A Mother in History,* offered a lengthy interview with Oswald's mother, who

Random House photo by Rudy Valenzuela

Above: Truman Capote, who wrote *In Cold Blood.* Below: A. E. Hotchner (left) with his friend Ernest Hemingway.

Random House

seemed to deny that her son committed the murder, while proclaiming that if he had, it was for the good of the country.

Biography and Autobiography. Apart from those books that make news or supplement news, it is generally agreed by both literary critics and those critics of another sort, the booksellers, that readers have a taste for biography and autobiography, and that today's writers in this field are topflight (another verification of the theory that great audiences are needed to produce great writers).

In the biography-autobiography category England supplied two important works on Sir Winston Churchill. The first volume of the official biography, *Winston S. Churchill: Youth 1874–1900,* written by his son, Randolph S. Churchill, appeared at the end of the year. Earlier the book *Churchill* from the diaries of Lord Moran, personal physician to the Prime Minister, aroused controversy over its revelations about the great man, and over the ethical question the book raised, based as it was on what some thought privileged material that Lord Moran had no right to make public.

Other European leaders either published their memoirs or were subjects of biographies. Konrad Adenauer published the first volume of his autobiography, *Memoirs, 1945–53,* as did Harold Macmillan in his *Winds of Change.* Many books appeared about Charles de Gaulle, among them *The Three Lives of Charles de Gaulle* by news commentator David Schoenbrun, and *De Gaulle* by the Nobel Prizewinning novelist François Mauriac.

There were two books about the late Secretary-General of the United Nations: *Hammarskjold* by Emery Kelen, and *Dag Hammarskjold: A Spiritual Portrait* by Sven Stolpe, a noted Swedish writer and a friend of Hammarskjold. His successor as secretary-general was also subject of a biography, *U Thant: The Search for Peace* by June Bingham.

There was no sign of a letup in books about John F. Kennedy. His White House Press Secretary, Pierre Salinger, wrote *With Kennedy,* a chatty, ingratiating, but not really important book. Paul B. Fay, Jr., a friend of JFK from Navy days in the Pacific, wrote *The Pleasure of His Company,* an account of his twenty-year friendship that emphasized the informal and unguarded moments.

Lyndon B. Johnson: The Exercise of Power, by Washington reporters Rowland Evans and Robert Novak, was a political biography hard to put down. It was primarily an inside view of the development and use of LBJ's famous powers of "persuasion."

Probably the most important literary biography of the year was the first volume of Robert Frost's authorized biography, *Robert Frost: The Early Years* by Lawrance Thompson, the man Frost invited to be his biographer about twenty years ago. But certainly *Mr. Clemens and Mark Twain,* by Justin Kaplan, ran a close second as it examined the two different, even contradictory, personalities in the great American writer.

John Dos Passos, in his memoirs *The Best Times,* offered a view of his own life and of many leading literary figures in the first half of the twentieth century, and Charles W. Morton, longtime associate editor of *The Atlantic,* wrote his autobiography, *It Has Its Charms . . . ,* giving a view of newspaper and magazine work during the same period of time.

The death of Somerset Maugham in 1965 prompted a strange family biography, *Somerset and All the Maughams* written by his nephew Robin Maugham, and a fascinating account of many meetings with the man, *Remembering Mr. Maugham* by Garson Kanin. Both books revealed Maugham as a talented, irascible, intriguing and unpleasant person.

Fiction. In general 1966 was not a distinguished year for fiction. Two novels by U.S. writers that received the most critical attention and praise were *Giles Goat-Boy* by John Barth and *The Fixer* by Bernard Malamud. Mr.

Novelist John Barth, author of *Giles Goat-Boy.*

Alex Gotfryd

Barth, who gained previous attention with his novel *The Sot-Weed Factor,* tells a wildly symbolic story that seems to defy brief and comprehensible summary. It is long, involved and difficult to read; whether it is a literary landmark of the stature of Joyce's *Ulysses,* as some claim, will take years to determine. Mr. Malamud's story of a Russian Jew falsely accused of killing a child in czarist Russia derives from an actual historical case (concerning which there was a nonfiction account published during the year: *Blood Accusation: The Strange History of the Beiliss Case* by Maurice Samuel).

Like Mr. Malamud, Walker Percy is a former winner of the National Book Award for fiction, and Mr. Percy also wrote one of the best novels of the year. His *The Last Gentleman* tells of a young Southerner trying to discover the way to break out of a shell and into a life of ordinary everyday living.

Other novels worth reading were *The Secret of Santa Vittoria* by Robert Crichton, the story of a small wine-making town in Italy, determined to save its treasure from the German soldiers sent there in 1943 to confiscate the wine; *The Embezzler* by Louis Auchincloss, a novel of an upper-class marriage and the husband's Wall Street downfall; and *Office Politics* by Wilfrid Sheed, a dissection of the maneuvering in a New York magazine's office when the editor's failing health seems to be forcing him out of his job.

In the Company of Eagles by Ernest K. Gann, a story of World War I flyers, was no great artistic achievement, but it was readable and concerned with an interesting period of the past. (The very time and people, incidentally, that Charles Schulz, creator of *Peanuts,* dealt with in trenchant style in his first novel, *Snoopy and the Red Baron.*)

A number of novelists, some well established and some with the beginning of a reputation, produced work that was a distinct disappointment when measured against their earlier novels. Edwin O'Connor's *All in the Family* was a return to Boston politics. As *The Last Hurrah* seemed to be suggested by Boston politician James Michael Curley, so *All in the Family* brought to mind the Kennedy family. John Hersey retold an indifferent version of the Faust legend in *Too Far to Walk.* John Knowles, remembered for his *A Separate Peace,* produced the inferior *Indian Summer.* Thomas Pynchon, author of the 1963 success *V,* received mild attention for his *The Crying of Lot 49.*

Two authors, one living and one dead, one American and one English, had three of their earlier novels published in single volumes. Evelyn Waugh's *Sword of Honour* contained his *Men at Arms, Officers and Gentlemen* and *The End of the Battle*; it may be the best English novel or group of novels about World War II. Conrad Richter's *The Awakening Land* contained his *The Trees, The Fields* and *The Town,* lasting novels about America's making.

John Updike's most recent short stories appeared in *The Music School*; as in the past, they were criticized for all sorts of reasons, but still are easily among the best being written today. Bruce Jay Friedman's collection, entitled *Black Angels,* consisted of black humor and way-out work; when they succeeded they were refreshingly effective, but not all of them succeeded. As usual, Ireland produced several fine collections of short stories. *The Heat of the Sun* was by the always-reliable Sean O'Faolain, and *The Gold in the Sea* is the second collection by Brian Friel. Friel's earlier *Saucer of Larks* and his play *Philadelphia, Here I Come!* established his name, and the present volume did nothing to diminish his reputation.

When the best short stories of the year are mentioned, *The Magic of Shirley Jackson* should not be overlooked. A volume of the late author's work selected by her husband, critic Stanely Edgar Hyman, it contained her famous story "The Lottery" along with other pieces impressive in their versatility.

Three novels from England were especially worth noting. Graham Greene's *The Comedians* was something of a comeback for a distinguished writer whose last few novels seemed to indicate a failing power. Some critics even called this story of confusion in Haiti his best work. Kingsley Amis' *The Anti-Death League* was a satiric spoof of spy stories, but with a deadly serious undercurrent. Mary Renault's *The Mask of Apollo* continued her distinguished series of historical novels based on the history of ancient Greece.

History. A number of popular historical works supplied the demand for books about World War I and II. Barbara Tuchman's *The Proud Tower* detailed the years leading up to World War I; it was not so big a seller as her earlier story of the outbreak of the war, *The Guns of August,* but it was an equally good book. *The Road to Sarajevo,* by Vladimir Dedijer, was an important account of the assassination of Archduke Franz Ferdinand and his wife, which touched off World War I. The end of World War II was treated by Cornelius Ryan in his *The Last Battle,* a masterfully pieced-together story of the battle for Berlin, and by John Toland in his *The Last 100 Days.*

Graham Greene's *The Comedians* was a 1966 success.

Cornelius Ryan's *The Last Battle* tells of Berlin's fall.

Two women dealt notably with early American history. Catherine Drinker Bowen did an excellent job of clarifying a complicated story in *Miracle at Philadelphia: The Story of the Constitutional Convention,* and the late Mari Sandoz was generally applauded on the posthumous publication of *The Battle of the Little Bighorn* for her objective and fresh account of what happened at Custer's famous last stand.

Jonathan Daniels' *The Time Between the Wars,* a competent but routine history of the American 1920's and 1930's, made front-page news across the country because a comparatively small section of the book revealed details of a little-known romance between Franklin D. Roosevelt and a prominent Eastern socialite.

Mary Renault specializes in historical novels.

Other Nonfiction. Of the many books on racial problems, three in particular were off the beaten track. George S. Schuyler, a Negro journalist who supported Barry Goldwater in his campaign for the presidency, wrote *Black and Conservative,* his autobiography. The editors of *Ebony* magazine invited a number of eminent Negro writers and scholars to contribute articles to a book they titled *The White Problem in America.* And Kyle Haselden, editor of the *Christian Century,* wrote *Mandate for White Christians.*

Criticism directed at American medicine was reflected in two books: *Condition Critical, Our Hospital Crisis* by Edwin P. Hoyt and *The Doctors,* a far-from-sympathetic study by M. L. Gross.

In books about religion, the God-is-dead discussion continued as earnestly as ever. Gabriel Vahanian, one of the Protestant theologians who touched off the controversy, contributed another book on the subject, *No Other God.* A staff writer for *The New Yorker* magazine, Ved Mehta, investigated the subject and the theologians involved in his book *The New Theologian.*

The end of the Roman Catholic Church's Ecumenical Council in December 1965 resulted in a flood of books interpreting the meaning of this renewal of Catholicism. *The Documents of Vatican II,* edited by Walter M. Abbott, S.J., contained English translations of all the decrees of the council along with commentaries on them by both Catholics and Protestants. *Paul Blanshard on Vatican II* was an analysis by the mellowed but still critical author of many attacks on the Catholic Church. Perhaps the best single-volume, overall view of the council appeared in Gary MacEoin's *What Happened at Rome?*.

LITERATURE: EUROPEAN

By MAX WYKES-JOYCE
Contributor, THE TIMES
(London) LITERARY SUPPLEMENT

In 1965, literature of significance was published in a number of countries, with many of the most exciting volumes the work of women. In 1966 most of the meaningful activity was by the British and French.

Exceptions, to write of these first, included a novel by the Italian Mario Soldati, *Two Cities* (the echo of Dickens one supposes is intentional). It is a study of the degeneration of a man and his character under Fascism. The Mexican Carlos Fuentes published *La Muerte de Artemio Cruz* (The Death of Artemio Cruz). A Greek romance in the modern manner by Nikos Athanassiadis, entitled *Young Nude,* may be summarized as "a boy, a girl and an island (Lesbos)."

The French and the British, as though to compensate, ranged widely in subject, style and manner, so that "literature" in 1966 may be interpreted to include memoirs, histories, a volume of letters, fantasies, a political appraisal, a book of essays, a volume on the theater.

Britain. This theater volume is by the former drama critic of *The Times* of London, Laurence Kitchin. His study, *Drama in the Sixties,* subtitled *Form and Interpretation,* is both extremely knowledgeable and extremely readable. It also throws light on thought and practice in the other arts, as well as brilliantly illuminating the craft of the stage.

The memoirs and the "books about" were a particularly rewarding group. Vyvyan Holland, Oscar Wilde's son, continued and concluded his autobiography in *Time Remembered.* He resumed his narrative at the point where his father's remains were taken from Bagneux to the famous Paris cemetery of Père-Lachaise.

The biography of Ernest Hemingway, *Papa Hemingway* by the U.S. author A. E. Hotchner, caused a great deal of controversy all over Europe. For quite different reasons so did Beverley Nichols' acid memoirs of Somerset Maugham, *A Case of Human Bondage.* Another writer to be anatomized was Arnold Bennett, about whom an excellent study, *Writer by Trade,* was written by Dudley Barker.

In Britain there were no wildly exciting newcomers. A number of established authors improved or maintained their reputations with fresh works, however. Charlotte Bingham, whose memoirs were one of the delights of 1965, wrote a straight novel, *Lucinda.* William Sansom produced another analysis of suburban calamity, *Goodbye.* Peter Everett created a scarifying fantasy, *The Fetch.* Jerzy Peterkiewicz, a British novelist writing in English despite his Polish birth, published a fantasy of past, present and future, *Inner Circle* (with brilliant illustrations by Francis Souza).

A number of miscellaneous works were all well worth attention. Nancy Mitford's biography of Louis XIV of France, *The Sun King,* was on the British best-seller list for much of the summer and autumn. Robert Blake's exhaustive life of *Disraeli* will supplant all former works on the statesman, not excluding that of André Maurois. Bryan Guinness in *The Girl with the Flower* made a collection of short stories ranging over more than thirty years. Michael Baldwin, already famed as poet, novelist and short-story writer, added *Sebastian, and Other Voices* to his credits.

The prize for the single most significant book of 1966 should perhaps go to John R. Harrison for his book of essays *The Reactionaries,* a study of W. B. Yeats, Wyndham Lewis, Ezra Pound, T. S. Eliot and D. H. Lawrence. It was one of the most seminal of the year's publications despite some disagreement with its basic premises and a humorless style.

France. Disguised as a novel and said to be about Van Gogh, Drieu la Rochelle's last book, unfinished at the time of the author's suicide, painfully reflected his own disturbed mental state. The *Mémoires de Dirk Raspe* (notice the identical initials of author and hero) was a sad book with which to terminate a career, but demonstrated that, whatever else perturbed him, La Rochelle had lost none of his literary skills.

Marguerite Duras produced *Le Vice-Consul,* a study of four men and one woman in a strange environment. Annabel Buffet, wife of the celebrated painter Bernard Buffet, and friend of Françoise Sagan, created a Sagan-like account of *moeurs contemporains, Midi à quatorze heures* (Noon at Two P.M.). Alain Bosquet wrote the narrative of an artist's soul-searchings, *La Confession Mexicaine.*

Newcomers to the novel in France included veteran film director Jean Renoir, son of the painter, with *Les Cahiers de Capitain Georges* (Captain George's Notebooks). Yves Buin wrote a book for young people by a night person, though, strictly speaking, *Les Environs de Minuit* was his second novel. Its punning title is impossible to translate. Florence Asie, a former post-office clerk, had her first novel, *Fascination,* compared to the writing of Alain-Fournier. It was highly commended by Simone de Beauvoir.

LITERATURE: MANCHESTER-KENNEDY BOOK.

During the summer and early fall of 1966, rumors circulated in the book trade of trouble between the Kennedy family and the author and publishing house selected to produce an authorized account of President Kennedy's assassination. In late fall, William Manchester, who wrote the book, *The Death of a President,* and the publishing house of Harper and Row were going ahead with plans for publication. Mrs. John F. Kennedy then demanded changes in the manuscript. Author Manchester had agreed to her okaying the book in an 11-point "Memorandum of Understanding" of March 1964. (At that time the Kennedys had decided to give one writer exclusive access to information concerning the tragedy.)

Magazine rights to the book had been sold to *Look* for $665,000; the magazine was advertising the appearance of the first installment when the affair broke into headlines with Mrs. Kennedy's decision to sue. On Dec. 16 she asked a New York court for an injunction against William Manchester, Harper and Row, and Cowles Communications, Inc., the publishers of *Look,* to prevent their publishing the book. In a statement to the press, Mrs. Kennedy described portions of the book as "tasteless and distorted," and as containing "inaccurate and unfair references to other individuals," the latter quotation referring to Manchester's portrayal of President Johnson.

Neither Mrs. Kennedy nor Robert Kennedy read Manchester's completed manuscript, but a number of their advisers informed them that Manchester had in places used bad judgment. The Kennedys insisted on deletions under their right of final approval. At this point, Manchester feared that the book would never be published, and at the repeated requests of Harper and Row, Robert Kennedy sent him a telegram, in July 1966, saying that the Kennedy family would place no obstacle in the way of publication. This was assumed to be the final approval needed, and led to plans for publication, to the Kennedys' insistence on deletions they had asked for, and ultimately to the lawsuit.

With presses already printing the issue of *Look* that contained the first installment, Cowles Communications, Inc., reached an out-of-court agreement on deletions to be made. Harper and Row announced its intention of fighting the suit, but in mid-January 1967 also came to an out-of-court settlement.

At the conclusion of the affair, a spokesman for Mrs. Kennedy said: "In restrospect the whole agreement to have this book was a mistake. In 1964 . . . it seemed like a good idea."

PAUL CUNEO

LITERATURE: MYSTERY FICTION.

The year 1966 may prove, in retrospect, to be the year when factual, rather than fictional, studies in murder came into their own with U.S. readers. Truman Capote's *In Cold Blood* became the all-time best seller of fact-crime. Gerold Frank's *The Boston Strangler* was almost as successful. Paul Holmes performed yeoman journalistic service by getting responsible book length accounts of notorious cases into print almost as fast as newspapers could publish the verdicts: *The Candy Murder Case,* about Florida's sensational Mossler trial, and *Retrial,* about the ultimate vindication of Dr. Sam Sheppard. Dr. Sheppard's own *Endure and Conquer* appeared with comparable speed.

England's contributions to the year's strong fact-crime shelf included Elwyn Jones' *The Last Two to Hang,* a fine concise study of the last victims of capital punishment in England, and Julian Symons' *A Pictorial History of Crime.*

Spy novels and so-called "gothic" (which has come to mean little more than *feminine*) romances continued their numerical domination of the fiction field, and even contributed a few of the year's better novels, such as Elliot West's sensitive and bitter novel of espionage, *The Night Is a Time for Listening;* Donald E. Westlake's gorgeous comedy, *The Spy in the Ointment;* and attractive romances by Janet Caird and Mary Elgin. And the formal detective story flourished in such able hands as those of Agatha Christie, Ngaio Marsh, Ross Macdonald, and Emma Lathen, with Nicolas Freeling (*The King of the Rainy Country*) and Dick Francis (*Odds Against*) demonstrating especially well how the detective story may also be an impressively substantial novel of character.

Important to the future of suspense fiction is the growing number of curious, grotesque novels which may be called "black humor" or "the mystery of the absurd." Remarkable in this strange subgenre were George Baxt's *A Queer Kind of Death,* Stanley Crawford's *Gascoyne,* and Mark McShane's *The Crimson Madness of Little Doom*—none of them quite like anything published before the mid-1960's.

The year saw at least five books about the late Ian Fleming, who will soon occupy more space in the subject catalog than in the author catalog. Most useful: John Pearson's comprehensive *The Life of Ian Fleming.* Most provocative: Ann Boyd's *The Devil with James Bond!,* a serious theological essay taking its text from Fleming.

ANTHONY BOUCHER
Mystery Reviewer
THE NEW YORK TIMES BOOK REVIEW

New post-office tower joins Big Ben in London's skyline.

LONDON. London, uniquely tradition-minded among the world's great cities, now finds itself struggling with those tough modern problems of traffic and growth which beset the newest of metropolises.

As 1966 dawned, London was launching, with boom of bells and lavish processions, the commemoration of Westminister Abbey's 900th anniversary. Throughout the year, Abbey celebrations included special services for groups such as lawyers, newsmen and public officials, plus exhibitions, lectures and musical interludes.

The stately Abbey, where some of England's great are entombed, and much of its history is enshrined, began on a lonely Thames marsh outside the London walls in 1065. Now the vastly enlarged Gothic edifice, visited by every London tourist, stands forth resplendent, the grime of centuries washed from its stonework, paint applied to every coat of arms, ironwork newly gilded.

London wrestled more and more with its mounting traffic congestion and sprawl. To 1965's proposal for a double-tiered Piccadilly Circus was added 1966's plan for a Trafalgar Square rebuilt and rebeautified in two levels, one for pedestrians, one for automobiles.

Looking ahead, city officials pondered whether to continue opting for more throughways and elevated motorways, following the example of Los Angeles, Calif., or whether to turn increasingly to public transportation, perhaps even restricting the entry of automobiles into London except on proven business necessity.

The Greater London Council unveiled its Traffic Survey aimed at the year 1981. This predicted that, although population would only slightly increase (8.8 million to 9.1 million), higher incomes would mean many more cars on the road, more delivery trucks and more shops and shopping centers. One study predicted that, whereas 5 years ago the number of vehicles crossing the Thames River was 600,000 daily, by 1981 the figure would be 2 million.

The Traffic Survey, costing £600,000, notes that public transport is improving. The underground Victoria Line and the Fleet Line will be soon completed. British Railways will run more commuter trains. But autos will increase their daily trips by at least 50 per cent.

New circular and "ring" roads are proposed and more urban underground parking. But London planners are realizing that their booming city, increasingly on wheels, could "seize up" into total immobility—as traffic has done on a few sleety winter nights recently—unless transport programs are diligently pushed.

WILLIAM H. STRINGER
London Bureau Chief
THE CHRISTIAN SCIENCE MONITOR

LOS ANGELES. A specter of new racial strife haunted Los Angeles in 1966 despite brilliant space-age achievements made by its scientists, and record skyscraper construction by its builders.

Advances in aerospace programs were made on many fronts. At nearby Pasadena, space engineers at the Jet Propulsion Laboratory guided Surveyor 1 satellite to a soft landing on the moon. And at North American Aviation workers perfected a three-man Apollo space capsule to carry America's first astronauts to the moon.

The city's skyline was changed with two 42-story structures—highest ever erected in the downtown area—plus smaller multistory buildings.

Millions of dollars and man-hours were devoted to a "crash program" aimed at averting a repetition of the 1965 Negro uprising in which 34 persons were killed. One leader in this program was John A. McCone, former director of the Central Intelligence Agency, who headed a six-member governor's commission to study causes of the riot and recommend steps against any recurrence.

While thousands of pages of testimony were recorded and evaluated, new incidents broke out. On March 15 two men were killed in a disorder in the Watts area. In May a Caucasian policeman's revolver discharged, killing a Negro drunk-driving suspect, and a coroner's inquest upheld his claim that the gun had gone off accidentally.

Meanwhile the once-stalled war-on-poverty program was stepped up. Programs were rushed through in an attempt to alleviate the Negro's reaction against poverty, humiliation and despair. They included job training and counseling, Head Start classes for the very young, Teen Post educational and recreational centers and others.

Guarded optimism was expressed by the McCone Commission in a report issued almost a year after its formation. The commission said "significant progress" had been made on most of its recommendations.

No one pretended all danger had passed. Violent outbreaks in other major cities, including nearby San Francisco, made civic leaders realize that there was no reason for complacency. But still there was more reason for hope. And significantly the most hopeful were those who had devoted their time to the problem.

One was H. C. (Chad) McClellan, head of a Chamber of Commerce-founded Management Council which called on private industry to fill job vacancies with unemployed from the Watts area. Within a year an estimated 12,000 persons from the riot area were working.

RICHARD F. MAIN
Reporter, LOS ANGELES TIMES

LOUISIANA. In the November elections, voters approved a constitutional amendment that will allow a governor to serve two four-year terms. . . . Harold Robert Perry, a Negro, became auxiliary bishop in the Roman Catholic archdiocese of New Orleans. . . . The state ranked first in U.S. production of salt and sulfur and second in production of oil and natural gas. . . . Shreveport will be the home of a Louisiana State University branch medical school.

McCORMACK, JOHN W. House Speaker McCormack succeeded in guiding the great bulk of President Johnson's program through his branch in the 1966 Congressional session, compiling one of the most productive records of any Democratic leader in history. He won passage of two heavily disputed bills which were killed in the Senate: a civil-rights measure containing an open-housing provision, and legislation to repeal section 14(b) of the Taft-Hartley law, which permits states to ban the union shop.

The Speaker told his colleagues as the session ended that it "has been every bit as outstanding, has been the scene of as much achievement as the first session" of the 89th Congress in 1965. The second session "has not been marked by the great breakthroughs that so

Wide World
House Speaker McCormack displays case of pens used by President Johnson to sign Great Society legislation.

distinguished the first," he conceded. But he said the 1966 session had been "responsibly engaged in fortifying the legislation passed last year and previous years, improving and adding to enacted programs, and carrying out one of its least celebrated and least obtrusive functions—that of overseeing the administration and execution of its legislative enactments."

McCormack proved to be a poor prophet in forecasting 1966 election returns: on Sept. 14, he predicted his party would gain 5 to 10 House seats but it lost 47. McCormack was elected to the House for the twentieth time from the 9th Massachusetts district Nov. 8; he had no opposition. He thus became the second-ranking House member in seniority.

JOSEPH W. HALL, JR.
Washington Bureau, THE ASSOCIATED PRESS

MAGAZINES. Following the record-breaking year of 1965, forecasters predicted that 1966 would be the "best year ever" for the magazine industry. Profitable reports were announced by all the major publishers. Even Curtis turned from red to black for the first time since 1961.

Advertising revenue passed the $1,000,000,-000 mark in 1965. Circulations, too, set records, with *Reader's Digest* exceeding 17 million, and *TV Guide* reaching 11.5 million. Advertising costs climbed, reflecting the larger guarantees and greater use of full-color pages to combat increased use of color on television.

Time Inc. reported its net income for 1965 at $33,544,000 on revenues of $455,309,000. Of this, *Life* accounted for a gross of $163,-208,795. For the first six months of 1966, profits were even higher.

Curtis reported profits of $368,000 for the first half of 1966. The firm sold timber and mineral lands for $24 million, reducing its bank debt and providing working capital.

The New Yorker, with a circulation of 470,-000, carried a record 6,092 pages of advertising and earned nearly $3 million on revenue of $22 million in 1965.

Magazines continued to stress the selective audience approach, offering more zoned editions. *Look* had 52 "Magazones," *Life* had 26. Some magazines offered New York and Los Angeles editions. *Time* provided special editions for college students, educators and doctors.

New periodicals appeared selective, designed for specific groups. *Time* reported on such magazines as *Atlanta, Greater Philadelphia, Los Angeles, Phoenix, San Diego* and *Seattle,* noting that these publications "have moved into a void left by many newspapers, which have either given up comprehensive local coverage or disappeared from the scene."

Titles indicated the appeal of some of the newcomers slated for 1966-67, including *Apartment Construction News, Clothes, Discoscene, Gal Friday, Hullabaloo, Hospital Medicine, Hospital Practice, Journal Miss, Lady-Fare, Meetings and Conventions, Men's Bazaar, Nutrition Today, Outdoors Calling, P.S., Pet Fair, Sport Fishing, Take Thou* and *Your Job Future.*

Look received the first National Magazine Award, sponsored by Columbia University and the American Society of Magazine Editors. Others cited for excellence were *Scientific American, Grade Teacher, Ebony, American Machinist, Fortune, Continuum, Life, Motive, The New Yorker, Time, TV Guide* and *Vogue.*

Robert Manning became the tenth editor of *The Atlantic,* now in its 109th year. *The Nation,* long a money-loser, acquired a new backer, James J. Storrow, Jr., of Boston. *The New Republic* was expected to "break even" as it turned more to facts, less to opinion.

"A milestone in printing technology" said the *Magazine Industry Newsletter* in reporting the use of a computer to set all the type for the *Journal of Chemical Documentation.*

The trend to more international editions continued, with a Spanish-language copy of *Good Housekeeping. Life* added *Life Asia,* printed in Tokyo, and announced plans for *Life Australia/Life New Zealand* to be printed

Peg Shull

In 1966, *Life* added *Life Asia; Good Housekeeping* was printed in Spanish; and *Family Circle* came out in German.

in Melbourne in 1967. *Family Circle* started a German-language version.

Circulation leaders were *Reader's Digest,* 17 million; *TV Guide,* 11.5; *McCall's,* 8.5; *Look,* 7.6; *Life* and *Family Circle,* 7.4; *Woman's Day,* 7; *Better Homes & Gardens* and *Ladies' Home Journal,* 6.7; and *The Saturday Evening Post,* 6.6. Then *Good Housekeeping, National Geographic, Redbook, American Home, Playboy, Time, American Legion Magazine, True, Boy's Life* and *True Story.*

"The printed word is holding its own against television and electronic communications" reported the *Magazine Industry Newsletter.* It appeared to be true.

WILLIAM H. TAFT
Professor of Journalism, UNIVERSITY OF MISSOURI

MAINE. The U.S. Department of the Interior announced July 31 that the Migratory Bird Commission had approved acquisition of two thousand acres of southeastern Maine marshlands as part of Coastal Maine National Wildlife Refuge. . . . As a result of November elections, no Republican will represent Maine in the U.S. House of Representatives. Kenneth Curtis (D) was chosen governor. . . . In June, voters turned down a $7 million bond issue for airport development.

MALAYSIA: COMMUNIST GUERRILLA PROBLEM

By DOUGLAS HYDE

Author, CONFRONTATION IN THE EAST

On the face of it Malaysia should be a peculiarly untroubled land. Its population of 11 million is relatively small. Huge areas remain under virgin forest waiting to be developed. The millions of rubber trees planted on the coastal plain of Malaya, and the tin mines which lie close to its cities, meet two essential needs of modern industrial society and so provide the cash for development.

The Malays, Chinese and Indians who make up the bulk of its multiracial society have traditionally lived together in peace. Malaysia's climate is such that anyone who has lived there can never help but yearn to return.

Here, indeed, one might reason, should be a haven of peace in a troubled world. But in 1966 the federation of Malaysia was still in its uneasy infancy. The Malayan heartland, itself a federation of 11 states, was given independence in 1957. Sarawak and Sabah, across the water on the coast of the huge Indonesian island of Borneo, gained their independence from British rule by joining Malaya. So in 1963 was created the new federation of Malaysia.

Malaysia is in an area where the ideological struggle which tears the world in two is being fought not with ideas but with guns. Vietnam is only a couple of hours' flying distance from Kuala Lumpur, the Malaysian capital.

Indonesia was already pursuing its policy of military and economic "confrontation," aimed first at preventing the formation of the new federation, and then, when Malaysia came into existence nonetheless, at "crushing" and destroying it. Thus Malaysia found itself subjected to two distinct external pressures, both of which encouraged the growth of insurrectionary movements: military infiltration from Indonesia, and a communist guerrilla war in a nearby country.

Malaysia Meets Two Threats. An illegal communist organization in Sarawak was just about to switch from clandestine political activity to "the armed struggle" when Indonesia's confrontation of Malaysia began. The threat of an Indonesian invasion of Malaysian territory, however, brought to the area some sixty thousand British Commonwealth troops. Sarawak's Communists had somewhat optimistically considered themselves ready to start a guerrilla war against the new Malaysian regime. They soon realized that they could not hope to win so long as scores of thousands of highly trained, well-equipped Commonwealth troops were active there. They encouraged hundreds of their younger members to cross the border into Indonesian territory, to receive training in guerrilla warfare from the Indonesian Army, which saw them as possible allies.

With the ending of confrontation in August 1966, British troops, at the Malaysian Government's request, immediately began to withdraw from Sabah and Sarawak. Intelligence reports in Sarawak showed that the communist organization planned an early return to the armed struggle, enriched now with a hard core of its members having been trained in the art of guerrilla warfare. Soon some of these were attempting to get back to their homeland.

The Government's response to the new threat was quick and stern. Its members were acutely conscious of the horrible example of neighboring Vietnam, and, moreover, all could remember the civil war which the Communist Party of Malaya started in 1948, and which dragged on for 12 years. They recalled how some years after that earlier rebellion began, decisive action was taken which robbed the Communists of that support from the civilian population living in the affected areas which every guerrilla movement must have if it is to succeed. Tens of thousands of the Chinese rural population, most of them "squatters," were moved into new, guarded villages.

The people who had been thus forcibly evacuated were taken to and from their work in armored trucks; every ounce of food going into the compounds was closely checked; everything possible was done to ensure that no one provide either food, intelligence or military aid to the insurgents. The Communists were denied their help, and they in turn were insulated against communist pressures.

It was this policy which the Kuala Lumpur Government in the summer of 1966 applied to Sarawak. The population in the villages most seriously under communist influences was moved into new ones, fortified against communist intrusion and under constant police surveillance. For security reasons, too, some of the population in Sarawak's remotest jungle areas was also moved.

Meanwhile the security police were given the job of discovering and frustrating the Communists' plans for going over to the armed struggle.

Just across the Malayan border in Thailand was another group of armed Communists. These were the remnant of the defeated communist army who were driven during the earlier Malayan emergency into the deep jungle of the northern end of the mainland peninsula. From there they had made their way over the border into the southernmost end of Thailand. For ten years they have maintained a relatively safe base in this border region. They have held their forces together against the time when some new opportunity enables them to resume the armed struggle.

Captured documents indicate that had the Malaysian security forces been totally engaged in warding off Indonesian intruders during the period of confrontation, and had not Commonwealth troops arrived in such numbers, the Communists, under their leader Chin Peng, would have fought "shoulder to shoulder" with the invaders. No such opportunity came.

Young Chinese of the extreme Left in Malaya did, however, seize the chance to make off to some nearby Indonesian islands, to be trained in guerrilla warfare, urban terrorism and sabotage. They formed a communist organization with its own "government-in-exile" on Indonesian territory. Communist sources claim that many of these were massacred during the wave of anticommunism which swept Indonesia after the abortive coup of 1965.

Some of those who went for training had already made their way back to the Malayan peninsula before the fateful coup occurred. Denied the chance to put their military training into practice, they set about trying to rebuild the local communist movement.

The Government's response was to root out and imprison those who had been to Indonesia and to detain all suspected active Communists. Consistently over the years the Kuala Lumpur Government, which is in the main composed of men of liberal outlook, has felt obliged to take action of a sort that would not be acceptable in a Western democracy in a period of normalcy. But the situation in southeast Asia is not normal today.

Social Reforms. Any new attempt at insurrection either in the Borneo territories or on the mainland would bring suffering to the whole of the people of Malaysia. It would involve the nation in great expense, and it would slow down the process of development which, despite all odds, has made Malaysia's standard of life the highest in southeast Asia.

Side by side with the punitive measures taken against the Communists has gone a vigorous attempt to develop the country as a whole, and the rural areas in particular, and so to destroy the roots of communism.

In Kuala Lumpur during the last successful years of the fight against the Communists who took to the gun in 1948, there was established a military operations room. There it was possible to see at a glance the progress being made in the fight against communist insurgency in every state, town and village of the land.

In the capital today there is another operations room. Almost exactly modeled on the earlier one, it shows the course of the fight against poverty and for a better life for the rural people.

The man with the ultimate responsibility for the Rural Development Plan is Tun Razak, deputy prime minister. Son of a noble family, he nevertheless was involved in the fight for his country's independence years ago. From that experience he learned that it is not enough to fight against something: you must be for something too.

The Prime Minister, Tunku Abdul Rahman, Tun Razak and their colleagues in government believe that a genuine victory against communism will never be achieved until the necessary social reforms are carried through. Given the chance to overcome their present difficulties and, by firm action, to keep the Communists under control, they believe that it should be possible to create in their southeast Asian country a society in which communism has lost its appeal.

283

MAO TSE-TUNG. Nineteen sixty-six was the year of Mao Tse-tung's apotheosis. He "disappeared" during the latter part of 1965, and despite rumors of his death he reappeared again about the beginning of spring. In the intervening period he evidently had developed plans for a "Cultural Revolution" and had prepared to launch it. The main theme of the Cultural Revolution, which began in force in April, was the study of Mao Tse-tung's thought and the growing deification of Mao himself.

Throughout 1966, Chinese newspapers and radio carried a constant stream of stories concerning the benefits to be gained by the "application" of Mao's thought to the practical problems of production and life. Excerpts from his writings were published in small red plastic-covered books, which became the symbol of the Red Guards, the chief agents of the Cultural Revolution. Widely distributed inside China, these books were prohibited from being sold abroad until late December. By the Oct. 1 anniversary of the establishment in 1949 of the communist regime in Peking, the apotheosis of Mao had reached new heights. Bookstores in Peking, under pressure from the Red Guards, removed all but Mao's writings from their shelves, and according to Polish sources his picture appeared at night in practically every window in the city, providing on the eve of the celebrations almost the only illumination in Peking.

Throughout the autumn, Mao himself appeared before mass demonstrations of Red Guards in Peking's great Square of Heavenly Peace. These appearances, where Mao never spoke (rumors in the West suggested he may have lost the power of speech because of a stroke), were the culmination of the Red Guards' indoctrination process. By the end of November, Mao had reviewed between 9 million and 11 million Red Guard youth in the Square.

Mao Tse-tung's exact position in Peking was unclear at year's end, and reports emanating from Eastern Europe by way of London suggested that he had been in fact the victim of a palace coup led by Lin Piao, minister of defense and now Mao's announced successor, who was said to be keeping the aging leader prisoner in order to use him as a front for a purge of Lin's opponents.

In addition to several public audiences with foreign dignitaries, Mao Tse-tung swam the Yangtze River in the first part of summer, evidently as a demonstration to the world that he was not only alive but healthy. According to Peking's announcement concerning the speed with which Mao covered the distance, he appears to have set a world's swimming record. Accordingly he was issued an invitation to compete in the 1968 Olympics, but to date he has not accepted. Several Western observers questioned whether Mao himself made the swim, suggesting that it may have been made by a double.

MARK MANCALL
Department of History, STANFORD UNIVERSITY

MARTIN, PAUL. As Canadian secretary of state for external affairs, Paul Martin intensified his efforts during 1966 to bring about an end to the war in Vietnam. A firm believer in quiet diplomacy, Martin held private talks with many world statesmen during the year. He suggested that the International Control Commission, of which Canada is a member, should take the initiative in getting negotiations

Mao Tse-tung waves to crowd at Peking rally.

Wide World

Canada's Paul Martin, making UN speech.

UPI

started. In November he conferred with Soviet leaders in Moscow and held talks in Warsaw and Rome.

As president of the NATO Ministerial Council, Martin presided over the Brussels meeting in June, and was given credit for suggesting a compromise that avoided a breach between France and other NATO members over the relocation of NATO headquarters. In the UN General Assembly in November, Martin broke with U.S. policy on the seating of China, and advocated a two-China policy, with Communist China replacing Nationalist China on the Security Council.

WILLIAM FRENCH
Literary Editor, TORONTO GLOBE AND MAIL

MARYLAND. Spiro T. Agnew (R) defeated George P. Mahoney for the governorship. . . . Some 1,000 inmates of Baltimore's Maryland Penitentiary rioted July 8, protesting brutality and living conditions. . . . Federal, state and local authorities formed a crime-fighting council in April. . . . White supremacists invaded a Negro sector of Baltimore July 28–29 and clashes ensued. . . . CORE spearheaded civil-rights movements in Baltimore.

MASSACHUSETTS. Attorney General Edward W. Brooke (R) was elected to the U.S. Senate Nov. 8. Brooke is the first Negro to serve in the U.S. Senate since Reconstruction. Also on Nov. 8, Gov. John A. Volpe (R) was re-elected, and voters ratified an amendment providing for a 3 per cent limited sales tax which had been passed by the legislature. . . . The legislature also passed a $150 million bond issue for water-pollution control and liberalized Massachusetts' 1879 birth-control law. . . . The state department of education underwent reorganization.

MEDICARE. On July 1, 1966, health insurance for those 65 years or older was introduced as a new dimension of protection under the U.S. social-security system.

On that date, 18.6 million elderly Americans became eligible to receive, as insured patients, basic hospital care and related health services under the hospital-insurance part of the new program. A total of 17.3 million had enrolled under the voluntary supplementary-medical-insurance program which would also pay for physicians' services and many other important medical services and supplies. At the present rate of growth of the population 65 and older, approximately 250,000 elderly Americans a year will be added to the number of those eligible for Medicare benefits.

Participation. Participation in the nation's health-care system is almost universal. As of July 1, 1966, there were some 6,600 participating hospitals, with 98 per cent of all the short-term, general-care hospital beds in the nation. Also taking part were 1,338 home health agencies, with some 400 additional such agencies in the process of developing or expanding their services so as to qualify for participation. It is anticipated that approximately 2,000 skilled nursing homes will have qualified to participate as extended-care facilities when that phase of the program begins on Jan. 1, 1967.

Early Experience. In the first four months of Medicare's operation there were almost 2,-500,000 hospital admissions of Medicare beneficiaries. Predictions that serious hospital overcrowding would accompany the beginning of the program failed to materialize.

Preliminary statistical projections, based on early program experience and weighted by seasonal hospital bed-occupancy rates, indicate that well over 5 million Medicare beneficiaries will receive inpatient hospital care during the first full year of the program. If the current average length of stay for this age-group remains constant, this will represent some 70 million days of hospital care under Medicare.

Between July 1 and Dec. 31, close to 105,-000 Medicare beneficiaries received home health services, a rapidly expanding dimension of health care of special importance to the elderly.

Statistics for the medical-insurance program, over the first 6 months of Medicare, are less indicative of the extent of protection this program affords. Under this program, the beneficiary must, in each calendar year, accumulate $50 in covered expenses—called the medical-insurance deductible—before the program begins paying 80 per cent of the reasonable charges for all additional covered services in that year. Thus, early figures do not accurately reflect the full scope of the medical-insurance program.

Features. The medical-insurance program is voluntary, requiring the payment of a $3 monthly premium (which is matched by the Federal treasury for each enrolled beneficiary). Approximately 1.8 million elderly Americans who were eligible for this supplementary program did not choose to enroll. The majority of these, however, are covered under the hospital-insurance program, which is financed primarily by withholdings from earnings during an individual's working years, and which does not require any current premium payments as does the medical-insurance program.

Under Medicare, the patient is at all times

MEDICARE

Who is covered? Almost everyone over 65—in a growing population.

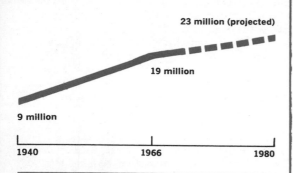

23 million (projected)

19 million

9 million

1940   1966   1980

How hospital insurance benefits are financed...

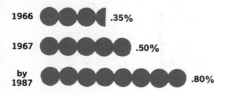

1966   .35%

1967   .50%

by 1987   .80%

of first $6,600 of yearly earnings paid by employer and employee.

How it will help the elderly... An example*

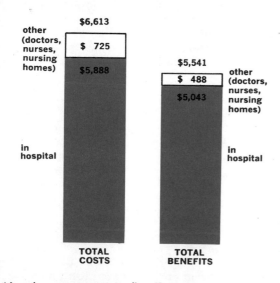

$6,613

other (doctors, nurses, nursing homes) $ 725

$5,888

in hospital

$5,541

other (doctors, nurses, nursing homes) $ 488

$5,043

in hospital

TOTAL COSTS   TOTAL BENEFITS

*A major-surgery case spending 49 days in a hospital and 30 more in a nursing home.

free to choose his own doctor. The law specifically states that no Federal officer or employee shall exercise any supervision or control over the practice of medicine or the manner in which medical services are provided.

One of the most unusual features of the Medicare program is its administrative use of intermediaries to carry out certain program functions, particularly the determination of reasonable costs and charges and the payment of claims. The law specifically provides that, wherever possible, prepayment plans and other health insurers should be utilized to carry out these program functions. Over 100 such organizations have been selected and have been operating as intermediaries since July 1, 1966. They represent a wide variety of organizations with experience as third-party payers, such as Blue Cross, a number of Blue Shield plans and a significant number of commercial insurers.

Benefits. Medicare was not intended to, and does not, provide health care or services. But it was intended to, and indeed does, help those who are 65 and older in paying the costs of high-quality health care. For the average person over 65, Medicare will pay well over 80 per cent of the costs of the services covered by the two insurance programs—and these services cover the major items of health expenses for most persons in that age-group: hospitalization, extended care and home health services, physicians' services and other essential medical services and supplies. Even against the total of *all* health-care expenses of the average older person—which includes dental care, eye care, prescription drugs and other items not covered under Medicare—coverage under the two health-insurance programs will, on the average, help pay over 50 per cent of the total health-care costs of the elderly.

Effect on Health Facilities. Many feel that one of the vulnerable points of the U.S. health-care system has been the assumption by that system of the burden of providing services and care for many charity cases. With Medicare paying on the basis of the reasonable costs and reasonable charges of providing health care for those 65 or older, rather than on a discount or fixed-schedule basis, the program will make a significant contribution to the financial stability and strength of the nation's health-care system. Filling the financial gap should provide substantial resources for upgrading health-care facilities in terms of both equipment and personnel, which will contribute to higher-quality health care for all age-groups.

ARTHUR E. HESS
Director, Bureau of Health Insurance
U.S. SOCIAL SECURITY ADMINISTRATION

MEDICINE

By LAWRENCE GALTON
Contributing Editor
FAMILY CIRCLE AND PARADE MAGAZINES

Even as Medicare, providing medical insurance for the aged, went into effect in mid-1966, another far-reaching new concept—a national program for preventive medicine—began to receive consideration in Washington. Under a Preventicare bill introduced into both houses of Congress, regional mass-screening programs would be set up to detect disease in advance of symptoms. An array of automated equipment, which could make such programs feasible, is already developed and available for use. Some of the equipment was demonstrated before a Senate committee.

One of the key elements is an electronic console that can split a thimbleful of blood into smaller specimens and automatically perform a dozen valuable tests (albumin, sugar level, and so on) at the rate of 500 an hour. Such a console is now at work at Duke University Medical Center.

Another important element is a special computer system, developed at the University of Wisconsin, which can take over from the doctor the time-consuming (up to 2 hours) task of getting a patient's full case history. The machine gives the patient operating instructions, registers answers to the questions it poses, probes further when an answer indicates some specific area needs further exploration.

Also demonstrated was a computer system capable of receiving electrocardiogram impulses from a patient and producing a diagnosis of heart condition in 15 seconds.

The need for making use of electronic advances, particularly in the area of preventive medicine, was underscored in reports to the Senate committee. They indicated, for example, that for each case of cervical cancer detected in city health clinics, 40 cases go undiagnosed, and for every case of diabetes diagnosed, 50 go undetected.

The problem is complex, the difficulties compounded by cost, apathy and shortages of medical personnel. Most Americans, if they feel well, are reluctant to take the time and pay the cost of regular periodic checkups. If the reluctance were overcome, and all reported for regular preventive-care examinations, physicians using conventional checkup techniques would have no time left to treat the critically ill.

University of Wisconsin

Doctors at the University of Wisconsin Medical Center with computer that takes patients' medical histories.

Automated screening promises to be a major contribution, many medical authorities believe, to the next great forward step in health care. This step is an all-out effort to prevent degenerative diseases, or at least to uncover their beginnings and make possible early treatment to arrest their progress. At the end of 1966 the expectation was that the Preventicare concept would receive careful consideration in the U.S. Congress during 1967.

During 1966 a number of promising clinical developments were reported—advances in understanding and treatment of major killing and crippling diseases and some hopeful specific preventive possibilities.

Heart Disease, Hypertension and Stroke

More than 500,000 U.S. citizens annually die of heart disease; many more are incapacitated. At many major medical centers, physicians and engineers have been collaborating in efforts to develop an artificial heart. Late in 1966 came the announcement of the development at Indiana University School of

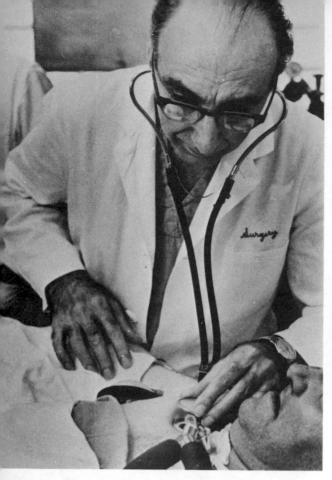

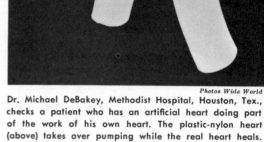

Dr. Michael DeBakey, Methodist Hospital, Houston, Tex., checks a patient who has an artificial heart doing part of the work of his own heart. The plastic-nylon heart (above) takes over pumping while the real heart heals.

Medicine of a mechanical device for total replacement of the human heart.

Already, heart-assist devices—mechanical pumps for easing temporarily the work load of diseased but not hopelessly damaged hearts —have been used in a few patients by Drs. Michael E. DeBakey of Methodist Hospital, Houston, and Adrian Kantrowitz of Maimonides Hospital, Brooklyn, N.Y.

The new Indiana device hopefully is applicable in cases in which maintenance of heart function cannot be expected even with use of such assistors. A 3-lb. metal and plastic unit designed to be implanted inside the chest, it has pumping chambers driven hydraulically by a miniature electric motor, with wire leads from the motor extending through the chest wall to portable batteries. After successful animal testing, the device is now considered far enough along in development to warrant early trial in heart patients who clearly have no other chance for survival.

During 1966, important new evidence of the value of physical activity in helping to prevent heart disease, and even in helping to ameliorate it once the condition has developed, was reported.

A study reported to the American Heart Association followed 8,000 men over a 10-year period and found that physically active men are (1) less likely to develop coronary heart disease before age 50 than their sedentary counterparts and (2) more likely to have a milder form if the disease strikes them. The incidence of heart disease was more than twice as great among the sedentary men (4.8 per cent) as among the physically active (1.9 per cent). And manifestation of the disease differed significantly. Active men were more prone to a milder form, angina pectoris (chest pain), than the sedentary who more often had fullblown heart attacks. In angina, the heart muscle gets needed blood, although with some difficulty. In a full-fledged heart attack, part of the muscle is deprived entirely of blood and may die.

Active men, the study suggests, get protection by gradual development of additional blood vessels to supply the heart in response to the stimulus of exercise. These extra vessels provide alternate routes to nourish the heart muscle if a major coronary artery is closed off by hardening (atherosclerosis).

Meanwhile, at Harper Hospital, Detroit, physicians investigated use of exercise as a therapeutic measure in 17 patients with angina so far advanced and severe that they could not walk more than half a block without an attack of pain and had to take 15 to 25 nitroglycerin tablets a day. In a special program, the men, aged 35 to 66, after taking nitroglycerin, which dilates the coronary arteries feeding the heart so more blood can get through, were given carefully supervised graded exercise on a treadmill. All showed improvement. The improvement continued later when daily exercises were carried out at home. No patient sustained further heart damage while on the graded exercise program, and all 17 resumed usual business or other activities. The fear that activity will cause pain deters many angina pectoris patients from being active, yet the Harper study suggests that carefully graduated activity can improve circulation and may also increase the ability of the heart muscle to absorb more vital oxygen from coronary blood flow.

Another noteworthy development during 1966 was a report linking heart disease, hypertension and stroke. Ever since 1949, a major long-term study has been going on in Framingham, Mass., under the auspices of the National Heart Institute. It follows 5,000 men and women, all of whom were free of circulatory disease in 1949. As the years go by and they fall ill or evidence of disease is uncovered during periodic examinations, it becomes possible to correlate various findings.

The latest Framingham report dealt with 86 instances of stroke and the finding that stroke is particularly likely to occur in hypertensive people—those who have high blood pressure alone or elevated pressure plus heart disease. There are indications from the study that hypertension accelerates hardening of the arteries, thereby raising the risk of stroke, and also that impaired heart function, even in the absence of hypertension, increases risk of stroke. Thus treatment for hypertension and preventive measures for heart disease promise to be of value as well in reducing the incidence of stroke.

A new advance against hypertension was reported by Georgetown University, Washington, D.C., physicians. A "crash" program was developed for people with severe hypertension that could not be managed with routine drug treatment. The program involves daily injections over a 20-day period of a special antihypertensive agent, diazoxide. In 87 per cent of a group of patients with severely elevated pressures that had not yielded to high, and even toxic, doses of oral drugs, hypertension was brought under control and complications such as heart failure, heart enlargement and eye hemorrhages cleared. Afterward, the patients returned to oral drug treatment.

Kidney Disease

Little more than a decade ago, chronic kidney failure was almost certain to lead to death from uremic poisoning. For lack of kidney function, toxic chemicals were not eliminated, and built up in the blood.

Then came the dialysis machine which can be used periodically to remove the toxic substances. But while its use has kept some patients alive and well, most candidates for dialysis treatment have not received its benefits because of the expense and complexity of the equipment. A typical machine costs $10,000, with operating cost running up to $5,000 a year.

Toward the end of 1966 came two hopeful new developments. Physicians at Cleveland Clinic reported the prospect of a relatively simple home dialyzer derived from an ordinary washing machine, expected to cost about $150, with annual expense of home operation estimated at $1,500. The device had been used successfully by clinic patients.

Meanwhile, Harvard University physicians reported finding that some patients may be spared need for dialyzer treatment through use of a special diet. It is basically a selected protein diet, designed to eliminate nonessential protein material. With protein intake reduced, Drs. Donald Snyder and John P. Merrill discovered, the body apparently resorts to making effective use of materials it otherwise discards in waste form and which, in uremia, accumulate in the blood. Of 14 patients tested, 10 responded.

Cancer

For retinoblastoma, an eye malignancy of childhood, standard treatment has been immediate removal of an affected eye. Now in many cases loss of the eye may be avoided. Stanford University physicians reported that over a six-year period they have used high-energy radiation to treat 15 eyes in 10 children. There have been no deaths, and every child but one has retained useful vision in the treated eye or eyes. High-energy radiation can be patterned into a pinpoint beam designed to kill a cancer while sparing the lens of the eye, the Stanford doctors reported. And while cure may not always be achieved, "it is now often possible to try at least once to cure by radiation without proceeding directly to eye removal."

Wilms' tumor, a kidney malignancy, is one of the most common childhood cancers. Over

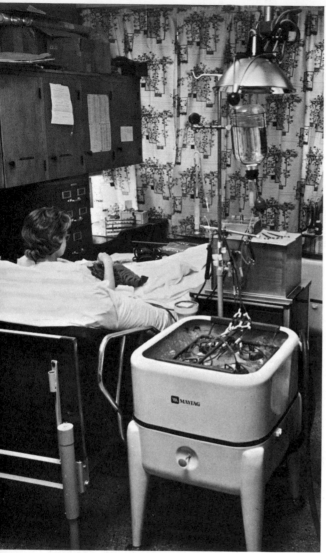

Cleveland Clinic

Kidney-disease patients use dialysis machines to remove toxic substances. In Cleveland (Ohio) Clinic, ordinary washing machines have been made into dialysis machines.

the past 10 years, earlier diagnosis, improved surgery and X-ray therapy have led to the saving of more and more lives. In 1966, Baylor University pediatricians reported a major gain through use of a drug, dactinomycin. Among children four weeks to seven years old when the tumor was diagnosed, 43 per cent treated by surgery and X ray were living, apparently free of malignancy, two years or more after treatment. Of others receiving the drug treatment in addition, 92 per cent are alive and apparently free of tumor. The drug seems to combat any small remaining "seeds" of cancer left after surgery and radiation.

Another promising development for some types of malignancy is the application of extreme cold, via an instrument in which liquid nitrogen circulates at −300°F.

Cryotherapy, as the freezing technique is called, appears to be effective in destroying many localized cancers, including some otherwise difficult to treat. Drs. A. A. Gage and F. C. Emmings of the State University of New York reported using it successfully in more than 60 patients with mouth, throat, skin, rectal and bone cancers. The growths in some cases had proved resistant to X-ray treatment; in others they could not be removed surgically without extensive loss of bone structure. In most cases, a single cryotherapy treatment was enough to cause malignant tissue to die and slough off within a few days.

Surgery

Several significant surgical advances were made in 1966. Johns Hopkins surgeons reported promising results in alleviating severe, otherwise unyielding pain—and in treating some diseases as well—with a new technique in which a tiny stainless steel rod (about 4/100-in. in diameter, 32/100-in. long) is implanted in a selected brain area.

Once in place, the rod serves as an "electroseed." It can be heated from outside by focusing radio waves of a specific frequency on it. The heating can be controlled so a very small area of tissue can be destroyed without affecting surrounding areas.

The technique has been used to free patients of previously intractable pain. It has helped control shaking palsy and some types of epilepsy. A major advantage of the procedure is that no further surgery is needed should symptoms recur after first treatment. The tiny rod can be reheated with radio waves to affect just enough more tissue to reestablish relief. One patient with severe shaking palsy has required, and benefited from, four exposures in a 2½-year period without damage to normal brain tissue.

For many of the two million victims of epilepsy in the United States, drugs and surgical techniques have made life more bearable. But others have not benefited because doctors have not been able to identify the trigger area in the brain that sets off their epileptic attacks. In particular, deeper areas of the brain, long suspected of being involved in some seizures, have been inaccessible.

In October, Duke University researchers reported finding a way to reach into the brain's inner sanctum and record seizures originating there. It involves introducing into the brain hairlike electrodes through a dime-size opening in the skull. The wound is closed and the electrodes left in place for several weeks. The procedure is painless; the patient remains in hospital and is ambulatory; and several times a day and during sleep at night recordings are made through electroencephalograph leads that are hooked up to the electrodes. After the study is completed, the electrodes are withdrawn painlessly.

The Duke researchers report that they have been able to confirm origin of seizures deep in the brain and establish the sites. They predict that the new knowledge will profoundly affect the lives of many epilepsy victims.

Cryotherapy, as already noted, is showing promise against some cancers. In addition, the use of extreme cold in place of a cutting scalpel to destroy diseased tissue was reported during 1966 to be valuable for other ailments.

University of California surgeons used the painless, virtually bloodless technique for tonsil removal. Applied twice for three minutes at a time, the supercold caused diseased tonsil tissue to disappear over a period of two to three weeks, and in no instance led to bleeding. Most patients requested their dinners the same evening they received treatment.

The same technique has been used to remove multiple nasal polyps. It has been of dramatic value in combating acromegaly, a disorder in which the face becomes misshapen, hands and feet are enlarged, and agonizing headaches occur. Acromegaly is caused by abnormal activity of the pituitary gland at the base of the brain. Freezing has been used to destroy part of the gland in 12 patients. Within a few weeks, facial coarseness began to disappear, hand and foot size decrease, and headache pain diminish.

Vaccines

During 1966, scientists at the National Institutes of Health announced the development of a vaccine that appears to be effective against rubella, or German measles. The scientists also reported promising preliminary results with an experimental vaccine against Mycoplasma pneumoniae, the major cause of primary atypical pneumonia. In addition they made a successful field trial of an oral vaccine against adenovirus 4 infections, main cause of acute respiratory disease at military training camps.

And from University of Chicago researchers came word of a new experimental vaccine that appears to be effective in providing protection against group A Streptococci. If results with the vaccine can be confirmed, rheumatic fever, the kidney infection glomerulonephritis and possibly other debilitating or fatal strep infections may be on the way out.

Other Developments

About four million women in the U.S. are using oral contraceptive pills. In June, 1966, the American Medical Association issued a report indicating that the pills were virtually 100 per cent effective. In August, the U.S. Food and Drug Administration also issued a report indicating that they seem to be safe.

In some families, staphylococcal infections of the skin and other sites are not just occasional problems but almost constantly recurring ones. One member gets an infection which clears after treatment. Then another becomes infected and is treated. But the trouble recurs in the first, and then again in the second, and perhaps in still other family members. New York Hospital-Cornell Medical Center physicians in 1966 reported a successful new approach to overcoming the recurring problem. Their method involves clearing with antibiotics any infection present in the family, then introducing harmless strains of bacteria into the noses of all family members. The "good" bacteria settle down, multiply, and keep the harmful types from reestablishing residence.

Also in 1966, dramatic healing of bedsores and skin ulcers, severe and long-resistant to all standard forms of treatment, was reported after application of ordinary gold leaf.

And on the psychiatric front, a report from Temple University Medical Center, Philadelphia, indicated that people with phobias—abnormal fears of heights, confined spaces, public speaking, and so on—often can be helped by a type of treatment somewhat akin, on the psychological level, to the desensitization treatment used to combat hay fever and other allergies. In allergy therapy, the objective is to build up resistance through injections of small, gradually increasing doses of troublesome pollens and other materials.

In phobia treatment, the patient identifies his fears, and lists in order of increasing severity the situations that provoke them. He is then taught a technique of deep muscle relaxation and, while relaxed, is presented with an imaginary situation based on the least fear-provoking item in his list. The situation is repeatedly presented until it no longer evokes fear.

Then stronger fear-provoking situations are presented until those most frightening in the past no longer arouse fear. When the patient stops reacting fearfully to imaginary situations, he is almost always freed of fear in real situations. Completed in about 11 sessions, the therapy helps 90 per cent of those treated.

METEOROLOGY. International aspects of meteorology dominated the list of significant developments in the science of the atmosphere during 1966. A global plan for weather services called the World Weather Watch, in preparation for almost three years, neared completion as the year ended, and was scheduled for presentation at the Meteorological Congress in April 1967 at the headquarters of the World Meteorological Organization in Geneva, Switzerland. The plan exploits many new elements of modern technology: a fully operational meteorological satellite system; high-speed telecommunications networks covering the entire world; and internationally designated world weather centers equipped with ultra-high-speed computers for processing and analyzing global weather data. It calls for implementation of these facilities during the period 1968–71.

Countries of the southern hemisphere, meeting in Wellington, New Zealand, in February 1966, took several significant steps toward the implementation of the World Weather Watch program. The conference endorsed the establishment of a world weather center in Melbourne, Australia, and designated Wellington as a regional center for the collection and processing of weather information. The session also began steps for a complete reorganization of weather telecommunications in the southwest Pacific, and arranged for a series of scientific meetings to explore methods of analysis and prediction of tropical disturbances, heavy rains and floods and weather phenomena of particular concern to agriculture in the region.

U.S. weather satellite ESSA 3 launched in October.
NASA

Upper-Air Exploration. At another meeting in Wiesbaden, Germany, during March, technical experts of the World Meteorological Organization established a comprehensive program for the exchange of weather reports from commercial aircraft throughout the northern hemisphere. While such reports have been distributed over small areas for a number of years, a hemispherical effort involving many countries has never before been undertaken. Results of a preliminary test of the program indicated that the large-scale exchange of aircraft weather information was extremely valuable, especially for the analysis of weather over the oceans and other areas where upper-air data are limited.

Exploration of the global upper air was undertaken by the French Météorologie Nationale in a series of experimental flights using camera-equipped balloons. Known as the COLOMBE project (Collecte d'Observations Météorologiques par Ballons Equilibrés), it utilized balloons designed to float at heights of 60,000 to 120,000 ft. They were equipped with photographic and television cameras to take pictures of the clouds over which they traveled. Initial experiments in February were carried out over the Pyrenees, but by July a balloon that had been launched in Landes, France, came down near Great Falls, Mont. Photographs of cloud systems obtained by the project provided excellent detail on cloud structure and texture.

In the Southern Hemisphere, another balloon program, called GHOST (Global Horizontal Sounding Technique), was tested and observed. A weather balloon released from New Zealand in April completely circled the globe in about 10 days. The balloon, carried by the winds, passed over South America, Australia and vast expanses of open ocean. It transmitted weather data at its flight altitude (about 40,000 ft.) as it traveled. In this manner a subsequent GHOST balloon made more than six trips around the globe before it finally burst and fell to earth. The project was a joint effort of the National Center for Atmospheric Research and Environmental Science Services Administration of the United States, the New Zealand Weather Service and an international group of observers.

Meteorological Satellites. The extremely successful weather satellite program, begun by the United States in 1960, continued its unbroken record of near-perfect launches in 1966. Two operational weather satellites called ESSA 1 and ESSA 2, which took their name from the initials of a newly established scientific agency, the Environmental Science Services Administration, were launched from Cape Kennedy, Fla., in February. These two satellites were followed by ESSA 3, launched from Vandenberg Air Force Base, Calif., in October. All three spacecraft provided useful weather information to the nations of the world.

Another meteorological satellite, designed for carrying out more sophisticated research projects, was launched from the Vandenberg site in May. This satellite, called Nimbus 2, was part of an advanced program being carried out by the Goddard Space Flight Center of the National Aeronautics and Space Administration. Weighing slightly over 900 lbs., Nimbus 2 was designed to take over 3,000 television pictures per day, and to measure the infrared outgoing radiation from the earth in five spectral bands. This latter information was used by meteorologists to calculate the heat energy emitted from the earth by carbon dioxide and water vapor in the atmosphere, and by the solid earth itself.

Also launched in 1966 was Cosmos 122 of the Soviet Union, the first weather satellite announced by that country. It was placed into orbit on June 25 on the occasion of French President Charles de Gaulle's visit. In compliance with a Soviet-American agreement made in 1963, the transmission of weather data from Cosmos 122 to the U.S. National Satellite Center in Suitland, Md., was initiated.

Clear-Air Turbulence. During the early days of flying, airmen looked forward with anticipation to the day when aircraft would be able to fly in the clear "smooth" air high above all clouds. At that time it was believed that turbulence occurred only in the lower atmosphere where strong vertical and horizontal winds could easily be detected, as in thunderstorms. As planes began to fly at high levels, however, pilots encountered severe turbulence in the clear air. This phenomenon could not be seen, and there was no known way of detecting it.

In 1966, however, scientists succeeded in observing clear-air turbulence in a visible form on a radar screen. Sponsored by the National Aeronautics and Space Administration and U.S. Air Force, a research study by the Johns Hopkins University Applied Physics Laboratory made use of the world's most powerful radar equipment, located at Wallops Island, Va., to detect this hitherto invisible menace. The turbulence was observed at altitudes up to 15,000 ft. Further work was initiated to carry the investigations to higher levels, and to develop radar equipment sufficiently light and compact to be carried in an airplane. Such equipment could provide a pilot with a radar "picture" of potential areas of clear-air turbulence in the plane's path so that danger could be avoided.

Because clear-air turbulence will be especially critical for supersonic transport flights between 40,000 and 100,000 ft., a National Committee for Clear Air Turbulence was created. Established by the Environmental Science Services Administration, the committee is responsible for a comprehensive program of research on clear-air turbulence, and for seeing that efforts of the U.S. Government in this field are adequately coordinated. Named as chairman of the committee was Maj. Gen. J. J. Catton, U.S. Air Force.

Weather Modification. Responding to the stimulus of critical scientific analyses of weather modification, meteorologists in 1966 placed emphasis on fundamental studies. In January, the primary topic of the annual meeting of the American Meteorological Society, in Denver, Colo., was the subject of weather modification. A keynote address by the U.S. Secretary of the Interior, Stewart L. Udall, called for greater support for research aimed at increasing precipitation in the arid lands of the western part of the United States and harnessing the excessive flood-producing rains in other regions.

As the year progressed, initial results of this research were reported. Several projects, taking into consideration the possible adverse effects of experimenting with the weather itself, made use of mathematical models of the atmosphere so that conceptual experiments could be tried first on electronic computers. One such study concluded that the seeding of tropical clouds with silver iodide or other artificial nucleating substances could indeed produce significant changes in the cloud structure. Continuation of work on this model is expected to reveal many facts about tropical hurricanes, and perhaps suggest ways in which they might be controlled.

In addition to such theoretical studies, field experiments were carried out extensively in the western United States. These included attempts to increase the precipitation from winter storms in the Rocky Mountains, to analyze the structure of summertime clouds in Wyoming, the Dakotas and Arizona, and to measure the moisture and other characteristics of thunderstorms in the Wasatch Range in Utah.

JACK C. THOMPSON
Assistant Professor, SAN JOSE STATE COLLEGE

MICHIGAN. Gov. George Romney (R) was reelected Nov. 8, and Robert P. Griffin (R) defeated former Gov. G. Mennen Williams for the U.S. Senate. . . . Automobile production fell 3.5 per cent below that of 1965. . . . Tourist business brought $1,000,000,000 into the state treasury. . . . Freighter *Daniel J. Morrell* sank in Lake Huron off Harbor Beach during a Nov. 29 snowstorm, killing 28. . . . The Public Bank of Detroit failed Oct. 12.

MIDDLE EAST

By JAMES FERON
Middle East Staff
THE NEW YORK TIMES

The Middle East saw a worsening of Arab-Israeli relations and a growing division within Arab ranks during 1966. The Israeli border was the scene of increasing tension during the year, with Arab sabotage followed by Israeli military retaliation. The most severe incident came Nov. 13 when two columns of Israeli armor moved six miles into Jordan to destroy homes in Es Samu, south of Hebron.

Inter-Arab affairs were dominated by King Faisal of Saudi Arabia, who challenged President Nasser of the U.A.R. in a contest that seemed to have less to do with ideology than with influence. The Saudi monarch's call for Islamic solidarity tended to divide the Arab world between Left and Right. Meanwhile, two internal wars, the Kurdish struggle for autonomy in Iraq and the Yemeni civil war, slowed down somewhat but remained unsolved. Arms continued to pour into the Middle East—to Jordan, Saudi Arabia, Iran, Turkey and Israel from the United States and Britain; to Syria, U.A.R. and (perhaps) Iraq from the U.S.S.R.

Twelve nations of the Arab League boycott conference voted to ban dealings with the Ford Motor Company, RCA and Coca-Cola for dealing with Israel. "Coke" was given nine months' grace to use up existing stocks.

Cyprus. The Cyprus problem seemed no nearer solution, although Greece and Turkey began private talks during the year in an effort to solve the island's ethnic conflict. Turkish Cypriots remained barricaded in two enclaves, one stretching from the northern sector of Nicosia to within a few miles of the northern coast, and the other inside the walled city of Famagusta on the east coast. In many villages, however, Turkish Cypriots and Greek Cypriots continued to till adjacent lands in peace.

Another dispute remained unresolved between President Makarios and General George Grivas, military leader of the rebellion against the British that led to independence. The fight was over control of the island's military garrison. Grivas, now head of the island's armed forces, continued to insist that he would take his orders only from Athens. Makarios thought Grivas should be in command only of the Greek soldiers on the island, with the Greek Cypriot units under the President's control. The President created a new storm at year's end

by buying arms from Czechoslovakia. Their potential use either against Turkish Cypriots or as part of the dispute with Gen. Grivas created new tensions in Athens and Ankara.

The United Nations peace-keeping force remained on the island, in its third year of extended temporary duty. It had a new commander, Maj. Gen. Ilmari Martola of Finland.

Iran. Iran's stronger ties with the Soviet Union, featuring an exchange of Russian-built steelworks for Iranian natural gas pumped across the border, threatened to reach into the sphere of armaments purchases. The United States had given the Teheran Government more than $700 million in military assistance since 1945, but with terms getting tougher the Shah of Iran hinted that he might consider purchase of Soviet missiles. He was dissuaded, however, and Washington agreed to sell Iran at least one squadron of F-4 Phantoms, the most advanced jet fighter in the American inventory. London indicated it would provide a destroyer, four corvettes and surface-to-air missiles.

The equipment will be used mainly to protect the Persian Gulf where a huge oil-loading terminal was opened in March, at Kharg Island. Virtually all of Iran's oil will flow through the facility at one of the fastest loading rates ever achieved, 10,000 tons a day and over.

A consortium of 17 oil companies that runs the Iranian oil industry agreed to a government demand that they increase the nation's oil production. Iranian leaders said they needed the extra revenue to finance a development boom.

Iraq. The nation's 45-year-old President, Abdul Salam Arif, was killed with two cabinet ministers and seven aides when his helicopter crashed Apr. 13 during a sandstorm. His brother, Maj. Gen. Abdul Rahman Arif, took over the presidency and with Premier Abdul Rahman al-Bazzaz moved slowly toward trying to find a peaceful end to the nation's biggest problem, the Kurdish rebellion. On Aug. 6 the Premier resigned unexpectedly and was replaced by a career army officer, Naji Taleb. The new Cabinet included three Kurds, but the peace offensive seemed to slow down as the year ended. The Kurds represent one million of Iraq's 8 million population and have been fighting for local autonomy in the country's mountainous northern sector for five years.

Israel. Economic and military problems troubled Israeli leaders during the year. The economic problems were signaled dramatically by May Day riots in some of the nation's development towns. Workers who had been recently laid off picked the traditional "workers' day" to indicate their displeasure. Finance

Minister Pinhas Sapir explained in Parliament that the nation was paying for years of "abundance and prosperity." He imposed new taxes to take some of the steam out of Israel's "overheated economy" and announced a three-year economic reform plan.

Israel's border with Jordan and Syria, two of her four Arab neighbors, became increasingly tense. Three times Israeli military units struck across the border, twice at Jordan and once at Syria, in raids intended as retaliation for 36 acts of sabotage by Arab infiltrators. The most spectacular incident followed the killing of three Israeli soldiers in November. The next day, eight Israeli tanks, a convoy of half-tracks and several hundred soldiers attacked Es Samu, a Jordanian village south of Hebron said by the Israelis to have harbored the terrorists. Houses were demolished; some lives were lost; and after a brief battle with units of the Arab Legion, the Israelis withdrew. The raid led to a United Nations Security Council censure. Premier Levi Eshkol said Israel's aim was simply to be left in peace.

Earlier in the year a dramatic and bizarre flight by a Tel Aviv café owner, Abie Nathan, to Port Said brought some comic relief to the Israeli-Arab situation. Armed only with a "peace petition" of 60,000 signatures, the former Israel Air Force and El Al pilot landed his 39-year-old biplane safely, was refused permission to see President Nasser and then sent home by bemused Egyptian authorities.

Premier Eshkol, who had been returned to office in November 1965, formed a broad coalition in January. He toured Africa in midyear, presided over the dedication of a new parliament building and announced the end of military rule for Israel's Arab population.

Jordan. King Hussein was severely shaken in the aftermath of a strong Israeli retaliation raid against the Hebron village of Es Samu on Nov. 13. Former Palestinians demanding arms to fight the Israelis created riots in several towns in western Jordan. Resentment against the King, who has refused to heed Arab extremist calls, increased the tension, but the Arab Legion remained loyal and restored order. The King stilled some of the complaints that he was inactive after the raid by ordering conscription. This move not only served as a response to Palestinian demands but it established governmental control over possibly unruly youth. The United States said it would airlift arms it had previously promised when it appeared that the pro-Western King might be endangered by Syria or the U.A.R.

Other Arab states offered to provide troops to ensure Jordan's "safety," but Hussein declined to admit them. The King dissolved his Government in December and set new elections for next April.

Jordan's economic growth continued, nevertheless, aided by a thriving tourist industry. The King, in May, laid the foundation stone of the Mokheiba Dam, part of the plan for diversion of the Jordan River.

Lebanon. Lebanon once again managed to remain generally above the turmoil of Arab rivalries during the year. Beirut drew unenviable attention, however, with the failure of Intra Bank, the nation's largest banking house. The Oct. 15 closure of the bank, which commanded a fifth of all Lebanese bank deposits and had extensive interests abroad, created instant repercussions in New York, London and other international financial centers. The bank's problem was laid to excessive involvement in

Israeli soldiers move six miles, into Jordan village of Es Samu, Nov. 13.

King Hussein greets Emperor Haile Selassie of Ethiopia.

Lebanese demonstrate against October bank holiday.

assets not easily convertible to cash, large withdrawals by major depositors in Kuwait and Saudi Arabia and a worldwide tight-money situation. The final blow came when Lebanon's Central Bank declined to provide temporary assistance. Youssef K. Beidas, chairman of the bank's board, was replaced by his deputy, Najib Salha. Small depositors began getting their money back by mid-December.

Premier Rashid Karami resigned in April, was replaced by Abdullah Yaffi, and then resumed the premiership in December.

Saudi Arabia. King Faisal's call for Islamic unity tended to split rather than unify the Arab world. At the same time, it enhanced Faisal's stature as a major Arab leader. The stately monarch visited several countries seeking support for his Islamic conference next year in Mecca. The more conservative governments, such as Iran and Jordan, followed Faisal's lead but the "revolutionaries" in Syria and the U.A.R. saw it as a call to reactionaries to turn back the forces of Arab socialism.

Faisal also visited the United States. He was treated royally in Washington, but officially snubbed in New York following a comment he made at a news conference while discussing the Arab boycott of American concerns trading with Israel. "Unfortunately," he said, "Jews support Israel and we consider those who provide assistance to our enemies as our own enemies." Later he said he meant Zionists, not Jews, but New York City's Mayor John Lindsay canceled an official dinner for the King.

South Arabian Federation. Terrorism continued to haunt this federation of sultanates, sheikdoms and the colony of Aden at the southern end of the Arabian Peninsula. The Federation is scheduled for independence in 1968, when the British plan to leave the 14,000-man military base at Aden and abandon their defense guarantees. As in Yemen, pro-Nasser and pro-Faisal forces are struggling for domination. Britain promised $125 million in arms subsidies to a Federation delegation that traveled to London. But the visiting officials said they would rather have the defense guarantees. It appeared that a United Nations presence might assist in the transition.

Syria. The Syrian Government moved sharply to the Left when the eighth coup since 1949 brought extremist members of the Baath Party to power in Damascus. The latest coup takeover, which featured a brief battle in the capital, ousted Lt. Gen. Amin el-Hafez as party chief, and returned to power two previously ousted officials: Nureddin al-Attassi as chief of state and Yussef Zayen as premier.

Within two months Zayen was in Moscow for talks and on April 25 it was announced that the Soviet Union would help Syria build a dam on the Euphrates River, paying $150 million, or half the cost. The long-envisaged hydroelectric project will double Syria's irrigated area and create a host of new industries.

By fall, the Syrian leaders had foiled a countercoup and were condemning Jordan and Israel for plots against Syria. Later Jordan came under fire after having offered political asylum to two dozen Syrians following the abortive coup. Syrian border units twice fought Israelis in major clashes near the Sea of Galilee. The Damascus Government openly proclaimed a "Peoples' War" against Israel and the Syrians were thought to be behind the marauders attacking Israeli border villages through Jordan.

Damascus authorities in December seized the pipeline that carries Iraqi Petroleum Company oil across Syria to the sea. The move followed an argument over Syrian demands for increased transit fees, but it was seen by some as an attempt to force Iraq to nationalize the foreign-owned oil company.

Turkey. Premier Süleyman Demirel, elected in October 1965, confounded Left-Wing critics by strengthening his position during the year. His Justice Party increased its majority in the midyear senatorial elections. Demirel's greater emphasis on private enterprise to get the country moving economically angered opposition members of the Republican People's Party who favored state planning. The Premier's friendly attitude toward foreign investment pleased Washington, but the Turkish leader also welcomed bids from the Soviet Union. An eight-day visit by Soviet Premier Kosygin, although coolly received, produced a year-end offer of capital assistance for several Turkish development projects.

Turkey remained firmly in the Western camp and an important member of NATO, although anti-American riots led by students broke out toward the end of the year on several occasions. One of the worst was in Adana where U.S. servicemen were attacked.

Gen. Cemal Gürsel, Turkey's president, died Sept. 14 after a seven-month coma. He was replaced by another career officer, the 66-year-old Gen. Cevdet Sunay.

A severe earthquake in eastern Turkey, near Varto, in August, killed 2,300 Turks and left 10,000 homeless.

United Arab Republic. A 5-year-old political split was mended to a degree in Cairo when President Nasser and the Syrian Premier, Yussef Zayen, signed a defense agreement. Syria was part of the U.A.R. from 1959 until 1961. The 1966 reconciliation was encouraged by the Soviet Premier, Aleksei N. Kosygin, whose Government aids both Arab states. The defense pact was seen as a means of providing a stronger front against the rising influence of Right-Wing Arab governments led by King Faisal of Saudi Arabia. It also served to bolster the shaky Syrian Government and acted as a restraint on the extremist Syrian leaders.

The U.A.R. suffered severe economic problems during the year. Although Cairo had received about $2,000,000,000 in military and economic assistance from Moscow since 1955, little more assistance seemed to be forthcoming after Kosygin's visit to Cairo in May. The United States, similarly, seemed to be taking a new look at Cairo's economic planning. American officials signed a six-month, $55 million Food for Peace agreement that was shorter, smaller and on tougher terms than usual. It expired in June and there was no word by year's end on what Washington planned to do about Cairo's request for an additional $150 million agreement. Similarly, there was no decision on a U.A.R. request for a $70 million loan from the International Monetary Fund.

President Nasser shuffled his Cabinet, naming Sidkyi Suliman, former head of the Aswan High Dam project, to replace Zakaria Mohieddin, as premier. His appointment signaled greater emphasis on economic planning. The Government did what it could, meanwhile, by cutting $100 million in development spending from a budget that originally called for $700 million in new investments. Cairo also was forced to sell $50 million in gold to relieve an acute foreign-exchange squeeze and unfavorable balance of trade.

President Nasser announced a $216 million project to widen and deepen the Suez Canal, a bid to accommodate the giant oil tankers that are being used with increasing frequency.

Work on reconstruction of the temples of Abu Simbel moved ahead of schedule with completion now set for 1967, well before the rising waters of the Nile, blocked by the nearly completed Aswan High Dam, cover the original sites.

The nation of 30 million people moved into population-control programs, financed to a considerable degree by Ford Foundation grants totaling $1 million. . . . A project of irrigating portions of the western desert moved ahead with 43,000 acres now fed by well water. Half the area is under cultivation.

Yemen. The civil war between Republican forces, backed by the U.A.R., and the Royalists, supported by Saudi Arabia, moved into its fourth year. A truce arranged in August 1965 was held intact with only occasional outbreaks of fighting. A split in the Republican camp was finally resolved in favor of the U.A.R.-backed Yemeni President, Abdullah al Salal. He assumed the premiership from Maj. Gen. Hassan al-Amryi and purged the more liberal "Yemen first" faction. By year's end the Egyptian Army seemed to be assuming direct rule of the Republican forces.

MINING. The world is experiencing a boom in minerals production, research and technology, partly as a result of the worldwide drive to increase trade. But the real impetus comes from expanding economies, and the knowledge that the world's booming population and growing industrialization are using up larger and larger supplies of metals. As a result, mankind may find that its "next frontier" is down, rather than upward in space.

Getting down to this next frontier will be accomplished by deeper underground mines; by development of open-pit mines in which waste removal will reach proportions undreamed of even a decade ago, and by the use of novel mining machines under remote-control operation. To achieve the needed production of new minerals and the reclaiming of minerals from industrial wastes will require a tremendous increase in the use of energy. By 1980, for example, the total use of energy in the United States will be double that of 1960, and such energy must cost substantially less than it does today. Twice as much coal, twice as much natural gas and two thirds as much oil will be consumed. It is no wonder that in 1966 the United States, Canada, France and Italy gave extra effort to the search for uranium reserves —looking ahead to an actual economic shortage of uranium fuels for nuclear reactors, which by the year 2000 will play a major role in production of electrical energy in the world.

An important factor in the consumption of both minerals and energy is the multiplication rate of use. In 1850, energy requirement for a single person in the United States was equal to 4 tons of coal per year; by 1961, each man, woman and child consumed an equivalent of 10 tons per year. Some experts believe this consumption will hit 30 tons' equivalent in 1970. This need for more coal is matched by forecasts for increased production of aluminium, steel, copper, zinc, lead, titanium, uranium, beryllium, magnesium, lithium, molybdenum, vanadium and other metals.

Meanwhile the output of sulfuric acid from pyrite and conventional sources will increase. The need for fertilizers, so that the world may feed itself, seems endless, and the dramatic programs for higher output of phosphate ores and potash are matched only by the great leap forward in nitrogen-plant construction.

New Mining Techniques

To achieve some of these production needs, mining engineers have been forced to discard some conservative approaches which had characterized the mining industry during the last thirty years—a conservatism induced by crumbling price structures for minerals, and by problems arising from huge post-World War II stockpiles and the switch from wartime to peacetime production.

Mining engineers now are borrowing from the oil and gas industry and from the construction industry, and they are developing new ideas on their own. Here are some new mining techniques.

Underground shaft "construction," or raising, is made easier by drilling large-diameter holes, which reduces time and expense in conventional timbering approaches. Actual manway, service and ventilation shafts are being sunk from the surface by huge drilling rigs analogous to the typical drilling equipment found in oil fields. The "mole," a mobile adaptation of such a drilling rig, is now employed in driving horizontal tunnels for water-reclamation purposes. Similar machines are in use in the world's coal industry to drive through shale and limestone formations that cannot be cut by conventional coal-mining equipment.

Remarkable machines to handle the ore and waste rock from the mining face underground have been devised in order to reduce manpower requirements, increase safety and speed excavation.

A machine developed in the last decade speeds the sinking of shafts necessary to the development of ore bodies. This novel device (an air-powered clamshell) emulates to perfection the action of the human hand and arm as they would dig a hole in the earth.

Twenty years ago an overburden of 700 or 800 feet would have posed major problems in

This tunnel-boring machine exerts a 1.4 million-lb. force.

Hughes Tool Company—Houston, Tex.

the open-pit mining of minerals of "low" value. Nowadays, however, mines go deeper, and overburdens of 1,000 to 1,500 feet of waste do not deter the mining engineer. Removal of waste presents few problems with the great advance in truck haulage (with 100-plus-ton vehicles); the lowering of blasting costs through employment of ammonium nitrates as against higher-cost explosives; the utilization of conveyor belts and large electric shovels.

Mining Industry's Contributions

Without the mining, metallurgical, geological and petroleum engineer, civilization as we know it would not exist. Its perpetuation depends upon the production by society of engineers who can advance, maintain and save this civilization. The new contrast in the color TV tube, emanating from rare-earth phosphors; mercury measuring devices on huge transcontinental pipelines; aluminum and copper in electrical transmission lines; delicate silver points of electrical appliances—these are but a few contributions of the mining industry.

The harvest of the land is renewable. But there is no second crop of minerals. For world civilization to maintain itself, it is essential that mining go deeper, down into the "next frontier." The mining industry can go deeper, and can serve mankind, through its use of capital outlays, important technological advances and great imagination.

ROGER V. PIERCE
Past President, AMERICAN INSTITUTE OF MINING,
METALLURGICAL AND PETROLEUM ENGINEERS

MINNESOTA. In November, Harold LeVander (R) defeated incumbent Karl F. Rolvaag of the Democratic-Farmer-Labor Party for the governorship. Earlier, Rolvaag, who had lost his party's endorsement for a second term to Lt. Gov. A. M. Keith, defeated Keith for nomination in a primary election. . . . Walter Mondale (D) was reelected to the U.S. Senate. . . . Gov. Rolvaag signed a compromise reapportionment bill May 18. . . . Employment in Minnesota reached an all-time high in June.

MISSILES AND ROCKETS. The highlight of 1966 in missilery/rocketry was the flight debut of a new launch vehicle that will figure prominently in the U.S. manned-lunar-landing program.

Saturn. Once known as Saturn 1B but now termed Uprated Saturn 1, the big superbooster made three flights during the year, all of them successful. The flights marked the start of the unmanned portion of the National Aeronautics and Space Administration's (NASA) Apollo project.

NASA

Uprated Saturn 1, a superbooster.

An interim vehicle between the Saturn 1 which completed its test program in 1965 and the Saturn 5 which will launch manned flights to the moon, Uprated Saturn 1 is a two-stage booster that stands 224 ft. tall when topped by its Apollo payload. Its lower stage is powered by eight liquid-propellant rocket engines producing a combined thrust of 1.6 million lb. The power plant for the upper stage is a single J-2 engine that burns high-energy, liquid-hydrogen fuel and develops a 200,000-lb. thrust. This combination permits the vehicle to boost about 18 tons into earth orbit, a payload adequate for manned Apollo missions for which the spacecraft is lightly fueled.

On its initial flight, Feb. 26, Uprated Saturn 1 carried an unmanned Apollo spacecraft, sending it on a short, suborbital path down the Atlantic Test Range. The flight was primarily a checkout of the new Apollo heat shield. The spacecraft was driven back toward earth at a very steep angle and a velocity of 28,000 ft. per sec. Although reentry velocity was far short of Apollo's lunar return speed, the flight provided the first of several checkpoints of the heat shield's performance.

The second Uprated Saturn 1 mission, launched July 5, was to check the upper stage, designated S-4B. S-4B is of particular importance because it is also the topmost stage of the Saturn 5 moonbooster. It stays with the Apollo in orbit, and must be restarted in space to provide the final thrust into lunar trajectory. The July mission, which was successful, involved a study of the behavior of liquid hydrogen in space and a reliability check of the restart capability.

A second heat-shield test was conducted on Aug. 25 on Uprated Saturn 1's third flight of the year. This time the booster sent the Apollo spacecraft into a different suborbital path, one that took it through three quarters of an orbit to a landing in the Pacific. The craft reentered the atmosphere in a long, flat trajectory at 28,000 ft. per sec., absorbing greater heat than it had on the initial flight because of longer exposure to atmospheric friction. Other checks, at the lunar mission reentry speed of 36,000 ft. per sec., must await the availability of the Saturn 5 booster.

At year-end, the latter vehicle was being readied for its initial flight. Saturn 5, at 364 ft., considerably taller than the Statue of Liberty, is capable of launching 120 tons into low earth orbit, or of sending a 95,000-lb. spacecraft to the moon. It consists of a basic S-1C stage composed of five F-1 rocket engines producing 1.5 million lbs. of thrust each, a second S-2 stage made up of five J-2 engines and the S-4B upper stage.

In addition to its July flight test, S-4B underwent ground test firings in 1966, as did the two lower stages late in the year. These tests set the stage for a first flight of the complete launch vehicle early in 1967. Saturn 5 was slated to launch lunar-mission dress-rehearsal flights of the fully fueled Apollo in 1968. In

the interim, Uprated Saturn 1 was to boost a series of manned earth-orbital Apollo missions for complete checkout of all of the spacecraft's systems.

Titan. Development of the prime military space booster, Titan 3-C, continued with three flights in 1966, all of them successful from the boost standpoint, although some trouble was experienced in attempts to inject payloads into orbit. On June 16, Titan 3-C launched a multiple payload consisting of one experimental satellite to test the gravity gradient system of spacecraft stabilization, together with the first increment of seven communications satellites in the Initial Defense Communication Satellite Program (IDCSP). All stages of Titan 3-C— the 470,000-lb.-thrust lower stage augmented by two 120-in.-diameter, 1,200,000-lb.-thrust solid rockets, a 100,000-lb.-thrust second stage and the 16,000-lb. Transtage—performed flawlessly and all satellites were properly injected into orbit. A second increment of eight IDCSP comsats was lost to service on an August launch of Titan 3-C, when malfunction of the payload fairing made it impossible for the satellites to separate from the booster.

On Titan 3-C's third 1966 flight, the sixth of its developmental program, the booster showed its versatility in an impressive display of space gymnastics involving a suborbital flight of one spacecraft and orbital insertion of three others. On Nov. 3, Titan 3-C lofted a five-spacecraft payload consisting of a modified Gemini capsule, a classified decoy experiment, two advanced comsats and a package of eight military/scientific experiments. It achieved an altitude of approximately 120 mi. The 16,000-lb.-thrust Transtage, or space "switch engine," was then nosed downward. Its twin engines fired briefly, accelerating the Gemini to earth orbital reentry velocity of 17,500 mi. per hr. and the Gemini plummeted into the Atlantic. This portion of the mission was a test of a new heat shield.

The Transtage then nosed upward and fired again for 40 sec., canceling the downward momentum and starting the remaining payloads toward an orbital altitude of 184 statute mi. At that altitude, the Transtage fired again for five sec. to circularize the orbit. The mission was marred by the failure of the classified satellite to eject, but the other spacecraft successfully achieved orbit.

In 1966, the Air Force initiated development of an improved model of the Titan 3 by increasing the length of the 120-in. solid motors that supplement the liquid-propellant rocket engine in the first stage. The solid motors are assembled in segments. The existing system has

Titan 3-C with multiple payload of eight satellites.

UPI

Long Tank Thor with upper stage undergoes vibration test.

five segments, while the Titan 3-M booster for the Manned Orbiting Laboratory will have seven. The additional segments will provide 400,000 extra lbs. of thrust for each of the solid strap-on motors, boosting total thrust in the solids from 2.4 million to 3.2 million lbs.

Lesser Rated Launch Vehicles. The lesser-rated launch vehicles are the less powerful boosters employed for orbiting of unmanned spacecraft. In 1966 the Air Force introduced a new one called Long Tank Thor. Latest of the Thor family of launch vehicles, which includes more than two dozen configurations, Long Tank Thor is self-descriptive: the volume of liquid propellant in its tanks has been increased to provide a longer burning time, hence greater payload capability. Long Tank Thor is 70 ft. long, compared to the 56-ft. standard version. With thrust-augmenting solid strap-on rockets, the new model can send 3,000 lbs. of payload into low-altitude earth orbit, a gain of 500 lbs.

A companion development by the Air Force was Burner 2, the first solid-fuel upper stage with full control and guidance capability. Designed for use with Thor, or any other launch vehicle used for small or medium payloads, Burner 2 features very precise control of flight rate and burnout velocity, offering more accurate injection of spacecraft into orbit or escape trajectories. Burner 2 was undergoing ground test in 1966, and the first Thor/Burner 2 was scheduled for flight late in the year.

Nuclear Rocket Development. In the field of nuclear-rocket propulsion, NASA and the Atomic Energy Commission (AEC), together with associated contractors, continued the "technology phase" of nuclear-rocket development, testing various system components aimed at eventual development of a nuclear-powered upper stage. The program is in three parts, one involving development of the reactor, another the engine and the third the complete stage. The latter part of the program is confined to studies, but in 1966 the reactor and engine projects were moving into advanced stages.

At the Nuclear Rocket Development Station in Nevada facilities were being prepared for a series of advanced tests, while component development work on the NERVA engine continued at the plant of the prime contractor, Aerojet-General Corp. The Joint NASA/AEC Space Nuclear Propulsion Office (SNPO) disclosed plans for a 1967 test of the 1,000-megawatt Phoebus 1B reactor and a NERVA technology reactor designated NRX-A6. Then, late in 1967, SNPO plans a ground test of the first experimental reactor-powered engine, a nonflyable system called XE. A successful test would be one of the last steps before initiation of hardware development of an operational flight engine. In developmental stages were a 5,000-megawatt Phoebus 2 reactor and a 200,-000-lb.-thrust NERVA 2 flight engine.

Missiles. The most notable step of 1966 in missiles was the October award of a contract

Artist's conception of SRAM, Short Range Attack Missile.

Wide World

to the Boeing Co. for development and production of the SRAM missile, long a paper-study item. SRAM stands for Short Range Attack Missile, a weapon intended for use with the Air Force's FB-111 bomber, which will carry four to six missiles. The weapon is also to be adaptable to the big, eight-jet B-52 strategic bomber. Designed to penetrate enemy defenses at low altitude, SRAM will be launched outside the range arc of enemy defensive weapons, permitting the launching airplane to "stand off" outside the defense line. SRAM will be inertially guided and powered by a solid-fuel rocket. It is slated for initial entry into the USAF's operational inventory in 1969.

Both the Air Force and the Navy were busy modernizing their prime offensive missile systems, Minuteman and Polaris, respectively. The USAF was rapidly emplacing the advanced Minuteman 2. By year-end about 140 of the improved 2 weapons had joined the 800 Minuteman 1's already operational. Minuteman 2 has a more powerful second-stage engine, an improved guidance system, greater range and payload and increased penetrability than its predecessor. A still more advanced Minuteman 3 was in developmental status. An eventual force of 1,000 Minuteman missiles is planned, but the Department of Defense did not disclose the composition with regard to models.

Similarly, the Navy neared completion of its program to modernize Polaris submarines by replacing the initial Polaris A1 with A2 and A3 versions. The latter, with a range of 2,500 nautical mi., are to arm 28 of 41 operational subs. The remaining 13 subs are to carry the 1,500-nautical-mi.-range A2. Withdrawn A1 was used in missile and space test programs.

The year passed without decision on operational deployment of the Nike-X antiballistic-missile system. The developmental effort continued on Nike-X's two types of missiles and associated radars, however, and construction was started on a new Nike-X test complex at Kwajalein Island in the Pacific. The two missiles in the Nike-X system are Sprint, a two-stage, high-acceleration weapon designed to intercept an enemy intercontinental ballistic missile (ICBM) at relatively low altitude, and Zeus, the long-range or high-altitude interceptor. Douglas Aircraft Co. was working on an improved version of Zeus, slightly longer and heavier than its predecessor and powered by three solid-propellant rocket engines. The extended range of the new model, said the contractor, would allow it to intercept ICBM warheads outside the earth's atmosphere.

Among other missiles in development or production status during 1966 were:

Poseidon, a close relative of the Navy's Polaris family, described as "eight times as effective as the A3 Polaris." Poseidon will have a range comparable to that of the A3, but it will have greater accuracy and twice the payload.

Sea Sparrow, under development for the U.S. Navy and the armed forces of NATO as a basic point defense missile system.

Viper, a small antitank weapon, first firings of which started in October 1966.

Interim ARM, Navy antiradiation missile designed to attack enemy electronic defenses.

JAMES J. HAGGERTY
Editor, AEROSPACE YEAR BOOK

MISSISSIPPI. Statewide prohibition ended June 30. . . . Tornadoes struck central Mississippi March 3–4, with Jackson hardest hit. . . . Civil-rights activity included James Meredith's voter-registration march; he was shot June 6 near Hernando. There was also racial violence in Grenada during the summer and fall. . . . Episcopal Bishop Duncan M. Gray died June 25.

MISSOURI. The Department of Labor announced Feb. 20 the extension to St. Louis of its experimental job program—an attack on hard-core unemployment. . . . In late May the Performing Arts Foundation of Kansas City sponsored a three-day international festival. . . . Some 140 deaths in St. Louis were attributed to a June-July heat wave. . . . CORE and Bi-State Transit System reached agreement March 3 ending a Negro boycott of St. Louis buses.

MONTANA. Senator Lee Metcalf (D) was re-elected Nov. 8. . . . Two state constitutional amendments called for flexible use of governmental structure in a national emergency, and for creation of Legislative Assembly electoral districts based on population rather than county lines. . . . Yellowtail Dam in the canyon of Bighorn River was completed in October. . . . Wheat production was lower than the 1965 output; employment in mining gained.

MONTREAL. The biggest day in many years for Canada's largest city was Oct. 14, 1966, when Montreal's new "Métro" carried its first passengers. The Métro is the most modern and possibly the most beautiful subway system in the world. Its swift (50 mph maximum speed) and almost silent rubber-tired trains are copies of those used on the newest lines of the Paris Métro in France, but its main claim to distinction lies in its 28 stations. Contracts for designing the stations were given to different architects who were encouraged to express individuality and commission artists and sculptors of their choice.

Two lines totaling 13 miles and 25 stations, all underground, were opened on Oct. 14. A third, 3-mile, line, from Montreal Island under the St. Lawrence River to the mainland, with a stop en route at the 1967 world exhibition (Expo 67), will enter service in April 1967. This will be almost exactly 5 years after the start of work on the $213 million system.

Nine days after the subway opened, Mayor Jean Drapeau was elected to his fourth term, with more than 90 per cent of the vote, an unprecedented endorsement of the man who brought the Métro and Expo to Montreal.

Transportation news was made on the international level. The Russian luxury liner *Alexandr Pushkin* made her first voyage from Leningrad to Montreal in April 1966 and completed her first season of six crossings in October—the first regular service between Russia and a North American port. In November, state-owned Canadian and Russian airlines inaugurated a twice-weekly Montreal-Moscow service, another North American first.

The city recorded another busy construction year. In addition to work on the site of Expo 67, the last major link of an expressway to speed tourists through the city to the exhibition was nearing completion. The Decarie Expressway included a 70-foot tunnel, 26 overpasses and the city's most elaborate multiple-level traffic interchange. Total cost: $80 million. At the east end of Montreal Island, workmen were putting the last touches to a new link with the mainland: a 6,451-foot tunnel and 1,500-foot bridge.

Canadian National Railways ordered a $15 million fleet of gas-turbine "super trains" which will travel between Montreal and Toronto at speeds up to 160 mph. The trains will go into service in June 1967, and travel the 330 miles between the 2 cities in 4 hours, cutting 1 hour from the CNR's diesel-powered Rapido service, which already is the fastest passenger train in North America.

The most serious of many labor disputes in the city in 1966 was a hospital-workers' strike which closed all major hospitals in the city for twenty days.

PETER DESBARATS
Editor in Chief, PARALLEL

MORO, ALDO. Italy's Premier Aldo Moro, 50, was beset by domestic problems in 1966, a year of confidence votes and shouting matches for the usually cool-headed southern Italian. During a November discussion of Italy's worst floods in centuries, communist Senators heckled Moro mercilessly for not going to the devastated city of Florence during the disasters. "Not heartlessness but a sense of responsibility held me in Rome!" Moro shouted back.

A bitter exchange between Moro and communist deputies stirred a near riot following a confidence vote on a minor bill in July. Hoping for defectors in the Premier's Christian Democratic Party, the opposition time and again demanded secret ballots on amendments to minor bills. Each time Moro called for an open-ballot confidence test. Earlier in the year, Moro had survived Italy's longest postwar political crisis.

Moro was humiliated in October when he could not muster a quorum on a confidence vote concerning the Government's five-year economic plan. Absent members of the Center-Left coalition, ridiculed publicly, showed up next day to defeat the communist-sponsored amendment.

During Parliament's debate of terrorism in Italy's German-speaking Alto Adige region, Moro was erudite, convincing and stern. He provided the note needed to satisfy irate Italians and still not come to a break with Austria.

Foreground: shell of Conference Hall, Council for Mutual Economic Aid, Moscow.

Tass from Sovfoto

The Premier was silent but obviously worried when the Socialists and Social Democrats, partners in his coalition, rejoined forces after 19 years' schism—thus threatening to become their own power.

ERNEST A. LOTITO
Rome Bureau, UNITED PRESS INTERNATIONAL

MOSCOW. Muscovites probably will look back on 1966 as a significant year in their old capital's history. Beneath the solid, seemingly unchanging exterior, the city was undergoing rapid change. Throughout the year, the city blossomed with towering cranes, symbols of an ambitious program of construction outlined by the Mayor, Chairman Vladimir F. Promyslov of the Moscow City Executive Committee. The plan called for construction of living quarters totaling 120,000 apartments, for a population still severely short of housing space. There would be 34 new school buildings, 400 new shops and public catering enterprises, 254 new communal service enterprises.

Longer-range plans, already being carried out, called for 8 new hotels, one of which would take up a city block in the area of Red Square and overshadow spectacular old St. Basil's Cathedral. New administrative buildings were planned or under construction along Kalinin Street. In an area near the U.S. Embassy, construction was under way on a skyscraper headquarters for the Council for Mutual Economic Aid (CMEA), the communist bloc's economic-collaboration organization. In addition, Moscow looked forward to a new television center, a new state art gallery and a new circus building. Even the style of building was changing. Once, all new residential building seemed low and squat, but now high-rise apartments are appearing.

Traffic was becoming more of a problem with each passing month, and promised to be even more so in the future with government plans to increase the output of automobiles for private use. There were only about 75,000 privately owned automobiles in the capital in 1966, but these and state-owned vehicles managed to clog the main arteries.

Mayor Promyslov, addressing the 23d Congress of the Soviet Communist Party in April 1966, predicted that Moscow soon would need many more gasoline stations, many spare-parts outlets, and a program for widening streets to accommodate new traffic. New pedestrian underpasses were opened at busy intersections.

Muscovites themselves were undergoing subtle changes. In the city's streets there seemed a far larger proportion of well-dressed people than in other years, and women particularly seemed more stylishly turned out. In the stores there were more consumer goods than the year before. Food supplies in the shops seemed plentiful and more varied than in the past.

Moscow was experimenting with a new system that likely would be extended to the rest of the nation. The city fathers hesitantly instituted a new system of planning which involved economic incentives to boost the quality and quantity of goods and services available to the public. By year's end, this system had extended to a score or more enterprises, and was expanding steadily as officials expressed pleasure at reports that it was bringing in significant profits.

WILLIAM L. RYAN
News Analyst, THE ASSOCIATED PRESS

MOTION PICTURES

By RICHARD L. COE
Film Critic
THE WASHINGTON POST

"Strike while the iron is hot" hardly applies to the major event of the U.S. film year, revision of the production code.

Adopted in 1930, the Motion Picture Code of Self-Regulation was the fundamental statement of the Motion Picture Association of America. But in the 36 years since its introduction, the studios, through antitrust proceedings, lost control of the theaters they once dominated. Foreign films exposed other mores. American life changed vastly. The code became almost as meaningless as it was hypocritical. How meaningful the revised code can become remains to be seen, but while some of its new freedoms may seem hedged, two new factors will have wide, lasting effects.

The code now promotes a long-disputed concept: its administration "will identify certain pictures as Suggested for Mature Audiences." Some revision of this sort had been rumbling for years. Otto Preminger broke the first barrier in 1953 when his wholly virtuous but outspoken comedy, *The Moon Is Blue,* was denied an MPAA seal of approval. When theaters, no longer controlled by the studios, proved willing to show this picture without a seal, the code's effect was shattered. Before his death in 1963, Eric Johnston, the longtime MPAA head, was pushing for change. His successor, Jack J. Valenti, made revision the first order of business. Going directly from his White House post as a special assistant to President Johnson, Valenti commanded the force to get agreement from the eight major producing members. (The creator of the first code, Will Hays, had become MPAA's first boss in a similarly august aura, moving directly from his postmaster general role in the Harding Cabinet.)

In the film world, as in contemporary politics, youth is a key factor: 44-year-old Valenti immediately stressed this in several areas, calling for development of young creative talent, cooperation with the National Council on the Arts' plan for an American Film Institute, and for more "adult films of excellence" which so conspicuously have been captivating the young, who like fine films from Europe.

Revised Code and *Virginia Woolf*. But it was an American picture that provided the first opportunity for Valenti to make a breakthrough, the adaptation of Edward Albee's Broadway play, *Who's Afraid of Virginia Woolf?*. Its producer, Jack Warner, had made it clear that the film would be released whether or not it got its seal, and that all exhibitors would be "prohibited from admitting anyone under the age of 18 unless accompanied by his parent." The picture got its Valenti-pushed seal as an "exceptional" case.

Thus, classification, so long opposed by American theater men, has slipped into official status in the nongovernmental "self-regulatory" agency. Whether the theater owners, or even parents, will cooperate is a question.

An established device in Britain, classification of certain films for adults only has been fought in the United States as a form of censorship. What is unfit for some children may be suitable for others, the argument goes; parents should decide. That some adult-only British pictures have wound up on television, for any child to see, presages what will happen in the States. As it happened, *Who's Afraid of Virginia Woolf?* proved a worthy choice for the new approach to classification. The film tingles with vitality; the dialogue bristles with contemporary acuity; and at Oscartime '67 both Elizabeth Taylor and Richard Burton will be leading contenders.

Ernest Lehman's screenplay cuts the long stage work by an hour's running time without damage to the whole. Mike Nichols, in his first film, showed a directorial eye so precise that the onetime revue comedian now has still another field for his gifts.

A 1966 film favorite: Who's Afraid of Virginia Woolf?
Warner Bros.

Zero Mostel and Jack Gilford star in *A Funny Thing Happened on the Way to the Forum;*
Eva Marie Saint, Carl Reiner and Alan Arkin are featured in *The Russians Are Coming.*

If the story seemed as enigmatic as its title to some, none could deny its vitality. A middle-aged couple, he a professor in the college headed by his wife's father, play host to a young instructor and his vacuous wife. Through a long evening of drinking, startling talk and harrowing insults, the host and his wife are revealed as pitiably dependent on each other for the illusions which make so many lives bearable.

For all its bitterness, the story of George and Martha is stirring for its insights, shown more unmistakably in the film than onstage. Nichols' final shot of two hands was the inspired, meaningful image for unuttered truth. Because Burton's was the finer performance, the picture seems more the story of George than of Martha, who had been the play's storm center. The roles gave the Burtons their finest screen moments and proved them worthy of their thumping stipends.

Comedies and Laugh-Weep Mix. Two other films received the SMA—Suggested for Mature Audiences—treatment, and both fell into categories that dominated the year: comedy and the laugh-weep mix.

In the latter category was England's *Alfie,* its hero for much of the time a laughable, amoral rogue. But as in other films of the laugh-weep mix, *Alfie* jolted into an episode of tragedy, and one left *Alfie* not with a laugh, but with sorrow for his self-inflicted plight.

In *Alfie* the previously inadmissible film material concerned an illegal operation. After trekking about with all kinds of "birds," whom

he treats with egoistic contempt, the hero forces a married woman (whose husband he knows) into getting rid of his own child. We see only his eyes as he looks at what we do not see, but the lesson could not be more maturely gripping, nor the sacredness of human life more awesomely expressed. Michael Caine's performance and the calm underplaying of the scene mark this as one of the year's finest screen dramas.

An outright comedy also received the SMA classification—*A Funny Thing Happened on the Way to the Forum.* Here the reason lay in the motion picture's frankly bawdy quality. But this particular bawdiness has been evident for centuries in the comedies of the Roman dramatist Plautus, from whose work this musical comedy stems.

A Funny Thing also stemmed from Broadway, where the book by Burt Shevelove and Larry Gelbart to music and lyrics by Stephen Sondheim flourished with the ineffable Zero Mostel, properly lured into the screen version along with Jack Gilford, also repeating his Broadway role. They are joined by a rare galaxy of comics, including Phil Silvers, Michael Hordern and the late Buster Keaton in his final screen role.

Director Richard Lester, who guided the Beatles' first two films, rockets this farce of a teeming, lusty old Rome with dazzling details. Even the Imperial City has novelty in that it no longer looks like the immaculate, gleaming city of biblical spectaculars, but like the brawling, vulgar maze it must have been. The hearty

In a scene from Billy Wilder's *The Fortune* Cookie, Walter Matthau (right) reads from lawsuit dealing with "injuries" suffered by Jack Lemmon (left).

rambunctiousness of *A Funny Thing,* which would have denied this comedy a seal, is the precise quality which is its virtue.

To *Virginia Woolf, Alfie* and *A Funny Thing,* the churches—especially the National Catholic Office for Motion Pictures—once would have been implacably opposed. While the church groups may not now approve them, the fact that they have been presented for what they are, "adult entertainment," is a battle church leaders have long tried to win.

The year's most refreshing tone was the laugh-weep mix typified by *Alfie.* Into that category had fallen *Darling,* for which Julie Christie won an Oscar in April 1966 for feminine-star performance. A third in the genre also came from Britain—*Morgan!,* on the surface a zany misadventure of a misfit who dreams of an easier life through old Tarzan-King Kong movies and his mother's Marxian fixation. The character's alienation, as expressed in David Warner's self-absorbed portrait, made this far more touching than farcical.

Several spirited American films also caught this vital contemporary quality. *A Thousand Clowns* found Jason Robards re-creating his stage portrait of a joking but disenchanted comedy writer. *A Fine Madness* presented versatile Sean Connery as an attractive genius unable to cope with present distractions. *The Fortune Cookie* gave Jack Lemmon and Walter Matthau farcical adventures with insurance policies, but also reflected how one man's fortune can be another's disaster.

The Russians Are Coming The Russians Are Coming imagined the rumors that would arise should a Soviet submarine make an innocent landing on the New England coast. The movie, from a Nathaniel Benchley story, did not miss the concomitant point—that sanity must preserve all from international misunderstandings.

Comedies dominated the successes; one wide stratum derived from the spy mania propelled by James Bond and TV's espionage series. There was a score of such comedies to keep Jerry Lewis, Dean Martin, Rowan and Martin, Horst Buchholz, David Niven, Robert Vaughn and David McCallum on the theater screens.

The best of the type, however, took pains to avoid making sense—a harum-scarum chase involving a professorial Gregory Peck and Middle East oil in *Arabesque;* a cocky Warren Beatty breaking into a playing-card factory, shattering gambling centers in *Kaleidoscope.* Technically glittering and with leading ladies such as Sophia Loren and Susannah York, both cliff-hangers chuckled at their plot holes, as did Dirk Bogarde's zany *Modesty Blaise.*

Our Man Flint introduced James Coburn as a sybaritic spy bound to have later adventures, and the same star (joined by Dick Shawn) provided broad fun about Italian warfare habits in *What Did You Do in the War, Daddy?.* Even the virtuous Audrey Hepburn took to thievery with Peter O'Toole in a spoof of the art world, *How to Steal a Million.*

More rigors of the card sharks, poker division, were amusingly exposed in *A Big Hand for the Little Lady,* with Joanne Woodward and Henry Fonda in fine fettle. Peter Glenville, who had revived it for the stage, had fashionable film fun with Feydeau and Desvallières' turn-of-the-century farce, *Hotel Paradiso*, abetted by Sir Alec Guinness, Gina Lollobrigida and Robert Morley.

Another prank stemmed from Bryan Forbes' use of a Robert Louis Stevenson story for Britain's wholly hilarious *The Wrong Box*, smartly employing Peter Sellers, Sir Ralph Richardson, John Mills, Peter Cook and the busy Mr. Caine.

Drama. Pure drama, as usual, was in the minority, but a few were strikingly fine. *Doctor Zhivago*, American-financed in Spain with a British director, David Lean, and an international cast, was inspired by the Pasternak novel and proved a surprisingly strong popular success. While Pasternak's well-known dispute with the Soviets undoubtedly had something to do with the general curiosity about the movie, the director's faithfulness to Pasternak's visual concepts and Robert Bolt's shrewd adaptation were the critical factors. Making the point that in the Soviet philosophy the individual must be sacrificed for the mass, the long picture had the curious quality of being almost a strain to sit through but immensely rewarding to reflect on afterward. Its superb photography and substantial performances (Miss Christie, Sir Alec, Omar Sharif and Tom Courtenay) made for serious conversation and six Academy Awards in 1966.

From Sweden came *Dear John*, an absorbing study of two lonely people, a freighter captain and a port waitress, in an impressively sensitive blend of the sensual and the spiritual. Czechoslovakia sent a touching study of an old lady enmeshed in the conquering Nazis' anti-Semitic drive, *The Shop on Main Street*. Ida Kaminska gave a memorable performance. Her importation from Poland for the central role revealed cooperation between iron-curtain studios.

Decisive performances by Charlton Heston and Sir Laurence Olivier brought the personal duel of General Gordon and the Sudan's Mahdi splendidly to the fore of spectacular settings in the sweeping *Khartoum*, its screenplay notable for adherence to historical fact. *King Rat*, with England's Courtenay and James Fox and the United States' George Segal, had director Forbes' skillful direction in a story about class consciousness in a Japanese prisoner-of-war camp. Although *A Patch of Blue*, with a theme of racial tolerance, was blatantly sentimental in writing and handling, it starred Sidney Poitier and provided Shelley Winters with an Oscar in the supporting-actress category.

Big Films and TV. *The Sound of Music*, which had opened in late 1965, had five Oscars, including those for best picture and best direction (Robert Wise). At U.S. box offices, by year's end a mere 120 of them, the musical was establishing itself as the most popular film ever made. Projecting present figures into future earnings, it is slated soon to pass the 26-year total grosses for *Gone with the Wind*. *The Sound of Music* also had the baleful effect of encouraging other films about nuns, Debbie Reynolds' *The Singing Nun* and Rosalind Russell's *The Trouble with Angels*, both of which were poor, Hayley Mills in the latter notwithstanding.

The Sound of Music gross brings up, again, the matter of TV. Big movies of the recent past can now command into the millions for one or two TV showings. *The Bridge on the River Kwai* cost ABC $2 million but brought the network 71 million viewers, impressive in the black magic of ratings. The $5 million 20th Century-Fox will receive for televising *Cleopatra* finally will get this behemoth out of the red. Metro's sale of 63 films (18 still to be produced) to CBS for $50 million includes such pre-code-revision scorchers as *Cat on a Hot Tin Roof* and *The Night of the Iguana*. All the film companies are up to their ears in TV, once viewed as a rival, but now a partner in the most amusing marriage since *The Taming of the Shrew* (which will be, by the by, the Burtons' 1967 "special").

Another film on the mammoth side was *Hawaii*, based on only part of James A. Michener's novel covering centuries of Pacific history. This distillation took seven years of planning. Ultimately George Roy Hill directed the screenplay by Daniel Taradash and Dalton Trumbo. The roles of a missionary, his wife and her admirer gave Max von Sydow, Julie Andrews and Richard Harris a monumental three hours' screen time.

Unusual Features and European Fare. Two effective films made up in novelty what they avoided in length. *Fantastic Voyage*, played with delicious credulity, imagined a submarine of scientists reduced to invisibility and injected into the bloodstream of an injured scientist. This motion picture promises to have the timeless appeal of *King Kong*. Also novel was *Seconds*, a scientific variation on *Faust*, wherein a middle-aged man gains Rock Hudson's body, and finds he is no happier than when he lived in Scarsdale. John Frankenheimer's direction was matched by James Wong Howe's atmospheric photography.

Not all the year's releases, mercifully, were blockbusters. Unpretentious ones of quality

Columbia Pictures Corp.

The Wrong Box. a British comedy, is based on a Robert Louis Stevenson story.

found audiences beyond ordinary dreams. Most impressive of U.S. sleepers was *The Endless Summer*, disarmingly modest but eloquently photogenic in following two young surfers to Africa, Australia and the Pacific in search of the perfect surfing waves.

India sent *Shakespeare Wallah*, presenting the new India from the viewpoint of a small family of English actors who long had offered the classics in Indian schools, the very minute-

ness of this specialized world stressing the subcontinent's throbbing changes.

Sweden's onetime actress, Mai Zetterling, showed her writing and directorial talents in *Loving Couples*, which opened in the United States just when repercussions from the Venice showings of her *Night Games* were echoing.

France's ebbing *nouvelle vague* underscored emptiness, a nadir being Tony Richardson's direction of a Genet story, *Mademoiselle*, with

Ida Kaminska in *The Shop on Main Street*.
Prominent Films

Max von Sydow, Julie Andrews and George Rose in *Hawaii*.
United Artists Corp.

Jeanne Moreau as an unattractive, sexually frustrated provincial, casting perversity *in excelsis*. Agnés Varda had an equally absurd story for her richly photographed *Le Bonheur,* and Claude Lelouch's *A Man and a Woman,* with Anouk Aimee and Jean-Louis Trintignant, was probably the best of the Gallic imports, though Sylvie created another fine old lady for Brecht's *The Shameless Old Lady*.

Italy's prime entry was the long-aborning Dino De Laurentiis production, *The Bible,* with a small-print phrase "in the beginning" tacked on after three dots to indicate that this Bible covered only from the first sentence through the story of Abraham and Isaac, as written in King James style by Christopher Fry. *The Bible* proved as drowsy as a Sunday afternoon. The Noah sequence, in which John Huston directed himself as the ark builder and at the same time doubled as the Voice of God, strived for but never reached the gentle humor of a similar episode in *The Green Pastures*.

Another part of the Bible inspired another Italian import, *The Gospel according to St. Matthew,* which had that home-movies quality which brings overpraise from the bored fashionable. Both this film and *The Bible* were inferior to the preceding year's *The Greatest Story Ever Told,* but, being foreign, they inspired more serious critical attention than George Stevens' visually striking film.

Strong in the European festivals, the too often platitudinous Soviet films have suffered recent American reverses. The only 1966 release to get much attention was the disappointing *Bolshoi Ballet '67,* a misnomer, for it was photographed four years earlier. The best of Japan proved a trio of grippingly eerie tales from Lafcadio Hearn under the title *Kwaidan*.

That there are too many film festivals is painfully clear: there are not enough quality pictures even from global supplies to satisfy first-showing requirements. There are now 175 of these international get-togethers.

As this report must suggest and for all the obvious changes from "the good old days," films (at higher prices, granted) are more booming than ever. By October, Department of Commerce figures forecast that the year's national film income would be over 1965's record-setting $1,205,000,000. Chipping away at the old "downtown" haunts, hundreds of new theaters pop up in easy-to-park-at shopping centers. Nothing reflects this motion-pictures boom more cogently than a year which found Wall Street arranging corporate alliances between the film companies and the food, oil and banking corporations.

MUSEUMS. Hardly a region in the United States escaped the sounds of the building of new museums or museum additions during 1966. There was a heavy increase in donors of funds and works of art. Affluence of the arts was evident everywhere. Despite the affluence, however, authorities did not expect an all-time high in 1966 construction to match that of 1964, when almost $75 million went into new buildings or new additions for museums.

East-coast museum construction was highlighted by the new location and facilities of the Whitney Museum of American Art, in New York City. Gifts and pledges of over $6.5 million virtually covered the cost of land and construction of the cantilevered granite building.

On the U.S. west coast, San Franciscans saw the opening of the $2,725,000 home for the Avery Brundage Collection of Oriental Art—a collection judged by many as the finest in the Western Hemisphere. The new 3-story Wing for Asian Art at the M. H. de Young Memorial Museum opened in June. Despite its size (100,000 square feet), less than ¼ of the near-legendary collection for which the building was designed can be displayed.

Other construction for art museums included work at: the Philadelphia Museum of Art ($445,000); the Memorial Art Gallery of the University of Rochester ($1.9 million); the Detroit Institute of Arts ($3,785,000); and dozens of others.

Science, not to be outdone by art, came in for its share of new construction when the Rochester Museum Association (New York) unveiled plans for a $1.4 million computerized space and star center, the Strasenburgh Planetarium, to be opened early in 1968.

Grants to museums from private foundations and organizations continued to increase, and ranged from money for new construction to money to salvage important photographic archives threatened with loss from aging.

Despite the seemingly easy surge of money for museums, the present economic distress of most U.S. museums remains serious. The Boston Museum of Fine Arts, for instance, ended a 50-year-old tradition of free admission. In July 1966 the Museum began charging all museum visitors an admission fee. Increased operating costs and mounting annual deficits have not been overcome by gifts and grants.

Typical of a large museum, the Boston Museum of Fine Arts' expenses include the costs of school for 1,200 students; maintenance of a reference library of over 150,000 volumes, a science laboratory and a corps of technicians for the preservation and restoration of works

Whitney Museum of American Art

Fourth floor gallery of New York City's new Whitney Museum of American Art.

of art; and an education program serving over 130,000 school children annually. In addition, substantial sums must be spent annually on repairs, improvements and maintenance. The cost of exhibiting and preserving the Museum's treasures is approximately $6,600 per day. In addition to this type of museum operating cost, museums must set aside money for acquisitions, salary commitments and utilities.

Today, approximately 25 per cent of U.S. museums charge admission fees ranging from 25 cents to $3.00. The number of museums charging admission fees increases each year. Thirty years ago, only 12 per cent of the museums in the United States charged fees.

During 1966 the U.S. Congress considered and passed a national museums bill. The bill was signed into law by President Johnson in October, and it goes a long way toward providing museums with funds needed for publications relating to the profession, training centers for personnel, and funds for in-service traveling and seminar programs. Such an act becomes official recognition by the government that U.S. museums are, in effect, educational institutions as well as guardians of the best of man's creative efforts.

N. CARL BAREFOOT, JR.
Director of Publications
AMERICAN ASSOCIATION OF MUSEUMS

New Wing for Asian Art at the M. H. de Young Memorial Museum in San Francisco.

M. H. de Young Memorial Museum

MUSIC

By WILLIAM BENDER
Music Critic
WORLD JOURNAL TRIBUNE

Few would dispute that the year 1966 belonged to the Metropolitan Opera. The Met reached one of the great turning points in its history, and quite understandably stole the show. It was also a good year for opera in general: the New York City Opera continued to emerge from the shadow of its older sister; new American operas by Carlisle Floyd, Gunther Schuller and Douglas Moore made strong impressions; and the other U.S. opera companies entrenched themselves deeper into the musical life of their country. Finally, in the nonoperatic sphere, the Ford Foundation enriched American symphonic life with a grant of $80.2 million to 61 orchestras in 33 states, the District of Columbia, and Puerto Rico.

The Metropolitan Opera. All year long, the Met was on the move. It traveled to Europe for the first time in half a century. It went to Newport, R.I., and linked arms with a jazz festival. It moved from its hallowed but antiquated old house at New York City's Broadway and 39th Street to a spectacularly equipped new home in Lincoln Center, 25 blocks north. In a field where glamour counts high, the old girl showed emphatically that she was still queen of all she surveyed, despite her 83 years. She had her artistic failures, but her triumphs were enormous, and in the final summing up, no one could deny that it was a year to remember for a long while to come.

Of the many big nights, the biggest was that of Sept. 16, when the doors of the new house—a $45.7 million structure—were formally opened with the premiere of an American opera commissioned for the occasion, Samuel Barber's *Antony and Cleopatra.* Alas, the opera was not a success. Barber, whose *Vanessa* had been done previously by the Met, had come up with a score that, unfortunately, lacked romance and passion, and that skimmed the surface of the love affair portrayed. In addition, Franco Zeffirelli's sets and costumes were gaudy and overdone. To be sure, one could only admire the sight of Cleopatra's barge sailing down a silver Nile almost the full 146 feet of the combined front and rear stages, and it was impressive to see the great Sphinx spin this way and that. But it was all simply too much, and the music, despite effective moments like Antony's suicide, was no justification for such largess.

The failure of *Antony* did not prevent a brilliant audience of 3,800—headed by Mrs. Lyndon B. Johnson, and sprinkled heavily with elite of society and the arts—from making a social success of the affair, or from enjoying the singing of Leontyne Price as Cleopatra, Justino Diaz as Antony, and Jess Thomas as Caesar.

Nor could it mar the triumph of the new Metropolitan Opera House itself. In a companion article, Herman Krawitz, assistant general manager of the Met, gives a detailed description of the structure. It should be sufficient to report here that the auditorium's sight lines are almost uniformly excellent, and that the acoustics—about which many fingers had been crossed—meet just about everyone's standards of what a good opera house ought to sound like. The orchestral blend is full and rich; the voices vault clearly off the stage.

As for the technical plant, just as *Antony* showed to what excesses it could be put, so the Met's first production ever of Richard Strauss' long, complex *Die Frau ohne Schatten* showed the wonders of which the house is capable. The work hops repeatedly between the realms of the real, the make-believe and the supernatural, and requires exceptional technical facility. Many hailed the stunning production as the most beautiful in the company's history. Karl Bohm conducted an exemplary cast headed by Leonie Rysanek, Christa Ludwig, Irene Dalis, Walter Berry. *Die Frau* was designed by Robert O'Hearn and directed by Nathaniel Merrill.

Of the two other new productions with which the Met opened the 1966–67 season, Amilcare Ponchielli's *La Gioconda* was a sparkling, fun-filled treatment of a less-than-momentous opera, but Giuseppe Verdi's *La Traviata* was disappointing because of Cecil Beaton's drab sets and costumes and a lackluster performance.

Quite a contrast was the evening of April 16, when the Met closed its old house. Dozens of legendary singers and conductors performed for an audience who paid as much as $200 a ticket. The faithful cheered and applauded, and then they wept openly with nostalgia when the singing stopped at 1:20 A.M. the next day.

At the conclusion of the regular season and spring tour, the Met went to Paris for a week's participation in the international festival Théâtre des Nations, directed by Jean-Louis Barrault and Madeleine Renaud. Starting May 31, the Met gave three performances each of Mozart's *Le Nozze di Figaro* and Rossini's *Il Barbiere di Siviglia.* It was the Met's way of honoring its hosts, since both operas had been based on plays by the French 18th-century playwright Beaumarchais. But although the Met's intentions were of the best, the productions were

FORD FOUNDATION GRANTS

MAJOR ORCHESTRAS
(budgets over $250,000 a year)

Atlanta Symphony	$1,750,000
Baltimore Symphony	1,750,000
Boston Symphony	2,500,000
Buffalo Philharmonic	1,750,000
Chicago Symphony	2,500,000
Cincinnati Symphony	2,500,000
Cleveland Orchestra	2,500,000
Dallas Symphony	2,500,000
Denver Symphony	1,750,000
Detroit Symphony*	1,500,000
Houston Symphony	2,500,000
Indianapolis Symphony	2,500,000
Kansas City Philharmonic	1,750,000
Los Angeles Philharmonic	2,500,000
Minneapolis Symphony	2,500,000
National Symphony (D.C.)	2,500,000
New Orleans Philharmonic	1,750,000
New York Philharmonic*	1,500,000
Philadelphia Orchestra	2,500,000
Pittsburgh Symphony	2,500,000
Rochester Philharmonic	1,750,000
St. Louis Symphony	2,500,000
San Antonio Symphony	1,750,000
San Francisco Symphony	2,500,000
Seattle Symphony	1,750,000

OTHER ORCHESTRAS

Orchestra	Amount	Orchestra	Amount
American Symphony (N.Y.)	1,500,000	North Carolina Symphony (Chapel Hill)	1,000,000
Birmingham Symphony	800,000	Oakland Symphony	1,350,000
Brooklyn Philharmonica	325,000	Oklahoma City Symphony	750,000
Columbus Symphony	600,000	Omaha Symphony	500,000
Festival Orchestra (N.Y.)	425,000	Phoenix Symphony	850,000
Florida Symphony (Orlando)	600,000	Portland (Ore.) Symphony	1,250,000
Fort Wayne Philharmonic	325,000	Puerto Rico Symphony	375,000
Hartford Symphony	1,350,000	Rhode Island Philharmonic (Providence)	500,000
Honolulu Symphony	1,100,000		
Hudson Valley Philharmonic (Poughkeepsie)	325,000	Richmond Symphony	650,000
Jacksonville Symphony	325,000	Sacramento Symphony	700,000
Kalamazoo Symphony	600,000	San Diego Symphony	600,000
Little Orchestra (N.Y.)	425,000	Shreveport Symphony	425,000
Louisville Orchestra	700,000	Syracuse Symphony	1,000,000
Memphis Symphony	500,000	Toledo Orchestra	650,000
Milwaukee Symphony**	1,250,000	Tulsa Philharmonic	600,000
Nashville Symphony	700,000	Utah Symphony	1,500,000
New Haven Symphony	600,000	Wichita Symphony	650,000
New Jersey Symphony (Newark)	650,000		

not. The reception inside the 1,200-seat Odéon-Théâtre de France had typical French volatility, but unfortunately in the wrong direction. The critics were unkind, and the audience booed more than one singer. As Harold C. Schonberg, who was there, wrote later in *The New York Times:* "It was clear that a terrible miscalculation had been made."

More successful, however, were the concert performances the Met gave of *La Bohème, Carmen, Lucia di Lammermoor,* and *Aïda* at Newport, in exchange for which the Newport Jazz Festival sent some of its best talent to the Met's summer home at New York City's Lewisohn Stadium. And, backtracking a bit, there was nothing wrong with the roster of impressive new artists introduced by the Met during 1965–66. They included singers such as Mirella Freni, Grace Bumbry, Montserrat Caballe, Nicolai Ghiaurov, James King, Sherrill Milnes, and Gianni Raimondi, as well as conductors Lamberto Gardelli, Zubin Mehta, and Francesco Molinari-Pradelli.

Other U.S. Opera Companies. The New York City Opera made news Feb. 22 when it opened shop in its new home, the New York State Theater, also in Lincoln Center. The occasion was enhanced by the resounding success of the company's production of a new opera from Argentina, Alberto Ginastera's *Don Rodrigo.* The work is a bold retelling of the story of the last of the Visigoth kings of Spain, and in mounting it the New York City Opera achieved the most ambitious undertaking in its 22-year history.

Although it was often stagy rather than theatrical, and though its use of the language of atonality was often repetitive and limited in vocabulary, *Don Rodrigo* did manage to consolidate many of the recent developments in contemporary composition. And that was something of immense importance for the world of music.

Of the New York City Opera's other new productions, outstanding were versions of Handel's *Julius Caesar* and Mozart's *The Magic Flute* during the fall season.

Elsewhere, the San Francisco and Chicago Lyric Opera Companies continued at their old stands, but it was the smaller and newer companies that got the headlines. The Metropolitan Opera's national touring company, composed of young artists, successfully completed its first season, and launched a second Sept. 15 at Indianapolis, Ind., with a repertory including *La Bohème, The Marriage of Figaro, La Traviata* and Britten's *The Rape of Lucretia.*

The University of Kansas gave the world premiere April 28 of Douglas Moore's *Carry Nation,* another of the composer's pleasing, homespun studies of colorful personalities in American life. The New Orleans Opera gave

The Saratoga Performing Arts Center, Saratoga Springs, N.Y.

the first performance of Carlisle Floyd's *Markheim* (based on a Robert Louis Stevenson story), which was found to be skillful and exciting.

On Feb. 23, the Hartt College of Music in Hartford, Conn., gave the American premiere of Werner Egk's generation-old *Peer Gynt*, and on April 6 the Opera Company of Boston gave the first staging in the United States of an even older work, Rameau's *Hippolyte et Aricie*. The latter event attracted a considerable amount of advance attention, but the production turned out to be unstylistic and disappointing. What was apparently the first New York staging of Mozart's *Idomeneo* was given Oct. 29 by the Brooklyn Academy Opera Theater Company under the direction of Boris Goldovsky.

European Opera and Festivals. While American companies were relying heavily on European composers for the bulk of their repertory, it took the Hamburg State Opera to give the premiere of *The Visitation* by Gunther Schuller, one of America's brightest younger composers. The work showed Schuller's continuing predilection for combining jazz and classical

elements, and the reception in Hamburg was most cordial. There was even talk of presenting the work during the company's forthcoming visit to the United States.

Another American to conquer Europe was Leonard Bernstein, who made a big hit in March with readings of Gustav Mahler in London. He also impressed Austria with a scintillating *Falstaff* at the Vienna Staatsoper. It starred Dietrich Fischer-Dieskau and Regina Resnik.

Salzburg gave a good reception to Hans Werner Henze's *The Bassarids* with libretto based by W.H. Auden and Chester Kallman on Euripides' *The Bacchae*. And the 16th postwar Bayreuth Festival came up with two exciting new conductors—the Frenchman Pierre Boulez, who led an unorthodox, but stimulating *Parsifal,* and the Hungarian Carl Mellis, who led *Tannhäuser.*

Benjamin Britten's current fascination with Japanese mystery plays was reflected by his *The Burning Fiery Furnace,* given its premiere in June at the Aldeburgh Festival, and his *Curlew River,* given its American premiere at

View of orchestra and balcony at Jesse H. Jones Hall, Houston, Tex.

the Caramoor Festival, Katonah, N.Y., the same month.

Contemporary Music Scene. The contemporary music scene was highlighted by a three-day festival of the music of Carl Ruggles at Bowdoin College in Maine. The Boston Symphony Orchestra under Jean Martinon climaxed the festival with a performance of Ruggles' *Sun Treader.* The entire event, and the distinguished audience it drew, indicated that Ruggles, now 90 and still the toughest of rugged individualists, may at last be coming into his own.

Elsewhere, Erich Leinsdorf and the Boston Symphony set a January date for the premiere of Elliott Carter's new, eagerly awaited Piano Concerto, commissioned by pianist Jacob Lateiner in conjunction with the Ford Foundation. Leonard Bernstein was commissioned to write a major "dramatic work" for the John F. Kennedy Center for the Performing Arts, and Virgil Thomson was commissioned to write an opera on the life of Lord Byron for the Metropolitan Opera.

After a two-year hiatus, the Pulitzer Prize in Music was reinstated. The winner was Leslie Bassett, a professor of music at the University of Michigan, and the work honored was his *Variations for Orchestra,* which had been performed by the Philadelphia Orchestra.

The revival of interest in some of the secondary composers of the Romantic and post-Romantic eras—Busoni, Alkan, Dussek—continued with the belated New York premiere of Busoni's Piano Concerto, a work of more than an hour's duration with a finale that includes a male chorus singing the text of Oehlenschlager's *Aladdin.* The Busoni Society sponsored the actual premiere in Carnegie Hall on Jan. 26, in which Gunnar Johansen was soloist with the American Symphony Orchestra. Pietro Scarpini came along the next month with George Szell and the Cleveland Orchestra and did it again.

Other new homes for the performing arts continued to open. On Oct. 2, the $6.7 million Jesse H. Jones Hall was opened as the new home of the Houston Symphony, Houston Grand Opera and the Houston Ballet Foundation. Sir John Barbirolli led the first concert the next day. In July, the Saratoga Performing Arts Center opened its doors as the new summer home of the Philadelphia Orchestra and the New York City Ballet.

The New York Philharmonic honored composer Igor Stravinsky with a three-week festival in July at Philharmonic Hall in Lincoln Center. Leonard Bernstein, music director of the orchestra, Ernest Ansermet, Robert Craft, Lukas

Igor Stravinsky conducts a rehearsal.

Foss, Kyril Kondrashin, and Stravinsky himself were the conductors. Mr. Foss supervised the entire program. The event reached a bit far at times in its attempt to relate Stravinsky's heritage to other composers, but there was no denying the unprecedented—and well deserved —nature of the event itself, or the impact of the final concert at which Stravinsky led an eloquent, marvelously controlled reading of his *Symphony of Psalms.*

Bernstein announced in November that he would retire as music director of the New York Philharmonic when his contract expires in 1969.

Labor disputes marred the activities of several orchestras, most notably the Metropolitan Opera orchestra and the Philadelphia Orchestra. The Met reached a settlement opening night, and Rudolf Bing announced it dramatically from the stage. But the Philadelphia had to cancel portions of its early season.

Finally, there was the Ford Foundation's huge $80.2 million grant to 61 U.S. symphony orchestras. It was the largest known act of philanthropy in the arts, and it was expected— through matching provisions—to pump an exhilarating $195 million into the country's symphonic life in the next 10 years. Some 14 major orchestras received $2.5 million each. That was top amount. The grants ranged on down to $325,000 each for five smaller organizations.

MUSIC: POPULAR

By JOHN S. WILSON
Free-Lance Music Writer

The predominant sound in popular music in 1966 was the bright, crisp, jaunty blend of Mexican mariachi and American honky-tonk put together by Herb Alpert and the Tijuana Brass. Alpert, a trumpeter, made his first record in 1962, using a home tape machine on which he dubbed in two trumpet parts himself, and then added sounds taped at a bullring in Tijuana, Mexico. Alpert's way of playing such catchy tunes as "The Lonely Bull," "Mexican Shuffle" and "Whipped Cream" did not begin to attract wide attention until 1965. Then the appeal of the Brass built up such momentum that they rolled into 1966 sweeping everything in popular music before them.

During the year, the 7-man group had 6 long-playing discs on the market, each of which was awarded a gold record (which signifies $1 million worth in sales). The records together added up to more than $11 million in sales.

Big 1966 sound: Herb Alpert and the Tijuana Brass.
Wide World

Inevitably, the Tijuana Brass sound was copied assiduously, even by as unlikely an ensemble as the Glenn Miller Orchestra (which managed to produce an attractive hybrid by mixing the Miller sound with the Brass sound and the cool jazz clarinet of the band's current leader, Buddy De Franco). The extent of the Tijuana Brass influence in 1966 could be heard in "A Taste of Honey," which had been a consistently popular tune for several years, usually played in a moody, atmospheric fashion. The Brass attacked it briskly, and midway everything stopped for several loud, tempo-setting bangs on a bass drum. Alpert had intended to delete these bangs from the recorded tape (they were used to get the band back on the beat after a slowdown) but they were left in, and all through 1966 they turned up in many other versions of "A Taste of Honey."

Besides Herb Alpert's American-Mexican musical potpourri, other blends cropped up during the year: raga-rock, which combined rock 'n' roll with an interest in Indian music stimulated by the sitar playing of Ravi Shankar, was espoused by the Byrds; folk-baroque took aim at both a revived following for baroque music and the established folk-music audience.

For two Sinatras—father Frank and daughter Nancy—1966 was a very good year. Frank Sinatra's career had been moving along quite satisfactorily, but his singing "Strangers in the Night" lifted him to a peak of singing popularity that he had not enjoyed for many years. Meanwhile Nancy was emerging as a potent singing star in her own right with "These Boots Are Made for Walking."

The war in Vietnam produced its first successful inspirational song, "The Ballad of the Green Berets," written and sung by S/Sgt Barry Sadler. But the most ubiquitous song of the year was the Academy Award winner, "The Shadow of Your Smile," written by Johnny Mandel and Paul Francis Webster for *The Sandpiper*.

One of the oddities of the year was the popular success of a West Coast housewife, billed simply as "Mrs. Miller," who sang pop hits with all the dire inaccuracy and blithe assurance that once made Florence Foster Jenkins a comic favorite of followers of classical music.

The Beatles and the Rolling Stones, each of which had three gold-record discs during the year, continued to hold their audiences. At the same time, a new group, the Monkees, was successfully launched both on recordings ("Last Train to Clarksville"), and a television series in which they followed the madcap trail the Beatles had blazed in their films.

MUSIC: THE NEW METROPOLITAN OPERA HOUSE

By HERMAN E. KRAWITZ
Assistant General Manager
METROPOLITAN OPERA

The new Metropolitan Opera House, the towering architectural triumph of Wallace K. Harrison, looms majestically on the horizon of New York City's Lincoln Center. The house's facade was designed so that a panoramic view of the romantic interior—with its upward-circling double staircase, glistening chandeliers and festive murals—could be viewed by passersby; so that those within the sweeping garnet-and-gold foyer, or at any one of the upper terraces, might look down upon the promenade and out through the arched windows to the Lincoln Center Plaza and city beyond.

Mr. Harrison's wish for an auditorium that would be free of columns and yet able to seat 3,800 persons led to the creation of 5 bays and 5 cantilevered arches soaring 96 feet above the plaza, forming barrel vaults between the proscenium arch in the auditorium and the east facade of the building. One hundred and fifty-six glass panels, randomly dispersed in a bronze grid, enhance the contours of supportive travertine columns. Continuous surfaces of closely spaced, precast concrete mullions envelop the north, south and west sides to the rhythmic reinforcement of bronze-colored glass panels.

Four times larger in cubic measure than the old Metropolitan Opera House on Broadway, the new Metropolitan has 16 times more square footage on the ground surface, with a length of 451 feet (the length of a 45-story skyscraper laid on its side). The width at the stage end of the house is 234 feet, the front facade 175 feet; the building rises to a height of 96 feet.

Because of the multitude of shapes in the auditorium, it would have been prohibitive from the standpoints of time and cost to execute the entire building in steel. Thus, the building was designed in two parts: the reinforced-concrete section east of the proscenium for the auditorium, lobby, promenade, restaurant and lounge areas; and the structural-steel section west of the proscenium for the extensive backstage facilities—scenic construction, storage, workshops, studios, rehearsal halls and offices.

A majestic grand staircase, originating on the concourse and extending up to the grand tier, records a masterful use of volume and space. This sculptured free form—molded of concrete, bordered by Italian Cremo marble, capped with hammered bronze rails and warmed by carpet of opera-house red—provides a series of subtly changing interior and exterior vistas, arrested and empowered by a pair of Chagall murals, with one Lehmbruck and two Maillol sculptures nearby.

The Auditorium

Approximately one third of the present house is occupied by the auditorium, whereas the auditorium in the old Met took up two thirds of that house's space. The height (front to rear), proscenium opening and width of the front portion of the new house's modified horseshoe are about the same as those of the first Metropolitan. A slight increase in seating capacity (179 more seats) and volume parallels a decrease in the distance between the rail of the orchestra pit and the face of the boxes. This realignment significantly contributes to the feeling of intimacy achieved in Mr. Harrison's hall, "built like a violin of wood."

Within the clearly contemporary mood of the auditorium, an ambience of warmth and grace, of serenity and splendor has been created. Carefully chosen materials of the traditional red, gold and ivory hues enrich Mr. Harrison's structural gem, replacing the ornate decorative features of the old house. The gold of the great curtain is echoed in a 72-foot-high, shell-shaped ceiling covered (except for the dome) with 23-karat-gold-leaf burnished concentric petals. Uniquely, the auditorium is completely isolated from its shell and therefore from the building itself, with the ceiling suspended on spring hangers, and the floor resting on a cork cushion. This technique, devised to eliminate extraneous sounds, has been extensively utilized throughout the building so that groups rehearsing simultaneously will not interfere with each other. The sunburst sprays of the crystal chandeliers in the auditorium (diameter of 17 feet) and grand foyer are continued not only by their own satellite clusters (20 in the former, 10 in the latter) but in all sources of illumination.

Lounges, Restaurants

Comfortably outfitted lounges and office areas are designated for members of the press. Public lounges have also been installed so that latecomers, particularly, can view a performance on closed-circuit television until admission into the auditorium is permitted. Two bars and three luxurious dining areas—the Opera Café on the plaza level, the Grand Tier Restaurant and the Top of the Met Restaurant at the pinnacle—add to the leisurely pleasure of opera going.

Main Stage and Backstage

Dimensions of the main stage (103 by 90 feet) are approximately the same as the first Met's. But additional side and rear stages, which can be wheeled onto the main platform replete with scenic arrangements, provide a composite area 6 times greater than that of the old house. Three double-decked hydraulic elevators on the main stage permit a set stored below to be raised to position when the scene on the main stage has served its purpose. The 7 sections of the main stage which can be terraced or interlocked in various combinations are also equipped with 52 trapdoors and 2 movable table lifts for transporting artists up to and below the stage. A labyrinth of electrical and mechanical systems supports this intricate stage complex.

The backstage world is also considerably larger than that of the original Metropolitan Opera House. The extent to which creature comforts have been accommodated in the dressing rooms, lounges and offices for each member of the company, staff and crew is reflected in the rooms assigned to the ballet and chorus. In these rooms, each person has an individual unit consisting of a makeup desk, locker and

Louis Mélançon

Above: Act II, scene 4, *Antony and Cleopatra*, Samuel Barber's opera that opened the new Met. Below: view of the house's twisting stairways, seen from top level of lobby.

Michael Rougier, ''LIFE'' magazine © Time Inc.

costume rack, with readily accessible lounge, rest-room and shower facilities for each group.

Of the 20 rehearsal rooms that exist (in addition to the 4 stage areas), 3 are of such substantial size that simulated stage performances can be enacted on them. If a marathon were planned, it would be possible to schedule 24 rehearsals at one time in various parts of the house, although such a tour de force was not part of the management's intention. Storage facilities, sufficient as repository for approximately three quarters of the season's repertory, are arranged so that delicate and intricate constructions such as the Pyramid and Sphinx in *Antony and Cleopatra* and the boat in *La Gioconda* need not be dismantled.

Backstage is also home for the scenic, electrical, prop, carpentry, tailor, wig and makeup shops. An electronic carillon system, a two-manual and pedal organ console, and an elaborate intercommunication system (of telephones, radios, speakers and closed-circuit television), which reaches every room in the house, are a few of the many other features of the updated backstage resources.

It would be a circus indeed if all available equipment were to be used in any one performance. Judicious selectivity in conjunction with artistic conviction can, however, provide unbounded opportunities for the creative forces involved on any one project.

Wide World

Tanzania President Nyerere greets President Nasser.

NASSER, GAMAL ABDEL. The President of the United Arab Republic remained the Arab world's most dominant figure in 1966, but his position was undermined by events at home and abroad.

The strongest challenge came from King Faisal of Saudi Arabia, an old foe with a new banner: "Islamic Solidarity." Faisal's apparent success in consolidating conservative Arab leadership was bitterly denounced by Nasser as an attack against the socialist regimes. The Egyptian leader caused cancellation of an Arab summit meeting rather than sit down with the Saudi monarch and his ally, King Hussein of Jordan. Faisal, meanwhile, moved ahead with his own plans for an Islamic summit meeting in Mecca in 1967.

Nasser renewed ties with Syria during the year, healing a breach created by Syria's withdrawal from the United Arab Republic in 1961 because of Egyptian domination. The Cairo and the Damascus governments, apparently brought together by a common ally, the Soviet Union, signed a military pact and agreed to take steps "toward political coordination."

Yemen remained the Cairo leader's thorniest foreign problem. A truce signed with Faisal, who has backed the Royalist forces in Yemen against the Nasser-aided Republican forces, remained in effect but more than 50,000 Egyptian soldiers stayed in the area adding to the drain on the Egyptian economy.

Nasser's greatest problem at home was economic. A visit in May by Soviet Premier Aleksei N. Kosygin was a personal triumph for the host, Mr. Nasser, but it failed to produce any noteworthy economic aid. American assistance, similarly, seemed to be drying up.

Nasser remained popular at home, although he was not free of the plots characteristic of the Middle East. Twenty Egyptian Army officers were reported at year's end to have been arrested on charges of plotting against him. Earlier in the year nearly 400 members of the Muslim Brotherhood, an extremist religious group, were arrested and charged with trying to revive the banned organization or plotting to overthrow the Government. Some were hanged.

JAMES FERON
Middle East Staff, THE NEW YORK TIMES

NATIONAL SCIENCE FOUNDATION. The U.S. government agency, the National Science Foundation, supports basic-research projects (primarily at colleges and universities), seeks better methods for the dissemination of scientific information and promotes improved science education in the United States.

In basic research during 1966, synthesis of a self-duplicating entity—ribonucleic acid, commonly known as RNA—was reported by a scientist at the University of Illinois. A Dartmouth College geological team discovered 720-million-year-old animal fossils that may solve the mystery of how advanced forms of life evolved on earth. A University of North Carolina scientist reported on his study of a possible new chemical catalyst that could play a vital role in the manufacture of fertilizer, a necessary tool for the production of foodstuffs.

Aided by an NSF grant, Carnegie Institution of Washington scientists have devised a new device that intensifies telescopic images, thereby enabling astronomers to study and photograph stellar objects, such as quasars, with greater speed and accuracy. Researchers at a number of institutions studied hormones and their related areas with the idea of obtaining a better understanding of chemical communicators.

During the summer of 1966, 23 separate research teams pooled their facilities and talents to concentrate on hailstorms in the Great Plains area. Project Whitetop, under the direction of the University of Chicago, studied the role of ice nuclei in the formation of precipitation in the Minnesota area. Results of this project indicate that such precipitation is heavily influenced by natural seeding from ice-crystal showers originating in high-level cloud decks.

NSF continued to provide fellowships for graduate students; institutes for elementary, secondary, and college teachers; seminars; research participation for undergraduates and high-ability secondary students. It also worked to improve science-course content.

NATIONAL SCIENCE FOUNDATION

GREAT BRITAIN

LIBERIA

Chet Reneson

NATIONS OF THE WORLD

Nation & Region	Population (in millions) [1]	Capital	Area—Sq. Mi. (approx.)	Heads of State & Government, Date Installed[3]
AFGHANISTAN, Cen. Asia	15.5	Kabul	250,000	Mohammed Záhir Shah, king—1933
				Mohammed Hashim Maiwandwal, premier—1965
ALBANIA, S.E. Europe	1.9	Tirana	11,097	Haxhi Lleshi, president of the presidium—1953
				Mehmet Shehu, premier—1954
ALGERIA, N. Africa	11.3	Algiers	846,124	Houari Boumedienne, president and prime minister—1965
ARGENTINA, S. America	22.7	Buenos Aires	1,084,359	Juan Carlos Ongania, president—1966
AUSTRALIA, S.W. Pacific	11.5	Canberra	2,948,366	Richard G. Casey, governor-general—1965
				Harold E. Holt, prime minister—1966
AUSTRIA, Cen. Europe	7.3	Vienna	32,375	Franz Jonas, president—1965
				Josef Klaus, chancellor—1964
BARBADOS, Caribbean	.246	Bridgetown	166	Errol W. Barrow, prime minister—1961
BELGIUM, W. Europe	9.5	Brussels	11,779	Baudouin I, king—1951
				Paul Vanden Boeynants, prime minister—1966
BHUTAN, Cen. Asia	.770	Tashi-Chho Punakha	18,000	Jigme Dorji Wangchuk, maharaja—1952
				Lhendup Dorji, prime minister—1964
BOLIVIA, S. America	3.7[2]	La Paz	412,777	René Barrientos, president—1966
BOTSWANA, S. Africa	.576[2]	Gaberones	222,000	Seretse Khama, president—1966
BRAZIL, S. America	83.9[2]	Brasilia	3,287,842	Artur da Costa e Silva, president-elect—1966
BULGARIA, S.E. Europe	8.2	Sofia	42,796	Georgi Traikov, president of the presidium—1964
				Todor Zhivkov, premier—1962
BURMA, S. E. Asia	24.7	Rangoon	261,757	Ne Win, chairman of the council of ministers—1962
BURUNDI, E. Africa	2.8	Usumbura	10,747	Michel Micombero, president—1966
CAMBODIA, S.E. Asia	6.3	Pnompenh	69,900	Prince Norodom Sihanouk, chief of state—1960
CAMEROUN, W. Africa	5.2	Yaoundé	193,681	Ahmadou Ahidjo, president—1960
CANADA, N. America	19.6	Ottawa	3,845,144	George Vanier, governor-general—1959
				Lester B. Pearson, prime minister—1963
CENTRAL AFRICAN REPUBLIC, Cen. Africa	1.4	Bangui	240,000	Jean Bedel Bokassa, president and premier—1966
CEYLON, S. Asia	11.2	Colombo	25,332	William Gopallawa, governor-general—1962
				Dudley Senanayake, premier—1965
CHAD, N. Cen. Africa	3.4	Fort-Lamy	485,750	François Tombalbaye, president—1960
CHILE, S. America	8.6	Santiago	286,396	Eduardo Frei Montalva, president—1964
CHINA, REPUBLIC (TAIWAN), Far East	12.7[2]	Taipei	13,886	Chiang Kai-shek, president—1950
				C. K. Yen, premier—1963
CHINA, PEOPLE'S REPUBLIC, Far East	700	Peking	3,800,000	Liu Shao-chi, chairman—1959
				Chou En-lai, premier—1949
COLOMBIA, S. America	17.8	Bogotá	439,828	Carlos Lleras Restrepo, president—1966
CONGO, DEM. REP. OF THE, S. Cen. Africa	16.0[2]	Kinshasa	904,754	Joseph Mobutu, president—1965
CONGO, REPUBLIC OF, W. Africa	.846	Brazzaville	134,749	Alphonse Massemba-Debat, president—1963
				Ambroise Noumazaly, premier—1966
COSTA RICA, Cen. America	1.5[2]	San José	19,650	José Joaquin Trejos, president—1966
CUBA, Caribbean	7.8[2]	Havana	44,218	Osvaldo Dorticós Torrado, president—1959
				Fidel Castro, premier—1959
CYPRUS, Middle East	.598[2]	Nicosia	3,572	Archbishop Makarios, president—1960
CZECHOSLOVAKIA, E. Cen. Europe	14.2	Prague	49,354	Antonin Novotny, president—1957
				Josef Lenart, premier—1963
DAHOMEY, W. Africa	2.4	Porto-Novo	45,560	Christophe Soglo, head of government—1965
DENMARK, N.W. Europe	4.8	Copenhagen	16,576	Frederik IX, king—1947
				Jens Otto Krag, prime minister—1962
DOMINICAN REPUBLIC, Caribbean	3.8[2]	Santo Domingo	19,129	Joaquin Balaguer, president—1966

[1]1965 estimate   [2]1966 estimate   [3]As of Dec. 31, 1966.

NATIONS OF THE WORLD

ETHIOPIA

TAIWAN

BRAZIL

Nation & Region	Population (in millions)[1]	Capital	Area—Sq. Mi. (approx.)	Heads of State & Government, Date Installed[3]
ECUADOR, S. America	5.2	Quito	108,478	Otto Arosemena Gomez, provisional president—1966
EL SALVADOR, Cen. America	2.9	San Salvador	13,176	Julio A. Rivera, president—1962
ETHIOPIA, N.E. Africa	22.6	Addis Ababa	395,000	Haile Selassie, emperor—1930
				Aklilou Abte Wold, premier—1966
FINLAND, N. Europe	4.6[2]	Helsinki	130,091	U. K. Kekkonen, president—1956
				Rafael Paasio, premier—1966
FRANCE, W. Europe	49.2[2]	Paris	212,659	Charles de Gaulle, president—1959
				Georges Pompidou, prime minister—1962
GABON, W. Cen. Africa	.462	Libreville	103,089	Léon M'ba, president—1960
GAMBIA, W. Africa	.330	Bathurst	4,000	John Paul, governor-general—1965
				D. K. Jawara, premier—1965
GERMAN DEMOCRATIC REPUBLIC (EAST GERMANY), N. Cen. Europe	17.0	East Berlin	41,635	Walter Ulbricht, chairman—1960
				Willi Stoph, premier—1964
GERMANY, FED. REPUBLIC (WEST GERMANY), N. Cen. Europe	57.1	Bonn	95,913	Heinrich Lübke, president—1959
				Kurt Georg Kiesinger, chancellor—1966
GHANA, W. Africa	7.7	Accra	92,100	Joseph A. Ankrah, chairman, National Liberation Council—1966
GREAT BRITAIN, W. Europe	54.4	London	94,279	Elizabeth II, queen—1952
				Harold Wilson, prime minister—1964
GREECE, S.E. Europe	8.5	Athens	51,182	Constantine II, king—1964
				Ioannis Paraskevopoulos, premier—1966
GUATEMALA, Cen. America	4.4	Guatemala City	42,042	Julio César Méndez Montenegro, president—1966
GUINEA, W. Africa	3.5	Conakry	95,350	Ahmed Sékou Touré, president—1958
GUYANA, S. America	.647	Georgetown	83,000	Forbes Burnham, prime minister—1965
HAITI, Caribbean	4.7	Port-au-Prince	10,714	François Duvalier, president—1957
HONDURAS, Cen. America	2.4[2]	Tegucigalpa	43,227	Oswaldo Lopez Arellano, president—1965
HUNGARY, E. Europe	10.2[2]	Budapest	35,902	István Dobi, president—1952
				Gyulla Kallai, premier—1965
ICELAND, N. Atlantic	.191	Reykjavik	39,758	Asgeir Asgeirsson, president—1952
				Bjarni Benediktsson, prime minister—1963
INDIA, S. Cen. Asia	483.0	New Delhi	1,262,275	S. Radhakrishnan, president—1962
				Indira Gandhi, prime minister—1966
INDONESIA, S.E. Asia	104.5	Jakarta	575,893	Sukarno, president—1949
				Suharto, chairman of the presidium—1966
IRAN, Middle East	23.4	Tehran	630,000	Mohammed Riza Pahlevi, shah—1941
				Amir Abass Hoveida, premier—1965
IRAQ, Middle East	7.2	Baghdad	168,040	Abdul Rahman Arif, president—1966
				Naji Taleb, premier—1966
IRELAND, W. Europe	2.9	Dublin	27,137	Eamon de Valera, president—1959
				Jack Lynch, prime minister—1966
ISRAEL, Middle East	2.6[2]	Jerusalem	8,050	Schneor Zalman Shazar, president—1963
				Levi Eshkol, premier—1963
ITALY, W. Europe	51.8[2]	Rome	116,224	Giuseppe Saragat, president—1964
				Aldo Moro, premier—1963
IVORY COAST, W. Africa	3.8	Abidjan	127,800	F. Houphouet-Boigny, president—1960
JAMAICA, Caribbean	1.8	Kingston	4,411	Clifford Campbell, governor-general—1965
				Alexander Bustamante, premier—1962
JAPAN, Far East	98.7[2]	Tokyo	140,680	Hirohito, emperor—1926
				Eisaku Sato, premier—1964
JORDAN, Middle East	2.0	Amman	37,000	Hussein I, king—1952
				Wasfi al-Tal, premier—1965
KENYA, E. Africa	9.4	Nairobi	224,960	Jomo Kenyatta, president—1964

SPAIN

CYPRUS

DOMINICAN REPUBLIC

Nation & Region	Population (in millions) [1]	Capital	Area—Sq. Mi. (approx.)	Heads of State & Government, Date Installed[3]
KOREA, PEOPLE'S DEM. REPUBLIC, Far East	12.1	Pyong Yang	47,861	Kim Il Sung, premier—1948
KOREA REPUBLIC, Far East	28.8[2]	Seoul	37,425	Chung Hee Park, president—1963
				Chung Il Kwon, premier—1964
KUWAIT, Middle East	.475	Kuwait	6,000	Sabah al-Salem al Sabah, head of state—1965
				Jaber al-Ahmed al-Jaber, premier—1965
LAOS, S.E. Asia	2.0	Vientiane	91,400	Savang Vatthana, king—1959
		Luang Prabang		Souvanna Phouma, premier—1962
LEBANON, Middle East	2.3	Beirut	3,927	Charles Hilu, president—1964
				Rashid Karami, prime minister—1966
LESOTHO, S. Africa	.745	Maseru	11,716	Moshoeshoe II, king—1966
				Leabua Jonathan, prime minister—1966
LIBERIA, W. Africa	1.1	Monrovia	43,000	William Tubman, president—1943
LIBYA, N. Africa	1.7[2]	Tripoli	680,000	Idriset Senussi I, king—1951
		Benghaz		Hussein Mazik, prime minister—1965
LIECHTENSTEIN, Cen. Europe	.018	Vaduz	62	Franz Josef II, prince—1938
				Gerald Batliner, prime minister—1962
LUXEMBOURG, W. Europe	.333	Luxembourg	999	Jean, grand duke—1964
				Pierre Werner, minister of state—1959
MALAGASY REPUBLIC, S.E. Africa	6.4	Tananarive	229,602	Philibert Tsiranana, president—1960
MALAWI, S.E. Africa	4.0	Zomba	47,949	Glyn S. Jones, governor-general—1965
				H. Kamuzu Banda, president—1966
MALAYSIA, S.E. Asia	9.4	Kuala Lumpur	129,000	Ismal Nasiruddin Shah, head of state—1965
				Tunku Abdul Rahman, premier—1963
MALDIVE ISLANDS, Off Cen. Asia	.098	Male	115	H. H. Al Amir Mohamed Farid Didi, sultan—1965
				Ibrahim Nasir, premier—1965
MALI, N.W. Africa	4.6	Bamako	465,000	Modibo Keita, president—1960
MALTA, Mediterranean	.316[2]	Valletta	122	Maurice Dorman, governor-general—1962
				Giorgio Borg Olivier, premier—1962
MAURITANIA, W. Africa	.920	Nouakchott	419,000	Moktar O. Daddah, premier and president—1958
MEXICO, N. America	42.2[2]	Mexico City	760,373	Gustavo Diaz Ordaz, president—1964
MONACO, W. Europe	.023	Monaco	0.578	Rainier III, prince—1949
MONGOLIAN PEOPLE'S REPUBLIC, E. Cen. Asia	1.1	Ulan Bator	1,000,000	Zhamsarangin Sambu, presidium president—1950
				Yumzhagin Tsedenbal, premier—1950
MOROCCO, N. Africa	13.3	Rabat	174,000	Hassan II, king—1961
MUSCAT AND OMAN, S.W. Asia	.565	Muscat	82,000	Said bin Taimur, sultan—1932
NEPAL, S. Cen. Asia	10.1	Katmandu	55,000	Mahendra Bir Bikram Shah Deva, king—1955
NETHERLANDS, N.W. Europe	12.4[2]	Amsterdam	15,800	Juliana, queen—1948
				Jelle Zijlstra, premier—1966
NEW ZEALAND, S.W. Pacific	2.7	Wellington	103,416	Bernard E. Fergusson, governor-general—1964
				K. J. Holyoake, prime minister—1960
NICARAGUA, Cen. America	1.7	Managua	57,145	Lorenzo Guerrero Gutierrez, president—1966
NIGER, W. Africa	3.4[2]	Niamey	489,000	Hamani Diori, president and premier—1960
NIGERIA, W. Africa	57.5	Lagos	357,000	Yakubu Gowon, chief of state—1966
NORWAY, N. Europe	3.7	Oslo	125,182	Olav V, king—1957
				Per Borten, prime minister—1965
PAKISTAN, S. Asia	102.9	Rawalpindi	365,907	M. Ayub Khan, president—1958
		Dacca		
PANAMA, Cen. America	1.3[2]	Panama	28,575	Marco A. Robles, president—1964
PARAGUAY, S. America	2.1[2]	Asunción	157,047	Alfredo Stroessner, president—1954
PERU, S. America	12.0[2]	Lima	514,059	Fernando Belaunde Terry, president—1963
PHILIPPINES, S.W. Pacific	33.5[2]	Quezon City	115,600	Ferdinand E. Marcos, president—1966
POLAND, E. Europe	31.6	Warsaw	120,359	Edward Ochab, chairman, council of state—1964
				Josef Cyrankiewicz, premier—1954

NEPAL

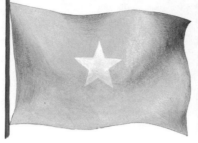

SOMALI REPUBLIC

CANADA

Nation & Region	Population (in millions) [1]	Capital	Area—Sq. Mi. (approx.)	Heads of State & Government, Date Installed[3]
PORTUGAL, W. Europe	9.2	Lisbon	35,409	A. D. Rodrigues Tomás, president—1958
				A. de Oliveira Salazar, premier—1932
RUMANIA, E. Europe	19.0	Bucharest	91,700	Chivu Stoica, chairman, state council—1965
				Ion Maurer, chairman, council of ministers—1961
RWANDA, Cen. Africa	3.1	Kigali	10,000	Gregoire Kayibanda, president and chief of government—1961
SAUDI ARABIA, Middle East	6.8	Riyadh	618,000	Faisal Ibn Abdul Aziz, king—1964
SENEGAL, W. Africa	3.5	Dakar	75,750	Léopold Senghor, president—1960
SIERRA LEONE, W. Africa	2.3	Freetown	27,968	Henry Boston, governor-general—1963
				Albert Margai, premier—1964
SINGAPORE, S.E. Asia	1.9	Singapore	224	Lee Kuan Yew, premier—1965
SOMALI REPUBLIC, E. Africa	2.5	Mogadishu	246,135	Aden Abdulla Osman, president—1961
				A. Haji Hussein, premier—1964
SOUTH AFRICA, S. Africa	17.9	Pretoria	472,359	Charles R. Swart, president—1961
		Capetown		Balthazar J. Vorster, prime minister—1966
SPAIN, W. Europe	31.9[2]	Madrid	194,232	Francisco Franco, chief of state—1938
SUDAN, N. Cen. Africa	13.9[2]	Khartoum	967,500	Ismail Al'Azhari, president, supreme council—1965
				Sayed Sadik al Mahdi, premier—1966
SWEDEN, N. Europe	7.8	Stockholm	173,423	Gustav VI, king—1950
				Tage Erlander, prime minister—1946
SWITZERLAND, W. Europe	5.9	Berne	15,944	Hans Schaffner, president—1966
SYRIA, Middle East	5.3	Damascus	66,063	Nureddin al-Attassi, chief of state—1966
				Yussef Zayen, premier—1966
TANZANIA, E. Africa	10.5	Dar es Salaam	363,000	Julius Nyerere, president—1964
THAILAND, S.E. Asia	30.6	Bangkok	198,000	Bhumbol Adulyadej (Rama IX), king—1946
				Thanom Kittikachorn, prime minister—1963
TOGO, W. Africa	1.7[2]	Lomé	22,000	Nicholas Grunitsky, president—1963
TRINIDAD AND TOBAGO, Caribbean	.975	Port of Spain	2,000	Solomon Hochoy, governor-general—1962
				Eric Williams, prime minister—1962
TUNISIA, N. Africa	4.7	Tunis	48,300	Habib Bourguiba, president—1957
TURKEY, Asia Minor and S.E. Europe	31.4	Ankara	296,185	Cevdet Sunay, president—1966
				Suleyman Demirel, prime minister—1965
UGANDA, E. Africa	7.6	Kampala	94,000	A. M. Obote, president—1966
U.S.S.R., Eurasia	231.9[2]	Moscow	8,600,000	Nikolai V. Podgorny, president of politburo—1965
				Aleksei N. Kosygin, premier—1964
UNITED ARAB REPUBLIC, N. Africa	29.6	Cairo	386,198	Gamal Abdel Nasser, president—1958
				Sidkyi Suliman, premier—1966
UNITED STATES, N. America	196.5[2]	Washington, D.C.	3,615,211	Lyndon B. Johnson, president—1963
UPPER VOLTA, W. Africa	4.9	Ouagadougou	105,900	Sangoule Lamizana, president—1966
URUGUAY, S. America	2.7[2]	Montevideo	72,152	Oscar D. Gestido, president-elect—1966
VATICAN CITY, W. Europe	.001	Vatican City	0.17	Paul VI, supreme pontiff—1963
VENEZUELA, S. America	9.0[2]	Caracas	352,141	Raul Leoni, president—1964
VIETNAM, DEMOCRATIC REPUBLIC, S.E. Asia	19.0	Hanoi	62,000	Ho Chi Minh, president—1945
				Pham Van Dong, premier—1955
VIETNAM, REPUBLIC, S.E. Asia	16.1	Saigon	65,000	Nguyen Cao Ky, premier—1965
				Nguyen Van Thieu, chief of state—1965
YEMEN, Middle East	5.0	Sana	75,000	Abdullah al-Salal, president and premier—1966
				Ahmed Mohammed Noman, premier—1965
YUGOSLAVIA, E. Europe	19.7[2]	Belgrade	99,000	Josip Broz Tito, president—1953
ZAMBIA, Cen. Africa	3.8	Lusaka	290,000	Kenneth Kaunda, president—1964

[1] 1965 estimate   [2] 1966 estimate   [3] As of Dec. 31, 1966

BARBADOS

Barbados, a Caribbean island of 166 square miles and close to 250,000 inhabitants, about 200 miles northeast of Trinidad and Tobago, became independent Nov. 30, after more than three centuries of British rule. The island is a constitutional monarchy within the British Commonwealth of Nations. Production of sugar accounts for over 90 per cent of the national income, and tourism is important, but the island faces grave problems of overpopulation and unemployment. Prime Minister Errol W. Barrow announced the country would seek membership in the Organization of American States. It was admitted to the UN Dec. 9.

BOTSWANA

Botswana, formerly Bechuanaland, joined the ranks of independent nations Sept. 30 after 81 years as a British protectorate. A landlocked country of 222,000 square miles and over half a million people, squeezed in between Rhodesia, South Africa and South West Africa, it has a republican Government headed by President Sir Seretse Khama. Its chief industries are cattle raising and dairying, but crop production is variable because of insufficient rainfall. The toughest problem of the new republic might prove to be its proximity to white-dominated South Africa and Rhodesia. Botswana remained within the Commonwealth of Nations; it was admitted to the UN Oct. 17.

GUYANA

Guyana, previously named British Guiana, became an independent nation May 26, after 152 years of colonial rule. Situated on the northeastern shore of South America, between Venezuela and Surinam, it has an area of 83,000 square miles and a population of 647,000. The country is a constitutional monarchy and a member of the Commonwealth of Nations. Forbes Burnham, a Negro, is the prime minister, but there is a powerful East Indian opposition party led by former Premier Cheddi B. Jagan. Agriculture and mining are the main industries, with sugar and bauxite the principal products. Guyana joined the UN Sept. 20.

LESOTHO

Lesotho was formerly called Basutoland. It became independent Oct. 4, having been a British colony for nearly a century. Tiny Lesotho is a mountainous area of 11,716 square miles, with a population of 745,000. It is completely encircled by South Africa, a fact that might present some future tensions. The chief economic activity is the raising of crops and livestock. Lesotho's King Moshoeshoe II was placed under house arrest late in 1966; Leabua Jonathan remained as prime minister. Lesotho was admitted to the UN Oct. 17.

NEBRASKA. Riots rocked Omaha's Near North Side, a Negro area, July 3–5. . . . In May, Sargent Shriver announced a Job Corps center for Lincoln. . . . Two major power failures struck Nebraska July 11. . . . The state conducted the most complete study of road and street needs in its history. . . . Plans proceeded for official centennial celebration commencing Mar. 1, 1967 (Statehood Day), and concluding Nov. 23, 1967. . . . N. T. Tiemann (R) defeated P. C. Sorensen for the governorship.

NEVADA. State legislation enabled University of Nevada regents to issue and sell certificates worth $5 million for school improvements. . . . Paul Laxalt (R) defeated incumbent Grant Sawyer for the governorship. . . . Contracts signed Oct. 27 entitle Southern California Edison Company to erect a $188 million thermal-electric plant on the Colorado River below Davis Dam.

NEW HAMPSHIRE. In November elections Gov. John W. King (D) won a third term, and Democratic Senator Thomas J. McIntyre was also reelected. Republicans, however, elected the state's 2 U.S. Representatives and regained control—4 to 1—of the Governor's Council. . . . Protesting the war in Vietnam, 50 pacifists marched on Portsmouth Naval Base on April 23.

NEW JERSEY. Gov. Richard J. Hughes signed a 3 per cent sales-tax bill Apr. 27. . . . Newark celebrated its tercentenary during 1966. . . . A Congressional redistricting bill passed on June 18. . . . A New Jersey Arts Council was established in July. . . . The Governor announced the start of a $30 million, three-year overhaul of railroad commuter service. . . . Clifford P. Case (R) retained his U.S. Senate seat in a victory over Warren W. Wilentz.

NEW MEXICO. In January the Federal Government announced plans for the sale of some Federal housing and facilities at Los Alamos. . . . A three-judge Federal court ruled unconstitutional a state-Senate reapportionment plan passed Feb. 16 by the state legislature; the court issued its own plan to be used in the 1966 elections. . . . Voters returned Clinton P. Anderson (D) to the Senate and elected David F. Cargo (R) governor.

NEWSPAPERS. The death on Aug. 15 of the *New York Herald Tribune* was the sad note in journalism in 1966. After a series of strikes, the death of the *Mirror* in 1963, and steadily increasing costs, New York publishers planned to combine the operations of the *Herald Tribune, Journal-American,* and the *World-Telegram and The Sun.* According to the merger agreement, the *Journal-American* and the *World-Telegram and The Sun* were to be combined into an afternoon paper, *The World Journal.* The *Herald Tribune* was to remain a daily morning paper, except on Sundays when it would merge with the *Journal-American* as *The World Journal and Tribune.* Immediately after its formation in April, the new company was hit by a strike.

After 113 days of discouraging negotiations with ten unions, John Hay Whitney, publisher of the *Tribune,* closed his paper. Innovations in makeup, editorial personnel changes, and circulations promotions had failed in recent years to bring the paper to the break-even point. Whitney also sold 45 per cent of his Paris *Herald Tribune* to the *Washington Post.*

Historians recalled the many famous men once with the *Herald* and the *Tribune,* established as separate papers in 1835 and 1841. The two papers had merged in 1924. The last issue was April 24, 1966.

The strike, longest against a major-city newspaper in the history of U.S. journalism, finally ended in September, and the new evening and Sunday paper, the *World Journal Tribune,* made its debut Sept. 12.

Developments outside New York

The newspaper business as a whole was a bright one despite the publicity given a passing paper. For the second year, the total circulation for dailies passed the 60 million mark. *Editor & Publisher International Yearbook* reported a total of 1,444 evening and 320 morning papers in 1966, eleven below 1965, but 15 more than twenty years ago when circulation was below 50 million.

New York's experiences reflected a trend, the steady growth of suburban papers. In Cocoa, Fla., the Gannett group started *Today,* competing with papers from Orlando and Miami. In Los Angeles, the *Times* continued to lead in space for news, features and advertising content, but it had competition from 28 suburban papers, plus some 250 weeklies and "throwaway" advertising papers.

It was an eventful news year. Mass murders captured the headlines, at times overshadowing the Vietnam conflict. Critics continued their pro and con attacks on the Vietnam coverage, while others complained of a "racial news gap." A welcome break from the tragic side came with the press coverage of the wedding of Luci B. Johnson, President Johnson's daughter.

THE TIMES

London to be new H.Q. for Nato

Mr. Thomson to pursue talks with allies today

FROM OUR DIPLOMATIC CORRESPONDENT

Mr. Brown at ...-Budget

Labour M.P.s want better deal for coal

Minister umpire on rival claims

Strike by seamen to go on

BIG DOLLAR SALE BY BRITAIN

$83m. U.S. oil released

12,000 WILL BE LAID OFF

Print inquiry Ld. Cameron

The *Times* of London changed its format in May with news, not advertising, on front page.

Wide World

The Supreme Court ordered a retrial for Dr. Sam Sheppard, who was convicted, in 1954, of murdering his wife, and sentenced to life in prison. In ordering the new trial the court was critical of the circuslike atmosphere of the trial, and the failure of the presiding judge to isolate the jurors from newsmen. Some editors feared this decision might hamper future coverage of crime stories and trials.

Sam Newhouse added to his group, acquiring the *Mobile* (Ala.) *Register* and *Press* and the *Pascagoula* (Miss.) *Chronicle,* bringing his total to 21. After six bitter years of fighting in Springfield, Mass., he obtained sole ownership of the papers there. Another struggle developed in Denver where Helen G. Bonfils, secretary-treasurer of the *Denver Post,* led a fight to prevent Newhouse from acquiring any more than the 15 per cent ownership he now has of the *Post.*

A critical shortage of trained personnel continued to plague newspapers, although journalism schools reported higher enrollments. The University of Missouri, with 523 students in 1965–66, led the 119 schools and departments, followed by Michigan State, Illinois, Florida, Georgia and Northwestern.

Some newspapers acquired other papers. Richmond Newspapers Inc. bought control of the *Tampa Tribune.* The *Kansas City Star* bought the *Great Bend* (Kans.) *Tribune.* At the same time, the *Star* announced plans to spend $10 million in plant modernization in Kansas City. Other papers, too, were expanding operations. In Chattanooga, *The Times* and *News-Free Press* ended 24 years of joint operations while plans were completed for a new paper there, *The Chattanooga Post,* which made its first appearance in August. In Chicago the Field papers met the suburban press competition by founding one of their own, the *Arlington Day.*

Advertising revenue passed $4,400,000,000 in 1965; newsprint consumption continued upward; and employment on dailies reached 346,-900, up 39 per cent in 20 years. The 5 cent paper was rapidly disappearing, with a dime required more and more.

Edward W. Barrett, dean of Columbia University's Journalism School, said, in discussing some of the mergers, "We're ending up with stronger papers doing a more comprehensive job."

And with the problems of inflation, international relations, outer space, the draft, Vietnam, civil rights, and other events, today's editors face a challenge greater than that of a century ago when Bennett and Greeley battled for the New York audience.

WILLIAM H. TAFT
Professor of Journalism
UNIVERSITY OF MISSOURI

NEW YORK. In the Nov. 8 gubernatorial election, Gov. Nelson A. Rockefeller defeated Frank O'Connor, a Democrat, Franklin D. Roosevelt, Jr., a Liberal, and Paul L. Adams, a Conservative. . . . In April, Gov. Rockefeller signed into law the state-medicare-plan bill and a new divorce bill. . . . State University drafted plans pledging some form of higher education to every high-school graduate in the state by 1974. . . . U.S. Supreme Court decision of June 13 invalidated a state law that required a 6th-grade education in an English-speaking school (or English literacy) as a requisite for voting.

NEW YORK CITY. For the first time in the city's history, subway and bus service for New York's eight million residents was stopped dead in 1966 by a labor dispute. The paralysis that began New Year's morning did not end for 12 days and not until after a costly settlement of between $52 and $72 million.

Pickets march during New York City newspaper strike.
Wide World

During the strike many New Yorkers could not get to their jobs; others did not get home from their work and housed themselves up in downtown hotels. Oldsters could not visit their doctors; everyone was angry, and the city's overall business suffered to the tune of $1,-000,000,000.

At about the time that the first motorman was walking off his job, John V. Lindsay, a young and handsome Congressman who had vowed to make New York a "fun city," was being sworn in as mayor. He became the first Republican inhabitant of Gracie Mansion since Fiorello H. La Guardia.

Other Strikes. But in many respects, 1966 was no "fun year" in New York City. A fare hike closely followed the transit strike to anger more people. To make matters still worse, an empty exchequer forced Mr. Lindsay to impose an income tax on city residents and commuters.

Starting with a two-week walkout of heavy-construction hoist and crane operators that tied up $1,400,000,000 of building in the city, the year saw several other strikes. Some 4,000 construction plumbers walked off their jobs in July and had not returned by year's end. More than $500 million in hospital, school and apartment construction was idled by that walkout.

The city also experienced a 140-day newspaper strike, the longest labor shutdown in American newspaper history. The strike of all 10 newspaper craft unions was against a new corporation that had been formed by the merger of the *Herald Tribune,* the *World-Telegram and The Sun,* and the *Journal-American.*

As a result of the long strike the city lost one of its oldest and most respected morning newspapers. Originally the new enterprise had planned to publish a morning newspaper as a continuation of the *Trib.* But this plan was abandoned on Aug. 15—the 114th day of the dispute. The strike was finally settled and a new newspaper, the *World Journal Tribune,* appeared on newsstands in mid-September.

Heat and Racial Tension. The year 1966 also produced one of the hottest summers in the city's history. On July 3, temperatures at Times Square hit 103°, the hottest for that date since the Weather Bureau began keeping records nearly a century ago. At La Guardia Airport, the mercury climbed to 107° on that day. Only once before—back in 1948—had the temperatures topped 100° for three days in a row.

As was to be expected, the heat brought with it the city's annual racial tensions—though these were not so bad as in years past. The sniper murder of a young boy in Brooklyn did, however, touch off a weekend of near

Mayor Lindsay (r) and retiring Park Commissioner Hoving Ice-skate in Central Park.

riots, calmed only by the deployment of troop-sized units of police to the area. A trial later freed a Negro youth accused of the slaying.

Scandal, Civilian Review Board, Other Developments. The year did not end until the Lindsay administration had seen one full-scale scandal in which a sizable number of Sanitation Department personnel were fired or suspended. They were accused of paying for promotions and for taking payoffs from private carting companies that dumped their refuse in city-owned property. Several inquiries also uncovered tragic conditions in the city's huge hospital system and more was to be heard on that matter in 1967.

The Mayor's cherished civilian-controlled board to review complaints against the police was roundly defeated at the polls in November after a heated campaign that had been punctuated with racial overtones.

In October, 12 city firemen lost their lives in a horrible fire on 23d Street.

There were, however, numerous improvements during the year. A new Metropolitan Opera House was opened at Lincoln Center, and an effort was made to clean up Times Square of undesirables. The stationing of a policeman in every subway train and station after 8 P.M., instituted in 1965, resulted in a drastic reduction of crime in the underground railway system in 1966.

And, while the Police Department—under its new commissioner Howard R. Leary—was towing away every car within sight from the midtown area (a step which greatly improved traffic and was to be expanded to 72nd Street), bike riders had Central Park to themselves every Sunday morning.

The New Yorkers who applauded the bike riding, the beer parties in Bryant Park and the "happenings" in parks throughout the city, lamented the loss, at the end of 1966, of the man who made this possible. Thomas P. F. Hoving, the city park commissioner and the man who did more than anyone else in 1966 to make New York City a "fun city," announced an impending move to the Metropolitan Museum of Art. He will be its director.

ROBERT E. DALLOS
Reporter, THE NEW YORK TIMES

NEW ZEALAND. Climaxing a year in which the political implications of international relationships and defense tended to overshadow domestic issues, Prime Minister Keith Holyoake's National Party was returned to office in triennial elections held Nov. 26. After expanding the national defense effort and promising to continue support for U.S. policies in Vietnam, the 62-year-old Prime Minister campaigned vigorously. His party—which could point to rising levels of prosperity over its six years in office—lost only one of the 45 seats it previously held in the 80-member Assembly.

Election Campaign. In emphasizing the value of the close association existing with the United States and Australia on southeast Asia policies, Holyoake stressed his party's support

Prime Minister Holyoake awaits Nov. 26 election returns.

for the concept of regional defense. Holyoake pointed out that both Australia and New Zealand would have to involve themselves more directly in the affairs of southeast Asia. His chief opponent, 43-year-old Norman Kirk, the Labor Party leader, promised to end conscription, to withdraw New Zealand's 150-man artillery battery from South Vietnam and to concentrate on increasing civilian aid to Saigon. The latter proposal was also espoused by Holyoake.

It was generally conceded that President Johnson's visit to New Zealand was a significant factor in consolidating political support for the U.S.-oriented National Party. The President's warm personality drew enthusiastic response from the people who flocked to see him in Wellington during his Oct. 19-20 visit.

The only party to improve its electoral position was the Social Credit Party, a monetary-reform group, which gained its first seat in Parliament. The unexpectedly strong vote for Social Credit candidates was interpreted as an indication of public concern over mounting economic stresses.

The Economic Situation. Personal earnings moved to higher levels and there was general business prosperity. However, there were also signs that strains produced by New Zealand's impressive rates of economic growth of recent years—involving a very high utilization of resources—were intensifying. A slow but persistent increase in consumer prices (rising at over 3 per cent a year since 1963) continued. Assisted by a greater number of women drawn into industry, the labor force expanded to more than a million people; one effect was an escalation of internal demand in line with greater wage payments, leading to a rising level of imports. In turn this produced a large current-account deficit in the balance of payments.

Favorable features of the economic scene were to be found in a general rise in production and in the high rate of investment outlays in export and import-replacement industries. The volume of factory production showed a solid rise, and farmers invested freely in improvements. Nevertheless, the growth recorded in gross national product (in real terms) slipped below the 5 per cent rate maintained in previous years.

For the year ended March 31 imports were £NZ 488 million ($1,366,000,000), an increase of 12 per cent over 1964-65, while export receipts at £NZ 429 million ($1,201,-000,000) showed only a slight increase. In spite of substantial external borrowing, and drawings from the International Monetary Fund, net overseas assets fell to £NZ 58 million ($162 million), a decline of £NZ 22 million ($62 million) in twelve months.

With the drain persisting, more stringent import controls were imposed at midyear, when curbs were placed on various forms of spending abroad. Funds available to importers were tightly rationed, travelers had their daily allowance abroad cut sharply, and New Zealanders were no longer permitted to sell private holdings abroad in order to secure foreign currency. In the field of monetary policy, credit was further restrained and interest rates on savings were increased. At the same time, the national budget provided for total government expenditure of £NZ 632 million ($1,769,000,000), representing a rise of 8 per cent over the previous year.

Longer-term prospects were enhanced by the successful renegotiation of commodity agreements in London. The agreements assured that most of New Zealand's primary products, apart from butter, would have unrestricted access to the British Market.

R. M. YOUNGER
Author, AUSTRALIA AND THE AUSTRALIANS

NOBEL PRIZES

Above: **CHEMISTRY** (about $60,000): ROBERT S. MULLIKEN (l), professor, University of Chicago. **PHYSICS** (about $60,000): ALFRED KASTLER, professor, Ecole Normale Supérieure, Paris. Below: **MEDICINE or PHYSIOLOGY** (about $60,000 shared): CHARLES HUGGINS (l), professor, University of Chicago; FRANCIS PEYTON ROUS, pathologist, Rockefeller University, New York City.

LITERATURE (about $60,000 shared): NELLY SACHS (l), Jewish poet who writes in German and lives in Stockholm; SHMUEL YOSEF AGNON, Hebrew writer who lives in Jerusalem.

NORTH ATLANTIC TREATY ORGANIZATION. For the North Atlantic Treaty Organization, 1966 was a climactic year in which it found itself unwanted by one of the principal European nations it was formed to protect. Its sharp rejection by France's President Charles de Gaulle set off a reexamination from which few expected the alliance fully to recover.

De Gaulle began his attack against the alliance's military organization on March 7 with a note to its largest member, the United States, which signaled a series of communications informing all of NATO that France was withdrawing from integrated military command on July 1, 1966, and expected all NATO headquarters and foreign—largely United States but also some Canadian—bases off French territory by April 1, 1967.

After much handwringing and official protestations of solidarity in the face of France's defection, the 14 remaining members of NATO proceeded to do just what De Gaulle ordered and even more. At a ministerial meeting in Brussels in June, it was decided that NATO's main military command on the Continent, Supreme Allied Headquarters, Europe, would move to Belgium. Lesser headquarters would be split between West Germany and the Netherlands. Even though De Gaulle did not oust the North Atlantic Council, at the edge of Paris' Bois de Boulogne, the council decided to move to Brussels.

De Gaulle's contention was that an integrated allied military force was outdated in light of a *détente* between the West and the Soviet Union, the main threat against which NATO was organized in 1949. De Gaulle also vowed that French forces would no longer be subordinate to any supranational command.

U.S. military jeeps leave France by rail in November.
UPI

De Gaulle's critics argued that if there was the beginning of a *détente* with Russia, it was precisely because of NATO's challenge to Soviet expansion, and that it was foolish to throw aside this guarantee of security. As for the alleged restraint of national forces within NATO, it was pointed out that the integration was largely on paper, to be implemented only in time of war.

The counterarguments did nothing to divert De Gaulle, nor did the cold fact that he was unilaterally breaking five treaties with the United States regarding the installation of American forces on French soil.

De Gaulle chose to strike at an opportune time, a time when other NATO members were chafing under the load of peacetime military obligations. Britain, faced with a worsening balance-of-payments problem, sent up warnings that it would be obliged to reduce its Army of the Rhine. West Germany, although contributing a healthy 12 divisions to NATO's European shield, said it could not see its way clear to cut America's European defense costs with offset purchases of more military hardware. Tiny Luxembourg was looking for ways to trim her defense costs.

As the year drew to a close, the United States, West Germany and Britain were in consultation on a basic reassessment of what sort of defense system was really needed for Western Europe, given a very real, if perhaps temporary, relaxation of tensions, and the development of more modern arms which lessens the pressing need for heavy manpower commitments along NATO's frontier with the Soviet bloc.

On Dec. 14, in Paris, 14 NATO nations agreed to set up a permanent nuclear-planning group of 7 nations. These 7 member nations—permanent and rotating—would determine Western nuclear policy and strategy.

DAVID M. MASON
Paris Bureau, THE ASSOCIATED PRESS

NORTH CAROLINA. President Johnson signed a bill March 10 authorizing establishment of Cape Lookout National Seashore. . . . Durham faculties were ordered desegregated July 5 by U.S. Court of Appeals. . . . Republicans won impressive victories in November's general election. . . . Seven new community colleges opened. . . . Chief Justice Emery B. Denny of the state Supreme Court resigned in February. . . . Cash farm income from crops declined.

NORTH DAKOTA. State elections gave Republicans their largest majorities since 1956: 83 (R) to 15 (D) in the House of Representatives, 44 (R) to 5 (D) in the Senate. . . . To develop new, small industries, the North Dakota Development Corporation was organized. . . . A 3-day March blizzard piled 34 inches of snow on the eastern part of the state, and an April flooding of the Red River seriously affected some 3,000 people in 16 counties.

NUCLEAR TESTING. Communist China conducted its third, fourth and fifth nuclear tests during 1966 at its Lob Nor test center. All indicated considerably greater progress by China toward an operational atomic-weapons system than was expected. The first Chinese test in 1964 was about a 20-kiloton nuclear device dropped from a tower; the second, in 1965, an atomic bomb dropped from an aircraft, of about the same yield.

The third, on May 9, 1966, was a device rated by the U.S. Atomic Energy Commission at over 200 kilotons, and estimated as a major step toward a hydrogen bomb. It contained enriched uranium, with no plutonium. The fourth test, Oct. 27, was a ballistic missile of about 20 KT's, with a range of about 400 mi. The fifth, on Dec. 28, had thermonuclear material estimated at 300 KT's. This led to speculation that China was testing a triple-stage fission-fusion-fission reaction, looking toward a high-yield, "dirty" fallout bomb.

French Tests. France also conducted a number of nuclear tests during 1966 at its new testing ground in the South Seas. It exploded a fission, plutonium atomic device from a tower at Mururoa Atoll in French Polynesia on July 2, reportedly its first test in the atmosphere since 1963.

President Charles de Gaulle witnessed a test at Mururoa on Sept. 11, from a cruiser reportedly 25 miles from the point of impact, of an aircraft-dropped atomic bomb. A Paris announcement said that the sixth and final A-test of the year, Oct. 4, and its predecessor, "contained plutonium and thermonuclear materials," but it was not a hydrogen bomb, which the French talk of having in 1968.

Underground Tests. The United States announced that it conducted 39 tests during 1966. The U.S. Atomic Energy Commission conducted 4 Plowshare (peaceful uses) tests, while announced "military-connected" tests included 22 low yield—under 20 KT's; 10 low-intermediate yield—20 to 200 KT's; and 2 intermediate-yield tests—200 KT's to a megaton. On Dec. 3, 1966, there also was a 350-ton test in a pre-prepared cavity near Hattiesburg, Miss., to learn more of the effect of muffling or "decoupling" an explosion.

Wide World

On Mururoa, a large balloon is ready Sept. 7 to carry a French nuclear device aloft, France's last 1966 A-test.

Although the United States made official announcement of only a few Russian underground tests in 1966, the U.S.S.R. undoubtedly made many more. U.S. officials believe that Soviet underground tests grew in number and were larger than U.S. tests. One Soviet test at Novaya Zemlya, on Oct. 27, was said to be over one megaton. On Dec. 20 the United States detonated an "intermediate" size explosion in Nevada. There was speculation that both this large test and the Soviet Oct. 27 test were linked to development of either an antimissile missile or a multiple-warhead ICBM.

The United States is working on foolproof scientific means for detecting underground tests to make possible a change in the 1963 treaty—barring atmospheric, space and underwater tests—to make a complete test-ban pact practicable. Russia opposes an underground test ban with on-site inspections, to check on suspected tests, which the United States insists be required. The Mississippi "decoupling" test, however, apparently showed that such techniques may make it extremely difficult to detect future underground tests, causing "cheating" to be easier.

Secretary of State Dean Rusk said in August that the three-year-old limited-test-ban treaty generally had been observed by its signatories. There had been, however, some minor technical violations, involving "venting" gases, which in small quantities reached the atmosphere from the underground and crossed national borders. Neither Red China nor France is a treaty signatory.

JOHN G. NORRIS
Assistant Foreign Editor
THE WASHINGTON POST

OCEANOGRAPHY. The Second International Oceanographic Congress was held at Moscow University in Moscow, May 30 to June 9, 1966, with 1,767 delegates from 57 countries attending. Since the majority of oceanographic research is being done in northern countries, most of the delegates were from the Soviet Union, Japan, northern Europe and North America. However, the presence of representatives from southern Europe, southern Asia, South America and Africa indicated a growing interest in marine science in these areas.

Convened by the Soviet Union's Academy of Sciences through special agreement between UNESCO and the Soviet Government, the congress had the support of the Special Committee on Oceanic Research, the Food and Agricultural Organization, the World Meteorological Organization and the International Atomic Energy Agency. The 490 papers presented during the congress gave evidence of a great deal of progress in oceanography throughout the world. In fact, the amount of oceanographic information assembled since the First International Congress in New York in 1959 is far larger than all such information gathered prior to that meeting. There follows a brief summary of outstanding reports presented at the 1966 congress.

Ocean and Atmosphere. The sea absorbs heat from the sun and loses heat to the atmosphere by radiation, conduction and evaporation. At the same time, the wind over the sea creates waves, stirs the waters and drives ocean currents. For many years this relationship between the sea and the atmosphere has been the subject of theoretical-physics research that would enable man to predict oceanographic and meteorological conditions. Heretofore, there have not been enough observations to verify the theories.

Since the 1959 congress, however, it has become possible to make continuous observations of air temperature, humidity, wind speed, sea and swell, sea temperature and ocean currents. The observations are made simultaneously from oceanographic towers, stable buoys (unaffected by waves) and fields of anchored and free-floating buoys. The vast masses of data can be analyzed with computers. On the bases of the research and observations, progress has been made toward forecasting oceanographic and marine meteorological conditions.

Ocean and Life. During the congress, interest focused on primary biological productivity: the conversion of carbon dioxide and water into carbohydrates in phytoplankton (single- and chain-celled plants such as algae). These phytoplankton are eaten by tiny animal plankton (zooplankton). The animal plankton are then eaten by small and larval fishes which in turn are food for larger fishes. Using radioactive carbon, it is possible to trace this process of ocean life from dissolved carbon dioxide to phytoplankton and on to larger fishes. The radioactive carbon also measures at each stage the efficiency of food utilization—the ratio of meat produced to the food eaten. Thus the productivity of sea regions in all parts of the world is being assessed.

Fisheries exploration has been extensive and intensive. U.S.S.R., Japan and the United States are conducting most of the exploration, and are rapidly exploiting new fish stocks as they are discovered. It is estimated that the present world fish catch of fifty million tons may be quadrupled by the end of the century, but further increase is unlikely.

Marine Geology. At the congress, marine-geology emphasis was on the structure of the earth's crust and the upper mantle under the oceans. Seabed exploration has been extended

Second International Oceanographic Congress opens.

Tass from Sovfoto

New oceanographic vessel, the *Oceanographer*, described as the largest U. S. vehicle ever built solely for ocean surveys and research, is commissioned in July 1966.

markedly. Both the U.S.S.R. and the United States have attempted to drill holes through the earth's crust (which is thinnest in the ocean bed) to the upper mantle in an effort to determine the character and structure of the earth's core. (In late August 1966 the U.S. Congress killed Project Mohole by failing to appropriate funds for it. The project was designed to probe through three miles of the ocean and three miles of the earth's crust.)

Classical Oceanography. The International Indian Ocean Expedition (1960–65) was the largest single oceanographic research ever undertaken. It was organized and coordinated by the Intergovernmental Oceanographic Commission. More than forty ships from about twenty nations took part surveying and resurveying the area. The expedition revealed the circulations, the properties and structure of the waters, the standing crops and rate of production of plankton, and seasonal variations. The monumental task of analyzing the data is proceeding.

The BOREAS leg of the ZETES expedition from Scripps Institution of Oceanography, La Jolla, Calif., made the first winter oceanographic survey of the western subarctic Pacific Ocean during February and March 1966. Using the most advanced sensing and sampling equipment and a shipboard computer, the expedition was able to present its results on completion of the cruise. This was the outstanding single ship effort reported at the congress.

New Researches. Some hitherto little-known areas of research were reported, such as radio ecology, which is the effect of radioactive materials on life-forms and communities in the sea. Other new research dealt with radioactivity of the oceans, optical and acoustical properties and effects in the sea (bioacoustics), and chemical history of the oceans.

Equipment. New Equipment shows the most spectacular advance in the field of oceanography. Many new oceanographic vessels have been built during the past seven years, most of them large, well equipped and specially designed. Several types of buoys have been developed which can be anchored in mid-ocean, or allowed to drift while they measure and record data or transmit data by radio to shore stations. The most spectacular buoys are in the form of long, thin ships which can be towed to sea and then upended to become a buoy with research laboratories and living accommodations.

Electronic devices now available can be lowered into the sea to measure temperature, salinity and dissolved oxygen. These and other devices allow easy, rapid collection of enormous amounts of data. Shipboard computers record, analyze and pass on the data to World Data Centers in Moscow and Washington, where they are available to researchers the world over.

JOHN P. TULLY
Oceanographic Consultant to the Chairman
FISHERIES RESEARCH BOARD OF CANADA

OHIO. Summer race riots occurred in Cleveland and Dayton. . . . To protest what they termed inadequate state welfare payments, welfare marchers made a 155-mi. walk from Cleveland to Columbus in June. . . . Gov. James A. Rhodes (R) was reelected by a record majority of 698,000. . . . In January, Springfield elected as its mayor Robert C. Henry, a Negro. . . . On Nov. 16, in Cleveland, Samuel H. Sheppard was found not guilty of murdering his wife in 1954.

OKLAHOMA. Eighty-one died in an airplane crash April 22 near Ardmore. . . . Tulsa hosted the 15th International Petroleum Exposition May 12–21. . . . Jayne Jayroe of Laverne was chosen Miss America. . . . Will Rogers World Airport Terminal, Oklahoma City, officially opened in December. . . . Dewey F. Bartlett (R) won the governorship. . . . The 31st state Legislature has 38 Democrats, 10 Republicans in the Senate; 74 Democrats, 25 Republicans in the House of Representatives. . . . Sen. Fred R. Harris (D) was reelected.

OREGON. Western Oregon suffered flooding Jan. 4–5 due to heavy rains and snows. . . . In fiscal 1965, Portland received 80 per cent of minimal entitlement of funds available through the Office of Equal Opportunity. . . . Gov. Mark O. Hatfield (R), a critic of the Vietnam war, won a U.S. Senate seat in November's election, and Tom McCall (R) was elected to replace him as governor. . . . Portland was the scene of "read-ins" for peace in Vietnam on March 4–5.

ORGANIZATION OF AMERICAN STATES. The year was one of transition for the Organization of American States (OAS), wracked by internal dissension over the Dominican crisis of 1965, and faced with the prospect of major 1967 developments which will include a summit meeting of American presidents.

In this period of transition, the hard-working OAS sought and partially attained two objectives—a solution of the Dominican conflict (which brought the organization considerable internal discord), and a streamlining of projected reforms aimed at making the inter-American system more dynamic and effective. Planned reform of the OAS charter was discussed in Panama in February, and differences in policy, stemming from disagreement between the United States and a Latin-American bloc, were conciliated at a meeting in Washington in June. The disagreement derived from Latin-American insistence that U.S. aid be placed on a firm, juridical basis, and that the United States agree to trade concessions the Latin Americans considered indispensable for their economic and social development.

The U.S. delegation in Panama insisted that it could not go along with the draft as proposed, because of the certainty it would be rejected by the U.S. Congress. The "conciliation" agreement finally reached in Washington smoothed over language of the agreement and placed it in a form designed to win Congressional approval.

The Third Inter-American Conference, scheduled to open in Buenos Aires in August, was to have given final approval to the proposed OAS reforms, but the conference was postponed after the Argentine military overthrew constitutional President Arturo U. Illia in late June. The meeting was tentatively slated to take place during the first quarter of 1967.

Another factor in the postponement of the Buenos Aires conference was the Argentine initiative, subscribed to by the United States, for a summit meeting of all American presidents. It was originally thought that such a meeting could be held in December, but unforeseen delays pushed the date ahead into 1967. At year's end OAS officials considered it likely that the summit meeting, as well as the Inter-American Conference, could be held in early 1967.

Preparations for the summit meeting went into full gear in October when the OAS Council called American foreign ministers to Washington to prepare formal convocation of the meeting. The Council also formed a special preparatory commission of nine economists to draft an agenda and bases for discussion for the summit meeting. The economists completed their work at a two-day, Nov. 25-26, meeting in Washington.

Basically, the summit agenda represents a consensus that the chiefs of state should adopt political decisions at the highest level to "recharge" the flagging Alliance for Progress, and step up to economic integration of Latin America.

Throughout most of 1966, the OAS studied repercussions which emanated from the so-called Tricontinental Solidarity Conference held in Havana in January. In late November the Council received and approved an extensive report on the subject, calling on member nations to prevent their nationals from visiting Cuba, and recommending frequent reunions and symposiums on the subject of communist subversion in the Americas.

FRANCIS L. MCCARTHY
Latin-America Editor
UNITED PRESS INTERNATIONAL

Campeau Construction Co. Ltd.
Model of Ottawa's new complex, Place de Ville, containing hotel (left) and office building.

OTTAWA. Canada's capital experienced growing pains and controversy in 1966 as physical changes swept the former old lumber town from one end to the other.

Controversy surrounded the approval of a new sports center in the south end of Ottawa, a project which will be completed in time for Canada's centennial in 1967. There were those who thought the money—more than $8 million—could be spent with better results on other projects. But the new stadium, with a seating capacity of 33,000, will bring the Grey Cup game to Ottawa in 1967 for the first time since 1940. Canadians shed all their inhibitions at this major sports event when the best from the east meets the best from the west in an annual football classic.

More controversy swirled around the breaking of the century-old building-heights bylaw in 1966—a stipulation that no building should go over a height of 150 feet. Ottawa planners had always thought anything higher would dwarf the nearby Parliament Buildings on Parliament Hill. But break the bylaw they did, with a hotel in the heart of the capital that will fill a city block, and which may well set a North American record for depth—80 feet down in solid rock, or 6 full stories underground. Height for the new Place de Ville, 250 feet, will no doubt set a trend. Other developers are now expected to ask for and get permission to erect buildings of similar heights.

Then there is the urban-renewal plan for Lower Town, that older portion of the city that for the most part has become worn out over the years. While the project has been approved in principle, it ran into an unexpected snag when a citizens' group objected to some phases of planning. It has now been set back for a three-month study.

Another older portion of the city, however, will soon take on new life. LeBreton Flats, which already has been cleared of homes and businesses, will be the site of a new $100 million Canadian Defense Headquarters.

And after much delay and more controversy, Ottawa Station, a brand-new $34 million passenger railway complex, opened in the southeastern part of the city. This will mean trains will no longer pass within hailing distance of Parliament Hill. The old Union Station, in use since 1916, probably will feel the wreckers' hammer in 1967, much to the dismay of a spirited group of citizens who wish to preserve the building. The removal of some of the tracks will make way for completion of the eastern arm of the Queensway, a high-speed elevated traffic artery, which passes through the heart of the city.

A Supreme Court of Canada decision with far-reaching implications was handed down in June. In effect, it means that the National Capital Commission—an appointed body responsible only to the Federal Cabinet—can expropriate any lands around the city it deems fit for the benefit or beautification of the capital. The NCC already has expropriated a ribbon of land, or Green Belt, up to eight miles wide around the capital on which nothing can be built without their express approval.

WILF BELL
THE OTTAWA CITIZEN

PAINTING AND SCULPTURE

By WILLIAM H. GERDTS
Associate Professor of Art
University of Maryland

The year 1966 was an active one in the arts in the United States and Canada, with a great number of diverse exhibitions, and the acquisition of a number of great paintings by leading museums.

U.S. Exhibitions. The increasing difficulty in borrowing old-master works was reflected in the fact that most of the major U.S. exhibitions concentrated upon the art of the last 150 years or upon the display of the institutions' own permanent collection. There were two great shows of two 19th-century giants. The first was the exhibition of the work of Joseph M. W. Turner in the spring at New York City's Museum of Modern Art. Included in this exhibition were many paintings borrowed from London's Tate Gallery. The second was the Manet show, which was seen in November at the Philadelphia Museum of Art.

A number of shows of 19th-century European art were more varied in their selection and were made up of works borrowed from private collections. In an already established tradition, several of these took place in two of the best-known commercial galleries in New York City. First, there was the show of "Impressionist Treasures" held at the Knoedler Galleries in January. Emphasizing work of the previous generation was the show of "Romantics and Realists" exhibited at Wildenstein's in the spring. The most heralded exhibition in this category, however, was the March showing at Washington's National Gallery of Art of the privately owned treasures of Mr. and Mrs. Paul Mellon and Mrs. Mellon Bruce. The exhibition stressed French art from Corot to Bonnard and included such famous works as Cézanne's *Boy in Red Vest*.

Joseph M. W. Turner's *San Giorgio from the Dogana, Venice: Sunrise*, watercolor, exhibited, New York City's Museum of Modern Art, 1966.

The British Museum, London

The great Norwegian expressionist Edvard Munch was the subject of a show early in 1966 at New York's Guggenheim Museum. It included work dating from the late 19th century well into the 20th. Among other early moderns who were the subject of major exhibitions was the French fauve, Henri Matisse. The University of California in Los Angeles inaugurated an exhibition of rarely seen works by Matisse in January. The show traveled across the United States to Boston's Museum of Fine Arts. New York's Museum of Modern Art held its own, smaller exhibition of Matisse's work during the summer. One of the major Canadian exhibitions was a complete survey of the painting of the founder of the Dutch de Stijl movement, Piet Mondrian, early in the year. A unique survey of 20th-century art took place in May in New York City, where ten commercial galleries surveyed developments in "Seven Decades 1895–1965."

American Art. American art, past and present, was the natural subject of a good many exhibitions in the United States throughout the year. Several institutions, following the lead of the Metropolitan Museum's giant exhibition of 1965, attempted to cover the complete history of U.S. painting and sculpture. The first of these was the show of "250 Years of American Art" at the Corcoran Gallery of Art in Washington, an interesting but spotty show drawn almost completely from its permanent collection. It was rather weak in the field of 20th-century art. The second was the inaugural exhibition of the Whitney Museum of American Art in New York City in their new Madison Avenue building. Although more of a loan exhibition, it was also one of the finest surveys of American art ever shown.

At the same time, more and more earlier American artists were the subject of perceptive examination. A number of them were painters whose work had been until lately little known or else somewhat neglected since their own times. The able mid-19th-century seascapist Fitz Hugh Lane was reassessed in an exhibition at the Lincoln, Mass., De Cordova Museum in the spring. At the same time, the National Collection of Fine Arts held a show of the grandiose, theatrical work of Frederic E. Church, featuring landscapes by this peripatetic painter of South America, the Arctic, the Mediterranean and the Middle East. John La Farge was seen in a small but sensitive show at the Graham Galleries in New York City in May. America's foremost woman artist, Mary Cassatt, was featured in a show at New York's Knoedler Galleries in February, with works borrowed mainly from the Cassatt family. This exhibition was a benefit for the National Collection of Fine Arts. In March, the Gallery of Modern Art in New York City held a giant survey of the work of the 20th-century realist George Bellows, a show that rather tended to confirm the opinion that Bellows' most vigorous painting dated from early in his career.

Contemporary Artists. Contemporary artists, European and American, were featured in many exhibitions, primarily of course those held in the galleries where they are represented. In addition to these, a number of outstanding one-man shows were seen. The major American sculptor Reuben Nakian, who had been a somewhat neglected figure, finally received his due in a fine showing of his monumental semiabstract work. Several shows featured two of the world's leading surrealists. One show, devoted to Salvador Dali and held at the Gallery of Modern Art in the spring, was so popular that it continued through the summer. A smaller, more tasteful show featured the work of René Magritte and took place in early spring at the Museum of Modern Art. The largest showing of the work of Andrew Wyeth, which began a museum tour at the Pennsylvania Academy of the Fine Arts in late September, proved that the field of contemporary realism was not neglected. Edward Kienholz' pop figure environments created a stir in April at the Los Angeles County Museum. City officials on the board of this institution attempted to ban the show on the basis of its purported pornographic content.

There was also a furor over the choices of artists to represent the United States at the Venice Biennale. The choices of first the curator and then the director of the Guggenheim Museum were superseded. The artists finally picked were pop artist Roy Lichtenstein, abstractionist Helen Frankenthaler, the hard-edge painter Ellsworth Kelly and the color abstractionist Jules Olitski. The commercialism and politics noted in the Biennale did not, in the long run, seem to warrant the controversy that had flared for some time before the exhibition opened.

New Movements. Two new movements in contemporary art received much notice and interest. Kinetic art—art involving actual movement of parts and components—was studied in the spring in two shows in California, one at the Art Gallery of the University of California in Berkeley, and the other at the San Francisco Museum. The second new movement was introduced at the brilliant and controversial show entitled "Primary Structures," which began in late April at the Jewish

Andrew Wyeth's *The Mill*
is executed in dry brush.

The Triumph of Marius, oil by Giovanni Battista Tiepolo,
hangs in the Metropolitan Museum of Art, New York City.
The Metropolitan Museum of Art, Rogers Fund, 1965

Museum. This show was concerned with abstract sculptural forms, totally impersonal and objective, monumental in scale and with architectural references.

Oriental Art and Major Drawings. A most welcome development during the year was the increase in major shows of Oriental art, partly due to the activities of the relatively new gallery of Asia House in New York. This institution showed "Treasures of the Kabul Museum" (in Afghanistan) early in the year. The great show of national art treasures of Japan was shown first at the Los Angeles County Art Museum, then at the Philadelphia Museum of Art and finally at the Royal Ontario Museum in Toronto. The National Gallery of Art in Washington held a number of major Oriental shows, including the "Art Treasures of Turkey" in June, and a show of small, exquisite bronzes, jades and ceramics from the collection of the King of Sweden, held in September. The M. H. de Young Memorial Museum in San Francisco doubled its size to accommodate the vast, great Oriental collection donated to them by Avery Brundage. The museum opened the Brundage wing in June.

Strangely, there was relatively little activity in the field of master drawings. The most important U.S. show was one of "Italian Renaissance Drawings" held in New York City at the Metropolitan Museum and sponsored by this institution and the Morgan Library. It is one in a series of such drawing shows that will be held. In early spring, a comprehensive show of 19th- and 20th-century Latin-Amer-

Jasper Francis Cropsey's oil painting *Autumn on the Hudson River* can be viewed in the National Gallery of Art in Washington, D.C.

ican art was held at the Yale University Art Gallery in New Haven.

Acquisitions. Some of the great acquisitions made by American museums in 1966 require particular mention. The Art Institute of Chicago acquired Coreggio's *Virgin and Child with St. John,* referred to as one of the major acquisitions ever made by that institution. One of the very few works by Raphael in the United States is his *St. Jerome Punishing the Heretic Sabinian,* a new addition to the collection of the North Carolina Museum in Raleigh. The Metropolitan Museum announced its acquisition of three major works by the 18th-century Venetian painter Tiepolo. The National Gallery in Washington acquired a number of major works, including a portrait by the French baroque painter Largillière, *Elizabeth Throckmorton;* Rubens' *David in the Lions' Den;* Vermeer's *A Lady Writing;* and a painting of *Saint George* ascribed to Roger van der Weyden.

The most spectacular acquisitions were made by the Cleveland Museum of Art, a series of works in all media and representing all cultures. Among these is a great drawing by Dürer of an arm for his figure of *Eve;* such paintings as Goya's *Infante Don Luis de Borbon,* Ribera's *The Death of Adonis,* Murillo's *Laban Searching for His Stolen Idols,* and Ingres' *Stratonice;* and a series of rare early Christian sculptures of the 3d and 4th century depicting such figures as Jonah and the Good Shepherd.

The plans for the National Portrait Gallery continued, and the nascent institution held its first show of its first acquisitions. The famous collector Joseph Hirshhorn gave his gigantic collection of 19th- and 20th-century art to the United States. The Johnson Wax Company also made a large donation in giving the Smithsonian Institution its collection, of contemporary American art, "Art U.S.A. Now."

New Monuments. The year 1966 also saw the unveiling of a number of public monuments by great contemporary artists. A major stabile by Alexander Calder was installed in May at the Massachusetts Institute of Technology. The city of Chicago received a giant abstract sculpture by Picasso in September. Art adorning the new Metropolitan Opera House in New York City, which opened in September, came from Raoul Dufy, Marc Chagall and Aristide Maillol.

Auctions. In the area of auction sales and prices, New York's Parke-Bernet Gallery announced its most profitable season ever. Among the major sales was that of the collection of G. David Thompson on March 23-24, which sold for about $2.5 million. In this sale a Braque still life sold for $120,000, a painting by Paul Klee for $80,000, and Rodin's *Balzac* for $70,000. The last went to the Rhode Island School of Design. Another major sale was that of the collection of the late Helena Rubinstein in April. Items at this sale grossed almost $3 million. The most spectacular price was that of $140,000 for Brancusi's *Bird in Flight.* The highest price paid during the year for a single painting was $616,-000, for Hubert van Eyck's *Saint George and the Dragon.*

Oval Form, bronze by Barbara Hepworth, exhibited at Battersea Park, London.

PAINTING AND SCULPTURE: EUROPEAN

By SHELDON WILLIAMS

London Correspondent, International Edition NEW YORK HERALD TRIBUNE-WASHINGTON POST

Very rarely does a museum make over most of its exhibition space to one item, but this is what the Moderna Museet in Stockholm did for *Hon,* the cooperative work of Niki de St. Phalle, Jean Tinguely and Per Olof Ultvedt, during the summer of 1966. To understand the museum's decision means going back a couple of years to the time it was decided to commission the three artists to make a visual demonstration of some kind. At first there was discussion whether this should be weighted in favor of Tinguely's exploding mobiles or should reflect the whimsical imagination of Mademoiselle de St. Phalle's collage monsters. Initially it looks as if she had her own way: the enormous body of *Hon* (She) was decorated on the outside with the sort of embellishments familiar in her later works; but inside *Hon* turned out to be a veritable hive of movement and mechanics and architectural fantasy, including a bar from which drinkers could jettison empty bottles down a chute to a machine which masticated them. There was even a small cinema showing an old Garbo movie. Yet *Hon* was much more than just an assembly of tricks and gimmicks.

Nineteen sixty-six was a big year for sculpture, notably the summer show at Sonsbeeg in Holland, the Italian Sculpture Exhibition in Edinburgh and the G.L.C. "Sculpture in the Park" Exhibition at Battersea Park, London. The triennial, open-air public exhibition at Battersea was distinguished in 1966 by being entirely the choice of one man—Alan Bowness. His control of the exhibits brought about a great improvement in the character of this great display. The sculptors were all British—with the single exception of David Smith (a compliment to this much-mourned American, paralleling his retrospective exhibition at the Tate). Simultaneously the exhibition was a demonstration of the new wave in British sculpture. Apart from Henry Moore and Dame Barbara Hepworth, all the artists showed signs of the influence that polychrome and plastic have recently exerted upon modernist British sculpture. This is the territory of Anthony Caro and Phillip King.

Strangely enough, the brilliant colors of these objects proved easily at home in the outdoor setting. Certainly, Moore's half-sized version of the Lincoln Center (New York) two-piece figure was imposing, mounted on a grassy knoll. And the glimpse of waterfowl swimming in single file across the lake, seen through the apertures of Barbara Hepworth's *Oval Form,* had the authoritative touch which one expects from the seniors of modern art. The Paolozzi group, with their dappled camouflage colors, set on their own gray square of concrete against the background of bushes, had all the excitement of carousel horses arrested for a moment before starting to rear and plunge on their restricted round.

Of the artists at the Venice Biennale, Günter Haese, with his golden cobweb mobiles, was well received, and British artists, as forecast, were able to carry off a number of prizes. But the real return to figuration—anyway in the view of the Venice jury—has not yet come to fruition. The signs and portents are still there —David Hockney won a Graphics Prize at the first Cracow Biennale for *Portrait of Kasmin,* as did Alan Davie, whose *Zurich Improvisation No. 8* can hardly claim to be a figurative label.

It still looks as if the real action is steering clear of Paris. The long-awaited display of Paul Guillaume's collection at the Orangerie turned out to be a disappointment; even the exhibition of French art treasures from American collections failed to excite the critics. The culture axis continues to swing between London and New York.

In London the Hallsborough Gallery showed the 6 frescoes in grisaille made by the Tiepolos to glorify the 600-year history of the Porto family. These larger-than-life frescoes were

miraculously removed from the walls of the Palazzo Porto (Vicenza), and sold to the famous Berlin collector Dr. Edouard Simon, who had a building specially designed to hold them. When, after World War I, inflation sent the mark crashing, Simon's fortune was so drastically reduced that he was forced to put the Tiepolos on the market. Shortly after the sale he took his own life.

The frescoes then passed into the collection of the Swedish multimillionaire Wenner-Gren, who also organized their display in a building specially constructed for the purpose. The 6 frescoes were purchased from Sotheby's by the Hallsborough Gallery on March 24, 1965, and were put on exhibition by the gallery a year later. In the interim, Hallsborough had 2 of the works cleaned so that the gold—hardly perceptible in the other 4—shone out as the Tiepolos had intended it to do, creating an even deeper illusion of bas-relief.

Lefebre Gallery from the collection of Mr. & Mrs. Alexander Hollander, Oak Ridge, Tenn.

Howard Wise Gallery, New York

Here are works by first-prize winners at the Venice Biennale competition. At the left is Robert Jacobsen's *Le Gnome,* made of found iron. Above is a sculpture by Julio Le Parc utilizing wood, light and aluminum and titled *Cylindre Continuel Lumière.* Below is a bronze sculpture by Etienne Martin, who titled it *Couple Goudron.*

Lefebre Gallery, New York

Paris' Eiffel Tower dwarfs new high-rise apartments.

PARIS. The French capital, an ever growing, ever more active metropolis, virtually completed its face-lifting in 1966, with most of its public monuments and private homes and business places cleaned of decades of grime. The Arch of Triumph, which dominates the broad Champs-Elysées, emerged as a brilliant buff-stone colossus with many of its reliefs resculptured by skilled artisans.

The Paris skyline was also being transformed as twenty- and thirty-floor *gratte-ciel* pierced the suburban skies. To the south, west and north, new housing developments and business blocks were going up, giving the ancient city a modern aspect which did not please many sentimentalists who were happy with the Eiffel Tower as the only marked panoramic irregularity. But Paris was rapidly growing out of its space limits, and planning boards went to work creating satellite cities and attempting to attract industry to provincial areas—a particularly difficult task because in so many senses, Paris is France.

American influence was evident in the new Paris, with the familiar formula of suburban housing developments springing up around supermarkets and shopping centers. The American drugstore idea was extended and embellished, with a restaurant-gift-shop-pharmacy establishment opening in the Opéra district and another in a western suburb. An English flavor was added to the Etoile district, with the Winston Churchill Pub, offering English breakfasts and beer. The elegantly modern architectural approach to these and other bars and eating places was making the traditional postwar mirror-and-plastic *bistros* look less and less attractive.

Traffic problems were eased somewhat with the creation of new subterranean parking lots in the Champs-Elysées district, and with the opening of a new segment of a Seineside freeway on the right bank.

Paris finally got a new hotel in 1966, its first since before World War II. The Hilton chain opened a luxury hotel very near the Eiffel Tower. Parisians kept the hotel's three restaurants filled, forgetting their frequently expressed impatience with American attempts at *haute cuisine*.

Despite the new buildings, Paris still had a housing shortage and a slum area, crowded with thousands of Portuguese, Spaniards and other foreign workers in Paris to benefit from wages higher than those back home.

A new morning newspaper turned up in Paris, but could not attract enough circulation from the six other main morning papers to last out a year.

DAVID M. MASON
Paris Bureau, THE ASSOCIATED PRESS

PARKS. In 1966 the National Park Service celebrated its golden anniversary. The Service was established as a bureau of the U.S. Department of the Interior by an Act of Congress on Aug. 25, 1916, signed by President Woodrow Wilson.

Many special events commemorating the anniversary were held in the various natural, historic and recreational units of the National Park System. These events, along with scores of others sponsored by civic, conservation, historical, business and other organizations across the United States, heightened public interest in, and use of, the nation's parklands.

At ceremonies held in Yellowstone National Park, Wyoming-Montana-Idaho, on Aug. 25, a special anniversary postage stamp was placed on sale for the first time. Yellowstone, established in 1872, was the world's first national park.

Portrayed on the stamp is the symbol of PARKSCAPE—U.S.A., the new, long-range program under which the National Park Service will mobilize its resources and capabilities to support the "new conservation" called for by President Johnson, which involves the total environment. PARKSCAPE—U.S.A. pledges *growth* in response to human need; *cooperation* with all those concerned with the quality of the environment in which we live; *innovation* in seeking the goals of the new conservation.

Mrs. Lyndon B. Johnson dedicated Point Reyes National Seashore, Calif., and Fort Davis National Historic Site, Tex. While in Texas, she visited Big Bend National Park where she, Secretary of the Interior Stewart L. Udall, and other members of her party journeyed down the Rio Grande aboard rubber rafts. Mrs. Johnson also visited Glen Canyon Recreation Area, Arizona-Utah, in connection with the dedication of Glen Canyon Dam, the third-highest dam in the world, built and administered by the Bureau of Reclamation of the U.S. Department of the Interior. Beautiful Lake Powell, formed by the dam, lies in the heart of the spectacular, 1,239,985-acre recreation area which is administered by the National Park Service under a cooperative agreement with the Bureau of Reclamation.

Cape Cod National Seashore, Mass., also was dedicated in 1966.

Canada's Prime Minister, Lester B. Pearson, and President Johnson laid the cornerstone for a new visitor center at the Roosevelt-Campobello International Park at ceremonies on Aug. 21. The park is located on Campobello Island in Canada's New Brunswick Province where the late President Franklin D. Roosevelt vacationed during the summertime.

On March 10, President Johnson signed legislation enacted by Congress authorizing the establishment of Cape Lookout National Seashore, N.C. This 30,000-acre area will conserve for public use and enjoyment a 58-mile chain of barrier islands of the celebrated Outer Banks extending from Ocracoke Inlet at the southern tip of Cape Hatteras National Seashore to Beaufort Inlet.

President Johnson also approved legislation enacted by Congress authorizing the establishment of the following areas:

Chamizal Treaty National Memorial, Tex., which honors the amicable settlement of the long-standing boundary dispute between Mexico and the United States over the Chamizal tract in the El Paso-Ciudad Juárez region.

Fort Union Trading Post National Historic Site, North Dakota-Montana, containing the remains of Fort Union, which in the 1800's was the principal fur-trading establishment on the Upper Missouri River and in the Northern Plains area.

George Rogers Clark National Historical Park, in Vincennes, Ind., containing the imposing memorial honoring the American Revolutionary hero. The memorial is near the site of Fort Sackville, the British fort captured by Clark following a surprise attack in 1779.

Guadalupe Mountains National Park, Texas, encompassing some of the most diversified and beautiful scenery in the Southwest.

San Juan Island National Historical Park, Washington, including sites associated with the boundary dispute between the United States and Great Britain during the mid-1800's.

Pictured Rocks National Lakeshore, Michigan, encompassing a portion of the Lake Superior shoreline, including 50-to-200-foot-high multicolored sandstone cliffs.

Bighorn Canyon National Recreation Area, Montana-Wyoming, including the reservoir formed by the construction of Yellowtail Dam by the Bureau of Reclamation.

President Johnson's boyhood home in Johnson City, Tex., was one of 15 sites declared eligible in 1966 for the registry of National Historical Landmarks.

Fourteen areas were declared eligible for designation as registered natural landmarks, among them picturesque Monhegan Island in the Atlantic off the coast of Maine, and the Great Swamp in Morris County, N.J.

These historical and natural landmarks are not units of the National Park System, but the National Park Service recognizes them with a certificate and marker which are presented to the owners.

As part of an extensive program of international cooperation, park administrators from the United States and 23 other countries participated in a 3-week course in the administration of national parks and equivalent reserves, conducted by the National Park Service and the School of Natural Resources of the University of Michigan.

Secretary of the Interior Udall named three new members to the Advisory Board on National Parks, Historic Sites, Buildings and Monuments—Dr. Bradford Washburn, director of the Museum of Sciences, Boston Society of Natural History, Boston, Mass.; Dr. Loren C. Eiseley, Department of Anthropology, University of Pennsylvania, Philadelphia, Penn.; and Dr. Durward L. Allen, Professor of Wildlife Ecology, Department of Forestry and Conservation, Purdue University, Lafayette, Ind.

GEORGE B. HARTZOG, JR.
Director, U.S. NATIONAL PARK SERVICE

PAUL VI, POPE. The search for peace in Vietnam was a major preoccupation of Pope Paul during 1966. He followed up his 1965 peace visit to the United Nations General Assembly with intensive diplomacy, and was credited with a significant role in achieving the Christmas cease-fire in 1965. And in pursuit of peace, he conferred not only with U.S. Ambassador to the United Nations Arthur Goldberg, but also granted a special audience to Soviet Foreign Minister Andrei Gromyko, who on his

Pope Paul VI visits Rome's City Hall April 16.

Wide World

April 27 visit became the highest-ranking communist official ever welcomed at the Vatican.

In his Easter message, Pope Paul begged for peace. He warned mankind against returning to the old world of "grasping, shortsighted schemes." In September, he issued a special encyclical letter calling on Catholics to pray for peace, and to be alive to the possibility that the war in southeast Asia could become "a more disastrous calamity." The Pope earlier sent a special mission to Vietnam but the findings of that diplomatic endeavor were not made public.

Paul VI in the course of Vatican Council II had removed the question of birth control and the population explosion from the agenda, and appointed a special commission to investigate it. The commission delivered its report to the Pope in June. The Pope waited until the Italian Gynecological Society met in Rome in October, when he said that the question is so complex that he was deferring his decision. Pending a further pronouncement on his part, he said, Catholics should maintain the church position against artificial birth control, laid down by Popes Pius XI and XII.

The most notable ecclesiastical visitor of the year at the Vatican was Archbishop of Canterbury Michael Ramsey, who in March became the first head of the Church of England to pay an official call on the bishop of Rome since the Anglican Reformation. The two ended their two-day conversation by jointly leading an ecumenical service.

In the same ecumenical vein, the Pope played a major role in the Vatican's encouragement of Catholic scholars to join with others in Bible translations for all.

In the course of the year, Paul VI urged bishops to step down by the age of 75. He also reduced the traditional Roman Catholic fast days to two: Ash Wednesday and Good Friday, and paved the way for the elimination of the age-old requirement that Catholics abstain from eating meat on Fridays. The bishops of many countries, Canada and the United States among them, later erased the Friday abstinence law from the books.

The Pope had taken steps to continue his visits abroad with a trip to Poland, where in 1966 the church was celebrating its 1,000th anniversary. But because of a church-state dispute in Poland, the Polish Government rejected the idea of such a trip. Pope Paul instead made excursions to central Italian villages where no pope had been for centuries.

PAUL W. McCLOSKEY
Former Assistant Foreign Editor
NATIONAL CATHOLIC WELFARE
CONFERENCE NEWS SERVICE

PEACE CORPS. In 1966—the Peace Corps' fifth year—the 25,000th volunteer left for overseas assignment, while the 10,000th volunteer to complete a two-year tour returned to the United States.

Interest in the Peace Corps during the year was so great that the organization recruited 1,000 more volunteers than it first expected. A record 10,000 would-be volunteers were trained during the program year, a 20 per cent increase over 1965 when about 8,500 were accepted.

During the summer of 1966, on more than 80 college and university campuses from Hawaii to southern Florida, the Peace Corps conducted the nation's largest summer school. Some 7,500 would-be volunteers trained for three months. Total Peace Corps strength by the end of the year was over 14,000.

Volunteers were sent during 1966 for the first time to Chad, Botswana (Bechuanaland) and Mauritania in Africa, Guyana and Paraguay in Latin America, and South Korea in the Far East, and Micronesia in the Pacific, bringing to 52 the total of Peace Corps host countries.

Education and community development continued to be the major focus of Peace Corps efforts (half of the volunteers are engaged in teaching, and a quarter in community development). During 1966, Peace Corps volunteers helped train 60,000 young teachers who will be responsible for the education of 10 million students. Impact in community development is harder to measure, but Bolivia provides an example: initial efforts there have blossomed into a national program that is putting hundreds of trained workers into the villages with Peace Corps volunteers at their side.

Important programs in agriculture and health also are under way. Twenty-one countries are getting help in modernizing agriculture. In Malawi a successful pilot tuberculosis-eradication program has demonstrated that Peace Corps volunteers—college generalists working with a few professionals—can make a significant contribution to the control of communicable disease. This has been followed by programs tackling a variety of diseases: malaria, filariasis and leprosy.

Among the more dramatic new projects undertaken by the organization during the year were:

India Agriculture. Following Prime Minister Gandhi's visit to the United States, the Peace Corps was asked to augment its operations in India to help alleviate that country's chronic food shortage. By the end of 1966 more than 1,100 of the 1,600 volunteers, who were serv-

Jack Vaughn, who succeeded Sargent Shriver as Peace Corps director in early 1966, meets with volunteers and students in Tanzania in April. Below, a volunteer and an Indian farmer work on a poultry-development project.

Photos Peace Corps

ing in India, were specializing in agriculture and nutrition.

Micronesia. In May, President Johnson transmitted a request from the UN for the assistance of Peace Corps volunteers as teachers, health workers and community-action workers to go to the U.S.-administered Trust Territory of the Pacific Islands. Some 3,000 applications were received in the few weeks following the announcement—a figure nearly ten times the Peace Corps' original expectation. The training programs were conducted in Hawaii and Florida. By year's end, about 400 volunteers were at work in Micronesia.

Eighteen other nations have set up their version of the Peace Corps or expanded existing programs of a similar nature.

JACK H. VAUGHN
Director, U.S. PEACE CORPS

PEARSON, LESTER B. Prime Minister of Canada Lester B. Pearson guided his minority Government through a tumultuous year in the House of Commons and managed to survive several crises without having to dissolve Parliament and call a general election. The problems that preoccupied him were espionage, widening labor troubles and inflation. His greatest success came in the international field: at two conferences of British Commonwealth prime ministers—one at Lagos, Nigeria, in January, the other in London in September— his diplomacy was given credit for averting a serious split between white and nonwhite Commonwealth nations over Rhodesia.

One espionage case involved a minor postal clerk in Vancouver, George Victor Spencer, who allegedly agreed to provide information about the post office to the Soviet Embassy in Ottawa. Spencer was discovered and fired, and two Soviet diplomats were expelled. Pearson refused requests of opposition parties in the House of Commons to hold an inquiry to ascertain if Spencer had been treated fairly; then took the unprecedented step of telephoning the spy suspect to find out if he wanted an investigation. He did, so Pearson ordered one. This

In August, Prime Minister Pearson and President Johnson met at Campobello Island, off the coast of New Brunswick.
Wide World

precipitated a cabinet crisis: in changing his mind, Pearson overruled his Minister of Justice, Lucien Cardin. Cardin resigned, then withdrew his resignation, only to bring about an even greater crisis. Goaded by the leader of the opposition Conservative Party, John Diefenbaker, Cardin accused Diefenbaker of ignoring a sex-and-security scandal during the previous Conservative administration. The resulting furor caused some of the wildest scenes ever witnessed in the House of Commons.

Pearson was accused of supplying the information to Cardin after combing through secret files of the Royal Canadian Mounted Police to find scandals with which to intimidate and embarrass the Opposition. Pearson confirmed that he had perused the files, but insisted that his motive was not political vengeance. The only reason he did it, he argued, was to discover if there had been any further attempts to subvert the course of justice similar to the 1964 scandal in which a cabinet aide was accused of offering a bribe to a lawyer in a criminal case. Pearson's explanation was upheld when an opposition motion of no confidence in him was defeated by a vote of 133 to 106. As a result of the two security cases, Pearson appointed a Royal Commission to inquire into all aspects of security.

Pearson also appointed a commission to examine labor law and labor disputes in Canada after a year of crippling strikes and union unrest. In June, Pearson intervened in a 5-week strike of Quebec longshoremen and facilitated a 30 per cent increase for the strikers. A threatened strike of St. Lawrence Seaway workers was narrowly averted when a government-directed settlement—again a 30 per cent increase—was accepted. Other unions adopted the 30 per cent figure as their goal; railway unions went on strike when they could not get it, and Pearson had to call a special session of Parliament to force the strikers back to work.

In August, President Lyndon Johnson invited Pearson to meet him at Campobello Island, off the coast of New Brunswick. They conferred for two hours.

WILLIAM FRENCH
Literary Editor, TORONTO GLOBE AND MAIL

PENNSYLVANIA. In March the United States' first atomic power station began operation at Peach Bottom, Pa. . . . The University of Pittsburgh became part of the state system of higher education. . . . Lt. Gov. Raymond Schafer (R) defeated Milton Shapp Nov. 8 for governor. . . . State Attorney General Walter E. Alessandroni and his wife died May 8 in a plane crash. Former Gov. David L. Lawrence died Nov. 21.

PHOTOGRAPHY

By JACOB DESCHIN
Camera Editor
THE NEW YORK TIMES

Rolleiflex SL66 (Rollei Honeywell in the United States).

Major attention was focused in 1966 on the debut of a new design by the makers of the Rolleiflex twin-lens reflex camera. Without abandoning the latter, which has had an international following since Franke & Heidecke, the German makers, introduced the camera in 1928, the company announced a single-lens reflex version to use the 120 film size. The camera was not expected to reach the United States until sometime in 1967.

The new camera is the Rolleiflex SL66, equipped with 80mm f/2.8 Planar lens and a focal-plane shutter with a speed range of 1 second to 1/1,000 and bulb. Interchangeable lenses will range from the wide-angle 50mm f/4 and will include 120mm, 150mm, 250mm, 500mm and 1,000mm lenses. The lenses can be reversed for optimum correction in close-up photography. The camera has an 8° tilt in front for increasing depth of field; interchangeable film backs; four interchangeable focusing screens, one with a range finder; and several other interesting features, among them an air brake to minimize camera shake when the reflex mirror swings up for the exposure.

Activity in the super-8 (format 50 per cent larger than the traditional double-8) field centered principally on projectors that offered users the best of both the old and the new in 8mm movies. That is, the dual-format super-8 8mm projector, which could be adapted by a simple adjustment either for the old 8mm size or the 50 per cent-larger super-8 frame.

Eastman Kodak's Kodak Instamatic M95 had, in addition to this feature, an ultrafast f/1.0 Kodak Projection Lens and could be adjusted to run at 6 frames per second for slowing down action, and at 54 frames for speeding it up.

Bell & Howell's contribution, the 8mm Autoload Projector, simplified the changeover from one film format to the other by means of a selector lever. The machine also has the novel convenience that both film formats can be spliced together on a single reel. A special cutout above and below the splice automatically stops the machine, enabling the user to shift the lever to the new format.

In the movie-camera field, Japan's Fuji introduced an advanced design in Single-8 or Instant Load 8mm, the Japanese counterpart of the super-8. The camera, the Instant Load Fujica Reflex Zoom Z-2, offers facilities for making fade-ins and fade-outs, lap dissolves, animation, double exposure, and time-lapse effects right in the camera. The effects are possible because of the special design of the Single-8 film cartridge: this permits rewinding the film for any desired length.

The growing acceptance of the Instamatic Kodapak design by the public and hence by manufacturers in the United States and abroad continued apace as companies brought out new inexpensive models. At the same time, the competing Rapid system introduced by Agfa in Germany and the United States, and adopted by other companies, made considerable headway. This was due to vigorous promotional activity.

A new addition to the flashcube line was the Kodak Instamatic 324 camera. A West German product made for Eastman Kodak, it has the relatively fast aperture of f/2.8. The camera also has automatic exposure control, daylight shutter speed of 1/125, which converts to 1/30 when using the flashcube, and focuses down to 2.5 feet.

Bell & Howell offered a slide projector with a preview screen that automatically shows the next slide to be projected. This feature gives the projectionist an opportunity to prepare his comments, if needed, before the slide is actually projected on the full screen. The innovation was incorporated in a machine with an autofocusing mechanism. After the first slide has been properly focused, all succeeding slides come into focus automatically by means of electronic control.

An innovation in the 35mm single-lens reflex field was the Konica Auto-Reflex, said to be the industry's "first fully automatic single-

Gerald Lauzze, a 14-year-old student at Gillette Road Junior H.S., Clay, N.Y., won a first award for his *Reflections* in the 1966 Scholastic Photography Awards contest.

lens reflex, with interchangeable lenses and a focal-plane shutter." The camera does not require matching the exposure-meter needle: one merely selects the film and shutter speed. The user can override the automatic feature.

New Darkroom Equipment

Several darkroom items stirred some interest. The Spiratone DoubLograM enlarger, for enlarging from 2¼ x 2¼ inches down to 35mm, has a pantograph system by which the enlarger head can be moved easily to project onto any part of the baseboard and even below the baseboard level. The enlarger itself remains stationary. It has a color head with a choice of glassless carriers, a 4-inch condenser and standard Leica-type threaded lens board.

A brighter darkroom was made possible by the introduction of the Amber Photo-Lite, a new kind of safelight source for darkrooms. It approaches the level of moderate room illumination, allowing the darkroom worker to move about more comfortably and efficiently in the darkroom than he can with the conventional safelight. Basically an ordinary white fluorescent tube, it is coated on the outside with a blend of six colors designed selectively to absorb certain colors and to transmit others.

Two print-developing units that required no darkroom were demonstrated. The Insta-Larger was to be on the market by the end of 1966. It is a fixed-focus combination enlarging and developing machine for making black-and-white 3½-inch-square pictures from Instamatic black-and-white or color negatives in 10 seconds for the one, in 60 for the other. Photo-Magic, an amateur contact-printing machine that took only 1 minute to develop a roll of 120 or 620 roll film and make prints from the negatives, was near completion at year's end.

The Brooks Instant Load Developing Kit introduced a slightly whimsical note in the darkroom category. This was a small tank for developing 35mm black-and-white film without removing the film from its cartridge. A one-shot solution was poured into the tank, and the cartridge was attached to the cap of the tank for agitating the solution during the 4 minutes combined developing-fixing time required. The film was then removed from the cartridge for washing and drying.

Exposure Meters

Two unusual exposure meters appeared. The Spotron Pentaview, a cadmium-sulfide spot meter with an acceptance angle of 10°, reads a field covering about the same area as a 250mm lens on a 35mm camera. The unit's prism finder system shows the area being read upright and unreversed. After the meter needle has been centered, the correct exposure is read from an external control dial.

A new Weston meter radically different from its predecessors, the Weston Ranger 9 incorporates an eye-level viewfinder that isolates an 18° area for spot reading. It is made in Newark, N.J., and measures "illumination at levels as low as distant candlelight or moonlight or as bright as noon sunlight." Provision was made to interchange the calculator dials, one of which would convert to Ansel Adams' zone system.

Other Developments

The Kodak Carousel Sound Synchronizer can be used with any model of the Kodak Carousel projector in conjunction with a standard stereo tape recorder. Sound is recorded on one track, and a change-slide signal is recorded on the second track. The sound is then played back as the pictures are projected. The operation is fully automatic and in complete synchronization with the previously recorded sound.

The principle of the electronic shutter reached the market in two Japanese cameras, both in the half-frame 35mm category. One was the Yashica Electro Half; the other, the motorized Olympus Pen-Em. Instead of the progressively spaced time intervals of the conventional mechanical shutter, the new shutters are controlled by a cadmium-sulfide cell that electronically computes the exact shutter speeds called for by the available light. These can be as short as 1/500 and as long as two minutes in the two cameras made available in 1966.

A new kind of flashcube helped solve a supply problem. There had been a scarcity of the sealed rotating flashcube that held 4 tiny AG-1 bulbs in separate reflectors and permitted exposure of 4 flash shots in quick succession. The flashcube had to be discarded after 4 flashes. The new flashcube is a permanent device in which flashed AG-1 bulbs are replaced with fresh bulbs.

A novel design in this category is the HIP "piggyback" device, in which reusable flashcube holders can be mounted on the camera one on top of the other to permit 8 instead of 4 flash shots in succession.

Moviemakers and color-slide enthusiasts were offered a new line of C-battery-operated tape-recorder equipment in new Norelco units made by the North American Philips Co., Inc. The compact cassette system that is the basis of the line has been adopted by 39 major companies throughout the world. Operation of the reel-to-reel system is contained permanently within the miniature cassettes. The tape is less than ¼-inch wide and plays at a speed of 1⅞ inches per second.

Shelby Wilson, 17, a student at Palo Verde High School, Tucson, Ariz., won a college scholarship grant in 1966 Scholastic Photography Awards contest for his portfolio of photographs, which included the above, On Serving.

PHYSICS. One of the wonderful things about physics is its scope. From the incredibly tiny particles that make up the nucleus of every atom to the incredibly large galaxies, no aspect of matter or its transformations is without interest to the physicist. Events of 1966, a small sampling of which is recorded below, gave fresh evidence of this breadth.

Within the Nucleus

One focus of physical-research effort in recent years has been on elementary particles. These are the smallest portions of matter known to man. Three of them, the electron, the proton and the neutron, are stable. They are the stuff out of which all atoms and hence all bulk matter are made. All of the remaining so-called elementary particles are not stable. They have extremely short lives (measured in millionths of millionths of a second) after the moment they are created in high-energy collisions at the target of one of the modern multibillion-volt atom smashers.

A prime task of physics in recent years has been to understand these elementary particles, to bring order out of the increasing number of which we are aware. No resolution of the problem came in 1966. Instead there came a further addition to the now-crowded "nuclear zoo." It was a new particle known simply as N*3245. It is the most massive nuclear particle yet found—more than three times heavier than the stable proton. Its lifetime is extremely short,

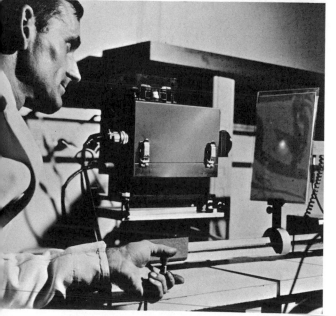

A technician activates a high-energy liquid laser.
General Telephone & Electronics Corporation

however, a fraction of a billionth of a billionth of a second. Indeed, like some other "nuclear-resonance" particles of this very short life, it is likely that this is not so much a distinct particle as an excited (superenergized) state of the proton itself.

At a somewhat larger size level—within the atomic nucleus rather than within its constituent protons and neutrons—1966 brought fresh progress and understanding. Here the picture is not nearly so dark as among the elementary particles. A great deal is known about the numbers and about the energy of the protons and neutrons within any particular nucleus. But much detail of their arrangement is missing.

In March 1966, research using a new measurement technique gave fresh insight into this matter of shape. The measurement, an indirect one, involves the capture of muons. Muons are one of the more stable of the unstable elementary particles mentioned above. The negatively charged muons are akin to the electrons that orbit the atomic nucleus, but about two hundred times heavier. This means that a muon can be captured in an orbit around the positively charged nucleus, and this orbit will lie much closer to the nucleus than an ordinary electron orbit. In fact, some of the time the muon will be within the nucleus itself. X rays emitted as the muon shifts from one orbit to another convey information about the muonic orbits around the nucleus. If these X rays could be measured with sufficient precision, physicists reasoned, new information could be gathered about the shape of nuclei. The new technique that has now made such precision measurement possible utilizes a special variation of semiconductor material, the sort from which transistors are made. These so-called lithium-drifted germanium detectors permitted researchers at the University of Chicago and at New York's Columbia University to gain new insight into the shape of the nuclei of lead and bismuth.

The year 1966 saw the new $114 million Stanford Linear Accelerator come into operation at full energy. Its beam of twenty billion-volt electrons provides another, if rather more costly, technique for investigating both the structure of nuclei and their constituent nucleons.

Among the Stars

The stars that crowd the night sky, and even the billions more that we can see only with the aid of optical telescopes, are not all the stellar objects. The relatively young science of radio astronomy has helped locate objects that emit no light but do give off radio waves. Even more recently it has been recognized that some

Lawrence Radiation Laboratory, Berkeley
This giant nuclear accelerator has a proton output of 800,000,000,000 particles per pulse.

stars can be "seen" only through the X rays they emit. To see the X rays, a satellite or rocket with X-ray detectors mounted aboard must be sent above the earth's atmosphere, which absorbs X rays. This sort of measurement, pioneered by a group from the U.S. Naval Research Laboratory, has led to the identification of X rays from our sun, from the Crab Nebula, and from at least ten other sources in the equatorial plane of our galaxy.

On March 8, 1966, an Aerobee rocket was used to measure a totally new sort of X-ray source. Called Sco X-1, the new source is located in the constellation Scorpio. What makes it different is that it is very concentrated—less than twenty seconds of arc in angular diameter. The experimenters, a combined group from the Massachusetts Institute of Technology and American Science and Engineering, Inc., feel that the new celestial body must be unlike any heretofore observed. It may be a proto-star, a star just being formed that radiates X rays as a result of the interaction of high-energy electrons and the magnetic field surrounding it.

In Man's Domain

Not all of the developments in physics are concerned with matters so esoteric. One bit of developmental physics, reported in February 1966, concerns the problem of hearing underwater. In air we are able to determine the direction from which a sound comes, because the ear closer to the sound hears it a thousandth of a second or so before the other. This difference in time of arrival is interpreted by our brains to give the direction of the source. Underwater this mechanism does not work. For one thing, the speed of sound is over four times faster than in air, and the delay between the receptions of a sound at our ears is correspondingly shortened. The brain cannot work with this briefer interval. Furthermore, underwater sounds go through the skull as much as directly into the ears. Skin divers hear as much through bone conduction as through their ears.

Physicists at CBS Laboratories in Stamford, Conn., found an answer to this problem. They developed a pair of microphones to receive the sound, and added appropriate electronic circuitry to increase the time delay and intensity to those corresponding to sounds received in air. These corrected signals are fed to an underwater diver through earphones, restoring his ability to determine the direction from which a sound comes.

No survey of annual developments in physics would be complete without at least a quick view of what is new with lasers, those remarkable sources of powerful and coherent light. One advance, revealed in the June 1966 issue of *Applied Optics,* was the development of a sun-powered laser. Using a crystal of yttrium-aluminum-garnet (YAG) onto which are focused the rays of the sun, one can get laser action that leads to intense, highly concentrated beams of infrared light.

In another development, a second type of liquid laser—the first to use an inorganic liquid—was developed at the Bayside laboratories of General Telephone & Electronics, Inc. It is one of the simplest lasers to make, requiring no complex crystal growth as for the solid-type laser. The chemical neodymium oxide is dissolved in selenium oxychloride, a liquid. This solution is then put into a tube, placed between suitable mirrors and exposed to a strong pulse of light from a flashtube. A pulse of laser light is produced between the mirrors.

DANIEL I. COOPER, Publisher
INTERNATIONAL SCIENCE AND TECHNOLOGY

POSTAL SERVICES:

NEW TECHNIQUES FOR BETTER MAIL SERVICE

By LAWRENCE F. O'BRIEN

U.S. Postmaster General

The greatest problem facing the Post Office Department today is the phenomenal increase in mail volume. Because of evidence that past methodology will not solve postal problems of the future, most of the department's programs are directed toward more efficient ways of handling volume mail.

Since 1961 the department has introduced a number of programs encouraging large mailers, responsible for about 75 per cent of total mail volume, to distribute their nonpriority mail throughout the working day instead of in bulk after 5 P.M. Nationwide Improved Mail Service (NIMS) was the first effort in this direction, and 20,000 business leaders, working in cooperation with the department through Mail Users' Councils, have turned NIMS into an effective system of scheduled mail. Growing out of NIMS were: (1) Accelerated Business Collection and Delivery (ABCD), permitting delivery, within certain delivery areas, by 3 P.M. of all first-class letters deposited in ABCD boxes by 11 A.M.; and (2) Vertical Improved Mail (VIM), designed to move mail through high-rise office and apartment buildings by conveyors operating from a central mailroom.

The ZIP Code

In July 1963, with the introduction of the Zoning Improvement Plan popularly known as ZIP Code, the department began possibly the most epochal postal program of all time. ZIP Code divides the country into 15 national areas, 552 sectional centers, and many local zones and delivery post offices. Like other NIMS programs, ZIP Code originally sought the cooperation of large mailers in converting their address files and presorting in ZIP Code sequence before placing mail in the postal stream.

Traditionally the great bulk of the department's domestic mail was transported by rail, and major railroad centers had been the massing, re-sorting and redistributing points for long distances. Until 1930, when the railroads furnished 10,000 trains to carry the mails, trains offered the fastest, cheapest transportation available. Today mail volume has virtually trebled, rising from 27,000,000,000 to 76,000,000,000 pieces annually. Ironically mail trains available to post offices have dropped by 90 per cent, or to fewer than 1,000, while millions of cars and trucks move over a network of highspeed inter- and intrastate roadways, and fledgling airlines have become a giant industry.

In July 1965, the Post Office Department opened the last of its 552 sectional centers, and set in motion a new transportation system to tie in with ZIP Code. Instead of the old railroad hubs, the sectional centers are strategically located to move mail by *every* type of transportation: rail, bus, truck, boat or plane.

In the fall of 1965, at the Detroit, Mich., post office, the department began operation of its first optical reading machine, capable of reading and sorting printed ZIP Coded addresses at the rate of 36,000 an hour. The scanner's memory system is geared to sort the mail for incoming, outgoing or local delivery at the flick of a switch. The machine, attached to a letter sorter, examines the face of each envelope (formerly a manual operation), locates the ZIP Code, and then instructs the sorter where to distribute each letter. Fourteen additional machines have been ordered for use in eight other major post offices.

Increasing use of ZIP Code by individuals has been requested. The Post Office Department conducted a national ZIP Code promotion week in the fall of 1966 and arranged to promote a year-round, nationwide educational campaign on ZIP Code. The Federal Government has announced regulations for full participation in ZIP Code. Multiple ZIP Codes have been reduced to single ones in 641 cities; all single-coded cities have ZIP Codes imprinted in postmarks; and slogans urging use of ZIP Code were ordered for the cancellation dies in 314 major post offices.

On July 1, 1965, the department issued regulations making it mandatory after January 1967 that commercial mailers presort second- and third-class volume mail by ZIP Code. Since then, each of the 250,000 second- and third-class permit holders have been personally notified of the deadline and offered assistance.

Computers and the Mails

During 1966, the Post Office Department aligned itself with the computer age, moving deeply into newly explored areas of planning, programing and budgeting. Long-range planning became integral to all basic activities of the department, from processing of the mail to enforcement of the postal law.

In the early months of 1966 there was created an Office of Planning to maintain close ties with private industry and research groups and to chart alternative programs in anticipating future needs of the department. This office —made up of specialists in engineering, physical sciences, and statistical and postal operations—will not be burdened with daily operational details. It will on the contrary be free to plan for the future, and provide leadership to meet rapidly increasing mail volume and tremendous problems of population growth, suburban sprawl, big-city bottlenecks and such.

In line with this modern concept of planning for the future, the department signed a $22.7 million contract in May 1966 for a source data system to be installed in 75 post offices and connected to two central computers. The system will supply operating officials with facts needed for proper decisions and eliminate many manual functions, such as labor distribution and reporting, recording of mail volume and collection of payroll data.

By the end of 1966, electronic data-processing systems in six postal-data centers were replaced with equipment keyed to heavier work-load requirements and more economical operation.

Highlighting the entry into the computer age was reorganization of the Office of Research and Engineering. With the department's support, Congress approved legislation providing a sixth assistant postmaster general to direct research-and-engineering activities. The department contracted with leading educational institutions to tap research advances in technology.

Further Changes

The Post Office Department undertook a massive program to accelerate mechanization and modernization of the postal system, particularly in the 109 post offices handling more than 60 per cent of the annual volume. In addition to the ZIP Code readers this accelerated mechanization will place 52 letter sorters in 30 cities, 130 edger-stacker machines in 80 cities, 11 semiautomatic sack-sorting machines in 8 cities, 17 parcel-post sorting machines in 3 cities, and 24 overhead equipment monitoring systems in 18 cities. The letter sorters separate more than a million letters an hour, distributing them to as many as 279 destination bins; facer-canceler machines

Post Office Department

Postmaster General O'Brien examines an optical scanner. It can sort 36,000 printed ZIP Coded addresses an hour.

use electric eyes to locate stamps, face all letters in the same direction and then cancel the stamps.

January 1966 saw the beginning of an intensive study to determine what can be done to improve mail service. The investigation, under a team of 200 postal inspectors, started with observations at the 76 largest post offices and has been expanded to all of the Post Office Department's 552 sectional centers. Postal inspectors checked out complaints, pinpointed bottlenecks and recommended solutions to delayed-mail problems. By April, significant advances had been scored in all phases of the investigation, and the program continued.

Starting in September 1966, the department began installation of 100 self-service postal units in major U.S. shopping centers. Scheduled service for parcel post now operates in 26 areas across the nation, offering faster and more reliable service for nearly 80 million people over a million square miles.

On Sept. 20 President Johnson signed into law a postal-reform bill, effective Jan. 15, 1967, designed to raise rates and to boost weight and size limits for parcel post. This legislation provides for a gradual increase in weight and size of parcels mailed from first-class post offices to 40 pounds and 84 inches by 1971.

POVERTY

By SARGENT SHRIVER
Director
U.S. OFFICE OF ECONOMIC OPPORTUNITY

Congress appropriated $1,500,000,000 to the Office of Economic Opportunity for the second year of its operation—July 1, 1965, through June 30, 1966. This money was used to continue existing OEO projects and to fund new projects to help eliminate the poverty afflicting more than 32 million Americans.

The Economic Opportunity Act of 1964 was passed by the U.S. Congress on Aug. 20, 1964. This act called for the creation of the Office of Economic Opportunity (OEO) to (1) establish new programs for the poor and (2) coordinate the antipoverty efforts of *all* Federal agencies. The combined national effort is called "the war on poverty."

Community Action. By June 1966, over 1,000 communities throughout the United States had organized public or private nonprofit agencies to administer programs especially designed to meet the needs of their communities. These programs (1) gave promise of eliminating the causes of poverty and (2) involved the poor in planning and operating the programs. The concept of "maximum feasible participation" of the poor was strongly supported by the Office of Economic Opportunity. Over 29 per cent of the members of the governing boards of the Community Action agencies were representatives of the poor.

Sargent Shriver, director of OEO.

Services provided through Community Action ranged from preschool programs to job opportunities for senior citizens. In addition to the community programs, special programs serving the needs of the poor throughout the nation were funded through Community Action. Upward Bound provides cultural enrichment and remedial tutoring to motivate high-school students from low-income families toward college. Over 20,000 students were enrolled in projects at 224 educational institutions, at a cost of $28 million. Legal assistance was provided to communities through 155 Legal Services projects costing $27 million. The Head Start preschool program provides educational experiences, health check-ups, and parental involvement for disadvantaged children, in preparation for their entering school. Over 575,000 children participated in the 1966 summer program, and almost 200,000 children participated in the year-round program. The total cost for all of Head Start in fiscal year 1966 was $180 million.

Foster Grandparents is one of several employment programs for the aged. In 1966, 2,194 men and women 60 years of age and older earned money and increased their feelings of self-respect by visiting with and providing concern and affection for 4,388 infants and children living in institutions. There were 33 Foster Grandparents projects funded at a cost of $5 million. Other programs for the aged in 1966 were Medicare Alert, Home Health Aides and Green Thumb. Over $9 million was granted for 8 new Health Centers, making a total of 9 centers operating in fiscal year 1966 to provide outpatient medical care for the poor. Neighborhood Multipurpose Centers were funded in communities throughout the country to provide information about new and existing poverty programs and to make available under one roof the services of many public and private agencies.

Community Action funds benefited Indians and migrant worker families, who are among our most poverty-stricken citizens. In fiscal year 1966, 78 grants were made to 100 Indian tribes at a cost of $12 million. Over 150,000 migrants benefited from 66 grants for migrant aid, authorized as Migrant Assistance programs and costing $25 million.

VISTA. Another major program is VISTA (Volunteers in Service to America), which functions as a domestic Peace Corps. VISTA volunteers were at work in 12 mental-health projects, 56 Indian reservations, 23 migrant camps, 31 Job Corps centers, 86 rural areas and 89 urban poverty areas at the close of the fiscal year. Thirty-six hundred volunteers, aged

18 through 85, were in service or training at that time, including 500 college students, known as VISTA Associates, who worked in Appalachia during the summer of 1966. A total of 450 volunteers reenlisted for further service at the end of their one-year commitment. OEO-obligated funds for VISTA in fiscal year 1966 totaled $16 million.

Job Corps. The Job Corps, for which $303 million was obligated in fiscal year 1966, provides a new opportunity for school dropouts aged 16 through 21, offering programs of education, job training and citizenship responsibility. During 1966, there were 106 Job Corps residential centers in operation in 40 states and Puerto Rico. Urban centers are located near cities, and smaller conservation centers are in rural areas. The conservation centers, administered by the Departments of the Interior and of Agriculture, provide training for such jobs as forestry, surveying and carpentry. The men's urban centers train for such fields as data processing and auto mechanics. At women's urban centers there are courses for secretaries, homemakers, beauticians and nurses' aides.

On June 30, 1966, there were 28,500 youths (25,900 men and 2,600 women) enrolled in the Job Corps. By June 1967, the Job Corps Centers will have a total enrollment of up to 45,000, and 23 per cent of the enrollees will be women. Since the first center opened, 6,566 youths have graduated from the Job Corps. Of these, 1,765 were placed in jobs, 314 returned to school and 679 entered the armed forces.

Delegated Programs. The remaining programs of the Office of Economic Opportunity are delegated to other Federal agencies for purposes of administration. The Neighborhood Youth Corps (NYC) is administered by the Department of Labor. During fiscal year 1966, the Neighborhood Youth Corps made available 528,000 jobs for youths 16 through 21 years of age who were still in school or had been out of school for at least 4 months. During the school year, 189,000 enrollees were in school, and worked up to 15 hours a week. The 99,000 out-of-school enrollees worked 32 to 35 hours a week and received up to eight hours a week of remedial instruction. The summer program enrolled 240,000 youths. Besides encouraging dropouts to return to school and providing income for needy youths, NYC has reduced juvenile crime and has prepared teen-agers for further employment opportunities. The obligated cost of this program was $271 million.

The Adult Basic Education program was administered by the Office of Education, Department of Health, Education, and Welfare, in fiscal year 1966. It aims to help the millions of adults who lack the basic skills of reading, writing and arithmetic. By June 1966, 45 states had their plans approved to provide elementary-level education classes for adults, training of teachers and development of instruction materials. Obligated costs totaled $35 million. Starting in fiscal year 1967, this program will be a part of the Office of Education, but other experimental adult basic education activities will be funded to local communities through Community Action.

The College Work Study program, transferred in 1965 to the Office of Education, was funded by OEO in fiscal year 1966. Beginning in fiscal year 1967, the program will be both funded and administered by the Office of Education. More than 1,100 institutions of higher learning have participated in College Work Study by administering part-time employment programs for needy college students.

The Work Experience program is administered by the Welfare Administration, Department of Health, Education, and Welfare. In fiscal year 1966, there were 147 new projects approved for 38,000 trainees, and renewals of 127 projects for 46,500 trainees. A total of $112 million was obligated for these programs, which give job training for unemployed heads of households with dependent children. During 1966, 13,800 people were placed in useful, income-producing jobs after finishing their Work Experience training.

The Rural Loans program is administered by the Farmers Home Administration of the Department of Agriculture. Loans of up to $2,500 are available to individuals living in communities of less than 5,500 people, for farm improvements, or small income-producing enterprises. In fiscal year 1966, 17,073 loans were made at a cost of $27.3 million. Loans to cooperatives serving rural poor are also available, and 391 such loans totaling $4.7 million were granted. Beginning in 1967, Indians living on reservations are also eligible to receive cooperative loans.

The program of Small Business Loans, administered by the Small Business Administration, made $17.3 million available through 1,651 Economic Opportunity loans of up to $15,000 each. The recipients of the loans each received technical assistance to help in the establishment or expansion of businesses.

In less than two years, more than eight million Americans have been served by programs of the Office of Economic Opportunity. New and promising ways to end the cycle of poverty will be inaugurated, until the "war on poverty" is won.

PRIZES AND AWARDS

ART, ARCHITECTURE AND MUSIC

American Institute of Architects
Gold Medal: KENZO TANGE, Japan
R. S. Reynolds Memorial Award ($25,000): HANS HOLLEIN for a specialty candle shop in Vienna
American Institute of Graphic Arts Medal: PAUL RAND, artist, author, teacher, pioneer in graphic design
Robert O. Anderson Aspen Award in the Humanities ($30,000): CONSTANTINOS A. DOXIADIS, Greek city planner
Dimitri Mitropoulos International Music Gold Medals ($5,000): SYLVIA CADUFF, Switzerland; WALTER GILLESSEN, Germany; JUAN PABLO IZQUIERDO, Chile; ALAIN LOMBARD, France
Leonie Sonning Prize ($7,500): BIRGIT NILSSON
National Academy of Design Awards
Benjamin Altman (Landscape) Prizes ($2,000 and $1,000): EDWARD BETTS for *Spanish Coast;* ANTONIO P. MARTINO for *West Manayunk*
Benjamin Altman (Figure) Prizes ($2,000 and $1,000): JOSEPH HIRSCH for *Heretic;* ROBERT PHILIPP for *Introspection*
National Academy of Recording Arts and Sciences Awards (Grammy Awards)
Single record: A TASTE OF HONEY, Herb Alpert and the Tijuana Brass
Album, nonclassical: SEPTEMBER OF MY YEARS, Frank Sinatra
Album, classical: HOROWITZ AT CARNEGIE HALL, Vladimir Horowitz
Song: THE SHADOW OF YOUR SMILE
Female vocal: MY NAME IS BARBRA, Barbra Streisand
Male vocal: IT WAS A VERY GOOD YEAR, Frank Sinatra
National Gallery of Art Awards ($500): JAMES S. ACKERMAN, Harvard; HELEN AUPPERLE, Idaho Falls, Idaho; EMMA L. BIPPUS, Toledo, Ohio; SIBYL BROWNE, San Antonio, Tex.; MARTHA CHRISTENSEN, Louisville, Ky.; HOWARD CONANT, New York University; VICTOR D'AMICO, New York City; CHARLES M. DORN, Washington, D.C.; J. EUGENE GRIGSBY, JR., Phoenix, Ariz.; ROBERT INGLEHART, University of Michigan; MARIE L. LARKIN, University of Missouri; FREDERICK M. LOGAN, University of Wisconsin; DORIS W. LOUGH, Seattle, Wash.; EDWARD MATILL, Pennsylvania State University; MARY ADELINE MCKIBBIN, University of Pittsburgh; ERWIN PANOFSKY, Princeton; JAMES A. PORTER, Howard University; OLGA M. SCHUBKEGEL, Hammond, Ind.; JULIA B. SCHWARTZ, Florida State University; GRACE S. SMITH, Houston, Tex.; JOHN and AURELIA SOCHA, Minneapolis, Minn.; WILBER MOORE STILWELL, University of South Dakota; RUTH J. STOLLE, Tripoli, Wis.; FREDERICK S. WIGHT, University of California (Los Angeles); EDWIN ZIEGFELD, Columbia University
National Institute of Arts and Letters Awards
Arnold W. Brunner Memorial Prize in Architecture ($1,000): ROMALDO GIURGOLA

Gold Medal for Music: VIRGIL THOMSON
Gold Medal for Sculpture: JACQUES LIPCHITZ
Marjorie Peabody Waite Award ($1,500): HARRY PARTCH, composer
Richard and Hinda Rosenthal Foundation Award ($2,000): HOWARD HACK, painter
Grants in art ($2,500 each): ROMARE BEARDEN; LEE BONTECOU; CARROLL CLOAR; RAY JOHNSON; EZIO MARTINELLI; KARL SCHRAG; RICHARD CLAUDE ZIEMANN
Grants in music: WALTER ASCHAFFENBURG; RICHARD HOFFMANN; JOHN MacIVOR PERKINS; RALPH SHAPEY

JOURNALISM

Albert Lasker Medical Journalism Awards ($2,500 each)
Magazine award: GERALD ASTOR, Look, for article "Stroke: Second Greatest Crippler"
Newspaper award: MRS. JOANN RODGERS and LOUIS LINLEY, The Baltimore News American, for series *Your Health and Medicine*
Television award: WABC-TV, for mental-retardation story *Who Will Tie My Shoe?*
Ayer Cup for "excellence of typography, makeup and printing": THE WASHINGTON POST
Heywood Broun Award of the American Newspaper Guild ($1,000): JOHN A. FRASCA, Tampa (Fla.) Tribune, for series that resulted in the freeing of an innocent man from prison
Overseas Press Club Awards
George Polk Memorial Award for foreign reporting: MORLEY SAFER, CBS News, two Vietnam films
Robert Capa Award for photography from abroad: LARRY BURROWS, Life, Vietnam coverage
E. W. Fairchild Award for business-news reporting from abroad: BERNARD NOSSITER, The Washington Post, reports on international monetary developments
Ed Stout Award for Latin-American article or report: TED YATES AND NBC NEWS TEAM, *Santo Domingo: War among Friends*
Special award: GEN. DAVID SARNOFF, RCA board chairman, "in high respect and gratitude" for his pioneering in electronic journalism
Reporting from abroad
Newspaper or wire service: RICHARD CRITCHFIELD, Washington Star, Vietnam series
Newspaper or wire-service photographic reporting: KYOICHI SAWADA, United Press International, Vietnam photo coverage
Television reporting: MORLEY SAFER, CBS News, Vietnam films
Radio reporting: RICHARD VALERIANI, NBC News, Dominican Republic civil-war coverage
Magazine reporting: MICHAEL MOK and PAUL

SCHUTZER, Life, Vietnam story "In They Go To the Reality of War"
Foreign-affairs interpretation
  Newspaper or wire service: JACK FOISIE, The Los Angeles Times, Vietnam reports
  Television: FRED FREED, NBC News, White Paper series *American White Paper: U. S. Foreign Policy*
  Radio: EDWARD P. MORGAN, ABC Radio, Eastern European reports
  Magazine: A. M. ROSENTHAL, The New York Times, Hiroshima and Warsaw ghetto articles
  Book: ROBERT SHAPLEN, *The Lost Revolution*

LITERATURE

American Library Association Awards
  Caldecott Medal for "most distinguished American picture book for children": NONNY HOGROGIAN, *Always Room for One More*
  Newbery Medal for "most distinguished contribution to American literature for children": ELIZABETH BORTON de TREVIÑO, *I, Juan de Pareja*
Bancroft Prizes for "best books in American history, American diplomacy and American international relations" ($4,000 each): RICHARD B. MORRIS, *The Peacemakers: The Great Powers and American Independence;* THEODORE W. FRIEND 3d, *Between Two Empires: The Ordeal of the Philippines, 1926-1946*
Thomas R. Coward Memorial Award ($15,000): GAVIN LAMBERT, *Norman's Letter*
Governor-General Awards for Canadian Literature ($2,500 each)
  English poetry and drama: ALFRED PURDY, *The Cariboo Horses*
  English nonfiction: JAMES EAYRS, *In Defence of Canada*
  French poetry and drama: GILLES VIGNEAULT, *Quand les bateaux s'en vont*
  French fiction: GÉRARD BESSETTE, *L'incubation*
  French nonfiction: ANDRÉ S. VACHON, *Le temps et l'espace dans l'oeuvre de Paul Claudel*
Grolier Award for "devoted attention to children's reading and books for young readers" ($1,000): MILDRED L. BATCHELDER, retired executive director of the American Library Association's Children's Services Division
Houghton Mifflin Literary Fellowship Award ($5,000): MARGARET WALKER, *Jubilee*
J. Morris Jones-World Book Encyclopedia-American Library Association Goals Award ($25,000): AMERICAN ASSOCIATION OF SCHOOL LIBRARIANS
Mystery Writers of America (Edgar Awards)
  Mystery novel: ADAM HALL (Elleston Trevor), *The Quiller Memorandum*
  Mystery verse: JOHN BALL, *In the Heat of the Night*
National Book Awards ($1,000 each)
  Fiction: KATHERINE ANNE PORTER, *The Collected Stories of Katherine Anne Porter*
  Poetry: JAMES DICKEY, *Buckdancer's Choice*
  Arts and Letters: JANET FLANNER, *Paris Journal (1944-1965)*
  History and Biography: ARTHUR M. SCHLESINGER, JR., *A Thousand Days: John F. Kennedy in the White House*
National Book Committee's National Medal for Literature ($5,000): EDMUND WILSON
National Institute of Arts and Letters Awards
  Richard and Hinda Rosenthal Foundation Award ($2,000): TOM COLE
  Fellowship in literature ($6,500): H. E. F. DONOHUE
  Loines Award for Poetry ($1,000): WILLIAM MEREDITH
  Grants in literature ($2,500 each): WILLIAM ALFRED, JOHN BARTH, JAMES DICKEY, SHIRLEY HAZZARD, JOSEPHINE HERBST, EDWIN HONIG, GARY SNYDER, M. B. TOLSON

MOTION PICTURES

Academy of Motion Picture Arts and Sciences Awards (Oscars)
  Film: THE SOUND OF MUSIC
  Actor: LEE MARVIN, *Cat Ballou*
  Actress: JULIE CHRISTIE, *Darling*
  Supporting actor: MARTIN BALSAM, *A Thousand Clowns*
  Supporting actress: SHELLEY WINTERS, *A Patch of Blue*
  Direction: ROBERT WISE, *The Sound of Music*
  Foreign-language film: THE SHOP ON MAIN STREET
  Documentary feature: THE ELEANOR ROOSEVELT STORY
  Original screenplay: FREDERICK RAPHAEL, *Darling*
  Adapted screenplay: ROBERT BOLT, *Doctor Zhivago*
  Film editing: WILLIAM REYNOLDS, *The Sound of Music*
  Cartoon: THE DOT AND THE LINE, Metro-Goldwyn-Mayer
  Song: THE SHADOW OF YOUR SMILE by Johnny Mandel and Paul Francis Webster, from *The Sandpiper*
  Original musical score: MAURICE JARRE, *Doctor Zhivago*
  Adapted score: IRWIN KOSTAL, *The Sound of Music*
  Irving Thalberg Award for excellence in motion-picture entertainment: WILLIAM WYLER
Cannes International Film Festival Awards
  Gold Palm Grand Prize: UN HOMME ET UNE FEMME (A Man and a Woman), France; SIGNORE E SIGNORI (The Birds, the Bees and the Italians), Italy
  Best actor: PER OSCARSON, *Faim* (Hunger), Denmark
  Best actress: VANESSA REDGRAVE, *Morgan!*, Great Britain
  Best direction: SERGE YOUTKEVITCH, *Lenin in Poland*, Soviet Union
  Best short: SKATERDATER by Noel Black, United States
  Special jury prize: ALFIE, Great Britain
  International critics prize: THE YOUNG TÖRLESS, West Germany; LA GUERRE EST FINIE (The War Is Over), France

PULITZER PRIZES

Letters and music ($500 each)
  Fiction: COLLECTED STORIES OF KATHERINE ANNE PORTER by Katherine Anne Porter
  Drama: no award
  History: LIFE OF THE MIND IN AMERICA by Perry Miller
  Biography: A THOUSAND DAYS: JOHN F. KENNEDY IN THE WHITE HOUSE by Arthur M. Schlesinger, Jr.
  Poetry: SELECTED POEMS by Richard Eberhart
  Nonfiction: WANDERING THROUGH WINTER by Edwin Way Teale
  Music: VARIATIONS FOR ORCHESTRA by Leslie Bassett
Journalism ($1,000 each except for public-service gold medal)
  Public service: BOSTON GLOBE for campaign to prevent confirmation of Francis X. Morrissey as a Federal district judge in Massachusetts
  Local reporting, deadline pressure: LOS ANGELES TIMES STAFF, for coverage of Watts riots
  Local reporting, no deadline pressure: JOHN A. FRASCA, Tampa (Fla.) Tribune, for investigation and reporting of two robberies that resulted in the freeing of an innocent man
  National reporting: HAYNES JOHNSON, Evening Star, Washington, D.C., for coverage of Selma, Ala., civil-rights conflict
  International reporting: PETER ARNETT, Associated Press, for coverage of Vietnam war
  Editorial writing: ROBERT LASCH, St. Louis Post-Dispatch, for distinguished editorial writing
  Cartoon: DON WRIGHT, Miami News
  News photography: KYOICHI SAWADA, United Press International, for photography of Vietnam war

SCIENCE

Albert and Mary Lasker Foundation Special Award for "outstanding contributions to the health of the American people" ($10,000): President LYNDON B. JOHNSON

American Chemical Society Awards

Priestley Medal "for distinguished services to chemistry": RALPH CONNOR, Rohm & Haas Company

Anselme Payen Award for "professional contributions to the science and chemical technology of cellulose and its allied products" ($1,000): WAYNE A. SISSON, American Viscose Division, FMC Corporation

Dexter Chemical Corporation Award in the history of chemistry ($1,000): EARLE R. CALEY, Ohio State University

E. V. Murphree Award in industrial and engineering chemistry ($1,000): ALFRED CLARK, Phillips Petroleum Company

James T. Grady Award in science writing ($1,000): IRVING S. BENGLESDORF, *Los Angeles Times*

Petroleum Chemistry Award ($5,000): ANDREW J. STREITWIESER, JR., University of California, Berkeley

Petroleum Research Fund "unrestricted" grants ($40,000 each): GEORGE A. OLAH, Western Reserve University; MAX T. ROGERS, Michigan State University; PAUL SCHLEYER, Princeton University; HERBERT L. TOOR, Carnegie Institute of Technology; HARRY M. WALBORSKY, Florida State University

William H. Nichols Medal for "outstanding contributions to the area of chemical thermodynamics": FREDERICK D. ROSSINI, Notre Dame University

American Institute of Aeronautics and Astronautics' Goddard Award ($10,000 shared): HANS J. P. von OHAIN, Aerospace Research Laboratory, Wright-Patterson Air Force Base; A. W. BLACKMAN, United Aircraft Research Laboratories; GEORGE D. LEWIS, United Aircraft Corporation

Fannie and John Hertz Foundation Award for achievement in the applied physical sciences ($20,000 shared): ALI JAVAN, Massachusetts Institute of Technology; THEODORE H. MAIMAN, Korad Corp. of Union Carbide

Franklin Institute Medals for outstanding careers in science

Franklin Medal: BRITTON CHANCE, University of Pennsylvania School of Medicine

Elliott Cresson Medal: EVERITT P. BLIZARD, National Laboratory, Oak Ridge, Tenn.; HERMAN F. MARK, Polytechnic Institute of Brooklyn, N.Y.

Edward Longstreth Medal: FREDERICK D. BRADDON, Sperry Rand Corporation

Francis J. Clamer Medal: LAWRENCE S. DARKEN, U.S. Steel Corporation

Frank P. Brown Medal: BOLT BERANEK AND NEWMAN INC.

Howard N. Potts Medal: ROBERT KUNIN, Rohm & Haas Co. Laboratories

John Price Wetherill Medal: HOWARD G. ROGERS, Polaroid Corporation

Stuart Ballantine Medal: JACK S. KILBY, Texas Instruments, Inc., and ROBERT N. NOYCE, Fairchild Camera and Instrument Corp.

Pacific Science Center's Arches of Science Award ($25,000): RENÉ JULES DUBOS, Rockefeller University

Paul Ehrlich and Ludwig Darmstaedter Prize ($25,000): FRANCIS PEYTON ROUS, Rockefeller University

Stouffer Prize in Medicine ($50,000 shared): HARRY GOLDBLATT, Mount Sinai Hospital, Cleveland, Ohio; ERNST KLENK, University of Cologne, West Germany

UNESCO Kalinga Prize for "popularization of natural sciences" (about $2,800): EUGENE RABINOWITCH, editor, *Bulletin of the Atomic Scientists*

U.S. Atomic Energy Commission's Enrico Fermi Award ($50,000 shared): OTTO HAHN, Göttingen, West Germany; LISE MEITNER, England; FRITZ STRASSMAN, West Germany

U.S. National Medal of Science: JOHN BARDEEN, University of Illinois; PETER DEBYE, Cornell University; HUGH DRYDEN, National Aeronautics and Space Administration; CLARENCE JOHNSON, Lockheed Aircraft Corporation; LEON LEDERMAN, Columbia University; WARREN LEWIS, Massachusetts Institute of Technology; FRANCIS PEYTON ROUS, Rockefeller University; WILLIAM RUBEY, University of California, Los Angeles; GEORGE SIMPSON, Harvard University; DONALD VAN SLYKE, Brookhaven National Laboratory; OSCAR ZARISKI, Harvard University

TELEVISION AND RADIO

George Foster Peabody Awards

Special award: MRS. LYNDON B. JOHNSON, *A Visit to Washington with Mrs. Lyndon B. Johnson on Behalf of a More Beautiful America*, ABC

Television entertainment: THE JULIE ANDREWS SHOW, NBC; FRANK SINATRA: A MAN AND HIS MUSIC, NBC; MY NAME IS BARBRA with Barbra Streisand, CBS

Television news: FRANK MCGEE, NBC; MORLEY SAFER, CBS; KTLA, Los Angeles

Education: NATIONAL EDUCATIONAL TELEVISION NETWORK

Youth and children's programs: A CHARLIE BROWN CHRISTMAS, CBS

Public service: CBS REPORTS: KKK—THE INVISIBLE EMPIRE

Innovation: THE NATIONAL DRIVERS TEST, CBS

Most inventive documentary: THE MYSTERY OF STONEHENGE, CBS

International understanding: XEROX CORPORATION, for sponsoring *The Making of the President, 1964, Let My People Go, The Louvre,* and U.N. dramas

Radio entertainment: MUSIC TILL DAWN, CBS

Special public service: WCCO, Minneapolis, for alerting and saving "millions suffering blizzards, floods and tornadoes"

National Academy of Television Arts and Sciences Awards (Emmy Awards)

Comedy series: THE DICK VAN DYKE SHOW, Carl Reiner, producer, CBS

Variety series: THE ANDY WILLIAMS SHOW, Bob Finkel, producer, NBC

Variety special: CHRYSLER PRESENTS THE BOB HOPE CHRISTMAS SPECIAL, Bob Hope, executive producer, NBC

Dramatic series: THE FUGITIVE, Alan Armer, producer, ABC

Dramatic program: AGES OF MAN, David Susskind and Daniel Melnick, producers, CBS

Musical program: FRANK SINATRA: A MAN AND HIS MUSIC, Dwight Hemion, producer, NBC

Children's program: A CHARLIE BROWN CHRISTMAS, Lee Mendelson and Bill Melendez, producers, CBS

Single dramatic performance by actor: CLIFF ROBERTSON, *The Game*, Bob Hope Presents the Chrysler Theater, NBC

Single dramatic performance by actress: SIMONE SIGNORET, *A Small Rebellion*, Bob Hope Presents the Chrysler Theater, NBC

Continued dramatic performance by actor: BILL COSBY, I Spy, NBC

Continued dramatic performance by actress: BARBARA STANWYCK, The Big Valley, ABC

Continued comedy performance by actor: DICK VAN DYKE, The Dick Van Dyke Show, CBS

Continued comedy performance by actress: MARY TYLER MOORE, The Dick Van Dyke Show, CBS

Dramatic performance by actor in supporting role: JAMES DALY, Eagle in a Cage, Hallmark Hall of Fame, NBC

Dramatic performance by actress in supporting role: LEE GRANT, Peyton Place, ABC

Comedy performance by actor in supporting role: DON KNOTTS, The Return of Barney Fife, The Andy Griffith Show, CBS

Comedy performance by actress in supporting role: ALICE PEARCE, Bewitched, ABC

News and documentaries: AMERICAN WHITE PAPER: UNITED STATES FOREIGN POLICY, Fred Freed, producer, NBC; KKK—THE INVISIBLE EMPIRE, David Lowe, producer, CBS; SENATE HEARINGS ON VIETNAM, Chet Hagan, producer, NBC

Daytime programing: CAMERA THREE, Dan Gallagher, producer, CBS; MUTUAL OF OMAHA'S WILD KINGDOM, Don Meier, producer, NBC

Sports: ABC WIDE WORLD OF SPORTS, Roone Arledge, executive producer; CBS GOLF CLASSIC, Frank Chirkinian, producer; SHELL'S WONDERFUL WORLD OF GOLF, Fred Raphael, producer, NBC

Educational television: JULIA CHILD, The French Chef, National Educational Television Network

Individual achievement: BURR TILLSTROM, Berlin Wall, That Was the Week That Was, NBC

Board of Trustees awards: XEROX CORPORATION; EDWARD R. MURROW

THEATER

Antoinette Perry Awards of the American Theater Wing (Tony Awards)
Drama: MARAT/SADE
Musical: MAN OF LA MANCHA
Actor, drama: HAL HOLBROOK, Mark Twain Tonight!
Actress, drama: ROSEMARY HARRIS, The Lion in Winter
Actor, musical: RICHARD KILEY, Man of La Mancha
Actress, musical: ANGELA LANSBURY, Mame
Supporting actor, drama: PATRICK MAGEE, Marat/Sade
Supporting actress, drama: ZOE CALDWELL, Slapstick Tragedy
Supporting actor, musical: FRANKIE MICHAELS, Mame
Supporting actress, musical: BEATRICE ARTHUR, Mame
Director, play: PETER BROOK, Marat/Sade
Director, musical: ALBERT MARRE, Man of La Mancha
Composer and lyricist, musical: MITCH LEIGH and JOE DARION, Man of La Mancha
Choreographer: BOB FOSSE, Sweet Charity

New York Critics Drama Desk-Vernon Rice Awards
Playwrights: JOHN ARDEN, Inadmissible Evidence; WILLIAM ALFRED, Hogan's Goat; DOUGLAS TURNER WARD, Day of Absence
Actor: KEVIN O'CONNOR, 6 from La Mama
Actress: IRENE DAILEY, Rooms; ELLEN STEWART, Café La Mama
Special citation: LIVING THEATER

New York Drama Critics Circle Awards
Best play: MARAT/SADE
Best musical: MAN OF LA MANCHA
Special citation: MARK TWAIN TONIGHT!

Outer Circle Awards
Best musical: MAN OF LA MANCHA
Best revue: WAIT A MINIM
Outstanding performers: GWEN VERDON, Sweet Charity; ANGELA LANSBURY and BEATRICE ARTHUR, Mame; DONAL DONNELLY and PATRICK BEDFORD, Philadelphia, Here I Come!
Director: PETER BROOK, Marat/Sade

Village Voice Off-Broadway Awards (Obies)
Best actor: DUSTIN HOFFMAN, The Journey of the Fifth Horse
Best actress: JANE WHITE, N.Y. Shakespeare Festival productions of Coriolanus and Love's Labor's Lost
Best play: THE JOURNEY OF THE FIFTH HORSE

WORLD AND NATIONAL SCENE

Freedom House Freedom Award: President LYNDON B. JOHNSON

Jawaharlal Nehru Award for International Understanding ($13,300): UN Secretary-General U THANT

Lenin Peace Prizes (about $28,000 each): MIGUEL ANGEL ASTURIAS, exiled Guatemalan writer; JOSEPH PETER COURTIS, Nigerian nationalist leader; GIACOMO MANZU, Italian sculptor; JAMSARANGÜN SAMBI, leader of the Mongolian Parliament; MIRIAM VIRE-TUOMINEN, Finnish member, World Council of Peace

Rockefeller Public Service Awards (each category $10,000)
Administration: Millard Cass, deputy undersecretary of labor
Foreign affairs or international operations: JOHN M. LEDDY, assistant secretary of state for European affairs
General welfare or national resources: DAVID D. THOMAS, deputy administrator, Federal Aviation Agency
Law, legislation or regulation: JOHN R. BLANDFORD, chief counsel, Committee on Armed Services, House of Representatives
Science, technology or engineering: EDWARD F. KNIPLING, director, Entomology Research Division, Agricultural Research Service, Department of Agriculture

U.S. National Security Medal: FRANK BYRON ROWLETT, former member, National Security Agency; Vice Admiral WILLIAM F. RABORN, Jr., former director, Central Intelligence Agency

U.S. President's Awards for Distinguished Federal Civilian Service: WILLIAM F. MCCANDLESS, assistant director for budget review, Bureau of the Budget; ELSON B. HELWIG, Armed Forces Institute of Pathology; ROBERT E. HOLLINGSWORTH, general manager, Atomic Energy Commission; H. REX LEE, governor, American Samoa; THOMAS C. MANN, former undersecretary of state for economic affairs; JAMES A. SHANNON, director, National Institutes of Health

PSYCHOLOGY. The extensive antipoverty programs undertaken by the U.S. Federal Government have raised a number of psychological issues. Often poverty, cultural disadvantage and relatively low intelligence accompany one another. In a technical society such as that of the United States, job opportunities are severely restricted for persons even in the dull-normal intellectual range. Psychologists have been concerned with finding out whether the cultural deprivation, found in many poverty homes, is a product of low intelligence, or whether it is a cause of intellectual disadvantage.

Over the past few years, a number of programs have been initiated to work extensively with culturally deprived preschool children, attempting to provide them with various types of intellectual stimulation. Milgram (Catholic University, Washington, D.C.), on the basis of a comprehensive evaluation of the various programs across the country, reports significant increments in tested IQ scores. These increments bring many deprived children to within the normal range in intelligence. Analysis of this evidence strongly suggests that cultural disadvantage can indeed retard intellectual development, and that remedial steps, if taken early enough, can reduce this retardation.

An investigation by Kamii and Radin (Ypsilanti, Mich., Public Schools) attempted to determine the particular types of intellectual difficulties found in culturally deprived children who were mildly retarded intellectually. These children, approximately 4 years of age, functioned at the mental level of the average 3-year-old. Comparing them with the average 3-year-old disclosed that by far the greatest deficiency in the deprived children occurred with simple, common-sense problems which involved understanding everyday language and required simple verbal answers. For example, most 3-year-olds can tell what you must do when you are thirsty. Almost all of the culturally deprived children with mental ages of 3 failed this problem.

Sigel (Merrill-Palmer Institute) finds that forming simple abstraction is another problem for the culturally deprived. For example, given a set of concrete objects, the deprived do almost as well as nondeprived children in sorting these in a logical fashion. However, given *pictures* of the identical objects, the deprived children can no longer perform the task. This is true despite the fact that they can label the contents of the pictures accurately.

The increments in IQ's of deprived children, produced by remedial work, appear to be due to increased ability to comprehend and use language in common-sense-type tasks and from improvement in specific skills such as arithmetic. Little improvement in more complex reasoning ability has been noted.

A related set of issues has been investigated by Whitman (Wayne State University, Detroit, Mich.) in a very provocative study. In reviewing previous research, Whitman found that while children of superior intelligence often excel in concept formation, the relationship is not strong, and in some cases intelligence appears to be irrelevant to such conceptual activity. Whitman hypothesized that the recent work by Kagan (Fels Institute) and others on "cognitive styles" might be a relevant factor in such conceptual activity. Some children are predisposed to respond to the descriptive aspects of situations, while other children respond to the more abstract aspects of the environment. Whitman found that the more intelligent children tend to have more abstract "styles," but the relationship is weak, so that many children of dull-average intelligence may also have abstract styles. Similarly some of the most intelligent children have descriptive styles. Whitman found that when the cognitive styles of the children being studied were compatible with the type of information to be processed, dull children performed as well on conceptual tasks as very intelligent children. The more intelligent children were superior in conceptual activity only when style and the type of information to be processed were incompatible.

This study appears to have important implications for both education and job placement. It suggests that even dull children can be helped to learn complex concepts if these are taught in terms of the child's cognitive style. Also it suggests that persons who score low on intelligence tests may be able to succeed in complex jobs if the type of reasoning involved in the job is compatible with their styles.

Finally, 1966 saw further advances in the study of biochemical factors in learning and intelligence. Vogel, Broverman, Draguns and Klaiber (Worcester State Hospital, Worcester, Mass.) have systematically reviewed the effects of glutamic acid. Systematic administrations of glutamic acid have been found to increase intelligence of mentally retarded children when accompanied by remedial classroom work. Apparently the drug permits better assimilation of new experiences. When mentally retarded children were given the drug without concomitant remedial work, no intellectual improvement occurred. Similarly, without the drug the remedial schooling was much less effective.

ELI SALTZ
Director, Cognitive Processes Center
WAYNE STATE UNIVERSITY

PUBLIC HEALTH: PHYSICAL FITNESS

By STAN MUSIAL
Consultant to the President on Physical Fitness

The Marshmallow Generation. The Soft Americans. Are We Becoming a Nation of Weaklings?

Such headlines were common a few years ago. They probably were due in part to the mixture of envy and despair which every older generation feels about its heirs. But they also were based on facts: (1) the increased incidence of obesity among U.S. boys and girls, and (2) test results showing these children's inferiority to European youngsters in physical strength, stamina and agility.

Such headlines are seen less often today, but many people still consider them appropriate. These people are relying on facts and observations gathered in the 1950's. Actually, today's generation of U.S. school children is the most fit of any since World War II.

Advances In Physical Fitness

During the 1957–58 school year, 10,000 U.S. children, representing a cross section of the nation, took the Youth Fitness Test, which consists of pull-ups, sit-ups, shuttle run, 50-yard dash, standing broad jump, softball throw and 600-yard run. The test was repeated in 1964-65 with a similar group—and with startling results. For example, the 15-year-old boys shaved 19 seconds off the 1957–58 average time for the 600-yard run and added 7 inches and 17 feet respectively to the average marks in the standing broad jump and the softball throw. Other boys, and the girls, did equally well.

Early in 1966 President Johnson established the Presidential Physical Fitness Award for boys and girls aged 10 through 17 years. To qualify, youngsters must score at or above the 85th percentile on all items of the Youth Fitness Test—marks that would have been respectable for varsity athletes a generation ago. Despite the rigorous standards, more than 10,-000 boys and girls won the award during the first weeks of the new program.

The level of physical fitness has improved markedly since 1960. Of the many reasons for the improvement, two stand out: (1) 24 of the 50 U.S. states strengthened their school physical-education requirements, and (2) the number of physical-education specialists employed by the schools shot up 26.3 per cent while school enrollments were going up only 14.5 per cent.

Typical of the stronger regulations is that adopted by Louisiana, which increased the minimum physical-education time requirement for junior and senior high schools from 120 to 150 minutes per week. Massachusetts made daily physical-education classes mandatory for all elementary- and secondary-school students. California previously was the only state with such a requirement.

Stronger teacher staffs, like stronger requirements, have meant more and better programs. A U.S. Office of Education survey shows that 37 per cent of all school children now have physical education 5 days a week, and another 21 per cent participate either 3 or 4 days a week. In junior high schools, more than 90 per cent of all students are involved in organized physical-activity programs.

In addition to being more fit, today's school children are being taught skills in such sports as swimming, tennis, badminton, golf and volleyball to enable them to enjoy physical activity as adults.

The President's Council on Physical Fitness

Many of these gains can be attributed to the President's Council on Physical Fitness, which for 5 years has conducted a nationwide advertising campaign alerting parents, school officials and children themselves to the fitness problem. The council also has distributed more than a half million books to the schools and has produced 6 films for their use.

During 1965–66 the council staged 8 regional physical-fitness clinics, demonstrating the newest teaching techniques and physical-condi-

COMPARISON RESULTS OF YOUTH FITNESS TESTS

LEGEND

1958 1965

50-YARD DASH
(11-year-old girls)

8.9 SECS.

8.4 SECS.

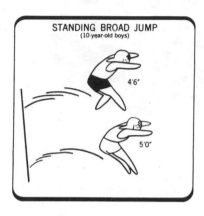

STANDING BROAD JUMP
(10-year-old boys)

4'6"

5'0"

600-YARD RUN
(14-year-old boys)

2 MINS., 30 SECS.

2 MINS., 6 SECS.

SITUPS
(16-year-old girls)

20

28

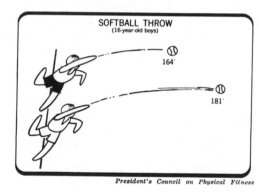

SOFTBALL THROW
(16-year-old boys)

164'

181'

President's Council on Physical Fitness

tioning methods. More than 16,000 leaders in education, medicine, recreation and state and local government attended.

One of the council's most promising programs is the Physical Fitness Demonstration Center project, launched in the fall of 1963 with 20 schools in 6 states. During the 1964–65 school year there were 110 Demonstration Center schools in 16 states, and they received 7,000 visitors, mostly teachers.

Demonstration Center schools must have model programs to be selected by the council and their state departments of education. Once selected, they invite visits and stage demonstrations for other schools seeking to improve their programs.

The council launched in 1966 a campaign urging all communities to open up their school-sports-and-fitness facilities for the after-hours and summer use of the people who live in the neighborhoods around them. The campaign was inspired by President Johnson's remarks at the national convention of the American Association of School Administrators Feb. 16, 1966:

"Tomorrow's school will be the center of community life, for the grown-ups as well as the children: 'a shopping center of human services.' It might have a community health clinic, a public library, a theater and recreation facilities.

"It will provide formal education for all citizens, and it will not close its doors any more at three o'clock. It will employ its buildings around the clock and its teachers around the year. We just cannot afford to have an $85,000,000,000 plant in this country open less than 30 per cent of the time."

PUBLIC HEALTH. Development of the first effective experimental vaccine against rubella (German measles), a major cause of birth defects, was one of the major events of 1966 in public health. The result of work by two scientists in the Division of Biologics Standards, National Institutes of Health, the vaccine appears to meet essential requirements: producing a nontransmissible disease and conferring long-term immunity.

NIH scientists also developed a simple, rapid and reliable blood test for detecting immunity to rubella. The major danger from rubella lies in the risk of transmission of the virus to the fetus during early pregnancy, resulting in birth defects. With the new test, physicians can determine within three hours whether an expectant mother has antibody protection against rubella.

New Health Programs. Several new health programs were initiated in 1966, with Medicare holding the spotlight. Benefiting some 19 million persons aged 65 and over, the hospitalization and home-health-care provisions became effective on July 1. Most of the aged had also enrolled in a separate, voluntary program which would help to pay for physicians' services.

Months of planning, including the development of conditions of participation for hospitals and other health facilities, preceded Medicare. An intensive effort was made to assure that participating hospitals were in compliance with Title VI of the Civil Rights Act of 1964. By July 1, over 6,600 hospitals had been studied and found to be extending health services without regard to race, color or national origin.

Development of Regional Medical Programs in heart disease, cancer and stroke was initiated with the awarding of first Federal grants for planning. These programs will unite major medical centers, clinical research centers and hospitals in cooperative programs of research and education and demonstrations of patient care. The purpose is to make the latest knowledge for diagnosis and treatment of these diseases widely available throughout the United States.

Funds became available in fiscal 1966 to initiate other activities authorized by recent legislation, including grants to modernize obsolete hospitals and to aid construction of teaching facilities in schools of professional nursing. The hospital modernization is a new emphasis in the Hill-Burton construction program. By Hill-Burton's 20th anniversary—Aug. 13, 1966 —the program had helped to add over 300,000 beds in hospitals and nursing homes.

The Public Health Service, which administers most Federal health programs, moved in 1966 toward a major reorganization that would enable it to carry out its responsibilities with greater effectiveness. In addition to the Office of the Surgeon General, it will have five operating bureaus: Bureau of Health Services, Bureau of Health Manpower, Bureau of Disease Prevention and Environmental Control, National Institute of Mental Health, and National Institutes of Health.

Congress approved two major health bills in 1966. The Allied Health Professions Personnel Training Act authorized a three-year program of support for the education of a wide range of professional and technical health personnel. It provides grants for various purposes, among them aid to universities, colleges and junior colleges in building or modernizing teaching facilities in centers for training allied health personnel.

The Comprehensive Health Planning and Public Health Services Amendments of 1966 authorize major changes in the pattern of Federal assistance to the states for public-health programs. One key provision establishes a two-year program of grants to the states to aid comprehensive health planning. To qualify, the states must establish a state planning agency and a council that represents its public and private health agencies, organizations and consumers. A second provision consolidates existing state grants for specific health activities, such as cancer control, into a single, flexible grant for health services.

Changes in previously passed legislation include an amendment to the Nurse Training Act

New Yorkers suffer from severe smog Nov. 24.
"The New York Times" (by Neal Boenzl)

which establishes a scholarship program for needy nursing students. Additional amendments to the Clean Air Act authorized a new program of grants to aid air pollution-control programs.

Epidemics, Pollution, Disease. The United States was free of major nationwide epidemics in 1966, although isolated outbreaks occurred. Dallas and Corpus Christi, Tex., were scenes of a late-summer outbreak of St. Louis encephalitis. For the first time since 1957, there was a national decline in reported primary and secondary syphilis cases—a drop of 3.3 per cent in the fiscal year.

In the area of environmental health, substantial progress was made toward control of air pollution. Under new Federal abatement powers, the Department of Health, Education, and Welfare established emission standards for cars and light trucks. The standards take effect with the 1968 models. Standards were also issued for control measures which will apply to all new Federal installations.

A National Conference on Air Pollution, held in mid-December, brought together government officials, leaders of business and industry, and representatives of many scientific and civic organizations in discussions of ways to improve the national effort to control air pollution.

Diseases caused by bacteria, viruses and other infectious microbes are, as a group, the leading cause of disability and time lost from work and school. Research progress in 1966 included early tests of experimental vaccines against three types of parainfluenza viruses, which cause croup and bronchopneumonia in infants and children. A major attack was launched against lung-crippling emphysema in which research teams at 10 major medical centers will seek to find causes of the disease.

Advances were made in many other fields of research, including cancer, diabetes, the heart and heart diseases, neurological diseases and human development.

WILLIAM H. STEWART, M.D.
Surgeon General, U.S. PUBLIC HEALTH SERVICE

PUERTO RICO. Legislation that would provide statehood for Puerto Rico was introduced in Congress on Sept. 22, 1966, by 10 congressmen. It was the first such proposal in seven years. Although the measure expired with the 89th Congress, it was assured reintroduction in 1967. Its author, Rep. Leo W. O'Brien (D-N.Y.), retired at the end of the year. Five Democrats and five Republicans introduced the measure, the first such bipartisan statehood bill.

The last bill calling for Puerto Rican statehood had been introduced in 1959 by the then Rep. Victor Anfuso (D-N.Y.). Both Anfuso's bill, and the companion measure introduced on Sept. 22, proposed a statehood referendum be held on the island.

On June 30 (end of the fiscal year), the island's industrialization program completed its fifth record-breaking year, chalking up a record of 412 plant promotions. The investment represented totaled more than $167 million and provided employment for 25,000 persons. It was the first time that Puerto Rico's Operation Bootstrap went over the 400 mark in new plants. The improvement over the record for new industries established during the preceding fiscal year was 18 per cent.

The construction industry surged over the $500 million mark to hit a record of $504.6 million during the year. A major increase was scored in public housing which rose by 29.5 per cent to $28.5 million. The construction value of the 1966–67 fiscal year was set by the Planning Board at an estimated $513.7 million.

The United States Information Agency (USIA) in October called on underdeveloped nations throughout the world to model their economic programs after Puerto Rico's Operation Bootstrap. Julio Garzon, chief of the USIA's Spanish-language staff, told newsmen that his agency was especially trying to impress countries in Latin America, Africa and Asia to follow in the footsteps of Puerto Rico.

The question of whether Puerto Ricans should be eligible for the U.S. draft was one of the most sensitive political issues on the island in 1966. Nationalist groups, always eager to support controversial issues that put the United States in a bad light, seized upon conscription as a *cause célèbre*. The antidraft campaign, however, was limited to a small, though highly vocal, minority, and failed to receive any broad public support.

FRANCIS L. MCCARTHY
Latin-America Editor
UNITED PRESS INTERNATIONAL

RADIO. The outstanding development in U.S. radio in 1966 was implementation of a Federal Communications Commission ruling concerning AM-FM stations. The FCC decreed that combined AM-FM stations in cities of over 100,000 population must program their FM service independently during a minimum of 50 per cent of the broadcast hours. While a few licensees were granted extensions to the end of the year, most stations introduced separate FM programming during 1966.

Permission of Roy Doty and "Business Week"

New Programming. The FCC ruling produced a colorful variety of new program services on FM stations around the United States. The CBS-owned FM stations introduced a music service which features the top hits of the 1950's and 1960's, in contrast to CBS AM stations which, for the most part, offer news and conversation. NBC-owned FM stations are programming classical music, supplementing a variety of services on NBC AM stations ranging from all-talk in New York to top-100 records in Cleveland. The ABC-owned FM stations took a variety of courses. In New York the ABC FM outlet programs classical and light jazz music, while in Chicago the FM service features play-by-play sports events, such as high-school football, not normally covered by radio. Major independent stations groups were no less inventive in separate FM programming. For example, Storer Broadcasting Company's Miami FM station broadcasts music similar to its AM service, but the FM service is full-time stereo.

AM radio also produced its share of new programming formats in 1966. Some AM country-music stations in large U.S. cities had strikingly successful audience ratings. All-news stations generally remained in an experimental phase during 1966, but formats stressing telephone-conversation programs and controversial speakers scored well in ratings.

Nineteen sixty-six proved again that radio's course today is the highly specialized program service directed to a specific audience. This course has been made possible by the great number of new stations licensed by the FCC since World War II.

Radio's Wide Appeal. There is no doubt that U.S. citizens like radio. There are about 25 per cent more radios than people in the country. In 1965 more than 31 million standard radios were sold, compared to 14 million in 1946, the last year before television joined radio in the U.S. living room. In 1966 there were over 240 million sets in working order throughout the nation. Today more than 60 per cent of U.S. homes have radio sets in a bedroom, and more than 50 per cent of all kitchens have radios. Over 90 per cent of all new cars are sold equipped with a radio. In the last few years more than 30 million tiny transistor sets have been sold.

Popularity of radio rests with its new value as a companion medium able to fit itself to the needs and demands of its listener. Radio news, information, weather and traffic reports, and entertainment programs have been tailored to attract all segments of the public. What is available on today's radio dial covers the complete spectrum of consumer tastes, attitudes and living patterns.

Radio's all-pervasiveness is demonstrated by results of a series of nationwide studies. The surveys found that, on the average, virtually all key consumer groups listen to radio at least 2 hours daily. Housewives average 2 hours 48 minutes' listening time each weekday, while professional men spend a daily 2 hours 10 minutes listening to the radio. Housewives with jobs hear their radios for 2½ hours per day.

Increased Advertising Revenue. Just as people continue to buy radio sets in record numbers, so too are advertisers—local, regional and national—increasing their investment in radio. Through its spot, network and local announcements, advertisers gave radio one of its most profitable years in 1966. The industry is moving rapidly toward its first $1,000,000,000 year. (Its volume in 1965 was a little less than $800 million.) Based on consumer acceptance of the medium and the great strides it is taking with advertisers, that goal will be realized by 1970.

LIONEL F. BAXTER
Vice-President, Radio Division
STORER BROADCASTING COMPANY

RECORDINGS

By STANLEY GREEN
Author and Lecturer

Nineteen hundred and sixty-six may well go down in the books as the year the record industry's leaders discovered America. Of course, American composers' works had been recorded in the past, but not until 1966 did the major record companies seem so willing to offer more than token releases devoted to the U.S. product. Foundation money helped and so did the near-saturation of classical European literature. But whatever the reason, it was an encouraging and long-due development.

Representative U.S. Composers. The spryest pacesetter was unquestionably Charles Ives, but since he died in 1954, he was hardly in a position to enjoy the sudden splurge of activities in his behalf. Ives was represented in 1966 by new releases of no less than all four of his symphonies: the charming, slightly derivative First, ably performed by Morton Gould and the Chicago Symphony (RCA Victor LM/LSC 2893); the wild but wonderful Second and the serenely compelling Third, both knowingly interpreted by Leonard Bernstein and the New York Philharmonic (Columbia ML 6289/ MS 6889 and ML 6243/ MS 6843); and, finally, the challenging, complex and practically unrecordable Fourth, heroically played by the American Symphony under Stokowski (Columbia ML 6175/ MS 6775). Also recom-

Leonard Bernstein conducts New York Philharmonic.
Columbia Records

mended: the *Robert Browning Overture,* conducted by William Strickland (CR1 (SD) 196), and Seymour Lipkin's reading of *The Fourth of July* (on the reverse of the Second Symphony) and Bernstein's of *The Unanswered Question* (on the reverse of the Third).

A venerable figure, Carl Ruggles, happily *was* able to enjoy his recent fame. His vivid, strongly dissonant *Sun-Treader* has finally been preserved in a gripping performance by Zoltan Rozsnyai and the Columbia Symphony (ML 6201/ MS 6801). Robert Helps' impressive First Symphony is the companion piece. Another commendable effort, the two-record set *New Music for the Piano* (RCA Victor LM/LSC 7042) finds Mr. Helps as piano soloist performing works by 24 Americans representing schools from the *arrière-* to the *avant-garde.*

Leonard Bernstein continues to be represented on records by his best and almost exclusive interpreter, Leonard Bernstein. On Columbia ML 6192/ MS 6792, he offers his deeply moving *Chichester Psalms* back to back with his youthfully brash ballet score *Facsimile;* on Columbia ML 6285/ MS 6885, it is his excitingly jazzy Symphony No. 2 (*The Age of Anxiety*) with Philippe Entremont as featured pianist. The composer leads the New York Philharmonic on all three. On the low-priced Heliodor label ((S) 25020), his rueful, satirical Broadway opera *Trouble in Tahiti* is brought back with loving care under Arthur Winograd's direction. Bernstein is also one fourth the composers represented on a Columbia disc (ML 6205/ MS 6805), *Meeting at the Summit,* which was assembled as a showcase for Benny Goodman's impeccable clarinet. In addition to the Bernstein item, *Prelude, Fugue and Riffs,* the collection displays attractive clarinet pieces by Aaron Copland, Morton Gould and Igor Stravinsky.

Copland's opera *The Tender Land*—also known as *The Tender Copland*—is an evocative breath of Americana, given a splendid, if abridged, production on Columbia ML 6214/ MS 6814. Copland himself conducts. The same composer's brilliant early creation *Dance Symphony* shares the RCA Victor album LM/LSC 2850 with Morton Gould's popular *Spirituals for Orchestra.* Both benefit from Gould's expert direction. Two other esteemed names in American music, Virgil Thomson and Howard Hanson, are fittingly represented on one disc, Mercury MG 50429/ SR 90429, by two appealing works—the former's *Symphony on a Hymn Tune* and the latter's *Four Psalms,* both conducted by Hanson. Among younger composers, Gunther Schuller deserves special mention for his imaginative *Seven Studies on Themes of Paul Klee,* performed by Erich Leinsdorf and the Boston Symphony (RCA Victor LM/LSC 2879). Stravinsky's superb ballet score *Agon* is on the reverse.

And European Masters. Modern American composers have all been influenced by a number of European pioneers, most of whom did not lack for recordings in 1966. Two versions of Bartok's soul-searing *Concerto for Orchestra* vie strongly for praise—George Szell's shining performance with the Cleveland Orchestra on Columbia ML 6215/ MS 6815, and Georg Solti's vigorous reading with the London Symphony on London CM 9469/ CS 6469. The Bartok *Miraculous Mandarin Suite* receives a miraculous interpretation by Eugene Ormandy and the Philadelphia Orchestra (Columbia ML 6189/ MS 6789), while his mystical, poignant *Bluebeard's Castle* is sung and played with consummate artistry under the direction of Istvan Kertesz (London 4158/ OSA 1158).

Other praiseworthy offerings were released during the year in the area of modern vocal music. That hypnotic nightmare of the musical stage, Alban Berg's *Wozzeck,* receives a performance that cuts to the heart of this chilling score on Deutsche Grammophon (13)8991/2. Evelyn Lear and Dietrich Fischer-Dieskau sing the leads. The exaltation of Stravinsky's *Symphony of Psalms* is captured by the Robert Shaw Chorale on RCA Victor LM/LSC 2822. One of Schoenberg's major vocal creations, *Gurrelieder,* is a prodigious work requiring the most exacting interpretation. Fortunately it receives just that on Deutsche Grammophon (13)8984/5, with Inge Borkh and a chorus and orchestra conducted by Rafael Kubelik. And from Benjamin Britten—via London A 4156/ OSA 1156—comes a rare, hauntingly beautiful operatic work, *Curlew River,* featuring inspired singing by Peter Pears and John Shirley-Quirk.

If you are looking for definitive—so far—performances of multirecorded vocal works of the twentieth century, your search should end happily with two Angel releases, both under the helm of Rafael Frühbeck de Burgos. On (S) 36333, it is the ever-fascinating *Carmina Burana* of Carl Orff, and on (S)BL 3672, the exciting *La Vida Breve* of Manuel de Falla, featuring the unsurpassable Victoria de los Angeles. Another look-no-further release for Falla fanciers is *El Retable de Maese Pedro* on Epic LC 3919/ BC 1319, a colorful, witty opera, presided over by the firm hand of conductor Pedro de Freitas Branco.

Sometimes the classical and the modern meet in a single work. Even that arch modernist

Deutsche Grammophon/Max Jacoby
Evelyn Lear and Dietrich Fischer-Dieskau sing leads on Grammophon's recording of Alban Berg's *Wozzeck.*

Igor Stravinsky was not above paying due homage to two of his heroes—Tchaikovsky, in the beguiling *Fairy's Kiss* (Columbia ML 6203/ MS 6803), and Pergolesi, in that intriguing "ballet in song," *Pulcinella* (Columbia ML 6281/ MS 6881). And on Angel (S) 36303, the old and the new meet in the pairing of Corelli's Concerto Grosso in F and Michael Tippett's splendid modern variations thereof, irresistibly performed by Yehudi Menuhin and the Bath Festival Orchestra. Listeners should not overlook Britten's corruscating *Variations on a Theme of Frank Bridge* on the other side.

Most of the year's releases continue, not surprisingly, to feature new interpretations of works in the standard repertory. Also not surprisingly, imaginative artists can make Bach, Beethoven and Brahms sound as fresh to modern ears as Berg, Britten and Bernstein. Take, for example, Glenn Gould, that most personal of pianists, whose remarkable technique and rare insight breathe new life into both Bach's *Well-Tempered Clavier* (*Book 1*) (Columbia D3L 333/ D3S 733) and Beethoven's *Emperor Concerto* (Columbia ML 6288/ MS 6888). Soviet pianist Vladimir Ashkenazy takes the Bach Concerto in D Minor at a bright, rhythmic clip, and fills the Chopin Concerto in F Minor with shimmering detail (London CM 9440/ CS 6440). The old master Artur Rubinstein has never sounded better than he does in the dazzling display he showers on Liszt's Piano Sonata and Schubert's *Wanderer Fantasy* (RCA Victor LM/LSC 2871). Deep gratitude is surely due Julius Katchen (and

London Records) for undertaking to record *all* of Brahms' piano literature in such arresting fashion. Among the delights are the *Hungarian Dances* (CM 9473/ CS 6473), the *Handel* and *Paganini Variations* (CM 9474/ CS 6474), and the *Schumann Variations* (CM 9477/ CS 6477). Another collection of variations, this time by Liszt, is beautifully traversed by Raymond Lewenthal in *The Operatic Liszt* on RCA Victor LM/LSC 2895.

The most auspicious recording debut? Easily, the palm goes to the Guarneri String Quartet, a new American group, which offers superlative versions of the Smetana *From My Life* Quartet and the Dvorak Quartet in A-flat (RCA Victor LM/LSC 2887), as well as the Mozart Quartets in B-flat and F (RCA Victor LM/LSC 2888). The always welcomed Juilliard String Quartet brings a bright-eyed, decidedly *ungemütlich* approach to Beethoven's *Rasumovsky Quartets* on Epic SC 6052/ BSC 152 and Schubert's Quartets in A Minor and G Minor on Epic LC 3913/ BC 1313.

Conductors. In the realm of conductors, Leonard Bernstein continues to lead the New York Philharmonic in performances that add new luster to even the most familiar works in the repertory. The Vivaldi *Four Seasons* (Columbia ML 6144/ MS 6744) fairly leaps from the speakers as it engulfs the listener in sparkling, dramatic sound. The Sibelius Fifth Symphony (Columbia ML 6149/ MS 6749) has never seemed so exuberant, while Beethoven's *Eroica Symphony* (Columbia ML 6174/ MS 6774) transmits all the wonder and excitement that the conductor so obviously feels about the music. Other men—in some rather internationalized combinations—are showing equal mettle on the podium. On RCA Victor LM/LSC 2884, Hollywood's André Previn takes the London Symphony through an effective performance of Tchaikovsky's *Little Russian* Symphony, a work that the French-born American, Lorin Maazel, leading the Vienna Philharmonic, has instilled with majestic sweep on London CM 9427/ CS 6427. India's Zubin Mehta cracks the whip over the same aggregation to produce a highly charged interpretation of Bruckner's Ninth Symphony (London CM 9462/ CS 6462), while the venturesome Australian, Denis Vaughan, not only steers the Orchestra of Naples through a totally satisfying reading of all of Schubert's symphonies, he even manages to finish the *Unfinished* (RCA Victor LM/LSC 6709).

Equally determined to tidy up a composer's loose ends is arranger Deryck Cooke, who undertook the formidable task of orchestrating Mahler's sketches for his unfinished Tenth

Symphony. His devotion to the task may be appreciated on Columbia M2L 335/ M2S 735, spotlighting an impassioned performance by the Philadelphia Orchestra under Ormandy. Other recordings of Mahler symphonies should find favor with the Mahlerites. Leinsdorf and the Boston Symphony bring strength and conviction to the vigorous Sixth (RCA Victor LM/LSC 7004); Bernstein and the New York Philharmonic shake up the enervating Seventh in a slambang performance (Columbia M2L 339/ M2S 739); Szell and the Cleveland Orchestra achieve positive grandeur in their firmly controlled version of the ever-appealing Fourth (Columbia ML 6233/ MS 6833); and, in a reissue, the late Bruno Walter and the Columbia Symphony bring nobility to the gallant Ninth (Columbia D3L 344/ D3S 744).

Opera. On the operatic stage, new approaches also illuminate old favorites. Under Leinsdorf's direction, Wagner's *Lohengrin* emerges with clarity and detail, and is especially blessed by Sandor Konya's singing of the title role (RCA Victor LM/LSC 6710). London's recording of Verdi's *Don Carlo* (A 4432/ OSA 1432), a powerfully persuasive job, benefits from the presence of the impressive Nicolai Ghiaurov. And the Angel release of Puccini's *Turandot* ((S) 3671) offers two superlative leads in Birgit Nilsson and Franco Corelli. Vocalists featured on highly recommended new collections include Montserrat Caballe (RCA Victor LM/LSC 2862, 2894 and 2910), Victoria de los Angeles (Angel (S) 36296 and (S) 36351), and Mirella Freni (Angel (S) 36268). But past operatic glories still have undiminished appeal. Angel's *The Genius of Puccini* ((S)BL 3683) is a most welcome compendium, and, most assuredly, so is RCA Victor's package *Opening Nights at the Metropolitan* (LM 6171), which holds, among other treasures, a nostalgic swatch of the famous gold curtain.

Pops, Jazz, Folk. U.S. domination of lighter musical forms is of course the rule rather than the exception. Broadway can still be counted upon to produce scores of quality, as, for example, the Alan Jay Lerner-Burton Lane *On a Clear Day You Can See Forever* (RCA Victor LOCD/LSOD 2006); or the Joe Darion-Mitch Leigh *Man of La Mancha* (Kapp (S) 4505); or the Dorothy Fields-Cy Coleman *Sweet Charity* (Columbia KOL 6500/ KOS 2900); or the Jerry Herman *Mame* (Columbia KOL 6600/ KOS 3000). Also from the general vicinity of New York's Times Square have come such laudable collections as Frank Sinatra's *My Kind of Broadway* (Reprise F (S) 1015), Woody Herman's *My Kind* of Broadway (Columbia CL 2357/ CS 9157) and Nancy Wilson's *From Broadway With Love* (Capitol (S)T 2433). Eminently worthy too are four discs highlighting the contributions of specific Broadway composers—the sparkling two-record salute to Howard Dietz and Arthur Schwartz (Evergreen (S) 6604/5), Harold Arlen's own *Harold Sings Arlen* (Columbia OL 6520/ OS 2920), plus two journeys into the unfamiliar, *Jerome Kern Revisited* (Columbia OL 6440/ OS 2840) and *George Gershwin Revisited* (MGM (S) 4375).

The area of nontheatrical pop music has a decidedly more international look. From Italy we hear the caressing tones of Emilo Pericone on *Il Mondo* (Warner Bros. W(S) 1622); from France, the intense emotionalism of composer-singer Jacques Brel (Reprise R (S) 6187); and from Brazil, the subtle approach of composer-singer Caymmi (Warner Bros. W(S) 1614). Trini Lopez, another south-of-the-border balladeer, is as infectious as ever on two Reprise albums, *Trini* (R (S) 6196) and the *Second Latin Album* (R (S) 6215). Less exotic fare may be sampled in a number of pleasurable albums—Barbra Streisand's *My Name Is Barbra, Two* (Columbia CL 2409/ CS 9209) and *Color Me Barbra* (Columbia CL 2478/ CS 9278), Jimmy Durante's *One of Those Songs* (Warner Bros. W(S) 1655), Shani Wallis' indisputable *I'm a Girl* (Kapp (S) 3472), *Nat King Cole at the Sands* (Capitol (S)MAS 2434), and Libby Morris' impressive recording debut, *Ad-Libby* (RCA Victor LPM/LSP 3506).

Jazz, that exclusively American product, is well represented by such treasures as Miles Davis' absorbing collection, *ESP* (Columbia CL 2350/ CS 9150), a worthy sampling of the great Earl Hines on *Spontaneous Explorations* (Contact (S) 2), and a compelling interpretation of Lalo Schifrin's *The New Continent* performed by Dizzy Gillespie (Limelight (S) 86022). As for jazz singing, Ray Charles, on *Live in Concert* (ABC Paramount (S) 500), is in a class by himself. Other recommended jazz releases: Kenny Burrell's *Guitar Forms* (Verve (6)8612), Herbie Mann's *Latin Mann* (Columbia CL 2388/ CS 9188), Chico Hamilton's *El Chico* (Impulse (S) 9102) and Duke Ellington's *Concert in the Virgin Islands* (Reprise R(S) 6185).

Great jazz performances of the past were made available again in highly commendable packages. From Columbia, *The Ellington Era, Vol. 2* (C3L 39) and *Billie Holiday—The Golden Years, Vol 2* (C3L 40), both filling serious gaps in the LP catalogue. From RCA

Reprise
Trini Lopez, a 1966 recording favorite in pop music.

Victor—via their significant Vintage series—have come reissues of performances by Fats Waller (*Valentine Stomp*, LPV 525), Dizzy Gillespie (LPV 530), and the Benny Goodman small groups (LPV 521).

The folk scene, both traditional and contemporary, received welcome representation and variety—all the way from Leadbelly's Library of Congress recordings on Elektra 301/2, to Bob Dylan's *Highway 61 Revisited* on Columbia CL 2389/ CS 9189. Also found within the broadening spectrum of folk music are such superior examples as Lightnin' Hopkins' *Lightnin' Strikes* (Verve/Folkways (S) 9022), Jackie Washington's *At Club 47* (Vanguard (7)9172), *The Peter, Paul and Mary Album* (Warner Bros. W(S) 1648) and Billy Edd Wheeler's *Goin' Town and Country* (Kapp (S) 3479). And don't overlook Amalia Rodrigues, the queen of the Portuguese *fado*, on Capitol T 10441.

Lastly, 1966 produced two oddities that happily defy rational musical designations. Whether they be classical, pop or camp, those newly discovered manuscripts by one P. D. Q. Bach (on Vanguard (7)9195) and his equally distinguished contemporaries, the Baroque Beatles (on Elektra (7)306), certainly helped make it a brighter year.

RELIGION

Judaism. For Judaism the problems of 1965 continued as the problems of 1966—somewhat sharper, pointed up, but the same problems nevertheless. The two main ones were assimilation and anti-Semitism.

A delegation from the Jewish War Veterans of America paid a call on President Johnson to tell him that their convention had passed a resolution backing his Vietnam policies. Following the visit, the veterans held a White House press conference. What the veterans' spokesman, Commander Malcolm A. Tarlov, said is in dispute. What one reporter said, and which Commander Tarlov denied, was that President Johnson could not understand why Jews opposed him on Vietnam when he has been so helpful, militarily, politically and economically, to Israel.

The U.S. Jewish community bridled. It was far from being monolithic on the subject of Vietnam. Few national organizations had taken an outright antiwar position; some had merely stated the right of Americans to dissent.

Reacting, Johnson called in the President of the mass organization B'nai B'rith, Dr. William A. Wexler, and the Executive Vice-President, Rabbi Jay Kaufman. Following the meeting, they issued a statement absolving President Johnson of indicting an entire community for the actions of some of its parts.

But this apparently was not satisfactory. The Conference of Presidents of Major National Jewish Organizations met with U.S. Ambassador to the United Nations Arthur Goldberg. He reassured the delegation that the President had not equated U.S. help to Israel with conformity to his policies. The delegation expressed its satisfaction, and there the matter rested.

At the top of the agenda of every major organization in 1966 was "assimilation." The question being asked was: "Jews have managed during these two millennia to survive all kinds of adversity; can they now survive affluence?" The matter is acute. The rate of intermarriage is growing, in the United States as well as elsewhere. In the Scandinavian countries, more than 50 per cent of the Jews marry outside their faith. The answer? Jewish leaders believe it to be more and better Jewish education, and there are now greater attempts to channel Jewish community funds into youth projects.

The situation of the Jews in the Soviet Union continued to obsess their coreligionists elsewhere. Some improvements have been noted: there were matzos for the Passover in Moscow, Leningrad and other large cities, whereas there had been none, by official fiat, in 1965. There was another promise that prayer books would be printed. A promise to reactivate the rabbinical seminary in Moscow was also made. Some books were published in Yiddish; the Yiddish periodical *Sovietish Heimland* has become a monthly and its pressrun increased. The drive against "economic crimes," and the pointed use of "Jewish names" in the accusations and executions, suddenly stopped. But there was evidence late in 1966 that the campaign against "economic criminals" had been resumed.

Generally, the demands on the Soviet Union, made by Jews and non-Jews alike, including Communists, were not met: there still were no Hebrew or Yiddish schools, no Jewish theater, no Yiddish newspapers—nothing to allow the Jews to live as a people.

Anti-Semitism continued to manifest itself crudely through continued swastika-smearing in many places in the world. In the United States the more polite kind of anti-Jewishness—the barring of Jews from certain jobs and industries—continued to be brought to light.

The United Hebrew Congregations of the British Commonwealth reached into New York for a Chief Rabbi—Rabbi Dr. Immanuel

President Johnson meets with Jewish War Veterans delegation at the White House Sept. 6.

Jewish War Veterans of America

Jakobovits of the Fifth Avenue Synagogue. He succeeds Rabbi Dr. Israel Brodie, who retired. With the announcement came word from one part of the British Orthodox community, the Federation of Synagogues, that it would not accept the Chief Rabbi's authority. The Federation appointed its own, Rabbi Dr. Eliezer W. Kirzner, and established its own rabbinical court to deal with questions of Jewish law.

In Brussels in July and August, the World Jewish Congress held its Plenary Assembly. Delegates from 57 countries, including Hungary, Rumania and Yugoslavia, attended. Among the features was a "dialogue" on Germany to which Dr. Eugen Gerstenmaier, the president of the West German Bundestag (lower house of Parliament) was invited.

In Germany itself, the trials of former Nazis accused of crimes against humanity went on. Most spectacular of these was the trial of officers and guards of the Auschwitz extermination camp, at which the whole horrible picture of what went on there was revealed.

Jewish women, organized in the International Council of Jewish Women, launched an appeal to the rabbis of the world to do something to ease their disabilities under Jewish religious law, particularly in matters of divorce.

In New York City, world Jewry and scholarship generally suffered a great loss when a fire destroyed priceless volumes and manuscripts in the library of the Jewish Theological Seminary of America. In New York State and elsewhere, "humane" laws were being introduced that Orthodox Jewish authorities believe strike at the root of shechita—ritual slaughter.

RICHARD YAFFE
Manager, American Bureau
THE LONDON JEWISH CHRONICLE

Protestantism. The Consultation on Church Union, formed as a result of a 1960 suggestion by Eugene Carson Blake, then stated clerk (or chief executive officer) of the United Presbyterian Church in the U.S.A., met in fifth annual session at Dallas in May. In 1966 eight bodies were formally represented. The Consultation adopted "principles of church union." Seeking a church truly evangelical, catholic and reformed, the Consultation also sent an open letter to the constituent members, stating that they sought a balance between discipline and freedom. The Presbyterian Church in the United States, with members mainly in the South, joined the Consultation in 1966. The others are the United Presbyterian Church in the U.S.A., the Protestant Episcopal Church, the Methodist Church, Christian Churches (Disciples of Christ), the United Church of Christ, the Evangelical United Brethren Church, and the African Methodist Episcopal Church. These have a present membership of 24 million persons.

The Seventh-day Adventists held a world conference in Detroit in June 1966, with representatives from the more than 1.6 million Adventists on all continents. This body observes Saturday as the Sabbath and expects the imminent return of Christ to earth.

The Southern Baptist Convention, demonstrating that it is no longer wholly a southern church, met in Detroit in May. At the convention, the Baptists decided to conduct a nationwide evangelistic campaign directed especially at the northern industrial centers and the spread of the "death of God" idea.

Richard Cardinal Cushing of Boston approved the publication in the United States of the full Revised Standard Version of the Bible, which is a translation completed in 1952 under Protestant auspices. Roman Catholic preferences were placed in footnotes only. This was only one step toward a common Bible for Protestants and Roman Catholics. Earlier in 1966 there appeared in Britain and the United States a Roman Catholic edition of the R.S.V. approved originally by Archbishop Gordon Gray of Scotland. This contained relatively few changes, requested by Catholic scholars of Britain, and to which the American translators gave ready assent.

The Church of Christ, Scientist celebrated the centenary of the first teaching of Christian Science by Mary Baker Eddy. Mrs. Eddy (1821–1910) sought to restore the lost art of healing. She began to teach after she reported recovering from a serious injury after reading about healing by Jesus in the Gospel of Matthew. Mrs. Eddy also taught that Christian Science could be applied to every human need. The Church of Christ, Scientist elected as its president Erwin D. Canham, editor in chief of *The Christian Science Monitor*, a newspaper published in Boston.

The General Assembly of the United Presbyterian Church in the U.S.A. met in Boston in May 1966 and adopted a *Contemporary Statement of Faith*. The *Statement* reaffirms the general historic Christian creeds and then adds a restatement of the traditional Calvinism. The new *Statement* is now referred to local presbyteries, and if two thirds approve, the next General Assembly, meeting in Portland, Ore., in 1967, will take final action.

Four Lutheran bodies approved the formation, beginning in January 1967, of a Lutheran Conference in the U.S.A., with headquarters in New York City.

I. M. Pei & Partners

Model of new church complex of the Church of Christ, Scientist, in Boston, Mass.

In 1966, 222 Protestant churches gave these figures to the *Yearbook of American Churches:* 296,406 local churches with 69,088,422 members; 239,743 pastors in charge of local churches, and a total of 335,461 clergymen; enrollment of 41,539,496 persons in Sunday Schools, including pupils and officers.

Both civil rights and Vietnam were subjects of considerable attention. Religious bodies expressing themselves were generally favorable to Negroes' demands, and a small minority of clergy took part in public marches and protests. However, the unity of the civil-rights movement was much disturbed because some Negro leaders opposed U.S. policy in Vietnam, and because declarations of "black power" revealed open splits among civil-rights organizations. Official church positions on Vietnam urged restraint, negotiation, and reliance on the United Nations, while a small minority of clergymen advocated U.S. withdrawal from Vietnam.

The National Council of Churches, with Protestant and Orthodox constituents, took the unusual step of appointing a Jesuit priest, Rev. David J. Bowman, S.J., of Loyola University, Chicago, to a full-time position in its Faith and Order Department.

The World Council of Churches, a group with over 200 Protestant and Orthodox Church bodies in 80 nations as constituents, elected as its general secretary Eugene Carson Blake. Dr. Blake, who was for 15 years chief executive officer of the United Presbyterian Church in the U.S.A., succeeds W. A. Visser't Hooft of the Netherlands.

BENSON Y. LANDIS
Former Editor, Yearbook of American Churches
NATIONAL COUNCIL OF CHURCHES

Roman Catholicism. Having closed the Second Vatican Ecumenical Council on Dec. 8, 1965, with a salute to the world which signaled an end of a defensive stance of four hundred years, the Roman Catholic Church in 1966 moved hesitantly to live up to this commitment.

Pope Paul VI at year's start was immersed in a series of attempts to bring about a negotiated settlement of the war in Vietnam. To get a wide variety of views, in the course of the year he met with a number of spokesmen, including Soviet Foreign Minister Andrei Gromyko. In September the Pope sought to refocus world opinion toward the cause of peace by issuing an encyclical letter on the subject.

The Pope also reinforced Roman Catholic participation in in-depth conversations with other Christians on topics ranging from Christian unity to cooperation in the relief of hunger and suffering. The Pope and Archbishop of Canterbury, Michael Ramsey, head of the worldwide Anglican Communion, met March 23–24, and concluded their historic conference.

The Vatican in 1966 modified its traditional stand on several issues. In February came an overhaul of laws requiring abstinence from meat on Fridays and certain other days, as well as fasting during Lent. Fast and abstinence days were reduced to two: the first day of Lent and Good Friday. In November, the National Conference of American Bishops announced that beginning Dec. 2, 1966, Catholics would no longer be obliged to abstain from meat on Fridays. The exceptions to the new rule would be Ash Wednesday and the Fridays of Lent. In announcing the dispensation, the bishops recommended that Catholics practice other penitential acts.

Cardinal Wyszynski marks 1,000 years of Christianity in Poland at Gniezno Cathedral.

Strictures concerning weddings between Catholics and other Christians were tempered by a decree issued in March. While maintaining the Roman legal view that a marriage involving a Roman Catholic is invalid if performed without the presence of a Roman Catholic priest, the Church withdrew retroactively the excommunication incurred by Catholics married in ceremonies at which non-Catholic ministers officiate. The decree was generally viewed by other churches as only a first step forward.

Rome's Doctrinal Congregation, the former Holy Office, announced in June that the Index of Forbidden Books no longer had "the force of ecclesiastical law."

Pope Paul in an official document in August suggested, but did not require, that bishops retire before the age of 75. Over 200 of the 2,600 bishops were already over 75. And the Pope received in the summer, but did not immediately act on, the long-awaited report of his commission on population and birth control.

Church-state relations were variable. In Spain, priests and Catholic lay people openly championed students' and workers' protests against the Government, especially in the Basque and Catalonian regions; priests in Barcelona were clubbed by police during one demonstration. In Poland, the Church promoted a long celebration of the 1,000th anniversary of the conversion of the Polish people to Christianity. The communist Government, charging that an exchange of letters by Polish and West German bishops promoting reconciliation was an instrusion into government affairs, used various tactics aimed at reducing the impact of the millennial celebration. Among other things, a planned visit by Pope Paul to Poland was rejected. In Yugoslavia, however, a signed accord ended a long church-state rift, and the communist Government agreed to welcome a permanent papal delegate.

Roman Catholicism in the United States witnessed new growth in the movement toward involvement of priests, nuns and laity in active roles in support of civil rights and social justice. There was extensive participation in demonstrations in behalf of farm workers in California and Texas, and for interracial justice elsewhere. In Chicago, nuns marching in favor of open housing were injured by bricks and other objects hurled by anti-integration forces in predominantly Catholic neighborhoods.

The U.S. Catholic school system, with over six million students, was the subject of probing. One study made under a Carnegie Foundation grant indicated that general education afforded by parochial schools was sound, but that the effectiveness of the religious training given was short of the mark. The largest Catholic university in the United States, St. John's University in New York City, was meanwhile the center of a bitter dispute during much of the year. Some 20 faculty members had been summarily dismissed, bringing charges of violation of academic freedom, and provoking extensive resignations.

According to the *Official Catholic Directory,* the U.S. Catholic population reached 46,246,175 by 1966. This was a gain of 605,574 in a year, as against 766,248 the previous year.

PAUL W. McCLOSKEY
Former Assistant Foreign Editor
NATIONAL CATHOLIC WELFARE
CONFERENCE NEWS SERVICE

REPUBLICAN PARTY. The decisive resurgence of the Republican Party in the 1966 elections certainly must rank among the historic landmarks of U.S. politics. After suffering a disastrous defeat *in depth* in the 1964 elections, the Grand Old Party surpassed even its fondest dreams by scoring a pyramidal victory *in depth* in 1966.

As this was written, the Republican Party had: outpolled the Democrats, nationwide, by more than 4 million votes, the Republicans recording 28.9 million and the Democrats 24.8 million; won a net gain of 47 seats in the U.S. House of Representatives; held all 33 seats in the U.S. Senate and picked up 3 additional seats. The GOP had also elected by popular vote the first Negro (Edward Brooke of Massachusetts) to the U.S. Senate since Reconstruction and also made significant gains among Negro, ethnic, labor and young voters in many sections of the nation; increased the number of Republican governorships from 17 to 25; gained over 700 state-legislative seats, increasing its national percentage from 32.6 in 1965 to 40.6. In addition, the party gained control of 17 state legislatures, compared to 6 prior to the election; increased its control of state Senates from 12, and 1 tie, to 18 and one tie; strengthened its position in the lower house of state legislatures by increasing its control from 8 to 23; and showed marked improvement in voting strength in the nation's largest cities.

The outcome of the 1966 elections is all the more noteworthy when considered in light of the party's desperate 1964 position. So devastating were the results of the 1964 elections that the GOP found itself severely split and in a dangerous state of shock.

One aspect of the party's dire condition was abundantly clear. The Republican Party could not make meaningful progress toward complete recovery until it was reunited. And, in order for the party to be united at the rank-and-file level, it must first be united at the top. For that reason, among others, the Republican Coordinating Committee was created.

The Coordinating Committee, which issued 18 position papers prior to the 1966 elections, is comprised of former President Dwight D. Eisenhower; former Republican presidential candidates Barry M. Goldwater, Richard M. Nixon, Thomas E. Dewey and Alfred M. Landon; party leaders in the Congress and on the Republican National Committee; and representatives of the Republican Governors Association and the Republican State Legislators Association. The Republican National Chairman is presiding officer of the Coordinating Committee. This committee became the vehicle through which unity was reestablished among the party's top leaders.

Then, in November of 1965, a highly significant development for the Republican Party took place when it made a phenomenal show of strength in many city elections. This showing was accompanied by a significant resurgence of support for Republican candidates among Negro voters.

These city victories gave a tremendous psychological lift to the party and to its leaders and workers. They also generated new hope for a Republican comeback in 1966. That hope mushroomed into political history on Nov. 8, 1966.

RAY C. BLISS
Chairman, REPUBLICAN NATIONAL COMMITTEE

RETAILING. Retailers have been quick to recognize that in a sense the U.S. population is getting younger. The fact is that almost half of all the people in the country are under 25 years of age. Young people between the ages of 14 and 24 constitute fully 18 per cent of the population. Teen-agers alone, it has been determined, represent $13,000,000,000 in disposable income annually and have a strong influence on the disposal of more than $30,000,000,000 aside from their own spending money.

Special attention is being given to the teen-age market of more than 25 million young people. Market research has established that teen-agers in almost one third of all American families influence the family purchases of foods, beverages, cars, apparel and many other items.

Merchants go all out to attract the teen-age customer. Small and large stores, for instance, engage rock 'n' roll bands, name singers and other celebrities to draw the young crowds. Does it work? Almost invariably the teen-agers, responding to what is commonly referred to as the "contemporary sound," stay on to buy apparel, accessories and cosmetics after the music has stopped.

All of the giant chains are placing more emphasis on the youth and young-family market. Chain stores like Sears Roebuck and Co. and Montgomery Ward & Co. are extending themselves to make their fashion apparel appealing to this market; the stores offer a broad range of services from decorator assistance through auto-care centers in order to attract the younger consumer as well as the older one.

Arnold Constable, Inc., a Fifth Avenue specialty department store in New York, with eight branches in suburban areas, has embarked on a million-dollar program of modernization with the specific object of bringing in

Fashion sketch, cutout archways accent Young Bendel floor, Henri Bendel, New York City.

the young customers. Almost all large stores have either completed or are undertaking similar programs.

Establishment of so-called *boutiques* within the framework of the department store is aimed at appealing to the younger groups. These range from shops for little boys and girls, to those selling sportswear for the swinging set; from shops offering matching ensembles (coats and suits) and dresses to the young matron, to men's specialty shops for her young husband.

A study by Scholastic Magazines, Inc., reveals that while teen-age girls represent 14 per cent of the U.S. population, they buy over 20 per cent of all women's apparel sold in the nation. It is estimated that they spend over $565 million for footwear and $850 million for back-to-school clothing. It is further estimated that teen-agers now own 20 per cent of all cars, and that 7 million have driver's licenses.

Young people marry earlier too. Over 40 per cent of all brides are teen-agers. More women marry at 18 than at any other age, and more wives have their first child in their 19th year than in any other time span, while 1 out of 6 teen-age wives has 2 or more children.

These young people, according to the magazine, expect to be able to purchase early in

Fashion show at Dayton's, Minneapolis, features clothes with a mod look.

their marriage many of the things that it took their parents and grandparents a lifetime to acquire.

A survey taken in the youth market indicates that among the 14 million high-school students in the nation, almost half have earned some income from jobs outside the home. The median weekly income for boys 15 to 18 is $11.50 a week, for girls in this age group, $6.88. Savings average $5.38 a week for boys going to high school and $1.81 for girls. It is estimated that 56 per cent of savings are for education and a large part for clothes. Boys spend proportionately more for automotive, entertainment, hobbies and sports equipment, while girls spend more than boys for food, grooming, cosmetics and gifts.

The smart retailer of course will not neglect customers in the older age groups. The highest income and spending power is in the 35 to 55 age group, and it is the middle-age purchaser who accounts for the major portion of expenditures.

Total purchases of all goods and services at retail, including automobiles, rose in 1966 to nearly $300,000,000,000, or about 8 per cent above the 1965 figure of $277,500,000,000. Volume would have been higher except for a lag in car sales felt during the summer months. The automobile industry was not able to exceed the 1965 sales record of more than 9 million new cars.

Undoubtedly, retailing in 1966 was affected by the hike in interest rates, a falling stock market in the middle of the year and an increase in withholding-tax rates. But counteracting these negative factors were the start of Medicare payments, the steady rise in personal income, and the second-stage excise-tax cuts.

The climate for small retailers has not improved with the ever-growing power of the large chains. It becomes more difficult for them to compete with the so-called mass merchandisers and discount-store operators. High costs of construction and mortgage money have cut down building of shopping centers, which afford the small specialty shop an opportunity to rent space.

There has also been a leveling off in the rate of increase of discount stores. Since 1960, the number of discount stores has risen by 140 per cent to bring the total to about 2,900 stores. From the standpoint of the number of stores, growth was much more rapid at the beginning of the decade than it is at present.

The number of stores increased by 34 per cent from 1960 to 1961 and by 40 per cent from 1961 to 1962. But in the following year, one of attrition for discounters, the increase was only 3 per cent. Since 1963, discount stores have been growing numerically at a rate of 8 to 11 per cent.

A discount store, according to *Discount Store News,* compiler of the figures, is one occupying space of at least 10,000 square feet, carrying full lines of both hard and soft goods that are sold at less than traditional markups.

HERBERT KOSHETZ
Assistant to the Business and Finance Editor
THE NEW YORK TIMES

RHODE ISLAND. Dr. Ray L. Heffner became Brown University's president July 1. . . . Work began in the spring to turn Goat Island (in Newport Harbor) into a recreational facility to be called Key Newport. The transformation will cost about $8 million. . . . Gov. John H. Chafee (R) and Sen. Claiborne Pell (D) were reelected in November. Democrats held on to control of the reapportioned state legislature. . . . President Johnson spoke in Kingston on Aug. 20.

ROME. The Eternal City began 1966 with its first city plan in 35 years. It dictated that Rome no longer would "spread like oil on water." New construction was aimed east to Pietralata, southeast to Centocelle and south to the satellite city, EUR. But despite these plans the year began badly.

Under extreme pressure, city fathers prematurely halted an experiment to turn a 12-block downtown area into a pedestrian island. Convinced that the idea was good, they vowed to try again in the Spanish Steps area and at Piazza Navona. In August they turned fashionable Via Veneto over to pedestrians from 9 P.M. to 4 A.M., and later talked of making it permanent.

To celebrate what some say was its 2,719th birthday, Rome gave itself an electronically controlled light system on Christopher Columbus Highway, leading to the beaches and EUR, and the 3d and 4th of 5 underpasses designed to shorten the trip from the railroad station to the Vatican. The 5 underpasses, located outside the ancient walls on Corso d'Italia, eliminate a dozen intersections and are altogether nearly 2 miles long. The longest, running 3,444 feet underground in front of Porta Pia, was inaugurated April 21. It did little to relieve traffic.

As if to compensate, the city redeclared war on car noise. Other wars included: the annual summer crackdown on beatniks loitering on the Spanish Steps, and one launched by the Tourist Department to keep ugly June 12 election posters out of tourist sight. The antinoise battle was least successful.

Wide World

UPI

Left: Roman traffic jam: cars clog the entrance to Cristoforo Colombo Highway. Right: Japanese Prime Minister Eisaku Sato.

Growing almost as fast as the number of vehicles was population, which passed 2.6 million—an increase of approximately 100,000 over 1965.

Twice in 1966, many Rome residents were without water. The second drought, wisely delayed until after elections, was for a laudable purpose: to insert new tunnel links in the aqueduct system. There was later more water flowing through the system—130 more gallons a second, the city boasted.

There was no boasting about the $1,200,-000,000 debt. On every appropriate occasion, Mayor Amerigo Petrucci said the only hope was to industrialize Rome's suburbs.

ERNEST A. LOTITO
Rome Bureau, UNITED PRESS INTERNATIONAL

SATO, EISAKU. The man who is Japan's conservative Liberal-Democratic Party president and premier had a hard year in 1966 but from all indications faces one more difficult still in 1967. Eisaku Sato's popularity plummeted to an all-time low for postwar prime ministers, and he himself was stricken by liver illness in the fall and recovered to find the socialist-led Opposition bitterly assailing several cabinet ministers appointed since a summertime's reshuffle. To try and remedy the situation, Sato scrapped a state visit to Russia and launched domestic tours to shore up the electorate.

One Diet man was forced to resign, criminally indicted for bribery, fraud and intimidation. Sato's transportation minister was junked (charged by the opposition with abuse of power and political favoritism), while his defense minister narrowly escaped, under heavy fire for alleged abuse of his position for electioneering. Sato himself was attacked on charges of tax irregularities.

The Premier withstood a determined threat by his Economic Planning Agency's Director General, Aiichiro Fujiyama, and was reelected Liberal-Democratic Party president Dec. 1. At year-end Sato faced the need to dissolve the Diet and call for Lower House nationwide elections in late January.

A socialist storm gathers, hopeful of advancing at the expense of the government party, even of toppling it from power. Beyond looms 1970, a crucial year for Japan when the U.S.-Japan Security Treaty could come up for revision or abrogation.

Sato met with many prominent visitors, from U.S. State Secretary Dean Rusk to Soviet Foreign Minister Andrei Gromyko. The Premier tried successfully to steer Japan from full-scale opposition to the Vietnam war toward tacit support of the U.S. position in southeast Asia, away from neutralism and toward continued prosperity and political stability through equal-partner relationship with Washington.

STUART GRIFFIN
East Asia Correspondent
THE LONDON OBSERVER FOREIGN NEWS SERVICE

SCANDINAVIA. For Scandinavia 1966 was a year of political shifts and of renewed hope that Western Europe's two rival trading blocs might be coming together.

The Political Situation. The Social Democratic parties of Denmark, Norway, Sweden and Finland have traditionally played a, if not the, key role in Scandinavian politics. But in 1966 the Norwegian Social Democrats were in the unaccustomed role of the Opposition while the Social Democrats in Denmark and Sweden were showing signs of fading popularity with the electorate.

However, in Finland just the reverse was true and the March parliamentary elections there undoubtedly constituted the biggest political upset of the year in Scandinavia. It had been expected that the Finnish Social Democrats would make heavy inroads into the support hitherto enjoyed by the governing non-socialist coalition, but the results far exceeded the expectations.

Dean Rusk (left) meets Finnish Premier Rafael Paasio.

In a triumph of landslide proportions the Social Democrats moved from third to leading position among Finnish parties. Although the Social Democrats had been excluded from successive government coalitions since 1958 because of Soviet antipathy to some of their leaders and policies, there was no denying them this time. Thus a new coalition Government, headed by Rafael Paasio, the Social Democratic Party chairman, was formed that included Communists for the first time since 1948.

In Sweden, where the Social Democrats have been in power almost without interruption for 34 years, Prime Minister Tage Erlander's Government got a rude shock in the September municipal elections. The Social Democrats won 42.8 per cent of the vote, a sharp drop of more than 8 per cent from the previous local elections four years ago. Mr. Erlander hinted that he might call a general election, but few observers thought he would do so before the next parliamentary elections scheduled for 1968.

As in Sweden, the Danish Social Democrats also have been ruling, although generally as a minority Government, almost uninterruptedly for 34 years. Signs earlier in the year of a slump in Social Democratic popularity prompted Prime Minister Jens Otto Krag to call national elections on Nov. 22, two years in advance of the regularly scheduled parliamentary elections.

The results confirmed the earlier forecasts. The Prime Minister and his Social Democrats won a renewed mandate but with a sharply reduced representation in Parliament. The big gains, however, were not registered by the nonsocialist parties but by the extreme Left-Wing Socialist People's Party led by a former Communist. But the Social Democrats still remained by far the largest party in the country.

In Norway the Social Democrats, who were knocked out of office in 1965 for the first time in 35 years, were discovering what it was like to be in the Opposition against the new non-socialist coalition Government headed by Prime Minister Per Borten, leader of the agrarian Center Party. It is still too early to tell whether this shift to the Right represents more than a temporary deviation from the traditional Norwegian voting pattern. The next parliamentary elections are scheduled for 1969.

The Economic Situation. If Scandinavia's economic problems with inflation and growing trade deficits undoubtedly contributed to voter discontent in 1966, the year also brought some hopeful economic news by way of London. British Prime Minister Harold Wilson's Labor Government indicated in November that it probably would make another attempt to take Britain into the European Economic Community, or Common Market. The first attempt was rebuffed in 1963 by President de Gaulle of France.

Western Europe accounts for about three quarters of Scandinavia's foreign trade. Sweden, Norway and especially Denmark, all members with Britain (and with Austria, Switzerland and Portugal) in the European Free Trade Association, have been pressing London to lead the way into the Common Market grouping of France, West Germany, Italy, the Netherlands, Belgium and Luxembourg.

Thus the news of Britain's initiative was generally well received in Scandinavia although no one was so sanguine as to believe that the possible merging of EFTA with the EEC would be either a quick or an easy matter.

Nonetheless, for Norway and Denmark, both members of the North Atlantic Alliance, to follow Britain into the Common Market would be politically painless. But not for neutralist Sweden. And even less so for Finland which, although an associate of EFTA, has to maintain the strictest neutrality between East and West because of her special position vis-à-vis the Soviet Union.

W. GRANGER BLAIR
Correspondent London Bureau
THE NEW YORK TIMES

SOCIALIST PARTIES. In 1966, democratic socialist parties affiliated with the Socialist International made an increasing impact on the political and social life and structure of European democracies.

Socialist Gains

Great Britain. The British Labor Party of Prime Minister Harold Wilson, in the parliamentary elections of March 31, elected 363 members to the House of Commons, an increase of 46 over the 1964 election, and 110 more than the Conservative Party.

West Germany. The German Social Democratic Party, led by Willy Brandt, mayor of West Berlin, accepted an invitation in late November to join the "grand coalition" Christian Democratic-Social Democratic Cabinet. In the new Cabinet, the first in which Social Democrats served since 1930, Brandt became vice-chancellor and foreign minister. During 1966 Social Democrats showed increased strength in state elections in North Rhine-Westphalia, Hamburg and Bavaria.

Finland. In the Finnish elections of March 20–21, the Social Democrats surprised many by adding 17 parliamentary seats to the 38 already held, while the Left-Wing Socialists increased their representation from 2 to 6, placing the Socialists first among the country's political forces. Rafael Paasio, Social Democrat, was thereupon called on to form a Government as a prime minister.

Denmark. Denmark's two socialist parties increased their combined parliamentary representation by 3 in Nov. 22 elections. The two parties received a total of 89 parliamentary seats: 69 for the Social Democrats (a loss of 7), 20 for the Left-Wing Socialists (a gain of 10). Social-democratic leader Jens Otto Krag continued as prime minister.

Italy. The socialist movement in Italy gained considerable strength with the reunification, after 19 years, of the socialist and social-democratic parties. Pietro Nenni, long leader of the Socialist Party, remained in the coalition government as vice-premier, while Giuseppe Saragat, a founder of the Democratic Socialist Party, continued as president.

France. France's Socialist Party continued to play an active role in the Federation of the Democratic Socialist Left and to prepare for 1967 parliamentary elections.

Socialist Losses and Other Developments

Western European Socialists, on the other hand, suffered losses during the year in Sweden, where the Social Democratic vote in local elections dropped by more than 8 per cent to 42.8 per cent of the total; in Austria where 74 Socialists were seated in Parliament, a drop of two, and where Socialists left the Cabinet,

becoming an Opposition party for the first time since the end of World War II; also in Belgium and the Netherlands, where the Socialist and Labor parties joined the countries' Opposition.

The Labor Party in New Zealand won in the national election the same number of seats—35—as in 1963; the Australian Labor Party won 41 seats, while the Liberal-Country alliance won 61. Both Australasian Labor parties continued as the chief opposition parties in their respective countries.

In Canada the New Democratic Party was represented in Parliament by 21 members under the leadership of T. C. Douglas, former premier of Saskatchewan.

The United States Socialist Party, a member of the Socialist International, was active during the year in the war against poverty and racial discrimination and in the campaign in behalf of a negotiated peace in South Vietnam. Norman Thomas continued as honorary chairman of the party, Darlington Hoopes as chairman.

The Socialist Party and Democratic Socialist Party in Japan served as the Government's most powerful Opposition movement.

Argentina's Government confiscated the property of the Socialist Party and of several other parties critical of the Government. The Accion Democratica Party, an observer member of the Social International, continued in control of Venezuela.

The Socialist International had over 50 affiliates during the year with a membership of over 10 million and a voting strength of over 60 million.

HARRY W. LAIDLER
Executive Director Emeritus
LEAGUE FOR INDUSTRIAL DEMOCRACY

SOUTH CAROLINA. Robert E. McNair (D), who had served 18 months as governor, won a 4-year term in November. Sen. Strom Thurmond (R) was reelected, and Ernest L. Hollings (D) will serve the remaining 2 years of the term of the late Sen. Olin D. Johnston.... In 1965 the state brought suit against the U.S. Attorney General over the 1965 Voting Rights Act. On March 7 the U.S. Supreme Court upheld seven major provisions of the act.

SOUTH DAKOTA. September was "See South Dakota Month."... On April 9 the South Dakota Supreme Court ruled that private and parochial schools be accepted as members of the State High School Interscholastic Activities Association.... Parts of the state were struck by two power failures July 11.... Republican incumbents Gov. Nils A. Boe and Sen. Karl E. Mundt retained their seats Nov. 8.

SOUTHEAST ASIA

By DEREK DAVIES
Editor, FAR EASTERN ECONOMIC REVIEW

Nineteen sixty-six was a year of violence in southeast Asia. The intensification of the bombing against North Vietnam, the mounting fury of the land war in the South as the Vietcong were brought to bay in their own strongholds, the wholesale massacre of Communists in Indonesia—itself the consequence of the brutal murder of six senior Indonesian generals—and the systematic assassination of officials in the northeast of Thailand as the Communists begin a campaign of subversion there . . . all are part of a pattern of strife and terror, as the struggle between militant communism and its opponents reached a new pitch of intensity. Only in the ending of confrontation between Indonesia and Malaysia was there a development toward stability, but even the benefits of this were nullified by deteriorating relations between Malaysia and Singapore.

Vietnam and Indonesia. In 1966 the Communists in Vietnam were on the defensive. The balance of power has gone almost full circle from the early months of 1965, when danger of a complete breakdown in the morale of the Vietnamese army made a communist victory in the south a distinct possibility. At that time the power and influence of the huge Indonesian Communist Party was growing daily, with the encouragement of President Sukarno.

But during 1966 the Vietcong failed to win any striking victories, and instead the cream of its regular forces was mauled in a series of bloody encounters in which the full force of the most destructive weaponry of the United States was turned against them. Moreover, the U.S. military buildup has ruled out the possibility of an outright communist victory. In early 1965 there were only 23,000 U.S. troops in South Vietnam, a year later 200,000, and at the end of 1966 almost 400,000.

In Indonesia the Communists suffered even more crippling setbacks. The ranks of the party were decimated by massacres on a terrifying scale. The precise number of Communists killed is not known, but the total is estimated to be at least 300,000. The destruction was not wrought by guns or napalm, but by a popular fury whipped up by religious fanatics, who had long resented the growth in influence of the Indonesian Communist Party.

This does not mean that communism is a spent force in southeast Asia. The massacres in Indonesia certainly obliterated the party's hold there, however. Not only has the full force of the army been employed in tracking down the communist leaders, but the organized fanaticism of religious leaders and their followers has wiped out the village communist organization. But the Communists still retain a firm hold in their strongholds—notably East and Central Java—and in view of the instability of Indonesian politics, they may well stage a comeback there sometime in the future.

The same is true of the Vietcong. Their losses in set-piece battles have blunted their offensive capacity, but the U.S./South Vietnamese leadership has yet to adopt a strategy that will succeed in bringing military forces to bear at the "grassroots." However, with the emphasis on the need for "social revolution" in the final communiqué of the October Manila Conference, and President Johnson's known support for this line, there were signs as 1966 ended that such a strategy would soon be adopted.

The immediate effect of the U.S. buildup was to stabilize the political situation within South Vietnam itself. Air Marshal Ky's Government remained in power throughout the year, and is now the longest-lived South Vietnamese Government since the fall of President Diem. Its resilience was tested by serious political crises. Ky had to overcome the discontent of members of his own Cabinet who accused him of regional discrimination in government appointments.

But the most serious challenge came in March when General Nguyen Chanh Thi, who had been dismissed from his Central Vietnam command for "warlordism," virtually seized power with the support of the Buddhists and defied Ky to unseat him. But the moderate Buddhists were won over by the Government's promise to hold elections to a constituent assembly, and Thi's control of central Vietnam was broken in May after several days of bloody fighting in Danang, the regional center.

The elections were duly held in September, and with a turnout of about 80 per cent of the population (even though the Vietcong urged the people to stay away), the outcome was regarded as a notable success.

Laos. In spite of escalation in Vietnam, the military situation in Laos remained calm—reflecting the unwillingness of the Communists to become embroiled on two fronts. Most military activities were confined to the Plain of Jars, where the communist Pathet Lao made headway at the expense of the neutralist forces under the command of General Kong Le. Kong Le himself returned to Thailand at the

Above: Farmer near Vientiane, Laos, plows field on experimental farm aided by UN Development Program and Food and Agriculture Organization. Right: Laos' Prince Souvanna Phouma at U.S. State Department.

end of October. If he carries out his declared intention of resigning his command, the neutralist army will undoubtedly break up.

The Laotian political scene was more lively. Prince Souvanna Phouma's tripartite Government (including royalist, neutralist and communist elements, although the Communists refuse to take up their ministerial portfolios) was under pressure from a Right-Wing faction, which demanded the dismissal of corrupt officials, and even called for the resignation of the Government. The Opposition took on a more definite form in September, when the 59-member Parliament rejected the budget, which forced the Government to dissolve Parliament and arrange for elections to be held on Jan. 1, 1967. But Prince Souvanna Phouma still remains indispensable. Without him the fragile structure of Laotian neutrality would disintegrate, with the accompanying danger of renewed conflict.

Laotian politics would not be complete without at least one attempted *coup d'état*, and this was duly made on Oct. 21, when General Thao Ma, who lost his job as air-force chief, launched his bombers against the headquarters of his army rival, General Ouane Ratikone. But the coup did not have any army backing, and General Ma fled to Thailand.

Thailand. The Vietnam policy of the United States was given solid support by Thailand. Realizing the close connection between developments in Vietnam, and communist subversion in Thailand's northeastern provinces (which was reported to be on the increase towards the end of the year), the Thais sent military equipment to Vietnam, and continued to permit U.S. bombers to operate from their bases. The U.S. military presence in Thailand increased, the total strength of U.S. forces estimated as being at least 30,000 by mid-1966.

Thailand's economy grew fast, but the Government has not yet succeeded in channeling the increased wealth to those sectors where it is most needed, particularly agriculture. At present urban wealth is accumulating rapidly, while rural incomes remain stagnant, an unhealthy condition for a country that may soon be the target of intense communist subversion.

Cambodia. The U.S. buildup had also given southeast Asian neutrals the opportunity to pursue a more liberal foreign policy. For instance, Prince Sihanouk of Cambodia has moderated his formerly "pro-Chinese" neutralism. Cambodia is anxious to restore relations with the United States from the all-time low reached in 1965 when Cambodia broke off diplomatic relations. In August the Prince agreed to meet Averell Harriman (President Johnson's roving ambassador) to discuss ways of improving relations between the two countries, but canceled the meeting after yet another Cambodian border village was bombed by South Vietnamese and U.S. aircraft. In September he made a similar proposal to the Thais (with whom relations were equally strained), which came to nothing, apparently owing to Thailand's refusal to admit that the border temple of Preah Vihear was on Cambodian territory, as decided by the International Court of Justice at The Hague.

The same trend can be detected in Cam-

Above: Fishing in Mekong River waters is big business following construction of Ubol Ratana Dam in northeast Thailand. Below: Prince Norodom Sihanouk of Cambodia.

bodia's internal politics. In October, General Lon Nol—known to be an advocate of a more moderate foreign policy—became prime minister, not by the personal appointment of the Prince (the procedure followed in the past) but by a vote in the Cambodian National Assembly. This suggests that the Prince does not want to be too closely associated with a Government that may make departures from his own policies.

But Sihanouk still maintained friendly relations with the Communists. During the year he received friendship delegations from China, and even arranged a summit meeting with President Ho Chi Minh and the President of the National Liberation Front (the political arm of the Vietcong). But there are signs that relations with the Communists are not so cordial as they used to be. Sihanouk is reported to be alarmed by the violence of the Great Cultural Revolution, and is disillusioned by the refusal of both the Chinese and the North Vietnamese to guarantee his border. The net result is that Cambodia's neutralism is becoming more broadly based.

Burma. The same is true of Burma's foreign policy. In the past, Burma's neutralism took the form of minimizing contacts with foreign powers. But in 1966 Burma was developing friendly relations with governments at all points on the political spectrum. In September, General Ne Win visited Washington and expressed "warm regard" for the United States. Burma was also anxious to be on good terms with her neighbors. The General made visits to Thailand, Japan and India, and, with the ending of confrontation between Indonesia and Malaysia, there will be opportunities for developing still other ties. But at the same time a genuine balance was preserved. Economic ties were strengthened with the U.S.S.R., Rumania and Czechoslovakia, and, in spite of the Cultural Revolution, there was no deterioration in relations with China.

The Burmese economy was subject to even stricter control when in January the Government took over the trade of nearly 500 essential commodities. In spite of some relaxation later in the year, the cost of living continued to rise, industrial production was stagnant and agricultural production actually fell.

Malaysia. For Malaysia, by far the most significant event in 1966 was the end of confrontation with Indonesia. Following the Bangkok accord of May (which laid down the conditions for peace), trade was resumed, and numerous delegations exchanged visits. But the *rapprochement* had disturbing overtones. There was talk about the ethnic and religious unity of the Malay race. This points to the danger that the Malays, backed up by their Indonesian coreligionists, may now feel less restraint in taking oppressive measures against the Malay Chinese community, and may be encouraged to adopt a more high-handed policy toward neighboring (Chinese) Singapore.

There were signs of this in 1966. For instance, any hope that the August 1965 separation between Malaysia and Singapore would facilitate cooperation between the two states has proved groundless. The Separation Agreement promised a defense treaty and a joint committee on economic cooperation; both have been ignored.

Moreover, petty rivalries have led to some absurd decisions. Malaysia plans to develop its own ports, although Singapore (the fifth largest port in the world) has the facilities to handle all Malaysia's export and import trade. The joint currency is to be abandoned, with the result that the backing for the two new currencies will be weaker. This new "confrontation" could, by hampering the economic development of both countries, be more harmful than the old.

Philippines. The year 1966 saw the installation of a new president in the Philippines—

Wide World

In New York City, Burma's U Thant (l), UN secretary-general, greets Burmese head of state, Gen. Ne Win.

Ferdinand Marcos, whose Nacionalista Party scored a landslide victory in the November 1965 presidential election. In 1966, President Marcos' major initiatives were in foreign affairs. In September he visited the United States, and, after talks with President Johnson, announced increased military and civil aid, and the reduction of the lease on U.S. bases from 99 to 25 years (disagreement on the length of the lease

Malaysian Deputy Premier Tun Abdul Razak (seated, l) and Indonesian Foreign Minister Adam Malik (seated, r) sign treaty ending 3 years' undeclared war between their nations.

UPI

Ferdinand E. Marcos, Philippine president and host of the 7-nation Manila Conference on war in Vietnam.

had long been an irritant in U.S.-Philippine relations). But Marocs' most important achievement was the convening of the seven-nation summit in Manila in October (attended by the United States, South Vietnam, South Korea, Thailand, Australia, New Zealand and the Philippines), which resulted in a vigorously worded communiqué outlining the allies' policy objectives in Vietnam, and offering to withdraw foreign troops from South Vietnam within six months after North Vietnam ends its infiltration and aggression.

The Philippines' long-standing economic problems remained unsolved. The price of rice continued to rise because of shortages, the economy's growth rate fell short of the planned total and the slow progress in the land-reform program led to increased communist insurgency in Central Luzon.

SOUTHEAST ASIA TREATY ORGANIZATION. At its 25th conference, held at Bangkok in December, military advisers of SEATO (Britain, United States, France, Pakistan, the Philippines, Thailand, Australia and New Zealand) "reaffirmed a determination to maintain and increase the effectiveness of SEATO in safeguarding the treaty area against communist subversion." But although 1966 was a year in which subversion posed a greater threat to southeast Asia than ever before—both in Thailand, a SEATO member, and South Vietnam (whose security is guaranteed by a "protocol" of the Treaty—in neither place was the communist threat met by collective action via SEATO.

Thailand has its own unilateral defense agreement with the United States—the Dean Rusk/Thanat Khoman agreement of 1962—which specifically bypasses SEATO by allow-

ing the United States to aid Thailand without the prior agreement of the other member countries. South Vietnam—which has received military aid from all the SEATO countries except Pakistan and France—has never requested aid under the SEATO treaty, nor has SEATO's planning machinery been used in allocating the aid that has actually been given.

This inactivity reflects differences among SEATO countries, which became apparent at the June Ministerial Conference in Canberra. On Vietnam, France's policies have long contradicted SEATO's official "containment" policy, and the French only sent observers to the June meeting. The Pakistanis disassociated themselves from the statement on Vietnam in the final communiqué, and, to emphasize its independence, the Pakistani Government welcomed Chou En-lai on an official visit just as the SEATO ministers were condemning China's expansionist ambitions in southeast Asia.

Moreover, there were signs of discontent among those members whose security was most in danger. The Philippines fulminated against France's continued membership. Thailand's Thanat Khoman blamed SEATO for the escalation of the war in Vietnam: "Emboldened by SEATO's impotence and lack of will to resist communist encroachments [the Communists] sought to deliver a *coup de grace* in South Vietnam." When Dean Rusk tried to present SEATO in a better light by arguing that the U.S. commitment in Vietnam was a "fundamental SEATO obligation," he was contradicted by the British, French and Pakistanis.

There has already been talk of altering the membership of SEATO, and this would be one way of achieving some unity. It is inconsistent that strongly anticommunist nations like South Korea and South Vietnam should not belong to the organization, and yet France and Pakistan should. But this would not overcome the potentially serious disagreement between the United States and Britain on Vietnam.

There are reports that the first draft of the SEATO declaration at the June conference met with strong disapproval from then British Foreign Secretary Michael Stewart, who substituted a second and more mildly worded draft. Moreover, the British disassociated themselves from the bombing of the Hanoi/Haiphong oil depots, and insisted that SEATO should not be involved in Vietnam. Britain is also under pressure to commit some of its troops formerly in Malaysia to Thailand. Another crisis could arise in SEATO if—on grounds of economy—Britain refuses to do this.

DEREK DAVIES

Editor, FAR EASTERN ECONOMIC REVIEW

SPACE

By JAMES J. HAGGERTY
Editor, AEROSPACE YEAR BOOK

Gemini. The space highlight of 1966 was unquestionably the U.S. Project Gemini, marked by five successful manned flights during the year and completion of the program with the Nov. 15 splashdown of Gemini 12.

Directed by the National Aeronautics and Space Administration (NASA), Gemini ranked as a 100 per cent successful program despite a variety of troubles, some major, some minor, which cropped up on every launch. The difficulties, however, generally only accented the versatility of the American space program. Although the troubles caused early termination of some flights, all missions qualified as successes.

Concluded in only two years, Gemini provided a wealth of space information and experience, and served well its objective of preparing the U.S. space community for the Apollo program, which is to culminate in a manned landing on the moon. In the course of 10 manned missions, Gemini astronauts learned how to maneuver from one orbital altitude to

UPI

Astronauts Neil Armstrong (l) and David Scott (r) return to Cape Kennedy following Gemini 8 flight.

Left: From Gemini 9 spacecraft a view of the augmented target docking adapter. Right: View from Gemini 10, moments before docking with Agena target vehicle.

Both photos NASA

Wide World
Gemini 11 photographs Australia from 850-mi. altitude.

another, and, to the limited extent of Gemini's capability, from one orbital plane to another. The astronauts scored the first rendezvous in space, then the first docking between 2 vehicles, and amassed considerable experience in this vital aspect of space flight. They learned how to live and maneuver outside their spacecraft, and compiled an impressive total of more than 9 hours outside or partially outside the Gemini capsule. They provided valuable in-

formation on the long-duration effects of weightlessness with one flight lasting 330 hr., 35 min., 17 sec. And Gemini produced a record altitude for manned flight, of more than 850 mi. Project Gemini boosted the total U.S. man-hours in space to 1,994 hr., 15 min., compared to the Soviet Union's 507 hr., 16 min.

The five 1966 flights were:

Gemini 8, March 16, Astronauts Neil Armstrong and David Scott. They achieved the first docking with another vehicle in space, an unmanned Agena target. This flight produced some anxious moments when a rocket thruster malfunctioned, and continued to fire after shutdown, throwing the coupled spacecraft into a violent spin. The astronauts successfully separated the craft and regained Gemini stabilization, but the planned 3-day mission was terminated.

Gemini 9, June 3–6, Thomas P. Stafford and Eugene Cernan. A shroud on the Agena target vehicle failed to separate, precluding docking exercises, but the astronauts were able to rendezvous 3 times with the target. Cernan conducted 2 hr., 9 min. of extravehicular activity (EVA). He became exhausted when he attempted to don a maneuvering backpack, however, and EVA was cut short. The mission continued through its planned 72 hr., 21 min.

Gemini 10, July 18–21, John W. Young and Michael Collins. This flight saw the first dual rendezvous, in which Young and Collins first

Astronaut Edwin Aldrin outside Gemini 12 during flight.
UPI

Astronaut Charles Conrad at Gemini 11 splashdown.
UPI

chased, caught and docked with the Agena launched the same day, then made a second rendezvous with the Agena still orbiting from the Gemini 8 flight. Collins went outside and, using a handgun, maneuvered over to the Agena. His EVA was cut, when fuel for Gemini's maneuvering rockets ran short.

Gemini 11, Sept. 12–15, Charles Conrad, Jr., and Richard Gordon, Jr. Conrad and Gordon accomplished the first "direct ascent" rendezvous, in which they caught the target vehicle within the first orbit. After docking, they used the 16,000-lb.-thrust Agena engine to boost the linked spacecraft to a record altitude of 850 mi. Once again there was trouble in the EVA portion of the mission. Gordon's vision was impaired by perspiration when his suit became overheated from excessive exertion. Exhausted, Gordon terminated his scheduled 107-min. space walk after 40 min.

Gemini 12, Nov. 11–15, James A. Lovell, Jr., and Edwin E. Aldrin, Jr. Project Gemini came to a successful conclusion as Aldrin demonstrated that EVA need not be a problem. His spacecraft was equipped with hand and foot holds that eased his movement around the outside of the spacecraft. Counting time spent partially outside—stand-up EVA in an open hatch —Aldrin became the all-time EVA champion with 5 hr., 37 min. Lovell and Aldrin made a third-orbit hookup with the Agena target, but fuel-pump trouble in the unmanned spacecraft wiped out a planned high-altitude flight. The remainder of the planned program was carried out, however, and the last of the Geminis landed after 94 hr., 33 min. Lovell, who had flown the 2-week-long Gemini 7 mission, became the world's most experienced spaceman with total flight time of 425 hr., 8 min.

U.S.S.R. The Soviet Union made no manned flights, but continued the unmanned portion of its program at a high level of activity. The U.S.S.R. lunar-exploration program, a dismal failure in 1965, scored 5 successes in as many

U.S. AND SOVIET MANNED ORBITAL FLIGHTS

ASTRONAUT	NATION	DATE	NO.OF CIRCUITS	FLIGHT TIME	CRAFT NAME
Gargarin	U.S.S.R.	April 12, 1961	1	1 hr. 48 mins.	Vostok 1
Titov	U.S.S.R.	Aug. 6–7, 1961	17.5	25 hrs. 18 mins.	Vostok 2
Glenn	U.S.	Feb. 20, 1962	3	4 hrs. 55 mins.	Friendship 7
Carpenter	U.S.	May 24, 1962	3	4 hrs. 56 mins.	Aurora 7
Nikolayev	U.S.S.R.	Aug. 11–15, 1962	64	94 hrs. 22 mins.	Vostok 3
Popovich	U.S.S.R.	Aug. 12–15, 1962	48	70 hrs. 57 mins.	Vostok 4
Schirra	U.S.	Oct. 3, 1962	6	9 hrs. 13 mins.	Sigma 7
Cooper	U.S.	May 15–16, 1963	22	34 hrs. 20 mins.	Faith 7
Bykovsky	U.S.S.R.	June 14–19, 1963	81	119 hrs. 6 mins.	Vostok 5
Tereshkova	U.S.S.R.	June 16–19, 1963	48	70 hrs. 50 mins.	Vostok 6
Feoktistov Komarov Yegorov	U.S.S.R.	Oct. 12–13, 1964	16	24 hrs. 17 mins.	Voskhod 1
Belyayev Leonov	U.S.S.R.	Mar. 18–19, 1965	17	26 hrs. 2 mins.	Voskhod 2
Grissom Young	U.S.	Mar. 23, 1965	3	4 hrs. 54 mins.	Gemini 3
McDivitt White	U.S.	June 3–7, 1965	62	97 hrs. 59 mins.	Gemini 4
Cooper Conrad	U.S.	Aug. 21–29, 1965	100	190 hrs. 56 mins.	Gemini 5
Schirra Stafford	U.S.	Dec. 15–16, 1965	16	25 hrs. 51 mins.	Gemini 6
Borman Lovell	U.S.	Dec. 4–18, 1965	206	330 hrs. 35 mins.	Gemini 7
Armstrong Scott	U.S.	Mar. 16, 1966	6½	10 hrs. 42 mins.	Gemini 8
Stafford Cernan	U.S.	June 3–6, 1966	46	72 hrs. 21 mins.	Gemini 9
Young Collins	U.S.	July 18–21, 1966	44	70 hrs. 47 mins.	Gemini 10
Conrad Gordon	U.S.	Sept. 12–15, 1966	45	71 hrs. 17 mins.	Gemini 11
Lovell Aldrin	U.S.	Nov. 11–15, 1966	59	94 hrs. 33 mins.	Gemini 12

attempts during 1966. The outstanding flight, from a technological standpoint, was that of Luna 9, launched Jan. 31. Luna 9 successfully "backed down" on a column of rocket thrust to become the first vehicle to make a "soft" landing on the moon. The spacecraft returned photos of the lunar surface for 3 days after its landing. Later in the year, the U.S.S.R. launched 4 lunar-orbiting spacecraft: Lunas 10, 11, 12 and 13. Lunas 10 and 11 carried only instruments for measuring the moon's surface and the near-moon space environment. Luna 12, however, was equipped with cameras to supplement the surface photography relayed by Luna 9. Luna 12 started sending excellent pictures in late October. Luna 13, launched at Christmastime, was a soft-lander containing both cameras and surface-sampling equipment.

The Soviet lack of success on unmanned interplanetary missions continued in 1966. Two Venus probes, Venera 2 and 3, launched in November 1965, reached the planet but failed to return data. They gave the U.S.S.R. an unenviable record of 14 failures in 14 attempts to fly by Venus and Mars.

The U.S.S.R. continued to launch its big Cosmos satellites at a frequency rate approximating that of 1965. Cosmos is a catchall designation for a variety of experiments in the scientific, military and applied-engineering fields. About 30 Cosmos spacecraft were launched during 1966.

Of particular interest was a special Cosmos designed for space/biological investigation. Cosmos 110, launched Feb. 22, carried 2 dogs named Veterok and Ugolyok. Each was enclosed in an aluminum canister equipped with food and with devices for waste disposal, environmental control, television and telemetry systems. The spacecraft itself contained a radiation shield to protect the animals against the high levels of radiation encountered in the lower portions of the Van Allen radiation belts, into which the spacecraft was deliberately guided. Cosmos 110 remained aloft for more than 22 days. Then it was deorbited and recovered in a land area of the Soviet Union. Although the dogs needed several days to regain full coordination, they apparently suffered little from radiation or the long duration of the flight, more than a week longer than any human flight.

The U.S.S.R. continued its development of a communications satellite (comsat) with the April 25 launch of the third of its Molniya series, Molniya 1C. The spacecraft was sent into a highly elliptical orbit with an apogee of more than 24,000 mi., phased so that the spacecraft reached apogee twice daily over the Soviet Union. Communications tests between Moscow and Vladivostok were conducted, and the comsat was later used in a joint Soviet/French color-television-transmission experiment. In addition, Molniya doubed as a me-

Russia's space dog Veterok is prepared for orbit.

Japan's Lambda-4S satellite measures 1.4 ft. in diameter.

Photos UPI

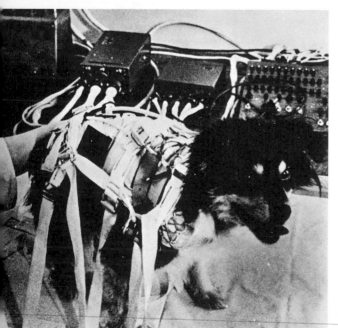

teorological satellite, sending cloud-cover photos taken from various altitudes.

France and Japan. France, which in 1965 became the third nation to launch a spacecraft by means of its own booster, continued its space program with the Feb. 17 launching of a DIA geodetic satellite. Boosted by the Diamant launch vehicle from the French complex at Hammaguir, Algeria, DIA successfully transmitted geodetic measurements to ground stations at Nice, France, and Beirut, Lebanon.

Later in the year, Japan sought to become the fourth nation to orbit a spacecraft with a home-developed launch vehicle. (The United Kingdom, Canada and Italy have built experimental packages that were launched by U.S. boosters.) On Sept. 26, the Japanese attempted to orbit a 57-lb. instrument package by means of a Lambda 4A-1 four-stage launch vehicle, but malfunction of the top stage canceled the effort. At the end of 1966, the Japanese were preparing another try with a new vehicle.

U.S. Lunar Flights. Aside from Gemini, the most important U.S. missions of the year were the unmanned lunar flights, with the two-fold aim of acquiring more scientific knowledge about the lunar environment, and of selecting sites for the manned landings to come. The United States launched 4 lunar flights, 2 soft landers and 2 orbiters, but 1 of the soft-landing attempts failed.

The first American soft lander, Surveyor 1, was launched May 30, to land 3 days later in the crater known as the Ocean of Storms within 10 miles of the aiming point. The spacecraft touched down on the surface at a descent rate of only 12 ft. per sec. Over the next 12 days, Surveyor 1 sent back to earth 10,338 high-quality photographs, then was shut down for the 2-week-long lunar night. Although the craft was not expected to survive the cold night, it proved still ready to accept earth commands on July 6, the second lunar day, and was able to send more than 800 additional photos. As late as Nov. 8, after 5 cold lunar nights, Surveyor was still able to respond to commands and relay some data, although it was no longer returning photos. A September Surveyor 2 mission failed. A malfunction of a control rocket at the time of the mid-course maneuver threw the spacecraft into a tumbling, off-course trajectory.

The first of the companion craft, Lunar Orbiter 1, was launched Aug. 10, and several days later was jockeyed into a low-altitude lunar orbit that at times dipped as close as 24 mi. to the surface. Equipped with 1 high- and 1 medium-resolution camera, Lunar Orbiter 1 operated flawlessly for 76 days, photographing

Lunar Orbiter 2's close-up of moon crater Copernicus.

some 2 million sq. mi. of the lunar surface, and in addition reporting millions of individual scientific measurements of the lunar environment taken by its battery of instruments. Low on rocket fuel for stabilization, the spacecraft was deliberately destroyed for fear its electrical system would interfere with signals from the second spacecraft of the series. Lunar Orbiter 1 was slowed by retro-rocket fired by earth command on Oct. 29. Deprived of orbital velocity, it crashed to the lunar surface, becoming the eleventh man-made vehicle to impact the moon. Lunar Orbiter 2, launched a week later, began photographing on Nov. 18.

Weather Satellites. The U.S.-pioneered meteorological-satellite (metrosat) system advanced another step during 1966 with the start of the first fully operational metrosats. The spacecraft in the network are of the Tiros type, which made 10 successful developmental flights in as many attempts during 1960-65. However, they carry a new designation—ESSA—for the sponsoring agency, the new Environmental Science Services Administration. Like the last models of Tiros, the ESSA spacecraft are drum-shaped with 2 cameras mounted on the rim of the drum, and facing exactly opposite directions. In orbit ESSA cartwheels, or rolls around its hub so that one or the other of the cameras is always facing earthward. Some of the ESSA satellites are equipped with the Automatic Picture Transmission (APT) system, which permits photo reception on the ground by simple, low-cost receiving equipment instead

Nimbus 2, NASA's 935-lb. weather satellite.

of the complex antennas and receivers employed by NASA and the U.S. Weather Bureau. APT allows any nation willing to expend about $30,000 to participate in the benefits of satellite weather reporting. ESSA plans to keep 1 APT-equipped spacecraft in orbit at all times.

The year saw 3 launches of operational ESSA satellites. ESSA 1, with a conventional camera system, started operating on Feb. 3.

Below: *Pageos*, a 100-ft.-diameter balloon, provides data for more precise mapping of the earth's surface. Right: Artist's concept of the Manned Orbiting Laboratory, which is about the size of a trailer house.

The APT-equipped ESSA 2 went into service Feb. 28. ESSA 3, launched Oct. 2 into near-polar orbit, photographs from altitudes above 800 mi., compared to about 500 mi. altitudes for ESSA 1.

In addition to the ESSA craft, NASA continued advanced development of the metrosat with the launch of Nimbus 2 on May 15. Like its 1964 predecessor, Nimbus 2 employs an approach different from that of Tiros/ESSA. Its 4 cameras, including 1 APT camera and 3 Vidicon cameras similar to the 2 cameras in ESSA 3, are mounted on the bottom of the spacecraft, but a stabilization system ensures that they always point toward earth. The May launch was successful, and Nimbus 2's photos are picked up by about 150 stations, including 44 APT stations in 26 foreign countries.

Communications Satellites. The United States also progressed further in development of advanced communications satellites for both civil and military use.

The first comsat launch of 1966, on June 16, was that of the military network known as the Initial Defense Communication Satellite Program, which is to operate as an interim system pending development of improved spacecraft. The first increment of the system consisted of 7 satellites carried aboard a Titan 3-C booster and ejected into random orbits one at a time. This batch was to be augmented later by at least 8, possibly 16, additional satellites. All 7 of the June-launched satellites operated successfully, and communications tests

were conducted between terminals at Fort Dix, N.J., California, England and Germany. An August attempt to send up a second increment failed because of booster malfunction.

On Oct. 26, the U.S. Communications Satellite Corporation, acting as manager for the 54-nation International Telecommunications Satellite Consortium (Intelsat), launched its newest spacecraft, Intelsat 2. Designed to serve as a transpacific communications link, Intelsat 2 was supposed to have been inserted into a synchronous equatorial orbit over the international date line. Trouble with the apogee motor, which provides the final kick into this orbit, resulted in a different trajectory: an elliptical orbit with an apogee of 23,306 mi., a perigee of 2,069 mi. and an inclination to the equator of about 17°. In this orbit the spacecraft is partially useful: it is simultaneously visible to stations in Washington and Hawaii. A second launch, most likely an attempt at achieving the originally desired position for transmissions between the United States and the Far East, was scheduled for early 1967.

Other Programs. In the U.S. national-geodetic-satellite program, the Army launched the sixth of its Secor series for precise map making on June 9. On June 23, NASA launched a one-of-a-kind satellite called *Pageos* for Passive Geodetic Satellite. *Pageos* is a 100-ft.-diameter balloon based on the design of Echo, used in earlier comsat tests. *Pageos'* purpose is to reflect sunlight from its Mylar/aluminum panels, providing an orbiting source of light whose exact position is known at all times. Photography of the space-based light source from ground installations over the estimated 5-year life of the spacecraft will aid in precise location of landmasses and other geographic points on earth with reference to each other.

During 1966, NASA launched 2 more of its large "observatory class" satellites but scored only 1 success. Astronomers all over the world were disappointed when the Orbiting Astronomical Observatory (OAO), which carried 7 telescopes to view some 200 stars from a position above the distorting influence of earth's atmosphere, failed to produce results after its April 8 launch. The 2-ton spacecraft was properly placed in near-circular orbit at an altitude of about 500 mi., but power supply was cut off by failure of OAO's primary battery.

NASA was more successful with the third of its Orbiting Geophysical Observatory (OGO) series, launched June 7. Carrying 21 experiments, the greatest number ever mounted on an unmanned U.S. spacecraft, OGO 3 went into a near-perfect, highly elliptical orbit that took the spacecraft at apogee to an altitude of more than 75,000 mi. The 21 experiments, covering cosmic rays, trapped radiation, magnetic fields, plasma, micrometeoroids, ionospheric investigation and optical and radio emission, all returned data.

The military services, particularly the U.S. Air Force, continued to launch classified payloads at the one-a-week rate that has been standard since 1964. The USAF also launched a series of unclassified small spacecraft, usually in multiples or as "piggyback" packages. Among them were experiments in zero gravity, thermal control, radiation research and gravity-gradient stabilization.

The United States progressed on its follow-on manned-space-flight programs, Apollo and the Manned Orbiting Laboratory (MOL). On Feb. 26 and Aug. 25, NASA conducted tests of unmanned but flight-rated Apollo spacecraft. The tests were suborbital flights, the first a short trip down the Atlantic Test Range, the second a path that took the spacecraft three quarters of the way around the world to a landing in the Pacific. The primary objective of both tests was investigation of the capabilities of the heat shield, which differs from that of Mercury and Gemini in that it must be able to withstand the higher reentry temperatures encountered on a lunar return trajectory. In addition, the two missions served to check out the systems of the Apollo Command and Service modules. The Lunar Module, third major component of the spacecraft, was not ready for flight test in 1966. Apollo passed its flight checks and was ready for the first manned flight early in 1967.

The first test of hardware in connection with the USAF's Manned Orbiting Laboratory took place late in the year. The MOL, designed for 2-man experimental missions of up to 45 days' duration, consists of a modified Gemini capsule together with a 41-ft.-long canister that serves as laboratory and living quarters. The Gemini is used only for launch and reentry. On Nov. 3, a Titan 3-C booster launched a secondhand Gemini together with a large cylinder simulating the MOL canister. Again the primary objective was check-out of the heat shield, installed on a capsule recovered from NASA's Gemini program. In the MOL, it is necessary to cut a hatch in the center of the heat shield, to allow passage from the Gemini into the canister. Because of this modification, the heat shield had to pass another test despite its unqualified success in the Gemini program. The new shield met USAF requirements. No further MOL flights were planned until 1968, when there is to be at least 1 more unmanned mission.

SPORTS Highlights

By HAROLD (SPIKE) CLAASSEN
Assistant General Sports Editor
THE ASSOCIATED PRESS

Jim Ryun, a human running machine nurtured on the plains of Kansas; Sandy Koufax, sore-armed pitcher with the Los Angeles Dodgers; Frank Robinson, a National League discard who presented Baltimore with a World Series championship; Pete Rozelle, pro football's commissioner who brought peace to the gridiron sport; and Buckpasser, who became racing's first three-year-old millionaire, were the names that blazed on the sports pages during 1966.

Jim Ryun. Ryun, a 19-year-old freshman at the University of Kansas, lowered the world record for the ½-mile run to 1 minute, 44.9 seconds in June and then brought the world

Buckpasser, Horse of the Year, wins Malibu Stakes; Drin is second, Kings Favor third.

record for the mile down to 3:51.3 in July. It was only 12 years ago that Roger Bannister of England clocked in at 3:59.4, shattering the myth of man's inability to run the mile in 4 minutes or less. Had Bannister been in the race at Berkeley, Calif., with Ryun and posted his epoch-making time, he would have finished an estimated 60 yards behind the Kansas strider.

Sandy Koufax. Koufax was in the headlines virtually the entire year. Before the baseball season began he combined with Don Drysdale, the towering right-handed pitcher with the Dodgers, to form baseball's first doubleheader holdout, missed 32 days of spring practice, and then accepted a reported $125,000 while Drysdale had to be satisfied with $100,000. Koufax, his arthritic left elbow quieted with medication and ice, clinched the pennant for the Dodgers with his 27th victory of the year; won the Cy Young Award as baseball's best pitcher for a third time; made a lackluster start in the World Series against the Orioles; and then announced his retirement at age 30 because the arthritis had become too painful. Koufax set 3 records in his last year. His 1.73 earned-run average gave him the National League honor for the fifth straight year; his 17 strike-outs made him the first pitcher ever to repulse more than 300 batters in 3 different seasons;

395

and his 27 victories was a new high for left-handed pitchers in the National League.

Frank Robinson. Baltimore, winner of the World Series in 4 straight games, was managed by Hank Bauer, but was led on the field by Robinson, a right fielder acquired from the Cincinnati Reds, who disposed of him "as an old 30" before the start of the season. The change in uniforms rejuvenated Robinson, who led the American League with a batting average of .316, drove in 122 runs and hit 49 home runs. These figures made him baseball's first Triple Crown batting champion since 1956, and he was voted the American League's Most Valuable Player. He received a similar distinction with the Reds in 1961, and is the only player ever to have been chosen MVP in both leagues.

Pete Rozelle and Football Developments. Ever since the American Football League began operations in 1960, it had been disdainfully ignored by the venerable National Football League, born in 1921, but suddenly in mid-summer the 2 professional circuits agreed to peace terms. During their 7 years of dollar-warfare, the price for player talent had mushroomed to the point that the Green Bay Packers paid Donny Anderson, former Texas Tech star, $600,000 merely to sign an NFL contract.

Although the merger cost him his job, Al Davis of the AFL brought about the peace. He was made commissioner of the young circuit after Joe Foss, who had presided at the league's birth, was ousted on April 7. Davis, then coach and general manager of the Oakland team, was named the next day, and soon became convinced that it was ridiculous to spend huge sums of money on untried collegians. Instead he began luring established NFL stars to come over to his league. When it became known that at least a dozen of NFL heroes were listening to his offers, the senior league quickly came up with a peace formula.

Rozelle became the commissioner of all pro football immediately, but other details were left blank until 1970 when the formal merger will take place. Until then the 2 leagues will continue independently because of television commitments, although the champions of the 2 leagues will meet each January for the world title.

Notre Dame, spurred along the way by a bevy of sophomores that included Jim Seymour and Terry Hanratty, and Michigan State dominated the college-football scene; they played a 10–10 tie on Nov. 19. Neither was eligible for a New Year's bowl game. The Irish always reject bowl bids, and the Spartans represented the Big Ten in the Rose Bowl a year earlier.

Buckpasser. Buckpasser, mighty son of Tom Fool, won 12 straight races and earned $1,-218,874 in 2 years to become the first three-year-old Thoroughbred to reach $1 million in purses. He did this despite his absence from the Triple Crown events—Kentucky Derby, Preakness and Belmont—because of a cracked hoof. The colt, owned by Ogden Phipps and trained by Eddie Neloy, was voted the Horse of the Year and set a world record in June by covering a mile in $1:32\frac{3}{5}$ in Chicago's Arlington Classic. His only defeat during 1966 came against a stablemate in his first start of the season. He won $649,921 during the year. His biggest purse was the $88,660 picked up in the Flamingo at Hialeah, where his presence frightened away so many rivals that the track management refused to accept bets on the outcome of the race.

In all, Buckpasser won 10 stakes. Neloy, training horses for the 3 segments of the Phipps family, saddled 43 stakes winners, 40 of them on the track and 3 in steeplechase events. This is a record, as was the $2.9 million the winners brought home.

Cassius Clay. Although Dick Tiger of Nigeria, who was the middleweight champion at the year's start and the light-heavyweight king at its close, was designated as the Fighter of the Year, much of the fistic limelight centered upon Cassius Clay (Muhammad Ali), the heavyweight champion. Clay, who broke off with his Louisville, Ky., backers for Muslim leadership, won all 5 of his fights during the year, 4 of them by knockouts. Only George Chuvalo, the Canadian champion, was able to last 15 rounds against Clay, who ran his string of pro victories to 26. Gradually Clay was earning grudging respect from ring experts on being a master craftsman.

Basketball. Although they had to struggle to do it, the Boston Celtics managed to win their eighth straight National Basketball Association championship. They were hard pressed to repulse Philadelphia in the Eastern Division play-offs and then were carried the full seven games of the title round by Los Angeles, Western champions. The decisive game went to the Celtics, 95–93.

Texas Western, represented by a team that listed only one native Texan, upset Kentucky, 72–65, for the collegiate title.

Golf. Billy Casper, former California fat man slimmed down to 185 pounds by numerous food allergies, won his second U.S. Open golf championship, at the expense of Arnold Palmer. Paired together for the final round over the heavily treed Olympic Club Course at San Francisco, the twosome reached the tenth tee

Left: Jim Ryun, University of Kansas, sets world record for the mile. Above: Dick Tiger (r) defeats Jose Torres for world light-heavyweight title.

Above: Swimming star Don Schollander of Yale. **Right:** American League Triple Crown winner Frank Robinson. **Below:** Montreal Canadiens defeat Red Wings for Stanley Cup.

Jack Nicklaus and caddie are jubilant after second consecutive victory in the Masters.

with Palmer leading by 7 strokes and day-dreaming of a possible record victory. By the time Palmer awakened on the final hole, he had frittered away his lead, and Casper pulled even at 278 strokes for 72 holes of play. The next day in an 18-hole play-off, Palmer was 2 up when the pair reached the tenth hole again. And again Palmer weakened and Casper charged in and beat the Pennsylvanian, 69 strokes to 73.

Jack Nicklaus won both the Masters, becoming the first player ever to win this spring headline event in successive years, and the British Open. He also combined with Palmer for a United States triumph in the Canada Cup matches, decided in 1966 at Tokyo.

Mrs. Don Carner of Seekonk, Mass., the former JoAnne Gunderson, regained the women's United States Amateur title by outlasting Mrs. Marlene Streit Stewart of Fonthill, Ont., in a 41-hole marathon that set a record for distance. Gloria Ehret of Danbury, Conn., won the Ladies PGA title, and Sandra Spuzich of Indianapolis, Ind., conquered the field in the Open.

Hockey. The Montreal Canadiens, after losing the first two Stanley Cup games to the Detroit Red Wings, won the next four, and retained hockey's most honored award. Closeness of the competition may be determined from the fact that the decisive game was won by Montreal, 3–2, in overtime.

Swimming. In swimming, Don Schollander of Yale and Lake Oswego, Ore., returned to his 1964 Olympic form after a lean year be-cause of illness and set world records in the 200- and 400-meter freestyle swims. He lowered the 400-meter mark to 4:11.6 at Lincoln, Neb., in the national AAU meet. This cut $6/10$ of a second from the mark he had established in Tokyo while winning 4 gold medals at the 1964 Olympic Games. The following night he was clocked in a fabulous 1:57.2 for the 200-meter freestyle, a full second faster than his pending world mark.

Tennis. It was another bleak year for Uncle Sam's nephews in world tennis, climaxed by a loss to Brazil in the North American interzone semifinal. The U.S. team was ahead 2–1 at Porto Alegre, Brazil, after the first two days' competition, but on the last day Edison Mandarino upset Dennis Ralston of Bakersfield, Calif., in five sets after Cliff Richey of San Angelo, Tex., lost to Thomas Koch. In individual play, American men failed to win a single major title, although Ralston advanced to the Wimbledon final where he was defeated by Manuel Santana of Spain in straight sets. (Ralston turned pro in December.) The U.S. singles final at Forest Hills, N.Y., was an all-Australia affair with Fred Stolle defeating John Newcombe for the crown.

Mrs. Larry King, the former Billie Jean Moffitt of Long Beach, Calif., captured the women's singles at Wimbledon in her sixth try. She downed Maria Bueno of Brazil, 6–3, 3–6, 6–1. However, the 22-year-old bride was eliminated early in the Forest Hills nationals, and Miss Bueno came through with a 6–3, 6–1 conquest of Nancy Richey for her fourth U.S. title.

BASEBALL

The story of major-league baseball in 1966 was largely the story of the Baltimore Orioles, who made a romp of the American League pennant race. The Orioles then annihilated the Los Angeles Dodgers in four straight World Series games to recoup spectacularly the fading dignity of the American League.

It was the year of an attendance explosion in both major leagues and the birth of three new stadiums. Individually it was the year of Hank Bauer among major-league managers, of Frank Robinson among the hitters and Sandy Koufax among the pitchers.

On the drearier side were the utter collapse of the Yankees into tenth place in the American League, and the tenth-place finish of the Chicago Cubs despite the arrival of Leo Durocher as their 1966 manager.

A startling postseason development came with the sudden announcement by Sandy Koufax that he was retiring from baseball. The game's highest-paid pitcher in history at $125,000 a year, 3-time winner of the Cy Young Award, author of 4 no-hitters, including a perfect game, elected to quit at the top after 12 years with the Dodgers. Koufax said it sorrowfully but bluntly: He did not choose to risk further injury to the pitching arm that had pained him

since 1964 when he hurt his left elbow sliding. He had been receiving cortisone injections after every pitching start and feared permanent loss of the use of his left arm. In his 12 seasons, Koufax compiled a 165-87 record.

From the outset of the season, the Orioles quickly exploited their trade of the previous winter which brought them Frank Robinson from the Cincinnati Reds, and by the time of the All-Star Game break in July they had a formidable league lead. With Robinson providing the power, the Orioles grabbed off the glory, much of it Robinson's own. He became the first Triple Crown winner since Mickey Mantle's 1956 feat of leading the American League in hitting, home runs and runs-batted-in.

The Orioles won their pennant by nine games, coasting. Minnesota dislodged the Detroit Tigers from second place in the final week of the season. There was no serious opposition to the Orioles in the last three months, so powerful was the hitting of the Baltimore team and its relief pitching.

Sandy Koufax, more than any other player, took the feeble-hitting Dodgers to the National League pennant. In a year when Don Drysdale was a disappointment, Koufax was a 27-9 winner on a club that was eighth in the league in runs-batted-in. The 30-year-old left-hander

Baltimore's Brooks Robinson leaps toward teammates as Orioles win World Series.

Wide World

FINAL MAJOR-LEAGUE STANDINGS

AMERICAN LEAGUE	WON	LOST	PER CENT	GAMES BEHIND	NATIONAL LEAGUE	WON	LOST	PER CENT	GAMES BEHIND
*Baltimore	97	63	.606	—	Los Angeles	95	67	.586	—
Minnesota	89	73	.549	9	San Francisco	93	68	.578	1½
Detroit	88	74	.543	10	Pittsburgh	92	70	.568	3
Chicago	83	79	.512	15	Philadelphia	87	75	.537	8
Cleveland	81	81	.500	17	Atlanta	85	77	.525	10
California	80	82	.494	18	St. Louis	83	79	.512	12
Kansas City	74	86	.463	23	Cincinnati	76	84	.475	18
Washington	71	88	.447	25½	Houston	72	90	.444	23
Boston	72	90	.444	26	New York	66	95	.410	28½
New York	70	89	.440	26½	Chicago	59	103	.364	36

*Won World Series, 4 games to 0

AMERICAN LEAGUE		NATIONAL LEAGUE
American League 1	All-Star Game	National League 2
F. Robinson (.316), Balt.	Batting Champion	M. Alou (.342), Pitts.
F. Robinson (49)	Home-Run Leader	H. Aaron (44), Atl.
G. Peters (2.03), Chi.	Leading Pitcher[1]	S. Koufax (1.73), L.A.
F. Robinson	Most Valuable Player	R. Clemente, Pitts.
T. Agee, Chi.	Rookie of the Year	T. Helms, Cinn.
F. Robinson (122)	Most Runs-batted-in	H. Aaron (127)

[1] Based on lowest earned-run average

pitched five shutouts despite a chronic arthritis condition in his elbow. The Dodgers outlasted the Pittsburgh Pirates and the San Francisco Giants to win the pennant in a final, frenzied September. The Giants slipped into second place one and a half games back, and one and a half games ahead of the third-place Pirates whose league-leading hitting suffered from a lack of pitching support.

The World Series. The World Series was a horror experience for the Dodgers from the first inning of the first game when Baltimore's two Robinsons, Frank and Brooks, hit consecutive home runs off Drysdale. The Dodgers narrowed the Baltimore lead to 4-2 in the third inning, never dreaming they would not score another run for the rest of the series and would make the record book as the most-shutout team in World Series history. Their next 33 consecutive innings of futility broke the previous record of 28 scoreless innings notched by New York Giants pitching in the 1905 series.

Baltimore pitching in the series was a succession of surprises. Bauer moved in a former castoff, Moe Drabowsky, as a relief pitcher in the third inning of the first game, and he allowed the Dodgers only one hit and no runs in gaining a 6-3 victory. The next day, Bauer produced a pitcher who could beat Koufax. Rookie Jim Palmer did it with a four-hitter. The second-game score was 6-0, but Koufax yielded only one earned run. In the fifth inning he was the victim of a sudden outbreak of errors by center fielder Willie Davis, who dropped two consecutive fly balls, then threw wild, to set a new World Series record of three errors in one inning. The Dodgers totaled six errors for the game, the only ones of the series.

For the third game, the Orioles produced another shutout pitcher, Wally Bunker, who needed only one swing of Paul Blair's home-run bat to break the Dodgers, 1-0. When the Orioles clinched the series in the fourth game it was with a string of back-to-back-to-back shutouts, with Dave McNally outpitching Drysdale, 1-0, in the finale. Frank Robinson's fourth-inning home run was the productive blow.

Among World Series records set in addition to the string of 33 scoreless innings by Baltimore pitching were these: lowest team batting average in series history, .142 of the Dodgers; fewest base hits by one team, 17 (Dodgers), by both teams, 41; highest fielding average, Baltimore's 1.000. Also a new World Series record was the players' share of the receipts, $1,044,042.65. Each Baltimore player received $11,683.04, each Dodger full share was $8,189.35.

Attendance. Attendance in the National League boomed to 15,036,491, a gain of 1,455,355 over 1965, with the Dodgers' 2,617,059 the high figure. For the first time since they came into the league in 1962, the New York Mets wrenched out of tenth place, finishing ninth. The Mets were second in attendance with a gain of 165,304 and a total of 1,933,693. Crowd losses at Cincinnati, Houston and Philadelphia were offset by the Atlanta franchise which, with a new stadium as an attraction, drew 1,539,801, an increase of 984,217 over the 1965 season in Milwaukee. A new stadium in St. Louis produced a plus of 471,779.

American League attendance shot up from 8,860,694 in 1965 to 10,166,738, with the California Angels' move to their new stadium in Anaheim as the greatest single factor. Paradoxically, the Angels, who finished sixth, led the league in attendance with 1,400,321.

The city of Milwaukee failed in its effort to defeat the transfer of the Braves' franchise to Atlanta. State Supreme Court overruled a decision by lower-court Judge Elmer Roller that the Braves' pullout was a violation of the state's antitrust laws. In vain, Milwaukee appealed to the Supreme Court of the United States.

League Leaders. Frank Robinson's heroics for the Orioles were expressed with his .316 batting average that dethroned Minnesota's Tony Oliva as league champion; his 49 home runs that far outstripped Harmon Killebrew's 39; and his 122 runs-batted-in which completed his Triple Crown conquest.

Jim Kaat, Minnesota Twins' left-hander, was the undisputed American League pitching leader with a 25-13 record. He outstripped Dennis McLain of Detroit, the only other 20-game winner in the American League. Juan

Marichal of the Giants crowded Koufax for the pitching honors in the National League with a 25-6 record. The National saw three other 20-game winners in Bob Gibson of the Cardinals (21-12), Gaylord Perry of the Giants (21-8) and Chris Short of the Phillies (20-10).

The Pittsburgh Pirates had a near-monopoly on the National League batting honors with three of its players among the first five. The Pirates' Matty Alou (.342) beat out his teammate, Danny Mota, and his brother, Felipe Alou of the Braves, for top honors. Roberto Clemente of the Pirates was also among the first five. Hank Aaron of the Braves led in home runs (44) and in runs-batted-in with 127. Lou Brock of the Cardinals replaced Maury Wills as the leading base stealer in the majors with 74 thefts. Willie Mays of the Giants broke Mel Ott's National League career home-run record of 511. On May 5, Mays hit the 512th homer of his career.

The Yankees and Managerial Changes. The Yankees were continual newsmakers during the year, chiefly for the futility which saw them lose 16 of their first 20 games and finish last for the first time since 1912. Manager Johnny Keane was released after the first 20 games of the season, and Ralph Houk was ordered out of the executive suite as general manager to take over as field manager. Other managerial changes in the American League occurred at Cleveland where Joe Adcock was appointed to succeed interim Manager George Strickland at the end of the season; and at Detroit where tragedy struck twice: the death of Manager Charley Dressen, a heart-attack victim, and the death of interim Manager Bob Swift of lung cancer. At the season's end, Mayo Smith was appointed the new Detroit manager. At Boston, Billy Herman was replaced by the Red Sox with Dick Williams.

In the National League, Bobby Bragan failed to last out the season as the Atlanta manager and was replaced by Bill Hitchcock, former manager of the Orioles. At Cincinnati, Don Heffner was let out in midseason with Dave Bristol as his replacement.

The Yankees' decaying empire passed completely into the ownership of the Columbia Broadcasting System, which purchased the remaining 10 per cent held by Dan Topping, who also resigned as president. To restore Yankee fortunes, CBS named Michael Burke as club president and Lee MacPhail as general manager and operating head. MacPhail was an assistant to Commissioner Eckert.

SHIRLEY POVICH
Sports Editor, THE WASHINGTON POST

James Drake for "Sports Illustrated" © *Time Inc.*

Texas Western defeats Kentucky for NCAA championship.

BASKETBALL

Throughout the many weeks of the 1965–66 basketball season when Texas Western was listed among the leaders in the college rankings, many scoffed, "Who or what is Texas Western?"

On March 19, 1966, these doubters found out. In a jammed field house in College Park, Md., the Miners from Texas Western—playing a contest that was presumed to be an anticlimax after the previous night's "big game"—handed mighty Kentucky a 72-65 beating in the championship final of the National Collegiate Athletic Association tournament.

It was an astonishing outcome. The idea of a little team from a little school in El Paso, Tex., overcoming one of the best squads ever put together by the fabled Adolph Rupp strained the imagination. True, both teams went into the title game with season records of 27–1. But there seemed little comparison between the big-name schedule that Kentucky had played and the list of largely unfamiliar schools on Texas Western's list. Rupp's Wildcats were 8-point favorites.

Some observers felt that Kentucky was defeated because it suffered a letdown after gaining an 83–79 victory over Duke in the previous night's semifinal. That game matched the top two squads in the final rankings by both Associated Press and United Press International, No. 1 Kentucky and No. 2 Duke.

The Wildcats and the Blue Devils did play a thriller. Despite the fact that Duke's top scorer, Bob Verga, was still recuperating from tonsilitis and was held to 4 points, the two powerhouses were tied at 71–71 with four minutes to go. Then a Wildcat trio of Larry Conley, Pat Riley and Louie Dampier teamed for 8 successive points and put Kentucky in charge. Dampier, a guard, was Kentucky's high scorer with 23 points. Conley, who also was ailing, was held to 10 but Riley had 19. Jack Marin had 29 for Duke.

In the other semifinal, No. 3-ranked Texas Western encountered plenty of trouble from Utah's Jerry Chambers, who poured in 38 points, but the Miners won 85–78. In the third-place game (which Duke took 79–77), Chambers added 32 more points and set an NCAA record of 143 points for the last four games of the national tournament. Clyde Lovellette of Kansas had scored 141 in 1952.

Just getting to College Park was a great achievement. After winning the Southeastern Conference, for instance, Kentucky had to turn back Big Ten champ Michigan in a regional final at Iowa City, Ia., 84–77 despite the efforts of all-American Cazzie Russell of Michigan. For Texas Western the struggle was even harder. In a regional semifinal the Miners got by Cincinnati 78–76 in overtime,

Then just a player: Boston's Bill Russell scores two.
"The New York Times"

with Willie Cager getting 6 points in the extra session for the winners. In the regional final Texas Western had to go two overtimes before gaining an 81–80 victory over Kansas.

If Cincy and Kansas were caught unawares, however, it was because they weren't reading the papers. Back on Dec. 30 Texas Western indicated it was a team to be reckoned with when it took on previously unbeaten Iowa in the Sun Carnival tournament, and whipped the Hawkeyes 86–68.

That was when other basketball powers were making themselves known. Providence won the Holiday Festival tournament in New York by topping Boston College 91–86 in the final. Jimmy Walker, a 6-foot-3 Providence guard, scored 50 points in that contest. Dayton's 6-11 Henry Finkel accounted for 44 points in the Sugar Bowl final, but Maryland topped Dayton 77–75 for that title.

Tournaments such as these, plus the regular-season games, brought attention to the standouts on the major powerhouses and led to the many all-American squads. AP and UPI agreed on four choices: Russell of Michigan, Dave Bing of Syracuse, Clyde Lee of Vanderbilt and Dave Schellhase of Purdue. They differed at one guard position, with AP naming Kentucky's Dampier, and UPI voters preferring Walker of Providence.

None of these players was a member of the teams that made the semifinals of the National Invitation Tournament, but it didn't detract from the quality of basketball played during it. Brigham Young turned back New York University 97–84 in the final. Villanova topped Army for third place 76–65. Villanova guard Bill Melchionni, who had 109 points in four games, was voted the tournament's most valuable player.

The NIT was over and all attention centered on Kentucky and Texas Western when they collided. The Miners did it with defense. Bobby Joe Hill, a 5-10 junior guard, stole the ball repeatedly and had 20 points. Hill was typical of the Miner team, although it had size too. Dave Lattin, 6-7, used his 246 pounds and had 16 points and 9 rebounds.

Professional Basketball

If college ball in 1965–66 is remembered for its surprises, the professional National Basketball Association season will have to be classed as another campaign in which form was followed despite thrills along the way.

True, the Boston Celtics' string of Eastern Division championships was terminated at nine by the Philadelphia 76ers and Wilt Chamberlain, but the Celtics atoned for the mistake quickly. They took the third-place Cincinnati Royals in a play-off, 3 games to 2, and then humbled the 76ers, 4 to 1.

In the Western Division the third-place St. Louis Hawks surprised by winning three straight from the second-place Baltimore Bullets, who were hampered by several injuries. The Hawks ran the division's final series to the full seven games before bowing to the first-place Los Angeles Lakers 130–121. St. Louis' Cliff Hagan, one of the NBA's top scorers, fired in 29 points as he wrapped up his playing career with this contest.

The Lakers got off to an excellent start in the championship series by beating the Celtics in Boston as Jerry West scored 41 points, and rejuvenated Elgin Baylor had 36.

The following day Boston coach Arnold (Red) Auerbach announced that Celtic defensive whiz Bill Russell would succeed him as coach the next season. Russell thus became the first Negro to head a major professional team. The Celts celebrated by winning the next three games from the Lakers: 129–109 in Boston, 120–106 and 122–117 in Los Angeles.

Coach Fred Schaus' Lakers did accomplish the unexpected by gaining a 121–117 victory at Boston and then evening the series by winning 123–115 in L.A. This provided Auerbach with an opportunity to light his final victory cigar before the home folks. In the final at Boston the Celtics achieved their ninth NBA championship in ten years by beating the Lakers 95–93.

BOB BROEG

Sports Editor, ST. LOUIS POST-DISPATCH

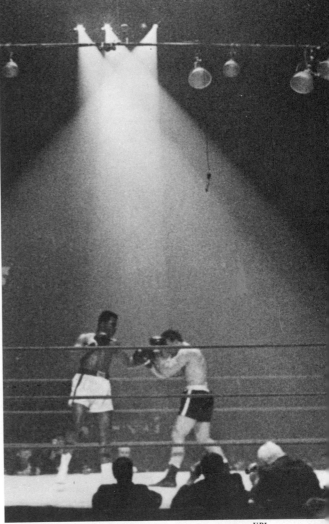

UPI

Heavyweight champ Cassius Clay defeats George Chuvalo.

BOXING

The World's Heavyweight Champion. Cassius Clay (Muhammad Ali) started 1966 in financial distress, married, brash, eligible for the draft, managed by a group of Kentucky millionaires and held in little respect by the boxing critics, although he was the world's heavyweight champion. By the end of the year, he had earned almost $2 million; had obtained a divorce; was jovial; still eligible for the draft but seeking an exemption as a minister; was managed by a member of the Muslim faith and was gaining consideration as one of the better heavyweight champions of the century.

His stature in midsummer was even lower than at the start of the year. Questioned about his draft status late in the winter, his answer of "I ain't mad at any of them Vietcongs" created so much ill will that the 24-year-old former Louisville resident was forced

BOXING

WORLD CHAMPIONS

Heavyweight: Cassius Clay, United States
Ernest Terrell, United States*
Light Heavyweight: Jose Torres, Puerto Rico
Middleweight: Emile Griffith, United States
Junior Middleweight: Ki Soo Kim, South Korea
Welterweight: Curtis Cokes, United States
Junior Welterweight: Sandro Lopopolo, Italy
Lightweight: Carlos Ortiz, Puerto Rico
Junior Lightweight: Gabriel (Flash) Elorde, Philippines
Featherweight: Vicente Saldivar, Mexico
Bantamweight: Masahiko (Fighting) Harada, Japan
Flyweight: Chartchai Chioni, Thailand
Horacio Accavallo, Argentina*

*Recognized by World Boxing Association

UNITED STATES AAU CHAMPIONS

112 pounds: Mickey Pirola
119 pounds: Jose Marquez
125 pounds: Robert Lozada
133 pounds: Ronnie Harris
139 pounds: James Wallington
147 pounds: Roland Pryor
156 pounds: John Howard
165 pounds: Martin Berzewski
178 pounds: John Griffin
Heavyweight: James Howard

to defend his title in such places as Toronto, London and Frankfurt, Germany.

Five times he fought and 5 times he won. Clay, in his lone U.S. appearance, closed out the year on Nov. 14 with an artistic display of punching power that brought a third-round technical-knockout triumph over Cleveland Williams in the Houston Astrodome before a record indoor crowd of 35,460. En route to his victory he had floored Williams 4 times. The knockout triumph was his fourth in a row. In 2 title defenses in London, he stopped Henry Cooper in 6 rounds on May 21 and Brian London in 3 on Aug. 6. Then, on Sept. 10 in Frankfurt, Clay knocked out Karl Mildenberger in 12 rounds. George Chuvalo, a husky and durable Canadian, was the only man to extend him to the 15-round limit. Clay, however, won their March 29 match in Toronto in decisive fashion.

Chuvalo substituted for Ernie Terrell of Chicago, recognized as the titleholder by the World Boxing Association. The Clay-Terrell bout was to have been staged in Madison Square Garden, but Terrell was refused a New York license because of his association with a man alleged to have underworld connection. Chicago was selected as the next site. However, the Illinois Athletic Commission vetoed it. The fight also was rejected by several other U.S. cities, then by Montreal and Verdun, Quebec, in Canada. The rejection followed severe criticism by political figures and veterans' organizations of Clay's remarks about the draft.

Terrell made one defense of his WBA crown and won by outpointing Doug Jones.

Other Championships. A slight case of fistic musical chairs prevailed among the champions in the weights immediately below the heavyweight division. Jose Torres of New York defended the light-heavyweight title three times early in the year, before he was unfrocked by 37-year-old Dick Tiger of Nigeria, who began the 1966 campaign as middleweight king in Madison Square Garden Dec. 16.

Tiger said after his April 25 loss to Emile Griffith of New York, then the welterweight titleholder, that he had weakened himself too much by sweating down to 160 pounds, the class limit. He weighed 167 for Torres, and his triumph over the 175-pound king won him Fighter of the Year honors.

After outpointing Tiger, Griffith was stripped of his 147-pound crown by the World Boxing Association, which ruled he could not hold two titles at the same time. Curtis Cokes, a Dallas veteran, won recognition as ruler of the welterweights by taking a decision from Manny Gonzales of Houston on Aug. 24.

One of the year's most controversial bouts involved lightweight champion Carlos Ortiz of New York and Sugar Ramos, a Cuban residing in Mexico City. The bout, on Oct. 22 in a Mexico City bullring, was stopped by referee Billy Conn in the fifth round, with Ramos bleeding profusely from a cut over his left eye. Conn declared Ortiz the winner by a technical knockout. Ortiz went to his dressing room, and refused to return when Ramon Velasques, secretary of the World Boxing Council, ruled that the fight should continue. After a ten-minute wait, Velasques declared Ramos the world champion. The WBC is confined almost entirely to Mexico and should not be confused with the WBA.

Conn's decision touched off a young riot before Velasques' ruling. The World Boxing Association later said that Ortiz was still its champion, while the World Boxing Council declared the title vacant.

Among the junior middleweights, Ki Soo Kim of South Korea took over from Nino Benvenuti of Italy, and Sandro Lopopolo of Italy moved to the junior-welterweight throne. Gabriel (Flash) Elorde of the Philippines held onto his junior-lightweight championship by outpointing Vicente Derado of Argentina on Oct. 22. In the lightest divisions, Fighting Harada of Japan still was the king of the bantamweights, while Chartchai Chioni of Thailand won the flyweight crown in Bangkok on Friday night, Dec. 30.

HAROLD (SPIKE) CLAASSEN
Assistant General Sports Editor
THE ASSOCIATED PRESS

Boyd Dowler scores touchdown for Green Bay as Packers defeat Dallas for NFL championship.

FOOTBALL

Football in 1966, both on the college level and in the professional ranks, achieved wider exposure, drew bigger crowds and was covered by the news media as never before.

The college game fattened on the resurgence of Notre Dame to a national championship in a year when the top-ten ratings and the "We're No. 1" syndrome commanded enormous attention from week to week.

Attendance at college games climbed for the thirteenth consecutive season, from a shade over 24 million in 1965 to 25,275,899 by actual head count. And the Notre Dame-Michigan State 10–10 tie drew the largest television audience ever to see a regularly scheduled college game (33 million viewers) as well as a record crowd of 80,011 at East Lansing, Mich.

Professional

Merger. For the pros, it was a year that saw peace settle on the rival National and American Football Leagues. The peace brought on a common draft of college players, the end of outrageous bidding for talent, and the establishment of a Super Bowl to determine a conclusive champion. Peace came to the pros in June of 1966, ending seven years of frantic competitive spending.

There had been some peaceful overtures and some dialogue between the leagues even before the New York Giants of the National League signed place-kicker Pete Gogolak of the Buffalo Bills of the American League. Gogolak had played out his option and was presumably free to negotiate with any team. The American League regarded the Giants' signing of Gogolak as a breach of ethics, even if the act had the approval of National League Commissioner Pete Rozelle.

Prodded by its own newly elected Commissioner, Al Davis, American League teams conducted secret negotiations with established stars of the National, including John Brodie of the San Francisco Forty-Niners, Roman Gabriel of the Los Angeles Rams and countless others.

The possibility of player losses, and the even greater danger of new franchises coming into cities where only one franchise now exists —cities such as Los Angeles, Chicago and Houston—accelerated the talk of the two leagues merging. Finally a wedding was arranged between the NFL and the AFL—a wedding of self-preservation to most of the owners; a shotgun wedding to a few opposed; but a wedding nonetheless, to be completed by 1970, when all present television contracts run out.

As the price for joining the older, more established National Football League, American League clubs, with emphasis on the Oakland Raiders and the New York Jets (because they are in head-to-head competition within their own cities), were assessed indemnities totaling an estimated $26.5 million.

Behind the scenes the chief arbitrators in the merger talks were Tex Schramm, president and general manager of the Dallas Cowboys of the NFL, and Lamar Hunt, president of the Kansas City Chiefs of the AFL.

However, not until Commissioner Rozelle, with the support of some Louisiana legislators, pushed through a rider to an anti-inflation bill (that exempted the merger from antitrust suits), was the wedding of the two leagues given the blessings of all concerned.

In advance of all these back-room maneuvers, the NFL's greatest running back, Jim Brown of Cleveland, had announced his retirement. And he made it stick.

Super Bowl. Green Bay won the NFL championship in a play-off with Dallas; Kansas City won the AFL title against Buffalo. And in the first Super Bowl, a designation credited to Lamar Hunt of Kansas City, Green Bay defeated Kansas City, 35 to 10. Playing in the Los Angeles Coliseum Jan. 15, before 63,000 spectators, the NFL champions did nothing to demean their image or that of their league.

For the first half, it was a ball game, Green Bay leading by 14–10, but the Chiefs ahead statistically. Then an interception of a pass by Kansas City's Len Dawson, picked off by Willie Wood, led to an early second-half Green Bay touchdown. It was no contest after that.

The game was seen on two television networks, CBS and NBC. Each winning player received $15,000; $7,500 went to each loser.

NFL Championship. For the fourth time in six years, the Green Bay Packers extended their domination of the NFL, with 34–27 victory over the Dallas Cowboys in the Cotton Bowl of Dallas on Jan. 1, 1967. It was a game in which the Cowboys fell 2 yards short of forcing the Packers into sudden-death overtime.

Green Bay struck hard and early; Dallas recovered its poise to tie; Green Bay surged ahead again, and seemingly had the game well in hand when the Cowboys, in 4 frantic final minutes, almost tied it up.

Quarterback Bart Starr of the Packers, the game's hero with 4 touchdown passes averaging 28 yards a throw, seemingly wrapped up the title late in the last quarter with a 28-yard TD toss to Max McGee. But Don Chandler's extra-point try was deflected, and Dallas, trailing by 14 points at 34–20, still was alive.

The Cowboys wiped out half of this deficit on a touchdown bomb from Don Meredith to Frank Clarke. And when Green Bay was forced to punt with 2 minutes left, there was still time for another Dallas drive.

The Cowboys almost pulled it off. Aided by a pass-interference call, they had a first down on the Green Bay 2. One rush was stopped. Then an off-side penalty put Dallas back on the 6. A second-down pass was dropped, and a third-down pass moved the ball to the 2. With fourth down, Meredith rolled out, Green Bay's Dave Robinson blitzed, and the pass was intercepted by Tom Brown in the end zone. That was the game, worth $8,500 to each of the Packers.

NFL Regular Season. This was basically the same Green Bay team that had taken the title from Cleveland the previous year, with this exception: Elijah Pitts had joined Jimmy Taylor as one of the two set backs, replacing Paul Hornung. The once Golden Boy of the Gridiron, suffering from a pinched nerve, played only a minor role for the Packers during the season, a season in which the Packers took the Western title by three games over Baltimore.

For Dallas, despite disappointment in the title game, it was a noteworthy rise to an Eastern title in its seventh operational year.

The Cowboys, under coach Tom Landry, had their severest competition from the St. Louis Cardinals, a team that might have finished on top but for an injury to quarterback Charley Johnson. Without Johnson, the Cardinals tumbled to fourth place behind Cleveland and Philadelphia.

The Cards did have the National League's rookie of the year in Johnny Roland, a superb runner who had achieved All-American honors at the University of Missouri for his defensive talents. Newborn Atlanta, with three victories, gave much of the credit for its limited success to rookie linebacker Tommy Nobis.

Late in the season, Pete Rozelle, now commissioner of both the National and the American League, announced a 16th NFL team for 1967 in New Orleans.

There was another announcement of major importance: Starting with 1967, and for the two succeeding seasons, the NFL would be broken down into four four-team divisions.

AFL Championship and Regular Season. In the American League, Buffalo took Eastern honors with the youngest pro coach, 34-year-old Joe Collier, who had succeeded Lou Saban.

Buffalo's front seven on defense stood out in a season in which the Bills lost their first two games, then a seemingly critical game to Boston, and still managed to finish on top when Boston dropped one to New York on the final weekend of the season.

The Bills also had the rookie of the year in Bobby Burnett of Arkansas, a running back. Boston in turn produced the player of the year in sophomore Jim Nance, who set an all-time AFL rushing record.

Elijah Pitts (r) drives into end zone for Green Bay touchdown in Super Bowl game.

Kansas City won in the West, sparked by the addition of rookie Mike Garrett, 1965's Heisman Trophy winner, and a young flanker, Otis Taylor. The Chiefs did not lose a road game.

The title game was played on the same day as the NFL showdown, Jan. 1, 1967, in rain-slick War Memorial Stadium. The Chiefs, favored by 3 points, defeated the Bills by 24. Quarterback Len Dawson's 2-touchdown passing and effective scrambling, the elusive running of Garrett, and the failure of the Bills to capitalize on their own chances made it something of a one-sided game.

It was 7–7 in the first period, but the Chiefs took a 17–7 lead at intermission and never were pressed. The final score: Kansas City 31, Buffalo 7. It was the first AFL title for Kansas City since their formation in 1962. Previously they had been known as the Dallas Texans under the same coach, Hank Stram.

College

The Ratings. Through most of the college-football season, the coaches' panel, which rates teams for the United Press International, and the writers and broadcasters, who assess the teams for The Associated Press, were in virtual agreement that Notre Dame, Michigan State and Alabama were the three best teams in the nation.

On Nov. 19, the one-two teams collided in what was popularly described as a natural, Notre Dame at Michigan State. The Irish had an 8–0 record; Michigan State was 9–0. For Duffy Daugherty's Spartans, this was a season finale. They were already Big Ten champs for the second straight year. Notre Dame, the glamour team with a sophomore forward-passing combination of Terry Hanratty at quarterback and Jim Seymour at end, still had another game to play, at Southern California.

Most valuable player of Sugar Bowl game: Alabama's Ken Stabler. Below: Notre Dame's Seymour (l) and Hanratty.

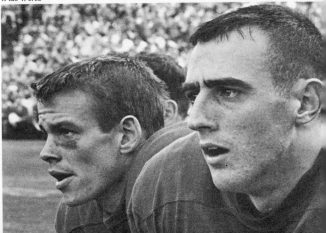

FOOTBALL

COLLEGE CONFERENCES

Atlantic: Clemson
Big Eight: Nebraska
Big Ten: Michigan State
Ivy League: Harvard, Princeton and Dartmouth (tie)
Mid-American: Western Michigan and Miami of Ohio (tie)
Missouri Valley: North Texas State and Tulsa (tie)
Pacific Athletic: USC
Southeastern: Georgia and Alabama (tie)
Southern: William & Mary and East Carolina (tie)
Southwest: SMU
Western Athletic: Wyoming
Yankee: Massachusetts

BOWL GAMES

Cotton Bowl: Georgia 24, SMU 9
Gator Bowl: Tennessee 18, Syracuse 12
Orange Bowl: Florida 27, Georgia Tech 12
Rose Bowl: Purdue 14, USC 13
Sugar Bowl: Alabama 34, Nebraska 7

PROFESSIONAL

American League Championship: Kansas City 31, Buffalo 7
National League Championship: Green Bay 34, Dallas 27
Super Bowl: Green Bay 35, Kansas City 10
Canada, Grey Cup: Saskatchewan Rough Riders

AMERICAN FOOTBALL LEAGUE FINAL STANDINGS

EASTERN DIVISION	WON	LOST	TIED	PER CENT	WESTERN DIVISION	WON	LOST	TIED	PER CENT
Buffalo	9	4	1	.692	Kansas City	11	2	1	.846
Boston	8	4	2	.667	Oakland	8	5	1	.615
New York	6	6	2	.500	San Diego	7	6	1	.538
Houston	3	11	0	.214	Denver	4	10	0	.286
Miami	3	11	0	.214					

NATIONAL FOOTBALL LEAGUE FINAL STANDINGS

EASTERN CONFERENCE	WON	LOST	TIED	PER CENT	WESTERN CONFERENCE	WON	LOST	TIED	PER CENT
Dallas	10	3	1	.769	Green Bay	12	2	0	.857
Cleveland	9	5	0	.643	Baltimore	9	5	0	.643
Philadelphia	9	5	0	.643	Los Angeles	8	6	0	.571
St. Louis	8	5	1	.615	San Francisco	6	6	2	.500
Washington	7	7	0	.500	Chicago	5	7	2	.417
Pittsburgh	5	8	1	.385	Minnesota	4	9	1	.308
Atlanta	3	11	0	.214	Detroit	4	9	1	.308
New York	1	12	1	.077					

Michigan State, quarterbacked by under-rated Jimmy Raye, forged a 10–0 lead and seemed to have the Irish in trouble. Suddenly Notre Dame was playing without three star regulars because of injuries, quarterback Hanratty, the runner Nick Eddy and top lineman George Goeddeke.

But the Irish came back to tie. Coach Ara Parseghian's kill-the-clock tactics in the final two minutes of the game brought on widespread criticism.

In the aftermath of this tie, Michigan State supplanted Notre Dame by a thin margin in the UPI poll, while the AP poll remained constant.

But a week later, after Notre Dame walloped the Trojans of Southern California, 51 to 0, there was agreement by both wire services that Notre Dame was No. 1. Previously USC had allowed only 63 points in 9 games.

In the coaches' poll, Georgia was fourth-rated, followed by UCLA, Purdue, Nebraska, Georgia Tech, Southern Methodist, and Miami of Florida.

Bowl Games. Alabama, the only major unbeaten and untied team in the nation, destroyed Nebraska, Big Eight champs, 34 to 7 in the Sugar Bowl, and was slightly put out by its No. 3 rating. But with the polls closed before the bowl games, it had to settle for that.

Because the Big Ten does not permit its Conference winner to make the Rose Bowl scene in consecutive years, Michigan State deferred to Purdue. The Boilermakers, in their first Pasadena visit, edged Southern Cal, 14–13.

Tennessee beat Syracuse in the Gator Bowl, 18–12, but the Orange, winners of the Lambert Trophy as best in the East, got a record-breaking rushing performance from Floyd Little.

Georgia won the Cotton Bowl game from Southern Methodist, 24 to 9, and in the Orange Bowl, under lights, Florida topped Georgia Tech, 27–12, though the luster of Steve Spurrier, at quarterback, was dimmed by that of his sophomore teammate, Larry Smith.

Award Winners. Spurrier won the Heisman award as the best college player of the year, with Bob Griese of Purdue, and Gary Beban of UCLA other prized quarterbacks. Michigan State's Bubba Smith was cited often as the lineman of the year, and Notre Dame dominated most All-America selections, with Nick Eddy, Pete Duranko, Jim Lynch, Tom Regner, Alan Page and Kevin Hardy frequently mentioned.

Army, under rookie coach Tom Cahill, beat Navy 20–7 in their annual rivalry. Cahill, who succeeded Paul Dietzel and led the Cadets to an 8–2 record, was voted the Coach of the Year in a national poll of coaches and of the Football Writers Association.

FRANK GIFFORD
DIRECTOR OF SPORTS, WCBS-TV

GOLF

Arnold Palmer has earned universal recognition and a record total of dollars during the past decade doing the positive things in golf. But during the 1966 season the Latrobe, Pa., business tycoon, who flies his own $750,000 jet plane, gained distinction in reverse with a playing collapse during the final round of the United States Open tournament in San Francisco that may haunt him always.

Palmer and Casper. Palmer, playing superbly, had a seven-stroke lead as he and Billy Casper, paired for the benefit of a 15,000-person gallery and untold millions of the television audience, stepped onto the tenth tee at

Above: Billy Casper, winner of U.S. Open. Right: Arnold Palmer misses putt during final round of the U.S. Open.

the Olympic Club to play the final nine holes for pro golf's most glittering title.

But here Palmer's game suddenly came apart completely while Casper, steady as an offshore breeze, moved closer and closer. Palmer, admitting that he had begun thinking of Ben Hogan's Open record of 268 strokes, went over par on four of the last five holes and finished with a 71 for a total of 278. Casper, who had preached at a Mormon church the night before, and who said he wanted only to finish a respectable second, came home with a 68—and also a four-round total of 278.

The play-off the following day saw Palmer throw off the effects of his collapse; he had a two-stroke lead as he and Casper again stepped onto the tenth tee. But once again Palmer began finding the trees with his tee shots and when the 18-hole play-off was over Casper was the winner by four strokes, 69 to 73.

It was a great season for Casper, the one-time roly-poly pro from San Diego. This was his second Open title. In addition, he was the year's leading money winner and topped the U.S. professionals in the Ryder Cup standings for the 1967 season's duel with Great Britain. His average of 70.2 strokes was the lowest among the pros who played over 65 rounds.

The devout Casper, always regarded as an outstanding putter, came into his own after a bevy of doctors discovered that he was highly allergic to a number of foods, and that his body was so sensitive it often reacted to the manner in which his meals were prepared. All his food must be cooked on electric stoves, and his menus now include such odd combina-

tions as avocado pears and buffalo steaks for breakfasts. He slimmed down to 175 pounds.

Nicklaus' Appearances. Play-offs also marked numerous other tournaments. Jack Nicklaus became the first player ever to win the Masters in successive years after he defeated Gay Brewer and Tommy Jacobs in a three-way play-off. Brewer made the additional round necessary when he three-putted the final green of the 72-hole tournament and posted a 288. In the play-off Nicklaus shot 70; Jacobs equaled the par of the Augusta, Ga., National course; while Brewer groped his way around in 78 strokes.

Another rich tournament to require a play-off was the World Series of Golf, a television-inspired golfing mint in which the winners of the Masters, U.S. and British Opens and the PGA, compete in a two-day event for a first prize of $50,000. With Nicklaus winner of both the Masters and the British Open, Gene Littler was invited to complete the foursome because he had won the 1965 Canadian Open. Casper competed as the U.S. Open winner and Al Geiberger as the PGA champion. Littler appeared on his way to the bank with the huge check until he fashioned a huge seven on the 625-yard sixteenth hole, known as the water hole, on the Firestone golf course at Akron, Ohio. That caused him to slip into a three-way tie with Nicklaus and Geiberger, but he sank a 22-foot putt in the play-off to win.

Geiberger, whose nervous tension is such that he munches on peanut-butter-and-jelly sandwiches during a round, was the winner of the PGA title over the same Akron course in

GOLF—1966 CHAMPIONS

INDIVIDUAL

MEN

Australian Open: Arnold Palmer
British Open: Jack Nicklaus
Canada Cup: George Knudson
Canadian Open: Don Massengale
Eisenhower Trophy: Ronald Shade
Masters: Jack Nicklaus
Pro Golfers' Association: Al Geiberger
Public Links: Monty Kaser
United States Amateur: Gary Cowan
United States Open: Billy Casper
World Match Play: Gary Player
World Series of Golf: Gene Littler

WOMEN

Canadian Amateur: Mrs. J. Douglas Streit
Canadian Open: Helen Gagnon
Pro Golfers' Association: Gloria Ehret
United States Amateur: Mrs. Donald R. Carner
United States Open: Sandra Spuzich
World Amateur: Mrs. J. Douglas Streit

TEAM

MEN

Canada Cup: United States
Eisenhower Trophy: Australia

WOMEN

Curtis Cup: United States
World Amateur: United States

mid-July, beating out Dudley Wysong by four strokes. Late in the year peace returned to the PGA when a compromise was reached on how the huge television sums should be spent.

International Competition; Other Items. In international competition, Nicklaus won the British Open, and he and Palmer combined for a score of 548, 32 strokes below par, for their four trips over the Yomiuri course just outside Tokyo that returned the Canada Cup to the United States. Individual honors at Tokyo went to George Knudson of Canada with 272, 16 strokes better than par.

Gary Cowan, an insurance salesman from Kitchener, Ont., defeated Deane Beman, an insurance salesman from Bethesda, Md., by a single stroke in still another play-off for the U.S. Amateur title at Ardmore, Pa.

The United States men amateurs finished second to Australia in the Eisenhower Trophy event, staged in Mexico City, while Uncle Sam's nieces repulsed Great Britain, 13-5, for the fourth straight time in Curtis Cup play. They then moved on to Mexico City where they took the first Women's World Amateur tournament, although Mrs. J. Douglas Streit of Canada took the individual honors.

For the first time ever three players finished the campaign with registered earnings of over $100,000. Casper banked $145,723.44; Palmer won 129,692.24; and Nicklaus $115,635.50.

HAROLD (SPIKE) CLAASSEN
Assistant General Sports Editor
THE ASSOCIATED PRESS

TENNIS

The year 1966 was a strange one in the world of tennis.

Major Championships. The four major titles (Wimbledon, Forest Hills, Australia and France) were won by four different men and by four different women. There was no standout in the amateur field as in the days of Bill Tilden, Don Budge or Helen Wills. Instead the Big Four trophies were chopped up into eight different pieces, with the lion's share going to Australia. A Spaniard, Manuel Santana, won the Wimbledon crown, but Aussies took the other titles—Roy Emerson won Australia, Tony Roche took France and Fred Stolle was the winner in the United States. In the women's events, four countries shared equally in the top prizes, with Margaret Smith taking her home title in Australia, England's Ann Jones winning in France, America's Billie Jean King taking the coveted Wimbledon title, and Brazil's Maria Bueno dominating at Forest Hills.

U.S. players had their ups and downs during the course of the 1966 season. Dennis Ralston, the U.S. No. 1 for the third consecutive year, reached his peak at Wimbledon (the unofficial world championships) where he got to the finals. Arthur Ashe had a brilliant early season, dropped out of tennis in June to enroll in an army training program and could not recapture his form in late season. In Australia he was magnificent, winning four of the five Australian state tournaments, and he reached the final of the Australian National Championships. Cliff Richey of San Angelo, Tex., won the U.S. National Clay Court Championships but fared less well on grass. Charles Pasarell of Puerto Rico, a student at UCLA, captured the U.S. National Indoors and the National Intercollegiates.

Two American women continued to share the major titles. Billie Jean King of Long Beach, Calif., took the U.S. National Indoors and the National Hard Courts, while Nancy Richey (Cliff's sister) won the National Clay Courts for the fourth consecutive year. Then Billie Jean scored the biggest triumph of her career when she beat Margaret Smith and Maria Bueno at Wimbledon. But Billie lost early at Forest Hills while Nancy reached the final before losing to Bueno. At the end of the year King was ranked No. 1 and Richey No. 2 in the United States.

Roy Emerson, the No. 1 player in the world in 1965, had an unfortunate season. He won the Australian title, was upset in the French championships by "unknown" François Jauffret, and seemed on his way to winning Wim-

UPI

A new member of pro tennis ranks: Fred Stolle.

bledon when he took a bad fall in the quarter-finals, which ruined his chances for successfully defending his title. Fred Stolle, many times a runner-up at the major tournaments, won his first big grass-court title when he took the U.S. championship over Ralston, Clark Graebner, Emerson and John Newcombe in that order. Stolle was rated No. 1 in the world for 1966.

The international women of the year were King, Bueno, Jones and Smith, but many young players also distinguished themselves. Rosemary Casals, an 18-year-old from San Francisco with one of the great tennis talents, had two wins over Billie Jean King, and played one of the best matches of the year against Bueno in the semifinals at Forest Hills. Kerry Melville of Australia was also outstanding.

Cup Competition. The stars of the Davis Cup were Brazil and India. Edison Mandarino and Thomas Koch, playing for Brazil, upset Spain and then defeated the United States in an interzone semifinal, which was played on clay in Porto Alegre. The tie was not decided until the fifth set of the fifth and last match, when Mandarino beat Ralston. Earlier Ralston had beaten Koch, and Ralston-Ashe had defeated Koch-Mandarino in the doubles, but Cliff Richey, playing No. 2 for the United States, lost both his singles matches. India, led by Ramanathan Krishman, Jaidip Mukerjea and Premjit Lall, beat Germany in one interzone semifinal and Brazil in the interzone final. Both of these ties were played on grass in India. The Davis Cup Challenge Round, held in Australia immediately after Christmas, was won by Australia over India, by a score of 4 to 1.

The Federation Cup, the women's equivalent of the Davis Cup, was played in Italy, and the United States was the winner. Billie Jean King and Julie Heldman played the singles, and King and Carole Graebner teamed in doubles. The Americans defeated France, England and Germany. Young Julie, playing her first Cup competition, was undefeated in all her matches. The Wightman Cup, an international competition between the United States and England, was once again won by the United States but only by the closest of margins, 4–3.

The Pros. There was also a great deal of activity in the professional game. Dennis Ralston joined the pro ranks late in December, followed a few weeks later by Fred Stolle. Rod Laver of Australia was a clear No. 1, but the ageless Pancho Gonzalez came out of retirement to play three major tournaments and succeeded in winning one of them—Wembley. Ken Rosewall of Australia, the former No. 1 professional, dropped to No. 2, with Spain's Andres Gimeno at No. 3.

Despite the fact that Pierre Barthes of France was the only new name on the pro tour during 1966's season, the professionals scored one of their biggest triumphs in an appearance at Madison Square Garden in New York City. Instead of their usual one-night stand, they played an entire tournament over a four-day period before thousands of pro fans. This was followed by an eight-week tournament circuit in the United States, then exhibitions and tournaments the rest of the year in Europe and South Africa.

GLADYS M. HELDMAN
Editor and Publisher, WORLD TENNIS

Peggy Fleming, Colorado Springs, Colo., wins world figure-skating championship. Below: France's Jean-Claude Killy.

John Pennel sets pole-vault record of 17 ft. 6¾ in.

SPORTS: SUMMARY OF

ARCHERY
U.S. Men's Champion: Hardy Ward
U.S. Women's Champion: Helen Thornton

AUTOMOBILE RACING
Australian Grand Prix: Graham Hill, Great Britain
Indianapolis 500: Graham Hill
Le Mans: Bruce McLaren and Chris Amon, New Zealand
U.S. Road Racing Championship: Chuck Parsons

BADMINTON
U.S. Men's Singles: Tan Aik Huang, Malaysia
U.S. Women's Singles: Judy Hashman, Great Britain

BOBSLEDDING
Two Man: Italy

BOWLING (American Bowling Congress)
CLASSIC
All-Events: Les Schissler
Doubles: J. Stefanich, A. Rogoznics
Singles: Les Schissler
Team: Ace Mitchell Shur Hooks, Akron, O.
REGULAR
All-Events: John Wilcox
Doubles: B. Kwiecien, T. Loiscano
Singles: Don Chapman
Team: Plaza Lanes, Sault Ste. Marie, Mich.

CANOEING
U.S. Canoe Singles: James O'Rourke
U.S. Kayak Singles: Jon Glair
U.S. Women's Kayak Singles: Marcia Smoke

CURLING
U.S. Champion: Fargo Club, N. D.
World Champion: Canada

CYCLING
U.S. Sprint Champion: Jack Disney
World Sprint Champion (Amateur): Daniel Morelson, France
World Sprint Champion (Professional): Beghetto, Italy

DOG SHOWS (Best in Show)
International: Ch. Fezziwig Raggedy Andy, old English sheepdog
Westminster: Ch. Zeloy Mooremaides Magic, wire fox terrier

FENCING
NCAA Team Champion: New York University

GYMNASTICS
NATIONAL AAU
All-Round: Makoto Sakamoto
Team: Southern Connecticut Gymnastics Club
Women's All-Round: Linda Metheny
Women's Team: Southern Illinois
NCAA TEAM: Southern Illinois

HANDBALL (U.S. Handball Association)
Four-Wall Singles: Paul Haber
Four-Wall Doubles: Bob Lindsay, Pete Tyson

HOCKEY
National League: Montreal Canadiens
Stanley Cup: Montreal Canadiens

HORSE RACING
Belmont Stakes: Amberoid
Kentucky Derby: Kauai King
Preakness Stakes: Kauai King

1966 WINNERS

ICE SKATING

FIGURE-SKATING CHAMPIONSHIPS
U.S. Men's: Scott Ethan Allen
U.S. Women's: Peggy Fleming
World Men's: Emmerich Danzer, Austria
World Women's: Peggy Fleming

SPEED-SKATING CHAMPIONSHIPS
U.S. Men's Indoor: Bill Lanigan
U.S. Men's Outdoor: Dick Wurster
U.S. Women's Indoor: Diane White
U.S. Women's Outdoor: Diane White
World Men's: Kees Verkerk, Netherlands
World Women's: Valentina Stenina, U.S.S.R.

JUDO
National AAU Team: Central Coast, San Jose, Calif.

LACROSSE
Intercollegiate: Navy

POLO
U.S. Open: Tulsa

RACQUETS
U.S. Open: Thomas Pugh, Great Britain

ROWING
Intercollegiate Rowing Assoc.: Wisconsin
U.S. Team: Union Boat Club, Boston

SKIING
NCAA TEAM: Denver

U.S. ALPINE CHAMPIONS
Giant Slalom: Jean-Claude Killy, France
Slalom: Guy Perillat, France

WORLD CHAMPIONS
Giant Slalom: Guy Perillat
Slalom: Carlo Senoner, Italy

SOCCER

U.S. CHAMPIONS
Cup of Champions: Santos, Brazil
National Challenge Cup: Philadelphia Nationals
National Collegiate: San Francisco

WORLD CUP: Great Britain

SOFTBALL
Men's Amateur Assoc.: Clearwater Bombers, Clearwater, Fla.

SWIMMING
Men's National Senior Indoor Team: Southern California
Men's National Senior Outdoor Team: Santa Clara Swim Club
NCAA Team: Southern California
Women's National Outdoor Team: Santa Clara Swim Club

TRACK AND FIELD
Intercollegiate AAAA Indoor Team: Maryland
Intercollegiate AAAA Outdoor Team: Maryland
Men's National Senior Indoor Team: Southern California Striders
Men's National Senior Outdoor Team: Southern California Striders
Women's National Outdoor Team: Tennessee State

VOLLEYBALL
Men: Sand and Sea, Santa Monica, Calif.
Women: Los Angeles Renegades

WEIGHT LIFTING
World Heavyweight: Leonid Zhabotinsky, U.S.S.R.

WRESTLING (World Free-Style)
Heavyweight: Aleksandr Ivanitsky, U.S.S.R.

Michael Barns

U.S. curling champion: Fargo Curling Club, N.D.

Evelyn Shafer

BEST DOG IN SHOW

Winner of Westminster Dog Show: Ch. Zeloy Mooremaides Magic. Below: Great Britain wins soccer's World Cup.

UPI

413

STEEL. U.S. steel producers established an all-time production record in 1966 by pouring 134 million net tons of ingots. They surpassed the previous record, set in 1965, by 2.5 million tons. The outlook for 1967 is for another good production year, approaching the 1966 record.

Some of steel's major markets—notably automobiles, residential construction and major household appliances—are expected to be a little softer in 1967 than in recent years. Demand from those market classifications should dip by several million tons. But increased military and military-related demands will at least partially offset losses in the automotive-housing-appliance markets.

Capital-goods demand will continue high, despite the suspension of the investment tax credit, the suspension of some accelerated depreciation policies and scarce and expensive financing. Capital-goods backlogs are high and most manufacturers should have a capacity year.

The outlook for agricultural demand is good. Railroad modernization will be at least as good as 1966. Production of containers, always an important steel market, will increase.

The metalworking industries as a group—the steel industry's biggest market—will mark a 6.5 per cent increase in dollar sales volume in 1967. If that increase is adjusted to compensate for anticipated price increases, the indicated gain in physical volume will be about 3 per cent.

Inventories of steel in manufacturers' plants at the start of 1967 were at a 2-year low, amounting to about 10.5 million tons. Pro-

ducers expect some inventory building by users toward the end of 1967 in anticipation of possible labor-dispute interruptions in 1968, when a new contract between the producers and the United Steelworkers of America must be negotiated.

Foreign Competition. Despite the promise of another heavy-volume year, the U.S. steel producers will be plagued by serious problems in 1967.

Rated first among those problems is the pressure of foreign competition. Foreign steel producers sold nearly 11 million tons of steel-mill products—equal to the yield of 16 million tons of ingots—in the United States in 1966. The outlook is about the same for 1967.

Imports to the United States hurt domestic producers not only in taking a sizable percentage of the market, but also in disrupting the domestic price structure. Often imported steel sells for $40 a ton under domestic quotations, holding domestic prices down.

Domestic prices have held remarkably level for the past eight years. Current steel prices are only 5 per cent above the average prevailing in the 1957-59 base period, despite huge increases in the hourly cost of labor, and in equipment and materials and services purchased by the mills. The result has been a continuing profit squeeze on the steel industry during a period of high-level operations. No immediate relief from this profit squeeze is in view, a situation reflected in the relatively low price of steel-company stocks.

World capacity for producing steel has been increasing much faster than world demand. The excess world capacity suggests continued

Armco's six-strand, low-level billet-casting machine.

Armco Steel Corporation

An 80-inch hot strip mill.

American Iron and Steel Institute

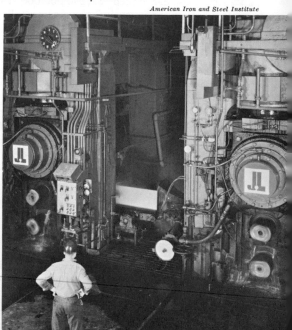

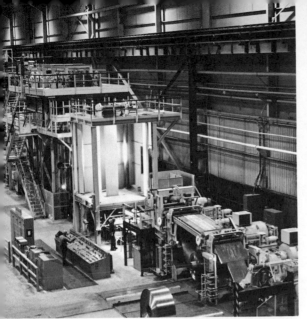

Bethlehem Steel's high-speed tinning line.

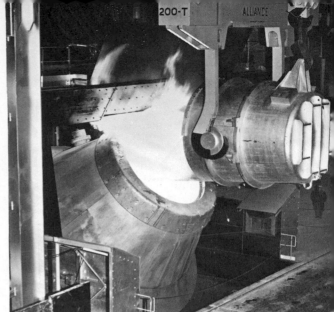

A basic oxygen furnace.

keen competition for world steel markets. High labor costs, and the absence of any government support for U.S. steel exports, places U.S. producers in a weak position to compete in the world market.

Meanwhile, new import threats appear. During 1966, the U.S.S.R. and its satellite countries shipped substantial quantities of pig iron into the United States. The price for pig iron from the communist countries was far below the domestic price, and the pig iron was purchased by some users in lieu of scrap iron and steel.

U.S. steelmakers recognize they must spend huge sums for new and more efficient equipment if they are to regain a competitive position in the world market. For 1966, the U.S. industry had earmarked $2,200,000,000 for modernization and capital expansion. The scarcity of manpower and of equipment held the actual expenditures to about $2,000,000,000. Plans are to spend another $2,000,000,000 in 1967 and in each year until 1970.

Technological Development. Technologically, the U.S. industry has been making large strides. Older open hearths have been and are being scrapped and replaced with the more efficient basic oxygen converters and larger electric furnaces.

Continuous casting (elimination of older methods of making semifinished steel for finishing mills) is undergoing an explosive growth. Eighteen installations were in operation at the end of 1966, eleven more will go on stream during 1967, and at least seven will be added in 1968. As recently as 1961, the United States had no commercial continuous casting.

All major companies in the United States have recently completed or are building large and efficient new hot-strip rolling mills. Most are controlled by on-line computers. To steel users, the new mills mean improved product availability and quality. Sheets rolled on them will be more uniform in width and gauge.

More cold rolling mills will be installed over the next several years to increase capacity for the quality sheets required by the automotive and appliance industries, which are expected to grow rapidly over the next decade.

Steelmakers continue to explore new technologies that may enable them to improve the quality of their product, or reduce costs, or both. Supplemental fuels for blast furnaces—natural gas, oil, coal and oil-and-coal slurries—reduce the requirements for more expensive coke and provide increased output. Computer controls for blast furnaces and basic oxygen furnaces are gaining in favor.

Experimentation continues in direct reduction of ores. Prereduced pellets (in which the iron content is raised to around 90 per cent) are under study by major companies. Research to date shows they are technically feasible and that they may be economically advantageous under certain conditions.

Over the longer range, one of the more exciting developments will be continuous steelmaking, but most U.S. firms believe this is a decade away for commercial applications. Meanwhile, all producers are working to improve strength, reduce weight and improve corrosion resistance.

WALTER J. CAMPBELL
Editor, STEEL

STOCK MARKET

By JOHN QUIRT
Free-Lance Financial Writer

Tight Credit. Wall Streeters will remember 1966 as the year tight credit hurt the stock market. Rising interest rates enhanced the attractiveness of bonds, bank savings certificates and other fixed-income securities; and all of them competed for the investor's money.

The competition grew more intense as the year wore on. Interest rates rose to where one could earn 5½ per cent on a savings certificate, almost that much on a government bond, and more than that in some West Coast loan associations; or, on the other hand, the investor could earn less return with more risk in a conservative blue-chip stock. As one market analyst wrote in August:

"This is not a hard choice for either the nickel-and-dime investor or the professional to make. Some pros who manage mutual-fund portfolios have been gradually selling blue chips and putting this same 'conservative money' instead into bonds; and a number of little guys are doing the same."

Tight credit also hurt the stock market in other ways. As the Federal Reserve System put the squeeze on banks, the banks raised the borrowing costs of brokerage firms, which in turn were forced to raise their lending charges to customers trading on credit or margin; these customers in some cases elected to unload stocks rather than pay premium interest rates to hold them.

More important was the overall economic effect of tight credit. When the banking authorities set out—as they did in 1966—to check inflation by making borrowed money more costly and more difficult to obtain, the result is usually not only a checking of inflation but also, eventually, at least slightly higher unemployment and lagging business profits. The anticipation of that happening in 1967 caused some investors to shy away from the stocks of companies that might feel the effects.

A number of big firms were beginning to report reduced profits late in the year, partly because of the credit squeeze, partly because inflationary wage demands were cutting into profit margins. Car and steel manufacturers were cutting back production, laying off workers, and lowering 1967 earnings forecasts; and there was open talk of the rest of industry following steel and automobiles in a general slowdown.

"This," one brokerage-firm economist wrote, "is the stuff recessions are made of. A sinking stock market does not always signal harder times ahead. But many investors have seen it happen before, and, in keeping their investment money in their pockets, they obviously are saying they see the possibility again."

Indeed fear that it all might turn into at least a mild recession worried the Street more with each passing month. It overshadowed, in the opinion of most experts, the fact that higher defense spending gave war-materials suppliers a decided lift. This meant the old bromide about Wall Street thriving on war was dealt another blow in 1966: the market continued dropping in the face of rising military spending and growing talk of an expanded war.

Nor did it help when the Federal Reserve began in December to make credit easier. Not even this otherwise encouraging economic news could draw the Street's attention away from the uncertainty of what lay ahead for manufacturers of consumer goods and business equipment. End-of-year comment stressed concern that the Johnson administration had caused credit to become unnecessarily and dangerously tight by failing to call early in the year for an anti-inflationary income-tax increase, and by underestimating the cost of Vietnam—either accidentally or deliberately—for fear of losing November votes. As one market analyst said:

"A lack of confidence in government economic policy has been added to Wall Street's worries. We feel we've been fooled; if we can't believe our own Government when it says the war should cost *approximately* such and such, then what can we believe? A lot of people are going to go slow in buying stocks until the administration wins back their confidence."

Drab Market Performance. Given this disquieting economic backdrop, the market's drab performance in 1966 is perhaps easier for the noninvestor to understand. Stock prices did not collapse in any burst of panic selling: they mostly drifted lower due to a lack of buying support. The Dow-Jones Industrial Average of 30 issues—mainly blue chips—finished the year down 183.74 points at 785.52; it dropped from its high of 995.15 on Feb. 9 to 735.74 during the trading session on Oct. 10, before bouncing back.

The Dow rail index dropped 44.51 to close the year at 202.97; the utility average closed down 16.45 at 136.18. On the New York Stock Exchange, 1,185 issues went down in price; 252 went up; trading volume rose to 1,900,-000,000 shares from 1,600,000,000 in 1965.

Among the blue chips, General Motors dropped from a high of 108¼ early in the

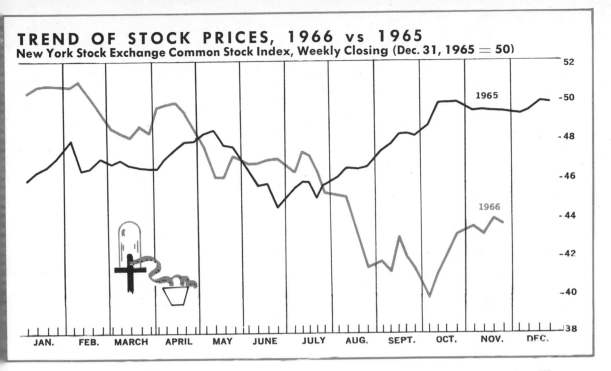

TREND OF STOCK PRICES, 1966 vs 1965
New York Stock Exchange Common Stock Index, Weekly Closing (Dec. 31, 1965 = 50)

1965

1966

52

-50

-48

-46

-44

-42

-40

38

JAN. FEB. MARCH APRIL MAY JUNE JULY AUG. SEPT. OCT. NOV. DEC.

year, to end 1966 at 65⅞; Chrysler fell from 61⅜ to 30¾; AT&T went from 63½ to an autumn low of 49¾ before recovering to close at 55. As in 1965, a handful of stocks outside the "conservative blue chip" category fared somewhat better. Polaroid gained 42⅛ to close at 158¾; Burroughs rose 37⅞ to finish at 87¾; Collins Radio climbed 9⅛ to a closing of 58⅜; Sperry Rand gained 7¾ on the year and finished at 29¾.

Investor's Dilemma. For many a small, cautious investor, this divergence between conservative and so-called performance stocks was not easy to accept. It conflicted with what he has been taught over the years—to accumulate solid equities in old, established industrial concerns, stash them away, and leave the gambling to speculators. It meant many conservative issues actually afforded poorer protection against inflation—and against the economic uncertainties of the new year—than did slightly more speculative stocks. It meant, moreover, that the worlds of risk-taking and defensive investment policy, for the second year in a row, came close to being turned upside down. As the senior partner in one brokerage firm put it:

"In the light of what's happening we need to reexamine carefully our old ideas about what's safe and what's risky; we need to remind ourselves that investing is not like following an old road map that can be memorized and obeyed blindly. That, of course, does not mean completely abandoning blue chips as

relics of some old and dying stock market. They will have their day again."

While conservative investors reacted to the market's split personality by sticking to their blue chips or pulling in their horns altogether, many less cautious investors tried to make money with an investment weapon normally reserved for the pros: the short sale. They sold borrowed stock in the hope of repurchasing it later at a lower price, and their short selling took on the trappings of an investment fad.

There was enough of it to cause roller-coaster price swings from day to day and week to week in the trading favorites. First they went down—five and ten points at a clip—bouncing back later as the short sellers scrambled for shares to cover or complete delivery on their sales. This yen for short selling disturbed veteran market observers. Analyst Bradbury Thurlow wrote:

"The old bull market was delightful in its way, but it was slow and one had to pick the right stocks. The new, bear-market money tree is much more fun. Positions are taken and abandoned with lightning rapidity, and no one need be burdened with dull knowledge about the stocks one is selling short. One merely looks at a chart, plunges in, and garners one's profit at the expense of the gullible optimists and investors, knowing that in the long run the basic trend of the market makes it impossible to be wrong.

"Short sellers are also given an important assist by the rumor mills, which dutifully re-project next year's earnings estimates down 10 per cent or more from the standard forecasts whenever a big block of stocks is thrown on the market. This is all highly stimulating to the participants, but must strike any unprejudiced observer as an authentic instance of mass madness."

But old ideas about what investment policy is safe and what is risky were not the only tenets that needed reexamining in 1966. In December the Securities and Exchange Commission disclosed that another supposedly sacrosanct institution was not above criticism. The SEC charged, in a lengthy report, that many mutual funds overcharge the investor, and called for a variety of reforms.

The commission asked Congress to pass a law lowering selling fees and eliminating the front-end-load plans, under which an investor buying on a contract stands to lose heavily if he backs out after a short time. The funds in turn struck back at the SEC, claiming that rising costs justify high fees, and arguing that the adverse publicity surrounding the SEC's report will hurt fund sales. As the year ended, it was clear that this dispute would wax hotter in 1967.

SUKARNO. President Sukarno's ambiguous relations with the leaders of "New Order" during 1966 highlighted the political uncertainties hanging over Indonesia's future. March saw Sukarno stripped of much of his power, and his close assistants removed from office; his

President Sukarno speaks, and strong man General Suharto looks over shoulder of a woman reporter.

UPI

cherished concept of Nasakom (a coalition of nationalist, religious and communist elements) formally destroyed; and the Government entrusted to Army Commander Suharto.

On the morning of March 11 the pressure of growing unrest which had earlier forced Sukarno to form an "Improved Dwikora Cabinet" reached a climax. At the news that "unidentified troops" were approaching the palace, Sukarno—accompanied by then Foreign Minister Subandrio and Third Deputy Premier Chairul Saleh—fled to Bogor. On March 12 he was "persuaded" to sign a declaration, handing over the reins of government to Suharto. Also on March 12, students and army units demonstrated their united enthusiasm for the New Order by parading down the streets of the capital. Even then, Sukarno stubbornly refused to sign the death warrant for his Nasakom concept. The formal dissolution of the PKI, Indonesia's Communist Party, was authorized by Suharto. This was followed by the arrest of Subandrio, Chairul Saleh and others.

The new leaders were committed to a gradual, legal reduction of Sukarno's once great powers. The MPRS (Provisional People's Consultative Congress), which held its fourth session in Jakarta in June and July, provided the obvious opportunity. But with the majority of its members—even after the Leftist purge—indebted to Sukarno for their positions, its steps against him were hesitant. The Ampera Cabinet, installed on July 28, was the result of a compromise between Suharto and Sukarno which recognized the former as chairman of the Cabinet Presidium, and the latter as prime minister.

In the ensuing months, Sukarno's speechmaking provided ample proof of his adherence to old views. He referred to his discredited doctrines and grandiose building schemes, unabashed over their growing unpopularity, and, dismissing his role in the breakdown of Indonesia's economy, blithely said that he was a nation builder, not bothered with filling bellies.

To the students, however, Sukarno represented the one remaining stumbling block to eliminating the corruption and economic mismanagement of the old regime. No longer satisfied to watch the gradual erosion of Sukarno's powers through "constitutionalization," by October the students had stepped up their campaign to force his resignation. Already there were dangerous signs that their growing impatience would provoke a showdown within the ranks of the New Order itself, a situation of which Sukarno would take adantage.

DEREK DAVIES
Editor, FAR EASTERN ECONOMIC REVIEW

SUPREME COURT 1966 — MAJOR DECISIONS

CHIEF JUSTICE: EARL WARREN (1953)

ASSOCIATE JUSTICES

HUGO L. BLACK (1937)
WILLIAM O. DOUGLAS (1939)
TOM C. CLARK (1949)

JOHN M. HARLAN (1955)
WILLIAM J. BRENNAN, JR. (1956)

POTTER STEWART (1958)
BYRON R. WHITE (1962)
ABE FORTAS (1965)

CASE	DATE	DECISION
UNITED STATES V JOHNSON	FEBRUARY 24	Constitutional provisions barring questioning of congressmen as to speeches made in either house held to require reversal of former Congressman's conviction of conspiring to defraud the United States where prosecution was dependent on extensive inquiry into background and motivation of speech in Congress. Vote 7-0 (Bl and Wh *np*).
SOUTH CAROLINA V KATZENBACH	MARCH 7	Provisions of Federal Voting Rights Act of 1965 (including those suspending state literacy and other voting tests, and requiring assignment of Federal examiners to list applicants entitled to vote) held constitutional as within the authority of Congress to enforce the Fifteenth Amendment's prohibition of racial discrimination. Vote 8-1 (Bl).
GINZBURG V UNITED STATES	MARCH 21	Conviction under Federal obscenity statute affirmed where, although literature distributed by accused through the mails was not itself obscene, evidence showed that accused, through mode of distribution and advertising of literature, exploited interests in titillation by pornography. Vote 5-4 (Bl, D, H, S).
COMMISSIONER OF INTERNAL REVENUE V TELLIER	MARCH 24	Taxpayer's expenses incurred in unsuccessful defense of criminal charge under Federal Securities Act held deductible, for Federal income-tax purposes, as ordinary and necessary business expense, where taxpayer was in securities business. Vote 9-0.
HARPER V VIRGINIA STATE BOARD OF ELECTIONS	MARCH 24	Virginia statute requiring payment of poll tax as voting qualification held to violate Federal Constitution's guaranty of equal protection of laws. Vote 6-3 (Bl, H, S).
UNITED STATES V PRICE	MARCH 28	Private individuals, as well as government authorities, held subject to criminal prosecution under Federal statutes barring interference with rights secured by the Federal Constitution. Vote 9-0.
JOSEPH E. SEAGRAM & SONS V HOSTETTER	APRIL 19	New York statute requiring liquor brand owners to affirm that prices on sales in New York do not exceed lowest prices on sales anywhere in the United States held valid. Vote 9-0.
UNITED STATES V GENERAL MOTORS CORP.	APRIL 28	Sherman Antitrust Act's prohibition of conspiracy in restraint of trade held violated by concerted action of automobile manufacturer, automobile dealers and dealers' associations designed to prevent sales of automobiles by discount houses. Vote 9-0.
SHEPPARD V MAXWELL	JUNE 6	Fair trial which due-process clause of Federal Constitution guarantees held denied defendant in Sheppard murder trial in Ohio where trial judge failed to protect defendant from prejudice resulting from presence and activities of press in courtroom. Vote 8-1 (Bl).
KATZENBACH V MORGAN	JUNE 13	Congress held not to have exceeded powers accorded by Fourteenth Amendment to Federal Constitution in providing, in Voting Rights Act of 1965, that right to vote in any election may not be denied applicant who, although unable to read or write English, has completed sixth primary grade in Puerto Rican school. Vote 7-2 (H, S).
MIRANDA V ARIZONA	JUNE 13	Federal Constitution held to bar state-court conviction of crime based upon statements and confessions of accused while in police custody, and at a time when accused was not informed of his right to counsel, right to remain silent, or possible use of his statements as evidence against him. Vote 5-4 (C, H, S, Wh).
SCHMERBER V CALIFORNIA	JUNE 20	Federal Constitution held not to bar state officials, acting without search warrant, from compelling arrested person to submit to blood-alcohol test, and using test results in obtaining drunk-driving conviction. Vote 5-4 (Wa, Bl, D, F).

ROBERT D. HURSH
Editor in Chief
BANCROFT WHITNEY COMPANY

Initials of dissenting justices in each case appear following vote. Justices not participating are indicated by *np*.

By the sea at Taipei, Chiang and sons Chiang Ching-kuo (c) and Chiang Wego (r).

TAIWAN. On March 21 and 22 Nationalist China's National Assembly elected Chiang Kai-shek to a fourth term as president and C. K. Yen to his first term as vice-president. Yen replaced Chen Cheng, who died during Chiang's third term. Yen is believed to belong to the political faction of Chiang Ching-kuo, the President's son and most likely successor. Yen's election was widely interpreted as clinching the succession for the younger Chiang.

In his semiannual report to the Legislative Yuan, Nationalist China's controlled Parliament, Yen, who is also premier, stated that the island's economy had kept pace during the first half of 1966 with "the rapid rate" of the two previous years. He further claimed that the objectives of the Economic Development Plan for 1966–68 had already been realized. With the end of American economic aid to Taiwan, many Nationalist Chinese economists had feared an economic recession, but the Pre-

mier's figures indicated that the recession had failed to develop. Commentators remarked that one reason was the widespread program of construction of new hotels, factories and housing. The Premier claimed that, despite droughts in the spring and torrential summer rains, the gross national product continued to increase during the first half of 1966 at a rate of 7.32 per cent, the same as in 1965. Taiwan's 1966 balance of trade was favorable: exports grew during the first half of the year by $13 million over the same period the previous year, while imports were down $4 million. New hospitals and clinics, and the spread of television and other indices pointed to a rise in the general standard of living.

Nevertheless, Taiwan continued to suffer a shortage of technical and professionally trained people. The island's best-educated youth continued to migrate abroad permanently, due to the lack of a political future on the island, and

In suburban Taipei, crowds enjoy an outing in Yangmingshan Park.

the fact that wages and salaries are so low that maintenance of a reasonable standard of living, even by local standards, requires dishonesty or moonlighting. Manual-labor wages in the first half of 1966 were less than $1 a day, while skilled masons and carpenters earned less than $2 a day. Government and army officials usually receive less than $50 a month. Consequently, as some observers noted, the economic boom has enlarged only the upper and upper-middle income groups. This was indicated by prices for new housing in 1966, when apartments sold for between $5,000 and $15,000, far out of the range of all but a tiny handful of the population.

Corruption continued to be a problem throughout the year, particularly in the parliamentary and policing institutions. Members of both the Legislative and Control Yuan (the auditing and civil-service branch of government) were arrested in connection with corruption cases, and the death sentence was imposed on one businessman involved in a scandal concerning bribery to government officials to lower import duties on soybean products.

In foreign affairs, Nationalist China continued to predict, as it has for the past seventeen years, the early downfall of the communist regime on the China mainland. Taiwan confronted in November its annual United Nations crisis, but Taipei's United Nations seat was saved at least for another year. President Lyndon Johnson's failure to visit Taiwan during his Asian trip was interpreted in some circles as indicative of declining American interest in the Chiang regime.

MARK MANCALL
Department of History, STANFORD UNIVERSITY

TARIFFS. The Kennedy Round—how is it going? This was the big question concerning tariffs in 1966.

Kennedy Round and GATT. The Kennedy Round took its name from the late President Kennedy, who was a strong advocate of expanding world trade by reducing trade barriers. The name describes current negotiations held under the General Agreement on Tariffs and Trade (GATT). GATT is an agreement among some 70 nations who are full members, and an additional 14 others who participate in GATT arrangements. Under GATT, these nations work together to cut trade restrictions and thereby promote greater commerce between countries.

The Kennedy Round of negotiations opened formally in May 1964, but the actual start at negotiating did not begin until April 1965. The goal of the negotiations is an across-the-board cut of 50 per cent in tariffs. From the beginning it was recognized that there would be exceptions to this general rule, and it was agreed that these would be limited to those exceptions considered necessary for national interest. Throughout most of 1965, GATT members worked to prepare their lists of exceptions.

In the closing months of 1965, GATT negotiations were stalled by a French boycott of the European Common Market (one of the major participants in the negotiations) and the resulting inability of the Common Market to participate in the bargaining on agricultural products. The latter comprised one of the key issues of the Kennedy Round. And the participation of the Common Market was regarded as essential to the success of the negotiations.

In January 1966, France ended its boycott, and it appeared that the Kennedy Round might start rolling again. At that time it was realized by many of those taking part in the negotiations that not only would they have to start, but that the pace would have to be stepped up. For, as a U.S. government official pointed out in early February, the authority for the United States to participate in the negotiations came from an act of Congress scheduled to expire in June 1967.

This official—William M. Roth, deputy special assistant for trade negotiations—offered the sobering observation: "We must get back to the hard bargaining by midspring. It will take another six months or so to negotiate the many fine points that give balance to the package. The deal must be set by early 1967 so that all necessary problems can be completed in time."

It was soon apparent that not only was the United States concerned about the pace of the negotiations, but that others were as well. In March, Eric Wyndham White, director general of GATT, expressed serious doubt on the successful conclusions of the Kennedy Round. He said that although progress had been made in the discussion concerning manufactured goods, the difficulty confronting Common Market members in agreeing on a common agricultural policy had been a major roadblock to negotiations.

Despite this warning of possible failure from Mr. White, the participants made little progress during the next several weeks. Press reports in April referred to the Kennedy Round in terms of uncertainty.

However, there were those who continued to look on the bright side. In May, Congressman Thomas Curtis said in Washington on his return from Geneva (site of the discussions) that he had found an increasing pace of negotiations. He thought the situation one ". . . in which many subjects are being simultaneously explored and in which there is reason for hope."

Perhaps the Congressman had reason for his optimism, for, during May, Common Market members agreed in part on their farm policy and set a deadline of July 1 for the completion of their final agreement. If this deadline could be met, the Common Market could then submit its agricultural proposals at Geneva.

In early June, the Common Market reached agreement on trade in grains, and U.S. observers took this as a hopeful sign that substantial progress in other agricultural areas might soon be made in the Kennedy Round. However, the July 1 deadline for the Common Market agreement on an agricultural policy passed without further accord. Despite this failure, many U.S. officials still remained optimistic. On July 8, a GATT official reported that chances of bringing the Kennedy Round negotiations to successful conclusion were better then than a few months earlier.

Shortly after this favorable report, the Director General of GATT proposed that negotiations be intensified after the August recess so that they could be concluded in early 1967. The timetable drawn up by Mr. White set September as the start of full-scale negotiations.

On July 24 the Common Market reached its long-awaited accord on agriculture, and it appeared that Mr. White's timetable might work. On July 27, the Common Market members reached final agreement on their Kennedy Round offers on agriculture. On Aug. 2, these were submitted at Geneva. Within a few days the United States countered with its final offers, and it looked as if serious bargaining could begin.

By early September, negotiators were hopeful that a package deal on reducing tariffs on both industrial and agricultural goods could be reached by Christmas. However, throughout October little progress was made, and the final outcome of the negotiations was still in doubt. As October drew to a close, a new deadline of Nov. 30 was set for the completion of preparations for the final negotiations in early 1967. But in late November a new delay, involving the Common Market, hit the trade talks and the outlook again became doubtful.

Prospects for the Kennedy Round's future could not be analyzed until the new year.

PETER F. GREENE
Editor, Dun & Bradstreet's
EXPORTERS' ENCYCLOPAEDIA

TAXATION

By JOSEPH D. HUTNYAN
Washington Bureau Chief
THE AMERICAN BANKER

U.S. Congressional tax activity during the early nineteen sixties dwelt mainly on the happy prospect of reducing the average citizen's financial obligation to his Government. This development pleased both the taxpayer, who liked having the extra money in his pocketbook, and the politician, who felt that he is the beneficiary when the voter-taxpayer is happy.

However, the gears of tax policy were reversed in 1966. Taxes went up, and most of the Congressional dialogue on the subject weighed the sober possibility of raising them even higher.

Why the change?

Two factors caused fiscal strategists to revise their thinking in 1966. The economic charts, which seemed to call for a tax decrease to stimulate the economy in previous years, now began reflecting a need for a tax rise to cool it down. Inflationary pressures, pushing up prices, suggested that it might be a good idea to extract some of the spending power that was propelling the unprecedented business boom.

The growing commitment of the United States in Vietnam was another reason why sentiment began to jell for a tax increase in 1966. Economists argued that this was the best means of financing U.S. involvement in the Asian conflict. It was pointed out that to raise the money through accelerated government borrowing merely would add to the inflationary forces in the money markets, which already were producing the highest interest rates in 40 years.

1966 Increase. Actually, the new tempo in tax policy was sounded the instant the clocks began to toll the midnight hour on the night of Dec. 31. When the nation's taxpayers awakened on New Year's Day, 1966, they were $4,200,000,000 deeper in debt to their Government.

This tax increase was far from being a surprise. It was a legacy of the 1965 Congressional session, which reshaped the Government's revenue structure to reflect new concepts in Federal responsibility. One such responsibility called for a program to care for the less-privileged persons in the United States. The 1965 Congress had made history by enacting into law the most sweeping expansion of social-security benefits since the depression years. The big package included establishment of Medicare—to help pay for the hospital and doctor bills of persons over 65. To finance these new benefits, the law provided for gradual increases over a 22-year period in social-security payroll taxes levied on employees and employers. The first of these social-security-tax increases—totaling $6,000,000,000—went into effect Jan. 1, 1966.

Excise Taxes. Some of the pain was taken out of this New Year's Day tax bite by a tax reduction which became effective at the same time. This was the second stage of the cutback in excise taxes also approved in 1965. Side by side with the $6,000,000,000 increase in social-security taxes, the law scheduled a $1,800,000,000 reduction in excises. On balance, then, the taxpayers' bill went up $4,200,-000,000 on Jan. 1.

Excise taxes are Federal sales taxes (ranging from 5 to 10 per cent) which had been placed on a variety of products and services in periods of national emergency during the past 25 years. Congress decided in 1965 that many of these levies were obsolete, and set up a schedule to repeal them. The $1,800,000,000 bundle that went off the books on Jan. 1 included excises on automobile parts; electric light bulbs; chewing tobacco and snuff; lubricating machine oil; and stock transfers. The excise tax on passenger autos was cut from 7 to 6 per cent, and the tax on telephone and teletypewriter service from 10 to 3 per cent.

The 1966 New Year's Day cut in excises had been authorized by a law passed months before that date. It became obvious later that if Congress had to do it all over again, it would not be quite so generous. Inflationary storm clouds already were gathering on the economic horizon when the 1966 reduction in excise taxes went into effect. The new spending power unleashed by the latest rebate was seen as just another aggravating factor. In addition, it was becoming obvious that the President would need every penny he could find to help pay for the war in Vietnam.

Mr. Johnson acted quickly. The new year was only two weeks old when he asked Congress to reimpose the tax rates on automobiles and telephones. Specifically he recommended jacking up the auto tax back to 7 per cent, while the telephone levy of 10 per cent would also be restored.

"Pay as you go." In a companion move, also intended to take some steam out of the economy and provide more revenue for defense, the President recommended legislation

Wide World
Senator Dirksen receives one of the pens with which President Johnson signed excise-tax cut.

to speed up tax collections for individuals and corporations. The idea was to put both classes of taxpayers on more of a pay-as-you-go schedule, and eliminate the fat tax bills that hit many Americans on April 15.

The overall result of the acceleration was that, effective May 1, millions of Americans discovered that a bigger chunk of their paychecks was being withheld for income taxes. For instance, a single wage earner making $200 a week found his weekly deduction for income taxes hiked from $26.20 to $35.80 after the speedup. A family of four receiving the same income began paying $23.20 a week in withholding, compared to $20.80 before the higher rates became effective.

Government tax officials estimated that the increases in the telephone and auto taxes, together with accelerated tax collections, would bring an extra $6,000,000,000 into the Treasury by July 1, 1967.

Congress sped the new tax bill through in record time, largely because it was relatively painless for most taxpayers. The quick action pleased the President, who observed: "Congress has demonstrated once again that we have the determination to meet our commitments abroad, and the capacity to rise to changing economic circumstances at home."

The Great Tax Debate. Republicans were less buoyant, contending that the early tax increase was only a down payment on a bigger and more unpopular general income-tax rise yet to come.

"Everybody in the Senate knows we are going to need another tax rise," observed Sen.

Norris Cotton (R-N.H.), "and it's coming just as surely as night follows day."

Sen. Cotton, as it turned out, was on the right track, but future events were to be somewhat less clear-cut than his simile suggested. What did follow must be considered one of the most spirited tax debates in U.S. history.

Throughout the next six months, as signs of inflation rose and fell, pressure for an income-tax increase ebbed and flowed. Economists, government officials and politicians were bitterly divided.

One month the tide of authoritative opinion would be rolling in favor of a tax rise; the next month, the consensus would be against it. President Johnson played his own private cat-and-mouse game with the issue: hinting at times that a tax increase was imminent, and giving the impression later that such an eventuality was highly remote.

Just about every American had some economic stake in this debate. The tax increase under discussion was an across-the-board raise which would have reached into every family in the nation. It did not, as in the case of more recent tax actions, deal just with excises or social-security taxes which affect only certain classes of taxpayers and involve comparatively small sums to the average wage earner.

Inflation and Legislation. By late summer it became evident that Mr. Johnson would not recommend a general income-tax increase. No doubt an important factor in this judgment was the upcoming election which Democrats were contemplating with apprehension.

Instead, Mr. Johnson chose to combat inflation by relying mainly on what has come to be known as "jawbone diplomacy." He urged businessmen to curb new plant spending. Government pressure was used to force price rollbacks in the aluminum, cigarette and molybdenum industries. Mr. Johnson prevailed on labor and management to hew to the noninflationary wage-price guidelines in contract settlements. The President also depended heavily on monetary policy to slow down the economy—a decision that angered some economists, who cited the high interest rates and the capital-starved mortgage market as proof that this device was carrying too much of the anti-inflation load.

When the "jawbone" approach met with only limited success, Mr. Johnson did recommend a tax increase—but one that applied only to the business community. He asked Congress to rescind until Jan. 1, 1968, a special 7 per cent tax credit for business investment and certain depreciation allowances, which business had been granted four years

ago. In a further move to fight inflation, he promised to stretch out or withhold a total of $3,000,000,000 in government appropriations. Again, Congress quickly complied.

The move was well received by many who felt the nation was in the grip of a roaring inflation. Others argued that the package was too little and too late.

Congress approved only one other significant tax proposal in 1966. This was a bill originally intended to liberalize tax laws for foreign investment in the United States, but it became so festooned with election-year amendments for special-interest groups that it was dubbed the "Christmas-Tree Bill." In addition to the foreign-investment provisions, the legislation was used as a vehicle for special tax concessions for a diverse group of taxpayers, including clay producers, oyster-shell dredgers, shale and slate producers, landlords, undertakers, authors, investors, doctors, dentists, inventors and lawyers.

It also included a special provision permitting a taxpayer to earmark $1.00 annually of his Federal taxes to be used to help finance presidential political campaigns.

Because of this, and the special-interest amendments, the "Christmas-Tree Bill" generated heated criticism in some quarters, but the legislation was enacted anyway.

From the standpoint of the tax issue, the year 1966 ended as it began: with the economists, government officials and politicians still debating the wisdom of enacting a general income-tax increase. The situation during December became infinitely more complex. Fresh estimates on defense expenditures increased the likelihood of a tax rise early in 1967, purely as a means of paying the mounting cost of the war in Vietnam. At the same time, some economists warned that weak spots were starting to show in the current business expansion, suggesting that a hefty tax jump might kick the economy into a recessionary spin.

This turn of events proved a troublesome paradox for the Democratic administration. Before the election, economic factors seemed to suggest the need for a tax increase, but political conditions were not conducive to such action. After the election, political considerations were less of a problem, but by then the economic signals were unclear.

This was the problem that Mr. Johnson faced as he began drafting his next budget. It was one that he was likely to resolve early in the new year, thus ending what historians may someday refer to as The Great Tax Debate of 1966.

TELEVISION

By RICK DU BROW
Television Critic
UNITED PRESS INTERNATIONAL

Search for New Patterns. One fact stood out above all others for television in 1966. The industry sought new patterns—to woo back the intelligentsia who had all but written off the commercial medium, and to rekindle enthusiasm in the loyal audience that had unmistakably indicated a lack of excitement about regular programing. Even at the networks, where most shows are judged primarily as marketing instruments and only secondarily for entertainment value, there was a feeling that the medium was at a dead end and had to seek new directions.

Thus a single drama—CBS' *Death of a Salesman*, which received excellent notices and a respectable rating against the top-ranked Bonanza series, a Western—touched off something of a renaissance in serious and experimental special programs. Thus a single weekly series, ABC Stage 67, which began in September and offered a mixture of original dramas, musicals and documentaries by respected creators, was clearly a temporary breakthrough in experimental broadcasts on a regular basis—despite mixed reviews.

Thus a single blockbuster movie, ABC's *The Bridge on the River Kwai*, drew an audience estimated by the network at 71 million persons and signaled a huge network spending spree for old films. Thus the Ford Foundation started a spirited debate with a revolutionary proposal that a domestic satellite system could save the networks millions in transmission charges, which in turn could be used to bolster a significant noncommercial educational-television apparatus. And thus, finally, there were nighttime broadcasts of baseball and football games as the networks tried various forms of programing that would hold the viewer for longer periods, and in a more involved way, in the prime entertainment hours.

Motion Pictures. Probably nothing in 1966 pleased and embarrassed the networks more than the success of the movies. It was pleasing because the films almost always got strong ratings, posed no problems with production and actors, and had a long waiting list of sponsors. It was embarrassing because the consistent audience preference for the motion pictures, as opposed to the competing series produced expressly for the networks, exposed the distinctly troubled condition of television's regular fare.

CBS-TV

Mildred Dunnock, Lee J. Cobb as Mr. and Mrs. Willy Loman in Arthur Miller's *Death of a Salesman*.

As the certainty of getting top ratings with movies mounted, the networks paid record prices for them, especially the blockbusters that could have enormous effect in the popularity battles with their corporate rivals. CBS paid $1 million for *The Music Man* and spread it over two nights. ABC paid $2 million for *The Bridge on the River Kwai*. ABC also paid $5 million for two future showings of the most expensive movie of all time, *Cleopatra*, with Elizabeth Taylor and Richard Burton. For the future, networks also booked such blockbuster motion pictures as *The Longest Day*, *Shane* and *Cat on a Hot Tin Roof*. And in the 1966–67 season that started in September, viewers could see such films as *Hans Christian Andersen*, *Breakfast at Tiffany's*, *Roman Holiday*, *The Defiant Ones*, *Rear Window*, *Fail Safe*, *The Country Girl* and *Lilies of the Field*.

Furthermore, television's power over movies was increased when a judge failed to uphold producer-director George Stevens' demand that commercials be banned from NBC's showing of his great film *A Place in the Sun*, based on Theodore Dreiser's *An American Tragedy*.

Stevens apparently felt that a former contractual arrangement gave him final approval of the presentation of the movie. The judge did make the significant ruling that the commercials could not be inserted in a way that would "emasculate" the artistic quality of the film— thus establishing the important idea that a creator's work and reputation were deserving of protection. But a subsequent ruling claimed that the film, as shown on NBC, did not have its quality destroyed—chiefly because the movie itself was so powerful. This technically left the door open to producers who might feel their films were not strong enough to survive the disabling effect of commercials.

The networks, with their new and future reliance on movies, also faced accompanying problems. For one, the supply of motion pictures in Hollywood vaults—that is, the better films—is running out. Television therefore arranged to have "original" two-hour movies made especially for the home screen. The feeling, however, is that, restricted in budgets and hampered by the medium's rules and regulations, these are more likely to have the quality of two-hour television shows.

To the family-minded TV industry, another problem of sorts is that the shortage of movies means using more and more foreign films. These films, often quite earthy, will make their way into the nation's living rooms. However, so great are the financial benefits of a film's appearing on American television that the content of some future foreign films is already reported to have been affected by this consideration.

Rush for Theatricals. The modest renaissance of theater "specials" for television, begun by *Death of a Salesman* and ABC Stage 67, was also aided by the increasingly exorbitant prices networks had to pay for remaining top movies. As the show-business newspaper *Variety* put it: "The way theatrical film prices are mounting, the economics of studio drama and features on TV are just about at the point of equalizing. If a drama costs $400,000 for a single run and can carry the rating momentum (and advertising lineup) of a feature showcase whose celluloid fare is $500,000 a shot, it becomes almost a bargain." The networks, of course, would retain possession of their own dramas.

At any rate, the rush for theatricals was on. ABC presented a splendid adaptation of the musical *Brigadoon*. The network announced it would offer a monthly Sunday Night at the Theater series, presenting such plays as *The Diary of Anne Frank* and *Dial M for Murder*.

CBS scheduled *The Glass Menagerie* with Shirley Booth; Hal Holbrook's one-man show, *Mark Twain Tonight!*; and Sir John Gielgud in Anton Chekhov's drama *Ivanov*, following his acclaimed two-part solo Shakespearean program, *Ages of Man,* on the same network early in 1966. A CBS Playhouse project of occasional "specials" was also announced, and England's Royal Shakespeare Company agreed to present *King Lear, Macbeth* and *A Midsummer Night's Dream* on the network during the two seasons starting in the fall of 1967.

NBC continued its Hallmark Hall of Fame productions—with such plays as *Barefoot in Athens*, *Blithe Spirit* and *Anastasia*—and revealed plans for a weekly Sunday afternoon experimental series. In addition, the broadcasting organization paid a record $112,500 for a new play by William Hanley, *Flesh and Blood,* and obtained rights to Peter Weiss' *The Investigation,* set in a courtroom and concerning the accused and witnesses of nazi horrors.

In short, what the networks hoped to do occasionally was far more newsworthy than what they were doing regularly. Offerings were far less impressive than what educational television did day in and day out—unfortunately, as yet, without a coast-to-coast hookup to make a national impact. Major steps for such an educational-TV hookup were planned for 1967 and 1968, however, and the Ford Foundation's do-

Julie Harris, Lynn Fontanne in NBC-TV's *Anastasia.*

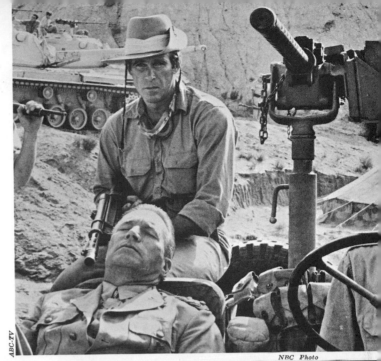

Here are scenes from three new series popular with viewers. Right: ABC's Rat Patrol, half-hour World War II action entry. Lower left: CBS' Family Affair deals with a bachelor and his valet and how they cope with three children. Lower right: NBC's Occasional Wife is about a bachelor who pretends to be married.

mestic satellite suggestion gave new impetus to the drive for a noncommercial fourth network as an alternative to the present system.

Regular-Series Fare. The early ratings of the 1966–67 season verified the missing enthusiasm and mediocre quality of the new regular-series fare. Almost all the popularly favored shows were standard veterans, such as Bonanza and the Red Skelton and Lucille Ball programs. The highest-rated new series was

ABC's Rat Patrol, a half-hour World War II action entry set in the North African desert. Strangely there was little outward public excitement about it, and very little critical interest, except mystery as to its success.

The three other new series that appeared to have gained ratings prominence were also half-hour productions: CBS' Family Affair, a comedy about a sophisticated bachelor and his valet who inherit several orphans; NBC's Occasional

427

Wife, a comedy about a young man who pretends to be married in order to get ahead in the baby-food firm he works for; and ABC's The Felony Squad, a detective story.

The new season brought disappointment to a number of veteran stars, some in comeback attempts, who tried to triumph over the weekly series grind. Jean Arthur, long retired, tried a situation comedy as a lady lawyer, but it failed quickly and was canceled. Milton Berle, once television's biggest headliner, returned in a variety hour, but the ratings were not there and he also was canceled. Garry Moore, too, came back in a variety series, but the public and critics agreed it lacked inspiration. Chill Wills turned up in a comedy Western, The Rounders, which did not last long. A Tammy Grimes comedy about a madcap heiress was short-lived.

One pair of veteran performers, however, updated and expanded their old series, and turned it into a rousing success. Jackie Gleason and Art Carney, as the bus driver and sewer worker of the classic television comedy episodes entitled The Honeymooners, reached new heights—critically and with the public—as their further adventures were presented in the form of hour-long "book musicals." Another old series, Dragnet, a highly popular police tale, was dusted off as a replacement. NBC's long-running Telephone Hour abandoned its standard variety form for lively documentaries about people and events in music.

The new generation of television performers, meanwhile, had a unique twist: offsprings of famous stars suddenly were being featured in their own series. Marlo Thomas, daughter of comedian Danny Thomas, portrayed an aspiring actress in a comedy entitled That Girl. Noel Harrison, son of actor Rex Harrison, was on view in a spy spoof called The Girl from U.N.C.L.E. David Carradine, son of actor John Carradine, played the title role in Shane, based on the Western film.

Several entertainment series gained unusual attention in 1966. Chiefly because of imaginative promotion, Batman, a tongue-in-cheek approach to the old comic strip, found huge popularity when it arrived in January. But by the end of the year it had slipped to routine status. Another program, Secret Agent, about a British spy, made a star of its leading man, Patrick McGoohan; showed that American audiences were not so provincially opposed to foreign accents as some network officials thought; and highlighted the increasing internationalization of U.S. home screens, with a host of English series in the forefront.

Departures, Standouts, Documentaries. A number of longtime series favorites, meanwhile,

bowed out. Among those to go were the Perry Mason mysteries, the Dick Van Dyke comedies, the Ben Casey and Dr. Kildare medical melodramas, and the Rawhide western adventures. The television public was shocked and saddened when a Rawhide star, Eric Fleming, drowned in a Peruvian river when his canoe capsized during filming of a movie.

Television 1966 was the recipient of another unforgettable one-woman show by Barbra Streisand. Frank Sinatra, an award winner for a 1965 one-man musical outing, returned too with an encore hour. Jack Paar ended his sabbatical with a hilarious revue about politics, A Funny Thing Happened on the Way to the White House. Simone Signoret dignified a crackling drama, A Small Rebellion, about an actress who tries to change a play because it affects her too deeply. And there were the documentaries —about car safety, the drug LSD, life along the Volga River, Beethoven, Stravinsky. President Johnson guided a tour of the central Texas hill country he calls home.

Yet most network documentaries in 1966 struck critics as innocuous, overcautious, "impartial" to the point of vacuity. Despite stepped-up coverage of the Vietnam war, there seemed little excitement or originality in commercial television's news. Ironically, perhaps the greatest interest in this area came when Fred Friendly, the respected president of CBS News, resigned because one of his superiors decided one day to put on comedy reruns instead of the Senate Vietnam hearings. NBC ran the hearings in full, probably the most influential news decision of the year because, as historian Arthur Schlesinger, Jr., noted, they had the effect, "for better or worse, of legitimatizing dissent."

Friendly, however, was still to be heard from. A man of vigor and principle, he had, in 1966, kept the CBS Reports series on its legs; used the Early Bird communications satellite for Town Meeting of the World discussions; presented lively, national audience-involvement tests on basic subjects such as health and taxes; and led in aggressive coverage of Vietnam. It was therefore not too surprising to learn, later in the year, after he had left CBS, that he was one of the architects of the Ford Foundation's domestic satellite proposal.

Thus television 1966. All network prime-time schedules were in color by autumn. Pay TV still stumbled along, with little accomplished. The sleeping giant was community antenna television, with its vast potential of interlocking systems—and the giant was awaking. Negroes got more and more prominent parts in programs. And movies were better than ever—on television.

TENNESSEE. Buford Ellington (D) was unopposed in the race for governor. Howard H. Baker, Jr., became the first Republican in Tennessee ever to win a U.S. Senate seat by popular vote. He defeated Gov. Frank G. Clement. . . . Memphis voted in a mayor-council form of government. . . . State Commissioner of Education J. Howard Warf announced in November that 29 per cent of the state's Negro public-school students attended integrated classes.

TEXAS. Charles J. Whitman, a 25-year-old student at the University of Texas, killed 14 persons from the University Tower Aug. 1. Later it was discovered that Whitman had also killed his mother and his wife. . . . Texas' poll tax was declared unconstitutional, and its plan to redistrict the state legislature was declared constitutional. . . . Sen. John G. Tower (R) was reelected Nov. 8. . . . Dr. Jack K. Williams, a dean and vice-president for academic affairs at Clemson University, Clemson, S.C., was named commissioner of higher education.

THANT, U. It was a year of decision for the 57-year-old former schoolteacher from Burma who would have liked to return to relative obscurity in his homeland. But he yielded to diplomatic importuning, the pressure of world public opinion and his own sense of duty and agreed to accept election to a second five-year term as United Nations secretary-general. Throughout 1966 Thant hinted that he intended to quit when his first term expired on Nov. 3. He announced formally on Sept. 1 that he had decided "not to offer myself for a second term."

Later, he agreed to remain until the end of the 21st General Assembly session, which adjourned Dec. 20. And it was not until the closing days of November that diplomatic activity, existing but quiescent during most of the year, stepped up to the point of persuading Thant to stay on.

Thant, notably never one to pull his diplomatic punches, gave a variety of frustrating reasons for wanting to quit. Foremost was his inability to budge the Vietnam war from the battlefield to the negotiating table. He did not deny published reports that the United States turned down a move he promoted toward negotiations—a move favorably received by North Vietnam. Nor did he move from his long-stated three-point proposal for ending the war: 1. Termination of the U.S. bombing of North Vietnam. 2. Descalation of military activities by both sides in South Vietnam. 3. Peace negotiations "among those actually doing the fighting," meaning inclusion of the Viet-

"The New York Times"

Saudi Arabia's Defense Minister Ibn Abdul Aziz, King Faisal and Secretary-General U Thant at UN in June.

cong and parent National Liberation Front in truce discussions. The United States went far toward accepting these when UN Ambassador Arthur J. Goldberg addressed the General Assembly on Sept. 22, but it demanded equalizing warfare concessions from North Vietnam.

Thant also expressed frustration at his inability to put the United Nations on a financially stable basis; to make it a potent force for peace (and peace-keeping); to achieve its universality (meaning inclusion of Communist China); to expand its economic activities and to "bridge the gulf between the giants" of East and West.

During 1966, Thant traveled extensively, pushing for his UN tenets. He made official visits to London, Paris and Moscow and was in frequent touch with U.S. officials in New York City.

When the diplomats evidently were convinced that Thant intended to leave his office, their behind-scenes activity boiled up. It was reported that Thant was assured privately of support for his efforts. The major powers were said to have assured him that he would not occupy the role of a "glorified clerk"—a term he had used in connection with his office.

On Dec. 2, the General Assembly, upon the unanimous recommendation of the Security Council, voted 120–0 (with one invalid ballot) to "appoint" Thant to a second term, due to expire Dec. 31, 1971. The tacit understanding, however, was that the little Burmese was free to resign at any time he felt he was not getting the cooperation promised in private discussions.

BRUCE W. MUNN
Chief UN Correspondent
UNITED PRESS INTERNATIONAL

THEATER

By HENRY POPKIN
Contributor on Theater
THE TIMES of London

Marat/Sade. In the U.S. theater in 1966, established dramatists faltered; musicals boomed; the British invasion continued; and the repertory companies flourished. But possibly the most important theatrical event occurred a few days before the beginning of the year. That was the opening on Broadway of a British production of a play with an interminable title, by Peter Weiss, a Swedish citizen who writes in German—*The Persecution and Assassination of Marat As Performed by the Inmates of the Asylum of Charenton under the Direction of the Marquis de Sade.* It opened December 27 and ran through the end of April. It earned extraordinarily favorable reviews, provoked innumerable debates and discussions and earned an astonishing amount of money for the Merrick Foundation and the Royal Shakespeare Company.

The production, by Peter Brook, was crammed full of violence, sensationalism, ingenuity—and meanings for our own day and our own public issues. Every one of the three dozen actors on the stage gave a performance, even the gibbering madmen of the asylum who had no lines. Best remembered were the most outrageous moments: the apparently naked Marat striding toward the back of the stage;

the buckets of paint (red, white, and blue) representing the blood of those who are guillotined; the final mad riot on stage that can be quelled only by the intervention of a stage manager in modern dress blowing a whistle; and the actors' slow, surly, derisive handclap—in response to the audience's applause at the final curtain.

The production was the culmination of Brook's years of work with his company in "theater of cruelty," reflecting the teachings of the French theatrical theorist Antonin Artaud. Also, this was a repertory company, the finest in the English-speaking world. It had begun in Stratford-on-Avon in 1960 and acquired an additional playhouse in London. Its excellence and its boldness made it a legend, and if, on an earlier American tour, its *King Lear* (also directed by Brook) did not win the attention it deserved, the reception of the *Marat/Sade* made up for this previous neglect of the Royal Shakespeare Company.

Before the year 1966 was out, the play was being performed in new productions around the country. Weiss himself visited the United States for the first time in spring to attend a meeting of the German intellectual organization Group 47 in Princeton, N.J. His grim documentary drama based on the Auschwitz trials, *The Investigation*, opened on Broadway in the fall.

Albee, Williams, Inge and Others. At the same time that Brook and Weiss were inaugurating a new kind of theater, three established American dramatists were disappointing their public. Edward Albee's first play of 1966 was

Actors of the Royal Shakespeare Company in Peter Weiss' Marat/Sade.

Sam Siegel
Brian Friel's *Philadelphia, Here I Come!*.

Miss Alix Jeffry
Edward Albee's *A Delicate Balance*.

Malcolm, based on James Purdy's novel about a precocious 15-year-old who dies, victimized by a bullying world, of "sexual hyperaesthesia." This strange little play, directed by Alan Schneider, lasted only seven performances. Albee took this failure gracefully and returned later in the year with an original play, *A Delicate Balance*, again with Schneider the director and featuring Jessica Tandy and Hume Cronyn. Amid a good deal of remarkably self-conscious conversation, we observe a household whose "delicate balance" is shaken by the arrival of two good friends who have been driven from their home by what is best described as cosmic fear. Their coming upsets the household, but they soon leave without resolving any problems, not even their own. Albee's strangely empty play did nothing to enhance the reputation of the author of *The Zoo Story* and *Who's Afraid of Virginia Woolf?*, and it did little to recall these plays.

The other two disappointing dramatists were Tennessee Williams and William Inge. Williams' new work was a double bill, *Slapstick Tragedy* (directed by Alan Schneider), in which Margaret Leighton played two mutilated women. The first play, *The Mutilated*, seemed to be a reworking of some of Williams' old themes in a familiar manner. *The Gnadiges Fraulein*, however, struck a new note of far-fetched farce with its account of a brave one-eyed woman who contends for cast-off fish with the vicious cocaloony bird. Possibly the first play was too familiar, and the second too unfamiliar; *Slapstick Tragedy* lasted only seven performances.

William Inge was only slightly more fortunate with *Where's Daddy?*. This comedy

about wayward youth—a young married couple who intend to get a divorce as soon as their baby is born—stated its problem rather obviously and demanded all-too-predictable answers. Like two earlier plays of the season, *Generation* and *The Impossible Years*, it appeared designed to calm troubled parents, but it did not enjoy the success of the other two comedies.

There were in fact no new American plays that made their mark on Broadway in 1966. The closest thing was James Goldman's *The Lion in Winter*, a rather labored, self-consciously modern play about the family life of Henry II of England. It owed much of the attention it received to Rosemary Harris' beautiful performance as Queen Eleanor of Aquitaine and to Robert Preston's dependable display of his vigorous personality as King Henry. *Wait until Dark* by Frederick Knott (who wrote *Dial M for Murder*) was a new play that succeeded, a thriller about a blind girl rather unnecessarily threatened with violence, but its author is British. Lee Remick returned from Hollywood to play the lead, and to give this play most of the little distinction it had.

Brian Friel's *Philadelphia, Here I Come!* is a relatively new play that succeeded, but its author is Irish, and the play had previously been seen in Ireland. This lively portrait of an Irish boy about to leave for America gave unmistakable proof of Friel's promise. Little of this promise was visible in the fall when Friel's new work, *The Loves of Cass McGuire*, arrived. In this play, Friel examined, with much less wit and point, the return to Ireland of an old woman who had spent most of her life in New York. Ruth Gordon's talents were—one might almost say "as usual"—wasted.

British Plays, Revivals. Inevitably, British productions were present on New York's Broadway: Jack Roffey's *Hostile Witness,* a not-very-thrilling courtroom drama with Ray Milland; *Wait a Minim!* a likable minor-league revue that originated in South Africa; Chekhov's *Ivanov* in a strangely bloodless staging that featured Sir John Gielgud and Vivien Leigh; Frank Marcus' *The Killing of Sister George,* a rather effective black comedy about a woman who is hard-boiled in real life but plays a beloved character on a BBC radio serial.

U.S. plays did stage one sort of comeback: old ones were revived. The Kaufman-Hart *You Can't Take It with You* continued its successful run from the previous year, and in the autumn Sir Tyrone Guthrie directed *Dinner at Eight* written by George S. Kaufman and Edna Ferber in 1932. Guthrie's star-filled cast (which included Walter Pidgeon, Arlene Francis, Pamela Tiffin, June Havoc and, in a bit part, Blanche Yurka) gave the impression of being a bit too much for this lightweight play. The New York City Center presented a series of modern American plays that included Clifford Odets' *The Country Girl* (with Jennifer Jones), Tennessee Williams' *The Rose Tattoo* (with Maureen Stapleton) and Maxwell Anderson's *Elizabeth the Queen* (with Judith Anderson).

Musicals. The big money-makers on Broadway continued to be the musicals, especially those that were successfully focused on a cap-

Courtesy: New York City Center
Dino Terranova and Maureen Stapleton appeared in a New York City Center revival of Williams' *The Rose Tattoo.*

Angela Lansbury sings and dances in the Broadway musical comedy *Mame,* based on the doings of Auntie Mame.

The Apple Tree is a three-part musical. Here Larry Blyden and Barbara Harris perform in "Passionella."

Above: Gwen Verdon (center) triumphed in *Sweet Charity*. Below: A scene from *Henry VI* as presented at the Stratford Shakespearean Festival, Stratford, Ont.

Peter Smith

tivating personality: *Mame* by Jerome Lawrence and Robert E. Lee, with songs by Jerry Herman (based of course upon the Lawrence-Lee *Auntie Mame*), featuring Angela Lansbury, who established an identity she had never won in her many films; Neil Simon's *Sweet Charity,* with music by Cy Coleman and lyrics by Dorothy Fields, an Americanized version of Federico Fellini's film *Nights of Cabiria,* drawing most of its appeal from Gwen Verdon's personal charm; and *The Apple Tree,* drawn by Jerry Bock and Sheldon Harnick from stories by Mark Twain, Frank R. Stockton and Jules

Feiffer, directed by Mike Nichols, but owing a unique debt to the ebullient Barbara Harris in the lead.

Off-Broadway. Remarkably little happened off-Broadway in 1966. Late 1965's principal hit attracted still more theatergoers. This was *Man of La Mancha*—book by Dale Wasserman, music by Mitch Leigh, lyrics by Joe Darion. Another show that made a big splash was a revue based on material from *Mad* magazine, *The Mad Revue.* Racine's *Phèdre,* acted by Beatrice Straight and Mildred Dunnock and directed by Paul-Emile Deiber of the Comédie

433

The Minnesota Theatre Company gave Shaw's *The Doctor's Dilemma* during its 1966 season.

The Minnesota Theatre Company

Française, created some astonishment by lasting for one hundred performances. More important in its way was Ronald Ribman's *The Journey of the Fifth Horse,* a brilliant, very free adaptation of Turgenev's *Diary of a Superfluous Man.* Presented by the American Place Theater, it had an encouraging reception.

Other U.S., Canadian and English Offerings. In New York the Lincoln Center Repertory Theater went its chosen way, staging excellent plays that were beyond the capacity of the company or its directors: Sartre's *The Condemned of Altona* and Brecht's *The Caucasian Chalk Circle,* which was its first popular success. Late in the year, the company, which had depended primarily upon actors who had accompanied the directors from San Francisco, announced that it would employ some stars. But the presence of Aline MacMahon and George Voskovec did not notably elevate the general level of performance in Ben Jonson's *The Alchemist.* In Minneapolis the Tyrone Guthrie Theater experienced its first year without Sir Tyrone. Under Douglas Campbell's direction, it had a competent season with *As You Like It,* Wilder's *The Skin of Our Teeth,* Strindberg's *The Dance of Death,* O'Neill's *S.S. Glencairn* and Shaw's *The Doctor's Dilemma.* The Shakespeare theater of Stratford, Ont., maintained its high standard with productions of *Henry V* (directed by Michael Langham), *Henry VI* (in John Barton's adaptation) and *Twelfth Night.* Ontario kept its lead over Stratford, Conn., where the high spot of the season was ironically not *Julius Caesar* or *Twelfth Night* or *Henry IV, Part Two* (retitled *Falstaff*) but John Houseman's production of T. S. Eliot's *Murder in the Cathedral.*

In England the great theater revival which began ten years ago showed signs of slowing down. The new plays by Arnold Wesker and John Osborne were disappointing. Wesker's *Their Very Own and Golden City* is an allegorical treatment of the author's difficulties in founding his popular theater, Center 42. Osborne's *A Bond Honoured,* an extremely controversial drama about a scoundrel who becomes a martyr, is freely adapted from a little-known play by Lope de Vega. The National Theater continued to stage a great variety of plays, including Osborne's *A Bond Honoured,* Feydeau's 19th-century farce *A Flea in Her Ear* (directed by Jacques Charon of the Comédie Française) and O'Casey's *Juno and the Paycock* (directed by Sir Laurence Olivier).

The Royal Shakespeare Company adopted a more conservative course at Stratford, where its only new productions were *Twelfth Night* and Cyril Tourneur's *The Revenger's Tragedy.* Its bolder policy in London was to stage the three most interesting plays of the previous season on the Continent: Slawomir Mrozek's *Tango* from Poland, Marguerite Duras' *Days in the Trees* from France, and Friedrich Dürrenmatt's *The Meteor* from Switzerland. The most popular was *Days in the Trees,* about a domineering mother, played with authority by Dame Peggy Ashcroft. (Madeleine Renaud had brilliantly created the role in Paris.) *Tango* proved controversial, but it drew an audience, and some of the hostile reviewers came to like it on second thought. *The Meteor,* about a great man who cannot die, while all the other characters around him are dying like flies, drew little praise in a production that effectively concealed its wit.

434

THEATER: DAVID MERRICK

By JAMES E. CHURCHILL, Jr.

During the 1966 calendar year, Broadway's David Merrick maintained the right to be known as the "Barnum of Broadway producers." Not only was he responsible for the previous season's big hits, but Merrick shows also dominated New York City's 1966 fall season.

In the 1965–66 season alone, four of Broadway's major hits were David Merrick productions: *Cactus Flower, Marat/Sade* (winner of a Tony Award as the year's best drama), *Inadmissible Evidence* and *Philadelphia, Here I Come!*. In addition, Merrick's *Hello, Dolly!*, in its third year on Broadway, was being presented by three road companies. Such big-name stars as Carol Channing, Ginger Rogers and Mary Martin have appeared in the title role of Dolly in New York, London, Chicago, Tokyo and even Saigon.

Merrick productions that opened in the fall of 1966 included: *I Do! I Do!,* a musical based on Jan de Hartog's *The Fourposter* starring Mary Martin and Robert Preston, and John Osborne's *A Patriot for Me*. A musical adaptation of Truman Capote's *Breakfast at Tiffany's* with Mary Tyler Moore and Richard Chamberlain closed before its New York opening.

Since the mid-1950's, David Merrick has produced approximately fifty shows, most of them financial successes. In 1961 he received a special Tony Award for "a fabulous production record." He is Broadway's most successful, most talked-about producer, and quite a personality in his own right.

For example, early in 1966, Merrick made the front page of *The New York Times* by canceling a preview of *Philadelphia, Here I Come!* to prevent *Times* drama critic Stanley Kaufmann from reviewing this performance of the show. In canceling the performance, Merrick had to refund an estimated $4,000 in ticket sales. He was also the subject of a 1966 *Time* magazine cover story, "The Presentation and Examination of the Be(a)st of Broadway As Published by the Writers and Editors of *Time*." The title of the *Time* story derived from the complete *Marat/Sade* title: *The Persecution and Assassination of Marat as Performed by the Inmates of the Asylum of Charenton Under the Direction of the Marquis de Sade.*

Background. David Merrick was born Nov. 27, 1911, in St. Louis, Mo., the youngest child of Samuel and Celia Margulois. After his parents' divorce, Merrick was brought up by his mother and married sisters. For amusement the shy young boy tried to see "everything live" that came to St. Louis. He attended St. Louis' Central High School, and Washington University as a scholarship student. At Washington, Merrick won second prize in a playwriting contest in which Tennessee Williams was a participant. From Washington University, Merrick transferred to St. Louis University where he obtained a law degree. During college Merrick

David Merrick, the "Barnum of Broadway producers," scans New York City's Broadway.

wrote and produced several campus productions. He also worked at odd jobs.

After practicing law for a while in St. Louis, Merrick moved to New York City. (Merrick never liked St. Louis, and even to this day he refuses to fly TWA from the East to the West Coast, for he believes that TWA flies over St. Louis.) Once in New York, Merrick changed his name from Margulois to Merrick, a combination of Margulois and Garrick—the name of the most famous eighteenth-century actor. He continued to practice law.

In 1940, Merrick engaged in his first theatrical venture, investing $5,000 in Herman Shumlin's The Male Animal. The investment brought him a $20,000 return. Merrick then worked for Shumlin as a playreader, press agent and general manager. By 1949, Merrick was ready to become a producer. In that year he staged Clutterbuck, which only broke even financially but gave him his Broadway baptism.

Merrick's first big Broadway production was the 1954 hit, Fanny, which ran for 888 performances. However, the success of the show must be attributed to David Merrick's first publicity stunt. Seeing that the show might have rough going after mediocre reviews by the critics, Merrick commissioned a sculptor to do a statue of the show's belly dancer, Nejla Ates. Placed in New York City's Central Park, the statue drew much attention, and the attention greatly lengthened the lines at the Fanny box office. So with Fanny, Merrick further developed what would become his two principal fortes: producing and publicity.

To publicize his next production, Thornton Wilder's The Matchmaker, Merrick had what appeared to be a monkey drive an antique British taxicab down Broadway. On top of the cab was a sign saying: "I am driving my master to see The Matchmaker." And to try and save Subways Are for Sleeping, Merrick sent seven men with names identical with those of New York City newspaper critics to previews of the show. After it opened, a full-page ad appeared in various newspapers, carrying the seven men's names, pictures and favorable reviews. In 1964, Merrick even persuaded President Lyndon B. Johnson to use "Hello, Dolly!" as the basis for his campaign song, "Hello, Lyndon!".

The Foundation. Tired of paying high taxes on his hits, Merrick in 1962 decided to invest his profits in the nonprofit David Merrick Foundation. From Foundation funds, Merrick can produce whatever shows he desires without financial risk. If a Foundation play is a flop, Merrick loses nothing; if, on the other hand, a Foundation play is a success, the profits can go back into the Foundation, or into an experimental theater that Merrick has established at Brandeis University.

Commenting on the Foundation, Merrick has said: "And even though I produce a Cactus Flower or a Hello, Dolly!, I still like to sponsor the unconventional, offbeat play. With a Cactus Flower or a Hello, Dolly! I can support my Foundation. Instead of turning over 70 per cent of my income in taxes I have been able to contribute and build up the Foundation. As a nonprofit operation it is able to offer the unusual production and, if successful in a particular venture, aid other worthwhile activities." Luther, Inadmissible Evidence, Marat/Sade, Philadelphia, Here I Come! and A Patriot for Me were Foundation productions.

David Merrick believes in two things—himself and the theater. "I love every minute of my life and I'm absolutely crazy about the theater!" He further believes that whatever is wrong with Broadway is the fault of The New York Times. He has been quoted as saying: "The Times wants to destroy Broadway. They boost off-Broadway, Lincoln Center—the tributary theater. Nothing is going to come out of that, or hardly anything." His ambition "is to have every one of Broadway's 31 theaters filled" with David Merrick shows. "I would like to be cited by the Justice Department for a monopoly." Then, David Merrick says, he can retire.

TOKYO. The world's most populous city, Tokyo, cannot stop growing. Some 11,021,579 Japanese call it home—3,226,416 households, averaging 3.4 persons. Men outnumber women 5,642,948 to 5,378,631.

Some 35,119—0.3 per cent—dwell on the Pacific's Izu Isles, part of Tokyo—though 180 watery miles from the recognized Ginza-Nihonbashi heart.

The only ways to build are up and out, for a burgeoning population aided by a booming economy. Tokyo programs a spate of skyscrapers pricking the smoggy sky to 30–35 stories. The building ceiling law, in existence since the "Great Kanto Earthquake" of Sept. 1, 1923, has been junked.

Metropolitan limits stretch into lush, adjacent, farmland countryside—into Chiba, Saitama and Kanagawa prefectures. Tokyo Bay is reclaimed. "Bedroom towns" mushroom 50–60 miles from Tokyo, and while factories and universities relocate, farmland acreage vanishes. Industry proliferates where rice once grew.

In 1966, Tokyo became the world's first great capital to install a computerized traffic system. Such a system, costing $150,000, was introduced for a small area of the Ginza district.

Tokyo faces, in April 1967 gubernatorial elections, a crucial showdown between Premier Eisaku Sato's conservative Liberal-Democratic Party and Socialist chairman Kozo Sasaki's Left-Wing Opposition. Neither man is "Edokko," a native-born Tokyoite.

STUART GRIFFIN
East Asia Correspondent, OBSERVER OF LONDON

TORONTO. Decisions were made during 1966 that will profoundly influence Toronto's political structure and physical appearance. Politically, metropolitan Toronto's 13-member municipal federation was dissolved, to be replaced on Jan. 1, 1967, with a strengthened and expanded central government. Boundaries of the city and its 12 suburbs were redrawn to form 6 boroughs, with the suburban boroughs holding the balance of power on the new council.

Progress was made in planning the largest urban-development scheme ever undertaken in Canada. The T. Eaton Company, Ltd., a department-store chain, proposes to spend $260 million during the next 15 years on replacing a ramshackle 20-acre warehouse area in downtown Toronto with several office towers—the tallest, 69 stories—a hotel and a new department store. Essential to its plan is the site on which the old City Hall stands. Opposition to demolition of the old Romanesque building, now used for municipal courts, was organized

"Business Week," (Michel Lambeth)

As part of a vast redevelopment plan for Toronto, a $30 million City Hall opened in September 1965.

on aesthetic and historical grounds by a citizens' group called Friends of the Old City Hall. But the Metropolitan Council agreed to give the Eaton Company a long-term lease on the site, and the building was doomed.

Chronic overcrowding of high-court facilities was relieved with the opening of a new $13,-650,000 courthouse adjacent to the Civic Square. On the square itself, a controversial Henry Moore abstract sculpture was installed in October. After the City Council voted against buying the $125,000 sculpture, Mayor Philip Givens raised $100,000 from private donors, and Moore agreed to reduce the price as a tribute to his friend the late Viljo Revell, Finnish architect who designed the new City Hall.

A ten-mile crosstown subway line, built at a cost of $200 million, was opened in February. Downtown redevelopment was stimulated by the decision of the Toronto-Dominion Bank to proceed immediately with the second phase of its Centre, a 46-story office tower adjacent to the 56-story tower nearing completion.

WILLIAM FRENCH
Literary Editor, TORONTO GLOBE AND MAIL

TRANSPORTATION

By FRED B. STAUFFER
Transportation Editor
WORLD JOURNAL TRIBUNE

The 1966 U.S. economic boom, with its large increase in the gross national product of goods and services, reflected corresponding advances in the transportation industry. Whatever is produced by industry or yielded by the nation's farms, mines and forests must move to market. Carriers by rail, air and highway faced up to the task, making the year one of the most prosperous on record for transport.

Bountiful crops and the demands of the Vietnam war effort contributed to the increased volume of business. Internal improvements and innovations in the many modes of transport bettered service to the public and boosted earnings well above those of the preceding year.

The record set by transportation in 1966 laid a firm foundation for continued growth in 1967 and beyond, provided that operating companies take full advantage of new and more economic equipment, other technological advances and improved managerial techniques. Contributing to the brighter view ahead is the prospect of a generally favorable regulatory climate and of relatively stable labor relations in most sectors of the industry. For the public, this means assurance of improving service in the movement of people as well as freight. For the investor, it means that transportation still is a growth industry.

U.S. Department of Transportation

The Federal Government recognized the vital role of transportation in the nation's life with the creation of the Department of Transportation, which on a cabinet level will unify many of the functions of more than 30 previously scattered agencies.

The new department—the fourth-largest in terms of number of personnel, and the fifth in terms of amount of annual expenditures—will require nearly 90,000 employees and total expenditures of about $5,500,000,000 a year.

The responsibilities of this consolidated body will be the policy-making, promotional, research and safety functions formerly vested in agencies dealing with rail, air and highway transportation. Economic and regulatory functions will continue to be exercised outside the new department by such agencies as the Interstate Commerce Commission, the Civil Aeronautics Board and the Federal Power Commission.

The history of the measure creating the department is interesting in itself. Although the idea of such a department had been broached frequently in the past, it first took on a concrete form as a proposal by the administration in a message to Congress in March 1966. Working with almost unprecedented speed in setting up a new department, the Senate and the House hammered out the necessary legislation in less than eight months.

Support for the new department came from most sections of the transportation industry as well as from business and industry in general, but there was some degree of dissension on what bodies and functions should be included. Much of this was dispelled by the decision to exclude economic regulatory power, such as the determination of rates and fares.

One exception to the general consolidation of transportation agencies was the Maritime Administration. Inclusion of this body had been urged by the President, but strong opposition was expressed by labor and other groups, and Congress rejected the proposal. In addition, Federal programs dealing with mass transit, a matter of large current interest, will remain with the Department of Housing and Urban Development. Some of the agencies of the new department will be transferred from other existing departments: Bureau of Public Roads from the Department of Commerce, Coast Guard from the Treasury Department.

Railroads

Changes in Fleets. Railroad capability to handle the ever-increasing volume of freight kept pace with the growth of traffic. The carriers and the private-car lines added some 100,000 new and rebuilt cars to the fleets in 1966, while retiring an estimated 80,000 units. Expenditures for freight cars mounted to $1,500,000,000 or more—up $200 million from 1965.

While the net addition thus was only around 20,000 cars, the expansion in terms of tonnage capacity was proportionately much greater as the larger and more-specialized types of equipment took to the rails. Better daily utilization also enhanced the industry's ability to meet the shippers' needs. In the locomotive field, the size of the fleets tended to diminish. Older types of diesels were withdrawn, replaced by fewer but larger and more powerful units that could haul long trains at what once were passenger-train speeds.

In spite of the physical improvements in the fleets, the problem of car shortages remained a sporadic but sometimes severe threat to efficient service. Such shortages usually are regional in character and arise from a variety of causes. For example, bumper grain crops in the Midwest will require more cars to move the harvest to storage or milling points; heavy demand for lumber in the construction industry may tax rail capacity in producing areas. When such exigencies coincide with great industrial production elsewhere, or with need to move Vietnam war supplies, the railroads can be in at least temporary trouble. Regulatory authorities take steps to ensure return of cars to affected areas. During 1966, increases in per diem charges—the rental charged by one road to another—also tended to alleviate the periodic shortages and stimulate buying of new cars.

Higher Speed in Mass-Transit Areas. Among the year's most outstanding developments in railroading was the progress made toward solution of the mass-transit problem around big urban centers, and the new attempts to woo travelers back to the rails with high-speed service in areas affected by great highway-traffic density. Both the mass-transit and the higher-speed programs were undertaken by the railroads themselves with the liberal aid of Federal, state and local funds.

Federal aid alone will provide $150 million a year through 1969 for research and development in the field of mass transit. Projects under way in the San Francisco Bay area, and the extension of an existing line to serve Cleveland's Hopkins Airport, are typical of moves made to provide passenger-transportation facilities off the highway on routes of heavy daily use. Such programs already have brought into being new, efficient and attractive equipment. Changes in roadway and station design accord with the modern mass-transit concept. Authorities in the field see need for projects of this sort at possibly a dozen points across the land.

Progress in the area of high-speed rail passenger transportation was equally spectacular.

This work was carried on by the Department of Commerce and the railroads as part of a 3-year, $90 million Federal program. In one instance, sleek streamliners, designed and built by the Budd Company, the United Aircraft Corporation and the Pullman-Standard division of Pullman Incorporated, will introduce aviation-type jet engines as the prime movers.

The most notable efforts to boost rail speeds are being made in the so-called Northeast Corridor between Boston and Washington, D.C. This is a route of some 400 miles through a metropolitan complex of which New York City is the center. The turbine-powered speedsters are slated for use on the Boston-New York sector.

Initial operations on the New York-Washington segment will use newly designed, electrically driven cars moving on new-laid, high-speed welded rail and protected by up-to-date signaling and other modern facilities. The Department of Commerce expenditure for this project is $9.6 million, with the Pennsylvania Railroad contributing at least as much. The speeds of these trains will range up to around 140 miles an hour. Travel time between terminals is expected to be reduced by as much as 1 hour. The Department of Commerce has said that if the experiment proves successful, the program may be extended to other metropolitan complexes.

Experimenting with costs and performance during the summer of 1966, the New York Central Railroad put on the rails in Ohio a rebuilt Budd RDC car on which 2 aircraft jet engines, geared to driving mechanisms at the wheels, had been mounted. This unique vehicle achieved an American rail-speed record of 183.85 miles an hour on a trip which company officials pronounced "comfortable." The experiment was regarded as a dramatic demonstration of the time that Central hopes to save, with

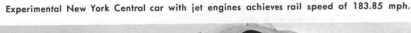

Experimental New York Central car with jet engines achieves rail speed of 183.85 mph.

New York Central

possibly more-conventional equipment, on passenger routes limited to around 200 miles. American railroaders note that the Japanese have set a fast pace for them to follow, but they hope they can reach comparable passenger speeds without building entirely new rail lines.

Problems of Mergers. Railroad mergers, widely urged in recent years as a means of salvation for individual companies and as a major step toward improvement of the industry, presented a more than usually confused picture in 1966.

In two principal cases which had been before it for several years, the Interstate Commerce Commission issued what appeared to be contradictory decisions. The commission authorized creation of the Pennsylvania-New York Central Transportation Co. by merger of the Pennsylvania and New York Central railroads. On the same day, it rejected the proposed merger of the Great Northern Railway, the Northern Pacific Railway and the Chicago, Burlington & Quincy, although the move had been approved by a commission examiner.

Management's pleasure over the Penn-Central approval was short-lived, for it was soon discovered that the paths of merger all too frequently lead from the ICC to the courts. In this instance, other railroads challenged the formation of the giant system, unless they also were taken care of, and carried the matter all the way to the U.S. Supreme Court. Following rejection of the so-called "Northerns" merger, the applicants asked the ICC for reconsideration, promising to satisfy some of the objections raised by the regulatory body with respect to competition in the territory.

While these formal ICC actions were being taken, merger-minded railroads, particularly in the Midwest, staged a series of marches and countermarches. No action was definitive, and the pattern of railroad ownership in the area grew more, rather than less, snarled.

The many and conflicting claims on the Chicago, Rock Island & Pacific Railroad were the highlight of ICC hearings. The Southern Pacific Co., the Union Pacific Railroad, the Chicago & North Western Railway, the Atchison, Topeka & Santa Fe Railway and the Denver & Rio Grande Western were all involved in proposals for carving up the Rock Island and for allotting the segments to other carriers. In the same area, the Missouri Pacific, seeking to control the Santa Fe, met strong resistance from an unwilling partner. The Santa Fe itself began, and then called off, merger discussions with the St. Louis-San Francisco Railway. The North Western proposed merger with the Milwaukee Road.

This ferment in the Midwest and Far West presented the ICC with a new set of merger problems at a time when the situation in the East had barely begun to clear. The commission can only approve or disapprove of specific merger proposals. It has no power to force railroads to consolidate according to patterns of an overall national plan.

The Piggyback Movement. Again in 1966, the piggyback movement of highway vehicles and containers on flatcars was a major feature of rail operations. Having passed the 1 million-car mark for the first time in 1965, piggyback loadings in 1966 mounted to 1.2 million or more. This traffic now accounts for only about 4 per cent of all rail transportation, but growth is greater than in most other areas of the industry, and the volume is expected to triple in the next decade. Railroaders estimate that piggyback handling of loaded and empty highway vehicles, sometimes two in a single flatcar, kept 2.5 million trucks off the highways in 1966. Motortruckers have found that the favorable piggyback rates for many relatively long hauls are really economic. At the same time, the railroads get back a good deal of profitable business that had been lost to the highway operators. More than 24,000 rail cars now are in piggyback service. Faster trains, often solidly piggyback, and more-efficient freight yards have attractively cut transport time, even for coast-to-coast movements.

Another important development in 1966 was the steadily increasing transportation of new automobiles in rack cars—flatcars with superimposed racks, each carrying 12 to 15 automobiles on 3 levels. The fleet of such cars available numbers more than 16,000 and is growing rapidly. Frequently, single trains of these cars carry as many as 1,800 automobiles from factory to buyer. In 1966, the number of new automobiles moving by rail was nearly 5 million, compared with 4.5 million in 1965.

Innovations and New Techniques. Contrary to some views, the railroad industry makes good use of innovations or adaptations of technological advances. One example is the rapidly growing function of computers in the far-flung electronic communications networks of the big rail systems. Once used by the industry only for such simple chores as improving accounting and payroll work, the computers are now employed to provide "real time"—up-to-the-minute information to shippers on the progress of cars—and they also give the rails copious data on which to base cost, rate and marketing decisions. The Association of American Railroads has set up a special department to coordinate individual carriers' efforts in the field.

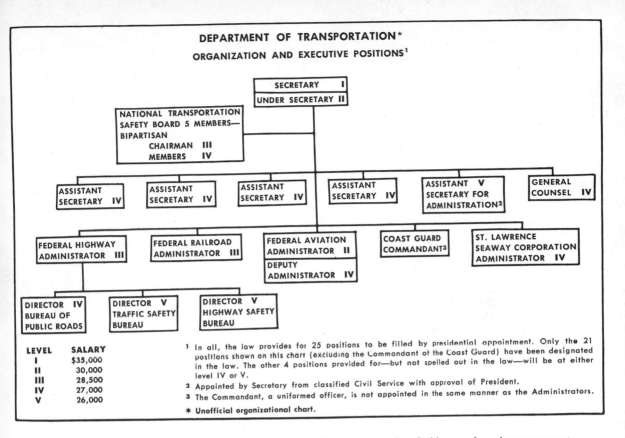

DEPARTMENT OF TRANSPORTATION*

ORGANIZATION AND EXECUTIVE POSITIONS[1]

LEVEL	SALARY
I	$35,000
II	30,000
III	28,500
IV	27,000
V	26,000

[1] In all, the law provides for 25 positions to be filled by presidential appointment. Only the 21 positions shown on this chart (excluding the Commandant of the Coast Guard) have been designated in the law. The other 4 positions provided for—but not spelled out in the law—will be at either level IV or V.

[2] Appointed by Secretary from classified Civil Service with approval of President.

[3] The Commandant, a uniformed officer, is not appointed in the same manner as the Administrators.

* Unofficial organizational chart.

Smaller in scope but equally novel is railroad adoption of a space-age tool—liquefied gases—for controlled cooling of perishables in transit. A small portion of the 115,000-car refrigerator fleet has been equipped with liquid-nitrogen cooling equipment. The advantage of this system, reported to be operating efficiently, is that it requires no moving parts or outside power source to provide temperatures down to minus 20° in hot weather. Similarly, the insulated cars prevent freezing of cargo when outside temperatures threaten.

Airlines

Air transportation, domestic and international, reached a new magnitude in 1966. Particularly rapid growth was achieved in the air-cargo business. Although it still constitutes only a small fraction of total airline business, the current growth rate indicates that within a relatively few years cargo will supply a substantial portion of both revenues and earnings. At least two factors contribute to this growth: availability of huge all-cargo jets and greater freight capacity in combined passenger and cargo planes. In the very near future, still larger aircraft are expected to increase the capacity which the industry is confident will be needed. Some warn, however, that ground handling facilities and techniques must keep pace with the demands of shippers for air movement of their goods.

In spite of a disastrous midyear strike, affecting 5 major carriers, the airlines in 1966 turned in an overall record performance, carrying an estimated 112 million passengers. The growth rate of the industry suggests that this figure will rise to 200 million by 1970. By that time, much of the $5,300,000,000 worth of flight equipment now on order will be in use, including the long-planned supersonic transports (SST's).

Trucking

The trucking industry, like the railroads, enjoyed a year of increased freight volume. Because of higher costs, however, profits were not so large as could have been expected. The two principal factors contributing to the rise of cost were wages—up about 3 per cent in a contract expiring in March 1967, when a further rise is threatened—and higher social-security payments. Two efforts to offset the advance in costs were upward revision of rates, particularly on small shipments not vulnerable to railroad competition, and the merger of small trucking units into larger and economically more stable companies. Widespread adaptation of computer techniques to the needs of the trucking business promises to keep costs at a reasonable level.

New Orleans Chamber of Commerce

Tourists in the United States can enjoy New Orleans' Mardi Gras (above), California's Disneyland (below)...

Walt Disney Productions

and a Colorado rodeo... *Rodeo Information Commission*

TRAVEL

By RICHARD JOSEPH
Travel Editor, ESQUIRE

Nineteen sixty-six saw a continuation of U.S. travel trends and problems that had made themselves evident all through the first half of the decade: a constant increase in American travel abroad, and a worsening of the "travel gap"—the difference between what Americans spend abroad, and what overseas visitors spend in the United States. (In 1965 the difference between the expenditures of 14 million Americans on foreign travel and those of a little over 1 million overseas visitors to the United States was $1,743,000,000.)

Washington economists blamed the travel gap for a large part of the balance-of-payments deficit—the fact that the United States is spending $1,337,000,000 more abroad than it is receiving—even though U.S. overseas expenditures include such enormous items as the Vietnam war, maintaining other forces and bases abroad, huge foreign-aid programs, and constantly increasing foreign investments.

The Vietnamese war had a braking effect on travel to Hong Kong and other parts of the Orient, for purely psychological reasons, since the conflict caused no disruption of travel facilities. Aside from this, citizens of the United States for the most part ignored the anti-foreign-travel propaganda, and set new records for travel to Europe, Latin America, Canada and even the Pacific (although here the rate of

and a Palm Springs, Calif., oasis . . .

increase slowed down somewhat) just as they have been doing for the past twenty years.

The strike of five major U.S. airlines during the height of the summer vacation season was a serious blow to domestic travel. Even so, more Americans spent more money in travel-ing around their own country than ever before. Obviously they are not just traveling *abroad* more: they are *traveling* more, due to longer vacations and more money to spend on them. Unless something catastrophic happens to the U.S. economy, these trends are not likely to change.

Most of the increased transatlantic travel continued to go to the airlines while the steam-ship companies more than made up for their decreased share in the transatlantic traffic with their booming cruise business.

As usual most U.S. railroads made no secret of their desire to secede from the pas-senger business. They followed their customary procedure of letting services deteriorate until travelers did not want to use them, and then used the passenger drop-off as an argument for further curtailment of service.

To Americans planning to travel abroad sometime in the future, the most important development continues to be the campaign to close the travel gap. If this campaign fails, some form of impediment to foreign travel will almost inevitably result. This may take the form of a whopping $50 to $100 exit tax, or a per diem tax on the time spent out of the country. Both steps have been under discussion in Washington. Members of President John-son's administration have constantly denied any intention to impede American travel

American Airlines

or the ski slopes of New Hampshire (above) . . .
or Hawaii's warm sun and warm welcome (below).

Hawaii Visitors Bureau

abroad, yet in testimony before a House sub-committee, John W. Black, director of the U.S. Travel Service, stated that the exit tax had been under consideration by the Treasury Department in 1965. He said, though, that the discussion had been classified as confidential.

Unfortunately there is considerable precedent for travel restrictions, even though they would reverse the U.S. policy of encouraging international travel, followed since the end of World War II.

In mid-1966, in an effort to correct its balance-of-payments deficit, the British Government imposed a limit of about $140 on the amount a British subject could take out of the country on a pleasure trip. And in September, Israel was reported planning to cut its citizens' overseas-travel allowance from $500 to $350 as part of an overall attempt to halt its outflow of hard currencies and reduce consumer spending. West Germany was also said to be considering travel restrictions for its nationals. Italy, France, the Netherlands, Sweden, Japan and many other countries all have travel restrictions of various degrees of severity.

Promoting U.S. Travel

U.S. efforts to close the travel gap by constructive measures have centered in two organizations, the U.S. Travel Service, a branch of the Department of Commerce,

charged with the Visit USA program designed to attract more visitors from abroad; and Discover America, Inc., a nonprofit group set up by private industry to stimulate domestic travel and make American tourist facilities more attractive both to U.S. vacationists and to visitors from abroad. Directors of Discover America, Inc., include representatives of airlines and the Association of American Railroads; plane, automobile and tire manufacturers; car-rental firms; and hotel chains.

At midyear the U.S. Travel Service reported about 379,000 visitors to the United States during the first 5 months of 1966, an increase of 14 per cent over the 1965 period. Director John W. Black predicted 1.2 million visitors in 1966, a gain of about 165,000 over the 1965 figure. The average visitor spends about $395, Black reported. (The British travel restrictions were a serious threat to the Visit USA program, as the United Kingdom was by far the most important European market for travel to the United States. Thus far, however, it appears that the rate of increase in foreign travelers will be maintained.)

Working quietly but effectively, the USTS has been instrumental in more than doubling the number of visitors from abroad since it started operations in 1961. In 1965, foreign tourists spent $1.4 million in the United States on American air and sea carriers.

More U.S. scenes: Sand and surf, Fort Lauderdale, Fla.
Florida Development Commission

and Arizona's Grand Canyon...
American Airlines

The USTS has to work quietly, because it is under constant attack from Congressional opponents who resent every dollar that goes into its limited budget. The character of this opposition is reflected in this colloquy between Director John Black and Representative John Rooney (D-N.Y.), chairman of the House Appropriations Subcommittee, at a budget hearing as reported in this transcript of the subcommittee proceedings:

MR. ROONEY. I suspect that it might have attracted attention, but did you recommend or approve the head of any of your offices riding around a foreign city on a motor scooter with a beatnik beard?

MR. BLACK. We did not approve the beard, sir. The beard was shaved back in 1963 at our orders.

MR. ROONEY. After it became practically a scandal with our personnel in the Palazzo Margherita on the Via Veneto.

MR. BLACK. I was not aware that it became a scandal. We did not like it in and of itself, and we told the man to shave it off.

MR. ROONEY. Where is that man now?

MR. BLACK. He is still in Rome, sir, beardless.

MR. ROONEY. But still riding the motor scooter?

MR. BLACK. Yes, you may be interested to know that after he bought the motor scooter the Ambassador in Rome saw it, and said "This is something I always wanted," and the Ambassador rode around the block on the Via Veneto on that same motor scooter.

MR. ROONEY. Highly interesting.

MR. BLACK. Scooters are a normal way of travel in Italy. I do not think it is improper for people to ride motor scooters in Rome.

All this went on during hearings on the Commerce Department request to have the USTS $3 million annual budget upped to $4.7 million.

Mr. Black stated that at least 12 countries, including small nations, such as Ireland and Greece, spend more money on travel promotion than does the United States, which, on a per capita or per-foreign-visitor basis, is near the bottom of the list. Expenditure for promoting the Visit USA program has remained at $3 million since the formation of USTS in 1961, while the budget for the Canadian Government Travel Bureau was being increased from $3 million in 1961 to $8 million in 1965. Senator Jacob A. Javits (R-N.Y.) introduced a bill late in 1965 to increase the USTS budget to $15 million, and the Travel Gap Study Group of the National Association of Manufacturers came up with a recommendation that the budget be increased substantially. Nevertheless, Mr. Rooney's subcommittee turned down the proposed increase.

Despite this handicap, the USTS campaign to attract more visitors and Discover America's drive to make U.S. travel more attractive are both gaining momentum. USTS has keyed its

and New York City's Rockefeller Center (l), colonial Williamsburg, Va. (r).

New York Convention & Visitors Bureau

Colonial Williamsburg

1967 campaign closely with the United Nations proclamation of 1967 as International Tourist Year, designed to dramatize travel as "the passport to peace" and travel's vital economic importance as the largest single item in world trade. (Travel was an $11,500,000,000 industry in 1965.) Discussion is now under way on possible reciprocal waiving of tourist visas during International Tourist Year, which could conceivably pave the way for eventual elimination of visa requirements for pleasure travel between friendly nations. USTS also hopes to convince many European and Latin-American travelers to take side trips within the United States on their way to and from Montreal's Expo 67, and its efforts should be helped by new regulations waiving visa requirements for visitors staying in the United States no more than five days en route to or from other destinations.

USTS is making its vigorous sales pitch out of offices in London, Paris, Frankfurt, Rome, Mexico City, São Paulo, Bogota, Sydney and Tokyo. USTS representatives call on thousands of travel agents and airline and steamship companies in their territories. In 1966 they handled hundreds of thousands of visits, phone calls and letters from people who wished to spend their holidays touring the United States.

Since there was no single event on which to base its promotion (such as the New York World's Fair in 1964-65, the Montreal fair in 1967 and the Olympic Games in Mexico City and the Hemisfair in San Antonio in 1968), USTS chose Festival USA '66 as its theme, focusing attention on the face of America at its best, happy and relaxed at the pageants, fairs, rodeos, carnivals, regattas, ceremonials and other special community events held throughout the country all year long. More than 19.5 million readers saw Festival USA advertisements in 49 publications in Europe, Latin America, the South Pacific and Japan.

Meanwhile, U.S. private industry was doing its part. Airlines, railroads and bus lines instituted special fares for overseas visitors; tour operators and travel agents cooperated on special Visit USA tour programs; and hotels added foreign-language personnel to aid visitors from abroad.

USTS is working with American Express in bringing leading overseas travel agents to the United States on familiarization tours, and with transatlantic airlines in setting up trips for European travel writers and other journalists. Turning their attention to business travel, USTS and Discover America, Inc., are working toward the holding of international congresses and meetings in the United States. The two organizations are also encouraging American firms operating abroad to bring foreign employees and associates to the United States for conventions, indoctrination tours and vacations and as prizes in sales and production incentive programs.

TRUMAN, HARRY S. Former President Harry Truman was honored during 1966 with the groundbreaking in July for the Truman Center for the Advancement of Peace at Hebrew University in Jerusalem. He had planned to attend the ceremony but decided against it on the advice of his doctor.

On Jan. 20, President Johnson flew to Independence, Mo., to participate in a ceremony at the Truman Library, launching the Truman center in Israel. Chief Justice Earl Warren also spoke. Truman, in a prepared speech delivered by a friend, stated "it is all too obvious that if we do not abolish war on this earth, then surely, one day, war will abolish us from the earth."

In May, for Truman's 82d birthday celebration, Johnson phoned the former chief executive to tell him of a proclamation he had issued extending "the admiration and gratitude of all our people" to the Missourian. In late July, Truman was forced to enter a hospital because of an intestinal disorder. He was discharged in August, however, and his doctors reported he was making a satisfactory recovery.

On Aug. 28, Truman caused a stir by issuing a statement expressing strong concern about the "tight money" situation facing the U.S. economy. He said the drastic rise in interest rates could lead to a "serious depression." The statement was hailed by critics of the administration's economic policies in Congress; these critics said Truman fought the Korean war without permitting soaring interest rates.

JOSEPH W. HALL, JR.
Washington Bureau, THE ASSOCIATED PRESS

The Trumans receive Medicare cards #1 and #2.
UPI

At Moscow parade schoolchildren join (l to r) Malinovsky, Brezhnev, Kosygin, Podgorny.

UNION OF SOVIET SOCIALIST REPUBLICS

By WILLIAM L. RYAN
Special Correspondent
THE ASSOCIATED PRESS

In the 49th year of communist power, the collective leadership of the Union of Soviet Socialist Republics rolled along a sometimes bumpy road with a look of stability. Overall, the year appeared more truly collective than any preceding one. Surely it was more so than the rule of Nikita S. Khrushchev who, holding the posts of premier and first secretary of the Communist Party, had considerably more personal power than either of the men who shared the two positions after Khrushchev's fall in October 1964.

Leonid Ilyich Brezhnev, bearing the resurrected title of general secretary of the party, and Aleksei Nikolayevich Kosygin, as chairman of the Council of Ministers, in many respects had turned the leadership inward to the pressing domestic problems of the Soviet Union. There was less emphasis in 1966 than ever before on the world goals of communism. Indeed, under the post-Khrushchev leadership, the U.S.S.R. appeared to seek stability abroad rather than violence, since the stability tended to make it less difficult for the party to concentrate on the task it had cut out for itself: to build the economy of the huge nation of 233 million to a point where it might hope to compete in most areas with the U.S. economy.

The Party

The 23d Congress. For the new regime, the year's most important event was the Soviet Communist Party's 23d Congress. It remained businesslike from start to finish, even though it was plagued by the deep split in world communism.

In advance of the Congress, there had been much speculation inside and outside the U.S.S.R. over signs of neo-Stalinism. The speculation increased when the Congress dropped the term "First Secretary" for its chief official, and returned to the title of "General Secretary"; Stalin had been the last to hold that title. Also, the Congress dropped the name Presidium for its ruling body, and returned to the Stalin-era term, Politburo. Neo-Stalinism, however, failed to materialize to any significant extent. General Secretary Brezhnev's powers plainly were even more limited than Khrushchev's had been. As for the Politburo, the smaller group of 11 full members was more manageable as a central policy-making body than the larger Presidium had been.

Top Men of the U.S.S.R. The Congress swept away much of the remnants of the Khrushchev era. Khrushchev himself was divested of all his posts. The Politburo now was made up of the general secretary, the premier and three "first" deputy premiers: K. T. Mazurov, A. P. Kirilenko and D. S. Polyansky; N. V. Podgorny, president of the Supreme Soviet (Parliament) Presidium and in effect U.S.S.R. president; M. A. Suslov, the veteran theoretician and party war-horse; G. I. Voronov, premier of the big Russian Federal Republic; A. N. Shelepin, a younger, rising star in the party firmament; P. Y. Shelest, party chief in the Ukrainian Republic; and A. Y. Pelshe, party chief in the Latvian Republic.

Alternates were P. N. Demichev, V. V. Grishin, V. P. Mzhavanadze of Georgia, S. R.

Rashidov of Uzbekistan, V. V. Shcherbitsky of the Ukraine, D. A. Kunayev of Kazakhstan, P. M. Masherov of Byelorussia and D. F. Ustinov, the Soviet arms czar.

To the powerful Central Committee Secretariat were named Brezhnev, as the general secretary, Suslov, Shelepin, Kirilenko, Demichev, Ustinov, Y. V. Andropov, who was responsible for relations with communist parties abroad; B. N. Ponomarev, chairman of the Central Committee's international department; I. V. Kapitonov, responsible for leadership cadres; and F. D. Kulakov, secretary for agriculture.

Pelshe was named to head the party control commission, now not nearly so powerful as it had been a year before under Shelepin. The party also named a central auditing commission of 65 members, with N. A. Murayeva as chairman.

The Congress approved the election of 195 full members and 165 alternates, a total of 360, to the Central Committee. At the last Congress, the 22d in 1961, there had been 175 full members and 155 alternates, a total of 330. The Congress disclosed that the party now was made up of 12 million members and alternates, a sharp rise from the time of the 22d Congress, when the total had been 9.7 million.

Two elder leaders were dropped from membership of the top ruling body. Anastas I. Mikoyan, 71, the durable survivor of many a convulsion in the Stalin and Khrushchev eras, stepped down from the Politburo, but he remained much in evidence, apparently as an adviser. Nikolai M. Shvernik, 78, a former president, also stepped down.

Ties with the old Bolsheviks were just about gone. Brezhnev, who had been a political commissar in the armed forces in Stalin's day, and Kosygin, who had been the youngest member of Stalin's Politburo, were among the last real links to the Stalin era itself. Much power was evident among younger men such as Shelepin, Polyansky and Mazurov.

Shelepin was one of the most-discussed figures in the leadership. A former secret-police chief, he emerged in 1966, according to the evidence, as a sort of czar over consumer-goods production. Since this was at the center of party and government attention, Shelepin could be counted, at 47, as a most important official and a leading contender to head the party at some future date. To all appearances, his main job was to concentrate on party work in the Secretariat and Politburo, the main seats of power in the Soviet Union.

In August, the Supreme Soviet of 1,517 deputies confirmed the reelection of Kosygin as chairman of the Council of Ministers (premier) on the nomination by Brezhnev. This appeared to underscore the stability and continuity of the post-Khrushchev regime. Mazurov, Polyansky and Kirilenko were reaffirmed as first deputy premiers. The session also approved the reappointment of a council of about 85 ministers.

The Government appeared to be, basically, a "Russia First" regime. Its attention was riveted on a program to build the domestic economy so it might measure up and effectively compete with capitalism, even if that meant using capitalist tools. Influence abroad would be sought with Soviet national interests in mind, first and foremost.

Ministers and economic bosses were warned that the U.S.S.R. was lagging in its bid to rival the U.S. economy. Kosygin, issuing the admonition, noted that the Government was far from satisfied with Soviet gains in agriculture and light industry, that improvement in quality and quantity of consumer goods was far too slow.

Ministers and economic bosses would be required to sweep away bureaucratic roadblocks. Profit and profitability would be the "supreme criteria of the economy." Kosygin supported such capitalist ideas as attractive packaging and "convincing advertising," to keep goods moving from the store shelves. He also called for more concentration on such measures as material incentives for workers and bonuses for farmers and industrial workers.

The Economy

The Liberman Reforms. The momentum of an economic-reform movement in the Soviet Union remained strong.

In April the 23d Congress ratified an economic-reform program aimed at overcoming such major ailments as chronic shortages of consumer goods and goods needed by industries. The principal target was the old bureaucracy, which had caused major distribution problems and enormous waste. In the past, the stress had been on quantity—meeting the fixed, bureaucratically decreed quotas—rather than on quality. Warehouses had been bursting with unsalable goods.

The views of one of the principal spokesmen for reform, Prof. Yevsei Liberman, were put to the test. Reform involved the use of market-economy principles, with less emphasis on centralized, bureaucratic planning. There was considerable opposition from the entrenched bureaucracy, and the Congress appeared to have been obliged to reach a sort of compromise, retaining centralized planning, but introducing more liberal rules based on free-market principles. At the same time, the Congress decided that an overhaul of the whole system of industrial planning was needed in order to bring in such new elements as material incentives and bonuses, and to eliminate petty bureaucratic domination over industrial management. Local managers would get broader authority to gauge their production in terms of salability, of supply and demand and, thus, of profitability. This fell short of Liberman's aims, but economic reformers considered the changes a victory.

Early Successes. The new system could be credited with some successes, notably in attitudes of factory managements. It appeared to encourage more efficient production. But the struggle continued between advocates of total centralization of planning and those supporting greater discretion at lower levels. Apprehension remained in high places that relaxation of centralized planning might be a long-range danger to Communist Party control over all aspects of Soviet life. Thus, the party continued to insist on some restrictive measures, tending to negate some of the gains. As a result, the success of the experiment was regarded as limited.

The reformers, nevertheless, must have had important party support. In September the monthly theoretical journal, *Kommunist,* came out in support of price flexibility. It backed the idea of freely fluctuating prices, and of a system reflecting supply and demand, distribution costs and production costs. It also seemed to back more independence and discretion for managers. All this, however, failed to remove a high degree of bashfulness among Soviet economists in discussion of money in terms of value.

Early in the year the Government had approved a decree transferring a group of enterprises to the new system of planning and economic stimulation. In that first group were 43 enterprises of 17 industrial ministries, assigned to work with new principles. Rates of deduction from profits to the personnel fund, the social-cultural fund, the housing-construction fund and the development fund were raised in order to encourage incentive. All showed increased productivity, permitting managers to cut staffs and production costs. There was heavy stress on sales and profits.

By midsummer 400 enterprises were involved in the new system. If the experiment was successful, the prospect was that all Soviet industry would be gradually shifted to the new order. A key to the system was that managers would make some important decisions themselves, taking into account local conditions and

Tass from Sovfoto
Fashion from Leningrad: a sports outfit for motoring.

demands, without having to refer everything to the center of authority in Moscow.

Record Grain Crop. At the 23d Congress, Kosygin contended that Khrushchev's Seven-Year Plan had included goals not economically justifiable. Thus, he said, targets for 1970 had to be lowered in certain industrial branches. The boast of catching up with and surpassing

Tractors ready for shipment from Kharkov Tractor Works.
UPI

the United States by 1970, so often voiced by Khrushchev, was forgotten. Instead, the Soviet press expressed some alarm over a drop in the growth rate of the economy.

Nevertheless, consumer-goods production was up. So were wages, by a modest percentage. There was an overall drop in industrial output, which did not, however, affect sensitive industries connected with national defense. There was no substantial narrowing of the gap between U.S. and Soviet gross national products. Soviet citizens seemed better off all the time, but their wants and demands grew apace, putting new pressure on the regime.

In agriculture, the picture looked far better than a year before. The Government said in September that grain harvest would be larger than the average—130 million metric tons—of the preceding five years. The actual harvest was even better. In October, the Ministry of Agriculture was able to announce that the grain crop would be a record 160–65 million metric tons, a 30 per cent increase over 1965.

Budget. In mid-December the Government announced a "guns before butter" budget for 1967 which promised to slow down the consumer-economy program in which the public had placed high hopes, even though stress once again was laid on consumer-goods production. Defense spending for 1967 would represent 13.2 per cent of the whole announced budget.

The defense spending would be the highest level for more than a decade, a total of 14,500,000,000 rubles. (Moscow values the ruble at $1.11.) This was an increase of 1,100,000,000 rubles, or 8 per cent, over the previous year. And, as a rule, publicly announced defense-spending figures are only about half what the Soviet Union puts out for military purposes.

All this reflected a hardening Soviet attitude toward the United States, much of it traceable to Vietnam. Announcing the budget, Finance Minister Vasily F. Garbuzov noted that because of U.S. policy, "the international situation is aggravated and the danger of new war is increased."

Garbuzov announced a total spending figure of 109,700,000,000 rubles and a total revenue of 110,100,000,000 for 1967, which, he said, would permit further increase in living standards while "strengthening the might of our state." He singled out agricultural production as the most important task for 1967, and a total of 13,500,000,000 rubles would be invested in that sector.

Deputy Premier Nikolai K. Baibakov, chairman of the State Planning Committee (Gosplan), conceded there would be shortages in the consumer sector of some goods such as timber, paper, chemicals and iron in the year to come, but pledged the Government to "improve the quality and assortment of consumer goods."

Total industrial production in 1966, Baibakov said, would show an 8.4 per cent increase over 1965, indicating the economy was off to a good start as the new Five-Year Plan began.

Social Problems

Drive Against Crime. The Soviet party and Government took a serious view of the growth of crime and "hooliganism" throughout the nation, and the concomitant problem: pressure from below for liberalization of the regime. Frequently, the press complained of the rising incidence of alcoholism, and some sociologists traced it to boredom among youth. Possibly this was a result of shorter workdays in factories. Some Soviet sociologists said there were not enough attractive pursuits for leisure time —that what was available in films, television and the like contained so much lecturing and badgering that these outlets were largely ignored in favor of antisocial forms of letting off steam.

The authorities mounted a new and determined drive on crime, particularly among youth. They decreed heavier penalties, speedier investigations and trials, increased police power for the militia and wider latitude for courts and prosecutors.

Pravda estimated that hooliganism accounted for 44 per cent of all offenses involving serious bodily injury. It complained that the crime wave caused widespread public nervousness. The press clamored for action against "drunken good-for-nothings." An experiment of the Khrushchev era with voluntary "people's militia" patrols had accomplished next to nothing. The most common crimes were murder, rape, robbery with violence, theft, bribery and juvenile delinquency. Severe penalties, including the firing squad, had failed to reduce the crime rate, which was all the more vexing for the fact that the party had proclaimed five years before, at the 22d Congress, that as the U.S.S.R. moved in the direction of communism, crime would become an anachronism. Instead, it was on the increase, and sharply.

In September a "Ministry of Public Order" was created to deal with such problems. Heading it, Nikolai A. Shchelokov, 56, became a sort of new-era police chief, successor to the Minister of Internal Affairs, but far from inspiring the terror that the initials MVD had evoked.

The regime worried, too, about intellectuals and their pressure for liberalization. In advance

Students at a New Year's ball held in the Kremlin, Moscow.

of the 23d Congress, a group of cultural leaders appealed to the party to guard against any return to the ways of Stalin. The appeal noted tendencies toward partial rehabilitation of Stalin's image. It deplored sentences imposed on Yuli Daniel and Andrei Sinyavsky, writers who in February had been sentenced to hard labor for exporting anti-Soviet writings. The press had denounced the two as hacks "consumed with hate for the Soviet system."

Intellectuals' Influence. The prosecution of the writers seemed one of a number of mea-

Soviet poet Yevgeny Yevtushenko made a U.S. tour in the fall of 1966. The picture below shows him giving a poetry recital at Queens College in New York City.
Both photos UPI

Russian youths jam Red Square protesting Vietnam War.

Rockets on display at May Day 1966 celebration, Red Square, Moscow.

sures to assert party control over the intellectuals. The party, however, failed to come up with a solution to the rising opposition among the younger generation to harsh party rule.

The appellant intellectuals, in fact, warned that measures such as the sentencing of the writers endangered the development of Soviet society whose people, they claimed, now were too mature to accept throwbacks to the Stalin "personality cult." In particular, they expressed worry about the impact on young people, but they also noted bad publicity abroad for the Soviet image. They would consider, they said, any tendency to rehabilitate Stalin as a surrender to the Red Chinese in the ideological dispute. Probably the appeal had an effect.

At the Congress there was no mention of the rehabilitation of Stalin. Only vague straws in the wind pointed to party worry about its authority. For all that, however, a cautious readjustment of Stalin's place in Soviet history was under way. Plays critical of the Stalin era disappeared from theaters. Stalin's excesses tended to be excused in the press, on the grounds that in the early days of Soviet power, iron discipline had been necessary.

The U.S.S.R.'s military establishment threw its weight into the argument against the liberals. Military publications demanded that So-

viet literature show "the greatness of our time," and that it stop questioning Stalin's motives for the things he did in wartime. The military press demanded more patriotic and military education of youth by artists and writers. Whatever the party did now, it appeared likely that it would have to accept as a fact the strong, influential forces among intellectuals who demanded a reasonable degree of individual freedom and the right to think for themselves. The writers' trial was a hint that the party feared its grip on the system was imperiled by searchers, questioners, the disillusioned, who wanted to remove the old taint of Russian barbarism so sharply silhouetted against the door of cultivated Western Europe.

Armed Forces

There was a suggestion of restiveness among Soviet military men because of Vietnam. The Americans were getting all the experience with the new gadgetry of war. Soviet surface-to-air missiles and MiG fighters had been less effective than they might have been against U.S. air power. This could cause apprehension about Soviet defenses.

On the other hand, there was a growing suspicion of Red China and worry over future threats from that direction. This was evident in a series of deliberate leaks about movement of Soviet troops to the China borders.

Soviet defenses, however, were still deployed in a manner suggesting that the potential enemies were in the West. The military announced that Moscow and Leningrad were being ringed by defensive-missile sites. According to Western intelligence, similar defenses were being constructed all over the U.S.S.R. to protect industrial areas, at which U.S. land-based and sea-based missiles might be aimed. The deployment suggested a Soviet attempt to ensure interception of hostile missiles hundreds of miles from target areas.

The Russians were estimated to have about 300 operational intercontinental ballistic missiles, 700 medium-range ballistic missiles and 150 fleet missiles, a small overall increase since 1965. The total rocket-force personnel under Marshal Nikolai I. Krylov was estimated at 200,000. The Air Force had about 10,000 operational aircraft and 500,000 men, no substantial change from 1965. The strategic bomber force was about 1,100; fighters numbered slightly under 5,000. Land forces showed no significant change, but there was a buildup of nuclear submarines to about 50, supplementing a conventional submarine fleet of 350, of which 40 could carry missiles. The total manpower of the forces was about 3,150,000, half of which were general-purpose ground and home-defense forces.

In midsummer there was evidence of disagreement in high places on the question of investment in defense. Despite increased emphasis on agriculture and consumer goods, the priority still went to heavy industry, which builds the sinews of armed might.

Science

Throughout 1966 there were no manned Soviet space shots. The last had been Voskhod 2 in March 1965. But the space program hinted at a determination to get a man on the moon, perhaps as early as 1968, and the Russians may have been concentrating on experiments with craft that ultimately would permit the realization of that goal.

Soviet scientists achieved history's first soft landing on the moon's surface in February with Luna 9, an unmanned space station. Its instruments reported intact, it sent back facsimile pictures. In April the Russians orbited Luna 10 around the moon, and in August sent up Luna 11, described as having "an entire orchestra of rocket engines." That 3,616-pound ship orbited the moon and sent back picture signals. Then, in October, Luna 12 sent back yet more pictures of the moon's surface. Pos-

Tass from Sovfoto

Photodiagram of Luna 12, launched October 1966.

sibly its orbit was closer to the moon's surface than that of any other spacecraft. Luna 13 soft-landed on the moon late in December.

Venus 3, launched in November 1965, reached the surface of the earth's sister planet in March, the news agency Tass said, but it seemed likely that the one-ton satellite crash-landed and burned. In July, Proton 3, a space laboratory weighing more than 12 tons, was launched on a mission to study spectra and charge composition of particles of high and super-high energies in cosmic rays. It was a continuation of a program begun in 1965.

Western scientists attached significance to three launchings beginning in September. The first was a large vehicle that exploded and broke into many pieces while in orbit. A second vehicle, launched early in November, also broke into pieces. The Russians announced neither of these shots publicly, but did announce a third. This was Cosmos 133, another in a long series of launchings begun in 1961. There was some thought that it was a test of a new sort of craft, possibly intended eventually to carry "cosmonauts."

Foreign Relations

Stability Sought. Soviet policy seemed to involve a quest for stability, not only in Western

Tass from Sovfoto

Above: Kosygin brought together India's Shastri (l) and Pakistan's Khan (r) for Tashkent summit meeting. Below: A Soviet delegation prepares to go to Hanoi. L to r: Suslov, Kirilenko, Shelepin, and Polyansky.

Sovfoto

Europe but in Asia as well. That did not signify abandonment of world-revolutionary goals, but it did indicate that national interests came first. Stability in Europe would permit the Russians to turn inward sufficiently to press ahead with internal economic development.

This was equally true with regard to Asia. Soviet efforts there clearly demonstrated that stability coincided with Russian national interest. Premier Kosygin was credited with a diplomatic coup when he brought together the leaders of India and Pakistan and persuaded them, at Tashkent in Uzbekistan, to put an end to their dangerous war over Kashmir.

The move enraged Red China, obviously wishing the Indo-Pakistani war to continue. To Peking, the Tashkent Agreement was a new indication of Soviet-U.S. plotting to contain Chinese ambitions. These suspicions were reinforced soon after when party chief Brezhnev, with an impressive delegation, went to the Mongolian People's Republic (Outer Mongolia) to conclude a mutual defense pact. Outer Mongolia is a buffer between U.S.S.R. and Red China. The agreement may have been pointed only at Peking, which had been trying to influence and subvert the Mongolians.

Thus, Soviet-Chinese relations, already near a breaking point, worsened even more. Soviet-Chinese trade was at its lowest point in 16 years. Export of Soviet petroleum products to China stopped completely and Peking turned to Rumania for such needs.

Yet another diplomatic thrust aggravated these relations. At the beginning of the year, Alexander N. Shelepin, member of the Soviet Politburo, went to communist North Vietnam. Promptly he was denounced by Peking as a tool of U.S.-Soviet plotting. The visit had coincided with a U.S. pause in the bombing of North Vietnam, and Red China's official party newspaper, *The People's Daily,* said: "The Soviet Union obviously was tipped off in one form or another by the United States about its pause in bombing, hoping the Soviet revisionists would exert influence to bring Hanoi to a conference."

Gains in the West. While Moscow's troubles with Peking complicated its problems in the world of communism, its soft-sell policy seemed to pay dividends in the West. It dimmed memories of the past and produced a widespread feeling that, so far as Western Europe was concerned, peace had broken out, and a prosperous public could go confidently about the business of easy living. Absence of tension in Europe helped a process threatening disintegration of the North Atlantic Treaty Organization, shaken by the withdrawal of France.

Kosygin (2d from l) at French hunting party hosted by De Gaulle (c).

Soviet policy in the West centered in France and President Charles de Gaulle. The latter went to Moscow in June for an 11-day visit, and he and Soviet leaders issued a joint statement saying their common goals included normalizing and developing relations among all European nations. They examined the Vietnam situation, agreed that it caused much concern, and supported a settlement based on the 1954 Geneva agreements, excluding all foreign intervention.

In December, Premier Kosygin paid a state visit to France. Once again the two sides agreed in general about Vietnam and the need for decreasing tensions. But Kosygin's visit fell far short of triumph. He failed to crack De Gaulle's opposition to recognizing Communist East Germany, nor did he find any way around the basic disagreement of the two on questions involving European security. The Russians contended that any move toward German reunification would fail unless East Germany was recognized by all as sovereign.

Soviet policy was sufficiently flexible to permit the Russians in December to agree to terms of a treaty, drafted in the United Nations, to bar weapons of mass destruction from craft orbiting the earth and from celestial bodies. The agreement was hailed as historic. For the Russians it meant also that another nail was driven into the coffin of communist unity, since the Chinese soon would point to it as another evidence of Soviet-U.S. collusion.

The Communist Bloc. Within the communist world, Soviet policy makers encountered vexing problems. Rumania in particular made it clear, during meetings of the Warsaw Pact nations, that it no longer considered Moscow the only source of authority for the whole world communist movement.

At the 9th Bulgarian Communist Party Congress, attended by representatives of 74 parties, and again at the 9th Hungarian Party Congress, attended by 32 foreign parties, Rumania balked at a Soviet effort to call a world communist conference, which could castigate the Chinese leadership. The move also was resisted by the Italians, Yugoslavs, Cubans, Japanese, North Koreans and North Vietnamese. A conference may be held in 1967, but it will probably move cautiously on any condemnation of China.

Moscow reentered the polemics arena with China late in November. It suggested that the stream of abuse from Peking had stretched Kremlin patience to the breaking point. The vigor of the attacks in *Pravda*, denouncing Mao Tse-tung as a splitter, was unmatched since the Khrushchev days.

As the year drew to a close, Soviet policy remained one of cautiously seeking to hold back tensions in Western Europe, and even of hesitant attention to U.S. approaches. But Moscow's dealings with Washington were complicated by Vietnam. The Soviet leaders were in a difficult position. A capitalist nation was attacking a communist one—North Vietnam. In such circumstances, the Russians felt obliged to turn back a number of appeals, such as those from the leaders of Britain and India, and from Secretary-General U Thant of the United Nations, to take the initiative in a search for a road to peace in Vietnam.

UNITED NATIONS

By BRUCE W. MUNN
Chief UN Correspondent
UNITED PRESS INTERNATIONAL

Southeast Asia, the Secretary-Generalship and sanctions were the United Nations keynotes during the year 1966.

Sanctions. On Dec. 16, 1966, the United Nations Security Council, for the first time in its history, voted mandatory economic sanctions against a government. It did so against Rhodesia's white minority Government, in rebellion against Britain. This represents a step that many believed might be decisive in the history of international organization.

In 1935, the League of Nations voted economic sanctions seeking to force Benito Mussolini's Italy to end its war against defenseless Ethiopia. The sanctions failed, and in due course, so did the League.

The UN founders put their emphasis on collective military security to keep offenders in line. The United Nations was able to use this means effectively in 1950 in Korea, because of the self-ordained absence of the Soviet Union.

The sanctions against Prime Minister Ian D. Smith's Rhodesia Government, sponsored in the Council by Britain, were adopted by an 11-0 vote, with the Soviet Union, France, Mali and Bulgaria abstaining. Sanctions provided for an embargo on 10 major cash-earning exports and a complete stoppage of oil imports into the rebellious African territory, which unilaterally had proclaimed its independence of Britain on Nov. 11, 1965.

African efforts to toughen the sanctions were voted down, and African diplomats openly expressed disappointment. Chief criticism was that the resolution—to which an amendment calling on Britain to use "all means" to enforce the sanctions was rejected—carried no penalty for failure to comply with the compulsory order of the Council. South Africa and Portugal, whose territory flanks Rhodesia on three sides, announced they would not enforce sanctions.

Vietnam. Virtually everyone in the various organs of the United Nations talked about the Vietnam war, but no one achieved anything to hasten its end.

The United States put the Vietnam conflict on the Security Council agenda in February, but no member showed inclination to discuss it and a formal debate was not held during the year.

Secretary-General Thant maintained throughout the year his standing three-point peace proposal calling for (1) an end to U.S. bombing of North Vietnam; (2) descalation of military activity by all sides in South Vietnam; (3) peace talks to include the Vietcong and its political parent, the National Liberation Front.

The United States went far toward accepting Thant's plan when Ambassador Arthur J.

Secretary-General Thant and U.S. Ambassador Arthur J. Goldberg confer at UN during Security Council's debate on Jordan's complaint of Israeli aggression.

United Nations

Afghanistan's Abdul Raham Pazhwak, president General Assembly, presides (c, rostrum).

Goldberg addressed the General Assembly on Sept. 22. Goldberg asked North Vietnam for assurances, "privately or otherwise," that it would effect a "corresponding and appropriate descalation" if the United States ended its bombing of the North. Goldberg also asked if, in response to a prior cessation of the U.S. bombing, North Vietnam would end its own "military activities against South Vietnam," and if it would agree to a timetable for phased withdrawal of "all external forces" from the South. Participation of the Vietcong in peace talks, he reiterated, would not be "an insurmountable obstacle."

There was no reply from Hanoi.

On Dec. 19, Goldberg, after a conference with President Johnson and Henry Cabot Lodge, U.S. ambassador to Saigon, formally asked Thant to "take whatever steps you consider necessary" to start Vietnam peace negotiations. Two days later, in response to a session-closing appeal by Assembly President Abdul Rahman Pazhwak of Afghanistan, he pledged U.S. readiness to "establish appropriate contacts" for truce talks.

As the year ended, Thant engaged in "quiet diplomacy"—on the substance of which he gave no hint—to carry out the U.S. appeal.

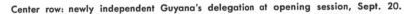

Center row: newly independent Guyana's delegation at opening session, Sept. 20.

In a letter to Goldberg on Dec. 30, the Secretary-General said that if the United States ended its bombing of North Vietnam, and all parties extended the New Year cease-fire, "I feel hopeful that thereafter some favorable developments may follow."

Goldberg replied, the next day, that the United States was ready to order "a prior end to all bombing of North Vietnam the moment there is an assurance, private or otherwise, that there would be a reciprocal response toward peace from North Vietnam."

Although the Security Council formally put Vietnam on its agenda, its major preoccupation of 1966 was a call to Britain to prevent ships from carrying oil destined for Rhodesia to the Mozambique port of Beira, and the continuing Arab-Israeli conflict.

In August, it rejected a resolution that would have condemned Israel's July 14 attack on Syria. On Nov. 4, the Soviet Union used its 104th veto—its first since 1964—to kill a resolution critical of Syria. On Nov. 25, the Council "censured" Israel for a major military action against Jordan, declaring further acts of reprisal would not be tolerated.

The Secretary-Generalship. Thant himself spent most of 1966 in indecision about serving another term as secretary-general. He decried his position, as a buffer between the big powers against whom he struck out from time to time with impartiality, as that of a "glorified clerk." He announced in September that he would not "offer himself" for a new term. He agreed later to serve to the end of the 1966 Assembly session, and finally, on Dec. 2, accepted appointment to a new term ending Dec. 31, 1971. His appointment was made by a 102-0 vote of the world parliament.

It was reported that Thant was free to resign whenever he felt he was not gaining the cooperation he demanded. Although there was no public announcement, it was reported that negotiations among the major Security Council powers brought general acceptance of Thant's demands for help in making the United Nations politically and financially stable, for transforming it into a potent peace-keeping force, for stepping up its economic activities, for seeking East-West *détente* and for giving Thant a generally free hand in peace initiatives.

Thant, as he said in his speech accepting a new term, pursued his Vietnam peace efforts in a "personal capacity"—meaning that he was not bound to report to any UN organ.

Despite the era of good feeling that followed Thant's December acceptance, little had been done toward furthering his goals by year-end.

The Assembly was unable to agree on the UN role in future peace-keeping activities or means to finance it, and the whole question was put off to a special session to be called by April 1967.

The UN deficit, variously estimated upwards from $30 million, remained. The expected voluntary contributions to erase it were still not forthcoming from the Soviet Union and France, the chief debtors whose refusal to pay Assembly-levied peace-keeping assessments created the political and financial crisis of 1964.

The General Assembly. The 21st General Assembly raced through a session of exactly three months, passing 115 resolutions on a 98-item agenda but making less impact than usual on the world's information media.

Its major achievements included:

Adoption of a resolution "terminating" the mandate over South-West Africa given South Africa by the League of Nations after World War I and appointing a 14-nation committee to determine the means by which the United Nations should take over the territory. The committee is to report to a special session to be held by April 1967. The vote was 114–2, with Portugal and South Africa voting against the resolution, and France, Malawi and the United Kingdom abstaining.

Refusal to seat Communist China and expel Chiang Kai-shek's Nationalist Chinese from the United Nations and all its agencies. The vote, contrasting with the 47–47 tie in 1965, was 57-46 with 17 abstentions. The Assembly also rejected a proposal for a year's study of a "two China" plan.

Unanimous agreement commending a U.S.-Soviet treaty on peaceful uses of outer space.

Approval of international covenants putting enforcement power behind the Universal Declaration of Human Rights adopted in 1948.

Creation of a UN Capital Development Fund to supplement existing sources of financial assistance to underdeveloped countries. The vote was 76–19 with 14 abstentions. But, significantly, the United States, Britain, France, the Soviet Union and virtually all the powers financially able to contribute to such a fund failed to vote in favor of its establishment.

Admission of Barbados, Botswana (formerly Bechuanaland), Lesotho (formerly Basutoland) and Guyana (formerly British Guiana), raising the UN membership to 122 countries but creating a growing unrest about the continued creation of "ministates" with voting rights equal to the greatest powers.

Welcoming Indonesia—the only country ever to quit the United Nations—back into the organization after a 21-month absence.

UNITED NATIONS MEMBERSHIP

SECURITY COUNCIL MEMBERS AND CHIEF REPRESENTATIVES
*Permanent members

ARGENTINA	José Maria Ruda	DENMARK	Hans R. Tabor	MALI	Moussa L. Keita
BRAZIL	José Sette Camara	ETHIOPIA	Lij E. Makonnen	NIGERIA	S. O. Adebo
BULGARIA	Milko Tarabanov	FRANCE*	Roger Seydoux	U.S.S.R.*	Nikolai T. Fedorenko
CANADA	George Ignatieff	INDIA	Gopalaswami Parthasarathi	UNITED KINGDOM*	Lord Caradon
CHINA*	Liu Chieh	JAPAN	Akira Matsui	UNITED STATES*	Arthur J. Goldberg

MEMBER NATIONS AND CHIEF REPRESENTATIVES

AFGHANISTAN	Abdul Rahman Pazhwak	KUWAIT	Rashid A. Al-Rashid
ALBANIA	Halim Budo	LAOS	Khamking Souvanlasy
ALGERIA	Tewfik Bouattoura	LEBANON	Georges Hakim
ARGENTINA	José Maria Ruda	LESOTHO	Albert Mohale
AUSTRALIA	Patrick Shaw	LIBERIA	Nathan Barnes
AUSTRIA	Kurt Waldheim	LIBYA	Wahbi El-Bouri
BARBADOS	vacant	LUXEMBOURG	Pierre Wurth
BELGIUM	Constant Schuurmans	MALAGASY REPUBLIC	Louis Rakotomalala
BOLIVIA	Fernando Ortiz Sanz	MALAWI	Bridger W. Katenga
BOTSWANA	Z. K. Matthews	MALAYSIA	Radhakrishna Ramani
BRAZIL	José Sette Camara	MALDIVE ISLANDS	Ahamed Hilmy Didi
BULGARIA	Milko Tarabanov	MALI	Moussa L. Keita
BURMA	U Soe Tin	MALTA	Arvid Pardo
BURUNDI	Terence Nsanze	MAURITANIA	Abdallahi Ould Daddah
BYELORUSSIAN S.S.R.	Guerodot G. Tchernouchtchenko	MEXICO	Francisco Cuevas Cancino
CAMBODIA	Huot Sambath	MONGOLIA	Jhambalyn Banzar
CAMEROUN	Joseph N. Owono	MOROCCO	Dey Ould Sidi Baba
CANADA	George Ignatieff	NEPAL	Padma B. Khatri
CENTRAL AFRICAN REP.	Michel Gallin-Douathe	NETHERLANDS	J. G. de Beus
CEYLON	Merenna Jayaratne	NEW ZEALAND	Frank Corner
CHAD	Boukar Abdoul	NICARAGUA	Guillermo Sevilla-Sacasa
CHILE	José Piñera Carvallo	NIGER	Issoufou S. Djermakoye
CHINA	Liu Chieh	NIGERIA	S. O. Adebo
COLOMBIA	Alfonso Patiño	NORWAY	Edvard Hambro
CONGO, DEM. REP. OF THE	Théodore Idzumbuir	PAKISTAN	Syed Amjad Ali
CONGO, REPUBLIC OF THE	Jonas Mouanza	PANAMA	Aquilino Boyd
COSTA RICA	Luis D. Tinoco	PARAGUAY	Miguel Solano Lopez
CUBA	Ricardo Alarcon Quesada	PERU	Carlos Mackehenie
CYPRUS	Zenon Rossides	PHILIPPINES	Salvador P. Lopez
CZECHOSLOVAKIA	Milan Klusak	POLAND	Bohdan Tomorowicz
DAHOMEY	Louis Ignacio-Pinto	PORTUGAL	Antonio Patricio
DENMARK	Hans R. Tabor	RUMANIA	Gheorghe Diaconescu
DOMINICAN REPUBLIC	José Ramón Rodriguez	RWANDA	Canisius Mudenge
ECUADOR	Leopoldo Benites	SAUDI ARABIA	Jamil M. Baroody
EL SALVADOR	Hector Escobar Serrano	SENEGAL	Ousmane Socé Diop
ETHIOPIA	Lij E. Makonnen	SIERRA LEONE	Gershon B. O. Collier
FINLAND	Max Jakobson	SINGAPORE	Abu Bakar bin Pawanchee
FRANCE	Roger Seydoux	SOMALIA	Abdulrahim A. Farah
GABON	Jacques Biyogho	SOUTH AFRICA	Matthys I. Botha
GAMBIA	Vacant	SPAIN	Manuel Aznar
GHANA	F. S. Arkhurst	SUDAN	Fakhreddine Mohamed
GREECE	Alexis S. Liatis	SWEDEN	Sverker C. Astrom
GUATEMALA	Ramón Cadena Hernandez	SYRIAN ARAB REP.	George J. Tomeh
GUINEA	Achkar Marof	TANZANIA	John W. S. Malecela
GUYANA	John Carter	THAILAND	Anand Panyarachun
HAITI	Carlet R. Auguste	TOGO	Robert Ajavon
HONDURAS	Humberto Lopez Villamil	TRINIDAD-TOBAGO	P. V. J. Solomon
HUNGARY	Károly Csatorday	TUNISIA	Taïeb Slim
ICELAND	Hannes Kjartansson	TURKEY	Orhan Eralp
INDIA	Gopalaswami Parthasarathi	UGANDA	Apollo K. Kironde
INDONESIA	Abdullah Kamil	UKRAINIAN S.S.R.	Sergei T. Shevchenko
IRAN	Mehdi Vakil	U.S.S.R.	Nikolai T. Fedorenko
IRAQ	Kadhim Khalaf	UNITED ARAB REPUBLIC	Mohamed A. El Kony
IRELAND	Cornelius C. Cremin	UNITED KINGDOM	Lord Caradon
ISRAEL	Michael S. Comay	UNITED STATES	Arthur J. Goldberg
ITALY	Piero Vinci	UPPER VOLTA	Tensoré P. Rouamba
IVORY COAST	Siméon Ake	URUGUAY	Pedro P. Berro
JAMAICA	E. R. Richardson	VENEZUELA	Pedro Zuloaga
JAPAN	Akira Matsui	YEMEN	Vacant
JORDAN	Muhammad H. El-Farra	YUGOSLAVIA	Danilo Lekic
KENYA	Burudi Nabwera	ZAMBIA	Joseph B. Mwemba

Source: United Nations as of January, 1967

UNITED STATES: THE WASHINGTON SCENE

By J. F. terHORST
Washington Bureau Chief
THE DETROIT NEWS

Washington began 1966 on a high note. The national capital, indeed the free world, was caught up in the fever of President Johnson's Texas-size peace offensive in Vietnam. The heavily Democratic 89th Congress was returning for its second session, seemingly ready to swallow another big chunk of Great Society legislation. The nation's economy was gliding along in the sixth consecutive year of unparalleled prosperity.

But 1966 ended far short of its dawning promise. The fighting raged on in sticky Vietnam, with a record number of American troops in the field and no signs of peace from Hanoi. A balky Congress thwarted and diluted some of Mr. Johnson's key proposals. The President's personal popularity skidded to a poll-time low. The November midterm elections produced a surprising Republican resurgence that cast shadows toward the 1968 White House race. At year's close, the President went to his ranch in Texas to recuperate from minor surgery, and to mull the need for Federal tax increases and massive cuts in his Great Society programs to meet war costs in Asia and inflation at home.

Thus if 1965 was the year that Washington was dominated by Lyndon Baines Johnson, then 1966 was the year it was unnerved by critics—particularly on Vietnam, civil rights and rising prices—critics within Congress and his own Democratic Party, on the college campuses and in the squalid big-city ghettos; critics on Wall Street, within organized labor and down on the farm.

The United States and Vietnam

Perhaps no single thing was so omnipresent in Washington in 1966 as the Vietnam war. Except when a domestic crisis flared briefly now and then, the war was the consuming interest not only of the White House, the State Department and the Pentagon but also of Congress, the political parties and the world's news media.

Peace Offensive. The year was but two days old when the White House let the nation in on a secret. Ever since Christmas 1965, American bombers had been absent from the skies over North Vietnam. The United States was engaged in the most far-reaching effort yet to achieve a peaceful settlement in Vietnam. President Johnson dispatched American diplomats to every point of possible influence in order to convince Hanoi that the bombing lull could be made permanent if it would only agree to talk peace. Roving Ambassador W. Averell Harriman went to Warsaw, Yugoslavia and India. McGeorge Bundy, then the President's chief White House foreign-affairs specialist, went to Ottawa.

United Nations Ambassador Arthur Goldberg called on Pope Paul VI and the leaders of the Italian, French and British governments. Vice-President Hubert H. Humphrey, making the first of two Asian trips, spread the word to Japan, the Philippines, Taiwan, South Korea. Ambassador Foy Kohler consulted urgently with the Kremlin. Assistant Secretary of State G. Mennen Williams flew off to see the African nations, and Undersecretary of State Thomas Mann hurried to Mexico City. "Everything the administration is doing is designed to bring about conditions in which peace is possible," White House News Secretary Bill D. Moyers told reporters.

For 37 days Mr. Johnson held back the bombers, but near the end of that period it became dismally clear that North Vietnam's Ho Chi Minh was not listening. In belligerent, denunciatory tones, Hanoi called it all a "trick" and renewed its original four points for any settlement: Not only must the United States stop "all acts of war" against North Vietnam, but it must cease its "aggression" in South Vietnam, withdraw all its forces, and let the Vietnamese people settle their differences themselves. Although Mr. Johnson and his emissaries had placed themselves repeatedly on record as willing to participate in talks, the administration hedged the one point which its allies and the neutral nations said was essential: a full bargaining role at the peace table for the Vietcong's political arm, the National Liberation Front of South Vietnam.

Fulbright, Honolulu and Humphrey. On Jan. 31, American fighter-bombers again streaked northward, to signal an end to the bombing lull. The bombing served also to signal an intensified round of "peace" demonstrations by antiwar groups across the country and in Washington, as well as the launching by Sen. William Fulbright (D-Ark.) of public, televised Senate Foreign Relations Committee hearings designed to quiz the Government's top policy makers on all aspects of U.S. intervention in Vietnam.

The timing of Fulbright's move disconcerted Mr. Johnson. For one thing, it drew attention away from the UN Security Council, before which the United States finally had taken the Vietnam war issue. More important, in the President's mind, the Fulbright hearings threatened to mar the one solid achievement of the peace offensive: the feeling in foreign capitals that Mr. Johnson had indeed done his best to end the war, and that it was Ho Chi Minh who balked.

So it seemed more than coincidence that almost at the outset of the klieg-lighted hearings, Mr. Johnson announced with fanfare that he would go to Honolulu Feb. 6–8 for a historic conference with South Vietnam's dapper Premier Nguyen Cao Ky and General William Westmoreland, top U.S. field commander, to review progress of the war and chart plans for the future. Surrounded by high aides of both governments in Hawaii, Mr. Johnson, Ky and the Vietnam chief of state, Nguyen Van Thieu, issued the Declaration of Honolulu, setting forth a coordinated plan to rebuild South Vietnam. Ky pledged to curb Vietnam's soaring inflation; work toward a civilian government to replace his military junta; and win the loyalty of the peasantry. But the mustachioed Ky also made plain to newsmen that his regime was not yet ready to accept a coalition government with the National Liberation Front or even to sit down with the NLF at a peace table.

To cap off his Honolulu excursion, his first trip as president outside the continental limits

Ambassador Harriman opens 1966 with peace tour.

of North America, Mr. Johnson sent Vice-President Humphrey off to Vietnam and nine other Asia-Pacific countries on a hastily arranged, 45,000-mile goodwill mission designed to reinforce the American commitment in that part of the world. To Democratic liberals' dismay, Humphrey began sounding hawkish about the war. When Sen. Robert F. Kennedy

Senate Foreign Relations Committee Chairman Fulbright with Defense Secretary McNamara.

Photos Wide World

Vice-President Humphrey and South Vietnam Premier Ky visit a school near Saigon Feb. 11.

(D-N.Y.) made a speech proposing that the NLF be admitted to any future coalition government in Vietnam, Humphrey fired back from New Zealand that this would be tantamount to "putting a fox in the chicken coop." It constituted one of many confrontations during the year between the administration and Kennedy, with Democratic dissenters from Johnsonian policy beginning to gravitate toward the boyish looking Kennedy as the new leader of liberalism in America.

Inside Vietnam. Whatever the source of the Vietnam debate, it was obvious that Washington's massive injection of manpower, matériel and money in the field was indeed turning the tide of battle. There were 190,000 American troops in Vietnam at year's beginning; by year's end there were nearly 400,000; and the expectation that another 100,000 or more would be added in 1967. At ever-increasing rates North Vietnamese army regulars infiltrated into the South via the tortuous Ho Chi Minh Trail and by elusive junks at night.

But the North Vietnamese and the Vietcong guerrillas were kept on the run almost everywhere by alert American forces. The enemy's monsoon offensive was thwarted. The aerial war escalated in intensity and degree. By mid-year, U.S. Navy and Air Force jets had struck their first blows at fuel dumps and communications near Hanoi and the big port of Haiphong, two cities previously untouched. By December,

American pilots were making daring raids on Hanoi's big railroad depot even as leaders on both sides of the 17th parallel agreed to observe three year-end holiday truces totaling eight days.

The price for military success came high. The U.S. death toll alone for 1966 was estimated at about five thousand men. While not yet spectacular, plane losses and the need for pilots caused the Air Force and Navy to accelerate pilot-training programs and to comb their ranks for deskmen with flying experience.

There was, in addition, the risk that an enraged Hanoi, as it seemed to threaten in July, might yet put captured American airmen on trial as war criminals and thereby provoke Washington and the nation into angry retaliation.

The administration learned to be patient with South Vietnam's internal politics. Ky nimbly survived a revolt of army forces loyal to ousted Lt. Gen. Nguyen Chanh Thi in the five northernmost provinces. While his American allies looked the other way, Ky's paratroopers moved in to capture Danang. Militant Buddhists rioted in late May, calling for Ky's ouster and burning the U.S. library and consulate in Hue. Five monks and nuns burned themselves to death to demonstrate their anti-Ky fervor, hoping to arouse the same kind of American revulsion that had helped in overthrowing President Diem in 1963. But this time

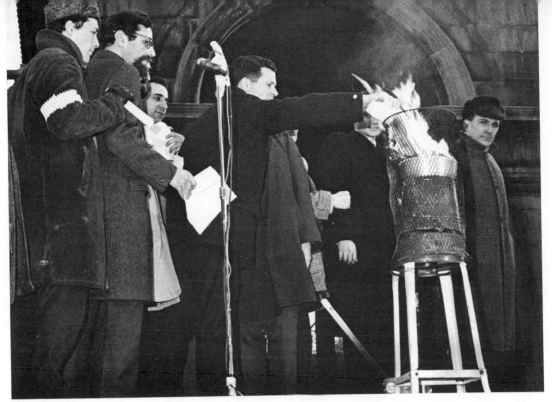

March 25 Vietnam-war protest: 17 men burn their military discharge and separation papers.

it did not work. Ky took much of the punch out of the Buddhist drive when he consented to the calling of Sept. 11 elections for a constituent assembly to write a new constitution for the country. The balloting was hailed as a triumph for the Saigon Government and the United States. Despite Vietcong terror and murder, some 80 per cent of the eligible voters participated in the election.

U.S. Antiwar Campaign. Meanwhile every dip and turn in the Vietnam war was reflected in continuing controversy on the U.S. front.

Senator Fulbright, in a Johns Hopkins University lecture, declared that the United States was "succumbing to the arrogance of power" by intervening in Vietnam. President Johnson responded sharply in a Princeton University speech. The exercise of power by America, he said, was " not arrogance but agony." He said the country was using its power "not willingly and recklessly" but "reluctantly and with great restraint."

Meanwhile scarcely a day went by without an antiwar demonstration some place in the land. New York City, Washington, Chicago, San Francisco and dozens of campuses from coast to coast were caught up in the fever. Some young men burned their military draft cards at rallies—and were promptly arrested by Federal agents for violating the law. More than 100 veterans of World War II appeared at the White House gates, seeking to return

their medals in protest against U.S. policy in Vietnam. The biggest demonstration in Washingston was the May 15 rally of at least 10,000 students and adults from around the country before the White House and at the Washington Monument grounds. Some youths of the "new Left" carried Vietcong flags, and signs terming Johnson a murderer.

In contrast to the potent and sedate nature of Fulbright's Vietnam policy inquiry, the House Un-American Activities Committee became embroiled in uproarious, capacity-crowd hearings on efforts of some Americans, a few admittedly communist, to aid the Vietcong enemy. At least 50 persons were arrested for disorderly conduct, including 12 witnesses, a lawyer for witnesses, and many collegiate spectators. One of those subpoenaed came dressed in a Revolutionary War uniform to symbolize that America itself "was born in revolution." Shouts of "get America out of Vietnam" rang out constantly during the hearings and through Capital Hill corridors.

In mid-October, Mr. Johnson dramatically suspended his plans to campaign for Democratic senators and congressmen in the November elections by taking a 17-day trip to Asia and the Pacific, highlighted by the Manila Conference of heads of 7 nations allied in the Vietnam war. The participants—South Vietnam, Australia, New Zealand, the Philippines, South Korea, Thailand and the United States

—agreed to quit Vietnam within 6 months of a North Vietnam decision to withdraw forces and halt subversion and terror in South Vietnam.

The International Front

On the international front outside of Vietnam, Washington found the scene generally tranquil, with no more than the usual problems but also with some decided pluses. The widening gulf between the Soviet Union and the Communist Chinese continued to prevent a unified Red course of action regarding Vietnam. Soviet Premier Aleksei Kosygin, in a Tashkent meeting with India's Prime Minister Lal Baladur Shastri and Pakistan's President Ayub Khan, effected a settlement of the Kashmir dispute which had flared into a brief war in mid-1965. A heart attack felled Shastri at the conclusion of the Tashkent talks, but concern for India's future abated somewhat with the selection of Mrs. Indira Gandhi, daughter of the subcontinent's revered leader, Jawaharlal Nehru, as the new prime minister.

French President de Gaulle, beginning his second seven-year term, showed his aversion to American dominance of NATO by announcing France would withdraw its military forces even while remaining a member of the Western alliance. All NATO units, including some sixty thousand U.S. citizens, would have to be removed from French soil before April 1, 1967. Mr. Johnson retained his equanimity. Although De Gaulle had "struck at the heart of the al-

U.S., Soviet leaders meet Oct. 10: (sitting) Soviet Foreign Minister Gromyko and President Johnson; (standing) Walt Rostow, Anatoly Dobrynin and Llewellyn Thompson.

UPI

liance," the President insisted the United States would continue to stand alongside other NATO members.

Washington noted with grim satisfaction the eclipse of Indonesia's President Sukarno, considered the Communists' stalking-horse in the Pacific, and with surprise and delight the election of pro-American Joaquin Balaguer as president of the Dominican Republic, still restless after U.S. intervention in the 1965 revolution there. Africa continued to dazzle Washington with a display of political gymnastics. For example, President Kwame Nkrumah was no sooner deposed as the dictatorial "messianic majesty" of Ghana than he turned up as co-ruler of Guinea—by invitation of President Sékou Touré.

Arab-Israeli friction plagued the Middle East most of the year, reaching the explosive point in November when an Israel army unit boldly crossed the Jordanian border in retaliation against guerrilla-type raids. The UN censured defiant Israel. Both the Soviet Union and the United States watched closely, if nervously. And in West Germany, in December, Kurt Georg Kiesinger was chosen chancellor.

An embarrassing military disclosure of the year was the Pentagon's belated confirmation of reports than an H-bomb had been lost off the Spanish coast, following the mid-January crash of a B-52 jet bomber. While atomic-energy experts and GI's combed the Spanish countryside for radioactivity, and while diplomats calmed the populace, U.S. Navy teams located the missing bomb on the sea bottom.

International problems, topped once more by the Vietnam war and the question of Red China admission, hung like a cloud over Washington and the United Nations when the UN's session opened in New York on Sept. 20. In a move to keep the war onus on Hanoi, Ambassador Arthur Goldberg again offered to halt the bombing and begin descalation of the fighting if North Vietnam would reciprocate. Goldberg also grasped the nettle of Vietcong representation at the peace table, saying this "would not be an insurmountable problem" for the United States. Although little happened on Vietnam to please President Johnson, the UN once again rejected membership for mainland China. Burma's U Thant finally agreed to serve a second five-year term as the UN's secretary-general, and on Dec. 8, U.S. and Soviet officials reached agreement at the UN on a treaty controlling exploration of space.

The U.S. Front

Legislation and Inflation. Mr. Johnson radiated confidence when he appeared before

U.S. Navy officers inspect hydrogen bomb recovered off Palomares, Spain, April 7.

Congress early in January with his State of the Union Message. The United States would stay in Vietnam, he announced, until aggression there had stopped—but it would also continue "building a great society here at home." His guns-and-butter policy would be based on a flourishing economy.

In the 5 previous years, Mr. Johnson proudly related, individual income after taxes had risen 33 per cent, farm income 40 per cent, and the nagging balance-of-trade deficit was down from $2,800,000,000 to $1,300,000,000. In his budget for fiscal 1966–67, he proposed Federal expenditures of $112,800,000,000 and estimated revenue at $111,000,000,000. The resulting $1,800,000,000 deficit, he said, would be the lowest in 7 years. To pay for the rising military commitment in Vietnam, he asked for an extra $5,800,000,000; to raise it he proposed a repeal of the automobile and telephone excise-tax reductions that had just taken effect Jan. 1, plus a step-up in the collection of corporate taxes and personal withholding taxes.

"We will not permit those who fire on us . . . in Vietnam to win a victory over the desires and intentions of the American people," the President told Congress. And to make good his pledge, he requested more money for the war on poverty, education and a host of Great Society measures enacted by Congress the year before. Mr. Johnson also surprised those who said there were no longer many liberal matters to place before Congress. He called for a four-year term for members of the House of Repre-

sentatives, a cabinet-level department of transportation, and a Federal highway-safety program. He called, as well, for a broad civil-rights bill. The bill would ban jury discrimination; interference with persons exercising their rights; and discrimination in the sale or rental of dwellings and apartments.

In spite of Mr. Johnson's rosy report to Congress on the health of the economy, it soon became apparent that the glow on its cheeks was a case of high money pressure. Early in February, the Federal Housing Administration gave bankers the right to raise the interest on FHA mortgages from 5¼ to 5½ per cent. To induce savings, the President increased interest on series E savings bonds from 3.75 to 4.15 per cent. A month later the nation's banks began charging businesses up to 5½ per cent interest on big loans. The stock market, reflecting investors' uncertainty, began a series of ups and downs—mostly downs—that lasted through the year. The rising cost of living worried Democratic officeholders and even Mr. Johnson. He told the housewives to "get out your lead pencil and put on your glasses," and inspect the price lists. He appealed to mayors and state governors to defer major projects and programs so as to relieve the competition for money. By autumn, homemakers were heeding the President's advice with a vim. Supermarkets from coast to coast were picketed by angry women.

The year 1966 also saw labor and management flout the White House's 3.2 per cent

The White House

Wide World

With Bill D. Moyers (l) departing from the White House staff in early 1967, President Johnson names George Christian (r) to take over for Moyers as press secretary Dec. 14.

guideline on wage and price increases. Big steel companies exceeded it in early August with a general boost in steel prices. The administration reacted unhappily, but Mr. Johnson did not try to force a rollback as President Kennedy had in 1962. The guideline was ignored again with government sanction when the International Association of Machinists reached a wage agreement Aug. 19 with five major airlines to end a costly 43-day strike.

March White House guest: India's Prime Minister Gandhi.

UPI

President Johnson was under tremendous pressure to take action to curb the inflationary spiral with a tax increase. No less a figure than William McChesney Martin, Federal Reserve Board chairman, said the time had come to slow down the economy's pulse "in a logical way," a "simple, clean-cut across-the-board increase" in income taxes. But the November election was coming on. The master politician in the White House deferred his decision, hoping the economic forces at work in the marketplace would decelerate on their own. Lawmakers on Capital Hill, up for reelection, were already chafing over Vietnam, civil-rights demonstrations and rising prices. Mr. Johnson's own popularity was slumping badly in the national polls. Many jittery Democrats in Congress were shying away from too close an identity with LBJ and some of his Great Society programs.

The same Congress that in 1965 had approved a record-breaking 68.9 per cent of Johnson's legislative requests was grumpy in 1966. In the end, it grudgingly approved 55.8 per cent of his proposals. Over and over again, the lawmakers met the President only halfway.

Congress voted to expand the war on poverty, but wrote in new restrictions on the program's handling. A controversial rent-subsidy bill was passed, but Mr. Johnson had to settle for a lower figure. A dramatic Demonstration Cities Bill, designed to test the country's ability to mount a coordinated attack on interrelated city problems, was approved without sufficient funds and without a ban on discrimination in the programs' housing category. Mr. Johnson's water-pollution-control bill was adopted, but the Government's request for enforcement powers was excluded.

There were some notable exceptions to the trend, however. A boost in the Federal minimum-wage law—which had failed in 1965—was passed in 1966. Congress also enacted bills that, for the first time, set safety standards for motor vehicles, and required states to establish highway-safety programs. But for the first time since he became president, Mr. Johnson was unable to persuade Congress, two-to-one Democratic, to approve a major civil-rights package. Nor would the lawmakers approve home rule for the District of Columbia, or repeal section 14(b) of the Taft-Hartley Act permitting states to ban union shops.

Civil Rights. Legislatively the civil-rights bill foundered on a rock named Everett McKinley Dirksen, the Republican orator from Illinois. Senate Minority Leader Dirksen could not be persuaded that the bill's open-housing provisions were constitutional. Without him to produce Republican votes, civil-rights Democrats simply lacked the necessary majority in the Senate. But politically speaking, the bill foundered because it was just too much emotional dynamite in an election year already made explosive by racial disorders and violence in some of the big cities, notably Chicago, Cleveland, Baltimore, Los Angeles and San Francisco.

Nineteen sixty-six was the year civil-rights leaders shifted their attention from Dixie and decided to "go north." They were out to break the insidious conditions of inequality that had produced the Negro ghettos, *de facto* school segregation, and unspoken but real discriminatory practices that prevailed in almost every social, geographic and economic stratum of urban life except the one at the bottom.

And 1966 was also the year that saw the movement beset by a dissension within its own ranks. Young, impatient hotbloods like Stokely Carmichael, new head of the militant Student Nonviolent Coordinating Committee, pushed for a social revolution with the cry "black power." The established civil-rights leaders, Dr. Martin Luther King, Jr., and Roy Wilkins, just as resolutely clung to the old, familiar theme of "we shall overcome." The black-power idea dismayed some whites within the civil-rights movement. Many lost their zeal for racial brotherhood. The northern strategy and the black-power concept struck hard in Congress and in the white residential communities of the big cities. Not a few Southern politicians found themselves enjoying the discomfiture of their erstwhile northern critics as the Negro marchers pushed forward.

Four marchers were killed and scores injured when Negro mobs went on a wild looting, shooting and burning spree in Cleveland in early summer. Illinois guardsmen were ordered out in Chicago where three nights of violence erupted in mid-July. Dr. King was struck on the head by a stone during a Negro march designed to break down housing barriers.

President Johnson spoke out forcefully at a news conference at the White House on July 20. He warned that although there is an oppressed Negro minority of 10 per cent, there is a white majority of 90 per cent, which is not Negro and has rights, too.

Elections. Against this backdrop—civil rights, the white backlash, Vietnam, inflation and Johnsonian-style government—the nationwide elections for Congress and a majority of governorships took place in 1966. The first sign of trouble for the Democrats was a massive falloff in Mr. Johnson's popularity among voters, as evidenced by polls. In January the Harris poll had credited the President with the approval of 67 per cent of the people. By October he had the approval of only 46 per cent.

The House makeup, going into the election, stood at 295 Democrats to 140 Republicans. In the Senate, where the lineup was 67 Democrats to 33 Republicans, 35 seats were on the 1966 ballot—20 of them held by Democrats and 15 by Republicans. Expectations were that the GOP might gain one or two. In neither chamber was there any real likelihood that the Democrats might lose majority control.

At the state level, 35 governorships also were up for balloting in 1966—20 of them held by Democrats and 15 by Republicans. In terms of party balance, there were 33 Democratic governors and 17 Republican governors in the 50 states. Republicans were hoping to pick up at least 4 more.

It was no secret in Washington early in the year that more than the usual political fortunes was at stake. A man who likes assurance in big doses, Mr. Johnson wanted a broad Democratic victory as vindication of his own Great Society performance. The Republicans needed to make a strong showing just to stay in the political ball game. Their own leaders warned aloud that another defeat like the one in 1964 could mark the GOP for extinction.

The President seized every opportunity to fly where he thought the voters needed to "press the flesh," his term for handshaking, and get a look at their chief executive. At the White House, every occasion—a bill-signing ceremony, visiting foreign dignitaries, a Congressional huddle, a chat with state officials, union leaders or businessmen—became an occasion for an LBJ-style news conference and a presi-

Former Vice-President Nixon and Sen. Dirksen at Capitol.

undertook weekend forays into New England, the Midwest and some of the border states, drawing large crowds at every stop. His spirits soared. But the most popular Democrat on the circuit was a nonadmirer of the President— Bobby Kennedy, adorned with a mop of hair and using the same hand motions and speaking patterns of his late brother. Johnson's crowds cheered; Kennedy's swooned. Johnson's message was, in effect, "LBJ's in the White House, all's right with the country." Kennedy's was: "We can do better." The Bobby phenomenon reached such a point that pollsters reported a majority of Democrats wanted him to run for president in 1968. Over and over, Kennedy had to knock down such talk with a pledge that he would support the Johnson-Humphrey ticket in 1968, and under no circumstances would he be a vice-presidential candidate on the Johnson ticket.

In October, with the polls reporting only 42 per cent approval of his handling of the Vietnam war, President Johnson cut short his political-campaign plans and took off Oct. 17 on his trip to Asia and the Far East.

When he returned Nov. 2, six days ahead of the election, he was expected to make a whirlwind campaign swing through at least a dozen states. But two days later Mr. Johnson told newsmen his doctors recommended surgery to repair the incision made when his gallbladder was removed. Furthermore, he said, the surgeons would remove a polyp from his vocal cords. Instead of campaigning, he went down to the ranch to rest before his Nov. 16 surgery.

There he was when the Nov. 8 election returns came in. The results showed a Republican resurgence that put the party in strong position to challenge the Democratic grip on the White House in 1968. Republicans gained 47 seats in

dential appearance before the television cameras of the various networks.

Republicans, meanwhile, were just as active. Former Vice-President Richard M. Nixon, a 1968 presidential prospect, and Rep. Gerald R. Ford of Michigan, House Minority Leader, spearheaded a "Booster Club" campaign to raise $2 million, and pick attractive candidates to run on the GOP ticket. Thanks to the new Republican Coordinating Committee, a cross-section group of state and national party leaders, the GOP came up with party positions on major issues, a device that created a semblance of unity, and, as Ford put it, "kept us from going off in ten different directions."

Mr. Johnson vowed he would visit all fifty states before the campaign year was over, but he never made it. In August and September he

New York's Senators Kennedy and Javits (r) with President Johnson in Syracuse Aug. 19.

the House, 3 seats in the Senate, took 8 governorships away from the Democrats and gained control of 9 additional state legislatures.

Some of the new comets in the GOP sky were actor Ronald Reagan, who defeated California's Gov. Edmund G. (Pat) Brown; handsome businessman Charles H. Percy, who beat the veteran liberal Sen. Paul Douglas of Illinois; and Massachusetts Attorney General Edward Brooke, the first Negro elected to the U.S. Senate since Reconstruction. All but Reagan are cast in the moderate-liberal mold.

Michigan's Gov. George Romney scored a smashing victory, his third in a row, and demonstrated enough pulling power to carry in a Republican senator and five new Republican candidates for Congress. Romney emerged as the front-runner in the GOP presidential sweepstakes for 1968. Ohio's Gov. James Rhodes won impressively, and New York Gov. Nelson A. Rockefeller gained a third term with surprising ease. In Arkansas, his brother Winthrop won the governorship by beating a Democratic segregationist.

The most novel Democratic victory was in Alabama, but the national party was not cheering. Mrs. Lurleen Wallace took over from her husband, Gov. George C. Wallace, the defiant segregationist who could not run to succeed himself. Wallace hailed her success by threatening to run as a third-party presidential candidate in 1968 if the two major parties do not nominate someone he likes.

The Democrats, in fact, lost every major contest in the country. Specific reasons were hard to nail down. Douglas said the white backlash hurt him in Illinois, yet Percy was an open-housing advocate. Oregon's Republican Gov. Mark Hatfield won a Senate seat in a contest with a Democrat who strongly backed Johnson policy in Vietnam, yet only after Hatfield blurred his original dovelike position. In the race for the Georgia governorship, neither Republican Howard (Bo) Callaway nor Democratic Lester Maddox, the segregationist restaurateur, garnered a majority, because of write-in votes for racially moderate Ellis Arnall, a former governor. The U.S. Supreme Court ruled Dec. 12 that the Georgia legislature should decide the winner. On Jan. 10, 1967, the legislature decided in favor of Maddox.

More significant than Republican numerical gains was the party's seizure of political control of statehouses in 5 of the 7 biggest states—those with more than half the electoral votes needed to elect a president—California, New York, Michigan, Ohio and Pennsylvania. The Democrats held only 2, Illinois and Texas, neither of which had governorships on the

Wide World
President Johnson, wearing Korean robe and Texas hat, chats with Korean farmer at Suwon, South Korea, Nov. 1.

November ballot. Additionally, the Republican gains included 2 governorships, 6 more House seats and 1 more Senate seat in the once solidly Democratic South.

Two Scandals. Republicans suggested—and Democrats denied—that the voters had been affected by political scandals involving Robert G. (Bobby) Baker, onetime Johnson aide in the Senate, and Sen. Thomas J. Dodd, Connecticut Democrat and LBJ friend.

Baker was indicted early in the year on Federal charges of tax evasion, conspiracy and fraud stemming from business deals dating back to his career as secretary to the Senate Democratic majority. In December the Government's case against him was jeopardized by the admission that the FBI bugged many of his telephone conversations with erstwhile business associates and others.

In early summer, Dodd was investigated by the Senate Ethics Committee on allegations that he used his official position to help a lobbyist friend, Julius Klein, a retired Army Reserve major general and foreign agent for German industries. Dodd also was alleged by former staff employees to have diverted campaign funds for his personal use. Dodd filed a $5 million, 14-count libel suit against columnists Drew Pearson and Jack Anderson but later reduced it to $2 million and 4 counts. By mid-December, neither the courts nor the Senate committee had ruled on the case.

Supreme Court Decisions. The U.S. Supreme Court posted several major decisions in 1966. It moved to curb the traffic in lewd publications by ruling that "titillating" advertisements could be used as proof that a publication was pornographic and therefore to be banned. The court also upheld the constitutional right of Communist Party members to refuse to register as such, and, in another move protecting the rights of arrested persons, ruled police-station confessions could not be used in a trial against a suspect unless he had been advised he could either remain silent or have a lawyer present at the interrogation. The high court likewise upheld the constitutionality of blood tests to determine whether motorists had been drinking.

Warren Report Questioned. The third anniversary of the Kennedy assassination was marked in November by fresh demands for a new inquiry into long-simmering doubts over whether Lee Harvey Oswald had acted alone, or was part of some conspiracy to kill the President. The doubts, fed by recent books critical of the Warren Commission's investigatory methods, culminated in *Life* magazine's conclusion that a new inquiry should be made by a second government panel. The magazine based its opinion on a 14-page analysis of a bystander's film of the shooting, and Texas Gov. John B. Connally's reassertion that, contrary to the *Warren Report,* he and Mr. Kennedy had not been struck by the same bullet. Sen. Richard B. Russell (D-Ga.), a member of the Warren Commission, conceded he had never been fully convinced that Oswald acted totally alone. Former presidential assistant Arthur M. Schlesinger, Jr., Sen. Russell B. Long (D-La.) and even *The New York Times* found the doubts sufficient to merit further official inquiry.

But there were also strong opinions on the other side. House Republican Leader Gerald R. Ford and former CIA Director Allen W. Dulles, both on the Warren Commission, said they had neither heard nor seen new evidence sufficient to justify a new inquiry or to change the conclusions of the Warren group. FBI Director J. Edgar Hoover declared "not one shred of evidence has been developed to link any other person in a conspiracy with Oswald to assassinate President Kennedy." Even Connally, while disputing the shot theory, insisted the Warren Commission's conclusion should be accepted as final. The only person in a position to reopen the case was President Johnson— and he said nothing.

The best summation of the problem was voiced by Russell, who, while recalling some of his personal doubts, nonetheless said: "It's easy to ask the questions; the problem is can you answer them?" Meanwhile, in Dallas, the courts ruled Jack Ruby sane, and the Texas Court of Criminal Appeals ordered him to stand trial for the police-station slaying of Oswald. Doctors in Dallas announced Dec. 10 that he had cancer. Ruby died Jan. 3, 1967, still insisting his shooting Oswald was an impulsive act to avenge Mr. Kennedy's murder.

And in 1967 . . . In a very real sense, all the major problems that occupied Washington in 1966 awaited solutions as the nation moved into 1967. Vietnam; inflation; taxes; civil rights; how far to advance the Great Society's goals for the 70 per cent of the population that lives in the urban centers—all these aspects of the "guns and/or butter" problem remained for President Johnson's attention. How he solves or attempts to solve them in 1967 would shape the 1968 presidential campaign and the role of the United States in the world.

At left: Sen. Thomas Dodd (D-Conn.), under investigation by Senate Ethics Committee, meets with attorneys June 27. At right: Texas' Gov. Connally discusses *Warren Report*.

Wide World

UPI

U.S. FEDERAL BUDGET 1967

WHERE THE MONEY COMES FROM

HOW THE MONEY IS SPENT

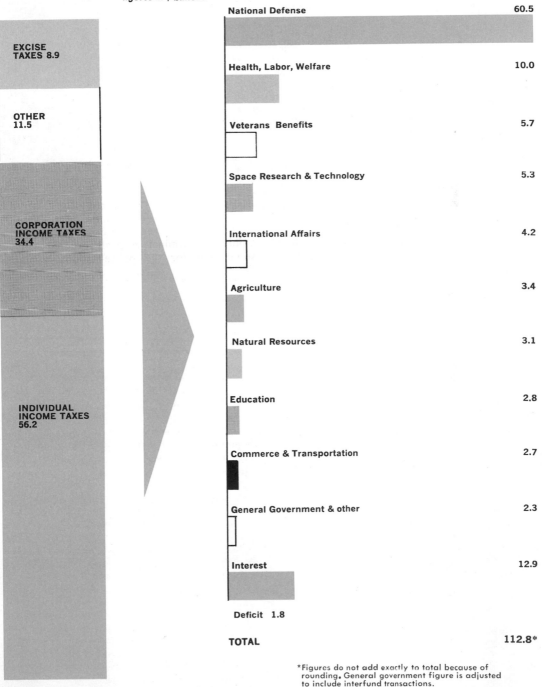

figures in $ billions

EXCISE TAXES 8.9

OTHER 11.5

CORPORATION INCOME TAXES 34.4

INDIVIDUAL INCOME TAXES 56.2

TOTAL   111.0

National Defense   60.5

Health, Labor, Welfare   10.0

Veterans Benefits   5.7

Space Research & Technology   5.3

International Affairs   4.2

Agriculture   3.4

Natural Resources   3.1

Education   2.8

Commerce & Transportation   2.7

General Government & other   2.3

Interest   12.9

Deficit 1.8

TOTAL   112.8*

*Figures do not add exactly to total because of rounding. General government figure is adjusted to include interfund transactions.

Source: Executive Office of the President, Bureau of the Budget

UNITED STATES GOVERNMENT

EXECUTIVE BRANCH

Lyndon Baines Johnson was elected president of the United States with the largest popular plurality in history on Nov. 3, 1964. He has served since Nov. 22, 1963, when he was sworn in as 36th president after the assassination of President John F. Kennedy. Following are major officials of the Government's executive branch as Mr. Johnson entered the fourth year of his presidency.

The Cabinet, composed of the heads of executive departments, is a creation of custom and tradition, goes back to Washington's day, and functions at the pleasure of the president. In 1966 the number of Cabinet posts was increased from eleven to twelve with the creation of the Department of Transportation. The various divisions of the Executive Office of the President were first established and defined under authority of the Reorganization Act of 1939.

President: Lyndon B. Johnson

Vice-President: Hubert H. Humphrey

EXECUTIVE OFFICE

THE WHITE HOUSE OFFICE
Press Secretary: George C. Christian
Counsel: Milton P. Semer
Armed Forces Aide: Lt. Col. James U. Cross, USAF
Physician: Vice Adm. G. G. Burkley, (MC) USN
Special Assistants to the President:

Joseph A. Califano, Jr.	Robert W. Komer
S. Douglass Cater, Jr.	David L. Lawrence
Donald F. Hornig	Walt W. Rostow
Robert E. Kinter	W. Marvin Watson

BUREAU OF THE BUDGET:
   Charles L. Schultze, dir.
COUNCIL OF ECONOMIC ADVISORS:
   Gardner Ackley, chm.
CENTRAL INTELLIGENCE AGENCY:
   Richard Helms, dir.
NATIONAL AERONAUTICS AND SPACE COUNCIL:
   Edward C. Welsh, exec. sec.
OFFICE OF ECONOMIC OPPORTUNITY:
   Sargent Shriver, dir.
OFFICE OF EMERGENCY PLANNING:
   Farris Bryant, dir.
OFFICE OF SCIENCE AND TECHNOLOGY:
   Donald F. Hornig, dir.
OFFICE OF TRADE NEGOTIATIONS:
   Vacant

INDEPENDENT AGENCIES

Atomic Energy Commission: Glenn T. Seaborg, chm.
Export-Import Bank: Harold F. Linder, pres. and chm.
Farm Credit Administration: Julian B. Thayer, gov.
Federal Communications Commission: Rosel H. Hyde, chm.
Federal Home Loan Bank Board: John E. Horne, chm.
Federal Maritime Commission: John Harllee, chm.
Federal Power Commission: Lee C. White, chm.
Federal Reserve System: Wm. McC. Martin, Jr., chm.
Federal Trade Commission: Paul Rand Dixon, chm.
General Services Administration: Lawson B. Knott, Jr., admin.
National Aeronautics and Space Administration: James E. Webb, adm.
National Labor Relations Board: Frank W. McCulloch, chm.
National Science Foundation: Leland J. Haworth, dir.
Securities and Exchange Commission: Manuel F. Cohen, chm.
Selective Service System: Lt. Gen. Lewis B. Hershey, dir.
Small Business Administration: Bernard L. Boutin, admin.
Tennessee Valley Authority: Aubrey J. Wagner, chm.
U.S. Arms Control and Disarmament Agency: William C. Foster, dir.
U.S. Civil Service Commission: John W. Macy, Jr., chm.
U.S. Information Agency: Leonard H. Marks, dir.
Veterans Administration: W. J. Driver, admin.

Chief Sources: United States Government Organization Manual 1966-67; Weekly Compilation of Presidential Documents

THE CABINET

SECRETARY OF STATE:
Dean Rusk

Ambassador-at-large: Ellsworth Bunker
Ambassador-at-large: W. Averell Harriman
Undersecretary of State: Nicholas deB. Katzenbach
Undersecretary for Political Affairs: Eugene V. Rostow
Chief of Protocol: James W. Symington
Counselor and Chm. of the Policy Planning Council: Robert Bowie
Agency for International Development: Wiliam S. Gaud, **adm.**
Peace Corps: Jack H. Vaughn, **dir.**
U.S. Representative to United Nations: Arthur J. Goldberg

SECRETARY OF THE TREASURY:
Henry H. Fowler

Undersecretary: Joseph W. Barr
Undersecretary for Monetary Affairs: Frederick L. Deming
Internal Revenue Service: Sheldon S. Cohen, **comm.**
Comptroller of the Currency: William B. Camp

SECRETARY OF DEFENSE:
Robert S. McNamara

Deputy Secretary: Cyrus R. Vance
Secretary of the Army: Stanley R. Resor
Secretary of the Navy: Paul H. Nitze
Secretary of the Air Force: Harold Brown
Chairman Joint Chiefs of Staff: Gen. Earle G. Wheeler

ATTORNEY GENERAL:
Ramsey Clark, Acting

Deputy Attorney General: Ramsey Clark
Solicitor General: Thurgood Marshall
Community Relations Service: Roger W. Wilkins, **dir.**
Director Federal Bureau of Investigation: J. Edgar Hoover
Commissioner of Immigration and Naturalization: Raymond F. Farrell

POSTMASTER GENERAL:
Lawrence O'Brien

Deputy Postmaster General: Frederick C. Belen

SECRETARY OF THE INTERIOR:
Stewart L. Udall

Undersecretary: John A. Carver, Jr.
Assistant Secretaries:
    Fish and Wildlife and Parks: Stanley A. Cain
    Mineral Resources: J. Cordell Moore
      Bureau of Mines: Walter R. Hibbard, Jr., **dir.**
    Public Land Management: Harry R. Anderson
      Indian Affairs Commissioner: Robert L. Bennett
      National Park Service: George B. Hartzog, Jr., **dir.**

SECRETARY OF AGRICULTURE:
Orville L. Freeman

Undersecretary: John A. Schnittker

SECRETARY OF COMMERCE:
John T. Connor

Undersecretary: vacant
Assistant Secretaries:
    Economic Affairs: William H. Shaw
    Bureau of the Census: A. Ross Eckler, **dir.**
    Science and Technology: J. Herbert Holloman
      Environmental Science Services Adm.: Robert M. White
      Commissioner of Patents: Edward J. Brenner
      National Bureau of Standards: Allen V. Astin, **dir.**

SECRETARY OF LABOR:
W. Willard Wirtz

Undersecretary: John F. Henning
Commissioner of Labor Statistics: Arthur M. Ross

SECRETARY OF HEALTH, EDUCATION, & WELFARE:
John W. Gardner

Undersecretary: Wilbur J. Cohen
Surgeon General, Public Health Service: William H. Stewart, M.D.
Commissioner of Education: Harold Howe, II
Commissioner of Social Security: Robert M. Ball
Commissioner of Food and Drugs: James L. Goddard, M.D.
Commissioner on Aging: William D. Bechill

SECRETARY OF HOUSING & URBAN DEVELOPMENT:
Robert C. Weaver

Undersecretary: Robert C. Wood

SECRETARY OF TRANSPORTATION:
Alan S. Boyd

UNITED STATES CONGRESS

SENATE
(64 DEMOCRATS, 36 REPUBLICANS)

President Pro Tempore: Carl Hayden (D-Ariz.)
Majority Leader: Mike Mansfield (D-Mont.)
Majority Whip: Russell B. Long (D-La.)
Minority Leader: Everett M. Dirksen (R-Ill.)
Minority Whip: Thomas H. Kuchel (R-Calif.)

HOUSE OF REPRESENTATIVES
(248 DEMOCRATS, 187 REPUBLICANS)

Speaker of the House: John W. McCormack (D-Mass.)
Majority Leader: Carl Albert (D-Okla.)
Majority Whip: Hale Boggs (D-La.)
Minority Leader: Gerald R. Ford (R-Mich.)
Minority Whip: Leslie C. Arends (R-Ill.)

COMMITTEE CHAIRMEN

Aeronautical and Space Sciences: Clinton P. Anderson (D-N.M.)
Agriculture and Forestry: Allen J. Ellender (D-La.)
Appropriations: Carl Hayden (D-Ariz.)
Armed Services: Richard B. Russell (D-Ga.)
Banking and Currency: John J. Sparkman (D-Ala.)
Commerce: Warren G. Magnuson (D-Wash.)
District of Columbia: Alan Bible (D-Nev.)
Finance: Russell B. Long (D-La.)
Foreign Relations: J. W. Fulbright (D-Ark.)
Government Operations: John L. McClellan (D-Ark.)
Interior and Insular Affairs: Henry M. Jackson (D-Wash.)
Judiciary: James O. Eastland (D-Miss.)
Labor and Public Welfare: Lister Hill (D-Ala.)
Post Office and Civil Service: Mike Monroney (D-Okla.)
Public Works: Jennings Randolph (D-W. Va.)
Rules and Administration: B. Everett Jordan (D-N.C.)

Agriculture: W. R. Poage (D-Tex.)
Appropriations: George H. Mahon (D-Tex.)
Armed Services: L. Mendel Rivers (D-S.C.)
Banking and Currency: Wright Patman (D-Tex.)
District of Columbia: John L. McMillan (D-S.C.)
Education and Labor: Carl D. Perkins (D-Ky.)
Foreign Affairs: Thomas E. Morgan (D-Pa.)
Government Operations: William L. Dawson (D-Ill.)
House Administration: Omar Burleson (D-Tex.)
Interior and Insular Affairs: Wayne N. Aspinall (D-Colo.)
Interstate and Foreign Commerce: Harley O. Staggers (D-W. Va.)
Judiciary: Emanuel Celler (D-N.Y.)
Merchant Marine and Fisheries: Edward A. Garmatz (D-Md.)
Post Office and Civil Service: Thaddeus J. Dulski (D-N.Y.)
Public Works: George H. Fallon (D-Md.)
Rules: William M. Colmer (D-Miss.)
Science and Astronautics: George P. Miller (D-Calif.)
Un-American Activities: Edwin E. Willis (D-La.)
Veterans' Affairs: Olin E. Teague (D-Tex.)
Ways and Means: Wilbur D. Mills (D-Ark.)

NINETIETH CONGRESS OF THE UNITED STATES

First Session

UNITED STATES SENATE

ALABAMA
Lister Hill (D)
John Sparkman (D)r

ALASKA
Ernest Gruening (D)
E. L. Bartlett (D)r

ARIZONA
Carl Hayden (D)
P. J. Fannin (R)

ARKANSAS
J. W. Fulbright (D)
J. L. McClellan (D)r

CALIFORNIA
T. H. Kuchel (R)
George Murphy (R)

COLORADO
P. H. Dominick (R)
Gordon Allott (R)r

CONNECTICUT
Abraham Ribicoff (D)
Thomas J. Dodd (D)

DELAWARE
J. J. Williams (R)
J. C. Boggs (R)r

FLORIDA
George A. Smathers (D)
S. L. Holland (D)

GEORGIA
H. E. Talmadge (D)
Richard B. Russell (D)r

HAWAII
D. K. Inouye (D)
Hiram L. Fong (R)

IDAHO
Frank Church (D)
Len B. Jordan (R)r

ILLINOIS
Everett M. Dirksen (R)
Charles H. Percy (R)e

INDIANA
Birch E. Bayh (D)
Vance Hartke (D)

IOWA
Bourke Hickenlooper (R)
Jack Miller (R)r

KANSAS
Frank Carlson (R)
James B. Pearson (R)r

KENTUCKY
Thruston Morton (R)
J. S. Cooper (R)r

LOUISIANA
Russell Long (D)
A. J. Ellender (D)l

MAINE
Margaret Chase Smith (R)r
Edmund Muskie (D)

MARYLAND
D. B. Brewster (D)
J. D. Tydings (D)

MASSACHUSETTS
Edward M. Kennedy (D)
E. W. Brook (R)e

MICHIGAN
Philip A. Hart (D)
R. P. Griffin (R)e

MINNESOTA
E. J. McCarthy (D)
Walter F. Mondale (D)r

MISSISSIPPI
James O. Eastland (D)r
John Stennis (D)

MISSOURI
Edward V. Long (D)
Stuart Symington (D)

MONTANA
Mike Mansfield (D)
Lee Metcalf (D)r

NEBRASKA
Roman Hruska (R)
Carl T. Curtis (R)r

NEVADA
Alan Bible (D)
Howard W. Cannon (D)

NEW HAMPSHIRE
Norris Cotton (R)
T. J. McIntyre (D)r

NEW JERSEY
Clifford Case (R)r
Harrison Williams, Jr. (D)

NEW MEXICO
C. P. Anderson (D)r
J. M. Montoya (D)

NEW YORK
Jacob K. Javits (R)
Robert F. Kennedy (D)

NORTH CAROLINA
Sam J. Ervin, Jr. (D)
B. E. Jordan (D)r

NORTH DAKOTA
Milton R. Young (R)
Quentin Burdick (D)

OHIO
Frank J. Lausche (D)
Stephen M. Young (D)

OKLAHOMA
Mike Monroney (D)
Fred R. Harris (D)r

OREGON
Wayne Morse (D)
Mark O. Hatfield (R)e

PENNSYLVANIA
Joseph S. Clark (D)
Hugh Scott (R)

RHODE ISLAND
John O. Pastore (D)
Claiborne Pell (D)r

SOUTH CAROLINA
Strom Thurmond (R)r
Ernest Hollings (D)l

SOUTH DAKOTA
G. S. McGovern (D)
Karl E. Mundt (R)r

TENNESSEE
Albert Gore (D)
H. H. Baker, Jr. (R)e

TEXAS
Ralph Yarborough (D)
John G. Tower (R)r

UTAH
Wallace F. Bennett (R)
Frank E. Moss (D)

VERMONT
George D. Aiken (R)
Winston L. Prouty (R)

VIRGINIA
H. F. Byrd, Jr. (D)l
W. B. Spong, Jr. (D)e

WASHINGTON
Warren G. Magnuson (D)
Henry Jackson (D)

WEST VIRGINIA
Jennings Randolph (D)r
Robert Byrd (D)

WISCONSIN
Gaylord Nelson (D)
William Proxmire (D)

WYOMING
Gale W. McGee (D)
C. P. Hansen (R)e

e = elected in 1966.
r = reelected in 1966.
l = elected in 1966 to fill unexpired term.

UNITED STATES HOUSE OF REPRESENTATIVES

ALABAMA
1. W. J. Edwards (R)
2. W. L. Dickinson (R)
3. George Andrews (D)
4. William Nichols (D)e
5. A. I. Selden (D)
6. John Buchanan, Jr. (R)
7. Tom Bevill (D)e
8. Robert Jones (D)

ALASKA
    H. W. Pollock (R)

ARIZONA
1. John Rhodes (R)
2. Morris Udall (D)
3. Sam Steiger (R)e

ARKANSAS
1. E. C. Gathings (D)
2. Wilbur Mills (D)
3. J. Hammerschmidt (R)e
4. David Pryor (D)e

CALIFORNIA
1. Don Clausen (R)
2. H. T. Johnson (D)
3. John Moss (D)
4. Robert Leggett (D)
5. Phillip Burton (D)
6. W. S. Mailliard (R)
7. J. Cohelan (D)
8. G. P. Miller (D)
9. Don Edwards (D)
10. C. S. Gubser (R)
11. J. A. Younger (R)
12. Burt Talcott (R)
13. C. M. Teague (R)
14. J. R. Waldie (D)
15. John McFall (D)
16. B. F. Sisk (D)
17. Cecil King (D)
18. R. B. Mathias (R)e
19. C. Holifield (D)
20. H. A. Smith (R)
21. A. F. Hawkins (D)
22. J. C. Corman (D)
23. Del Clawson (R)
24. G. P. Lipscomb (R)
25. Charles Wiggins (R)e
26. Thomas Rees (D)
27. E. Reinecke (R)
28. Alphonzo Bell (R)
29. G. E. Brown, Jr. (D)
30. E. R. Roybal (D)
31. C. H. Wilson (D)
32. Craig Hosmer (R)
33. Jerry Pettis (R)e
34. R. T. Hanna (D)
35. J. B. Utt (R)
36. Bob Wilson (R)
37. L. Van Deerlin (D)
38. J. V. Tunney (D)

COLORADO
1. Byron G. Rogers (D)
2. D. G. Brotzman (R)e
3. Frank Evans (D)
4. W. N. Aspinall (D)

CONNECTICUT
1. E. Q. Daddario (D)
2. W. L. St. Onge (D)
3. R. N. Giaimo (D)
4. Donald Irwin (D)
5. J. S. Monagan (D)
6. T. J. Meskill (R)e

DELAWARE
    W. V. Roth, Jr. (R)e

FLORIDA
1. R. L. F. Sikes (D)
2. Don Fuqua (D)
3. C. E. Bennett (D)
4. A. S. Herlong (D)
5. E. J. Gurney (R)
6. Sam Gibbons (D)
7. James Haley (D)
8. W. C. Cramer (R)
9. Paul G. Rogers (D)
10. J. H. Burke (R)e
11. Claude Pepper (D)
12. D. B. Fascell (D)

GEORGIA
1. G. E. Hagan (D)
2. M. O'Neal (D)
3. Jack Brinkley (D)e
4. B. B. Blackburn (R)e
5. S. F. Thompson (R)e
6. J. J. Flynt, Jr. (D)
7. J. W. Davis (D)
8. W. S. Stuckey (D)e
9. Phil Landrum (D)
10. R. G. Stephens (D)

HAWAII
    S. Matsunaga (D)
    P. Mink (D)

IDAHO
1. J. A. McClure (R)e
2. G. V. Hansen (R)

ILLINOIS
1. W. L. Dawson (D)
2. B. O'Hara (D)
3. W. T. Murphy (D)
4. E. J. Derwinski (R)
5. J. C. Kluczynski (D)
6. Dan Ronan (D)
7. F. Annunzio (D)
8. D. Rostenkowski (D)
9. Sidney Yates (D)
10. H. R. Collier (R)
11. R. C. Pucinski (D)
12. R. McClory (R)
13. D. Rumsfeld (R)
14. J. N. Erlenborn (R)
15. C. T. Reid (R)
16. J. B. Anderson (R)
17. L. C. Arends (R)
18. R. H. Michel (R)
19. T. F. Railsback (R)e
20. Paul Findley (R)
21. Kenneth Gray (D)
22. W. L. Springer (R)
23. George Shipley (D)
24. Melvin Price (D)

INDIANA
1. Ray Madden (D)
2. C. A. Halleck (R)
3. J. Brademas (D)
4. Ross Adair (R)
5. J. E. Roush (D)
6. W. G. Bray (R)
7. John Myers (R)e
8. Roger Zion (R)e
9. L. H. Hamilton (D)
10. R. L. Roudebush (R)
11. A. Jacobs, Jr. (D)

IOWA
1. Fred Schwengel (R)e
2. John Culver (D)
3. H. R. Gross (R)
4. John H. Kyl (R)e
5. Neal Smith (D)
6. Wiley Mayne (R)e
7. W. J. Scherle (R)e

KANSAS
1. Robert Dole (R)
2. C. L. Mize (R)
3. Larry Winn, Jr. (R)e
4. G. E. Shriver (R)
5. Joe Skubitz (R)

KENTUCKY
1. F. Stubblefield (D)
2. W. H. Natcher (D)
3. W. O. Cowger (R)e
4. Gene Snyder (R)
5. Tim L. Carter (R)
6. J. C. Watts (D)
7. Carl Perkins (D)

LOUISIANA
1. F. E. Hebert (D)
2. Hale Boggs (D)
3. Edwin Willis (D)
4. J. Waggoner, Jr. (D)
5. Otto Passman (D)
6. J. R. Rarick (D)e
7. Edwin Edwards (D)
8. S. O. Long (D)

MAINE
1. Peter Kyros (D)e
2. W. D. Hathaway (D)

MARYLAND
1. R. C. B. Morton (R)
2. C. D. Long (D)
3. E. A. Garmatz (D)
4. G. H. Fallon (D)
5. Hervey Machen (D)
6. C. Mathias, Jr. (R)
7. S. N. Friedel (D)
8. Gilbert Gude (R)

MASSACHUSETTS
1. Silvio Conte (R)
2. E. P. Boland (D)
3. P. J. Philbin (D)
4. H. D. Donohue (D)
5. F. B. Morse (R)
6. W. H. Bates (R)
7. T. H. Macdonald (D)
8. T. P. O'Neill, Jr. (D)
9. J. McCormack (D)
10. M. Heckler (R)e
11. James Burke (D)
12. H. Keith (R)

MICHIGAN
1. J. J. Conyers, Jr. (D)
2. Marvin Esch (R)e
3. G. E. Brown (R)e
4. E. Hutchinson (R)
5. G. R. Ford (R)
6. C. Chamberlain (R)
7. D. W. Riegle, Jr. (R)e
8. James Harvey (R)
9. G. Vander Jagt (R)e
10. E. A. Cederberg (R)
11. Philip Ruppe (R)e
12. J. G. O'Hara (D)
13. C. C. Diggs, Jr. (D)
14. L. N. Nedzi (D)
15. W. D. Ford (D)
16. J. D. Dingell (D)
17. M. W. Griffiths (D)
18. W. S. Broomfield (R)
19. J. H. McDonald (R)e

MINNESOTA
1. Albert Quie (R)
2. Ancher Nelsen (R)
3. C. MacGregor (R)
4. J. E. Karth (D)
5. D. M. Fraser (D)
6. John M. Zwach (R)e
7. Odin Langen (R)
8. John Blatnik (D)

MISSISSIPPI
1. T. Abernethy (D)
2. J. L. Whitten (D)
3. J. B. Williams (D)
4. G. V. Montgomery (D)e
5. W. M. Colmer (D)

MISSOURI
1. Frank Karsten (D)
2. T. B. Curtis (R)
3. L. K. Sullivan (D)
4. W. J. Randall (D)
5. R. Bolling (D)
6. W. R. Hull, Jr. (D)
7. D. G. Hall (D)
8. R. H. Ichord (D)
9. W. L. Hungate (D)
10. Paul C. Jones (D)

MONTANA
1. Arnold Olsen (D)
2. J. F. Battin (R)

NEBRASKA
1. R. V. Denney (R)e
2. G. Cunningham (R)
3. Dave Martin (R)

NEVADA
W. S. Baring (D)

NEW HAMPSHIRE
1. L. C. Wyman (R)e
2. J. C. Cleveland (R)

NEW JERSEY
1. John E. Hunt (R)e
2. C. W. Sandman, Jr. (R)e
3. J. J. Howard (D)
4. F. Thompson, Jr. (D)
5. P. Frelinghuysen (R)
6. W. T. Cahill (R)
7. W. B. Widnall (R)
8. C. S. Joelson (D)
9. H. Helstoski (D)
10. Peter Rodino, Jr. (D)
11. J. G. Minish (D)
12. F. P. Dwyer (R)
13. C. E. Gallagher (D)
14. D. V. Daniels (D)
15. E. J. Patten (D)

NEW MEXICO
T. G. Morris (D)
E. S. J. Walker (D)

NEW YORK
1. Otis G. Pike (D)
2. J. R. Grover, Jr. (R)
3. Lester Wolff (D)
4. John Wydler (R)
5. Herbert Tenzer (D)
6. S. Halpern (R)
7. J. P. Addabbo (D)
8. B. S. Rosenthal (D)
9. J. J. Delaney (D)
10. E. Celler (D)
11. F. J. Brasco (D)e
12. Edna F. Kelly (D)
13. A. J. Multer (D)
14. J. J. Rooney (D)
15. H. L. Carey (D)
16. J. M. Murphy (D)
17. T. Kupferman (R)
18. A. C. Powell (D) [1]
19. L. Farbstein (D)
20. W. F. Ryan (D)
21. J. H. Scheuer (D)
22. J. H. Gilbert (D)
23. J. B. Bingham (D)
24. Paul A. Fino (R)
25. R. L. Ottinger (D)
26. Ogden Reid (R)
27. John G. Dow (D)
28. J. Y. Resnick (D)
29. D. E. Button, Jr. (R)e
30. C. J. King (R)
31. R. C. McEwen (R)
32. A. Pirnie (R)
33. H. W. Robison (R)
34. J. M. Hanley (D)
35. S. S. Stratton (D)
36. Frank Horton (R)
37. B. B. Conable, Jr. (R)
38. C. E. Goodell (R)
39. R. D. McCarthy (D)
40. H. P. Smith III (R)
41. T. J. Dulski (D)

NORTH CAROLINA
1. W. B. Jones (D)
2. L. H. Fountain (D)
3. D. N. Henderson (D)
4. J. C. Gardner (R)e
5. N. Galifianakis (D)
6. H. R. Kornegay (D)
7. Alton Lennon (D)
8. C. R. Jonas (R)
9. J. T. Broyhill (R)
10. B. L. Whitener (D)
11. Roy A. Taylor (D)

NORTH DAKOTA
1. Mark Andrews (R)
2. T. S. Kleppe (R)e

OHIO
1. R. A. Taft, Jr. (R)e
2. D. D. Clancy (R)
3. C. W. Whalen, Jr. (R)e
4. W. McCulloch (R)
5. D. L. Latta (R)
6. W. H. Harsha (R)
7. C. J. Brown, Jr. (R)
8. J. E. Betts (R)
9. T. L. Ashley (D)
10. C. E. Miller (R)e
11. J. W. Stanton (R)
12. S. L. Devine (R)
13. C. A. Mosher (R)
14. W. H. Ayres (R)
15. C. P. Wylie (R)e
16. Frank T. Bow (R)
17. J. M. Ashbrook (R)
18. Wayne Hays (D)
19. M. J. Kirwan (D)
20. M. A. Feighan (D)
21. Charles Vanik (D)
22. F. P. Bolton (R)
23. W. E. Minshall (R)
24. D. E. Lukens (R)e

OKLAHOMA
1. Page Belcher (R)
2. Ed Edmondson (D)
3. Carl Albert (D)
4. Tom Steed (D)
5. John Jarman (D)
6. J. V. Smith (R)e

OREGON
1. Wendell Wyatt (R)
2. Al Ullman (D)
3. Edith Green (D)
4. J. Dellenback (R)e

PENNSYLVANIA
1. W. A. Barrett (D)
2. R. N. C. Nix (D)
3. James Byrne (D)
4. J. Eilberg (D)e
5. W. J. Green (D)
6. George Rhodes (D)
7. L. G. Williams (R)
8. E. G. Biester, Jr. (R)e
9. G. R. Watkins (R)
10. J. M. McDade (R)
11. Daniel Flood (D)
12. J. I. Whalley (R)
13. R. S. Schweiker (R)
14. W. S. Moorhead (D)
15. Fred Rooney (D)
16. E. D. Eshleman (R)e
17. H. Schneebeli (R)
18. R. J. Corbett (R)
19. G. A. Goodling (R)e
20. E. J. Holland (D)
21. John H. Dent (D)
22. John P. Saylor (R)
23. A. W. Johnson (R)
24. J. P. Vigorito (D)
25. Frank M. Clark (D)
26. T. E. Morgan (D)
27. J. G. Fulton (R)

RHODE ISLAND
1. F. J. St. Germain (D)
2. J. E. Fogarty (D) [2]

SOUTH CAROLINA
1. L. M. Rivers (D)
2. Albert Watson (R)
3. W. J. B. Dorn (D)
4. R. T. Ashmore (D)
5. T. S. Gettys (D)
6. J. L. McMillan (D)

SOUTH DAKOTA
1. Ben Reifel (R)
2. E. Y. Berry (R)

TENNESSEE
1. J. H. Quillen (R)
2. John J. Duncan (R)
3. W. E. Brock III (R)
4. Joe L. Evins (D)
5. R. Fulton (D)
6. W. R. Anderson (D)
7. Ray Blanton (D)e
8. R. A. Everett (D)
9. D. Kuykendall (R)e

TEXAS
1. W. Patman (D)
2. John Dowdy (D)
3. Joe Pool (D)
4. Ray Roberts (D)
5. Earle Cabell (D)
6. Olin Teague (D)
7. George Bush (R)e
8. R. C. Eckhardt (D)e
9. Jack Brooks (D)
10. J. J. Pickle (D)
11. W. R. Poage (D)
12. Jim Wright (D)
13. G. Purcell (D)
14. John Young (D)
15. E. de la Garza (D)
16. Richard White (D)
17. Omar Burleson (D)
18. Robert Price (R)e
19. George Mahon (D)
20. H. Gonzalez (D)
21. O. C. Fisher (D)
22. Bob Casey (D)
23. A. Kazen (D)e

UTAH
1. L. J. Burton (R)
2. Sherman Lloyd (R)e

VERMONT
R. T. Stafford (R)

VIRGINIA
1. T. N. Downing (D)
2. Porter Hardy, Jr. (D)
3. D. Satterfield III (D)
4. W. M. Abbitt (D)
5. William M. Tuck (D)
6. Richard Poff (R)
7. J. O. Marsh, Jr. (D)e
8. W. L. Scott (R)e
9. W. C. Wampler (R)e
10. Joel Broyhill (R)

WASHINGTON
1. T. M. Pelly (R)
2. Lloyd Meeds (D)
3. J. B. Hansen (D)
4. Catherine May (R)
5. T. S. Foley (D)
6. Floyd Hicks (D)
7. Brock Adams (D)

WEST VIRGINIA
1. Arch Moore, Jr. (R)
2. H. O. Staggers (D)
3. J. M. Slack, Jr. (D)
4. Ken Hechler (D)
5. James Kee (D)

WISCONSIN
1. H. C. Schadeberg (R)e
2. R. Kastenmeier (D)
3. V. W. Thomson (R)
4. C. J. Zablocki (D)
5. Henry Reuss (D)
6. W. A. Steiger (R)e
7. Melvin Laird (R)
8. John Byrnes (R)
9. Glenn Davis (R)
10. A. E. O'Konski (R)

WYOMING
W. H. Harrison (R)e

Numbers indicate Congressional districts; no numbers indicate Congressmen-at-large.
e = newly elected in 1966; others reelected.   [1] denied seat pending investigation   [2] died Jan. 10, 1967

URBAN DEVELOPMENT

By ROBERT C. WEAVER
U.S. Secretary of Housing
and Urban Development

The census of 1920 signified that the United States had become an urban nation. It revealed that for the first time in U.S. history more people lived in urban communities than on farms. During the past five decades urbanization has become the principal factor shaping the American way of life.

It is estimated that 70 per cent of the U.S. population presently lives in urban communities. This amounts to about 140 million of nearly 200 million residents. By the year 2000 —only 33 years away—urban areas will account for over three fourths of the total population, and will number some 260 million. This means that the urban population will nearly double by the end of the century. In these 33 years almost as many new houses, schools, hospitals and other facilities as presently exist in all U.S. cities and towns must be provided. This will offer the opportunity to make the nation's cities better, more efficient, and more satisfying places in which to live.

Becoming an urban nation has presented new problems and conditions that require the very best of planning and programming. The United States is faced with the challenge of polluted water supplies and watersheds. Eighty million automobiles and a burgeoning industrial complex are making the air unfit to breathe. The journey to work has become a harrowing daily ordeal for millions of commuters. The centers of cities are losing their attractiveness, and tending to become ethnic and low-income ghettos.

Modern Housing Legislation

Modern housing legislation entered the statute books as measures to counteract the U.S. depression of the 1930's. The first piece of Federal legislation intended to correct the blighted condition of cities was passed in 1949. Successive acts of Congress during the 1950's and since 1960 expanded the scope of Federal aids available to urban communities. Additional housing legislation focused increasingly upon the requirements of families whose incomes could not enable them to compete effectively in the private housing market. A broad array of community development aids offered help to communities to cope with problems of adequate water supply, sewers and transportation.

The year 1965 marked an important milestone in housing legislation when Congress established the Department of Housing and Urban Development (HUD). This provided cabinet representation to the various housing and urban-affairs programs of the Federal Government, and gave recognition to the importance that urban problems claim in society and

Public housing for low-income families, Washington, D.C.

"Instant rehabilitation": prefab unit fits into tenement.

A 12-acre urban-renewal project in the heart of downtown Hartford, Conn.

the economy. The newly created department absorbed all responsibilities and programs of its predecessor agency, the Housing and Home Finance Agency. Furthermore, it was charged, by law and executive order, to assume leadership in fostering the development and orderly growth of urban areas and to coordinate the other U.S. urban development programs.

The urban communities and their residents are provided with a diversity of programs to improve their present conditions and to keep pace with growing needs. Some of the more important programs in HUD are:

. . . in the area of housing, programs of mortgage insurance for privately financed rental and sales housing: below-market-rate-of-interest programs to house lower-middle-income families, including development of specially designed housing for the elderly; and public and private housing programs under which Federal annual contributions or rent supplements permit low-income families to be accommodated in housing at rents they can afford.

. . . in the area of urban renewal, programs for clearance and redevelopment of blighted areas; planning grants for metropolitan areas and smaller communities; grants in urban renewal areas of concentrated code enforcement; direct below-market-rate-of-interest loans for housing rehabilitation; and rehabilitation grants to low-income home owners in urban renewal areas.

. . . in the field of community facilities, grants for water and sewer development; interest-free advances to plan needed public

works; loans for public works to smaller localities; transportation loans and grants; and grants for neighborhood centers.

In order to assure that the maximum benefits will be derived from these and other Federal grant-in-aid programs, it is essential that they be utilized in a comprehensive and coordinated fashion to improve the lives of the poor, as well as their urban environment. Toward that end, President Johnson proposed the Demonstration Cities Program. Passed by Congress in October 1966, the program will provide $900 million in supplementary grant funds, over a two-year period, to assist cities to enlist all of their available public and private resources in a concerted attack upon the concomitant problems of slum and poverty.

The goals of HUD are constantly evolving in recognition of new problems and changing conditions. A present emphasis is to obtain more effective coordination of urban-physical-development programs with human-resource-development programs. This is reflected in the Demonstration Cities legislation, wherein whole neighborhoods and sections of a city will be exposed to optimally coordinated programs of housing and family improvement. An allied emphasis stresses rehabilitation of existing housing resources in order to minimize family displacement and to retain the character and strength of viable neighborhoods. It is expected that HUD will continue to adapt itself to changing conditions in its long-run effort to achieve the U.S. goal of ". . . a decent home and suitable living environment for every American family. . . ."

UTAH. Completion of Kennecott Copper Corporation's expansion program will boost the company's Utah copper production by 100,000 tons a year. Kennecott spent $100 million enlarging its facilities 20 mi. west of Salt Lake City. . . . Sargent Shriver, director of Office of Economic Opportunity, announced March 31 that Thiokol Chemical Corp. would operate a men's Job Corps Center in Clearfield.

VANCOUVER. The most significant 1966 event in the city of Vancouver, British Columbia, was the settlement of a 30-year dispute which has retarded the development of the port and has caused a marked deterioration of 1½ miles of valuable waterfront property. The National Harbours Board, which administers the port, and the Canadian Pacific Railway agreed to settle the problem of the ownership of tidewaters land out of court by splitting the disputed water frontage equally between them.

$23 million Simon Fraser University near Vancouver.
Ted Spiegel, Rapho Guillumette "Time" magazine. © *Time Inc.*

The railway retains the piers and property west of Burrard Street, which is on shallow water suitable for marine-oriented real-estate development, and the NHB assumes control over the tidelands east to Centennial Pier, which is in an area of deep-sea shipping berths. With this settled, the CPR revealed plans for a $200 million commercial and residential development backed by the railway, Woodward Stores, and Grosvenor-Laing Development Company. The NHB plans to build a $50 million dock extending from Granville Street to Centennial Pier and extending 300 yards into the harbor. It will provide the desperately needed mammoth berths for the new breed of giant bulk-cargo carriers which have found the port's facilities inadequate in the past.

The port was plagued by a 10-week strike of grain handlers, and a chronic shortage of boxcars for hauling grain from the prairies. Even so, grain shipments fell to only a shade under 200 million bushels in the 1965–66 crop year, and Vancouver remains one of the world's great grain ports. The export of 685,000 tons of potash has also made it the world's leading potash port. With additional shipments of pulp, paper, lumber, sulfur and coal, Vancouver maintained its position as the greatest dry-cargo port on the Pacific Coast of the Americas.

The Federal Government exchanged several acres of city beach property for the major part of a city-owned downtown block on which the Canadian Broadcasting Corporation will build a $10 million regional headquarters. The city will construct a $1.5 million museum-planetarium complex in a beach-park setting on its newly acquired land.

In the provincial election of Sept. 12, 1966, the metropolitan area returned 7 Social Crediters, 8 New Democrats (Social Democrats) and 5 Liberals, a slightly Leftward swing from its previous support of the Right-Wing Social Credit government. In the Federal Parliament the area is represented by 9 Liberals and 5 New Democrats.

JOSEPH C. LAWRENCE
Department of History
UNIVERSITY OF BRITISH COLUMBIA

VANIER, GEORGES P. Governor-General of Canada Georges P. Vanier was forced to cancel his public engagements for the last two months of the year due to illness. He was taken to the hospital in Ottawa late in October with influenza, and while there a urinary obstruction was discovered and corrected surgically.

Until then, the 78-year-old representative of Queen Elizabeth II had had another busy year of ceremonial functions. In January he read the Speech from the Throne to open the first session of the 27th Parliament. In May he made an extensive tour of the Maritime Provinces, during which he and Madame Vanier were awarded honorary degrees by St. Mary's University, Halifax. His annual garden party in June was attended by 3,500 guests.

WILLIAM FRENCH
Literary Editor, TORONTO GLOBE AND MAIL

VERMONT. President Johnson visited Burlington Aug. 20. . . . Gov. Philip H. Hoff testified May 23 that he opposed "any waterway project that adds to the pollution problem in Lake Champlain." The Governor appeared before a commission studying a proposed seaway. . . . Hoff, the state's first Democratic governor since 1853, was endorsed for a third two-year term Nov. 8. Incumbent Robert T. Stafford (R) won a fourth term as U.S. Representative.

VETERANS. Veterans' organizations in 1966 hailed the enactment of PL 89-358, the GI Bill of Rights for post-Korean veterans, as they moved to bring these veterans into their membership ranks and sought greater assistance for disabled veterans, their dependents and survivors. In general, veterans' groups supported the Johnson administration in its Vietnam policy, but the American Veterans Committee (AVC) qualified that support.

Some veterans' groups were concerned about the "phasing out" of national cemeteries; among those in vigorous opposition were the American Legion and the Veterans of Foreign Wars. The veterans' organizations continued their efforts to obtain higher benefits for veterans, and rejected any diminution of veterans' preference. An exception was the AVC, which has always maintained that what is good for the country is good for the veteran.

The American Legion elected John E. Davis, former governor of North Dakota, as national commander at its convention in Washington, D.C. President Johnson was the chief speaker. Basic programs of Americanism, child welfare, rehabilitation and national security were set up for the future. The Legion's Vietnam Relief Fund, which collected $120,000 for the Vietnamese people, is one of the major projects. At its convention the Legion opened its doors to Vietnam veterans.

At a special convention in February 1966 the AVC reaffirmed its traditional interest in civil rights, civil liberties, equality of opportunity and the war against poverty. It reelected John S. Stillman as national chairman. The AVC sponsored a National Conference on the Draft in November for a full discussion of the Selective Service System. AVC sought an end to discrimination in off-base housing and supported the civil-rights bill of 1966. It also opened its doors to Vietnam veterans.

A. Leo Anderson of Washington, D.C., was elected national commander of the American Veterans of World War II (AMVETS) at a convention in Columbus, Ohio. During 1966, AMVETS dedicated its new national headquarters in Washington and opened its membership to any veteran who had served honorably in the armed forces since Sept. 16, 1940.

The Veterans of Foreign Wars elected Leslie M. Fry as their national commander at a convention in New York City. Chief speakers were former Vice-President Richard M. Nixon, Secretary of State Dean Rusk, and Secretary of Defense Robert S. McNamara. Meeting in Miami Beach, Fla., in August, the Blinded Veterans Association (BVA) reelected James Hyde, Jr., as national president. Gen. Lewis B. Hershey, director of Selective Service, spoke. The BVA has represented blinded veterans for 21 years.

The Disabled American Veterans elected John W. Unger as national commander at an August convention in New York City, and heard Vice-President Hubert Humphrey speak. The organization adopted resolutions supporting a bill for judicial review of veterans' claims and more equitable adjustment in certain statutory wards for disabled veterans, and opposed any watering down of Veterans Preference. The Military Order of the Purple Heart elected John Burgess of Daytona Beach, Fla., as its national commander, and the Catholic War Veterans reelected Martin G. Riley to their top position. The Jewish War Veterans elected Malcolm Tarlov as their new commander.

At their Detroit convention, the Paralyzed Veterans of America (PVA) named Leslie Burghof as national chairman. The prime legislative goal of the PVA for 1967 is revision of the social-security law. The organization wants to raise disability retirement payments, to permit dual payment of veteran pension and social security and to extend Medicare provisions to those under 65 who are totally disabled.

Representatives of the U.S. Council of the WVF attended a meeting of the Governing Council of the 22 million-member federation in Toronto, Canada, in the spring. Judge Hubert L. Will of Chicago is chairman of the U.S. Council; members are: Amvets, AVC, BVA, DAV, Military Order of the Purple Heart and PVA.

JUNE A. WILLENZ
Executive Director
AMERICAN VETERANS COMMITTEE

VIETNAM

By JOHN HUGHES
Far Eastern Correspondent
THE CHRISTIAN SCIENCE MONITOR

For Americans, 1966 in Vietnam was a year of continuing hope and anguish.

The hope stemmed from the undisputable fact that the military position of the United States and its allies was much improved in Vietnam during the year. The anguish derived from the fact that this improvement was wrought with higher casualties and cost.

Meanwhile neither North Vietnam nor the Vietcong gave any sign they were ready to sue for peace. And on the nonmilitary front, the governments of both the United States and South Vietnam remained challenged by a variety of economic and political problems as they pursued the Vietnam campaign.

The War

Escalation. At the end of 1965, United States troop strength in South Vietnam was around 200,000. By the end of 1966 this figure had nearly doubled, not counting some 50,000 men offshore in vessels of the Seventh Fleet.

Thus during 1966 the American commitment rose above that of the U.S. commitment in the Korean war—327,000 troops at its peak.

With more U.S. troops in action, casualties took a sharp upward curve. In March, U.S. dead for the first time exceeded South Vietnamese dead: 95 Americans killed in one week, as compared with 67 South Vietnamese. In the air war, the United States lost more than 400 planes during the year, the bulk of them knocked down by intense ground fire.

Early in 1966 it became clear that the year was to be one of escalation. Throughout January there was a lull in air strikes against North Vietnam as President Johnson launched an intense peace offensive. But with no response from Hanoi, U.S. planes on Jan. 31 again screamed northward against North Vietnam after a bombing pause of 37 days.

Ho Bo Operations. Meanwhile, with the launching of a ground operation in January against the Ho Bo woods, some 25 miles northwest of Saigon, by the U.S. 173d Airborne Brigade, troops of the First Infantry (or Big Red One) Division and the Royal Australian Regiment, it seemed evident that American forces had begun a new role in South Vietnam.

The previous year, as U.S. troops rolled into the country, the official story was that they would be used for securing base areas, thus freeing South Vietnamese troops for action against the enemy. But with the Ho Bo operation, as American troops slashed their way into a Vietcong stronghold unvisited for years by South Vietnamese forces, it was clear that American troops from now on would be used as shock troops for cracking hard-core Vietcong areas. South Vietnamese units would follow, and ultimately behind them would come police and civilian officials to pacify the areas freed of communist control, and consolidate government authority over them.

It also became clear that, with more troops available, the U.S. commander, Gen. William C. Westmoreland, was embarking on a series of spoiling operations, designed to keep the Vietcong and North Vietnamese units off-balance, and thus thwarting their plans for a general offensive.

This strategy apparently proved successful, for the traditional communist offensive—under cover of the monsoon rains which ground American aircraft—failed to materialize. Instead, by the end of the year, the North Vietnamese were apparently trying to shorten their lines of communication by infiltrating troops directly through the Demilitarized Zone which divides North Vietnam from South. After a series of bloody battles to gain high points commanding these infiltration routes, U.S. Marines in I Corps, the northernmost corps area in South Vietnam, were redeployed to counter any major thrust through the zone by North Vietnamese troops.

Vietcong. Nevertheless, although the Vietcong and North Vietnamese suffered military reverses during the year, there seemed plenty of fight left in them. Despite the American decision in June to bomb oil dumps and installations in the vicinity of Hanoi and Haiphong, North Vietnamese infiltration into South Vietnam continued at a high rate throughout the year. Notwithstanding their supply problems, the North Vietnamese boosted their total of regular troops fighting in South Vietnam to some fifty thousand by the end of 1966.

Truce Proposals. Throughout the year the North Vietnamese and their Chinese Communist mentors maintained a hard-line position on negotiations with the Americans and South Vietnamese to end the war. The Communists insisted on complete withdrawal of U.S. troops prior to peace talks. In this position they seemed backed by France's President de Gaulle, who made virtually the same point in a speech in Pnompenh, Cambodia, in September.

The terms remained unacceptable to the United States, which spelled out its own position anew at the Manila Conference in October. Gathered with its Vietnam war allies, the United States offered to withdraw American troops from Vietnam within six months in exchange for a corresponding pullback by the Communists. The American offer was quickly brushed aside in both Hanoi and Peking.

Meanwhile if the United States had succeeded during the year in blunting the communist military drive, the outlook on South Vietnam's political and economic fronts remained far from satisfactory.

Politics and the Economy

Honolulu Conference. In February, South Vietnam's Premier Nguyen Cao Ky met with President Johnson in Honolulu for top-level policy talks. The conference indicated the U.S. President's personal interest in various vital, nonmilitary aspects of the war. Indeed, President Johnson assigned a number of experts and specialists to watchdog progress and report back to him at regular intervals. A follow-up conference was planned.

But though both sides left Honolulu in a flurry of promises of good intentions, problems both political and economic dragged on.

Fresh from Honolulu with President Johnson's endorsement about him, Air Vice-Marshal Ky was almost immediately plunged into new political crisis with the Buddhists at home; so much so that the projected follow-up conference at Honolulu several months later was canceled and never did take place.

Ky and the Buddhists. Shortly after his return, Premier Ky quarreled violently with Gen. Nguyen Chanh Thi, the swashbuckling paratrooper who commanded I Corps. One of South Vietnam's four corps areas, this northern area of strong regional loyalties is the site of the ancient imperial capital of Hue. General Thi was himself born in Hue, was popular in the area and had cultivated close contacts with the organized Buddhist church.

After an angry confrontation, Premier Ky fired General Thi. There was immediate pro-Thi reaction in Hue and Danang, the area's two major cities. The Buddhists moved swiftly to exploit the situation, having been cool to Premier Ky's military regime for months.

In particular, the Buddhists had been demanding a return to civilian government—a government in which the Buddhists presumably hoped to win major political influence. Premier Ky had promised such a return to civilian rule in principle, but the Buddhists argued that the two-year timetable he had set was too leisurely.

Thus General Thi's ouster touched off major antigovernment demonstrations in Danang and Hue. The "struggle forces," as the rebel forces called themselves, virtually took over the northernmost region of South Vietnam. Premier Ky reacted angrily. He charged that the city of Danang had been taken over by the Vietcong. To many, this speech smacked of extreme irresponsibility. That the Communists had tried to infiltrate the "struggle forces," nobody doubted. But to suggest that the whole rebel movement was communist organized and dominated seemed an evasion of the realities of the situation.

The Buddhists piled on the pressure by launching a new and grisly wave of suicides by fire. The militant Buddhist leader, Tri Quang, issued a series of urgent appeals to President Johnson to disassociate the United States from Premier Ky's regime. Officially the United States maintained that the political crisis was an internal affair of South Vietnam in which it could not intervene. Privately the United States helped shore up Premier Ky. Thus the rebels launched a series of sharp little anti-American demonstrations, sacking the United States Information Service center in Hue.

Finally, Premier Ky moved troops into Danang and later Hue, crushing the revolt. But he had agreed, under pressures, to hold vital elections in South Vietnam by Sept. 11.

In the aftermath of the revolt the Buddhists were bitter and divided. Tri Quang embarked on a long hunger strike in protest against the Government, gathering hard-line Buddhists about him. Others rallied to the more moderate leadership of Tam Chau, prepared to compromise and negotiate with the Government.

Elections and Aftermath. But though the Buddhist campaign to topple the Ky Government had failed, the elections scheduled for September did take place. Organizational problems were considerable. Clearly, there could be no voting in areas under Vietcong control. In areas held to be under government administration, neither communist nor "neutralist" candidates were allowed to run. Nevertheless, of about 5.2 million South Vietnamese considered eligible to vote, 4.2 million went to the polls.

The Vietcong failed, as they had threatened, to disrupt the election.

The outcome was a 117-member assembly—116 men and 1 woman—whose task was to draft within 6 months a new constitution for South Vietnam. Then would follow another election, held on the basis of that constitution, to produce a representative assembly with legislative powers. However, some observers speculated that the assembly elected to draft the constitution might itself assume larger powers as the months passed.

Chiefs of seven nations sign Manila Declaration, setting forth plan to end Vietnam war.

Early meetings of the assembly were marred by procedural wrangling, and a fight over the chairmanship. This was eventually resolved with the election of Phan Khac Suu, a former chief of state and elder statesman in South Vietnam.

Meanwhile another political crisis erupted on the eve of Premier Ky's departure for the Manila Conference in October. Seven ministers in his Cabinet, all of them from the southern provinces of South Vietnam, threatened to resign on grounds they were being discriminated against by ministers and officials from other parts of the country. Premier Ky managed to head off the political revolt until after Manila. But even after patching things up, his regime was harried by the problems of regionalism.

Economic and Pacification Developments. On the economic front the South Vietnamese Government took a bold decision to devalue its currency in June. Experts, however, explained that this only bought the country a breathing space. It could not in itself solve the nation's basic economic ills. Roaring inflation remained the major problem.

Meanwhile, despite the execution in March of a Chinese businessman, Ta Vinh, for war profiteering, there remained a vast amount of racketeering and corruption.

Despite intensive efforts to clear South Vietnam's ports, clogged with incoming military matériel and goods, the country wrestled with a logistics jam-up for much of the year. Off Saigon port, thirty ships at a time waited their opportunity to unload. Even when port experts cut down the waiting time for unloading, huge tonnages were simply stored in warehouses or lighters after being unloaded from incoming freighters and still did not clear the port.

On the pacification front, the South Vietnamese Government admitted it had suffered serious problems with its training program for Revolutionary Development cadres—the teams of experts assigned to outmaneuver the Communists at winning the loyalty of villagers and peasants. There were flaws in both the recruiting and training process. But by year's end, the Government claimed it had largely eliminated these, and that the pacification campaign was beginning to pick up speed.

In December, however, the Vietcong indicated they still had a deadly punch. In a series of daring raids they hit the Saigon airport, within the very boundaries of the capital city.

Gen. Westmoreland at his side, President Johnson greets troops at Camranh Bay, Vietnam.

Vietnam war: (above) blast of a mortar crew; (upper right) infantry attack on Vietcong supply base; (right) Vietcong terrorists wrecking rail line.

U.S. motor patrol passes through Vietnam village.

Medic aids wounded comrade during heavy battle.

Above: U.S. 1st Infantry Division evacuates Vietnamese peasants to refugee center north of Saigon. Left: Buddhists scurry as tear-gas grenade falls in Saigon street. Below: Catholic chaplain conducts services for men in the field.

Candidate for constituent assembly campaigns in Saigon.   Vietnamese boy trails U.S. infantrymen.

Wide World

Above: South Vietnamese civilians move through flooded streets of Mekong Delta town in Chau Doc Province. Right: During bombardment, Vietnamese mother and three children hide in swamp. Below: Fieldworkers carry soil to fill in war-torn land in South Vietnam.

Wide World

Sampans, barges, freighters fill Saigon's busy port.

Wide World

In Saigon, a proprietress and her black-market stock.

North Vietnam scenes: President Ho Chi Minh visits troops, while below . . .

North Vietnam girls practice hand-to-hand combat; women pass bombed Haiphong building . . .

and a Red China-Hanoi rail link north of Hanoi is knocked out by U.S. bombers.

Wide World

The Harry F. Byrds, son and father.

VIRGINIA. Harry F. Byrd, Sr., died Oct. 20 in Berryville. Democrat Harry F. Byrd, Jr., won a November election to fill his father's U.S. Senate term. . . . The General Assembly voted a sales tax designed for educational purposes. . . . The highway program received additional funds for completion of a four-lane arterial system by 1975. . . . The assembly passed a child-abuse law and also raised unemployment compensation from $36 to $42 per week.

WASHINGTON. In June, President Johnson signed a bill authorizing $390 million for a third power plant at Grand Coulee Dam on the Columbia River in Washington. . . . Studies were under way to investigate the possibilities of building a canal from the Puget Sound to Gray's Harbor and of constructing a bridge over the Puget Sound between the east shore and the Olympic Peninsula. . . . Voters rejected Nov. 8 a Congressional redistricting measure, passed by the state Legislature in 1965.

WASHINGTON, D.C. Largely through the efforts of President and Mrs. Johnson, Washington captured a prize in 1966 sought by many other cities: the Joseph H. Hirshhorn collection of paintings and sculpture. The President announced in May that the New York collector had agreed to give his works of art, valued at $25 million, to the Smithsonian Institution for the American people. Included were 4,000 paintings and drawings and 1,500 pieces of sculpture.

The gift was contingent upon agreement by the Government to build a $15 million Joseph H. Hirshhorn Museum and Sculpture Garden on the Mall in the center of Washington. Johnson promptly submitted legislation to authorize this expenditure. The agreement with Hirshhorn provided that the legislation must be enacted by 1968. Some opposition arose because the site chosen for the museum would involve tearing down the Armed Forces Medical Museum. But the President promised this would be relocated on a suitable site. The National Park Service announced the Hirshhorn Museum and Sculpture Garden would be an important part of a 10-year development program for the Washington area, which included a new master plan for the Mall. Congress passed the bill near the end of the 1966 session.

The program was presented as an outgrowth of Mrs. Johnson's beautification efforts for the national capital. The Mall plan called for the elimination of all temporary buildings, formal landscaping, and large plantings of trees and shrubs. There were some protests, however, that it would give the Mall a too-cluttered look and destroy long-range vistas. Thousands of flowering trees, plants and shrubs were planted in Washington during 1966 as a part of the beautification drive. But some of these suffered badly as the area went through a sixth successive summer of drought.

The National Capital Planning Commission voted during the year to proceed with the interstate-system freeway program for the District of Columbia.

There were two serious disturbances caused mostly by Washington Negro youths during 1966, one at the Glen Echo, Md., amusement park in April, and the other at a police precinct station in southeast Washington in August. Citizens committees were named in both instances to investigate the causes, and to make recommendations for improving the conditions which contributed to the incidents.

On Nov. 13, President Johnson announced that he was vetoing a bill, passed by Congress in October, to revise the District of Columbia criminal code. The bill provided that confessions would not necessarily be inadmissible simply because they had been obtained during the first six hours of a person's interrogation. Furthermore, the bill allowed suspects to be detained for up to four hours before they had to be released or charged with a crime. In addition it provided for detention of material witnesses and established mandatory minimum sentences for several crimes.

JOSEPH W. HALL, JR.
Washington Bureau, THE ASSOCIATED PRESS

WEATHER

By JOHN O. ELLIS

Meteorologist, U.S. ENVIRONMENTAL
SCIENCE SERVICES ADMINISTRATION

The weather for 1966 varied from severe cold in the midwestern United States in January and March to extensive heat in the Midwest and Northeast in June and July. The West and Northeast suffered from the drought, while heavy rains caused flooding in Texas and the Southeast. Blizzards hit the Plains States in February, tornadoes struck in March, April and September, and hurricane Alma swept over Florida in June.

January to March. During January there were record low temperatures in the Midwest and a succession of coastal storms throughout the East. It was the coldest January since 1950 at many stations in the Dakotas and Minnesota. Record low temperatures occurred in the mid-South and southern Atlantic coastal areas. Though it was very dry over the Southwest and Northeast, the Southeast had considerable precipitation. Baton Rouge, La., had its wettest January since 1925. Snow with blizzard conditions, the worst since 1958, hit the Northeast, and heavy rains fell farther south at the end of the month. Record January snows fell in the Carolinas, Virginia, northern New York and New England. Oswego, N.Y., claimed a record fall of 101 in. of snow in the three-day period, Jan. 30 to Feb. 1.

Though warm and cold spells alternated in February, temperatures generally were more moderate than in January. This moderating trend continued into March with above normal temperatures over most of the country. However, a record cold spell occurred in February in northern Minnesota with temperatures dipping into the −40°s F.

The western half of the United States was generally dry, but the East, particularly the Southeast, more than made up for it. Rain fell in record amounts for February in most of the South. Heavy rains continued in the Southeast early in March. Snowmelt, rainfall and ice jams combined to yield flood conditions in the upper Midwest. This spread southward along the Mississippi and Missouri rivers with heavy local and lowland flooding.

In March, blizzard conditions occurred in the northern Great Plains and in the north-central states, prolonging flood conditions. The storm over the Great Plains was one of the most damaging on record. Strong winds and heavy snow over a long duration caused several deaths and severe livestock loss.

Thunderstorms and tornadoes appeared along the east coast during the mild weather in mid-February. The most notable severe storm was the Jackson, Miss., tornado on Mar. 3, the worst in 30 years. In early April, severe tornadoes struck central Florida.

While the storms in January and February hindered activity in the Northeast, they did help alleviate, if only temporarily, the meteorological drought conditions that had persisted for the previous four years. The extreme dry conditions over the central belt of the nation extended into the Northeast again in March, reintensifying the drought. The water supplies of the large metropolitan areas did improve temporarily, however, from snowmelt. Snow in the Far West, the source of the warm-season water supply, was below average in almost all sections. Stations reported the driest March since the 1890's and early 1900's.

Spring. April showers in 1966 were late from New England to New Mexico, arriving the latter part of the month. In the Southwest and West the dry conditions that began in March continued on through April and May. In northeastern Texas, however, a storm dumped 10 to 12 in. of rain in two days, 15 in. in three days in some areas, causing severe flash floods. Heavy rains continued in northeastern Texas into the second week of May, resulting in record flood conditions. Dallas recorded 12.4 in. in nine days.

The Southeast was dry in April, a change from the wet conditions of earlier in the year. April afforded the New England area a dry spell after moderate precipitation in recent months. May was a dry month in the upper Great Lakes area and west of the Mississippi. Cheyenne, Wyo., had the driest May since 1871.

Spring came late, especially in the South. Snow fell over a wide area from the Rockies through the Northern Plains to the Great Lakes in mid-April. A freeze extending from the Great Lakes to the Virginias around May 10 caused considerable damage to fruits and vegetables. Cold conditions for the month set numerous records for that area.

In June most of the area east of the Mississippi River was deficient in rainfall. Florida was the exception with an accumulation of 20 in. of rain. Most of it came from Alma, the first hurricane of the season. This was a new record, for it was the earliest in the season that a hurricane had moved over a U.S. coastline. It was also the earliest incidence of the formation of a hurricane in 15 years. While

Alma brought $5 million damage and four deaths to Florida, she brought much needed rains to the northeastern areas that lay in her path.

On June 8 a severe tornado struck Topeka, Kans., causing numerous deaths, many injuries and much property damage. June began with cold air moving over the eastern half of the country, setting low-temperature records in 35 cities.

Summer. Toward the end of June a heat wave began over the north-central and northeastern states. It continued well into the third week of July, breaking numerous records in the Northeast and Midwest. In Oklahoma there were 20 consecutive days of 100° F. or more. St. Louis had 100° F. temperatures for six straight days, with 69 deaths attributed to the heat. Washington, D.C., set a new record for June, July and August, with 63 days over 90° F.

From Nevada and Utah north through Idaho and Montana dry conditions persisted through July, August and September. Helena, Mont., set an 86-year record for dryness for the period January through August. Despite beneficial rains that fell in September, moisture was still short in a belt from southwestern Idaho southwestward through Nevada into California.

Temperatures for August were cool in the central United States, but warm along the Pacific coast and in the Northeast. The heat set records in central and southern California. Nineteen consecutive days of 100° F. baked Fresno. Rains again deluged Nebraska and South Dakota, and in Texas and New Mexico rains caused extensive property and crop damage.

Through July, August and the beginning of September, hot humid conditions prevailed in the East and the drought intensified in the Great Basin, Midwest and Northeast. After mid-September, heavy rains fell over the eastern seaboard from the Gulf of Mexico to New England, right over the heart of the drought area. Rain also fell in the Great Basin and some sections of the Midwest. With these rains came an end to the water shortages in most soils, lakes and reservoirs.

Cold air pushed down over the Northeast in the middle of September, setting low temperature records for so early in the season— 40° F. at Richmond, Va., on the 17th. In the Far West, high-temperature records were set —109° F. at Red Bluff, Calif., on the 29th, the highest late-season temperature since 1877.

Autumn. Hurricane Inez lasted from Sept. 21 to Oct. 11 in the northern Caribbean, Florida Straits and the Gulf of Mexico. Though its effect on the United States was limited to southern Florida, this storm was unusual because of its long life, its large extent and its erratic path on Oct. 3. While damage in Florida was only $5 million and 3 lives lost, throughout its entire course more than one thousand people were killed, and damage exceeded $200 million.

The final week of September again gave substantial rains to the mid-Atlantic and northeastern areas. Rains after mid-October again benefited the drought area from Virginia to Connecticut. In the West, precipitation was only 50 per cent of normal from the central Great Plains southwestward.

The first large-scale cold-air intrusion of the season came in mid-October after a major storm developed in Montana. This brought blizzard conditions over the Great Plains northeastward to the Great Lakes. Tornadoes and severe thunderstorms, heavy winds and hail occurred. One tornado virtually destroyed Belmond, Iowa, the most destructive late-season tornado to have occurred in the state.

In early November a storm system brought cold weather and record early snows to the central United States. Topeka, Kans., had 10° F., an early season record, while New Orleans, La., had 28° F. In coastal California, desert winds gave Los Angeles a 101° F. temperature, an 82-year November record. San Diego broke a 95-year record with 97° F. In early November a storm from the Great Lakes to the South brought record early snows to Kentucky and Tennessee. This was followed by the coldest weather of the season in the north-central United States.

During the first half of November, substantial rains fell from the Ohio-Mississippi valley eastward. The latter half of November was unusually mild in most areas—up to 20° above normal for a weekly average. Over the month, dry weather continued from Idaho, Nevada and Southern California to the Midwest. Around Thanksgiving a stagnant high-pressure cell caused air pollution to reach dangerous levels in some sections of the Northeast.

December. By early December, cold weather swept over the central and eastern states. Precipitation occurred daily in the Pacific Northwest most of the month and for the first 10 days west of the Divide. The heaviest rains of 1966 fell in Utah and Nevada. By Dec. 10, strong southerly winds brought record high temperatures to the eastern United States; Trenton, N.J., set a high for 101 years' observation with 72°F. Snowstorms occurred from the mid-United States eastward the latter half of December. One storm brought the area from Arkansas northeastward a white Christmas.

WEATHER: JET STREAMS, PLANETARY WAVES AND WEATHER PATTERNS

By A. JAMES WAGNER
Extended Forecast Division
U.S. WEATHER BUREAU

The earth's atmosphere is in a continual state of change. It behaves like a restless fluid, progressing from one state to another, often with surprising rapidity. The changes in the atmosphere can be followed by means of synoptic weather maps, simplified versions of which are published in many newspapers and displayed on TV weather programs. A synoptic weather map is like a snapshot of the atmosphere at a particular instant of time. The patterns shown on these maps consist of the familiar fronts, air masses and high- and low-pressure areas, which are related to certain types of weather events.

Ground and Atmosphere. The fronts and pressure systems actually describe the weather only at or near the surface of the earth. Since the lowest layer of the atmosphere is the part in which we live and carry on most of our activities, we are naturally most concerned with weather near the ground. However, meteorologists—those who study and forecast weather—are just as interested in the behavior of the layer of the atmosphere aloft. This is because weather—together with the behavior of the fronts, lows and highs—is influenced by conditions in the atmosphere at least up to several miles above earth's surface.

Jet Streams and Planetary Waves. The difference in temperature between the tropics and the polar regions produces broad bands of westerly winds which encircle the earth in both hemispheres. The winds reach their greatest velocity—as much as 200 miles per hour or more—at altitudes of 5 to 7 miles. These upper-level winds, the core of which is called the jet stream, do not always blow straight from the west, but usually meander from north to south and back again several times, like a globe-girdling river of air. The large-scale undulations of the upper winds, which extend for thousands of miles, are called planetary (or long) waves. Since fronts usually are found near and below the jet stream, and the highs and lows tend to be steered by it, the surface weather is influenced by conditions aloft.

Jet streams are strongest in winter, when the temperature difference between the pole and equator is greatest. For this reason, weather systems generally move faster in winter than in summer, and the increased contrast between cold and warm air leads to larger and more intense storms. The normal position of the jet stream varies with the season, being farthest north in late summer, farthest south in late winter. Prevailing storm tracks undergo a similar variation through the year.

The geographical positions of the planetary waves are influenced by the nature of the earth's underlying surface. A mountain range will often slow the jet down, or cause it to split in two parts which later come together again. Areas of abnormally warm or cold water at the ocean surface seem to be related to the position of the jet stream, although it is difficult to tell to what extent the water temperature affects the atmosphere, and how much the weather systems associated with the upper winds change the water temperature. The atmosphere and oceans are continually interacting with each other in a complex manner.

The predominant type of weather over a period of time in a particular locality depends on the prevailing position and orientation of the jet stream. If it is several hundred miles to the north, storms will be infrequent and the weather will be dry. If one of the planetary waves is positioned so that a ridge (or northward extension) is to the west, and a trough (or southward dip) is to the east, the weather will be predominantly cold and dry. One can see that the prevailing air flow aloft will then be from the northwest, and the flow will transport relatively cold and dry air into the area from the north. Similarly, if the planetary wave shifts so that the upper-level winds come from the southwest, relatively warm, humid air is brought northward from the tropics, resulting in warm and wet weather.

Since the prevailing planetary waves change more slowly than the daily weather systems which move through them, the average weather in a given locality over an extended period of time may often depart considerably from the normal when the position or north-south displacement of the planetary waves is abnormal. These departures from normal can be computed for a period of anywhere from a day to several seasons or years. The weather and its abnormalities will display characteristic but not unique relationships to the prevailing position of the planetary waves regardless of the length of time over which the

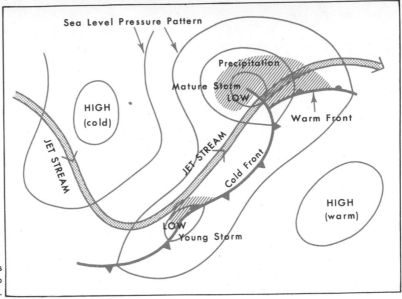

Typical relationship of fronts and surface weather systems to the position of the jet stream.

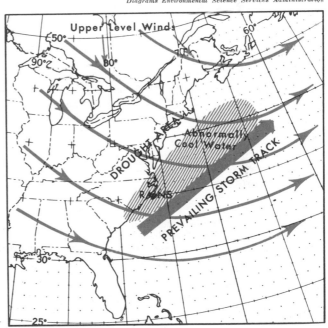

Storm track and upper-level winds that prevailed during the drought period of 1962–66.

average is taken. Thus, if over a period of several seasons, the position of a planetary-wave trough is farther east of a given area than normal, the weather will be cooler and drier than usual in that part of the world.

A good example of this has occurred over the northeastern United States for the past five years, particularly during the spring and summer. The trough in the planetary waves usually near the coast has been farther east over the western Atlantic. As a result, storms that normally bring rain to the coast have been steered farther out to sea, with serious drought

resulting. The greater-than-normal amount of cool, dry air moving over the area from Canada toward the ocean has in turn helped reduce water temperatures to below normal off the Middle Atlantic Coast. The cool water is favorable to maintaining the trough off the coast, and also releases less moisture to air blowing toward the land than warm water would, thus intensifying the drought. However, factors elsewhere in the atmosphere are always at work changing the planetary waves, so that eventually a more normal sequence of wet and dry weather will be restored.

WEST VIRGINIA. An explosion in a soft-coal mine near Mt. Hope killed seven and injured two on July 23.... The state suffered its worst drought since 1930; water reserves declined alarmingly.... Jennings Randolph (D) retained his U.S. Senate seat in November. John D. Rockefeller IV won election to the House of Delegates from Kanawha County. Rockefeller originally came to the state to work in the Appalachian Youth program. A Democrat, Rockefeller announced in late November his engagement to Sharon Percy, daughter of Senator Charles Percy (R-Ill.).

WILSON, HAROLD. For Great Britain's Prime Minister Harold Wilson, what might have been a year of political ease and surging prosperity became, instead, a year of struggle on two crisis issues: the failing economy and the dispute with Rhodesia.

Mr. Wilson's shrewd campaigning in the March general election—virtually on the theme "you never had it so good"—boosted the Labor majority in Parliament from three to ninety-seven. Yet almost immediately the pound was under attack and Rhodesia was again troublesome. When 1966 was finished, few Britons were neutral about Harold Wilson and his management.

To admirers, this sharp Yorkshireman was still the "modern minded" leader who was successfully revising Britain's Victorian economy, and who was facing down Rhodesia's racists while avoiding a perilous confrontation with South Africa.

To these people, he was the Churchillian statesman who refused to scuttle Britain's "east of Suez" role, who still sees his country as a world power, who maintains a working alliance with the United States, and who will take Britain into the European Common Market when its own special needs receive adequate consideration.

Admirers saw Mr. Wilson as the smart politician who holds Parliament under almost-mesmeric sway, who denounces the Conservatives with withering scorn, and who is rebuilding the Labor Party as the aggregation of the middle-road "consensus," where most voters reside.

To critical Britons, however, Mr. Wilson is a very different person.

He is the gimmicks man, who operates by razzle-dazzle, who aims to be all things to all people, who relies on noise and bustle instead of solid achievement. He is the author of "instant" policy, who has no program beyond tomorrow morning, whether for reshaping the economy or handling Rhodesia.

The Prime Minister, to these detractors, is the mismanager who wrecked the British economy by applying the brake pedal too hard when the economy began to overheat, who has transformed a mild run on the pound into serious deflation with over half a million unemployed. He is the unstatesman who, by applying harsh sanctions against Rhodesia, is threatening a ruinous trade war—and perhaps eventually the use of military force—against all of southern Africa.

Mr. Wilson's friends and foes alike admit that his permanent image will be largely determined by how Britain climbs out of its economic freeze, and how the Rhodesia crisis is resolved.

The Prime Minister meanwhile sought to enhance his statesman's role by traveling twice to Moscow, in February and July. Main topic each time: Vietnam. Russian reaction each time: noncommittal. But Mr. Wilson kept President Johnson carefully informed regarding Soviet viewpoints. And he kept his own Left-Wing Laborites relatively quiet by such gestures toward Vietnam peace.

At year's end Mr. Wilson was still telling newsmen that by the next general election, in 1970, Britain would again be marvelously prosperous and Labor would be reelected handily.

WILLIAM H. STRINGER
London Bureau Chief
THE CHRISTIAN SCIENCE MONITOR

WISCONSIN. The state Legislature instituted a program to combat water pollution, and also authorized the state to borrow up to $26.5 million for highway construction. A 1-cent-per-gallon increase in gasoline tax will finance the borrowing.... Gov. Warren P. Knowles (R) won reelection.... Milwaukee NAACP headquarters was bombed Aug. 9.... A state constitutional amendment, passed in November, reduced new voters' residency requirement from one year to six months.... The Legislature passed a bill that will preserve the Wolf River as a scenic area.

WYOMING. Although some rural residents protested combining rural with urban areas in several multimember Senate districts, the U.S. Supreme Court on Feb. 28 approved reapportionment of the state Senate.... On Oct. 15, President Johnson signed a bill making Bighorn Canyon National Recreation Area a national park. The park is comprised of 63,300 acres in Montana and Wyoming.... S. K. Hathaway (R) won the November race for governor; C. P. Hansen (R) gained a U.S. Senate seat.

ZOOS. Zoological gardens enjoyed another prosperous year during 1966, and old attendance records were shattered in many cities. A new zoo was officially opened in Los Angeles, and construction on new zoo buildings and exhibits throughout the United States probably reached a new high. Many rare animals of species vanishing in the wild were bred in captivity, and the importance of research on captive collections became increasingly apparent. Probably the zoo story that had widest U.S. circulation during the year concerned the plight of a group of more than 50 rare and valuable hoofed animals brought by ship to the United States and refused entry. For a time it seemed they would have to be destroyed.

The U.S. Department of Agriculture has long been charged with the task of protecting the U.S. dairy and cattle industry from alien diseases, and elaborate regulations to prevent the importation of hoof-and-mouth disease and rinderpest have been in effect for many years. All ruminant (cud-chewing) animals destined for zoological gardens must be held first in an approved quarantine station overseas for 60 days. If a properly accredited veterinarian certifies to their good health they may then be shipped to the United States, but they must be held for an additional 30 days at the government quarantine station at Clifton, N.J.

In the case of the 50 rare animals the problem arose from a technicality. Under the regulations "direct shipment" is required. The Department of Agriculture stipulates that "direct" requires a ship to sail without other stops from the port of embarkation to the United States, but in shipping circles "direct shipment" is interpreted as meaning that the cargo will not be unloaded or transshipped. En route to New York the vessel carrying the rare animals had stopped at several ports where infectious diseases may or may not have been present. The Department of Agriculture held that the shipment was considered as contaminated and could not be landed. Because of the great expense involved, the shipping line was unable to comply with the suggestion that the animals be taken back to Africa. Someone made the unfortunate remark that the ship should be put out to sea and the animals should be dumped overboard.

That was enough to raise a storm of protest, and very shortly humane societies, conservation organizations, congressmen, government officials, and representatives of the American Association of Zoological Parks and Aquariums were involved in efforts to save the animals. A plan was worked out to quarantine them at Fort Slocum on an island near New York

An okapi and her male offspring at the Copenhagen Zoo.

Soviet and British giant pandas meet at Moscow Zoo.

Ten-day-old dwarf hippopotamus at Copenhagen Zoo.

Harbor, with the animal dealers, the zoos for whom the animals were destined, and the Government sharing the expense. There was one unhappy result, however. The shipping line, the principal one plying between East Africa and New York, will no longer accept ruminants as cargo, which will make the importation of some of the most important kinds of animals more difficult and more expensive.

These problems point up the fact that buying animals for a zoo is not like shopping for groceries at a supermarket. A few kinds of small animals—including monkeys, cage birds, and baby turtles—can be purchased at virtually any pet store, but elaborate preparations must often be made before some of the large and rare animals can be imported. In practice most importations are handled by professional animal dealers, some of whom have their own collecting stations in Africa or other parts of the world. Few zoos are sufficiently rich or well-staffed to send their own expeditions into the field.

New Buildings and Exhibits. New buildings and exhibits were completed in many zoos. Among the more unusual were a natural-habitat cage for mandrills at the New York Zoological Park replete with a fiber-glass replica of a giant tropical tree, a new gibbon display at the San Diego Zoo, additions to the Farm-in-the-Zoo at Chicago's Lincoln Park Zoo, and an unusual building at the Fort Worth Zoo where visitors may see such normally behind-the-scenes activities as the preparation of food for the animals and autopsies of animals that have died in the collection. The Brookfield Zoo, in suburban Chicago, announced plans for a $5.5 million renovation and expansion program.

Rare Births. Among rare animals born were two gorillas at the Dallas Zoo, a proboscis monkey at San Diego, orangutans at Philadelphia and Washington, an Adélie penguin at Milwaukee, and the fifth elephant baby in recent years at Portland, Ore. The Arabian oryx herd at Phoenix, Ariz., established to preserve this nearly extinct animal, has now increased by eight; seven were males, but the eighth was a female. The London, England, Zoo sent its female giant panda to Moscow to be bred to the Soviet Union's male. These are the only two giant pandas outside the bamboo curtain. The New York Zoological Park sent its female gerenuk (antelope) to San Diego for a similar purpose.

Conservation and Research Activities. Conservation continued to occupy a large part of the agenda in zoo circles. Most zoos, in order to discourage the smuggling of orangutans, monkey-eating eagles, Galapagos tortoises, and lion marmosets—all of which are getting dangerously rare in nature—have pledged not to purchase or otherwise acquire such animals unless they have been legally exported under the laws of nations where they have their native homes. Other animals may soon be placed on the embargoed list.

Research has long been considered an important function of many large zoological gardens. The Penrose Research Laboratory at the Philadelphia Zoo (established 1901) has kept autopsy records on all animals that died in its collection and made many valuable contributions to the health and husbandry of captive animals. Currently there is great interest in studying the behavior of zoo animals as social groups, not only in Philadelphia, where a project is under way in collaboration with the University of Pennsylvania, but in several other zoos that are cooperating with various institutions of learning. Elaborate plans at the National Zoological Park in Washington for research on a very broad scale are currently being translated into laboratories and offices where it is hoped to attract scientists from a variety of disciplines.

Two items of unusual interest occurred during 1966. The San Diego Zoo celebrated its 50th anniversary with a year-long series of meetings and events. It featured an international conference on the role of zoos in the conservation of wild animals. The zoo in Frankfurt am Main, Germany, began the training of young Africans so that they could return to their native countries as directors of the zoos that have been newly created in Africa.

ROGER CONANT
Director, PHILADELPHIA ZOOLOGICAL GARDEN

INDEX